CONQUERING THE FEAR OF DEATH

CONQUERING THE FEAR OF DEATH

An exposition of I Corinthians 15,
based upon the original Greek text

by
Spiros Zodhiates, Th.D.

AMG PUBLISHERS
Chattanooga, TN 37421

Reprinted 1982
ISBN 0-89957-500-5

Dedicated to My Brother in the Flesh and in the Lord

Argos Zodhiates

Whose testimony led me to Christ and whose

encouragement the dedication of my life

to the ministry of the Gospel.

CONTENTS

Contents

Contents

Contents

Contents

Contents

PREFACE

As a Greek I have an unbounded curiosity, an itch to know the whys and wherefores of everything, and more especially of Scripture in its practical application to life. Some of the questions that intrigued me were, Am I really going to have a new body after death, after my spirit has lived its separate disembodied existence in the life to come? On what can I base such a belief? How can I, a thinking individual, accept as true something that is outside the common experience of man?

In this respect I was no different from the Corinthian Greeks who posed the question, "How are the dead raised up? and with what body do they come?" (I Cor. 15:35).

Paul had an answer for them and for me, but again I asked, Is it a valid one? Can I depend on it? Can you? Now Paul never accepted anything on an *a priori* basis in this matter. He was no gullible dupe, but an intelligent syllogist, a careful logician. He decided to start with the facts of history. The Christians of his day believed that Christ had risen from the dead. Very well, he says in effect, let's examine the historical evidence. In the end he came to the conclusion that the bodily resurrection of Jesus Christ was an indisputable historical reality. In this 15th chapter of I Corinthians he marshals the evidence.

Can thinking men believe in the resurrection of Christ? To say it couldn't have happened, without thoroughly examining the historical data, is only to reveal irrational ignorance and prejudice. Not too many years ago many persons held the opinion that man would never reach the moon. They may have thought themselves great thinkers, but they now stand corrected by history. So does anyone who declares that Jesus could not have risen from the dead. Here is the evidence in the 15th chapter of I Corinthians, analyzed in all its convincing detail from the Greek text.

We can take one step further by acknowledging that history can repeat itself. And who is more competent to tell us whether or not we may expect something similar to happen in our own experience than the One who was the first to rise from the dead? Let no one make the second mistake of assuming that his own resurrection is impossible. The One who gave us our corruptible bodies can give us incorruptible ones. "But God giveth it a body as it hath pleased him" (I Cor. 15:38). God the Son proved His ability to reveal to men that which they could not discover for themselves, that is, His own resurrection. Take a look back: Christ arose; take a look forward: we shall all be made alive.

Paul, under the inspiration of the Holy Spirit, probes further into the nature of the resurrection body—a fascinating study which he parallels with natural phenomena. And he ends this chapter—surely one of the hardest to understand and interpret in the entire New Testament—with the practical application of the certainty of our resurrection by declaring it to be the inspiration for us to abound in the work of the Lord. If you believe that your body is going to be raised, he says, you will be willing to subject it to even the most tiring labor for the Lord now.

It took me four years to study this great chapter and write as exhaustive an analysis and interpretation of it as I could. May the reader of these studies find as much spiritual profit and blessing in them as I derived from writing them.

SPIROS ZODHIATES

WELL-BALANCED CHRISTIANS

"Moreover, brethren, I declare unto you the gospel which I preached unto you, which also ye have received, and wherein ye stand" (I Cor. 15:1).

Suppose your home were on fire; what would you rescue first—your money, your jewelry, some treasured possession? No, your first thought would be for human lives, those who are near and dear to you, for without them all other possessions would be dust and ashes.

A proper sense of values is an excellent balance wheel in the machinery of life, and nowhere more so than in our Christian conduct and witness. What shall we give first place in our lives, and what shall we relegate to a subordinate position?

The Apostle Paul suggests an answer by the way he closes his discussion of the matter of "gifts" in the 14th chapter of First Corinthians. To possess any of the gifts of the Holy Spirit—preaching, teaching, wisdom, knowledge, and so on—is cause for thankfulness to God; but to overrate or underrate the importance of any gift is to distort the Gospel to that extent. The burden on Paul's heart, as he writes to the Corinthians at greater length than to any of the other churches, is for Christians to put first things first, lest by our behavior (especially in public worship) we give others the idea that God is the author of confusion and disorder. Therefore, as he closes his discussion on gifts in First Corinthians 14:40, he lays down this basic rule for Christian behavior: "Let all things be done decently and in order."

We can imagine him saying this with a sigh of relief, as this matter had become very irksome to him and disruptive of Christian unity. "Let us now proceed," he says in effect, "to that which is of primary importance to us as Christians—the fact of the resurrection of Jesus Christ, and our belief in Him and in life after death."

I must confess that I, too, experience a sense of relief as I turn from the discussion of gifts and tongues and enter upon what is really the cornerstone of our faith. Like Paul, I spoke not by choice but of necessity. The same imbalance that disrupted the Corinthian church is in danger of permeating the church of our own era, the pushing of minor gifts to the forefront, which results in a distortion of the whole truth of God. As we examine the Scriptures, how can we fail to be persuaded that the resurrection of the Lord Jesus Christ and our own future resurrection are of infinitely greater significance than the matter of speaking in an unknown tongue? Just compare the few references to tongues in the New Testament with the great number of references to the resurrection, to achieve a proper sense of proportion in this matter.

Now, in chapter 15, Paul presents the contrast between the unimportant matter of tongues and that which is all-important, the Gospel. The word "moreover" with which the first verse begins is *de* in Greek, which in this context might better be rendered "but." "But, brethren, I declare unto you the gospel which I preached unto you, which also ye have received, and wherein ye stand." Paul's argument, reduced to its essentials, is, "I have told you all that is needful about

— 4 —

such matters as tongues and the behavior of your women in church, but now I remind you that this is not the Gospel."

It should be noted that the same particle, *de*, is used in the previous verse (I Cor. 14:40), but unfortunately was omitted here by the translators of the Authorized Version. They simply rendered it, "Let all things be done decently and in order," when actually it should read, "*But* let all things be done decently and in order." This 40th verse stands in contrast to verse 39, which says, "Wherefore, brethren, covet to prophesy, and forbid not to speak with tongues. *But* [*de*]—" this is only permissible if it is done in an orderly fashion and does not produce confusion. The *de* (but) that provides the contrast between verses 39 and 40 of chapter 14 is followed by the *de* (but) of the first verse of chapter 15, which provides the contrast between the two chapters, and in fact between the two total arguments.

"But, brethren, I declare unto you the gospel which I preached unto you." The Greek word *gnoorizoo*, coming as it does from the same root as the word *gnoosis*, meaning "knowledge," might ordinarily be translated, "I make known unto you." Yet in this context we see also that Paul is making known the Gospel to them obviously again, by way of a reminder of what he had previously declared to them. This was not the first time that Paul had made known the Gospel to them. Hence we may paraphrase this as follows: "But, brethren, I am making known unto you the gospel which I preached unto you, as a reminder." This fact is further substantiated by the aorist tense and indi-

cative mood of the verb "preached," *eueengelisameen.*
Paul takes the Corinthians back to the time when he
journeyed from Athens to preach the Gospel in Corinth, as recorded in the 18th chapter of Acts. Actually
the verb translated "preached" here is the verbal form
of the noun "Gospel" (*euangelion*), which is limited in
New Testament usage to Gospel preaching only.

Paul does not refer in this chapter to tongues or
to any of the other gifts of which the Corinthians were
so proud, and which they were giving such undue prom-
inence. "Let me remind you of the gospel which I
preached to you," he says to them. And he did not
do this in an unknown tongue, for the verb he uses,
gnoorizoo, "I make known," involves thought and understandable speech. A look at Acts 18 will reveal
Paul's first preaching effort in Corinth. In verse 4
we read, "And he [Paul] reasoned in the synagogue
every sabbath, and persuaded the Jews and the
Greeks." The two verbs, "reasoned" (*dielegeto*) and
"persuaded" (*epeithen*) show that he used his mind
and spoke in a language the people could understand.
And what were the results? The chief ruler of the
synagogue, Crispus, was converted, and so, it would
seem, was his successor, Sosthenes, after his unsuccess-
ful court suit against Paul. (See I Cor. 1:1.) Nowhere
does the account mention Paul's speaking in an unknown tongue.

I was deeply distressed to read a pamphlet by the
leader of an organization that deals with foreign university students when they come to the United States,
in which he intimated that these students would more
readily come to Christ if those who witnessed to them

were enabled by the Holy Spirit to speak to them in their own languages. There is no question in my mind that God could do this if it were His will. But these foreign students coming here all know English, so that what this leader was asking for, in effect, was a sign or miracle to convince unbelievers. Isn't the Holy Spirit able to witness to them through the English language? Would they actually believe more readily if they heard the Gospel proclaimed to them in their native tongue by someone who had not previously learned the language? More likely they would suspect a trick, for a man who is disposed to believe will do so whenever and however the Holy Spirit speaks to his heart, and the man who is not disposed to believe will find reasons for rejecting even the miraculous.

In the story of the rich man and Lazarus (Luke 16), you remember that the rich man who suffered torments in Hades wanted Father Abraham to send someone from the dead to warn his brothers to repent. He thought that such a miraculous manifestation would make all the difference. But though God desires all men to be saved, He has His own methods of dealing with men's hearts, and does not accede to our frantic requests for a miracle to convince them. That is why Abraham was moved to reply, "If they hear not Moses and the prophets, neither will they be persuaded, though one rose from the dead" (Luke 16:31).

We are never to tempt God by asking for a sign. We are to take Him at His Word, recognizing that we are called to a life of faith here below, and that to ask for "sight" is a confession of unbelief, as well as being outside the will of God for this life. The Bible plainly states that God has chosen through what unbelieving men consider the "foolishness" of preaching to save the world, and not by signs and wonders (I Cor. 1:21).

REMEMBER YOUR FIRST LOVE

"Moreover, brethren, I declare unto you the gospel which I preached unto you, which also ye have received, and wherein ye stand" (I Cor. 15:1).

When John Wesley was returning from America to England, he wrote in his journal, "I have a fair summer religion. I can talk well; nay, and believe myself, while no danger is near: but let death look me in the face, and my spirit is troubled." That was before his true conversion in a little room in Aldersgate Street. "I felt," he said, "my heart strangely warmed. I felt I did trust in Christ, Christ alone for salvation." After that joyful experience of Christ as his Saviour, his whole heart was aflame with burning love and he knew the inward peace that passes understanding. He became fearless in the face of difficulties and often met the peril of death itself with serene joy. He passed at last into the presence of his Lord with the repeated words on his lips, as he lay dying, "The best of all is, that God is with us." (See C. F. Andrew's *Christ in the Silence*, pp. 271-2.)

When Paul writes to the Corinthians of "the gospel which I preached unto you," it is not hearsay that he is passing on to them but what he actually and personally knows. He had received and experienced the Gospel (I Cor. 15:3), and this authenticates his witness and gives him the right to preach it to others. Pity the preacher who tries to tell others the way of salvation when he has never experienced it himself. Buchsel remarks that orthodoxy can be learned from others, but living faith must be a matter of personal experience. The Lord sent out His disciples, saying, "And ye also shall bear witness, because ye have been with me from the beginning" (John 15:27). He only is a witness who speaks of what he has seen with his own eyes, heard with his own ears, and handled with his own hands. Orthodoxy apart from saving faith is merely another form of rationalism.

Paul's initial preaching to the Corinthians was in the power of the Holy Spirit, in a language that they could understand and that Paul knew. He presented the Gospel to them intelligently and persuasively, and the Holy Spirit used it to convert sinners, among them Paul's foremost persecutors. Now Paul reminds them of this Gospel that they had received. The verb *parelabete*, "ye have received," indicates an exercise of the will. The Gospel is never forced on people. Once the Gospel is preached, it is the hearers' responsibility to accept it or reject it.

Though God is omnipotent, He does not choose to disregard man's own choice. God can never be held responsible for anyone's rejection of the Gospel, nor can anyone take credit for his own reception of it. Salvation is all of God's grace and initiative. Probably there were many in Corinth who heard the Gospel and did not receive it. It is not to them that Paul addresses this chapter but to those who received and believed his message. That is why he calls them "brethren." For people to become brethren in Christ, they must first become children of the same Father. There can be no common brotherhood without common Fatherhood, for

"As many as received him [Christ], to them gave he power to become the sons of God" (John 1:12).

The aorist active tense of the verb *parelabete*, "received," indicates that the Gospel was accepted at some definite time, and that since then it has been the possession of those who received it. The implied meaning is, "Ye received and now have as your very own this gospel which I preached unto you." The compound form *elabete* ("took or received" prefixed by the preposition "from") gives this verb the connotation of a welcome reception. The Corinthians not only received the Gospel from the Apostle Paul, they welcomed it. It is still with them now as Paul writes to them.

But the Gospel is not just a message to be received and welcomed; it is a foundation to stand on. Paul calls it "the gospel which I preached unto you, which also ye have received, and wherein ye stand." Actually the Greek verb *hesteekate* (perfect tense) means "ye have stood and therefore now continue to stand." Just as a towering tree has its roots in time past in a little beginning—a seed planted in the ground—so, Paul reminds these Corinthian Christians, they stand where they stand because of that initial reception of the Gospel which he preached to them.

It is a heartwarming thing for us to remember the person or persons who first witnessed to us and from whom we received the Gospel. No matter how far advanced we may be from that small beginning, we should remember with gratitude the human means of our spiritual birth. This is the attitude Paul wants to instill in the Corinthian Christians. He had the authority borne of love to commend them, correct them, and establish them further in their most holy faith. "Don't divorce your present standing from your past planting and rooting," he seems to be saying. "You wouldn't be standing on the Gospel if it were not for my coming to preach it to you."

Despite the many defects in their Christian behavior, the Apostle indirectly commends the Corinthian believers for standing on the same Gospel that he had preached to them. He recognizes that there is danger of their shifting as a visible local church, and in fact had to reprove the Galatians for this very thing. "I marvel that ye are so soon removed from him [Christ] that called you into the grace of Christ unto another gospel," he says sorrowfully in Galatians 1:6. What he means is, "I would have you remember what sort of reception you once gave to the Gospel that I preached to you. It is the same Gospel that I preach to you still. The change is in yourselves. If the Gospel is not the same to you as a society of believers now as it was then, might it not be well for you as a fellowship to look back and ask yourselves how I preached it then, and how you received it then?"

How long has it been since you, as a church or as an individual, looked back to the beginning of your Christian experience? Do you remember how you welcomed the Gospel then? Do you give it the same welcome now? This does not mean that we are to reject any new suggestion of our enquiring spirits and shut our eyes to new light that may come in the context of the Gospel-revelation of God's Word. But as we examine the new, let us recall the Lord's dealings with our souls and our own experience under them. Before we indiscriminately accept the new, we are exhorted to consider what sort of Gospel once satisfied us, what sort of Gospel we once received. "No man also having drunk old wine straightway desireth new: for he saith, The old is better" (Luke 5:39).

Paul was conscious of the fact that old truths, precious and saving though they may be, may become commonplace, for the local church as well as for individuals. Guard against this danger, he advises the Corinthians and us. If your heart has become cold, your conscience callous, your reactions listless as you go through the motions of your customary religious exercises, it is time to heed the warning of the Lord Jesus Christ to the church of Ephesus, "I have somewhat against thee, because thou hast left thy first love. Remember therefore from whence thou art fallen, and repent, and do the first works" (Rev. 2:4, 5). Be alarmed if the plain Gospel, setting forth man's utter ruin and helplessness, and God's free and full salvation, fails to impress you and you feel it is trite and tiresome. Those who tire of the wholesome water of life and seek a more sophisticated drink often become intoxicated with their own cleverness instead of God's goodness, and end up promoting their own glory instead of God's.

WHAT IS SAVING FAITH?

"By which also ye are saved, if ye keep in memory what I preached unto you, unless ye have believed in vain" (I Cor. 15:2).

Sometimes it seems that the worst thing you can say about a belief, a way of life, or a moral code nowadays is that it is "old." Old masterpieces of art become more valuable with age; ancient manuscripts are handled with veneration; old ruins are great tourist attractions; but to many the Ten Commandments have become passe. Men will touch an early Gutenberg Bible with awe, while they reject its contents as irrelevant to the needs of modern man. Of course, this is not an attitude peculiar to the 20th Century. It is as old as the Garden of Eden. "Yea, hath God said?" is the prime doubt insinuated into men's hearts since Eve first listened to the serpent (Gen. 3:1).

The Apostle Paul felt it necessary, therefore, to warn the Corinthians as a local church not only against the danger of letting the Gospel become an old, worn-out story to them, but also against letting the so-called new refinements of philosophy concerning the cardinal doctrine of the resurrection undermine the stabilizing effects of the old Gospel. These new systems of thought that would bring doubt as to the truth of the resurrection may rock us, but the old Gospel is the rock that will enable us to stand firm against the recurring waves of each new "ism" that assaults us.

Paul reminded the Corinthians of the definite historic past in which he had preached the Gospel to them (*eueengelisameen*, in the aorist tense and indicative mood) and which they had welcomed (*parelabete*); then spoke of its effect on and relationship to the present (the Gospel "wherein ye stand" or "have stood"); and finally brought them up to the present (the Gospel "by which ye are saved"). The Greek verb for "ye are saved," *soozesthe*, actually means "ye are being saved." It is the present indicative form of the verb, which refers to continuous action. Paul speaks of their salvation as having its roots in the past, when they first received the Gospel, but as being continually operative throughout their lives. The Christ presented to us in the Gospel has saved us in the past, saves us now, and will ever save us. Salvation is not static, it is dynamic and ever progressing. Once it begins in us, it never ends. The first breath of air drawn in by a newborn baby successfully launches it on its earthly life, but this is just the beginning of a process that requires him to continue to draw in air moment by moment for the sustaining of that life. Our daily salvation from the power of evil can only be accomplished through the same Gospel that saved us initially.

The first and main verb of verses 1 and 2 is *gnoorizoo*, "I declare, make known, or remind you." What was it that Paul wanted to remind the Corinthians of? It was "the gospel which I preached unto you." Then after telling them that they have stood and are standing because of the Gospel, he says to them, "by which also ye are being saved if ye keep on holding fast in what manner I preached the gospel unto you." Hence by way of summary we observe that Paul said in effect, "I first of all made known to you the gospel, and secondly you must hold it fast in the manner in which I preached it to you." *Tini logoo* is used to help indicate manner here, but its basic meaning is "reason, intelligence, and the expression of intelligence." Paul reminds the Corinthians not only of the content of the Gospel but also of the intelligent manner in which he had presented it to them. And he will proceed to demonstrate to them in his forthcoming arguments on the resurrection how intelligent the presentation of the Gospel can be. Man does not have to bypass his mind or close his eyes to receive the Gospel. The genius of the Gospel is that it is for everyone, from the most primitive tribesman to the most highly intellectual product of our civilization. But for all classes of men to accept it intelligently, we must present it in a manner worthy of intelligent acceptance.

We must keep in mind the connection between the historical account of Paul's visit to Corinth as recorded in Acts 18 and his subsequent letters to the Corinthian Christians. The word used in Acts 18:4 to describe Paul's method of preaching in Corinth is *dielegeto*, the same word basically as *logoo*, used in I Corinthians 15:2. "And he reasoned in the synagogue," we read in Acts; and then, later, when he wrote to these same people, he reminds them of the intelligent manner in which he presented the Gospel to them. He spoke to them in understandable human language with the full use of his God-given intelligence.

After reminding them of the Gospel that saved them, Paul qualifies his words by adding, "if ye keep in memory what I preached unto you." It is my belief, after a careful study of this passage, that the translation "if ye keep in memory" leaves much to be desired. This clause, *ei katechete* in Greek, literally means "if ye hold or possess." The verb *katechoo* is a compound made up of the preposition *kata*, meaning "down," and the verb *echoo*, meaning "have." It means to possess securely, to hold, to keep. If they held or possessed what? There is no object of the verb, yet since the object right along has been the Gospel, it is safe to assume that the Apostle is referring to the same object. "If ye hold or possess the gospel," or "If ye keep on holding or possessing the gospel."

Why does Paul add this hypothetical clause? No doubt he had reason to believe that some of these Corinthians merely thought they had the Gospel, when in reality they did not. Many people are deluded into thinking they are Christians, when actually they have not accepted the Gospel at all. What *is* the Gospel in essence? It is the good news that though all men were and are sinners, and therefore under sentence of death, Christ paid the penalty for their sins on the cross, so that all who would come to Him in faith and repentance, and accept His atonement for their sins, might be delivered from death and receive eternal life.

From the argument that follows about the resurrection in the 15th chapter of First Corinthians, we can safely deduce that Paul believes men cannot claim to be Christians, possessing the Gospel, and at the same time doubt the fact of the resurrection of the Lord Jesus Christ and the general resurrection that follows.

"You are saved if you possess the Gospel I preached unto you," Paul's argument goes, "unless ye have believed in vain." This follows on the heels of the previous hypothesis. If you do not now possess the Gospel, then you must have believed in vain. Does this mean that the Gospel was ineffective and without result in their lives? Not at all. In verse 1 the Apostle very clearly sets forth the order of operation of the Gospel: "I preached it, you welcomed it, you have stood on it, and it is continuously the means of your salvation." If you don't possess it now, that means that you exercised the wrong kind of faith and therefore believed in vain. Perhaps it was merely intellectual assent, an acknowledgment that Jesus Christ is indeed the Son of God who died for the sins of the world, but your heart was not in it and so it did not transform your life. The Apostle James describes this kind of faith when he says, "Thou believest that there is one God; thou doest well: the devils also believe, and tremble" (James 2:19). (See the author's *The Labor of Love*, pp. 25-31, Eerdmans: 1960).

Paul wants to make it clear that the kind of faith he will be speaking about in the ensuing verses is not an empty profession of belief without a corresponding life of holiness, but faith resulting in the works of faithfulness or fidelity to God and man, that is, a living, operative faith. What kind of faith is yours? If it has made no change in your attitudes and actions, bringing them ever more closely into conformity to the Gospel of Jesus Christ, then you have good reason to doubt its validity.

THE SCRIPTURES: HANDLE WITH CARE!

"For I delivered unto you first of all that which I also received" (I Cor. 15:3a).

Perhaps the most frustrating patients a doctor has to deal with are those who consult him about their ailments, receive a diagnosis, accept his prescription, have it filled by their druggist, and then, after a few doses, stop taking the medicine. Sometimes they even have the effrontery to blame the doctor because they feel no better!

The Apostle Paul must have felt something like these doctors when he wrote his First Epistle to the Corinthians. It was apparent that some in the Corinthian Church did not possess the Gospel because they had believed in vain. Paul was intent on absolving not only the Gospel but also himself from any blame for the ineffectiveness of anyone's belief.

You recall that in the parable of the sower, the difference in results was due to the variety of the ground on which the seed fell. The sower and the seed were the same in each case. It is how the Gospel is accepted that makes the difference. If the Gospel was not productive in the lives of some of the Corinthians, it was their own fault. Paul clears himself of blame in chapter 15, verse 3, when he says, "For I delivered unto you first of all that which I also received."

The doctrinal implications of this verse are most important. First, Paul makes it clear that he did not add anything to the Gospel of Jesus Christ. "I delivered . . . that which I . . . received." Received from whom? Not the Church, that is evident. He did not receive the Gospel from the first ecclesiastical apostolic council of Jerusalem, but from the Lord Jesus Christ Himself. Even as an apostle, Paul had no authority to add anything to the Gospel. The source is the Lord Jesus Christ alone. Likewise, no church, denomination, group, or individual has any authority to add to or subtract from the Gospel as originally proclaimed by the Lord Jesus Christ. Paul did not make the Gospel, but the Gospel made Paul.

It is deceptive and blasphemous for anyone to claim that Scripture, that which constitutes the Gospel, which bears the approval of the Lord Jesus Christ, was either originated by the Church or is subservient to the Church (and by that they mean their own church) because the Church came before the Scriptures. If it were not for Christ and the Gospel He proclaimed, there would be no Church, and no church can truly be the Church of Jesus Christ that is not founded on the Lord Himself and His teachings as found in the Scriptures and validated by Him.

The Lord told His disciples that all truth, in order to be truth, must originate from Him, even that revealed by the Holy Spirit. "I have yet many things to say unto you," He declared, "but ye cannot bear them now. Howbeit when he, the Spirit of truth, is come, he will guide you into all truth: for he shall not speak of himself; but *whatsoever he shall hear*, that shall he speak: and he will shew you things to come. He shall glorify me: for *he shall receive of mine*, and shall shew it unto you" (John 16:12-14).

Furthermore He declared that the Holy Spirit was

to be faithful in transmitting the message of the Lord Jesus Christ: "But the Comforter, which is the Holy Ghost, whom the Father will send in my name, he shall teach you all things, and bring all things to your remembrance, *whatsoever I have said unto you*" (John 14:26). And in John 15:26, in speaking of the Holy Spirit, the Lord says, "He shall testify of me."

If the Lord Jesus requires faithfulness of transmittal of His will and words even from the Holy Spirit, how much more must He require it of those human beings whom He selected to transmit His message. Because He expected such absolute fidelity from His disciples and apostles in this matter, He gave them authority to speak on His behalf. That is why He said, "He that heareth you heareth me; and he that despiseth you despiseth me" (Luke 10:16). This authority was based on the assumption that they would act as faithful conveyors of His truth and not as innovators of their own concepts of truth.

This authority was given only to those who were personally called by the Lord (John 6:70) and who followed His earthly life and ministry (John 15:27). The Scriptures transmitted by those who had this personal knowledge of the Lord, with its inherent authority, were to be maintained intact and unaltered by all who later formed the Body of Christ. The Apostles first preached this Gospel meticulously and faithfully by word of mouth. It was complete as they themselves received it from the Lord. So that it might not later be altered through oral transmission, they wrote it down. Jude exhorted the Christians "that ye should earnestly contend for the faith which was *once* delivered unto the saints" (v. 3). The word translated "once" in Greek is *hapax*, which could better be rendered "once and for all."

No additions to or subtractions from the apostolic teaching were permitted. Faithful preservation was commanded. "That good thing which was committed unto thee keep by the Holy Ghost which dwelleth in us," wrote Paul to young Timothy (II Tim. 1:14). We read of the first disciples, "And they continued stedfastly in the apostles' doctrine and fellowship" (Acts 2:42). Paul says that those who have entered the household of God "are built upon the foundation of the apostles and prophets, Jesus Christ himself being the chief corner stone" (Eph. 2:20).

But how could Paul claim to be an apostle, that is, one who had personal knowledge of Christ and was called by Him during our Lord's earthly life and ministry? Paul was not even a believer when our Lord walked this earth. How could he say, then, "I delivered unto you first of all that which I also received?" The Lord revealed Himself in a special and supernatural way to Paul on the road to Damascus. That is why Paul can say, "Am I not an apostle? . . . have I not seen Jesus Christ our Lord?" (I Cor. 9:1). *Seeing the Lord was a prerequisite of apostleship.* That is why Paul challenged some of the Corinthians who were falsely claiming apostolic authority, "Are all apostles?" (I Cor. 12:29). The implication, of course, was that they were not.

Paul further pledges Timothy to a faithful transmittal of what he had taught him. "And the things that thou hast heard of me among many witnesses, the same commit thou to faithful men, who shall be able to teach others also" (II Tim. 2:2). The all-important thing was that the teaching of the Lord should be faithfully transmitted by the apostles, those who personally saw the Lord. If any later teaching of a person or church disagrees with this apostolic teaching, it is to be rejected as false. "But though we, or an angel from heaven, preach any other gospel unto you than that which we have preached unto you, let him be accursed" (Gal. 1:8).

The story is told of an overzealous preacher back in the 1800's, that in order to convince his congregation that the current hairstyle of women, featuring an elaborate topknot, was un-Scriptural, he preached a sermon on "Topknot, come down," alleging that he took his text from Matthew 24:17. When the curious in his congregation looked up the text afterward, they found that it was part of the Lord's discourse on the last days, and read in full, "Let him which is on the house top not come down." This is amusing, of course, but it serves to illustrate a dangerous practice—that of tampering with Scripture. Scripture is so often misquoted and misapplied that we must constantly be on our guard. The best way to do this is to become so thoroughly grounded in the Word of God ourselves that we shall not be misled.

IS RELIGIOUS TRADITION AS VALID AS SCRIPTURE?

"For I delivered unto you first of all that which I also received" (I Cor. 15:3a).

The way some people handle Scripture is similar to the way that Procrustes, an unscrupulous innkeeper of ancient times, treated the travelers who came to lodge at his house. Instead of accepting them as God had made them, he would make their stature conform to the size of his bed, either by stretching them out if they were too short, or cutting some part of them off if they were too long. Let us beware of the heretical tendency, either in others or ourselves, of adding to or subtracting from the Scriptures in order to accommodate our own point of view, or to promote any supposed new truth that bursts upon the scene from time to time.

When the Apostle Paul first delivered the Gospel to the people of Corinth, it was not in his written epistles, which came later, but in oral form—in the sermons he preached to them during the course of the eighteen months that he spent in Corinth at the end of his second missionary journey (Acts 18:11). These sermons were their introduction to Christianity, but we have no written record of their content. Paul was greatly concerned that what he delivered to the people might be preserved without adulteration. We see this in Second Thessalonians 2:15, where he writes, "Therefore, brethren, stand fast, and hold the *traditions* which ye have been taught, whether *by word*, or *our epistle*."

Much misunderstanding clusters around the word "traditions." Some Christian churches consider these as extra-Biblical teachings, doctrines formulated not by Christ and the Apostles but by the Church, by men and councils that followed the apostolic era. But clearly this could not be what the Apostle Paul meant by "traditions" here. If we look at the opening word in the original Greek of First Corinthians 15:3, we find it is *paredooka*, "I delivered." "For I delivered unto you," says Paul, "that which I also received" (that is, the Gospel). This is the same word to which "tradition" (*paradosis*) is related in Second Thessalonians 2:15. Thus we see that the noun *paradosis*, "tradition," actually means "that which is delivered." In the sense in which it is used in the New Testament, it is not to be taken to mean the pronouncements of a church, a denomination, a council, or a man, but as the revelation of God delivered by a specific apostle. The teaching of the Lord Jesus is the tradition of the Lord Jesus. The tradition of the apostles is that which was delivered by the apostles. It is not a nebulous or abstract thing, but a very concrete one.

The teaching of the Lord Jesus and the apostles was delivered in two ways, orally and in written form. It is a mistake to call the oral teaching "tradition" and the written teaching "Scriptures." It is all tradition in that it was delivered directly by the Lord Jesus and the apostles.

How careful Paul is, as he writes to the Corinthians, to keep the record straight. "For I delivered unto you first of all that which I also received." He wanted to dispel any impression that his teaching originated with himself. Even as the apostle to whom the Lord Jesus appeared individually and miraculously after His ascension, he disclaimed any thought of setting himself up as the originator of what he taught. He was acting as Christ's transmitting agent. How deceived, then, are those men who have subsequently claimed an authority that the Apostle Paul would not arrogate to himself .

Since it is obvious that a great deal of what Christ and the apostles taught was not written down, should we conclude that the Scriptures as we have them are sufficient and complete? Or shall we accept the unwritten traditions that have grown up since that time as having equal force and authority? Professing Christianity is divided on this important issue. One branch claims that the Church is the final authority, that it existed before the Bible (referring particularly to the New Testament), and therefore puts the stamp of authority on the Bible, and not vice versa. The opposing branch says that the Bible is our absolute authority, and that no church has the right to add to or subtract from the written Word of God. Any oral tradition must be subservient to the written tradition; if it disagrees with Scripture it must be rejected as spurious.

The preaching of the apostles was considered fundamental, adequate, and complete by the early Christians. That they considered it a criterion of genuineness is shown by Acts 2:42, "And they continued stedfastly in *the apostles' doctrine* and fellowship." Years afterward, when Paul wrote to the Ephesians, he told them they were "built upon the foundation of the apostles and prophets, Jesus Christ himself being the chief corner stone" (Eph. 2:20). Many and various were the teachings that sprang up at that time, introduced by men other than the apostles. But if these were not in agreement with the apostolic teaching of which Christ was the cornerstone, they were to be rejected.

It is interesting to note that when the Epistle to the Ephesians was written around A.D. 60-61, the following books of the New Testament had been completed: James, Galatians, Mark, First and Second Thessalonians, probably Matthew, First and Second Corinthians, Romans, Colossians, Philemon, Philippians, Luke, and the Acts. The book we are studying now, First Corinthians, was written in A.D. 55, at which time heresies had begun to arise such as Gnosticism and legalism; although God knows what else was about to erupt, as we see from Paul's own prediction to the Ephesian elders that "of your own selves shall men arise, speaking perverse things, to draw away disciples after them" (Acts 20:30). Paul's First Epistle to the Corinthians is one of the first New Testament books written. Only the two short letters to the Thessalonians were penned before it, the Gospels and other Epistles being written afterward. (See *International Standard Bible Encyclopedia*.)

The Church of Jesus Christ, that is, those believers who lived during apostolic times and later, was never commissioned or given the liberty to add to or subtract from what had been committed to the apostles by the Lord Jesus Christ. In writing to Timothy, Paul says, "That good thing which was committed unto thee keep by the Holy Ghost which dwelleth in us" (II Tim. 1:14). The only responsibility of the true Church of Jesus Christ as far as its teaching is concerned is to transmit exactly what Christ and His immediately commissioned apostles taught, without alteration. "And the things that thou hast heard of me among many witnesses, *the same* commit thou to faithful men, who shall be able to teach others also" (II Tim. 2:2). The way of salvation has been sealed once and for all, and no church, council, or individual may add anything or subtract anything. If an apostle of the stature of Paul said, "But though we, or an angel from heaven, preach any other gospel unto you than that which we have preached unto you, let him be accursed" (Gal. 1:8), who are we to presume to tamper with what has been revealed?

The Lord Jesus Christ never appealed to tradition outside the Scriptures, and in fact condemned the Pharisees, saying, "Thus have ye made the commandment of God of none effect by your tradition" (Matt. 15:6). The unreliability of oral transmission necessitated the Scriptures. It was in the Old Testament that the people of Christ's day looked to find out about the coming Messiah, not to oral tradition. "Ye search the scriptures, for in them ye think ye have eternal life," said Christ, "and these are they that testify of me" (John 5:39). Far from denying their belief that the Scriptures were the source of teaching about eternal life, Christ emphatically declared that they did indeed speak of Him, who is the way, the truth, and the life.

The apostles never referred to the fulfillment of oral prophecies, but always of those contained in the

Old Testament Scriptures, even if originally oral. John in his Gospel acknowledges that not everything that Christ said and did was written down, but what was necessary for salvation was written (John 20:30, 31). Therefore what was not written could not have been as important as what was written. In the matter of choice, the written would stand as against the oral. The written tradition, the Scriptures, is our criterion or yardstick. Any oral teaching concerning Christianity must be measured against it. When Paul preached to the Bereans, they did exactly that; they examined the oral teachings of Paul in the light of the written teachings of the Old Testament. They "searched the scriptures daily, whether those things were so" (Acts 17:11). That is what we must do in formulating our own faith and determining the genuineness of any doctrines we are called upon to accept.

THE MAN WHO DIED FOR YOU

"For I delivered unto you first of all that which I also received, how that Christ died for our sins according to the scriptures" (I Cor. 15:3).

During the funeral procession of Abraham Lincoln, a Negro mother, standing behind the crowd of white people, held her baby high above her head as the martyred President's body pa**ed, and said, "Take a long look at him, son; that's the man who died for you."

That's what the Apostle Paul said in effect when he wrote to the Corinthian Christians; it is what he says to all Christians: "Take a long look at Christ. He is the one who died for you." Will you do that? And may I especially invite all of you to whom Christ's death still means nothing personally to take a long look? That look may show you the liberty you have unknowingly desired and the peace of heart that you cannot find anywhere or in any thing.

That Christ died is a proven historical fact. It took place around A.D. 30, as recorded by the pagan historian Tacitus, who wrote seventy or eighty years afterward that one Christ was put to death under Tiberius by Pontius Pilate. Two other ancient historians, Suetonius and Pliny, also refer to Him. And here in First Corinthians we have a letter written by the Apostle Paul in A.D. 55, whose genuineness is admitted even by some skeptical liberal historians and theologians. Christ did die. But how are we to account for this event? Why has it made such a stir down through the course of twenty centuries?

We find this historical event, along with our Lord's resurrection, to be the central and most conspicuous fact of the New Testament. One-fourth of the Gospels are devoted to the story of Christ's death. A thousand interesting events of His career are passed over, a thousand discourses are never mentioned, in order that there may be abundant room for the telling of His death. This is very strange indeed, if Jesus was nothing but an illustrious teacher.

In fact, in the letters that make up the last half of the New Testament, there is scarcely a quotation from the lips of Jesus. Again, how strange, if Jesus was only the world's greatest teacher. These letters seem not at all concerned with the fact that He was a teacher or reformer, but they are saturated with references to His death and its significance. What is the reason for this particular emphasis? A study of the New Testament will convince us that Jesus had trained His disciples to see in His sufferings and death the climax of God's revelation of love to the world. The keynote of the whole Gospel story is struck by John the Baptist in his bold declaration about Christ, "Behold the Lamb of God, which taketh away the sin of the world" (John 1:29). The lamb in Palestine was a notable sacrificial animal, used in ceremonial atonement for sin.

As soon as Jesus began His public ministry, He began to refer in enigmatic phrases to His death. He did not declare it openly, for people's minds at large were not yet prepared to regard the Messiah as a sacrificial lamb but as an earthly king. However, the thought of His death was wrapped up inside of all Jesus said. When Nicodemus came to Him at night to talk with Him about His work, Jesus said to him, "As Moses lifted up the serpent in the wilderness, even so must the Son of man be lifted up" (John 3:14), referring to His hanging on the cross.

The Lord went into the temple and drove out the money changers who had made it a den of thieves; and when an angry mob gathered He calmly said, "Destroy this temple, and in three days I will raise it up" (John 2:19). The mob thought He referred to the temple building, but He really spoke of the sanctuary of His body, its death and resurrection. While in Capernaum He said, "The bread that I will give is my flesh, which I will give for the life of the world" (John 6:51). In Jerusalem He said, "I am the good shepherd: the good shepherd giveth his life for the sheep" (John 10:11). To the Greeks who came to see Him, He said, "I, if I be lifted up from the earth, will draw all men unto me" (John 12:32). The people to whom He thus spoke could hardly understand Him, but later they realized that He was referring to His crucifixion.

To His nearest friends, however, Jesus spoke more openly. "From that time forth," said Matthew, "began Jesus to shew unto his disciples, how that he must go unto Jerusalem, and suffer many things . . . and be killed" (Matt. 16:21). It is surprising how many times it is stated in the Gospels that Jesus told His disciples He must be killed. "The Son of man came not to be ministered unto, but to minister, and to give his life a ransom for many" (Matt. 20:28). "Ye know that after two days is the feast of the passover, and the Son of man is betrayed to be crucified" (Matt. 26:2). "This is my body which is given for you" (Luke 22:19). "This is my blood of the new testament, which is shed for many for the remission of sins" (Matt. 26:28). It is evident that the Lord Jesus wanted to impress very firmly upon His followers the fact that He was laying down His life for them.

The Apostle Paul also stresses Christ's death in his Epistles: "For I delivered unto you first of all that which I also received," he writes to the Corinthian believers, "how that Christ died for our sins according to the scriptures" (I Cor. 15:3). The Greek verb *apethanen*, "died," is in the aorist tense, indicative mood, which indicates that Christ did this once and for all, in the realm of history. As far as He is concerned, it is over and done with. He will not do it again. It was a positive, absolute fact, engraved in immortal letters on the tablets of time, which no discussion or argument could ever wipe out. But Paul is not merely teaching history here but doctrine. It is the purpose for which Christ died that makes His crucifixion of vital importance to you and me. "Christ died for our sins" is the burden of Paul's message. It is a statement that revolutionizes life.

It was not merely Herod and Pontius Pilate, the Gentiles and the people of Israel, who put Christ to death, but our sins, yours, mine, everybody's. It was the sin of all of us that slew Him.

In His own person, He took upon Himself the guilt and the punishment for our sins. Having borne our sins, He relieves us of their burden. He died *for* our

— 33 —

sins that we might not have to die *in* our sins. He consented to be slain by our sins, that they might not slay us. The Apostle Paul states this clearly when he says, "Christ died for our sins." The preposition "for" is the translation of the Greek word *huper*, which here means "by reason of, for the sake of, on account of." To die for our sins is to be subjected to the curse of the law; it is to bear the wrath of the lawgiver and judge. It is to suffer what Christ suffered when He uttered that exceedingly bitter cry, "My God, my God, why hast thou forsaken me?" (Matt. 27:46).

There were three attitudes displayed by those who watched Christ. Some, like the soldiers, regarded His sufferings with apathy and indifference. A second group—the priests, Pharisees, and various mockers—cried out "Away with him!" Their attitude was one of hatred. And the third group, a small one, was composed of those who viewed Christ's death with wholehearted sympathy. Some of them would gladly have taken His place if they could.

Apathy, antipathy, sympathy! Where do you fit in? With the soldiers, with the mockers, or with the disciples? Are you indifferent to Him, do you hate Him, or do you love Him? He died for your sins, that you might live eternally. The choice is yours, to take Him by simple faith and dependence as your Saviour and be freed from the guilt, the power, and the penalty of sin.

WHICH SAVES — CHRIST'S LIFE OR HIS DEATH?

"Christ died for our sins according to the scriptures" (I Cor. 15:3b).

The mother of Bernard M. Baruch, adviser to presidents, often attended the services of those great preachers, Thomas Dixon and Henry Ward Beecher. Someone asked her, "How is it that you, a Jewess, go into a church where the worship of Christ is part of the creed?" She replied, "If He was not divine, all His actions, His life, and His death were." The question for any sincere man to ask is this: "Has there been another person like Him, who lived like Him, who died the way He did, who rose from the dead by His own power, and who was seen by many after His resurrection?"

Paul, in writing to the Corinthians, wants to make one thing known to them: "I declare unto you the Gospel," he tells them in First Corinthians 15:1, adding the clause, "which I delivered unto you" in verse 3. That these two are connected is evident in the Greek, for the relative pronoun *ho* with which verse 3 begins agrees with the neuter gender of the word *euangelion*, "the gospel."

So that there should be no misunderstanding as to what the Gospel is, Paul proceeds to mention four items about Christ that constitute the Gospel, in verses 3-8.

1) "That Christ died for our sins according to the Scriptures;

2) "And that he was buried,

3) "And that he rose again the third day according to the scriptures:

4) "And that he was seen of Cephas, then of the twelve: after that, he was seen of above five hundred brethren at once; of whom the greater part remain unto this present, but some are fallen asleep. After that, he was seen of James; then of all the apostles. And last of all he was seen of me also, as of one born out of due time."

It is significant that the Apostle Paul does not make reference here to the life of the Lord Jesus Christ, wonderful and unique though it was. Why? Because His life was necessary only to achieve the purpose for which He was born—which was to die. His death and not His life was the ultimate aim of His incarnation. It was His death that reconciled man to God, and not His life. If it were not for the necessity of His death in effecting the forgiveness of our sins and our reconciliation to God, Christ could simply have lived out His life, with all its miracles, signs, and wonders, and then ascended into heaven. The Lord did not have to die in the same sense that you and I must die. He died because He chose to, and that choice was not suicide but sacrifice. His death was necessary for us, and His life was necessary for His death. If we expect people to be saved from their sins, we must always preach the death of Christ. The knowledge or even the imitation of His life cannot save anyone.

But what about Paul's statement in Romans 5:10, "We shall be saved by his life"? Isn't this a contradiction of First Corinthians 15:3, where he says, "Christ died for our sins"? Not if we take into consideration the whole of Romans 5:10. By taking part of a verse out of context, you can prove almost anything, but this is an ignorant and deceiving way of handling the Word of God. Listen to the whole of Romans 5:10: "For if, when we were enemies, we were reconciled to God by the death of his Son, much more, being reconciled, we shall be saved by his life." Paul states clearly that as enemies and strangers to God the only way we can become reconciled to Him is through the death of His Son, the Lord Jesus Christ. That death brings us life— the life of Christ; for Christ did not remain dead, He rose again; and it is not a dead Christ who now indwells us, but the living Christ in His resurrection power.

It is this indwelling of the living Christ in the heart of the former enemy of God, who has been reconciled through the death of Christ, to which the Apostle refers. In fact, the Greek text of the last clause of Romans 5:10 should rather be translated, "We shall be saved *in* his life," that is, His resurrection life and His intercession as Mediator. Paul leaves no room for anyone to believe that because we have been saved by the death of Christ, our Lord is still dead. Praise God, He is very much alive. It is this which the Apostle sets out to prove in this great 15th chapter of First Corinthians.

Of course, the word "save" (*soozoo* in Greek) must not always be taken to mean salvation in the sense of redemption from our original sin, when as individuals we first appropriated the death of Christ in our conversion experience. Many times it refers to His power to deliver us from the power and dominion of sin. If I may put it this way: The death of Christ saves us from *sin*, while His life gives us victory over *sins*, because of the victory of His resurrection and intercession. Only as we are in Christ's life, and Christ is our life, do we experience this wonderful victory over the sins that so easily beset us in this world.

More particularly in Romans 5:9 and 10 Paul speaks of two kinds of salvation — the first from the penalty of sin and the second from the dominion of sin. The first is accomplished through the death of Christ and the second through the living Christ. But the verb in both verses is *sootheesometha*, "we shall be saved," in the future passive tense, indicating that there is a time coming when the living Christ will save us from a fate that will befall others. This is brought out clearly in verse 9b, "We shall be saved from wrath through him." This is the wrath of God's judgment upon all who have not been reconciled to Him. Those who have been reconciled to Him by the death of Christ are the only ones who will also be saved from the judgment of God.

Thus we find that the Gospel that Paul preached is not a Gospel that declares that every person who ever lived shall ultimately be saved. It is, however, the Gospel of universal offer, stating that "whosoever will" may come (Rev. 22:17), but at the same time it is the Gospel of individual acceptance and then of individual judgment. And the good news (which is what the word "Gospel" really means) is that we need not live in dreadful anticipation of God's wrath which will one day be revealed. There is escape from it here and now. This escape not only delivers us from the wrath of a future judgment but also gives us victory in every encounter with sin, because Christ ever lives to make intercession for us. "We shall be saved in his life." The joy of such victory can be almost as great as that original experience of being reconciled to God. But it is possible (although in the power of the living Christ and through the Holy Spirit it could be avoided) that we may not always be victorious over sins of commission, omission, and disposition. What then? What avails the death or the life of Christ? "The blood of Jesus Christ his Son cleanseth us from all sin" (I John 1:7). That is, it cleanses us from all sin when we first believe, and from every subsequent defeat that we may suffer from the enemy of our souls, the devil—or his best ally, self.

A brilliant young college student contracted polio. "With such a misfortune, how can you be so cheerful?" asked a friend. "How can you face the world so confidently and without bitterness?" Smiling, the young man said, "You see, it never touched my heart." Having once been cleansed by the blood of the Lamb of God, this young man was possessed by the risen, living Christ. Any temptation from without or within was met by the new tenant of his heart, Jesus Christ.

As Vance Havner says, "If we resist the devil without first submitting ourselves to God, he will fly at us and not from us." "Submit yourselves therefore to God. Resist the devil, and he will flee from you" (James 4:7). You may have been saved by the death of Christ, but are you experiencing constant and recurring salvation in His life?

A PREDICTED AND PURPOSEFUL DEATH

"Christ died for our sins according to the scriptures; and . . . he was buried, and . . . he rose again the third day according to the scriptures" (I Cor. 15:3b, 4).

When you and I were born into the world, our birth was anticipated for only a few months in advance. And though we must all die, no one will be able to tell us in advance exactly how and when this event will take place. The purpose of our life will not be fulfilled in our dying, but will have been realized during the course of our years on earth. This is the normal and anticipated course of human life.

With one exception, that is. Christ's birth, death, burial, and resurrection were the confirmation and fulfillment of special predictions given by God centuries before and recorded in the Old Testament. And the purpose of Christ's life was fulfilled in His death on the cross, when He paid the penalty of man's sin and made it possible for him to be reconciled to God.

Why does the Apostle Paul so emphatically refer twice to the fact that Christ's death, burial, and resurrection took place "according to the scriptures"? It is not only that the Scriptures authenticate Christ as the Messiah, but that Christ's supernatural conception and birth, His miracle-working life, and His death, burial, and resurrection place the seal of authority on the Old Testament Scriptures.

The Lord often chided the religionists of His day for their oral traditions, but He never chided them for their belief in the Scriptures which were given to them by inspiration. Everything the Lord Jesus did and said lent authority to the Scriptures of the Old Testament. And they merit that authority precisely because of the fact that the Lord Jesus Christ is the central and most authoritative person of history. Only if a human being could have the same record as the Lord Jesus would he have the right to ascribe supreme authority to a book. Paul himself could not have accepted the testimony of the Old Testament Scriptures in relation to Christ, had it not been for the authentication of the supernatural character of the Lord Jesus.

The Lord Jesus referred to the Old Testament Scriptures to show that they had inherent authority in all that they announced. And since they were true about all that concerned Himself, they must be true in their totality. It was the Lord who said, "Behold, we go up to Jerusalem, and all things that are written by the prophets concerning the Son of man shall be accomplished. For he shall be delivered unto the Gentiles, and shall be mocked, and spitefully entreated, and spitted on: and they shall scourge him, and put him to death: and the third day he shall rise again" (Luke 18:31-33). Observe that the Lord did not speak of any oral tradition about these things, but of those "things that are written by the prophets." The Lord never lent His sanction to oral traditions but only to those things written once for all by the prophets.

Christ's enemies would never knowingly and willingly have done anything that would enhance Christ's authority. If they had known the prophesied details of His birth and death, they would have done their best to see that they were not fulfilled. They would not have crucified Him, but would have put Him to death in some other way, thus disproving that His death was a fulfillment of prophecy. Yet they did what they did in spite of themselves, for God could not be thwarted, and the authority of His Word must be vindicated even by His enemies.

The connection of the Old Testament prophecies with the Lord Jesus Christ, and with His death in particular, is not merely historical but doctrinal. True, He did die in Jerusalem on a cross, as prophesied; but the reason for His death was also prophesied. Paul's purpose in referring to the Old Testament Scriptures was not merely to prove the historical authenticity of both Christ and the Old Testament, but to indicate the place which the great truth "that he died for our sins" holds in the moral government of God. It was that event that gave birth to Christianity. Christ died; and in consequence of that fact, an old religion of works was shown to be inadequate, and the religion of faith, which was the religion even of Old Testament greats such as Abraham, was fulfilled and made permanent.

But the doctrine, "Christ died for our sins," lifts the fact of Christ's death out of the category of a mere historical event and makes it the embodiment or enacting of the supreme principle in the divine administration. It was "according to the scriptures" that Christ died for our sins, because it was according to the fixed, unalterable rule of the moral government of God, based on His eternal plan that His only Son of the same substance as Himself should once and for all atone perfectly for the sins of men, to which the Scriptures throughout are intended to bear testimony.

The logical conclusion of all this is that he who would save sinners must do so by dying for their sins. This principle is announced throughout the Scriptures, beginning with Genesis 3:15, when God said to the serpent, "I will put enmity between thee and the woman, and between thy seed and her seed; it shall bruise thy head, and thou shalt bruise his heel."

From the beginning, also, the rite of animal sacrifice, accompanied by confession of guilt over the victim's head, proclaimed the same universal, invariable, and indispensable law, that "without shedding of blood is no remission" (Heb. 9:22), that is, the laying down of the life of the innocent for the guilty. Sinners can be saved only through a substitute dying for their sins. The whole Levitical institute, with its vicarious priesthood, its ceremonial ordinances, its continual offering of daily, weekly, monthly, and annual sacrifices of slaughtered victims on behalf of the unclean, kept up the instinctive sense of that righteous rule of the divine government which requires death as the penalty for sin, and the hope also that ere long the rule would have its climactic accomplishment in a worthy ransom being found thus to die. Read the 53rd chapter of Isaiah for a clear picture of Him who was to be wounded for our transgressions and bruised for our iniquities.

The degree of the punishment imposed for any evil is an indication of the degree of that evil. Death is usually the ultimate punishment, and death by crucifixion is the worst of the death punishments (see Deut. 21:22, 23, Gal. 3:13). Therefore the evil for which this punishment is divinely imposed must be the worst. "The wages of sin is death" (Rom. 6:23). Thus the death of Christ asserts and vindicates the exceeding evil and demerit of man's sin. It also indicates the inevitable certainty of judgment and the impossibility of escape otherwise than through the shedding of blood.

Some people say they find it impossible to believe that a loving God would permit the existence of hell. Logically, then, they must believe that everybody goes to heaven, including Judas Iscariot and Hitler. Since they would not be fit for heaven, God would have to re-condition them. This is to do away with values altogether, and with the whole concept of God's integrity and man's responsibility.

Mercy could not and cannot cancel divine justice. The claims of divine law must be met or anarchy reigns. God's love for the sinner cannot overlook His righteous dealing with the transgression of the sinner. None of the attributes of God cancels another. God's law must stand. Somebody must die for your sin— either you or a worthy substitute. Christ—God come down to earth in the form of man—took your place on the cross and died for you. Thus God's justice is satisfied, His law for the redemption of the sinner is fulfilled, and at the same time you are set free if you will accept the work and sacrifice of Christ on your behalf.

An elderly man became so worried and fidgety in court that his lawyer, thinking to comfort him, said, "Don't worry, Charlie, I'll see that you get justice." "It's not justice I need," replied Charlie, "it's mercy!"

As you stand before the bar of God, what is it that you really want? Is it justice? That means death because of your sins. But if with a repentant heart you seek mercy, you can have it, for "Christ died for our sins according to the scriptures."

A FUNERAL FORETOLD IN DETAIL

"He was buried . . . ." (I Cor. 15:4a).

When heroes and leaders die, assembled multitudes follow them to their graves. But when the Son of God died, not even His disciples attended His funeral procession. "He was buried," says the Apostle Paul in First Corinthians 15:4. He does not tell us by whom and under what circumstances. But that one word in Greek, *etaphee,* "He was buried," is most comprehensive. Paul invites us to attend the funeral of the Lord Jesus Christ. Whom shall we find there? In the very first hour of His sufferings, the disciples had all forsaken Him and fled, and now that He is dead they leave His body to be mourned over and buried by others. We may take comfort from the thought that, though our closest relatives and friends may desert us in the hour of our greatest suffering and need, we can have faith in God to provide in totally unexpected quarters those who will love us and stand by us.

Who was it that proved to be faithful to the Lord in the hour of His death? A few humble women, and two men—Nicodemus, a ruler of the Jews, and Joseph of Arimathea, who were both afraid to acknowledge the Saviour when He was living and manifesting His greatness and miracle-working power. But now, when the glory appears to have departed, they are at the cross to avow their attachment to Him, and they prove fearless in testifying of their love. One goes boldly to Pilate, and from him to the cross, to claim the body of Jesus; the other brings costly spices to embalm it; and both, in company with the women, lay Him in His grave.

As we follow this little procession to the place of burial, we notice that it is evening—the evening before the sabbath on which the feast of the passover was celebrated, and consequently a season of special devotion. It was "the Jews' preparation day" (John 19:42), and the people were now attending the temple service; but Joseph, Nicodemus, and the women were not among them. They absented themselves in order to perform a necessary act of charit' and love. But as soon as the burial was completed, they rested in accordance with the commandment. All their love for Christ could not bring them back to His tomb until the sabbath was ended; and then, "early, when it was yet dark" (John 20:1), the impatient women came again to the sepulcher to express their grief. Thus did they indulge the ardor of their affection, and at the same time admonish us that we are bound to suppress the strongest and noblest feelings of our nature rather than violate the commands of God.

Where was Christ buried? In a most appropriate place—in a garden on the very hill on which He was crucified. There was a peculiar propriety in laying the Saviour there. It was right that the place where He suffered the greatest shame should be the first scene of His glory; that He should triumph over death on that very hill on which He submitted for a season to its power.

His tomb, we are told, was "a new sepulchre, wherein was never man yet laid" (John 19:41). This was a necessary precaution, lest His enemies claim after His resurrection that it was someone else's body that had come forth from it. This tomb "was hewn in a stone" (Luke 23:53), and a great stone was rolled across the doorway and securely sealed. A body could not be spirited away from such a tomb by an underground passage, or removed by His disciples under the noses of the Roman guard stationed in front of it.

Here, then, a few sorrowful friends laid the mangled body of Jesus, consigning to a sepulcher the One whom they had hoped to see on a throne. Oh, the depth of the Saviour's humiliation! Here we witness the Prince of life, who holds in His hand the keys of hell and of death, and in whom we all "live, and move, and have our being," brought to the dust of death in a borrowed grave. Yet with what loving reverence was He attended and His body prepared for burial. Surely the decent solemnities of a funeral are not displeasing to God. There is a respect due to the body, especially that of a Christian as the temple wherein God has been served and honored. It is designed to be rebuilt in another world, and it ought not to be cast away like common dust in this one.

Since Christ's body was to be raised to life in three days, why was it necessary that it be committed to the grave at all? Why could it not have remained in the home of Joseph of Arimathea as safely as in his sepulcher? The reason is stated by Paul: "He was buried, and . . . he rose again the third day according to the scriptures." The phrase "according to the scriptures" applies both to the burial and to the resurrection. Christ was buried in this manner so that the prophecies concerning Him as the Messiah should be fulfilled. So minute and precise were these prophecies that they not only foretold His incarnation, His passion, and the glorious resurrection that was to follow, but also His burial and the very mode and circumstance of it. His burial in the heart of the earth was prefigured by Jonah's enforced stay for three days and three nights inside the great fish; and Isaiah had expressly declared concerning Him, that He "made his grave with the wicked, and with the rich in his death" (Isa. 53:9).

Under the circumstances, it seemed humanly impossible for these prophecies concerning Christ's burial to be fulfilled. The Roman law, under which the Saviour was put to death, allowed no interment to the bodies of those who died on the cross; and lest any pitying hand should take their bodies from the tree and cover them with earth, a guard was usually stationed around them for several days.

We are accordingly told by Matthew that the centurion, and those that were with him, still remained on the hill of Calvary, watching Jesus, after He had given up the ghost (Matt. 27:50-56). And even if this difficulty could be surmounted, there was another obstacle to be removed before He could have an honorable burial. The Jews had a public burial place for all who died as criminals, and if any interment were allowed to Jesus by the Romans, this pit appeared to be the only grave in which His countrymen would allow Him to rest.

But what are difficulties and obstacles to God? He caused the very people who crucified His Son to prepare the way for the fulfillment of the prophecies that proved His deity and condemned their unbelief. The

Jewish law required that malefactors should be buried on the day of their execution; and to prevent their city from being ceremonially unclean on the succeeding sabbath, certain men besought Pilate that the sufferings of the dying criminals might be ended and their bodies taken down. Pilate granted their request, and no sooner was it granted than the rich and honorable Joseph of Arimathea came forward to rescue the body of Christ from the hands of His enemies and to lay Him in his own new tomb. What infinite wisdom foretold these details; what infinite power fulfilled them! A mighty God never lacks means and instruments to fulfill His purposes. He often passes by those whom we might expect to be employed in His service and singles out others who will perform His will with the greatest glory to Himself.

You and I, who were not there the day Christ died, may find it easy to condemn the cowardice of His disciples. But if we are honest with ourselves we must admit that sometimes we show no more courage in following Him openly today. The preaching of the cross is still an offense to those who make a god out of such beggarly elements of this world as money, power, human reason. Yet we dare preach nothing else to them if we are to be faithful to the purpose for which Christ died—the salvation of men's souls.

CONQUERING OUR FEAR OF DEATH

"Christ died for our sins according to the scriptures; and ... he was buried, and ... he rose again the third day according to the scriptures" (I Cor. 15:3, 4).

"What did you do to our daughter?" asked a Moslem woman whose child had died at the age of sixteen. "We did nothing," answered a Christian missionary. "Oh, yes, you did," persisted the mother. "She died smiling. Our people do not die like that." The girl had found Christ and believed in Him a few months before. Fear of death had gone. Hope, giving birth to joy, had replaced it.

How differently unbelievers regard death. The grave to them is the end of all hope. Sir Thomas Scott, an atheist, in dying said, "Until this moment I thought there was neither a God nor a hell. Now I know and feel that there are both, and I am doomed to perdition by the just judgment of the Almighty." And M. F. Rich, another atheist, cried, "I have given my immortality for gold; and its weight sinks me into an endless, hopeless, helpless hell!"

When the Apostle Paul wrote his great treatise on the resurrection of the Lord Jesus, why do you suppose he felt it necessary to emphasize that "he was buried"? Wouldn't a dead person ordinarily be buried? Paul's motive was not only to prove that Christ's burial fulfilled the prophecies of the Old Testament about Him, but that it also proved the reality of His death. Without real physical death, there could have been no resurrection. Had Christ been restored to life on the cross, or while His body was in the possession of His friends, it might have been said that He had never really died; that though life appeared to be extinct within Him, the vital principle still remained. His burial guarded against all such insinuations.

May it not also be that Christ was buried so that through His burial He could bring comfort to His people in the prospect of death? We shrink from the silence and darkness of the grave, and need some special source of comfort to support our trembling steps on their way to it. Now Christ assures us that we may venture securely where He has gone unhurt before. To the unconverted man, the region of death is a land of darkness; but when the Christian beholds his Redeemer entering it as his Forerunner, and passing through it in triumph to a world of light, he no longer heeds the gloom. Instead he sings with David, "Though I walk through the valley of the shadow of death, I will fear no evil: for thou art with me" (Ps. 23:4).

Christ crossed the river of death and the grave so that you and I as believers, whose sins have been forgiven, may not have to cross that river alone. The story is told of a shepherd who tried to induce his sheep to cross a swiftly flowing stream. Sheep are naturally afraid of rapidly running water, and he could not get them to cross until he picked up a lamb and stepped with it into the river, bearing it carefully and tenderly to the opposite shore. When the mother saw her lamb had gone, she forgot her fear and stepped into the rushing current and was soon safely on the other side. All the rest of the flock followed her leadership. Thus we follow our leader, Christ, and those of our loved ones whom He has already carried safely over to the other shore.

As we Christians attend the funeral of someone who was near and dear to us, what are our feelings? Grief, of course, but also sorrow for all the injuries we have done him and the pain we have given him. Every act of kindness to him is remembered and every impatient word lamented. And has the buried Jesus received no injuries at our hands, and endured no pain on our account? All His suffering was inflicted by us because sins past, present, and future were all one to Him, in that He bore the weight of all sin from the dawn of time until time itself shall be no more. Our sins made Him a man of sorrows; and when He was stricken and afflicted, we sharpened His anguish by hiding our faces from Him, despising and rejecting Him. Oh, let us look on Him whom we have pierced, and mourn!

But at the grave of Christ we may also experience joy, because in His death, as in the death of a loved one, there is aroused in us a desire to be where He is and to behold His glory. We may take comfort in the words of Christ as He spoke of His death to His friends. "Let not your heart be troubled: ye believe in God, believe also in me. In my Father's house are many mansions: if it were not so, I would have told you. I go to prepare a place for you. And if I go and prepare a place for you, I will come again, and receive you unto myself; that where I am, there ye may be also" (John 14:1-3).

This desire to be with Christ, which Paul so often

expressed, ought to cause us to be prepared for that great meeting. It is a sobering reflection that where the body of Jesus went, our bodies must also go. We are all heirs of the grave, and must sooner or later reap our inheritance.

But the thought is robbed of its gloom by the knowledge that it was only Christ's body that was interred, not His soul or spirit. This He gave up to His Father. "He said, It is finished: and he bowed his head, and gave up the ghost" (John 19:30). The Lord, like us, had a soul and a body, an immaterial and a material part. "My soul," He said to His disciples, "is exceeding sorrowful, even unto death" (Matt. 26:38). That soul of Christ that made atonement for our sins, that precious life of Christ that was laid down for us, was happily reunited to the body of our Lord! Death had been conquered by Him for us. In Him, those who believe and receive Him conquer death and the grave!

Have you ever wondered what an atheist can have to say at a deathbed? It must surely be an awkward place for him. A man who thinks this world is all must find it hard to find anything comforting to say to a loved one who is slipping away from life. How consoling if he were to say to his wife, to his child, to his mother, "We are about to part, and to part forever. But don't let that disturb you. Let me remind you that it is a universal law. You are nothing but a chance-composition of organic molecules, nor am I anything more. We shall never have individual consciousness again. But let me tell you, for your comfort, that you will pass into new forms, and sublimely, though unconsciously, last forever!"

By contrast the Christian can speak of dying as home-going; he looks forward to exchanging the sufferings and limitations of earth for the perfection of heaven; and anticipates seeing his loved ones who have gone before, and a future reunion with those who will come after. Above all he knows that he will be in the presence of Jesus Christ, whom he has loved so long without seeing Him. This is what robs death of its fears for the Christian. And this is what Christ secured for us in conquering death.

> Thou knowest He died not for Himself,
>   nor for Himself arose;
> Millions of souls were in His heart,
>   and thee for one He chose.
> Upon the palms of His pierced hands
>   engraven was thy name;
> He for thy cleansing had prepared
>   His water and His flame.
> Sure thou with Him art risen: and now
>   with Him thou must go forth,
> And He will lend thy sick soul health,
>   thy strivings might and worth.
>
>   — KEBLE

WHAT HAPPENS TO THE BODY AND SOUL AFTER DEATH?

"For I delivered unto you first of all that which I also received, how that Christ died for our sins according to the scriptures; and that he was buried, and that he rose again the third day according to, the scriptures"
(I Cor. 15:3, 4).

"When my son died, something died in me," confided a sad-faced woman to a close friend. This is a common reaction to the death of a loved one. When Christ died and was buried, His disciples were crushed with grief. All they had lived for and hoped for was gone; they were hunted men, and they hid themselves for fear. Yet in that death and burial of the Son of God lay their only salvation, as they were to realize later. The burial of the dead Christ was not only a historical event. It had doctrinal significance, a moral purpose in the eternal sovereign plan of God's government.

In the first three verses of the 15th chapter of First Corinthians, we have seen that the primary purpose of Christ's death was redemptive. He took our place on the cross, paying the divinely decreed death penalty for our sins, that we might be set free from the necessity of dying for our own sins, and in our sins. To those who will accept Him as their divine Substitute, He thus becomes the way of eternal salvation.

Secondly, we see that the burial of the believer is symbolized in baptism, as Paul indicates in Romans 6:2-4: "How shall we, that are dead to sin, live any longer therein? Know ye not, that so many of us as were baptized into Jesus Christ were baptized into his death? Therefore we are buried with him by baptism into death: that like as Christ was raised up from the dead by the glory of the Father, even so we also should walk in newness of life."

Again Paul stresses the moral value of our burial with Christ in Colossians 2:11, 12, when he says, "In whom also ye are circumcised with the circumcision made without hands, in putting off the body of the sins of the flesh by the circumcision of Christ: buried with him in baptism, wherein also ye are risen with him through the faith of the operation of God, who hath raised him from the dead."

These are the only two passages of Scripture where the burial of Christ is mentioned in a doctrinal manner. They indicate to us that once we have been redeemed from our sins through Christ's death, burial, and resurrection, our sinful nature is positionally buried and can be buried in actuality, even as was the body of Christ bearing our sins. The Lord provided forgiveness of sin, and as we are buried with Him in our sinful nature we can enjoy victory over sin.

On the Day of Atonement, under the Mosaic Law, two goats were required to typify the work of Christ. One goat was slain and its blood sprinkled as a means of purification and cleansing. The other was used as the "scapegoat," that is, the imputed sins of the people were laid upon it and it was led away into the wilderness to be seen no more. Accordingly, as L. S. Chafer tells us, in Christ's death for the unsaved He not only provided the blood which is efficacious for the cleansing and the judgment of sin, but He also actually took away sin by that same sacrificial blood (John 1:29, Heb. 9:26; 10:4, 9, 12). That final disposition of sin is attested to in His burial. He went into the tomb as a sin offering unto death. He came out completely unrelated to the burden of sin. Such is the doctrinal significance of the words, "and . . . was buried" (I Cor. 15:4).

Later on in this 15th chapter, in discussing the burial of the believer's body even as Christ's body was buried, the Apostle uses the term "sown" instead of "buried." In fact, Paul never seems to use the words "bury" or "burial" in connection with the entombment of believers as such. Romans 6:4 and Colossians 2:12 refer to our judicial burial with Christ. The words "bury" or "burial" seem never to be used in the New Testament in connection with the entombment of a true believer who has died since Christ rose from the dead. The believer's body following death is said to be sown or to sleep, but never to be buried. "It is sown in corruption; it is raised in incorruption: it is sown in dishonour; it is raised in glory: it is sown in weakness; it is raised in power: it is sown a natural body; it is raised a spiritual body" (I Cor. 15:42-44). The only difference between the buried body of Christ and ours is that His did not undergo corruption, while ours does.

By his use of the term "sown" instead of "buried," Paul shows us that the body of the believer, even as Christ's body, is not forgotten in the grave by God. It is sown in the ground as seed is sown. No farmer sows seed to forget it. He sows it in expectation of reaping a crop of far greater worth than the bare seed that was placed there. The believer's body, even as Christ's, must be raised, and will at length be raised at the coming of Christ. (See I Thess. 4:13-18. Also see L. S. Chafer, *Systematic Theology*, Vol. VII, pp. 63-4.)

Our bodies are sown in the ground, but as believers in Christ our souls go immediately to heaven. It is in heaven that Christ's Spirit and His risen body now abide. This to mortal man is an invisible, an untried, an unknown world. We believe it is real because the Lord of heaven came to reveal it to us, even in its generalities.

We read in the first chapter of Acts that after Christ's ascension to heaven, the disciples asked the Lord to choose a successor to Judas Iscariot, who "by transgression fell, that he might go to his own place" (v. 25). At death, each of us goes "to his own place." As Joseph Exell says, in commenting on this verse, "Wicked people need no 'sending to hell,' since they go there of their own accord. The gulf which divides heaven from hell is one of moral unlikeness, and as people have sought the company that suited them here, so they will find themselves in congenial society hereafter. The sinner makes his own damnation, and he cannot blame God with it hereafter."

A father who did not believe in future punishment for sins was telling his children the story of "The Babes in the Wood," when a shrewd little boy looked up and asked, "What became of the little children?" "Oh, they went to heaven, of course!" was the prompt reply. "And what became of the wicked uncle?" It was a poser, and for some moments the father was silent. Finally he said, "Why, he went to heaven, too." "Oh, that's too bad," said the boy, "because I'm afraid he'll kill them all over again." Here is logic in a nutshell, which no wishful thinking can overturn.

Men and women may be divided into three classes — the holy, the utterly depraved, and the in-between. We have little difficulty in seeing that for those who are holy because they have been cleansed in Christ's blood, and love Him and all that pertains to His Kingdom, heaven will be their "own place." Likewise, for the utterly depraved, who reject God and His laws, we can understand why hell should be their "own place." But for those who occupy a medium position, who are more or less moral, what is their "own place" after death? There is only one principle that can make heaven their "own place," and that is affinity with Him who lives in heaven, spiritual union with God in Christ, through the cleansing and regeneration of the Holy Spirit while they are here on earth—thus making them fit for that inheritance of light. (See Joseph Exell, *The Biblical Illustrator*, "Acts," pp. 102-5.)

Everybody goes to his own place. What lies beyond for you depends upon what you do with Jesus Christ in this life—the One who died, was buried, and rose again for you.

THE RESURRECTION—THE BASIS OF CHRISTIANITY

"He was buried, and . . . he rose again the third day according to the scriptures" (I Cor. 15:4).

A missionary wishing to teach a group of Moslems the truth of the resurrection of Christ, said, "I am traveling and come to a place where two roads meet. I look for a guide and see two men: one dead, and the other alive. Which should I ask for direction, the dead or the living?" "The living, of course," answered the people. "Then," said the missionary, "why send me to Mohammed, who is dead, instead of to Christ, who is alive?"

In the first four verses of the 15th chapter of First Corinthians, the Apostle Paul mentions three things about the Lord Jesus Christ: His death, His burial, and His resurrection. The death and burial are mentioned primarily as prerequisites to the resurrection, and for their doctrinal significance.

What made the apostles definitely and finally sure that Jesus was the Son of God, the divinely appointed Messiah, God made manifest in the flesh, was His resurrection. He was "declared to be the Son of God with power," Paul says, "by the resurrection from the dead" (see Rom. 1:4). Christianity and the Church would never have come into being except for the apostles' belief in the Messiahship of Jesus. His death and burial did not contribute to this belief. It was what happened on the third day that made them sure of it. Had things ended at the cross and the tomb, the world would have heard no suggestion that Jesus was the Son of God.

But the hope that had been shattered by the cross revived and became a certainty as a result of the resurrection. To no other doctrine does Paul devote so much space as this.

Observe that the Apostle does not say that *Jesus* died, was buried, and rose again, but that *Christ* underwent these experiences. Why Christ and not Jesus? Because Christ is the name of an office, His Messianic mediatorial office. It means "the anointed one," from the Greek verb *chrioo*, which has primarily a sacred meaning. He was anointed of God, appointed to bear our sins. His death, burial, and resurrection are the fulfillment of God's eternal plan for man's salvation.

We note a significant shift of tense in one of the Greek verbs here. The verbs *apethanen*, "he died," and *etaphee*, "he was buried," are in the aorist tense, active voice, indicative mood, referring to a historic event in the past. But the verb *egeegertai*, translated "he rose," is in the perfect middle or passive tense, which refers to an event having taken place in the past whose effects are evident in the present. It might better be expressed in English by our present perfect tense, "he has risen." The connotation of the Greek verb is that He continues to live.

Paul wrote these statements about twenty-five years after the crucifixion and before any of the Gospel narratives were written. The authorship and date of First Corinthians are among the least disputed of the books of the New Testament. What we find reflected here is the state of things around A.D. 55. The universal Christian teaching, accepted by all the Christian communities, though denied by some members of the Corinthian church, was belief in the resurrection of Jesus Christ. The evidence of First Corinthians is undeniable, because there was a large and formidable body of men in the early Christian Church who were bitterly antagonistic to Paul and who would have been only too glad to convict him, if they could, of any misrepresentation of the usual notions, or divergence from the usual type of teaching. So we may take it as undeniable that the representation of this chapter is historically true; and that within five-and-twenty years of the death of Jesus Christ every Christian community and every Christian teacher believed in and proclaimed the fact of the resurrection.

In an atmosphere so inimical to Paul, could he have successfully introduced between the date of the crucifixion of Christ and twenty-five years later an innovation of such proportions as the resurrection? That is harder to believe than the resurrection itself. Unless the belief that Jesus Christ had risen from the dead originated immediately after the time of His death, the Church would never have sprung up at all. His followers fell to pieces at His crucifixion, as the spokes fall out of a wheel when the hub is removed. What drew them together again into a purposeful and vigorous body of believers? Could a dead Christ ever have been the basis of a living Church? The existence of the Church demands, as a prerequisite, an initial belief in the resurrection. The contemporary Biblical evidence is therefore vital and is sufficiently established.

Now what is the fact of the resurrection? Some say that what actually happened to the body of Christ is unimportant, as long as His Spirit lives on. One of these, Harnack, says, "If the resurrection meant nothing but that a deceased body of flesh and blood came to life again, we should make short work of this tradition." Well, nobody claims that this is all that Scripture teaches concerning the significance of the resurrection. This is simply the historical fact which is the basis for belief in a now-living Christ. We do not maintain either that the resurrection is nothing more than flesh and bones coming alive again. It includes this fact, but it goes beyond it. It seems that Christ's resurrected body may have been bloodless, for "flesh and blood cannot inherit the kingdom of God" (I Cor. 15:50). This is given further weight by Christ's own words to the disciples after His resurrection: "Behold my hands and my feet, that it is I myself: handle me, and see; for a spirit hath not flesh and bones [He does not say 'blood'], as ye see me have" (Luke 24:39).

Like all pious Jews, the disciples at least believed in the survival of the spirit and the future resurrection of the body. They would need no assurance that in that sense Jesus was immortal. To assert that the resurrection means nothing more than a spiritual survival, even with the hope of a future bodily resurrection, is to say that the apostles spent their strength and risked their lives in claiming for Jesus what everyone freely granted in the case of Moses, David, Elijah, Isaiah, and every other good and holy man. But no one can read the New Testament without seeing that the essence of the resurrection story is this: that the apostles claimed for Jesus something that differentiated Him from every other person—however great and good—in human history, something that put Him in a class absolutely by Himself. They do not say simply that His spirit survived—that went without saying. What they say is that, at a certain specific point of time, the morning of the third day, Jesus Christ Himself came back to them. They saw Him and spoke to Him, and subsequently touched Him. They recognized His face and form.

People who say the bodily resurrection does not matter miss the entire point of the narrative. It was not a "subtle spiritual influence" that the apostles talked about. It was not for the mere helpfulness of such an influence that they risked their lives to bear witness. What they announced to the world was this: On the third day the grave was empty, and Jesus Himself, in the totality of His personality, in body and spirit, came back to them. That was the stupendous fact upon which the Christian Church was based; that is the stupendous fact upon which it still stands.

Christianity is not, as some think, a philosophy, a system of moral rules or speculative and ideal doctrines, but stupendous facts relating to a person, out of which flow all its implications. Christ died, He was buried, He rose again, says the Apostle Paul; the central substance of his preaching was Christ. In this respect Christianity differs from all other religious systems: it centers in the person of its Author and cannot exist apart from Him. The teachings of Confucius, of Socrates, of Plato, of Aristotle, or any other teacher, are the same without their authors as with them. Not so with Christianity. If we leave Christ out, it is nothing, no longer to be distinguished from other systems of ordinary philosophers. It is our relationship to Christ that determines whether we are Christians or not. What Scripture teaches about Him is the Gospel, and on our acceptance of this depends our salvation. The center and substance of Christianity is this person, the God-man Jesus Christ—and no preaching, no Gospel, no faith that does not above all present and embrace this Person and what relates exclusively to Him is essentially Christian.

(See Joseph A. Seiss, *Lectures on the Epistles*, pp. 268-80; J. D. Jones, *Things Most Surely Believed*, pp. 84-8; Alexander Maclaren, *I & II Corinthians*, pp. 195-200.)

WAS THE RESURRECTION "WISHFUL THINKING"?

"He rose again the third day according to the scriptures" (I Cor. 15:4).

Two eminent Englishmen, Gilbert West and Lord Littleton, agreed that Christianity should be destroyed. They further agreed that to do this they must disprove the resurrection of Jesus and explain the conversion of Saul in a way that met the demands of skepticism. West assumed the task of getting rid of the resurrection and Littleton that of disposing of the story of Saul's miraculous conversion on the Damascus road. After more than a year, they came together to compare notes, when they found to their mutual surprise and delight that each had been converted to Christianity as a result of his independent research. The resurrection withstood the test of unfriendly but honest investigation, as did also Saul's conversion. May I challenge you not to dismiss them lightly, but to carry on your own personal research with all the mental powers you possess. If, as Christians claim, the Scripture is God-breathed, then the more it is examined the more it will give a sense of self-authentication and inner persuasion to the one who examines it.

Paul was not afraid of Corinthian skepticism and rationalism. In his day, Corinth was a heathen city, many of whose rationalists and materialists sought to strike at the roots of this new religion that had sprung up, by discrediting the resurrection of Jesus Christ. If the resurrection of Christ is disproved or discredited, then the virgin birth becomes incredible and the claims of Christ to be the Son of God are the products of an unsound mind. His death could certainly not avail for the remission of men's sins if the resurrection did not confirm that He was more than a man.

The Book of the Acts contains thirteen sermons delivered to non-believers. Of these, eight or so mention the resurrection of Christ or of the body and the other five or so imply and presuppose it. Paul himself, as the great Apostle to the Gentiles, is the product of the power of Christ's resurrection.

The question is, did the Lord Jesus Christ physically rise from the dead never to die again? We are in court trying to find the truth about this claim. Let us call in the witnesses. But before we admit their testimony, let us first establish their trustworthiness. Few would doubt the honesty of the disciples. Their detractors may brand them fanatics and possibly mistaken, but at least the best scholars agree that the disciples really believed that Christ had risen from the dead. Their critics tell us that they mistook a subjective experience for an objective fact.

One of them puts it this way: "The great myth of Christ's bodily revival is due to the belief on the part of the disciples that such a soul could not become extinct. It was that faith that produced the visions of which the Scripture record tells us." Others, again, tell us that it was the visions that created the faith. The body of Christ, they say, was not raised except in the minds of His followers.

Thus, according to the noted infidel Renan, belief in the resurrection is simply the result of the great creative power of love and enthusiasm. "Heroes," he says, "do not die. That adored Master had filled the circle of which He was the center with joy and hope; could they be content to let Him rot in the tomb?" The empty tomb (whose emptiness he does not explain) helped to make them liable to hallucination. The actual process began with Mary Magdalene. She was an "imaginative creature," we are told. In the dim dawn of morning she saw a man in the garden, and she imagined he was Jesus. The miracle of love was accomplished, and to Mary's vivid imagination and passionate heart the resurrection had become a fact. Mary, they tell us, set an example that was infectious. After she imagined she had seen Christ, others imagined they saw Him too, until the whole company of disciples imagined they had seen Him, and so the stories of the resurrection appearances arose.

Let us now look at the facts, as given in the infallible revelation of Scripture, and determine from them alone whether this theory of subjective hallucination can stand. Before people take to seeing visions, there must be, as indeed the advocates of the theory presuppose, enthusiasm, expectancy, prepossession. Before anyone could imagine he had seen Christ alive, the wish to see Him, the expectation of seeing Him, must already have taken possession of the mind.

Were the disciples expecting Christ to rise? Hardly. According to the record their mood was one of despondency and despair; they gave up everything for lost when they saw Jesus dead on the cross and buried in Joseph's grave. Even the "imaginative" Mary came to the grave expecting to find only the dead body of

Jesus, and when she found the tomb empty all she "imagined" was that the gardener might have taken the body away. Far from expecting the resurrection, the disciples were utterly skeptical about it; the reports of the women seemed to them to be but "idle tales" (Luke 24:11). Thomas declined to believe, even on the testimony of his fellow disciples. When Christ appeared to them, He had to reproach them all with unbelief and hardness of heart. In a word, the temper necessary to make the vision-theory possible was conspicuous by its absence.

Besides, though one person might see a vision, it is incredible that a large number of persons, for several weeks, and in different places, should be subject to the same hallucination. This theory assumes that the disciples, who were sane and sober men at other times, suddenly took both singly and conjointly to seeing phantoms; it assumes that these visions ceased just as suddenly as they began; it assumes that, without inquiry, the disciples accepted these visions as realities; it assumes that they accepted from a phantom of their own imagination instructions with regard to their future work in the world. What assumptions these are, and what a tax they put on our powers of belief! This vision theory and any other such fanciful attempt to explain away the resurrection is crushed before the fact of the empty tomb. How shall we account for it?

A few weeks after the crucifixion, Peter preached boldly on the resurrection in Jerusalem. Later we find Peter and John before the Sanhedrin, where Peter declares "Jesus Christ of Nazareth, whom ye crucified [hath] God raised from the dead" (Acts 4:10). Why did not the unbelievers expose this as a lie, by producing the body of Jesus, thereby crushing the whole phantasy of the resurrection imposture? They did not because they could not. The grave was empty and nobody could produce a dead body that did not exist.

Perhaps, say some, the disciples had hidden the body of Jesus. This was impossible because of the heavy guard of Roman soldiers. It would also necessarily conclude that all the disciples were dishonest. Would not one have revolted against such a deception? There were no benefits to be gained as a result of such a conspiracy. The consequences were persecution and death. To assume that the disciples preached a resurrection while all the time the body of Christ was in their possession is to say, not that they were honestly mistaken but that they were deliberate and willful impostors. Nobody who reads the life of the disciples would conclude that they were crafty and deceitful men.

Thus, if the Jews or the Romans had the body of Christ, their desire to discredit the resurrection story would have led them to produce it. And if the disciples had it, their consciences would have prodded them into confessing their deception. The empty tomb is indisputable proof that Jesus rose and that the resurrection was not the product of wishful thinking. (See J. D. Jones, *Things Most Surely Believed*, pp. 95-100.)

CAN WE TRUST THE WITNESSES OF THE RESURRECTION?

"He rose again the third day according to the scriptures" (I Cor. 15:4).

The court hearing on the resurrection of Jesus Christ, and the claim that He was seen alive after His crucifixion and burial by many witnesses, has now been reconvened. We saw at the last session that we could reject the counterclaim of the plaintiffs in the world's self-styled court, that Christ rose only as a vision in the imagination of the disciples and others. Too many people saw the empty tomb and would be moved to ask, as a matter of simple logic, why those who denied the resurrection could not produce the body of Jesus. And if the disciples had hidden the body, how ridiculous that they should lie, and then risk their lives in support of that lie. Who would be willing to suffer and die for what they *knew* to be a historical fallacy?

Now we proceed to hear further evidence from the defendants, men and women who claimed to have seen Christ, talked with Him, and touched Him after He rose from the dead. No man actually saw Christ rise; no man could see Christ rise perhaps and live; but since He actually died and was buried, and the tomb was so carefully sealed and guarded, the fact that it was found empty by witnesses and that Christ was seen alive by many shows that He did indeed rise, though the event was too sacred for human eyes.

The first question that we as jurors have the right to ask is, "Are these witnesses trustworthy?" Nobody sincerely questions that they told the truth as it appeared to them. But are they competent? A witness in a court of law must give evidence of his trustworthiness and competence before what he says can be accepted as valid. The defect in the testimony of these First-Century Christians, who were special Biblical witnesses, if there is any, must arise from weakness or from willfulness in the witnesses. Did they lack knowledge, were they mistaken, did they lack honesty? Paul in this 15th chapter of First Corinthians seeks to render our faith reasonable and our infidelity inexcusable by giving us a self-consistent, watertight witness.

Although one or two witnesses ordinarily suffice for a decision in even the most serious court cases, the testimony in the case of the resurrection becomes indisputable because of the great number of firsthand witnesses involved. Paul records that "He was seen of Cephas, then of the twelve: after that, he was seen of above five hundred brethren at once; of whom the greater part remain unto this present [A.D. 55]. . . . After that, he was seen of James; then of all the apostles. And last of all he was seen of me also, as of one born out of due time" (I Cor. 15:5-8). "This Jesus," say the twelve apostles, "hath God raised up, whereof we all are witnesses." (See Acts 2:14, 32; 1:22; 10:39.) These twelve took it upon themselves to attest this matter, in addition to many others who were able and ready to do it.

Another strong point in their favor is that these witnesses were no strangers to Jesus, but persons most familiarly acquainted with Him "from the beginning," who went out and in with Him over the course of His three-year ministry, from His baptism to His ascension. (See John 15:27, Acts 1:21, 22.) They could not be mistaken in the identity of the One whom they claimed rose from the dead.

Their testimony was not based on rumor or hearsay, but on personal verification. They were eyewitnesses (Luke 1:2), as fully informed as their senses could make them, and more profoundly informed by the Holy Spirit's inspiration as to the significance of these things. "For we cannot but speak the things which we have seen and heard," they said (Acts 4:20). "That . . . which we have heard, which we have looked upon, and our hands have handled of the Word of life . . . declare we unto you" (I John 1:1, 3). This is John the beloved disciple speaking, who was in constant attendance upon his Master.

And Peter affirms his personal knowledge of the resurrection in these words: "For we have not followed cunningly devised fables, when we made known unto you the power and coming of our Lord Jesus Christ, but were eyewitnesses of his majesty" (II Pet. 1:16).

These disciples saw and heard the risen Christ, not just once but repeatedly, not just in passing or at a distance but close at hand, in intimate fellowship, often conversing with him. Peter tells us that the disciples ate and drank with Him after He rose from the dead (Acts 10:41). Luke, who was a companion of the disciples, says, "To whom also he shewed himself alive after his passion by many infallible proofs, being seen of them forty days, and speaking of the things pertaining to the kingdom of God" (Acts 1:3).

Paul, who knew the disciples so well, says of them, "And he was seen many days of them which came up with him from Galilee to Jerusalem, who are his witnesses unto the people" (Acts 13:31). Two of the witnesses, John and Matthew, relate in their writings conversations with the risen Christ.

The story of the resurrection was not readily believed by those who heard of it from others, and this would be especially true in the case of an educated physician like Luke. The words of the first eyewitnesses of the resurrection seemed to the disciples as idle tales. They did not believe them. They had to go to see for themselves (Luke 24:11, 12). Christ even let them touch His body to feel the marks of the crucifixion. He demonstrated that He was the very same person who had lived with them and died before them. "They were terrified and affrighted," Scripture tells us, "and supposed that they had seen a spirit. . . . And while they yet believed not for joy, and wondered, he said unto them, Have you here any meat?" (Luke 24:37, 41).

This certainly is what made the disciples bold witnesses of the resurrection of Jesus Christ. It was an unchallengeable fact. That is why "they spake the word of God with boldness. . . . And with great power gave the apostles witness of the resurrection of the Lord Jesus" (Acts 4:31, 33).

Thus we see that the resurrection of Jesus Christ could be more than substantiated by the physical senses of the disciples. So many of them, over such a length of time, can hardly be discredited. If the apostles imagined they saw their Friend and Master, with whom they had associated for so long, when they actually did not see Him; that they heard Him conversing lengthily with them, when actually they did not hear Him; that they walked, ate, and drank with Him, that they touched and felt Him, when actually there was no one present, what assurance can we have of the credibility of our senses in regard to physical phenomena? What testimony can be of any validity or use? As a matter of fact, many unbelieving philosophies and non-Christian religions do indeed reject the credibility of the senses in regard to physical phenomena. This ought not to surprise us, for if the heart of man rejects God's supernatural revelation, it will also reject His revelation of creation. Man will then doubt its reality. If this be so, he cannot be sure of the validity of anything, including the evidence of his senses. He cannot even lay claim to being an empiricist or a positivist any more. He cannot even say that he believes only what his five senses tell him, for by his own admission he is not even sure of that.

If Scripture be rejected, what other testimony can be relied on? The simple answer is that ultimately no testimony to any kind of reality exists, for men are fallible. We are again driven to skepticism in all matters, great and small. It is a known fact that testimony in a human court cannot always be trusted, nor can any merely human testimony. Think of the innocent who are punished and the guilty who go free.

We must, therefore, conclude that the testimony is impregnable, because the witnesses cannot be accounted ignorant or mistaken in this case. Neither can they be rejected on the grounds of insufficient numbers or incompetency.

WHY SUFFER FOR A LIE?

"He rose again. . . ." (I Cor. 15:4).

So far, in our study of the evidence for the resurrection of the Lord Jesus Christ, we have been looking into the credibility of the witnesses. Our examination has shown us that they were at the very least honest men, who were sincerely convinced that what they claimed was true. In addition to this we have seen that there were far too many of them to be deceived by a fantasy induced by wishful thinking, and that in any event the actual physical tests of their senses—sight, hearing, touch—preclude any such visionary explanation of the risen Christ. Furthermore, we have demonstrated that these men were competent to identify Christ, having associated with Him far too long and intimately to be fooled by an impostor or a hallucination.

Now let us look a little further into the allegation that the disciples, for purposes of their own, fabricated the resurrection story, having previously taken the body of Christ from the tomb and hidden it. We must examine the character of the witnesses to determine whether they were capable of such deceit. Let us assume for the sake of argument that they circulated a false story for a good purpose, out of a mistaken notion perhaps that they were honoring the memory of such a wonderful man as Jesus in this way; or that they could not admit that they had been mistaken in believing Him to be the Messiah. We must try to find out whether they have willfully deceived us and imposed upon the world a falsehood as a fact.

First of all, let us examine their teachings. What do these show about their character? We find that they constantly denounced dishonesty and deceit. They encouraged all kinds of goodness, truthfulness, sincerity, humility, and equity. This was part and parcel of that religion which their testimony about the resurrection was intended to confirm. They utterly condemned all malice, falsehood, craft, and hypocrisy. They never indicated in any way that the end justifies the means. One of their number, John, stated that those who were "without," that is, unbelievers, included such wicked men as "sorcerers, and whoremongers, and murderers, and idolaters, and whosoever loveth and maketh a lie" (Rev. 22:15). It is very hard to believe that men who made such statements could deliberately conceive and execute a plot that would impose a lie upon their own generation and generations to come concerning the resurrection of the Lord Jesus Christ. Listen to what those with most authority among them have to say:

The first to speak is Paul: "Putting away lying, speak every man truth with his neighbor," he tells the Ephesian Church (Eph. 4:25). Now Peter: "Wherefore laying aside all malice, all guile, and hypocrisies, and envies, and all evil speakings, as newborn babes, desire the sincere milk of the word, that ye may grow thereby" (I Pet. 2:1, 2). And John, who sternly warns, "All liars shall have their part in the lake which burneth with fire and brimstone" (Rev. 21:8). This could not have been the language of men who were liars themselves, conscious of being impostors and hypocrites. Deliberate deceit could hardly so denounce itself.

However, it is possible in some instances for men to preach one thing and practice another. What is the record of the disciples? We find their lives to be examples of virtue, goodness, and sincerity. Their practice agreed with their doctrine. Appealing to those who had observed their conduct they could say, "Ye are witnesses, and God also, how holily and justly and unblameably we behaved ourselves among you . . . how we exhorted and comforted and charged every one of you . . . that ye would walk worthy of God" (I Thess. 2:10-12). And Paul could say to the Corinthians without fear of contradiction, "We have renounced the hidden things of dishonesty, not walking in craftiness, nor handling the word of God deceitfully; but by manifestation of the truth commending ourselves to every man's conscience in the sight of God" (II Cor. 4:2).

For the sake of what they knew to be a lie, these disciples would not have bridled their sinful appetites and passions, or have borne adversities, imprisonments, beatings, and death so calmly. They would not have expressed such forgiving kindness toward those who persecuted them. Why should they spend a lifetime in defense of a deliberate deceit on behalf of a dead man, when it could only bring them hardship and suffering —even death? Listen to them tell about their lives: "Even unto this present hour we both hunger, and thirst, and are naked, and are buffeted, and have no certain dwellingplace; and labour, working with our own hands: being reviled, we bless; being persecuted, we suffer it: being defamed, we intreat: we are made as the filth of the world, and are the offscouring of all things unto this day" (I Cor. 4:11-13). They willingly accepted and embraced all this—for what? For the sake of a patent lie? Incredible.

Men will lie for the sake of personal profit, to gain some advantage or to get out of trouble, but hardly to get themselves knowingly into trouble. If the disciples started out by telling a lie, they might be expected to give it up when they saw what personal damage it resulted in. But not only did they not cease bearing testimony to the resurrection, they rejoiced in being counted worthy to suffer for the sake of the living Christ.

They knew that He for whom they suffered had told them they would undergo tribulation here on earth, but they also knew that He had promised to bless them richly in the world to come. Their motive for accepting their sufferings was the satisfaction of their conscience and of God. As Paul says, "For our rejoicing is this, the testimony of our conscience, that in simplicity and godly sincerity, not with fleshly wisdom, but by the grace of God, we have had our conversation in the world" (II Cor. 1:12). This was the principle that moved them. They suffered for conscience' sake and for God.

But they also hoped for the glory of heaven. In speaking of their heavenly inheritance, Paul says, "We are . . . joint-heirs with Christ; if so be that we suffer with him, that we may be also glorified together" (Rom. 8:16, 17). Did Paul expect God to reward him for propagating a lie? Of course not. If the disciples knew the Lord Jesus had not really risen from the dead, they would certainly not be so stupid as to believe He was worth suffering for or that He could possibly reward them hereafter. No, these disciples were thoroughly persuaded that the Lord Jesus was indeed the Son of God, who died for their sake, was raised again, and would reward them with eternal bliss — because they beheld Him in His resurrected bodily form.

And how could anyone think these witnesses were capable of perpetrating and sustaining such a monstrous fraud? They were not of noble birth, not wealthy, had no worldly interests, no education to speak of, no social status, no outstanding endowments of mind. They were fishermen, publicans, laborers, who were called unlearned and ignorant men (Acts 4:13). Yet the wisdom of their peculiar message defied any rational opposition.

Furthermore, how could such a lie have spread and prospered so readily in spite of persecution? How is it that thousands of Jews who were "zealots of the law" (Acts 21:20) believed in the resurrection? They had full opportunity of examining the matter to the bottom. Yet these believing Jews were convinced that the empty tomb was not a plot but a miracle. Why? Because God's truth, though prosecuted with vigorous integrity and constancy, is supported by divine protection and therefore invincible, as we plainly see on reading the Acts of the Apostles. It withstood the skepticism of those who might in this case have been considered its natural enemies. "And the word of God increased; and the number of the disciples multiplied in Jerusalem greatly; and a great company of the priests were obedient to the faith" (Acts 6:7). It took more than a false rumor to convince them.

Over the course of the centuries, a lie would certainly have collapsed of its own weight, or gone under through lack of vitality in the face of persecution. Gamaliel's advice to the Sanhedrin puts the matter in a nutshell: "If this counsel or this work be of men, it will come to nought: but if it be of God, ye cannot overthrow it; lest haply ye be found even to fight against God" (Acts 5:38, 39). Since it has not come to nought in twenty centuries, we believe God has vindicated it in the eyes of all men in every generation who in utter sincerity have opened their hearts and minds to the truth.

HOW LONG WAS CHRIST DEAD?

"He rose again the third day according to the scriptures" (I Cor. 15:4).

Our belief in the resurrection of Jesus Christ is strengthened by the fact that it was predicted many centuries before by the prophets, as well as by Christ Himself before His death. Show me anyone who can make such a prophecy beforehand and then fulfill it, and I will believe all other claims he may make and follow him to the death.

The resurrection of Christ was also foreshadowed in types in the Old Testament. That is, God used events, people, and things as divinely chosen illustrations to teach His people about His grace and saving power, which were ultimately and fully to be revealed in Christ. Types in general are God's object lessons, prefiguring things to come.

For instance, Abraham was asked by God to sacrifice his son Isaac, even as God would one day sacrifice His own Son on our behalf. But as Abraham's dagger was poised over Isaac's breast, God told Abraham to spare him, thus foreshadowing the deliverance of Christ from death. (See Genesis 22 and Hebrews 11:17-19.)

Another type of the resurrection of Christ is the deliverance of Joseph from the dungeon in which he found himself because of the treachery of his brothers (Gen. 41:14). Yet another is Jonah's delivery from the interior of the great fish (Jon. 1:17; 2:10). The Lord referred to this Himself when He said, "For as

Jonas was three days and three nights in the whale's belly; so shall the Son of man be three days and three nights in the heart of the earth" (Matt. 12:40).

This expression, "three days and three nights," brings up a problem of chronology. How could the Lord Jesus have said that He would remain in the grave "three days and three nights," when He actually spent only two nights in the grave? Some persons think the difficulty can be solved by setting Wednesday or Thursday as the day of the crucifixion, instead of Friday, but this seemingly easy solution cannot stand close scrutiny.

This point may seem of minor consequence, but its implications can be of the gravest concern. The veracity and verifiability of our Lord's word hinge upon it. I remember once that I was not able to lead a young man to place his faith in Christ until I had straightened out this point of Bible chronology for him. For that reason I am going into the matter in some detail here.

The question as to how long Jesus remained in the tomb would never have arisen had not some modern readers misunderstood the common ancient method of counting time called "inclusive reckoning." By this method, any fraction of a day or year at the beginning or end of a given period was included as a whole day or year. A classic Biblical example of this is found in II Kings 18:9, 10, in which a war was dated as beginning and ending during certain years of the reign of Hezekiah, King of Judah, and Hoshea, King of Israel. These verses say that the war began in the 4th year of Hezekiah's reign and the 7th year of

Hoshea's, and ended in the 6th year of Hezekiah and the 9th year of Hoshea. How long would you reckon that this war lasted? You would simply subtract four from six, or seven from nine, and say that the war lasted two years. The Bible, however, describes the closing date of this war as "at the end of three years." The writer evidently counted the 4th to the 6th year of Hezekiah's reign as "four, five, six," and the 7th to the 9th of Hoshea's as "seven, eight, nine" — three years inclusively. (Remember, these kings ruled simultaneously, but over two different kingdoms.)

The modern western method of reckoning a person's age is to say that a child is not one year old until he has lived twelve full months from the date of his birth, and he remains one year old all through his second year until his next birthday, when he becomes two. This was not the Biblical method of reckoning. In Genesis 7:6, 11, we find that Noah was considered 600 years old in the 600th year of his life, while according to our reckoning he was still only 599. Japanese people up until recently called a child one year old on January first who had been born at any time during the preceding twelve months. Thus even a baby born in December was called a year old on January first. The Chinese still follow this method.

Getting back to the question of what Christ meant by the three days and three nights that He prophesied He would remain "in the heart of the earth," the Bible lists several periods of "three days" that ended during, not at the close of, the third day, and thus covered less than 72 hours. (See Gen. 42:17-19; I Kings 12:5, 12; II Chron. 10:5, 12.) This method of reckoning was common in ancient Egypt, Greece, and Rome, and is still found in the Far East today.

Why, then, do we feel that we have to interpret Jesus' words according to the Western method of reckoning, allowing 24 full hours to a day, when He was speaking to people who thoroughly understood that any part of a day was counted as a unit in reckoning time? By common usage His hearers would count the three days successively as 1) the day of crucifixion (Friday), 2) the day after that event (Saturday), and 3) the "third" day after (or Sunday), though by modern count this would be the second day after. We cannot insist that, because Jesus said that He would rise after three days (Mark 8:31), He therefore meant, in modern fashion, after the end of the third full day, or 72 hours, for that would be equivalent to "on the fourth day," in usage then contemporary.

But we are not left with a mere obvious deduction as to what Jesus meant and understood by "third day." We have evidence from His own lips that He did indeed reckon time according to the ancient Hebrew method. In speaking of Herod on one occasion, He said, "Go ye, and tell that fox, Behold, I cast out devils, and I do cures to day and to morrow, and the third day I shall be perfected. Nevertheless I must walk to day, and to morrow, and the day following: for it cannot be that a prophet perish out of Jerusalem" (Luke 13:32, 33). He equated the third day with the day after to-morrow, the third day counted inclusively.

Since Scripture tells us that Christ arose on the first day of the week (Sunday), we have only to count back to the preceding Friday to establish the day of the crucifixion. This is in exact accord with Luke's statement that the women left the embalming unfinished on the day of preparation as the sabbath drew on, and rested the sabbath day according to the commandment before returning on the first day of the week. If Christ had been crucified on Wednesday, making the sabbath mentioned here merely a ceremonial sabbath, the women would hardly have waited several days to return.

The usual formula that our Lord employed in speaking of His resurrection was that "he should rise on the third day." The expression "three days and three nights" that He used only in Matthew 12:40 was meant to tie in with the quotation He gave from Jonah 1:17. The Hebrew expression for three days and three nights was likewise used generally and indefinitely for three days simply. This is manifestly the case here. Jesus was dead part of the first, all of the second, and part of the third day. In the Jerusalem Talmud, it is said "that a day and night together make up an *ownah* (*nuchtheemeron* in Greek, meaning "night and day"), and that any part of such a period is counted as a whole. (See *The Greek Testament*, by Henry Alford, D.D., Vol. I, Chicago: Moody Press, p. 133.)

To understand the way of salvation and how to live the Christian life, we can rely on our English translations of the Bible as being fully comprehensible and sufficient. But to understand many disputed points, it is necessary to examine the historical background and the original Hebrew or Greek of the Bible to determine just what was in the minds of the various authors, as they wrote under divine inspiration. To try to understand some of these disputed points by using our modern Western culture, language, and customs as a point of reference is to becloud rather than to clarify the issue.

WHO SAW CHRIST'S RISEN BODY?

"He rose again the third day . . . and . . . he was seen" (I Cor. 15:4, 5).

We have seen that not only was the resurrection of Jesus Christ foreshadowed in divinely appointed types; it was also foretold in prophecy. Lord Rochester, who was described by one of his biographers as "a great wit, a great sinner, and a great penitent," was for many years an out-and-out atheist, who spent a large portion of his time in ridiculing the Bible. Then one day he read the 53rd chapter of Isaiah, which prophesies the coming of the Messiah and His sacrificial atonement for sin. Through it, the Holy Spirit pierced his pretenses, and led him to a humble acknowledgment of Christ as Saviour and Lord.

In Psalm 16:10 we read, "For thou wilt not leave my soul in hell [*sheol, hadees*]; neither wilt thou suffer thine Holy One to see corruption." The Apostle Paul testified before King Agrippa that the sufferings and resurrection of the Lord had been foretold. "I continue unto this day," he said, "witnessing both to small and great, saying none other things than those which the prophets and Moses did say should come: that Christ should suffer, and that he should be the first that should rise from the dead" (Acts 26:22, 23). These prophecies appear in Isaiah 9:7 and 53:10: "Of the increase of his government and peace there shall be no end" (not even the cross could bring an end to it); and "when thou shalt make his soul an offering for sin . . . he shall prolong his days" (a prophecy fulfilled by the resurrection of Christ, in spite of all His enemies could do).

That Christ did rise according to the Scriptures is attested by "many infallible proofs":

1) By the eyewitnesses who saw Him. Those recorded in Scripture are Mary Magdalene (Mark 16:9), Cleopas and his companions on the way to Emmaus (Luke 24:13-31), all the disciples but Thomas (John 20:19-24), Thomas himself later on (John 20:26), five hundred people at one time (I Cor. 15:6), all the disciples (Luke 24:36-51, Acts 10:41, 42), and Paul (I Cor. 15:8).

2) By the testimony of His enemies. The soldiers who had been stationed to guard the tomb actually saw the angel roll back the stone from the door (Matt. 28:2-4). When some of them came and told the chief priests and elders what they had seen, they were bribed to say that Jesus' disciples had stolen His body while the guards slept (vv. 11-13). As St. Chrysostom says, "Truth certified by the enemies shines."

3) By angels who testified to the fact that Christ had risen from the dead (Luke 24:4-7).

4) By God Himself, who authenticated the faith of those who believed in the resurrection by miracles and by enabling the apostles to preach, propagate, and die for the Gospel. "And with great power gave the apostles witness of the resurrection of the Lord Jesus: and great grace was upon them all" (Acts 4:33).

Paul, in First Corinthians 15:5-8, lists six instances in which the risen Christ appeared to eyewitnesses: 1) Cephas (Peter), 2) The twelve, 3) five hundred people at once, 4) James, 5) all the apostles, 6) Paul himself.

It may at first seem strange that Paul does not refer to the material evidences of the resurrection, such as the empty tomb and the graveclothes. Perhaps he felt these were not enough thoroughly to convince a critical mind. Something more was needed by way of confirmation to refute the claim of Christ's enemies that His body had been secretly removed by His disciples.

In Luke 24:24 we read, "And certain of them which were with us went to the sepulchre, and found it even so as the women had said: but him they saw not." It took more than that to convince them He had risen from the dead. In fact, the first conclusion that Mary Magdalene came to on seeing the stone removed from the door of the tomb was, "They have taken away the Lord . . . and we know not where they have laid him" (John 20:2). No, the empty tomb of itself was not proof indisputable. Therefore Paul moves on to the ultimate and irrefutable proof of witnesses who actually saw the Lord after His resurrection.

"He was seen of Cephas [Peter]," he says in First Corinthians 15:5. The verb "was seen" (A.V.) here is *oophthee* in Greek, the passive aorist, third person singular form of the verb *horaoo*. This is the verb from which we derive our English words "optician, optometrist," etc. It refers to the physical eye and what it sees. Primarily it refers to bodily vision.

Thus Paul tells the Corinthians here that the witnesses he calls upon actually saw the physical body of Jesus Christ with their physical eyes. It was not His Spirit only that rose from the dead, but His body also. He possessed the same outward physical characteristics after His resurrection as before, so that He could be identified by those who knew Him. To confirm this, the Lord permitted Thomas, in the presence of the other disciples, to touch His side and hands, that he might be fully convinced (see John 20:27). Of course, the post-resurrection body of Christ was different in many ways from the body He had before the resurrection. It was a "glorified body," the nature of which Paul discusses later in this great chapter. Nevertheless, it was a body that could be felt and seen, and that could eat (Luke 24:39-43), a fact that Christ demonstrated to prove His physical resurrection.

The meaning of the verb *oophthee*, "was seen," however, goes beyond mere physical sight. It also connotes seeing with the mind, perceiving, knowing. What good is physical sight if you cannot comprehend the nature of what you see? Paul wants us to realize first that the witnesses saw with their physical eyes the physical body of Jesus risen from the dead, and secondly that they recognized Him.

This verb, *horao*, is also used of mental or spiritual perception without the prerequisite of physical sight. It is so used in John 6:46, "Not that any man hath seen [*heeoraken*] the Father, save he which is of God, he hath seen the Father." But in First Corinthians 15:5-8, the word cannot refer to mental sight only. How could 500 persons at the same time and in the same place have had one and the same vision? Or how could Thomas have touched a body that did not exist? And we cannot disregard the record that Christ ate in the presence of His disciples.

The testimony of the witnesses whom Paul produces is quite precise. The aorist tense of the verb *oophthee*, "was seen," indicates that these witnesses saw Jesus Christ after His resurrection at certain specific times in history. If they were to be questioned individually, they could give exact dates and places.

The verb *oophthee* here might better be rendered "showed Himself, or appeared" than "was seen." In the first century, the aorist passive often took on a middle or reflexive force. (See *A Grammar of the Greek New Testament*, by A. T. Robertson, p. 816f.) This form of the verb *horaoo* is used especially in connection with the appearances of the Lord after His resurrection (Luke 24:34, Acts 9:17; 13:31; 26:16, I Cor. 15:5-8, I Tim. 3:16). This indicates that the initiative lay with Christ rather than with the viewers. They did not conjure up this sight, but He showed Himself to them in each specific instance. If He had not done so, they could not have seen Him or understood who He was.

It is always so in our human relations with God. We cannot reach up to Him; it is He who must reach down to us. We can make no human discoveries of God; we can only receive divine revelations. In Christ's resurrection appearances, He showed Himself only to those whom He chose. He did not, for instance, allow His enemies or the idly curious to view Him at will during the forty days of His earthly post-resurrection life. He was seen because He allowed Himself to be seen at times and to people chosen by Himself. Christ was sovereign after His resurrection as He always has been and always will be, because He is God the Son.

SUFFICIENT PROOF OF THE RESURRECTION

"He was seen . . . ." (I Cor. 15:5a).

In defense of the reality of the resurrection of Jesus Christ, the Apostle Paul places great importance on the fact that He was seen by many witnesses. The list that he submits is not exhaustive. It does not include all the persons mentioned in the Gospel narratives. But it includes enough to establish the fact as incontrovertible. That is all a court requires, not that all possible witnesses be called, but that there be sufficient witnesses to establish the facts.

The resurrection of Christ is the keystone of Christianity. At the battle of Waterloo, Napoleon said that a certain stone house was the key to the whole situation; that if he could take that house, victory was certain. Against that house he hurled all his forces, but the men were driven back every time. If he had taken that house, Waterloo might now stand as a French victory. So today, the enemies of Christ hurl all their forces against Christ's resurrection, knowing that, if they can disprove that, they will have secured victory for the forces of hell.

Paul is too careful a master builder of the faith to place reliance on a weak keystone. Thus, in addition to citing the evidence of typology and prophecy for the resurrection, he makes an appeal to the senses. He meets the scientists and skeptics on their own ground. Christ rose from the dead, you say? Then there must be those who saw Him. Produce the witnesses, establish their reliability, furnish their evidence, and the question of Christ's survival after death is settled once for all.

If such evidence does not convince, then nothing can. The senses have testified to Christ's survival, as well as reason. The resurrection is a demonstrated historical fact. It can be proven like any other alleged event by an appeal to human witnesses. Hear the evidence from trustworthy human lips, and the reality of any phenomenon, however wonderful and inexplicable, is authenticated. Skepticism now means unwillingness to be convinced by reason. Doubt is now akin to sin.

To discredit the testimony of trustworthy human witnesses is to make advance in knowledge of any kind impossible. We have seen sheer intellectual blindness hinder progress in the past—as when men ridiculed the notion that the earth was round and revolved in space, or when the theory that germs caused disease was rejected without weighing the evidence. We fear it is in similar fashion that skeptics reject the resurrection today. They refuse to examine and evaluate the evidence in accordance with sound scientific principles.

As Paul writes this epistle, some twenty-five years after the resurrection, he mentions that a great number of these witnesses to it are still alive. Any inquirer who wanted further details of their testimony could investigate for himself. Paul's is the first written account of the resurrection, the Gospels and all others appearing later.

That Paul went to so much pains to convince the Corinthians of the reality of the resurrection implies that a significant number of them had serious doubts about it. It was not that the testimony of the eyewitnesses was insufficient, but their presupposition that such a resurrection was a natural impossibility, that was the stumbling-block (vv. 12 and 13). But it is most unscientific to let presuppositions exclude facts and reliable observations. Paul does not attempt to prove the reliability or the sufficiency of the actual witnesses. His purpose is to dispel the idea that Christ could not have risen because the resurrection of the dead is impossible.

Evidently the Corinthians failed to recognize that the uniformity of nature does not preclude higher manifestations of power by Him who is the Master of nature. Many persons once ridiculed the notion that man would ever travel in space. But the fact that so many astronauts have done so no longer makes it possible to hold such presuppositions. To declare that something is impossible on the ground that it controverts our present knowledge of the laws of nature is to put the law above the Lawgiver. No scientist dare say what is possible or impossible in an absolute sense. Humility is the mark of the truly great scientist or philosopher. A miracle—such as the resurrection—is not a violation of nature's laws. It may simply be a method unknown to us by which God operates to bring to expression some loftier purposes of His own. The hypothesis of uniformity is merely a generalization from past experience that must of necessity be incomplete. We must all confess with Paul, "Now I know in part" (I Cor. 13:12). No one can determine what his future experience will be. It is in the keeping of God, who can at any time alter the natural in order to reveal Himself to man. Whether things that transcend our usual knowledge have actually happened can be learned only by authoritative evidence. Naturally, such evidence must be in harmony with Scripture and attested to by witnesses whose characters are unimpeachable.

The significant question, then, in reference to the resurrection, is whether these witnesses, by the fact that they saw the risen Christ, provide sufficient evidence that God did restore Him to life. If adequate testimony is forthcoming, then the reality of the occurrence is beyond dispute. We are compelled to acknowledge that in this case, for some reason, the general law has been superseded by a higher law. If a worthy reason for this departure is discoverable, we can have no legitimate reason for refusing to accept the new statement of fact. The witnesses, in harmony with the prophecies of Scripture, establish it.

And what was God's reason for this exception to the general rule? Why should the body of Jesus not have decayed like other human bodies at death? Why should He be raised from the dead? It is as one preacher has said, "Jesus Christ is the standing proof that God has interfered in the affairs of this world." His resurrection is the supreme illustration of this. Testimony to this irrefutably establishes its historical validity. All depends upon the significance of the miracle and the quality of the evidence produced.

How was the Lord Jesus Christ raised? By the power of God, "according to the working of his mighty power, which he wrought in Christ, when he raised him from the dead" (Eph. 1:19, 20). Galatians 1:1 speaks of "God the Father, who raised him from the dead."

And Jesus Christ equated His own power with the power of God when He said, "Destroy this temple, and in three days I will raise it up . . . . He spake of the temple of his body. . . . I lay down my life, that I might take it again. No man taketh it from me, but I lay it down of myself. I have power to lay it down, and I have power to take it again" (John 2:19, 21; 10:17, 18). He did not say "My Father" in these instances but "I," thus demonstrating His deity. "When therefore he was risen from the dead, his disciples remembered that he had said this unto them; and they believed the scripture" (John 2:22).

The resurrection, then, was a demonstration of the power of God, of His authority to control and supersede the laws of nature, and of the deity of Jesus Christ.

INDIVIDUAL AND GROUP WITNESS TO
THE RESURRECTION

"He was seen of Cephas [Peter], then of the twelve" (I Cor. 15:5).

An assistant to a great chemist accidentally knocked a silver cup into a vat of acid. It was immediately dissolved, to the horror of the workman. But the chemist came in, put a certain chemical into the vat, and in a moment every particle of silver was precipitated to the bottom. The shapeless mass was lifted out and sent to the silversmith, and the cup was restored to its original shape. If a human genius can do a thing like this, why should we doubt that God can restore a sin-ruined life to beauty and usefulness?

Take the Apostle Peter, for instance, whom Paul mentions first in his list of witnesses to the resurrection of Jesus Christ. Among all the disciples, there was none sadder than Peter on Easter morning. The disciple who had said to his Lord that if all others forsook Him, he would not, had denied him at the first challenge outside the place of judgment. On the day of the crucifixion, he was not at the foot of the cross with John and the three Mary's. It is even doubtful that he was with the apostles who followed the scene of the crucifixion from afar. He not only denied his Master but he deserted Him. This was the man who said, "If I should die with thee, I will not deny thee in any wise" (Mark 14:31). It is true that the disciples had all said this, but our Lord had especially warned Peter and foretold his denial. How weak the strongest of us are!

Peter had denied his Lord, but Jesus had "turned, and looked upon Peter," and, pierced by that look, "Peter went out, and wept bitterly" (Luke 22:61, 62). In the hour of his trial, after all his promises, after his Master's warnings, he had failed. What must have been Peter's thoughts? It would not have seemed so hard to bear if he could only have told his Lord of his bitter sorrow, of his deep penitence; but after having denied Him, he had silently to see Him dragged away to suffer the greatest ignominy, and to die a malefactor's death.

Nobody needed the Lord Jesus on Easter Day so much as Peter. And so, after first rewarding Mary Magdalene's love, our Lord then blessed Peter's penitence. Luke alludes to this personal appearance, which must have taken place on the first day. "The Lord is risen indeed, and hath appeared to Simon [Peter]" (Luke 24:34). Mark also quotes the angel's command to the women at the tomb, "Tell his disciples and Peter that he goeth before you into Galilee" (Mark 16:7). It is evident that the Lord singled out Peter for special attention during His post-resurrection life. True, Mary Magdalene was the first person to see the risen Lord, but Paul mentions no women by name in his list of witnesses, although we may presume that they would be included in the 500 who saw Him. Paul selected only such names as would be well known to the Corinthians either in person or by reputation. The word "brethren," however, should not be construed as limiting the group to men only, but is used in a generic sense.

Although we do not know the content of the conversation between the risen Lord and Peter, we are told of its results in Peter's life. Strangely enough, of the appearances on Easter Day, this seems to be the only one of which we are told no details; and yet from this very silence we may learn the lesson that all real penitence must be in secret, that a veil must ever be drawn over the outpouring of the sin-laden soul, of the burdened heart, at the feet of the Lord Jesus. Preacher, minister, priest, never divulge to anyone that secret conversation between a penitent and yourself. We ministers of the Gospel cannot help but hear the stories of sorrow. But those stories must ever remain between us and God.

Sinner, put yourself at the foot of the cross. Behold our Lord dying there. Realize how much you have sinned against Him. Think of all your cowardice, your disloyalty, your lack of love. Pray Him to give you penitence. He will not only grant your petition but will also make Himself known to you as the risen Lord. He is living now. You can open your heart to Him as Peter did, who then became one of the first witnesses of the resurrection. With such a background, how could Peter help but write, "Blessed be the God and Father of our Lord Jesus Christ, which according to his abundant mercy hath begotten us again unto a lively hope by the resurrection of Jesus Christ from the dead"? (I Pet. 1:3). The resurrection of the Lord is your hope, too.

From the witness of an individual, Paul then proceeds to the witness of a group, from the leader of the twelve disciples of Christ to the group itself. "He was seen of Cephas, then of the twelve" (I Cor. 15:5). The same verb is used for both clauses. *Oophthee*, "was seen," with the inherent meaning of "He chose to appear to," is to be understood in the second clause. This appearance is described in John 20:19-21 and Luke 24:36-43. Actually, only ten of the disciples were present. Neither Judas nor Thomas was there. Why, then, does Paul speak of "the twelve"? This designation became synonymous with the term "the disciples," before Judas defected; just as the term "the eleven" was used to refer to the group after Judas betrayed Christ and was no longer with them. It designated the group as a whole, and did not refer to the actual number who might or might not be present in any given instance. Luke 24:33 is a case in point. Speaking of the men who had seen the Lord on the road to Emmaus and then returned to Jerusalem, it says, "They . . . found the eleven gathered together," although since Thomas was not present there were actually only ten. Whether the terms "the twelve" or "the eleven" are used, they refer not to the exact number within the group but to the group itself.

As an example, if I were to speak of the Senate of the United States as "those one hundred men on Capitol Hill who voted on such and such a day for a certain bill," even though only ninety-nine senators were present on that occasion, would I be wrong? Of course not, because I was speaking of the Senate as a group, and not of individual members.

Actually, as Luke 24:33 tells us, these ten disciples were not alone. Luke refers to "them that were with them." Probably Mary Magdalene was there, for she had gone to them after her conversation with the risen

Lord. "Mary Magdalene came and told the disciples that she had seen the Lord, and that he had spoken these things unto her" (John 20:18). No doubt others were there, too. And yet when Paul refers to this appearance of the Lord on the evening of resurrection day, he does not speak of these "others" but only of the twelve as a group, that is, the disciples of the Lord. Not only did Peter, their leader, see Him, but subsequently his colleagues also, those who were there. They are the ones who knew Christ best and whose testimony could stand. Paul is careful not to overstate the evidence. He gives only what is sufficient to establish the fact.

As Paul proceeds from the witness of one individual to that of a group, we see that Christ's religion is not for the individual only, it is also for man as a race, for society; and though the Church of Christ is made up of individual members, it is itself the aggregate of those members. The risen Christ is the hope of each individual believer, but He is also the hope of His Church. We must never lose sight of the fact that we are members of a body, as Paul so eloquently tells us in the 12th chapter of First Corinthians. "For as the body is one, and hath many members, and all the members of that one body, being many, are one body: so also is Christ" (v. 12).

500 WITNESSES AT ONCE

"After that, he was seen of above five hundred brethren at once. . . ." (I Cor. 15:6).

Christianity is primarily a "go and tell" religion. It spreads through both individual and corporate witness. When the Apostle Paul wants to strengthen the case for the bodily resurrection of Jesus Christ, he calls in the witnesses who actually saw, spoke with, and touched the Lord Jesus after His resurrection. First he mentions Peter, then the twelve, and now he calls in a group of 500 "brethren," who assembled most probably in Galilee. Matthew tells us that after Jesus' resurrection He appeared to Mary Magdalene and the other Mary, and told them, "Be not afraid: go tell my brethren that they go into Galilee, and there shall they see me" (Matt. 28:10). If this were to be a meeting of the disciples only, it could very well have been held in Judea, in Jerusalem, or in Capernaum. But in the hill country of Galilee the Lord could meet with a much larger number without their attracting undue notice.

As soon as the Lord had appointed the time and place of meeting, we may be sure it spread with great eagerness and secrecy from one believer to another. As Professor Henry B. Swete says, "How on the appointed day those who received it flocked, two or three from a village, a dozen or a score from a walled town, to the appointed place upon the hills. It may have been some of these who had not seen the risen Lord hitherto, that were doubtful at first of the identity of the person who appeared to them. But if so, their doubts vanished before His words, and when Saint Paul wrote his first letter to Corinth, some twenty-five years after the resurrection, there were still more than two hundred and fifty living eye-witnesses of that day's wonder. The Apostle makes much of such a 'cloud of witnesses,' as well he might; for even if the Eleven could be deceived or deceivers, was it credible that their error or their fraud would be shared by so great a company? Some there must have been among them who, as the days went on, would have exposed the imposture or betrayed their doubts. But if any doubts of this kind had arisen, it would have been dangerous for the Apostle to appeal to the survivors of the five hundred in a letter written to Corinth, where he had enemies who were in frequent communication with Jerusalem." (H. B. Swete, *The Appearances of our Lord after the Passion*, MacMillan, 1910, pp. 82-5.)

None of the Gospel writers records that so many believers saw the risen Lord. But Paul mentions them because of the great number who saw Him *all at one time*. This is what the Greek word *ephapax* means here. Often it means "once for all." Actually both meanings are true in this instance. The 500 believers together saw the risen Christ once for all. It is doubtful whether Paul adds up the various persons who saw the risen Christ at different places and different times. The importance of this piece of evidence is that these 500 witnesses were all together in one place at one time. The apologetic value of this consisted in the fact that it was impossible for so many to be deceived in thinking that they saw if they actually did not see Him. And to clinch the argument he adds, "of whom the greatest part remain unto this present, but some are fallen asleep." It is as if the Apostle were saying, "You can go and ask them, if you like: there they are, still in great numbers." (Godet.)

It is indeed unusual that more than half these men were still living when Paul wrote this Epistle. People then had a shorter life expectancy than today. One would ordinarily expect the greater part to have died during this twenty-five-year post-resurrection period. As Alexander Maclaren suggests, "Possibly there was some divine intervention which supernaturally prolonged the lives of these witnesses, in order that their testimony might be more lasting."

"The greatest part remain," says Paul. The Greek word for "remain" is *menousin*, from the verb *menoo*, meaning "to stay, often in the special sense live, dwell, lodge." This is the word that the Lord used in John 15:3 when He says, "Abide in me, and I in you." It is the word that the two disciples used at Emmaus when they besought the Lord to "abide" with them. It carries with it the thought of restfulness and quietness. These men, after having had the greatest vision any human could have, that of the risen Christ, went back to their daily tasks to witness in their daily lives of what the risen Lord can do for sinful men.

The word *menousin*, "remain," when used transitively, may also be rendered "wait." All vigorous and vital Christian life must have in it, as a very important element of its vitality, the onward look which is confident of the coming of the Lord from heaven. The vision of the risen Christ brought hope and expectancy into the lives of these men and women. We cannot live without hope. A nation without hope is doomed, and a Christian without hope would perish.

Paul, in writing to the Thessalonians, describes the Christian life as "to serve the living and true God; and to wait for his Son from heaven, whom he raised from the dead" (I Thess. 1:9, 10). The resurrection has for its consequences, its sequel and corollary, first the ascension; then the long period of time during which Jesus Christ is absent, but still in His invisible divine presence rules the world; and finally, His coming again in that same body in which the disciples saw Him depart from them. And no Christian life is up to the level of its privileges, nor has any Christian faith grasped the whole articles of its creed, except that which sets in the very center of all its visions of the future that great thought—He shall come again.

Questions of chronology have nothing to do with that. It stands there before us, the certain fact, made certain and inevitable by the past facts of the cross and the grave and Olivet. He has come, He will come; He has gone, He will come back. And for us the life that we live in the flesh ought to be a life of waiting for God's Son from heaven, and of patient, confident expectancy that when He shall be manifested we also shall be manifested with Him in glory.

So much, then, for life—calm, persistent in every duty, and animated by that blessed and far-off, but certain, hope, and all of these founded upon the vision and the faith of a risen Lord. What have fears and cares and distractions and faint-heartedness and gloomy sorrow to do with the eyes that have beheld the Christ, and with the lives that are based on faith in the risen Lord?

(See Alexander Maclaren, *Expositions of Holy Scripture, I Corinthians*, pp. 209-10.)

DEATH IS ONLY A SLEEP

". . . but some are fallen asleep" (I Cor. 15:6c).

Have you ever been so tired that you could hardly wait to fall into bed? We all have, at one time or another. What a wonderful feeling it is to lay your weary body down and close your eyes in sleep. The very word sleep has a pleasant, soothing quality about it. And yet sleep is coupled in the Bible more than once with the one subject that humans dread most, and which they leave out of their conversation as too upsetting to contemplate. That subject is "death." We wince when we speak of it and wince when we hear it.

That is why we are greatly intrigued by the phrase the Apostle Paul employs, in speaking of the 500 witnesses who saw Jesus Christ after His resurrection. Writing about twenty-five years after this event, he says that more than half of these men are still living, "but some are fallen asleep." Why did Paul use this term, instead of plainly stating that they were dead? Is it because he hesitated to call a spade a spade, and therefore employed a euphemism to soften the ugly word? Not at all. He used the most appropriate term for this experience for the Christian, in view of the reality of the resurrection of the body of the Lord Jesus Christ.

The New Testament often speaks of man's natural death as sleep. Perhaps it is this designation that has caused some to refer to death as soul sleep. We shall see, however, that this term refers only to the sleep of the body and not of the soul.

The Greek verb used for "sleep" in First Corinthians 15:6 is *ekoimeetheesan*, the aorist passive form of the verb *koimaoo*, the middle and passive forms of which are used intransitively. The primary meaning of the word is the natural sleep in which we spend one-third of our lives. This word is used of death because, in death as in sleep, according to Scriptural usage, we lie down only to get up later. Also, in death as in sleep, the body is stilled, calm, and tranquil.

Now, when we sleep, although our bodily senses are shut off from conscious contact with the world around us, our mind or soul is still active. Scientists who have measured men's mental activity while sleeping have found that everyone has several dreams a night. Some men even solve problems in their sleep and wake up in the morning understanding more about some perplexing situation than when they went to bed. When you sleep, the real you is still there, even though your body is "dead to the world." In using the term for death that denotes natural sleep, Paul intends us to understand that the resurrection pertains to the body and not to the soul, for it is the body only that falls asleep in death; the soul retains consciousness.

Scripture never says of the Lord Jesus Christ that He "fell asleep," but that He "died" (I Cor. 15:3). Yet referring to those who die with faith in Him, it says that they fall asleep. Although Scripture tells us that the Lord is "the firstfruits of them that have fallen asleep" (I Cor. 15:20), it does not say that He Himself fell asleep. Why is this?

We believe that God in His omniscience, foreseeing that there would be much doubt concerning the reality of Christ's death, inspired the Biblical writers to use the most careful phraseology here. The Moslems, for instance, claim that Jesus did not actually die; and many rationalists have tried desperately to prove the same thing. Just imagine how much stronger their case would be if Scripture had said that the Lord Jesus fell asleep during the three days that He was in the grave. No, this term commonly used of Christian death was never applied to the death of Jesus Christ.

The term "falling asleep" was used to describe the death even of saints who died before the Lord Jesus came to earth (Matt. 27:52, Acts 13:36). It was used of Lazarus while the Lord was on earth (John 11:11). And it was used of believers who died after Christ's ascension (Acts 7:60; I Cor. 11:30; 15:6; I Thess. 4:13-15; II Pet. 3:4). But the Lord never predicted that He Himself would fall asleep for three days and then wake up.

The Lord's death and resurrection have a definite bearing on our own death and resurrection, and this is expressed by the symbolism of sleep when referring to our physical death as children of God. It is remarkable and beautiful to note that the New Testament scarcely ever employs the terms dying and death to denote the separation of body and spirit. It keeps those grim words for that which is death in reality—the separation of the soul from God—and only exceptionally uses them for the shadow and symbol, the physical fact of man's parting from the house in which he has dwelt on earth. But Christianity and the world use this metaphor for death for directly opposite reasons. The world is so afraid of dying that it dare not name the grim and ugly thing. The Christian faith is so little afraid of death that it does not think such an event worth calling by the name, but terms it merely falling asleep. This is not to say that all Christians have achieved perfect peace of heart and mind with respect to death, but the closer they come to Christ and the more deeply immersed they become in the Word of God, the less death seems to them the end of life and the more they comprehend it as a falling asleep from which they awake to experience the supreme fullness of life in Christ for all eternity.

Even when the circumstances of leaving this earth are painful and violent, the Bible still employs the term "falling asleep." Is it not striking that the first Christian martyr, Stephen, kneeling outside the city, bruised by stones and dying a bloody death, should have been said to fall asleep? If ever there was an instance in which the gentle metaphor seemed inappropriate, it was that cruel death, amid a howling crowd who pelted him with rocks. But yet, "when he said this, he fell asleep" (Acts 7:60). If that be true of such a death, no physical pains of any kind make the gentle word inappropriate for anyone. (See Alexander Maclaren, *Expositions of Holy Scripture, I Corinthians*, pp. 211-12.)

The thought of death as sleep is not merely a Christian idea. The Jews were perfectly familiar with it, for they spoke of their dead as sleeping with their fathers (Deut. 31:16, II Sam. 7:12, I Kings 2:10, Job 7:21). You will find sleep employed as a symbol of death in the philosophy of Greece, in all poetry, and in most of the world's prose literature. It is interesting to note that in the post-Christian era, by the middle of the third century if not earlier, the Greeks called their cemeteries *koimeeteeria*, "sleeping places." It is from this Greek word that we derive our English word "cemetery."

However, the Lord Jesus Christ and the Apostle Paul were not speaking as mere poets or philosophers but were using the language of intense reality. Because of the reality of Christ's resurrection, death is only a sleep, for in Him our resurrection and waking are sure.

John Donne has said it beautifully in his moving poem, *Death, Be Not Proud:*

For those whom thou think'st thou dost overthrow
Die not, poor Death; nor yet canst thou kill me.

* * *

One short sleep past, we wake eternally,
And Death shall be no more; Death, thou shalt die!

OUR AWAKENING FROM THE SLEEP OF DEATH

". . . but some are fallen asleep" (I Cor. 15:6c).

A family moved into a home in the country, and shortly afterward heard that it was supposed to have a haunted room. The father, determined to put a stop to the superstition, said he would sleep in that room. He did so, and the next morning he came down smiling. "There," he said, "I told you. There is nothing to be afraid of there." "Oh, Daddy," sighed his little daughter in relief, "I was afraid you would never wake up!"

The universal use of the symbolism of sleep for death—in religion, philosophy, poetry, literature—indicates that man inherently believes and hopes that death does not end all, but that there will be an awakening from that sleep. Christ slept in that haunted room for us and emerged from it on Easter morning to show us that there was nothing to fear.

Even in natural slumber we lie down with the expectation that we shall rise refreshed to live for another day. Sleep as a symbol of death suggests continuous and conscious existence. There are some who teach that between death and the resurrection lies a period of unconsciousness or even of non-existence. But a man asleep is still himself, still conscious of his identity even in dreams. In sleep he is shut out of immediate touch with the world around him; but the mysterious consciousness of personal identity survives the passage from waking to sleep.

To those that see by faith the risen Christ, death is transformed into a sleep. A great Greek dramatist could ask, "What if death is only a sleep?" But the thought brought him no comfort. By contrast, he who has seen the risen Christ knows of a certainty that the dead sleep to wake. To him the metaphor of sleep that Christ uses with regard to Lazarus' death or that of the daughter of Jairus carries with it the hope of continuity of life. He who sleeps still lives. It is so in the natural course of our lives and it is so in death, though of course the body is lifeless and eventually corrupts and disintegrates. In spite of this, its resurrection is certain. David fell asleep and saw corruption (Acts 13:36). He who sleeps also rests from his labors and renews his strength. And he who sleeps wakes. We kiss our children goodnight without fear, expecting to meet them in the morning. And as Christians, we kiss our loved ones goodnight when this life is over and confidently look forward to meeting them in the next.

Yes, death is a sleep to those who believe in Christ —a quiet falling asleep, with a dear Face bending over our closing eyes like a mother over her child's bed, and the same Face meeting us when we open them in the morning of heaven.

A young wife, after a long and painful illness, which she bore with great courage and patience, thus fell asleep. Just before she closed her eyes, she turned to her husband and said, "The name death ought to be abolished. It is like going away for a holiday to a beautiful place, to meet beautiful people. I only wish you were going, too." That is what death should be for the Christian—a quiet lying down in peace to sleep, in the joyous confidence of a bright awakening. Let us but receive and believe the good news that Paul proclaimed to the Corinthians, "that Christ died for our sins according to the scriptures; and that he was buried, and that he rose again" (I Cor. 15:3 and 4), and life will be to us a patient and expectant waiting for Him, and then a falling asleep—that "blessed sleep from which none ever wakes to weep." (See *The Sermons of Bishop Chavasse*, pp. 165-6.)

Those who lived in the pre-Christian era had this hope of sleep and waking, but Christ came to confirm it by His death and resurrection, thus showing that it is certainly going to be so. There is no conjecture about it. As He rose from the dead, so shall we rise. And as there is a resurrection for the believer, so there must be an analogous resurrection for the unbeliever, in that they likewise will consciously exist endlessly. It was our Lord Himself who said, "Marvel not at this: for the hour is coming, in the which all that are in the graves shall hear his [the Son's] voice, and shall come forth; they that have done good, unto the resurrection of life; and they that have done evil, unto the resurrection of damnation" (John 5:28, 29). Believer or unbeliever, never think that the Lord is through with you when your body falls asleep in death.

We have no proof of immortality apart from the open grave of the Lord Jesus Christ. Every other foundation is too weak to bear the weight of such a superstructure. No heathen hope, no philosophical argument will stand up or will persuade anybody who is committed to materialism that it is absolutely certain the dead will rise; nothing but the fact of the resurrection of Jesus Christ. He rose; therefore death is not the end of individual existence. He rose; therefore life beyond death is certain for humanity. Our belief in the resurrection of all men stands on a rock and not on sand. It is based, not on mere hope and logical deduction, but on the historical fact and the proclamation of Him who earned through His resurrection the right to be trusted in what He said about us and about what was going to happen to us.

Again we want to emphasize that it is the body and not the soul that is asleep during death. The metaphor of sleep for death points to a similarity between a sleeping body and a dead body. Restfulness and peace normally characterize both. The object of the metaphor is to suggest that, as the sleeper does not cease to exist despite his withdrawal from the realm in which those who remain awake can communicate with him, and that, as sleep is known to be temporary, the death of the body is not the end of existence and is also temporary.

If we carefully analyze the Greek word *koimaomai* (intransitive), "to fall asleep," we shall see that it refers to the body only. It is derived from the verb *keimai*, which means "to lie down." This is the opposite of the word *anisteemi*, "to raise up," from which we get the noun *anastasis*, "resurrection." *Anisteemi*, "to raise up," comes from *ana*, meaning "up," and *histeemi*, "to cause to stand." The word *anastasis*, "resurrection," in the New Testament is used of the body only. Another Greek word, *katheudoo*, also meaning "sleep," is used in Daniel 12:2 (Septuagint), to describe "them that sleep," and it also occurs in I Thessalonians 5:6. In Daniel it refers to those who are "in the dust of the earth," which could not possibly mean the soul of man, since it is the body that lies in the dust. In Genesis 3:19 we read, "In the sweat of thy face shalt thou eat bread, till thou return unto the ground; for out of it wast thou taken: for dust thou art, and unto dust shalt thou return." What part of man was taken from the ground? It was not his soul but his body. The spirit of man returns to God who gave it (Eccles. 12:7, Acts 7:59).

Jesus Christ warned His disciples, "Fear not them which kill the body, but are not able to kill the soul: but rather fear him which is able to destroy both soul and body in hell" (Matt. 10:28). The Greek word translated "destroy" does not mean to annihilate the soul and body but implies rather a resultant state of ruination, a being undone, a state of utter wretchedness and misery. The Christian does not fear death as the end of everything because he knows that, though his body sleeps in the dust of the earth, his soul goes to be with God, who "breathed into his nostrils the breath of life; and man became a living soul" (Gen. 2:7).

In Longfellow's poem, *A Psalm of Life*, he affirms his faith in these memorable lines:

> Life is real! Life is earnest!
> And the grave is not its goal;
> Dust thou art, to dust returnest,
> Was not spoken of the soul.

Let us never forget that, while the body is a jewel case that must be kept in serviceable condition, the true treasure is the soul within. It is a poor sense of values that cares more for the case than for the jewel.

WHERE ARE THE DEAD?

". . . but some are fallen asleep" (I Cor. 15:6c).

Some persons are so anxious to have tangible proof of survival after death that they consult spirit mediums in an effort to make contact with loved ones who have passed away. Without going into the whole subject of spiritism, let me say that the Bible flatly condemns it, and that any so-called results in evoking the spirits of the dead are either outright frauds or the work of demonic forces. God has called us to walk by faith in Him and His Word, which tells us that we shall be in communion with our departed loved ones only when we ourselves go to be with the Lord.

But though the soul does not, after the death of the body, give any signs of its continued existence to those who remain, it does not follow that the soul has died also, or that it has passed into an unconscious and inactive state. We believe, on the basis of what the Lord Jesus Christ taught and the entire Bible sustains, that the soul leaves the body at death and goes right on with the activities of its intellectual and spiritual life, as perfectly as or even more so than it did when it was confined and limited by a mortal body. Of course, our eternal resurrection bodies will not at all limit the activities of the soul but will rather enhance them.

He who rose from the dead is our only trustworthy revelation in these matters. Since He is unique in His resurrection, He has the right to be unique in the revelation He gives us of the after world. The Lord intimated time and again that Abraham, Isaac, and Jacob, although dead for hundreds of years, were still living and actively conscious as far as their souls were concerned.

"But as touching the resurrection of the dead," Jesus told the Sadducees, "have ye not read that which was spoken unto you by God, saying, "I am the God of Abraham, and the God of Isaac, and the God of Jacob? God is not the God of the dead, but of the living" (Matt. 22:31, 32). In the account of Lazarus and the rich man, both died; one was carried by angels into Abraham's bosom, and the other awoke in hades, being in torment. The Lord plainly disclosed that they were living and conscious after death (Luke 16:19-31). He promised the penitent thief on the cross that he should be with Him in paradise; and that, too, on the very day in which both died (Luke 23:43).

Paul said that he desired to depart and be with Christ. He thought of his home in the body as an absence from the Lord, and he was willing to be absent from the body that he might be present with the Lord. He had no thought that death would extinguish his mental life or for a moment suspend its activity. He expected at death to quit the body and pass into the personal presence of Christ, in a sense not possible to him while in the body (II Cor. 5:6, 8).

The Bible teaches that when the physical frame of the Christian, "our earthly house of this tabernacle" (II Cor. 5:1), is dissolved and returns to the dust, the spiritual part of his highly complex being, the seat of personality, departs to be with Christ (Phil. 1:23). And since that state is described as "far better" than our present state of joy in communion with God and of happy activity in His service, it is evident that the word "sleep," where applied to departed Christians, is not intended to convey the idea that the spirit is unconscious. (See *Expository Dictionary of New Testament Words*, W. E. Vine, p. 81.)

The Scriptures very clearly distinguish between our body-life and our soul-life. We are not to confound the two, or to regard them as identical, or to make the soul either the product of or absolutely dependent upon the body. What we lose in death is our body-life; and what we retain after death is our soul-life. It is the body that "falls asleep," not the soul. Our present corruptible body is the home of the soul while we live on this earth, but it is not essential to the soul's existence or activity. The conscience, the reason, the affections, the memory, all the higher faculties of the soul are certainly not creations of the material body. They are spiritual powers and, as such, are proven and taught by the unique Christ to be undestroyed and unharmed by death.

The mourners at a funeral were startled when the organ broke into the triumphant strains of the *Hallelujah Chorus*. The pastor explained that this had been the last request of the deceased, a godly woman who rejoiced at the assurance that she would go to be immediately with the Lord.

"I would not have you to be ignorant, brethren," wrote Paul to the Thessalonians, "concerning them which are asleep, that ye sorrow not, even as others which have no hope. For if we believe that Jesus died and rose again, even so them also which sleep in Jesus will God bring with him" (I Thess. 4:13, 14). These words are full of comfort to Christians whose loved ones have died "in the Lord." They may have deep sorrow when laying them away in the grave; they will surely miss their presence; but their grief is not hopeless. Hope takes the despair out of their sorrow and substitutes for it the good cheer of the anticipated reunion that will some day take place in heaven.

God, in His Word, has furnished the basis for this hope. Christians believe and know that Christ died and rose from the dead as "the firstfruits of them that have fallen asleep" (I Cor. 15:20). They believe, upon the authority of this Word, that God will bring with Him those who, when they died, were believers in Jesus and who in this sense sleep in Him. They are assured that this risen and ascended Jesus will, at the appointed time, come in the clouds of heaven, and all the holy angels with Him; that while believers then living shall be changed, the dead in Christ will in the twinkling of an eye be raised incorruptible; that the sleeping believers will be raised first; that the living changed and the risen dead will be caught up together to meet the Lord in the air; that both will ever be with the Lord, and that then the corruptible will put on incorruption, and the mortal will put on immortality.

These stupendous miracles of the Resurrection Day are disclosed in the Bible; and Christians firmly believe them to be God's revelation. It is not more certain that Christ died and rose again, and then ascended into heaven, than that He will come again, and that these miracles will take place. Those that sleep in Jesus shall rise from the dead, shall meet their Lord in the air, and so shall ever be with the Lord.

We need not perplex our minds with curious questions we cannot answer. The Apostle Paul tells us that we need not ask, "How are the dead raised up? and with what body do they come?" (I Cor. 15:35.) It is enough to know that, in the resurrection of the dead, that which was sown in corruption will be raised in incorruption; that which was sown in dishonor will be raised in glory; that which was sown in weakness will be raised in power; that which was sown a natural body will be raised a spiritual body. (See I Cor. 15:42-44.)

Those disembodied spirits that went to be with the Lord Jesus at the touch of death are waiting to be clothed with a spiritual (that is, an incorruptible) body at the final resurrection. Though now we see through a glass, darkly, we nevertheless thank God for the information He has given concerning those who sleep in Jesus. It is our joy to know that those who died in the Lord are blessed, that they rest from their labors, and that their works follow them. It is our joy to know that the clouds that now hide them from our sight will one day be dispersed, that we and they together shall be forever united in heaven, "and so shall we ever be with the Lord."

WHY CHRIST APPEARED TO HIS BROTHER JAMES

"After that, he was seen of James. . . ."

(I Cor. 15:7a).

When the bodies of two missing children were found in a wooded area of New York State some time ago, the police called the mother in to make positive identification. Whenever the question of identity arises, the testimony of a close relative bears the most weight.

Thus, after the resurrection of Jesus Christ, who would be better qualified to testify that this was indeed He in the flesh than a member of His own family? Therefore, in order to leave no doubt whatever as to His identity, the Lord, after appearing to some 500 believers in Galilee, appeared to His brother James.

The Apostle Paul is the only one who refers to this incident. All evidence points to the fact that the James he mentions was the eldest brother of the Lord Jesus. We assume he was the eldest because in the list of Jesus' earthly brothers found in Matthew 13:55 he is named first: "James, and Joses, and Simon, and Judas."

Why did Jesus so signally favor James with a special revelation of His resurrection? Why did He appear to Him singly? As we study the life of James, we find good reasons for this, even apart from the fact that he would be an unimpeachable witness to Jesus' identity.

John 7:5 tells us that during His earthly ministry, "Neither did his brethren believe in him." The Lord

Jesus in a unique agony of soul wept over unrepentant Jerusalem; but may it not be that He shed even more bitter tears over a family in Nazareth, His own human family with whom He had spent a total of thirty years? No doubt Mary and Joseph were believers; but His brothers and sisters found it difficult to swallow the claims of their elder half-brother to deity and Messiahship.

The Lord Jesus, as a human being, had a special love for His earthly family. He would be most unnatural if He had not, for as a man He was in all respects like us except that He was sinless. Surely, then, He loved His family and did not wish them to perish eternally. He would do anything to win them to Himself, short of forcing them to believe. This He could not do, even as a father cannot impose his moral will on a child.

But at least He could appear to one member of His earthly family after His resurrection in the confident expectation that they would believe. And indeed this seems to have been the result, for we read that, after His ascension, His earthly half-brothers and His mother Mary gathered together with the eleven (Acts 1:14). James even became a prominent leader in the early Christian Church (Acts 21:18). It is evident, then, that a complete change of attitude on the part of Jesus' relatives took place after His resurrection. Such a change, as H. B. Swete says, can only have been due to the belief that He had risen from the dead, and had thus proved Himself to be the Messiah.

This special appearance to a relative cannot be devalued with the criticism that a relative will naturally stand up for his own. This is true only if the relative is in agreement with the one whose integrity and claims are being questioned. We see this in the case of those communist children who, encouraged by the State, have denounced their own parents as deviating from communist principles and practice. Paul, therefore, speaks of this special appearance of the risen Christ to James to show that even a disagreeing relative could not help but testify to the fact that the One whom he saw stand before him was his own brother, the Lord Jesus.

But there is another reason for this special revelation. Paul mentions three private manifestations, and it is wonderfully significant that each of them was granted to a man who had wronged Jesus yet subsequently became a leader in the Church. Peter had denied his Master; James had doubted His claims and had wished to put Him under restraint as insane; and Paul had done his utmost to exterminate His influence from the earth.

It was exquisitely fit that Peter, whose sin had been one of cowardice and denial of his Lord, should have been allowed to confess his sin and receive forgiveness face to face with his dear Lord.

Paul has given reasons for the revelation of Christ to himself, and all of them could very well apply also in the case of James. The first was that God chose to call Paul. Peter, in the house of Cornelius, explained God's sovereign ways thus: "Him [Christ] God raised up the third day, and shewed him openly; not to all the people, but unto witnesses chosen before of God, even to us, who did eat and drink with him after he rose from the dead" (Acts 10:40, 41).

As the Lord chose Paul, so did He choose James, who became a foremost witness to the people of Israel for many years, and who finally sealed his testimony with his blood. The special calling of men by God is always set before us in the light of consequent sacrificial service. Abraham was blessed in order that he might become a blessing. The prophets were not granted oracles and visions for their secret enlightenment but that they might become instructors to the people.

It was thus that Christ selected His twelve disciples. "Ye have not chosen me," He said to them, "but I have chosen you, and ordained you, that ye should go and bring forth fruit, and that your fruit should remain" (John 15:16). May it not be that as the Lord appeared to James He said to him, "I have chosen you, not merely because you are my brother, but because I need you to be my witness to Jerusalem and to the nations of the world"?

The Lord, having lived with James for many years, naturally knew the honesty and qualities of His brother. James was commonly called "the just" and apparently he had merited this appellation through his straight-forward conduct. He had been a doubter of Jesus' higher claims, but no sign of jealousy or ill-will can be detected in his conduct.

And what a level-headed leader James proved to be at the first apostolic council held in Jerusalem. Galatians 1:18 tells us that three years after his conversion Paul went up to Jerusalem to visit Peter. It was probably then that he met James and was told by both Peter and James how they had seen the risen Lord.

Nothing is disclosed, however, of the nature of their meeting with the risen Christ nor divulged of their conversation with Him. Probably what transpired was considered too sacred to reveal. And it may be that it would not have added anything to the establishment of the truth that Jesus had indeed risen from the dead. There are conversations and appearances of the Lord to individuals that must remain forever between the individual and his Lord. It is amazing that James in his epistle never even alludes to the personal appearance of the Lord to him or to anything He said. It must have been humbling to him, as it probably was to Peter, and as we know it was to Saul of Tarsus.

Perhaps at eventide, soon after the more public appearing to the 500 disciples on the mountain, the Lord came to the old home at Nazareth to meet with James. What was uttered then we do not know and dare not speculate. If the world needed those words, they would have been recorded. It would be wiser for us to consider whether we could bear Christ to come and speak to us alone about our past relations with Him.

Let us rejoice, however, that to every disciple, no matter how sinful and inconsistent, is given the privilege of having private communication with Him who knows each sheep by name; from whom nothing is hidden, and from whose saving love nothing can separate us except an evil heart of unbelief that loves darkness rather than light. With regard to salvation, Christ has no secret doctrine to impart. His message from above is the same to every creature—the same to you and me as it was to Peter who denied Him, to Saul who persecuted Him, and to James who doubted Him.

We need not envy these men their special revelation. If we take the Bible, and shut our door, we may be alone with Christ; and if after reading His words we will shut the Book and incline our ears to listen to His still small voice, we shall know what faults He is reproving, what faithless doubts He chides, what sins He will forgive, what counsel He is offering us for the days to come, and what commandments He is seeking to rewrite upon our hearts.

(See T. Vincent Tymms, "The Private Relationships of Christ," in *The Christian World Pulpit*, Vol. 70, pp. 316-18.)

A DIVINELY ORDAINED MISCARRIAGE

"After that, he was seen of James; then of all the apostles.   And last of all he was seen of me also, as of one born out of due time" (I Cor. 15:7, 8).

Above all others, the Lord Jesus wanted His own disciples to be absolutely sure of His resurrection. Thus He appeared to them more than once.   When Paul lists the witnesses to the resurrection in First Corinthians 15, he mentions "the twelve" in verse 5 and "all the apostles" in verse 7.   Although this latter group certainly included "the twelve," it may also have included James, the Lord's brother.   In Galatians 1:19 we find Paul saying, "But other of the apostles saw I none, save James the Lord's brother."

Essentially the apostles were "the twelve" to whom Paul referred in verse 5.   But why call them "the twelve" in verse 5 and "the apostles" in verse 7?   It may have been to show that the fact of the resurrection changed these men from mere disciples to apostles. A disciple is one who sits and learns from a teacher; an apostle is "one who is sent," one who goes forth to tell what he has learned.

Now, since Paul's own revelation of Christ on the Damascus road is mentioned immediately afterward (v. 8), this appearance to all the apostles may have been the final one before Christ's ascension.   At the end of the list of those who saw the risen Christ, Paul says, "And last of all he was seen of me also, as of one born out of due time."   He stands to give his own personal evidence in court.   With all the others whom

Paul lists as witnesses of the resurrected Christ, it was a matter of recognizing someone they knew before, but not so with Saul of Tarsus. He was a stranger and an avowed enemy.

Why does Paul leave his testimony to the very end of the list of witnesses? Because, at the time when Paul wrote these words, he was the last of the apostles to whom the risen Christ chose to appear. It was only after Paul's death that the Lord appeared to John on the island of Patmos.

Paul refers to appearances that had as their specific purpose the proof of Christ's resurrection. This is the dominant theme of the whole 15th chapter of First Corinthians. That is why we say that the appearance Paul refers to here must be the one on the road to Damascus described in Acts 9, 22, and 26. This was a special appearance of the Lord to Paul for the purpose of winning him to Himself. Of course, Paul saw the Lord as He appeared to him on subsequent occasions (Acts 22:18; 27:23; II Cor. 12:2-4); but these were subjective experiences. The appearance on the Damascus road was objective and to a certain degree analogous to the appearance of the risen Christ to the eleven disciples and the other believers whom Paul lists. It was a unique appearance in that it occurred not merely after the resurrection but after the ascension.

"And to me he appeared" might be a better rendering of this verse. How much that expression, "and to me," hides in it. It can sober the mind of the wildest skeptic. If the character of Paul can be reasonably deduced from his writings, we know what a great, strong, sane, spiritual man he was. By any reasonable method of deduction, we should find Paul to be one of the last men to base all his hopes for this life and the next upon an uncertainty. It was no will-o-the-wisp that induced him to forsake the religion of his fathers, and all his hopes among his own people, to become a persecuted follower of the despised Nazarene, and to undergo suffering and labors for the Jesus whom he had persecuted. It is no small evidence of the resurrection of Jesus that this man looked upon the risen Christ and was satisfied. (See *The Mysteries of Grace*, by John Thomas, pp. 87-8.) When Paul says solemnly, and stakes his life upon it, "And last of all he appeared to me also," no reasonable man can fail to be impressed.

Observe that the verb Paul uses is the one he has used right along to describe the appearances of our Lord after His resurrection. It is *oophthee*, from the verb *horaoo*, which means not only to see with one's physical eyes but also to comprehend what one sees. It is to see intelligently, spiritually as well as mentally. Peter, the twelve, the 500 believers, the apostles, James, all saw a physical form when they saw Christ after His resurrection, and they were able to make an intelligent identification. They knew He was Jesus.

When the Lord appeared to Saul on the road to Damascus, did he know who was speaking to him? Not at first, until Christ told him. The extraordinary light and noise caused Saul to attribute the occurrence to a higher power, to God Himself, for he called the One who said to him, "Saul, Saul, why persecutest thou me?" by the name of "Lord." But he was puzzled as to His identity, for he asked, "Who art thou, Lord?" And the Lord said, "I am Jesus whom thou persecutest"

(Acts 9:5). Paul had never seen Jesus in the flesh and had no way of recognizing Him. Now he saw Him in His risen, glorified body, and in this sense it was a physical manifestation and a personal identification. This appearance to Paul was somewhat different from the appearances to the disciples and other believers before Christ's ascension, in that the Lord did not stand before Paul on the Damascus road and submit Himself to Paul's touch, or show him His hands and side. As H. B. Swete says, "If a form were seen in the blinding light, it was an appearance in the sky, not on the earth."

But this appearance was fully objective and not a mere subjective ecstasy. The physical brightness was seen not only by Paul but by his whole party. They saw the blinding light that shone supernaturally. They even heard a voice, probably as thunder. In Acts 9:7 we read, "And the men which journeyed with him stood speechless, hearing a voice, but seeing no man." This in no way contradicts Paul's account in Acts 22:9, when he says, "And they that were with me saw indeed the light, and were afraid; but they heard not the voice of him that spake to me." This qualifies what voice they did not hear, the particular speech addressed especially to Paul. It simply means they did not understand what was being said.

In Acts 26:14 Paul says, "And when we were all fallen to the earth, I heard a voice speaking unto me." That voice was for him only to hear and understand, even as it was for him only to see the One speaking. When Paul speaks of this sight of the ascended Christ, in First Corinthians 15, he in no way indicates that

Christ was seen by the rest of the party on the road to Damascus. If they had seen Him as Paul did, they too would probably have been mentioned as witnesses to the resurrection. Very likely they did not even believe, for, if they did, it seems to me that we would have some record of it.

Paul uses a unique expression to describe his conversion. The English has it "as of one born out of due time." In the Greek it is *hoosperei too ektroomati*, "as if it concerned an untimely birth." Even to this day in Modern Greek we continue to use the ancient related word *ektroosis* for "miscarriage." Paul's birth into the body of Christ's apostles and fellow-believers was out of due course. "It was no natural process of ordinary development which brought him from one sphere of existence into another. He was suddenly forcibly ejected, in an abnormal way, all immature, into another order of life and thought" (Sabatier, as quoted by W. J. Sparrow-Simpson in *Our Lord's Resurrection*, p. 120). God acted supernaturally to bring about this abrupt transition to make Saul the meanest of all into Paul the greatest of all. God knows how to work out of due course. Accept such interventions of God. Most persons come into the kingdom through the regular course of childbirth, but others are brought in by miscarriage. God in His sovereign wisdom chooses not only whom He saves but also how He saves them.

REMEMBER WHAT YOU ONCE WERE

"For I am the least of the apostles, that am not meet to be called an apostle, because I persecuted the church of God" (I Cor. 15:9).

You and I usually hate to have our faults corrected. It seems that men have an inborn aversion to reproof, and often react to it with resentment and a spirit of retaliation.

As we read the epistles of Paul to the Corinthians, we observe that he did not hesitate to condemn them in love and to correct them. Some of them could not accept this and were stung to resentment. Since they could find nothing in Paul's character or teaching to justify counter-condemnation, they resorted to depreciation of his authority by declaring that he was not really an apostle. That is why Paul stresses his title to apostleship more frequently in his First Epistle to the Corinthians than in any of his other writings. (See 1:1; 4:9; 9:1, 2, 5; 15:9.) Since this is one of Paul's earliest epistles, his experience with the Corinthians no doubt is what motivated his emphasis upon his office in subsequent epistles. Notice that he starts many of them with a claim to apostleship. (See Rom. 1:1, II Cor. 1:1, Gal. 1:1, Eph. 1:1, Col. 1:1, I Th. 2:6, I Tim. 1:1; 2:7, II Tim. 1:1, 11, Tit. 1:1.)

In describing his encounter with the Lord Jesus after His resurrection, Paul uses the same verb (*oophthee*, "was seen") that he used in describing Christ's appearance to the disciples, to Peter, to James, and to the 500 believers in Galilee (I Cor. 15:5-8). And yet this appearance was distinctly different in that the Lord did not submit Himself to Paul's sense of touch, nor was physical recognition involved, as with Thomas and the other disciples. Yet Paul bases his claim to apostleship on the assumption that the appearance of the resurrected Christ to him had the same value as Christ's appearance to the other apostles.

That is why, immediately after Paul's statement that the Lord appeared to him after His resurrection (v. 8), he adds, "For I am the least of the apostles, that am not meet to be called an apostle, because I persecuted the church of God" (v. 9).

His claim is that he is an apostle, even though, on his own admission, he was unfit to become one. The first indication of this is his use of the word *ektrooma*, "untimely birth, or miscarriage." This Greek word conveys the idea of unfitness for life. Harnack believes that Paul is taking a term of abuse hurled at him by his opponents to call in question his apostolic office, and using it to signify that he is truly unworthy of this office because, when the other disciples and apostles saw the Lord, Paul was persecuting Him in His earthly community. *Ektrooma*, "a man born out of due time," was a current term of abuse with a religious application. (See G. Kittel, *Theological Dictionary of the New Testament*, Vol. II, Eerdmans, 1964, pp. 465-6.)

Paul further evidences his sense of unworthiness to be an apostle by the use of the word *kamoi*, meaning "and to me" or "to me also," in verse 8: "And last of all he appeared to me also." He places himself in a class of his own. He was agonizingly conscious of his past record of persecution of the Church of God, and recognized that it was only by the grace of God that he was what he was (v. 10). That is why he never ceased to wonder at the marvel of his salvation, and only second to that at the fact of his apostleship. That is why he says, "And unto me he appeared . . . making me an apostle by his grace." Paul was lost in wonder, love, and praise when he thought of his apostleship, for of all men he seemed the least worthy of this high honor and dignity.

Indeed, in one place he calls his apostleship a "grace." "Unto me, who am less than the least of all saints, is this grace given, that I should preach among the Gentiles the unsearchable riches of Christ" (Eph. 3:8). How was it that he who was less than the least of all saints became an apostle? By God's grace. Grace did more than save Paul; it brought him to honor and dignity. "Also to me the Lord appeared." That's all one needs to accomplish great things for God. Paul recognizes that all that he became and all that he accomplished were the result of that first encounter with the risen Christ.

Paul wanted all the Corinthian believers to realize that he was actually an apostle, and that it was by divine appointment. Just as he had had nothing to do with his salvation, he had nothing to do with his being made an apostle. It was not a matter of pride with him; in fact, he put himself at the foot of the apostolic ladder. "For I am the least of the apostles." The Greek word translated "least" is *elachistos*, which came to be a true superlative of the adjective "small" (*mikros*) in the development of the Greek language.

Note that Paul refers to a specific group of known apostles: "I am the least of *the* apostles." The apostolic office was established and sealed. All the apostles were known, and their number was not to be added to. Only those could claim apostleship who had been specifically called by Christ and had seen Him in the way the Twelve and Paul had seen Him after His resurrection. Any person who might claim apostleship in future would have to meet these qualifications.

Paul could very well have expressed his humility by saying, "I am the least apostle" (i.e., the humblest or lowest), instead of "I am the least of *the* apostles." The least of "the" apostles was greater than the greatest apostle among us. You and I are little apostles, but none of us can claim that he is even the least of "the" apostles. We must not usurp an office that does not belong to us. We are apostles only in the secondary sense that the Lord has sent us forth to preach the Gospel, or to witness in various ways, which is true of all believers; but we cannot qualify on the ground of having been called of the Lord to serve Him in His lifetime and having seen Him after His resurrection.

"I am not worthy to be called an apostle," Paul declares. The present infinitive *kaleisthai*, "to be called," is in the passive voice, indicating that he was called an apostle by others. The apostolic group not only accepted him as one of themselves but also called him by that title, as did others in the larger Christian community. This form could also be taken as middle voice. In this sense *kaleisthai* means "to call myself" (i.e., an apostle). Paul considered the title too lofty; but in order for his deeds and words to have the authority of the written Word of God, he had to be one of "the" apostles, even though it were the least.

But the reason Paul gives for his unfitness to be called an apostle is the stigma of the past, not the present: "Because I persecuted the church of God." He considered that he had committed a grave crime. Having experienced the glory of the Gospel of the grace of God, he could never forget the damage he had done to Christianity. Paul experienced the power of God in his life through a special appearance of Jesus Christ. He knew that this power was capable of destroying him, and that this was what he deserved. But instead it saved him. That is why he could write with such certainty that the power of God is unto salvation and not unto destruction (Rom. 1:16). Paul never lost sight of the fact that on the Damascus road God gave him, not what he deserved but what he needed, not destruction but redemption. How then could he pride himself on anything but the grace of God, the undeserved favor of the Almighty?

Has God saved you, cleansed you from sin, given you the privilege of serving Him, and given you a position of respect among the Christian community? Are you proud of your reputation and accomplishments as a Christian? Check that pride as a presumptuous sin; for, if it were not for the grace of God, you would be a lost and hell-deserving sinner. Marvel instead at the condescension of God in extending mercy to you while you were yet in your sins, and serve Him in the humble consciousness that it is by grace alone you stand.

LOOK AT YOURSELF AS YOU REALLY ARE

"But by the grace of God I am what I am"
(I Cor. 15:10a).

Have you heard the fable of the woodpecker who was pecking away at the trunk of a dead tree when it was struck by lightning? Although the trunk was splintered, the woodpecker flew away unharmed. Looking back he exclaimed, "Look what I did!"

The Apostle Paul was no such woodpecker. As he looked back he could only say, "See what God did!" He was not blind to the change for the better in his heart and life, but he did not make the mistake of taking credit for it himself. "By the grace of God I am what I am," said Paul, rejoicing in the mercy and favor of God that had saved, cleansed, and called him to be an apostle. He knew he was standing on the Rock of Ages. He knew of his heavenly position in Christ. But the higher one's position in Christ, the deeper and darker the pit seems from which he has been rescued. Jewelers make exquisite forms from precious metals, but God makes His precious things from base materials. He has not selected the best, but quite often the worst of men to be the monuments of His grace.

It was a Pharisee in the temple who prayed, saying, "God, I thank thee, that I am not as other men are" (Luke 18:11). Although he ostensibly gave thanks to God, his whole attitude was one of self-congratulation. Paul was a Pharisee, too, and there was a time when he boasted of his own standing and attainments: "Of the stock of Israel, of the tribe of

Benjamin, an Hebrew of the Hebrews; as touching the law, a Pharisee; concerning zeal, persecuting the church; touching the righteousness which is in the law, blameless" (Phil. 3:5, 6).

But there came a day when those things that Paul had counted gain, and in which he gloried, were regarded as refuse compared with what he had found in the Gospel of Jesus Christ. His experience of actually seeing the ascended Christ on the Damascus road thoroughly revolutionized his life, giving it a new center, new standards, and a new aim. From then on, he does not boast of what he has attained but of what he has obtained by the grace of God, manifested and mediated in and through the Lord Jesus Christ. Thus, when he utters the words, "But by the grace of God I am what I am," it is the privileges and possessions that belonged to him in Christ that he has in mind.

Paul realized that grace does not stand upon a distant mountain-top and call on the sinner to climb up its heights that he may obtain heaven; it comes down into the valley in quest of him and lifts him out of the mire. God in His grace does not offer to complete the work, if the sinner will only begin it by doing what he can; this grace or unmerited favor takes the whole work in hand from first to last, presupposing his total helplessness. As Bonar says, God's grace does not bargain with the sinner, that if he will throw off a few sins, and put forth some efforts after better things, God will step up and relieve him of the rest by forgiving and cleansing him: God's grace comes up to him at once, with nothing short of complete forgiveness as the starting-point of all his efforts to be holy.

We have noted that the word "least," in the phrase, "the least of the apostles," is the superlative of the adjective *mikros*, meaning "small." This gives us an insight into the fact that Paul did not consider any apostle great on his own merits. All are small, and I am the smallest of all, is Paul's thought here. They are greater than I, but let us not forget that we are all little men whom the grace of God has lifted and filled. What humbling language Paul uses to help us see that we should not glory in any greatness of our own. He does not say, "They are great, and I am less great, or the least of the greatest," but "I am the smallest of the small."

Despite his humility, Paul never minimizes the office he holds. He speaks with the authority of an apostle, conscious that through him God speaks to men. He stands as man before God, and represents God to men. This is a very sobering realization for him. You and I do not have the rank or authority of apostleship in this unique sense. That was limited to those who were personally called by Christ, and who saw Him after His resurrection. But in a more general sense we are Christ's apostles. We, too, should be conscious of the fact that men judge God by us, and that we are His messengers to them.

A young minister, when about to be ordained, confessed that at one period of his life he was well on his way to becoming an infidel. "But," said he, "there was one argument in favor of Christianity that I could never refute—the consistent Christian life of my father." Are you that consistent Christian influence to your family? This does not mean that you will brag about your Christianity. Instead you will admit that you esteem yourself the least of all Christians, and that it is only God's grace that gives you the ability to live a godly life and the authority to speak for Him. An Eastern proverb says, "I am not the rose, but I have been with the rose, and therefore I am sweet." It is only as we dwell with Christ, the Rose of Sharon, that others will be blessed by His fragrance through us.

Paul does not parade his attainments or his achievements as being intrinsically his own. This does not mean that he was ignorant, or pretended ignorance of what he could do. It was the same apostle who said, "I can do all things through Christ" (Phil. 4:13). He was conscious of the power of Christ in and through him to accomplish mighty things.

There is no harm in recognizing your God-given abilities. The harm lies in thinking that they make you a very fine fellow and that your accomplishments are so great as to set you above your fellows. To know that the grace of God has saved you is part and parcel of the work of grace. But to boast of your goodness as compared to the sinfulness of other Christians is presumption. Think less of who you are than of what you are by the grace of God.

Most men who have been chosen and empowered to do a great work for God have been aware that they could do it. But the less we think about ourselves in the process the better. The more we recognize how dependent we are upon the grace of God to accomplish His purposes, the less likely we are to become touchily self-assertive or to misuse the powers He has given us. We must acknowledge as Paul did that we are only reservoirs of God's grace and nothing more. "What hast thou that thou didst not receive? now if thou didst receive it, why dost thou glory, as if thou hadst not received it?" (I Cor. 4:7). Also, like Paul, we must give up the attempt to determine what we really are; for however clearly we may know our own powers and achievements, it is hard for us to estimate the relations of these to our whole character.

The truth of the matter is that Paul was so full of the capabilities of the grace of God that he did not know where to begin and where to end. Great men don't usually boast. They achieve. It is small men who become puffed up over their accomplishments. Self-conceit is not a disease peculiar to ten-talented people, but it is far more likely to be found among those with one talent. A young man received a medal at school, presented to him in a flowery speech praising the greatness of his accomplishment. Proudly the student repeated the words to his mother. Then he asked her, "How many great men are there in the world, anyhow?" "One less than you think," replied the wise woman.

As Paul says in Romans 12:3, "For I say, through the grace given unto me, to every man that is among you, not to think of himself more highly than he ought to think; but to think soberly, according as God hath dealt to every man the measure of faith." In calling himself the least of the apostles, Paul surely followed his own advice.

SELF-CONCEIT, SELF-CONTEMPT, OR TRUE SELF-APPRAISAL?

"But by the grace of God I am what I am"
(I Cor. 15:10a).

It is a good thing to know who and what you are. Many people don't. The advice of Socrates, "Know thyself," must be the starting point for any man who wants to use his abilities to the fullest. Psychiatry makes self-knowledge the first requirement for liberating a man from crippling personality defects. But the challenge of the Gospel makes knowledge of one's sin the prerequisite of repentance, forgiveness, and new life in Christ. If you don't know you're a sinner, you'll never seek a Saviour. If you are saved, you will recognize that you are a citizen of a new country, the Kingdom of Heaven. Knowledge of self and its abilities enables you to reflect and to decide wisely. It is not necessary for a man to be ignorant, or to pretend ignorance, of his abilities. To hide your talents is hypocrisy of the worst kind. The whole structure of society is based on what each of its members can do. You must have a realistic understanding of what you can and cannot do, or both you and your fellow men will suffer.

When Paul said, "By the grace of God I am what I am," he was not expressing self-satisfaction. He recognized the operations of God's grace in his heart and life, but he did not feel that all the work that grace could do had been accomplished. He acknowledged what God's grace had done in him thus far, but realized that there was much more for grace to accomplish. No person is more difficult to get along with than the man who feels that he is a finished product of grace.

Knowing what we have received from God does not give us a license to compare ourselves favorably with others. It was presumptuous for the Pharisee in the temple to pray as he did, "God I thank thee that I am not as other men are" (Luke 18:11). And yet it was right and fitting for a former Pharisee, Paul, to say, "By the grace of God I am what I am." The one was making a comparison that elevated himself in his own eyes and that sought to commend himself to God for his blamelessness. Paul never ceased to blame himself for his unworthiness or to feel that he was exempted from the battle with sin, even after he had experienced the grace of God in victory over that sin.

A young convert on the foreign field was given a position of trust in the mission station. He violated that trust by stealing. The missionaries were distressed. "Why did you take what didn't belong to you?" they asked. "It wasn't I who stole; it was grandfather in my bones!" he replied. That was his way of referring to his old nature. In time he became an overcoming Christian. When asked, "How is grandfather in your bones?" he would reply, "Well, grandfather in the bones isn't dead yet, but he doesn't get about as he used to."

Paul recognized this dual character of the Christian when he wrote in Romans 7:17, "Now then it is no more I that do it, but sin that dwelleth in me." But this sin that was still in him like an unwanted guest could not defeat the predominant grace of God. When

Paul said, "By the grace of God I am what I am," he certainly did not intend to convey the idea that that was all he was ever going to be. Self-satisfaction was the fault of the Pharisee whom Christ condemned, but not of the Apostle Paul. It is a most dangerous state into which to fall. What was the condemnation of the Laodicean Church but that they prided themselves on what they were and felt that they needed nothing. But the Lord said to them, "Thou . . . knowest not that thou art wretched, and miserable, and poor, and blind, and naked" (Rev. 3:17).

Self-satisfaction is a great hindrance to progress. The self-satisfied man is not motivated to learn anything. He may get worse, but he cannot get better until he gets rid of his overweening self-esteem. Our Lord found only one class on whom His teaching and example were wasted. They were not the criminals or even the covetous money-makers. Zaccheus and Matthew, the publicans, obeyed His call. But it was pre-eminently the dyed-in-the-wool self-satisfied religionists, those from whom most might have been expected, who learned nothing because they felt they had nothing to learn.

A friend of the great Danish sculptor Thorwaldsen found him in a depressed state one day and asked the reason. "My genius is decaying," he replied. "Here is my statue of Christ, which is the first of my works which has satisfied me. Hitherto I have never come near the idea in my mind. I shall have no more great thoughts."

Self-satisfaction is usually the result of setting our standards too low. That's what you do when you compare your righteousness with that of others. Don't be satisfied merely with having a tombstone that reads, "He lived respected and died lamented," but adopt the standard Paul had, not only for himself, but also for all his comrades: "Till we all come in the unity of the faith, and of the knowledge of the Son of God, unto a perfect man, unto the measure of the stature of the fulness of Christ" (Eph. 4:13). "Be ye therefore perfect, even as your Father which is in heaven is perfect" (Matt. 5:48). Perfection is absolute only in God. In humans, it is relative. It is the fulfillment of that kind and degree of excellence that God meant each of us to exhibit. But in a sense the standard is absolute, for it is one that we can never suppose for a moment we have reached. Those who have scoffed at Christian humility as a weak virtue, unfitting us to take a manly and active part in life, have totally misunderstood its nature.

We can see from Paul's language about himself how far humility is from self-contempt. Pride and self-contempt are alike in this, that they forbid any attempt at improvement. They are alike in this also, that they blind us to reality. There is a false humility to which inexperienced Christians are sometimes prone, which consists in beating themselves up, a feeling that they are so unworthy that it is right, and even acceptable before God, to hate themselves. But this leads to hopelessness and morbidity, and is far removed from the spiritual health that comes from believing that we have received the forgiveness of God in Christ, and that we now have His grace to give us the victory over our sins.

The proud man cannot see things as they are because he is always standing in his own light. And self-contempt prevents a man from seeking and cheerfully undertaking the work that God means him to do. True humility is not hopeless about itself, because although we have no power of ourselves to help ourselves, our sufficiency is of God. Paul knew that he was a fellow-worker with God—the most glorious and inspiring thought that can animate a human heart. At other times he knew that he was wrestling against the powers of evil within him as well as without. The more clearly we perceive the opportunities of doing good that God has placed in our hands, the more we shall feel our own need of praying with the publican, "God be merciful to me a sinner" (Luke 18:12), when we remember how many of these opportunities we have allowed to slip, and how often, alas, we have done positive harm instead of good.

(See J. G. Greenhough, *Sunset Thoughts*, Arthur H. Stockwell, London, pp. 140-1; and "The Sin of Self-Satisfaction," in *The Christian World Pulpit*, Vol. 108, pp. 121-2.)

A realistic self-appraisal, then, sees and acknowledges our sinful nature, but at the same time, if we have come into a saving relationship with Jesus Christ, it rejoices over the fact that the grace of God in us is sufficient to give us the victory over sin and to enable us to fulfill God's purposes for our lives.

THE FORCES THAT SHAPE OUR LIVES

"But by the grace of God I am what I am"
(I Cor. 15:10a).

When one child in a family turns out badly, and another turns out well, where does the responsibility lie? We can never be conscious of all the forces that have shaped us into what we are. The Apostle Paul could say, "By the grace of God I am what I am." By this he meant that God was to be praised for anything good that was in him, since God is good. Conversely we must conclude that God is not to be held blameworthy for the evil in men.

However, it is not only the believer who can say, "By the grace of God I am what I am," but also, to a certain degree, the unbeliever. All the operations of nature are the operations of God, and both believers and unbelievers share in their benefits. God is in the common events of every day, just as certainly as He is in the great spiritual experiences of life. He is all in all. He uses men to further His purposes even when they do not know Him. He orders their path and preserves them in life. They are as good as they are and no worse than what they are only by divine permission and grace. Our breath, the beating of our heart, are in His hands. "In him we live, and move, and have our being" (Acts 17:28).

Those who take no account of God's power claim that each man's moral condition is determined by one of three causes, or a combination of them: heredity, environment, and the exercise of his will. Materialists sometimes want to rule out the will, claiming that everything is determined by heredity and environment. This is materialistic fatalism, a philosophy that believes man is not at all responsible for his destiny.

No one would deny that we owe much to heredity. Just how much is a mystery that puzzles the wisest. Heredity plays the strangest of freaks. It is continually upsetting expectations and laughing our predictions to scorn. A wise father sometimes begets a foolish child, and the son of a stupid man may be a genius. The gifts of great men are rarely transmitted to their children. The qualities of good men do not always reappear in those they leave behind them.

Still, we owe something, oftentimes very much, to our parents, and to good parents we owe more than we can perhaps appreciate. Our best qualities, as well as some of our worst, had their beginnings, at least, in those who gave us birth. A man who had a drunken father or mother is terribly handicapped in the moral race; and to have the blood of God-fearing men and women in our veins is better than titles and wealth.

Consider the outstanding Murray family of South Africa. The father of the family, Andrew Murray the first, was a young Scotch missionary. He wooed and won a Dutch girl of Huguenot extraction, who became the mother of his seventeen children, twelve of whom lived to grow up and bless the world. The total number of ministers in the family, either directly or by marriage, in the last generation was forty-two. Others became missionaries, and three grandsons became members of the South African Parliament. Of the original family, five sons were ministers, and the daughters wives of pastors and heads of educational establishments; the best known, outside of South Africa, being the beloved Dr. Andrew Murray, his father's namesake. "Never," remarked a friend of the family, "were children more fortunate in their mother. Hers was one of those sweet, persuasive natures which mould and guide and bless without seeming to know it themselves. When asked, 'How did you bring up such a wonderful family?' she replied, 'Oh, I do not know; I did not do anything.' But everyone else knew, if she did not. She just lived herself the life she wanted her boys and girls to live. Her life was hid with Christ in God; and they, through her, saw the beauty of holiness." Heredity and environment combined provided a most favorable background for the children.

While heredity counts for something, environment and training count for more. Weak men are almost wholly shaped by their surroundings, and only the very strongest can overcome an unfavorable environment. Our morals are generally the morals of those among whom we live. It is terribly hard to be clean, upright, and sober when all about us is sordid and vile. Pity the children who are born into such an environment.

It is our duty as Christians to work for the betterment of man's environment everywhere. But we must not be so naive as to believe that a good environment will turn sinners into saints, or make corrupt men sound. Men once fell in paradise and would fall again; but a good environment would help to keep thousands on a decent level who go down to the depths. Many a degraded and criminal person would have some right to say, "My environment made me what I am."

A communist was haranguing a group of listeners in Columbus Circle, in New York City. In extolling the so-called virtues of communism, he cried out, "Communism can put a new suit on a man!" One of God's children, ever on the alert to turn any situation in such a way as to bring glory to his Lord, said in a clear, earnest voice, "And Christ can put a new man in the new suit!" "Therefore, if any man be in Christ, he is a new creature" (II Cor. 5:17).

But man's own self has to be reckoned with. He possesses the power to choose good or evil. Man is more than a brute whose instincts come by descent and who has no discernment of right and wrong. He has some power to see and strive after better things. By God's grace, Christians are continually overcoming their inherited tendencies through faith, energy, and prayer. Good men occasionally come from wretched and defiled homes, even as a silver coin is sometimes found shining in the gutter. The moral realm is full of surprises. If a man *will*, then by the help of God he *may*. There is in each of us the double possibility of rising or falling, and that is the only thing that makes us accountable to God.

Heredity, environment, and the little or much that each one contributes himself—these three are found in the making or marring of every life. But there is something more: there is God. He is the only One who can really make your life worthwhile; He is the One who can give you peace and joy that spring from His regenerating grace. Your rejecting of this grace can only result in the marring of your life.

"By the grace of God I am what I am." Anything

good in me I owe to Him. If I have been shaped for good by heredity or environment, it was God who determined these, and therefore I can still say, "By the grace of God I am what I am."

But be very careful lest you are still in a state of sin in spite of the grace of God that has surrounded both your heredity and environment. Have you gone wrong in very defiance of God's grace? Are you one for whom no excuse can be found on the grounds of heredity and environment? Your parents, perhaps, were the salt of the earth. Your home was a nursery of faith and virtues. And yet look at how low you have sunk in your moral perversity. You are inexcusable. You have thrown away the faith of your home, trampled on prayer, dishonored your parents. Remember that God's punishment will be proportionate to the opportunities of grace He has given you.

God gives each man an opportunity in His own sovereign way, and each man will be judged as to what he has done with that God-given opportunity of grace. Perhaps the greatest sinners in God's sight are those who might have been saved but have rejected His grace. The most terrible judgment for any man is that which he will one day have to pronounce on himself: "In spite of the grace of God I am what I am." (See J. G. Greenhough, *Sunset Thoughts*, pp. 141-8.)

Paul's heredity and environment were Pharisaism, and he was saved in spite of them. God can save you, too, no matter how impossible your background and how filthy or fanatical your environment. No heredity and no environment places anyone outside the reach of the grace of God.

JUST WHAT IS THE GRACE OF GOD?

"But by the grace of God I am what I am: and his grace which was bestowed upon me was not in vain; but I laboured more abundantly than they all: yet not I, but the grace of God which was with me"

(I Cor. 15:10).

Perhaps the most painful discovery we can make as children is that, though each one of us is by nature the center of his own universe, it does not revolve about us as its pivot. With what screams of outrage a spoiled baby reacts when his parents first decide to let him "cry it out." How disturbed an only child often becomes when a new baby displaces him as the center of interest in the home. And even in the Christian life, how painful it is to the immature soul to outgrow the tendency to see itself as the sole object of God's love and care, to make itself the object of its own contemplation, and to see all else as related to itself. Such a self-centered, self-concerned soul, trying to feed upon itself, must inevitably suffer both the pangs of unsatisfied hunger and a contraction and narrowing of itself, rather than the healthful growth and activity that come from centering upon God.

When we come to the 10th verse of First Corinthians 15, we find its whole emphasis is embodied in the expression, "By the grace of God." It centers not on Paul and his claim to apostleship, the great transformation that occurred in his life, or his accomplishments for God, but on the grace of God. Anyone reading the epistles of Paul will find that he teaches not a man-centered but a God-centered religion. God is at the hub of the universe and everything else is in the periphery. This is the difference between Biblical revelation and humanism. It is God who creates, God who provides, God who sustains, God who re-creates. It is God at the center. Man does not discover God but accepts or rejects God's revelation of Himself. It is God who takes the initiative and God who accepts our response to His love.

If you want to be miserable, think of yourself as being at the center of the universe. It has been well said that without God the world is simply a place where men sit and hear each other groan. Charles Kingsley said, "If you want to be miserable, think much about yourself, about what you want, what you like, what respect people ought to pay you, and what people think of you." The prescription of Christianity is just the reverse. Put God in the center and you will find yourself in your proper place. Put yourself in the center and you will be a misfit. Examine your estimate of yourself in relation to the universe. Get out of the center and then you won't seem to carry all its burdens.

A political leader, disturbed at the state of his nation, could not sleep. His aide, who saw him tossing and turning in bed, gathered up enough courage to venture, "Sir, don't you think that God governed the world before you came into it?" "Undoubtedly," was the reply. "And don't you think He will govern it quite as well when you are gone out of it?" "Certainly." "Then don't you think you may trust Him to govern it properly as long as you live?" No answer. But it wasn't long before the political leader fell asleep. Your sleep cannot help being disturbed if you place yourself at the center. Only as you place God there and trust Him to order things aright will you have peace of heart.

An inscription on a church speaks the mind of Paul: "Without God, without all; with God, enough." That's what Paul meant when he said, "By the grace of God I am what I am." His was not the philosophical postulate of Descartes: "I am; therefore God is," but rather the Biblical principle, "God is; therefore I am. Furthermore, I am what I am because God is what He is, a God of grace."

The whole secret of Christianity is found in one word, "grace." Into no other religion does the element of grace enter so consistently. It is not found in the Judaism that can only see the law. The law of Moses requires an eye for an eye, a tooth for a tooth, an exact debit and credit account of human conduct, a reward proportionate to desert, even to the fraction of a fraction, a mechanical concept of morality and virtue. Happily, the Old Testament really contains both law and Gospel, as does all Scripture, although in the Old Testament the Gospel is not fully explicit.

We find no real grace in pagan religions. In Buddhism we see the despairing effort of the human heart to cleanse itself, to extirpate self, to annihilate the energies that it cannot reconcile or harmonize. In all the systems of religious thought, man is left to work out his salvation as best he can. He may attain this or that reward by his own great effort, but nothing is given him. A road-map to the eternal city is put into his hands, but nothing is said about how he is to make the journey; there is nothing to supplement or inspire his own flagging energies.

But with its first word to man, Christianity changes everything. It tells us of One born to save us; of God setting Himself to do for us what we cannot do for ourselves; of eternal life, not as something attained but as a free gift. And behold, all is changed. In a moment Christ gives us what we could not have attained in a hundred lifetimes. The grace of God is the miraculous touch of God set upon human life; grace, something given and not earned; grace that covers our sins and gives us mystic inward renewal. Grace deflects the great engine of natural law and works upon the soul by supernatural means. Grace, out of barren natures, out of Pharisees, apostates, persecutors, and blind reactionaries, creates the new man that is after the image of Jesus Christ; and this man, astonished at the miracle, can only say, "It is by the grace of God that I am what I am."

Now what is this grace of God? Paul here is speaking of that specific grace that goes beyond the common providence of God. The Lord of the universe sends rain on the just and the unjust; He gives breath to the believer and the unbeliever. Paul was the recipient of God's grace in this limited sense even before his conversion on the road to Damascus. But certainly he became a different creature after this conversion experience, which he assigns to the miraculous special grace of God. He is therefore referring here not to the common providential care of God for all His creatures, but to the saving, redemptive, transforming special grace of God in the heart of the one who is led to believe on Jesus Christ.

Grace is love with a special direction to it. While all grace is love, not all love is grace. Love can be shown by an equal for an equal, by a higher for a lower, or by a lower for a higher. But the love that is grace can only be shown by the highest—God—for a lower—sinful man. We can love God, but it would be a blasphemous impertinence to talk about our being gracious to Him. God, however, is gracious to us. Saving grace is love that flows down; it is love that stoops; it is the love of the Highest for the lowest.

Then, too, grace is a gift, a benevolence that expresses the magnanimity of God. It may be explained for us in two Scripture passages and an incident.

In writing to the Romans, Paul says, "The wages of sin is death; but the gift of God is eternal life" (Rom. 6:23). Here you have a threefold contrast: sin and God, life and death, wages and a gift. All men have earned death by committing sin, but you cannot earn eternal life; that is a gift, the divine magnanimity of grace interfering on man's behalf.

Again it is said in John's Gospel, "The law was given by Moses, but grace and truth came by Jesus Christ" (John 1:17). Here is the same thought. Under the law you do something and you receive the due reward of your deed; but Christ reveals the magnanimity of God in a grace which puts the law aside and overwhelms man with unmerited mercies.

And when Christ stands up to preach His first sermon in the little synagogue at Nazareth, you have an incident that illumines the whole scene and gives you the keynote to Christianity. Do you remember that incident—the awe and wonder that fall upon the congregation as Jesus begins to speak, the sense they feel of something indefinably holy and benignant in Him as He reads, with a thrill of emphasis never heard before, the great words of Isaiah, "The Spirit of the Lord is upon me, because he hath anointed me to preach the gospel to the poor; he hath sent me to heal the brokenhearted, to preach deliverance to the captives, and recovering of sight to the blind, to set at liberty them that are bruised, to preach the acceptable year of the Lord" (Luke 4:18, 19). It was as though an apparition of perfect goodness and perfect love stood before them, and they marveled.

Yet in a moment their wonder changed to bitterness, rancor, and murderous hatred, and they sought to cast Jesus headlong from the brink of the hill on which their city was built. Why? Simply because of two things that Jesus said, two plain historical facts that He recalled. One was that in the days of Elisha, God had passed over the many widows of Israel to show mercy to a widow who was a heathen, a woman of Sarepta. The other was that God had passed over the many lepers in Israel to show mercy to a man who was a heathen, Naaman the Syrian.

Why did that make them so angry? What was there in the statement that encouraged in them such a murderous outbreak of hatred? It was the declaration of the Gospel of the grace of God made by Jesus Christ in His first sermon, grace that cannot be bought, merited, or earned; grace that came unsought to the alien and to the heathen; grace that took no account of ancestry or even of moral worth or unworthiness in men, but had mercy on whom it would have mercy. Christ proclaimed grace as the magnanimity of God triumphing over reason and tradition. The law had come by Moses; now grace had come by Jesus Christ. That was the message of the Lord Jesus, and that is the one message of the Gospel still—the message that God out of His fathomless love interferes to save men, and does this with a total disregard of their supposed claims upon Him; for we are saved by grace, and grace is a gift.

Did not the whole life of the Lord Jesus exhibit this spirit? Was He not the friend of publicans and sinners? Did He not choose His comrades, not for their worthiness but for their need? Did Saul of Tarsus have even the least claim upon that Jesus whom he persecuted? Yet the Lord came to him; the divine magnanimity sought him out, even him. Thus Paul looks back with tears of astonished happiness and says, "By the grace of God I am what I am."

(See W. J. Dawson's "The Grace of God," in *The Christian World Pulpit*, Vol. 52, pp. 200-2.)

LET'S AGREE ON THE FACTS

"Whether it were I or they, so we preach, and so ye believed" (I Cor. 15:11).

Truth is truth, no matter who preaches it. We are sometimes tempted to attach ourselves to the one who proclaims it rather than to the truth itself. We develop such a strong regard for some radio preacher, evangelist, or church pastor that we subconsciously relegate Jesus Christ to second place.

This is nothing new. Some of the first-century Christians attached themselves to personalities: some to Paul, some to Apollos, some to Cephas. This is what occasioned Paul's searching question: "Is Christ divided? was Paul crucified for you? or were ye baptized in the name of Paul?" (I Cor. 1:13).

The Corinthian church seems to have been unhappily affected by Greek culture and heathen practices. No other church of that day is said to have been guilty of such gross sins and inconsistent testimony. Party spirit and faction, which were the curses of Greek civic life, had likewise crept into the church.

In writing to the Corinthians to correct these conditions, Paul asserts his apostleship, which gave him the authority to speak for God. In proclaiming truths that some found unpalatable, and in correcting their disorderly worship practices, it was natural that he met with resistance. Some were inclined to revolt against Paul by asserting that most of what he taught was peculiar to himself, that it was not general apostolic teaching but was in fact heresy.

This is the way far too many people seek to rationalize their rejection of any truths that they do not like. They reject them as peculiarities of the one who taught them, and travel blithely on their own opinionated way. They justify the rightness of their rejection by downgrading the faithful preacher or looking for one who is more lenient in his views.

The Apostle Paul had an answer for the Corinthians who were looking for a way out in certain matters of doctrine and conduct, as well as for their modern counterparts. He says, "Whether it were I or they, so we preach, and so ye believed." That is, whether I, Paul, tell you these basic truths, or whether the other apostles preach them, there is unity in the apostolic teaching. I am not preaching something peculiar to myself but what is common to all the apostles. Since he had just spoken of himself as being also an apostle to whom the risen Lord had revealed Himself, the pronoun "I" should be understood as meaning "I, as an apostle."

There was common agreement among the apostles as to the essential doctrines of Christianity. True, these men were different from one another. Their methods and expressions varied. They may even have disagreed on some minor points (when not involved in the composition of Scripture under the direct inspiration of the Holy Spirit), but they all stood on the one Rock, the Lord Jesus Christ. The word "so," in the clause "so we preach," refers to the authoritative summary of the Gospel that Paul has just given in the preceding verses.

Christianity from the doctrinal viewpoint consists of certain facts that, like foundation stones, sustain the whole weight of the edifice of faith. Its distinctive creed is primarily a proclamation of those facts. They were the substance of the apostles' teaching and, if they were disproved, the foundation of the Christian religion would crumble.

These basic truths are the core of the Gospel proclamation. These are the substructure. The Christian Church is the superstructure. Each of us in the superstructure may live a little differently. We may decorate our own apartment, so to speak, with a variety of colors and furnishings, but we all stand on one and the same foundation. And as long as we do, we must have a basic fellowship together. The Christian Church has always been one, in spite of its divergent expressions of the same basic historic faith. Identity of expression does not always mean identity of belief, and diversity of expression does not necessarily mean disagreement on what is basic to the Gospel. Unfortunately, we who stand on the same foundation of Christian faith sometimes tend to emphasize our differences rather than what we have in common, and thus feel that we have no reason for coming together. How refreshing it would be if a minister of one denomination had enough of the spirit of Paul to say of the faithful preachers of the Gospel of other denominations, "Whether it were I or they, so we preach, and so ye believed."

A guard at a mental institution, who had been left in charge of several hundred patients, was approached by a visitor who said, "I should think it would be dangerous for you to be left in charge of so many mental patients. If they got together, they could soon make short work of you."

"Yes," agreed the guard, "but if they could get together they wouldn't be here in the first place." Of course, the reason they can't cooperate is that they are all deranged.

Sometimes I think the world must wonder if we Christians who fight one another are not spiritually deranged. Our common basic faith ought to unite us in one great fellowship of believers, without any sacrifice of individual modes of expression in our various churches. We are one in Christ when we believe and proclaim the Gospel, as set forth in Paul's resume' of apostolic teaching.

Wouldn't it be a refreshing change to concentrate on the beliefs that unite all true Christians rather than on the minor differences that divide them? What did the apostles hold essential; what was the Gospel that they agreed should be preached and believed? In First Corinthians 15:3 and 4, Paul gives us the foundation stones of the Christian faith:

1) That Christ died for our sins according to the Scriptures;

2) That He was buried,

3) And that He rose again the third day. This is the Gospel. This is the foundation, the substructure of Christianity. There was not the least dissension about it among the early apostles. Anyone who did not believe these facts could not be considered a Christian, nor can such a person be counted a Christian today.

Observe that in these declarations we have a central figure, the Lord Jesus Christ. They speak of three events about this historical person: His death, burial, and resurrection. They speak of One foretold hundreds of years before He came into the world, whose death, burial, and resurrection were not the result of chance but were predicted and typified in the Old Testament.

But the Gospel goes beyond mere assent to these facts about the person of Jesus Christ. No one can be saved merely by believing that Jesus died, was buried, and rose again. There was a purpose in these events, which each of us must personally relate to himself. Paul says that Christ died "for our sins." This changes history to personal redemption. Christ's death must be personally appropriated by faith so that you and I may not have to die for our sins. The death of Christ would do you no more good than the death of any other martyr if you did not believe it was meant for you, and appropriate it for yourself.

Two friends went for a boatride. The boat upset. The river was swift and deep. The man to whom the boat belonged had taken two life-belts along. He says, "I put one on, but my friend laid his down beside him. When we were thrown into the river, my life-belt soon brought me to the top, but my friend never came up again." Christ's death, like the life-belt, will not save you unless, by faith in Him, you put it on, that is, apply it to its intended purpose, which is to rescue you from eternal loss.

THE ONLY WAY TO BE SAVED

"So we preach, and so ye believed" (I Cor. 15:11).

What is the first thing you must believe in order to be a Christian? The Apostle Paul declares this to be the fact that Jesus Christ came into the world and died on the cross to save us from our sins. Unless a person accepts this basic fact, he is not entitled to call himself a Christian.

Take that man who came up to a minister at the close of the service and said, "I do not see any necessity for the blood of Christ in my salvation. I can be saved without believing in His shed blood."

"Very well," said the minister. "How, then, do you propose to be saved?"

"By following His example," was the answer. "That is enough for any man."

"I suppose it is," said the minister. "And that is what you propose to do?"

"I do, and I am sure that that is enough."

"Very well. I am sure that you want to begin right. The Word of God tells us how to do that. I read here concerning Christ, 'Who did no sin, neither was guile found in his mouth.' I suppose that you can say that of yourself, too?"

The man became visibly embarrassed. "Well," he said, "I cannot say that exactly. I have sometimes sinned."

"In that case you do not need an Example, but a Saviour; and the only way of salvation is by His shed blood."

The foundational belief of Christianity, common to all who can rightfully claim the name of Christian, is that the basic reason for which Christ came into the world and died on the cross was to save us from our sins. Because of His atonement, we can come to Him in repentance and be assured of forgiveness. But such forgiveness to be effective must be divine. Sin is an offense against God, and none but God can pardon it. God's forgiveness requires a God to grant it; and no man can do this for Him. Even the enemies of Christ confessed that only God can forgive sins (Mark 2:7). The Scriptures represent Christ as dying to atone for our sins. Therefore He who is presented as able to forgive sins must be God Himself. And that Christ was. He was God the Son, who came into the world to die for us.

They miss the point entirely who present Him as a merely human teacher, albeit the greatest who ever lived. The advocates of such teaching are not truly Christians. Christ did not come merely to teach or to show by example how sinlessly a dedicated human being could live. He came in order to secure man's forgiveness, and before He became man He had to be co-equal and co-eternal with God the Father, in order to be able to accomplish such a cosmic and eternal purpose.

Remember one other thing: the resurrection was not the actual payment for our sin but was the confirmation of the sufficiency of Christ's death to save anyone who would believe. To this all the apostles bear witness, that Christ's death was for the remission of sins.

We have noted previously that Paul encountered

opposition in the early Church. Some of this arose because the Judaizers in the Church, while not as a rule objecting to the Gospel he preached, insisted that Gentile believers could not appropriate the death of Christ without first undergoing the rite of circumcision. In their view, the Gospel belonged to the Jews, and those outside the Hebrew family had first to go through the gate of circumcision to be eligible for its benefits. None of these enemies of Paul, however, ever proclaimed that anyone could be saved other than through the blood of the Lord Jesus.

The Apostles Peter and Paul, although real individualists, agreed on this basic issue, for Peter says that we are "redeemed . . . with the precious blood of Christ, as of a lamb without blemish and without spot" (I Pet. 1:18, 19), and referring to Christ he says, "who his own self bare our sins in his own body on the tree" (I Pet. 2:24).

And John joins him in ascribing glory "unto him that loved us, and washed us from our sins in his own blood" (Rev. 1:5). Again he says of Christ, "Thou wast slain, and hast redeemed us to God by thy blood" (Rev. 5:9).

Paul spoke truly of the united front of the apostles, in spite of his differences with some of them on minor points not involving apostolic inspiration, when he said, "Whether it were I or they, so we preach." It was this kind of preaching that caused the Corinthians to believe. It was resultful, fruitful preaching. "So we preach," says Paul. The verb here is in the present indicative, which expresses continuity of action. "Thus we continue preaching." And as a result of this preaching, he tells the Corinthians, "so ye believed." The verb *episteusate* is in the aorist tense, active voice, indicative mood, which indicates some definite time in the past. There was a time when, hearing this Gospel, the Corinthians said, "We believe Christ died for our sins." Paul implies here that this kind of preaching, this Gospel, is the only one that stimulates belief. Therefore we must continue to preach it.

Is your preaching in the apostolic tradition, fellow preacher? What does it accomplish? Does it lead people to repent? Do they respond with a definite faith in Christ that makes them new creatures? How many believe as a result of your preaching? If sinners are not finding salvation in Christ, it may be that you are not preaching that Christ died for our sins according to the Scriptures, that He was buried, and that He rose again. Preach that in its fullness and you may be sure that souls will be saved.

Don't be afraid of being branded narrow-minded if you preach the Gospel. The laws of cause and effect are always narrow in their requirements for man's use, if he is to reach a certain goal. There is no room for broadmindedness in the technique of experiments in the chemical laboratory. Water, for instance, is composed of two parts hydrogen and one part oxygen. Any deviation from that formula is unthinkable. No one would think of calling you narrow-minded because you insisted on breathing only air. Nor is there room for broad-mindedness in applied mathematics. In geometry, calculus, or trigonometry there is no allowance for variations from exact accuracy; the solution of a problem is either right or wrong. There is no room for broad-mindedness in repairing a car: the mechanic says that the piston rings must fit the cylinder walls within one-thousandth part of an inch, and that's that. We could go on multiplying examples *ad infinitum* to show that life from this standpoint is always narrow in its requirements for reaching definite goals.

Why, then, do we expect God to be broad-minded about the way we must be saved? He has said that there is but one way, through the death of Christ. Don't be ashamed to preach it. A man with a mind as brilliant as Paul's wasn't. Why should you or I be?

On the cornerstone of a beautiful new church were inscribed the words, "We preach Christ crucified." Later, a vine was planted at the same corner, which in time covered part of the stone, so that the passers-by could only discern the words, "We preach." Is that what has happened in your church? There is preaching, but of what kind? Is the blood of Jesus Christ ever mentioned? Are souls cleansed by it? Or have the vines of pseudo-intellectualism eliminated the cross and left nothing but empty eloquence, which leaves people unaffected and still in their sins?

A minister who had two weeks' vacation enjoyed himself by going to services in some of the great churches of London. He listened to one of the most brilliant and popular men who had ever occupied a pulpit. He was spellbound by the silver-tongued oratory of another. Then he went to hear a mission preacher, a man of moderate learning and rude eloquence. That service left the most lasting impression on his mind. "What did you think of him?" a friend asked. "Well, of course," he replied, "for style and all that, he is not to be mentioned in the same breath with the other two preachers, but, do you know, that man made me feel like a scamp!"

"We preach . . . ye believed," said Paul. And they were still standing in that faith years later. Remember how Paul begins this 15th chapter of First Corinthians: "I declare unto you the gospel which I preached unto you, which also ye have received, and wherein ye stand." This was effective preaching that produced effective belief, which stood the test of time. The sacrifice of Christ is effective once and for all. True, the Corinthians had their spiritual battles, but Paul wanted to impress them with the fact that He who had begun a good work in them was able to bring it to completion.

> Before the cross in awe I stand,
> Beholding brow and pierced hand;
> For me it was He bled and died,
> No other price for sin beside
>   Could pay the price for me.
>
> His precious blood, there flowing red,
> Was love's best gift, most freely shed;
> No one but He the price could pay,
> Or save from death and point the way
>   For sinners, you and me.
>
> And as I gaze, I seem to hear
> Him gently say, "My son, draw near;
> New life I give and power withal,
> Free unto all who on Me call,
>   Now and eternally."
>   — ERNEST O. SELLERS

ONLY ONE GOSPEL

"Whether it were I or they, so we preach, and so ye believed" (I Cor. 15:11).

You hear so many confusing voices today—over the air, in the pulpit, in the press—that you hardly know what to believe. Especially is this true with regard to religion, where the public is often too inclined to be moved by specious oratory to ask for the facts.

For instance, you may hear it stated that the Apostle Paul taught an entirely different kind of Christianity than Jesus Christ proclaimed. Is this a responsible statement, backed up by facts; or is it merely an opinion voiced by those who would like to get out from under the authority of apostolic teaching, even as some in the Corinthian church in the first century?

Anyone who studies the Scriptures must agree that the apostles were unanimous in their belief in and proclamation of the fact that Christ came to shed His blood for the remission of our sins. Why this unanimity, if it were not in harmony with what Christ taught? Could these men who were so close to Him during His earthly ministry have misunderstood the purpose of God's incarnation in Jesus Christ, His death, life, and resurrection? Or is there a unity between Christ's teaching and theirs? The answer is a categorical yes. If this were not so, we would have to retrace our steps from A.D. 56 or 57, when Paul wrote the First Epistle to the Corinthians, and find out at what stages between A.D. 33 and 56 such a persistent and unified front of apostolic teaching was built. You will not find any record of change during this period. The teaching about the basic purpose of Christ's incarnation is unaltered from the beginning. Even if Paul were under a misapprehension about this doctrine, wouldn't at least some of the other apostles have gotten it straight? We grant that in a group it is possible for some to misunderstand a few things, but hardly everyone. The apostles were men of diverse backgrounds, temperament, and outlook, which makes unanimity in a major error highly improbable if not impossible. If Paul is wrong, surely one dissenting voice among the apostles would have been heard, if not more.

Furthermore, Christ surely would not have allowed His purpose in coming into the world to be defeated by a misapprehension. In His omniscience, knowing the possibility of such a misunderstanding, He would surely have guarded His apostles against it. Otherwise He would knowingly be encouraging deceit, which is certainly contrary to His holy and guileless character.

Read the Gospels carefully and notice how much space is devoted to the account of Christ's death. No other event of His career is spoken of in such detail as His death and the incidents that led to it. Take time to analyze some of His sayings, such as,

"Destroy this temple, and in three days I will raise it up" (John 2:19).

"As Moses lifted up the serpent in the wilderness, even so must the Son of man be lifted up" (John 3:14).

"The bread that I will give is my flesh, which I will give for the life of the world" (John 6:51).

"The Son of man came not to be ministered unto,

but to minister, and to give his life a ransom for many" (Mark 10:45).

"Take, eat: this is my body, which is broken for you: this do in remembrance of me" (I Cor. 11:24).

"This cup is my blood of the new testament, which is shed for many for the remission of sins" (Matt. 26:28).

"This do ye, as oft as ye drink it, in remembrance of me" (I Cor. 11:25).

What do these sayings indicate but that "Christ died for our sins according to the scriptures," as Paul declares in First Corinthians 15:3, and as Peter and John declare in their epistles? The apostles preached what they had been personal witnesses of.

True, the apostles speak more explicitly of the doctrine of Christ's death. This is only to be expected, since they wrote by the Holy Spirit's inspiration after the event and could understand it more fully. More is written of history than prophecy. As Alexander Maclaren says: "He Himself warned His disciples against accepting His own words prior to the Cross, as the conclusive and ultimate revelation. 'I have many things to say unto you, but you cannot carry them now.' There was need that the Cross should be a fact before it was evolved into a doctrine."

Life for men begins with the cross of Jesus Christ. This is what opens the way for growth and maturity. Christianity cannot be conceived apart from the cross of Christ. No teaching of Christ or of the apostles will meet your need apart from this basic life-giving fact that Jesus died for your sins. If some churches are powerless, it is usually because they have rejected the cross. Do you believe in the cross of Christ, not merely as a historical event but as an act performed by God to redeem you from your sin?

A young woman who was hopelessly ill recalled a Scripture verse that she had heard in health: "He was wounded for our transgressions, he was bruised for our iniquities: the chastisement of our peace was upon him; and with his stripes we are healed" (Isa. 53:5). She was led of the Holy Spirit to rest in Him of whom it spoke for her salvation. A friend said to her one day, "I am afraid you suffer very greatly." "Yes," she said, "but," pointing to her hand, "there is no nail there. He had the nails; I have the peace." Laying her hand on her forehead she said, "There are no thorns here. He had the thorns; I have the peace." Touching her side she said, "There is no spear here. He had the spear; I have the peace."

Do you have that peace that was bought for you on the cross of Calvary? Christ died so that each of us may know the peace of sins forgiven.

(See Alexander Maclaren, *Triumphant Certainties*, Christian Commonwealth Publishing Co., Ltd., London, pp. 140-151.)

It is the voice of Jesus that I hear;
His are the hands stretched out to draw me near,
And His the blood that can for all atone,
And set me faultless there before the throne.
Yea, Thou wilt answer for me, righteous Lord;
Thine all the merits, mine the great reward;
Thine the sharp thorns, and mine the golden
    crown;
Mine the life won, and thine the life laid down.
— S. J. STONE

BELIEVING DOESN'T MAKE IT SO

"Now if Christ be preached that he rose from the dead, how say some among you that there is no resurrection of the dead?" (I Cor. 15:12).

The quest for emotional security is so strong in some people that they will accept a philosophy or a religion on the ground that it does them good, whether they are fully convinced of its authenticity or not. How do such people face the all-important doctrine of the resurrection of Jesus Christ? If faith in it makes them feel good, they will say they do not care about the historical basis of the resurrection; all that matters to them is their belief. But the advantages of believing do not necessarily prove that what we believe is true.

Of course the Gospel satisfies people, but that isn't what proves it to be true. Nor is everything that seems to satisfy a man's religious hunger necessarily the Gospel, any more than whatever satisfies his physical hunger is necessarily nutritionally sound food. There are countless thousands of so-called Christian sects whose adherents are relatively happy in following certain beliefs, but this does not make their beliefs either Christian or true. The value of food is judged by its ingredients, not by our individual tastes; and the truth of the Gospel is judged not by how we feel about Christ, but by who Christ actually was and what He did.

Jesus Christ predicted that He would rise from the dead. Did He or did He not? If He did, He was all that He claimed to be. If He did not, then He was a deceiver or a deluded visionary, and belief in a liar or a lunatic can do nobody any ultimate good. Even the happy feeling derived from belief in false teaching is a snare and a deception.

Truth has objective reality. In verses 1 through 11 of First Corinthians 15, the Apostle Paul has proved that the Lord Jesus rose from the dead by producing eye-witnesses. Now, from verse 12 on, he proceeds to set forth the results that would follow from a denial of Christ's resurrection. His purpose is not to prove the historical veracity of the resurrection—which he has already done—but to show that belief in the resurrection is absolutely essential to all real Christian faith. If anyone professes a Christian faith that is not based on the historical fact of Christ's resurrection, it is not true Christianity. Thus, what Paul is about to prove is not what some have mistakenly assumed—the veracity of the fact judged from the consequences of its denial —but that any belief is non-Christian that is not based on the resurrection of Christ.

"Now if Christ be preached that he rose from the dead, how say some among you that there is no resurrection of the dead?" What is Paul's argument in this verse? The other apostles and I preach that Christ rose from the dead. We preach it because we were among the eye-witnesses who saw Christ after His resurrection. It is a historical fact, or we wouldn't be preaching it. This is the gospel I preached to you in the first place, which you believed and by which you are saved, unless your faith is worthless. If you believe that Christ rose, how can you say there is no resurrection? (And by inference, if you do not, how can you call yourself Christian?)

— 177 —

Paul was a true scientist. He did not start with a general notion or theory and then look around for arguments to support it. No, he started with facts, with personal observation and the evidence of others. We observe, we experiment, we conclude. That's the scientific method. But what were some of the Corinthians doing? They were saying that because it was impossible, to their way of thinking, that something should have happened, they would not believe in it, even though it was historically proved to have happened. The scientific method is not to propound a theory and then reject any facts that do not square with it. Yet a school of thought in Corinth was saying, "The resurrection from the dead is impossible [they did not say why]; therefore Christ could not have risen, no matter what the evidence to the contrary." Others among them did believe in the resurrection of Christ but could not accept the necessary corollary of a general resurrection of the dead.

A person with that type of mentality flatly states, "Never mind the facts; I believe what I choose to believe. There is no resurrection of the dead; therefore Christ did not rise." But Paul argues that the resurrection of Christ and the belief in a general resurrection are intimately and inseparably connected. They stand or fall together. This is his fundamental thesis.

The sad thing is that seemingly intelligent people often resort to this type of reasoning. Yet if they took this same attitude toward other historically attested facts they would be regarded as anything but intelligent. That is why Paul asks in some surprise, "How say some among you that there is no resurrection of the dead?" How can you come to this conclusion, if you believe in the fact of Christ's resurrection? And if you do not, you must have believed in vain; your faith is worthless.

Why does Paul say, "Now if Christ be preached that he rose from the dead," instead of "If it is believed that Christ rose from the dead"? Because he and the other apostles preached what they firmly believed, and Paul is indirectly appealing to the sense of respect which he and they enjoyed among the Corinthians. It is as if he were saying, "Do you think that I would preach such a thing as the resurrection of Christ if it were not so?"

This preaching was definite and general among the apostles. Observe that the verb *keerussetai*, "we preach," is in the present passive indicative and agrees with the tense of the same verb in verse 11, "So we preach, and so ye believed." By this present passive indicative Paul covers the whole span of time. Christ's resurrection was preached right after it happened, it has been preached ever since, and it will continue to be preached. No one could disprove the fact then, nor can they now. It has been proved true, and that is why we continue to preach it, Paul contends. If it were not true, we wouldn't be preaching it.

Yet belief in a mere fact will not save a man's soul. Observe how Paul expresses himself in verse 12: "Now if *Christ* be preached that he rose from the dead." It is not the mere fact that is preached but the person of Jesus Christ. The fact of the resurrection is not what saves men from their sins, but the Lord Jesus Christ Himself. "Now if Christ be preached"—Christ is the center, and the resurrection is the central fact about Him. "He rose from among the dead ones" would be a more accurate translation here. Paul's thought is that, if Christ had remained among the dead, His claims about Himself would have been discredited, and I would not preach the Gospel. The verb *egeegertai*, "rose," is a deponent verb in the perfect tense, which indicates that the Lord was not acted upon by some power outside Himself: He rose on His own initiative, He was not merely raised. But, someone may object, it says elsewhere in the Bible that God raised Him from the dead. How could it be said that He rose of His own power and volition, and at the same time that God raised Him? It was only possible because He Himself was God in the flesh. It is a proof of His deity. What He *was* made what He *did* possible.

"How say some among you that there is no resurrection of the dead?" asks Paul. In the Greek text, the word "say" here is *legousin*, which comes from *logos*, meaning "word, intelligence." *Legoo*, "I say," is expressive of thought. Paul's question, then, might be rephrased, "How can you logically say that there is no resurrection of the dead, since it has been proven that Christ rose?" Paul appeals to their intelligence, showing that it is folly to reach a conclusion that ignores a proven fact. It would not be a logical conclusion, but a presumptive general theory arrived at from limited data. Knowledge observes facts. Here is the fact: Christ rose from the dead. Let's carry it to its logical conclusion, says Paul in verse 13: "But if there be no resurrection of the dead, then is Christ not risen." You can't have it both ways. Can there be any Christian faith without the resurrection of Christ? We'll consider this in our next study, as we discuss verse 14.

WHO IS A CHRISTIAN?

"If Christ be not risen, then is our preaching vain, and your faith is also vain" (I Cor. 15:14).

From what Paul said in his First Epistle to the Corinthians, it seems that some at Corinth went so far as to deny that Christ rose from the dead, so strong were they in their presumption that the dead cannot rise. And yet they still felt entitled to call themselves Christians. This Paul would not tolerate. If you do not believe that Christ rose from the dead, he tells them, your faith is vain, worthless.

The persons with whom Paul is arguing here could not have been converts from Judaism to Christianity, for although the sect of the Sadducees rejected a belief in the resurrection of the dead, the Orthodox Jew or Pharisee believed in it so firmly that at times it led to acts of martyrdom (II Maccabees VII, 9, 11, 14, 23).

On the other hand, to the pagan Greek, the idea of a resurrection of the dead was new and unwelcome. The idea of the immortality of the soul appears in Greek literature only as an occasional speculation, but the resurrection of man's body was wholly foreign to Greek habits of thinking. When Paul began to preach the resurrection at Athens, his hearers missed the point so completely that they supposed that the word for "resurrection" was the name of a new deity. "He seemeth to be a setter forth of strange gods," they said, "because he preached unto them Jesus, and the resurrection" (Acts 17:18).

When converts from Greek paganism entered the Church of Christ, some of them still held these deeply rooted prejudices. These contributed largely to the systems of fantastic error that took definite forms in the second century after Christ, and are collectively known as Gnosticism. Ten years after writing to the Corinthians, Paul mentions to his pupil Timothy two Greek teachers at Ephesus, Hymenaeus and Philetus, "who concerning the truth have erred, saying that the resurrection is past already" (II Tim. 2:17, 18). What did they mean by this? The resurrection, they taught, was to be understood figuratively. The individual is resurrected in one of two ways: 1) In life, as when man's spirit turns from its sin and lives in righteousness, overcoming the evil tendencies of the body, thus experiencing resurrection; or 2) in keeping with the Greek concept of the supremacy of the spirit, when literal death comes, and the spirit is liberated from the body, then man may be said to experience his resurrection. The Corinthian doubter felt that to believe in a resurrection from the grave was to debase a sublime spiritual truth into a meager material impossibility.

This was the Greek feeling, in secret rebellion against the faith but not wishing to come to an open break, and so attempting an explanation which might keep the terminology of a Christian profession and yet reject the realities that those terms were meant to convey. Unfortunately much of our modern Christianity, so-called, is of this caliber. It lacks a vibrant, clear-cut belief that Christ's body rose from the dead. It is the privilege of any preacher or individual not to believe it, but honesty should compel him to discard the name Christian.

At Corinth we see the same feeling at work, but the Corinthians were recent converts, some of whom did not know what a revelation from God meant and involved. They thought it was much like one of their own philosophies, something to be reviewed, discussed, partly accepted, partly rejected, at their pleasure. There was much in Christianity that they liked and accepted, without difficulty and even with enthusiasm. Their modern counterparts accept the moral teaching of Christianity but in many cases reject its basic doctrines: the deity of Christ, His substitutionary death for our sins, His resurrection and our own bodily resurrection. Though they enthusiastically call themselves Christian, Paul states that they are not really entitled to do so. Christianity is either accepted in whole or it is not accepted at all. A partial, selective Christianity is spurious. No one is a Christian who does not believe in the bodily resurrection of Christ and his own resurrection to follow.

Some of the new Greek converts in Corinth could not tolerate "the resurrection of the dead." They asked in scorn, "How are the dead raised up? and with what body do they come?" (I Cor. 15:35), as if such questions had only to be raised in order to show all sensible people how absurd it was to expect an answer. Their difficulties arose out of their physical speculations, their ideas of the nature and destiny of beings. But they did not imagine that in denying the resurrection of the dead they were trifling with essential Christianity, or doing anything more or worse than rejecting a coarse dogma of Jewish origin.

This is the background of the objectors to the resurrection. Paul meets them head on. They could not merely reject the resurrection as a presumed physical impossibility. Facts cannot be discarded because they do not fit a theory. If there is no resurrection, says Paul, then you must logically say that Christ never rose. It is doubtful that all of these objectors wanted to go that far.

Paul proceeds to point out to them the consequences of such rejection. He does not want to prove the resurrection from a study of the horror of the consequences of such rejection, but simply to point out to these thoughtless Corinthians what the consequences of their attitude would be. The moral values of the historical fact of the resurrection were so highly esteemed that if they became fully conscious of them they would reconsider their basic position. They were ignorantly undermining the foundation even while they enjoyed the wonder of the building in which they dwelt.

If any of the Corinthians were prepared to accept the consequences of rejecting the resurrection, Paul felt they might as well come right out and say so. They may have flattered themselves that they still retained a firm hold upon all that was essential in Christianity, that they had only given up legendary additions to the simple story of the life of Christ, additions which their Greek science had pronounced impossible. They were still willing to believe in a Christ who displayed before the eyes of men a perfect example, who did many works of wonder and of love, who taught a heavenly doctrine, who died a cruel and shameful death. But the assertion that, being dead and buried, "He rose again the third day according to the scriptures," was, they thought, a superstitious, even though apostolic, addition to the simple truth. It was no part of the fragment of Christian teaching that approved itself to their order of intelligence as being really fundamental; and they dismissed it as unimportant, if not untrue.

It is to these persons that Paul says solemnly, "If Christ be not risen, then is our preaching vain, and your faith is also vain" (I Cor. 15:14). These Corinthians might still claim the honors and risks of the Christian name, differing from the apostles, they thought, only in being more clear-sighted and better informed. But Paul will allow nothing of the kind. He will not let them deceive themselves in a matter of such momentous import. To deny or ignore Christ's resurrection is to abandon Christianity. It is to give up the very core and heart of the faith. The beliefs that remain may have an interest of their own, but it is the sort of interest that belongs to a corpse. It may remind us of the past, but it no longer has any place in the land of the living.

MUST A CHRISTIAN BELIEVE
IN THE RESURRECTION?

"And if Christ be not risen, then is our preaching vain" (I Cor. 15:14).

The Bible teaches that only certain persons have the right to call themselves Christian. Not every non-Jew, non-Buddhist, non-Muslim can automatically be labeled "Christian." Not even every person affiliated with a Protestant, Catholic, or Eastern Orthodox church has a right to the title. Is this mere hair-splitting? No, for the Apostle Paul states in unmistakable terms that he who rejects the historic bodily resurrection of Jesus Christ cannot be considered a Christian and has no right to call himself one. That would eliminate many who call themselves Christian merely because they accept the moral teachings of Christ, though they reject His resurrection as a pious myth.

But why is belief in Jesus' resurrection so important? Because it is this foundation fact on which Christianity rests as unique among all religions. In what other religion has the founder substantiated his claim to reveal God and the supernatural by rising from the dead? None.

If any of the apostles had been asked how they knew that Jesus was the promised Messiah, God manifest in the flesh, the Saviour of the world, by whose teaching and life men were to be enlightened and by whose blood men were to be redeemed, they would have answered, "Because He rose from the dead." Over and over in their sermons, as recorded in the Acts of the

Apostles (2:22-36; 3:12-16; 4:10-12, 33; 5:29-32; 10:34-43; 13:16-41), the fact of the resurrection stands out as the proof of His uniqueness and deity. They considered it God's visible interference with the order of nature in order to certify the true mission and claims of Jesus. The Lord had told them that they would be fully persuaded of His identity as God made manifest in the flesh as a result of His coming resurrection. He foretold even the day of His resurrection. He spoke like God and acted like Him. But the apostles would never have accepted Him as such and preached Him as such if He had not risen as He had predicted.

Not only is the resurrection the foundation stone of Christianity, it is the basis on which we believe in the judgment to come. The judgment is no harder to believe in than the resurrection would have been before it occurred. Christ promised both, and the fulfillment of His promise concerning the one is a guarantee of the fulfillment of the other.

When Paul spoke to the people of Athens about the judgment, they thought him a dreamer. He proclaimed, "He [God] will judge the world in righteousness by that man whom he hath ordained [i.e., Jesus Christ]" (Acts 17:31). Naturally he expected objections and ridicule from such a skeptical audience, so he met them before they were even expressed. He told them that the proof of the certainty of this judgment to come is what has already happened—the resurrection of Christ's body. Of this God "hath given assurance unto all men in that he hath raised him [Jesus] from the dead" (Acts 17:31). The resurrection made everything else the apostles preached believable. On the other hand, if the resurrection of Christ did not take place, nothing that He said or did, or that the apostles preached about Him, is believable.

The religion founded by Jesus Christ has many teachings in common with other religions of the world. But it has other truths special and peculiar to Christianity, which it shares with no other religion. Eminent among these is the resurrection from the dead. True, other religions have entertained, with more or less clearness, notions of the immortality of the soul. And the ancient Egyptians even showed an awareness of the ultimate reunion of the soul with its revivified body. But none of these notions unfold, as does Paul in First Corinthians 15, the characteristics of the risen body or the risen life of everlasting holiness. What is more important, it is Christianity alone that has furnished a historic illustration and example of the risen life—in the person of the Lord Jesus Christ.

The entire structure of the Christian doctrine of the resurrection stands or falls with the personal bodily resurrection of the historic Christ. This is the foundation upon which all Christian teachings of the resurrection are built and rest. In the long history of the world, there has been no other resurrection to an incorruptible and immortal life. In this respect our Lord's resurrection is unique. All other resurrections have been resurrections to mortal and corruptible states. Individuals have been raised, as Lazarus was, only to die again. Only of Christ can it be said that, "being raised from the dead [he] dieth no more; death hath no more dominion over him" (Rom. 6:9). Christ is the only illustration and example yet given to the world of a complete and deathless resurrection. The world knows nothing whatever concerning the risen body and the risen life except what is taught by the resurrection of Jesus Christ. Everything, therefore, hinges upon the trustworthiness of this sole instance. If the resurrection of Jesus Christ is factually true, our faith is founded upon a rock; if it is not true, our faith is founded only on sand.

But some persons have said that they believe in the efficacy of Christ's death for the remission of sins, but not in His bodily resurrection. Can anyone logically sustain such a viewpoint? Let us see what becomes of the death of Christ if it was not followed by His resurrection. It then falls into the category of a purely human event, no different in character from the death of any other high-minded and disinterested man for a cause to which he is attached. It may still have the importance of a great moral example, of devotion to truth, charity, and justice. Even this is questionable, however, in the case of one who claimed he would rise from the dead, and then did not. But in any event, how can the death of a mere man, whose body has mouldered in his grave, be a power in earth and heaven, mighty to cleanse from guilt, and to win for the sinner pardon from God?

No one would think of speaking of Paul, or any of the saints of God, as dying "for the ungodly." But of Christ Paul says, "For when we were yet without strength, in due time Christ died for the ungodly" (Rom. 5:6). And Peter says of Christ, "Who his own self bare our sins in his own body on the tree, that we, being dead to sins, should live unto righteousness: by whose stripes ye were healed" (I Pet. 2:24). Who would dare to say that Christians are "reconciled to God by the death of" Paul (see Rom. 5:10), or that by him they had "received the atonement" (Rom. 5:11), or that Paul or any other man is a "propitiation for our sins: and not for ours only, but also for the sins of the whole world" (I John 2:2)?

Every believer in Christ feels the shocking impropriety of applying this language to any other than the Lord Jesus Christ, the Redeemer. Why? Because He alone was God in the flesh, and this fact is attested not only by His death but also by His resurrection. "Ye were not redeemed with corruptible things," exclaims Peter, "as silver and gold" (or, we would add, as the blood of a merely human victim), "but with the precious blood of Christ, as of a lamb without blemish and without spot" (I Pet. 1:18, 19).

How do we know that the sufferer on Calvary was God's own Son? The answer is, by the resurrection. This lifted Jesus' death to an altogether different level from that of any human sufferer. If, however, the resurrection is denied, all the apostolic language about the atonement becomes a tissue of mystical exaggerations, which, when applied to the death of Jesus as a mere man, are worse than unintelligible. The Corinthians who denied the resurrection might not have seen this consequence at once. But it is evident that their faith in the atonement was already undermined by their disbelief in the resurrection of the crucified Christ. Otherwise Paul would not have needed to reiterate the basic elements of the Gospel to them. (See I Cor. 15:3, 4.)

ARE THE WORDS OF A DEAD CHRIST
WORTH ANYTHING?

———◆———

"And if Christ be not risen, then . . . your faith is also vain" (I Cor. 15:14a, c).

Many persons admire Christ's life and teachings who do not see the necessity of believing in His bodily resurrection. They attempt to retain the ethics of Christianity without accepting the facts out of which the ethics grow and from which they draw all their nourishment.

The Apostle Paul, however, did not regard Christ as being simply a great moral teacher like Confucius or Socrates. The moral teachings of such philosophers did not depend in the least upon what happened to them after their death. If Christ had been simply a great moral teacher, His bodily resurrection would not be emphasized in Scripture as the fundamental fact upon which the Christian faith rests.

And on similar grounds, Paul did not regard Christ merely as one who set a beautiful moral example, as Buddha or Zoroaster is reputed to have done. If Buddha or Zoroaster perished forever at their death, the moral beauty of their human example would not be dimmed. Bodily resurrection is not essential to a moral example.

In the third place, it is evident that Paul did not regard Christ primarily as a prophet who revealed the will of God, as Mohammed is regarded by his followers. The Moslems accept Christ as a mere prophet, no more. But Mohammed did not have to rise from the dead in order to complete his supposed revelation. If Christ were no more than a prophet, His resurrection would not be essential to the acceptance of Christianity.

Christ was indeed a great moral teacher, a beautiful example, a prophet who revealed the will of God; but He was much more than that, as Scripture plainly demonstrates.

We may go one step further and say that the death of Christ can have no comparison with the death of purely human martyrs. Some have argued that others beside Christ gave up their lives as patriots, as martyrs for the truth, as friends of the human race. Socrates, for instance, drank the fatal hemlock. But such comparisons are altogether misleading, because no man except Christ ever took upon Himself the sins of the human race in his death. No founder of any religion, no martyr, ever claimed that through his death the world could be saved, as Scripture so clearly states of Christ. Christ's great work was to avert the wrath of Divine Righteousness by bearing the burden of our guilt. That was done in Gethsemane and on Calvary. He Himself said, "It is finished" (John 19:30), and the atoning work was done. He alone "bare our sins in his own body on the tree" (I Pet. 2:24). It is absolutely essential to emphasize this difference in the death of Christ, in an age of comparative religions, in order to exhibit the immeasurable superiority of the true faith.

To confirm His substitutionary death for our sins, Christ rose from the dead. In this He is absolutely unparalleled and unapproachable. And it is to this especially that Paul refers in the text when he declares in the strongest possible terms that, if Christ did not rise from the dead, Christianity, in the only sense in which he or any of his brother apostles understood it, was a dream and a delusion. He was thinking of the cardinal and fundamental fact that Jesus Christ rose from the dead in order to share His resurrection life with us. Christ Himself, referring to this unique peculiarity and glory of the Christian religion, said shortly before His death, "I will not leave you comfortless: I will come to you. Yet a little while, and the world seeth me no more; but ye see me: because I live, ye shall live also. At that day ye shall know that I am in my Father, and ye in me, and I in you" (John 14:18-20).

Those outside Christianity often mistakenly think that Christianity is a matter of opinion. To the true Christian, however, it is invariably a matter of vital experience. It is Christ in us and we in Christ. If Christ had merely set us a perfect example of unselfishness, it would have been worse than useless; for in our own strength and with our own natural moral resources we would have been incapable of imitating Him. What is the use of mocking us with an unattainable ideal? A command which we cannot obey is both absurd and irritating. If Christ had merely made an atonement for our sins and offered us forgiveness, we might well inquire, "What is the use of forgiving my sins if I am to continue living in the same condition of moral helplessness as before? I shall begin at once to sin again; and my last state will be worse than my first."

"I am come," Christ said, "that they might have

life, and that they might have it more abundantly" (John 10:10). He offers not only to forgive our sins but also to renew our natures, so that when we are forgiven we shall not be under a miserable necessity of sinking again into the depths of sin. He comes not merely to forgive us but also to change us so radically that old things pass away, all things become new, and in the strong but literally correct language of Paul we become "a new creation" (II Cor. 5:17). (See Hugh Price Hughes, *The Philanthropy of God*, pp. 175-184. Also, H. P. Liddon, *Easter in St. Paul's*, pp. 25-33.)

As genuine Christianity consists of a living union between Jesus Christ and a converted man, it cannot exist unless Christ is now alive. Our Lord illustrated this fundamental fact when He said, "I am the vine, ye are the branches" (John 15:5). The genuine Christian is as truly united to Jesus Christ as the branch is to the vine, and as truly receives his life from Christ as the branch receiving its life-giving sap from the vine. It would be useless to graft a living branch into a dead vine. It is equally impossible to unite a living man to a dead Christ. If Christ were dead, Paul could not say, "I live; yet not I, but Christ liveth in me" (Gal. 2:20).

Paul's answer to those who claim they have faith in Christ's life and teachings apart from His resurrection would be that it does not take faith to recognize the beauty of a man's life. There is no need to exercise faith in the self-evident. Faith is the acceptance of the unseen upon sufficient testimony. It is a venture, warranted indeed, but not by experience. Its proper object is something that lies outside the range of our experience. You and I do not need faith, or anything but ordinary judgment and common moral sense, to do justice to the good sayings and good actions of any one of the many excellent persons who may be named as having died some twenty or thirty years ago. We know enough about them on very good evidence to enable us to give full play to our admiration, and we admire them accordingly. It would be absurd to call them objects of faith. Thus, if all there is to Christianity is Christ's moral precepts and life to be admired and imitated, He is not necessarily the object of faith at all. In fact, it is a misnomer to speak of this as "the Christian faith," for as we stated previously, it takes no faith to recognize the quality and worth of a person's words and works.

Paul would have said that faith, by which the soul takes possession of the Invisible, is not needed for such an emasculated version of Christianity as some of the Corinthians seemed to hold. And he would have gone one step further by pointing out that to deny the resurrection, and at the same time to profess to admire the words of Christ or the example of Christ, is a logical impossibility.

Why? Because our Lord more than once, when challenged for a sign or warrant of His claims, said that He would be put to death and rise again the third day (John 2:18, 19, Matt. 12:38-40). Observe how the Lord insisted on "the third day." There is a precision in the announcement that forbids a figurative interpretation of this language. It could not be satisfied by the remote triumph of His name or doctrine, while His body mouldered in the grave. It is impossible to admire some of His best-attested words if we deny His resurrection. It is impossible to admire His example, for it would then be to admire the life of a liar, a deceiver, or a deluded madman. Do you profess to admire what Christ taught? But He taught that He would rise from the dead on the third day! How can you get around that?

If Christianity be faith in Christ's teachings and example, then we must accept all that He taught. Otherwise our brand of so-called Christianity is really faith in our own ability to pick and choose which of His words are worthy of acceptance and which we may reject with impunity. Paul clearly saw the trap into which the sophistry of the Corinthians had led them when he warned them, "If Christ be not risen, then . . . your faith is also vain." All the words of Christ rise or fall together.

WAS CHRIST'S RESURRECTION CONTRARY
TO THE LAWS OF NATURE?

"And if Christ be not risen, then . . . your faith is also vain" (I Cor. 15:14a, c).

Nobody places too much faith in a man's estimate of his own worth, especially if he makes great claims. That is why Paul states, "We preach not ourselves," in II Corinthians 4:5. But Paul's Master, the Lord Jesus Christ, without blinking an eye, and in a steady voice, says, "I am the way, the truth, and the life" (John 14:6). "Come unto me, all ye that labour and are heavy laden" (Matt. 11:28). "I am the light of the world" (John 8:12). "I am the true vine" (John 15:1). "I am the good shepherd. . . . All that ever came before me are thieves and robbers" (John 10:11, 8).

The constant, reiterated self-assertion of Jesus Christ—in the face of His own precepts about the beauty of being humble, self-forgetting, and retiring —can be explained only by the inward necessity laid upon Him by His divine personality, of which His resurrection was a visible witness to the world. Deny His resurrection, and you will discover that His character, as we have it in the Gospels, requires "reconstruction" if it is not to be met by the moral sense of man with a judgment very different indeed from that of sympathy and admiration.

The objection to the resurrection does not always come from those who are immoral and whose rejection of this foundational doctrine of Christianity is made an excuse for a life of degeneracy. There are many earnest, conscientious persons who find insuperable difficulty in accepting the fact of Christ's resurrection. It is a fact so wonderful, so awful, so glorious, so altogether unique in majesty and sublimity; it is, moreover, a fact so utterly unlike anything that the world has ever witnessed either before or since; both science and religion are so helplessly unable to supply any parallel to it; that multitudes of thoughtful people shrink from accepting, and even utterly reject, this occurrence.

And sometimes their rejection may possibly be more honest than other people's acceptance of Christ's resurrection. We refer, of course, to those who profess to believe in Christ's resurrection yet show not the least sign of the power of His resurrection in their daily lives. Yet, if the resurrection is a fact at all, it is the greatest of all facts, possessing the greatest of all influences. There is power in the resurrection (Phil. 3:10). To profess, therefore, to accept the fact, without ever displaying the influence, is less honest than to reject the fact altogether. People may honestly reject the resurrection because they are not satisfied with its evidences; or are staggered by the vastness of its significance and splendor; or are hesitant in giving credence to an unparalleled event that has happened once, and only once, in the history of the world; but no one can honestly accept the resurrection who does not show forth, in daily life, the proof of its deep and perpetual power.

However, having said all that can in fairness be said on the side of those who do entertain honest doubts regarding the resurrection, it would certainly seem that the difficulties of honest doubt are greater than the difficulties of honest faith. Men stagger at belief in the resurrection of Jesus Christ, who, if they studied the evidences more carefully, might more reasonably stagger at their unbelief.

This is a world of progress, for God is a God who produces progress in His plan of grace for the world. And the Bible is a book of progress in the unfolding of God's revelation. The fact that no religion previous to Christianity has furnished us with evidence of a resurrection to incorruptible life, instead of being a stumbling block, ought to fall in with our expectation of progress in God's revelation to man, as contained in Scripture. Christianity, as the culmination of that revelation, should contain illuminations brighter and more heavenly than any of the religions that preceded it.

Furthermore, the inherent wonder of the resurrection is not greater than the inherent wonder of many everyday occurrences. Consider the lilies, how they grow; the glory of the spring, how it arises from the nakedness of winter; the caterpillar, how it changes into a butterfly; the egg, how it is transformed into a bird. Let us not be like that youngster who watched over four beautiful little eggs in a nest in her garden, only to cry out in alarm that the eggs were ruined one day when she found the shells broken. "No, Amy, the eggs are not spoiled," her brother comforted her. "The best part of them has taken wings and flown away." In our reluctance to believe what we suppose to be an unnatural occurrence, let us not reject the workings of a higher law than we have yet known, as demonstrated in the resurrection of Christ from the dead.

It is not so much the inherent wonder of the resurrection, but its non-recurrence, that is the obstacle to belief; for every day we observe, without wonder, phenomena more wonderful than the resurrection. In itself, and apart from the frequency of its occurrence, a birth is more marvelous than a resurrection. It is more marvelous that a life should begin to be, that a human soul should ever inhabit a human body at all, than that after the interruption of death it should resume its habitation.

Yet reflection should convince us that the non-recurrence of the resurrection, instead of being an evidence of its unreasonable and unnatural character, is just the opposite. Think about it. Why is it that there has been only one resurrection to incorruptible life in the long history of mankind? Simply because, during the whole course of that long history, there has been only one Christ. It was the perfections of His holiness and the prerogatives of His Sonship that made death the unnatural thing that should have happened to Him and that made His resurrection a necessity. Death is the consequence of sin. But Christ was perfect and sinless. As God's only Son, He came not to die on His own account but on behalf of all sinners, past, present, and future. This accomplished, death could no more hold Him prisoner.

Surely, unless we deny that Jesus is the Son of God, the very incarnation of God Himself, we can hardly brush aside the resurrection as an impossibility.

Our resurrection, when it takes place, will be a stupendous miracle; but Christ's resurrection is in this respect really no miracle. It would have been a stupendous and incredible miracle had He *not* risen. If the Son of God has indeed taken human flesh, then which is more reasonable—to believe that His body never saw corruption, or to believe that His body is eternally dead? And if the latter supposition be, in a very high degree, unnatural and irrational, then "How say some among you that there is no resurrection of the dead?"

To those who affirm that the resurrection of Christ goes contrary to the laws of nature, who is to say what is natural in this case? We base our ideas of what is natural on the frequency and predictability of occurrence. But since there has been only one Christ, we have no means of judging what would be natural in His case except from what actually happened to Him. According to all evidence, He rose again. Therefore we assume that in the case of the sinless Son of Man, who was also the Son of God, the resurrection is not contrary to, but in keeping with, the laws of nature. To us who believe in the incarnation, the resurrection of the Christ is thus not so much a miracle as a kind of logical necessity; an event in full and perfect harmony with all the circumstances of the case.

WHAT IF YOU DON'T BELIEVE
IN THE RESURRECTION?

"And if Christ be not risen, then is our preaching vain, and your faith is also vain" (I Cor. 15:14).

An overweight woman once remarked to a friend who suggested that she diet, "You'll never convince me that food has anything to do with it." Because she loved to eat too much, she chose to believe that her weight problem had a mysterious and unfathomable basis. But she could not choose the consequence of her choice, which was that she put on weight.

It is the privilege of anyone to choose what he will or will not believe, but he cannot change the laws of cause and effect. Thus, anyone is free to reject the resurrection of Jesus Christ, but he is not free to reject the consequences of his rejection. I am free to sin but I am not free to choose the consequences of my choice. Those are determined by a power outside myself. Men are the discoverers of the physical and spiritual world, not the makers of them. He who made the world also predetermined the consequences of disobedience or obedience to the laws He instituted.

A sincere and heartfelt belief in the resurrection of Jesus Christ results in a transformed life, a faith that saves, a hope that looks forward to personal resurrection.

But what are the consequences of rejecting the resurrection? First, you are faced with the alternative that Christianity is based on a falsehood, that Christ and His apostles were deceivers. No other alternative is possible. It will not do to say that the apostles, in the frenzy of their enthusiasm after the death of Christ, imagined that their Lord was risen. Apart from the resurrection, what would engender such enthusiasm? Apart from the resurrection, their Master had proved a failure whose pretensions had been unmasked by the catastrophe of the cross. The apostles were in no enthusiastic mood after the victory of the Sanhedrin, the crucifixion of their leader, and the complete overthrow of their long-cherished Messianic hopes. On the contrary, they were in a state of utmost despondency, terror, and gloom. To say, therefore, that the resurrection was an illusion of enthusiastic devotees is to invert the historical order of events by substituting the effect for the cause. It is to say that their enthusiasm caused the idea of the resurrection, instead of the fact of the resurrection producing their enthusiasm.

Moreover the apostles themselves completely refuted any such irrational explanation. For in this First Epistle to the Corinthians (the authenticity of which no honest scholarly critic has ventured to assail) Paul, having enumerated a considerable catalogue of the risen Christ's appearances (vv. 5-7) to persons still alive at the time of his writing, proceeds in verse 15 to the plain issue—either Christ is risen or the apostles were bearing false witness to God.

Paul knew that the Corinthians would see the absurdity of these logical and necessary consequences of not believing in the resurrection of Christ. Unbelief must often be shown to be absurd and illogical. To make sweeping statements of a generalized nature, to say flatly that there is no God, for instance, or that there is no resurrection, reduces you to the necessity of accepting certain absurd conclusions.

Paul tells the Corinthians that, if they state that there is no resurrection of the body, they are also stating that Christ did not rise. This puts them in the position of denying a fact attested by the apostles and hundreds of other eye-witnesses. Only an absurd person will deny a fact. Furthermore, says Paul, if Christ did not rise, then our preaching is empty, your faith is empty, and we are found false witnesses of God. Do you see where your unbelief in the resurrection takes you? It wipes out the witness of Scripture, the whole Christian faith that is based on Christ's resurrection, and the credibility of the very disciples who were chosen by our Lord to preach the Gospel after His departure.

It is quite possible that the Corinthians were objecting only to the general future resurrection preached by the apostles and not particularly to the resurrection of Jesus Christ. It never dawned on them that their general unbelief would lead to this particular disbelief. It is doubtful that the Corinthians were real unbelievers. Their Christian faith seems to have been very precious to them, and Paul knew that they would never willingly relinquish that faith for the sake of a speculation concerning the resurrection. They just did not fully realize the seriousness of their intellectual and philosophical speculations.

Thus we could not say that Paul is here forcing his readers to choose between the acceptance of one particular doctrine and the rejection of the Christian faith as a whole. He knew what the effect of his words would be on those whom he addressed; he was satisfied that they loved their faith better than their speculations and that they would accept the resurrection of Jesus Christ once they found that to reject it was to reject the basis of Christianity.

A serious operation in logic was needed, but the Apostle knew that his patients could bear it. He seeks to lead them to give up their erroneous thinking about the resurrection by reducing the principle of this error to an absurdity, which, once presented to a Christian believer, would be indignantly set aside.

Paul's argument has some practical lessons for us. We are forced to the conclusion that we are not at liberty to choose only what we like and consider believable of what God has revealed. We cannot be the judges once God has spoken. Christian truth must be accepted as a whole or we do violence to the whole concept of Christianity. God does not open His bag of merchandise, as it were, and give us the privilege of picking out what we like. Such an attitude on our part would be quite unreasonable, simply because all revealed truth rests on the same ground and recommends itself equally to the balanced mind. Such an attitude would also be irreverent, because to reject any part of revelation is to tell the Divine Revealer that He has set before the mind of His creature that which is either unnecessary or incredible.

At the same time, we recognize that some truths may be rejected with less ruin to the entire fabric of faith than others, just as certain limbs of the human body may be amputated without destroying life, although they impair its beauty and usefulness, while others—the head, for example—cannot be parted with without instant death. Thus, too, mistakes may be made about some minor doctrines or the meaning of certain portions of Scripture, without necessarily leading to fatal consequences. But to reject the resurrection is to cut at the root of Christian belief; it is to cease, as far as thought and faith go, to be a Christian at all. A Christ who never rose from His grave is not the Christ of the Bible or of Christendom.

Each of us must seriously ask ourselves, "What does the resurrection of Christ mean to me? How much of my life, of my thoughts, of my resolve, is influenced by it? Suppose Christ had not risen. What would I have lost?" Try to estimate the difference in your thought and life that the absence of this truth would involve. Suppose the resurrection of Jesus Christ were withdrawn from the Bible and from the Creed. How would it affect your hold of other Christian truths? How would it change your thoughts about the future, about the world unseen, about death, about all that is to follow after death? How would it touch your thoughts and feelings throughout each day, as they move around the Person of an unseen but present Lord and Saviour? If you answer these questions honestly, you may form a tolerably fair estimate of the value of your faith in Christ's resurrection at this moment.

If we do indeed believe that He is risen, such a stupendous faith does and must mold thought, feeling, resolve, in many and various ways. If we do believe that He is risen and living, then we know that to part with this faith would affect the life of our spirits, just as the extinction of the sun's light and warmth in the heavens would affect all beings that live and grow on this earth. If Jesus Christ the Risen One is indeed the object of our faith, then our religion is not merely the critical study of an ancient literature but a vitally distinct thing; it is the communion of our spirits with the living God. It is faith in His resurrection that marks our present relations to Jesus Christ as altogether different from those that we have to the famous dead who in past years have filled the thoughts and governed the history of mankind. To believe in the risen Christ is to live under a sky that is ever bright. It is to believe that He is "alive for evermore . . . and has the keys of hell and of death" (Rev. 1:18).

CHRISTIAN PREACHING MUST CENTER IN THE RESURRECTION

". . . then is our preaching vain" (I Cor. 15:14b).

A peasant once traded a bag of nuts for some books he wanted, but the bookseller got the worst of the bargain, for later when he cracked the shells he found they were all empty. What good is a nut that contains no kernel? That is what apostolic preaching would be like without the resurrection. "If Christ be not risen, then is our preaching vain," said Paul.

The Greek word translated "vain" in verse 14 is *kenon* (neuter nominative singular of *kenos*) and *kenee* (feminine nominative singular). Verse 17 repeats the second part of verse 14, with the exception that the Greek word is not *kenee* but *mataia*. The repetition is purposeful. *Kenos (ee)* means "empty, hollow, devoid of reality." *Mataios (a)* means "wanting in result, fruitless, futile." This latter is the same word used in Titus 3:9, "But avoid foolish questions, and genealogies, and contentions, and strivings about the law; for they are unprofitable and vain [*mataioi*]."

"Then is our preaching vain." The word "preaching" here is *keerugma*, which refers not to the delivery of the sermon but to its content. Our preaching is without content if Christ did not rise. If that be the case, why bother preaching at all?

Observe that Paul does not say "my preaching" but "our preaching," stressing once again the unanimity of the apostles which he has proclaimed in verse 11: "Therefore whether it were I or they, so we preach, and so ye believed." He wants the Corinthians to realize that this is not merely his own personal conclusion but that of all the apostles. He associates himself with the older apostles who had seen the Lord Jesus on earth, and more especially after His resurrection. He and they alike had been preaching a message to the world which, if Christ had not really risen from the grave, was empty, mere words and phrases without substance or soul. In reality the Corinthians who denied the general resurrection had no intention of casting any slur upon the teaching of the apostles, much less of bringing it to such utter discredit. They did not realize what they were doing. They had no idea that by implication they were proclaiming to the world that the teaching of the apostles was only an insubstantial dream.

It was Paul's duty to undeceive them, as it is that of all faithful ministers of the Gospel to undeceive anyone who claims that there is no resurrection. As their denial must logically include the resurrection of Christ, this would be fatal to the claim of the apostles to be serious teachers of God's revelation. For if there was any one truth upon which the apostles had staked their credit as messengers of God, it was the truth that Christ had risen from the dead. His resurrection was the instrument by which they effectively made their way to popular attention. His resurrection was the proof of the truth of what they had to say; it was, in fact, the most important part of what they had to say.

Two months had not passed since Christ's resurrection before the apostles began to preach it, with the confidence of men who knew that they would not be successfully contradicted, and that their assertion had everything to gain by inquiry. One could be an apostle only if he had seen the risen Christ and thus bear personal testimony in his preaching to the fact that Christ had risen from the dead. And, when Mathias was chosen to fill the place left vacant by Judas, Peter thus defined an apostle's work: "one . . . ordained to be a witness with us of his [Christ's] resurrection" (Acts 1:22).

We find that the reported sermons of Paul and Peter reflect this. The whole point of the first sermon Peter ever preached in the Church of Christ, as he was surrounded by the eleven apostles on the Day of Pentecost, was that the resurrection, to which he and his brother apostles could bear witness, had been actually prophesied by David in Psalm 16 (Acts 2:22-36).

Again, how does Peter explain the miracle of the healing of the lame man at the Beautiful Gate of the Temple, in the two addresses that he delivered, first to the assembled spectators, and next when he was arrested and brought before the Sanhedrin? In both he refers the miracle to the power of Jesus Christ; living because risen, and risen although slain on the cross (Acts 3:12-16; 4:8-12).

The resurrection of Jesus is the clue to the mystery that so baffled the Jews and their elders, that poor unlettered men could work such miracles and win such influence. Again, when numerous conversions had taken place, and the apostles were arrested a second time and charged with having filled Jerusalem with their doctrine, what is Peter's defense? He says that the apostles cannot help it; the resurrection is a fact that lays a necessity upon them. "Peter and the other apostles answered and said, We ought to obey God rather than men. The God of our fathers raised up Jesus, whom ye slew" (Acts 5:29, 30).

Once more, when Peter is instructing the heathen soldier, Cornelius, and other inquirers, what is his main argument? "The Jews," he says, "slew [Jesus] and hanged [him] on a tree: him God raised up the third day, and shewed him openly; not to all the people, but unto witnesses chosen before of God, even to us, who did eat and drink with him after he rose from the dead" (Acts 10:39-41).

Look also at the reported sermons of Paul. He had not seen the risen Christ before the ascension. But he knew what the other apostles had seen. And he himself had a personal encounter with Jesus Christ after His resurrection, in the Damascus-road experience.

Consider Paul's great discourse delivered in the synagogue of Antioch of Pisidia (Acts 13:16-41). Everything he says in it leads up to Christ's resurrection. Christ was slain because of the pressure put upon Pilate by the Jews; Christ was raised by God the Father from the dead and seen many days by those who came up with Him from Galilee to Jerusalem. Paul then shows that all this agrees with prophecy, as the Jews understood it, in the Psalms and in Jeremiah.

Read Paul's speech on Mars Hill in Athens (Acts 17:22-31). All God's previous dealings with mankind, so he contends, had led up to the apostolic preaching of repentance. And repentance was necessary because judgment was coming; and the Judge was to be a man ordained by God, "whereof," he adds, "he hath given assurance unto all men, in that he hath raised him from the dead" (v. 31). That is Paul's own account, when put upon his defense, of his general teaching.

Studying the early teachings of the apostles, we see that they centered in and rested upon the resurrection of Jesus Christ. The resurrection was not only their reason for teaching at all; it was also the main substance of what they taught. If they were deceived as to its reality, their teaching had neither basis nor substance; their exhortations, their apologies, their appeals, their entreaties, their interpretations of prophecy, their account of the facts before them, their anticipations as to the future, all become a confused and irrational array of phrases, which might better die and be forgotten as soon as possible.

Paul presents the stern words of First Corinthians 15:15 as the necessary consequence of what any preacher would be who engaged in such empty preaching. "Yes, and we are found false witnesses of God; because we have testified of God that he raised up Christ: whom he raised not up, if so be that the dead rise not." If there is no resurrection, Paul tells the Corinthians, then our preaching is empty and we are deceivers. He knew they would never believe this; and by presenting such a strong argument he was persuaded that they would rather forsake their speculations than entertain the thought that he and the other apostles were deceiving them by preaching a deliberate falsehood.

It was because of Paul's saintly reputation among the Corinthians that he could appeal first to them, not on the basis of their faith derived from their belief in the resurrection but on the basis of the integrity of apostolic character; and since he was the only apostle who ever preached among them, it was to his own integrity that he appealed.

Is our integrity such that it becomes one of the strongest points in our witness to our belief in the resurrected Christ?

Stanley, who went to Africa to find Livingstone, later wrote that at that time he was "as prejudiced against religion as the worst infidel in London." But after he had found Livingstone and observed his dedicated life for some months, he said, "Little by little seeing his piety, his gentleness, his zeal, his earnestness, and how he went quietly about his business, I was converted through him, although he had not tried in any way to do it."

IS CHRIST DEAD?

"Yea, and we are found false witnesses of God; because we have testified of God that he raised up Christ: whom he raised not up, if so be that the dead rise not. For if the dead rise not, then is not Christ raised: And if Christ be not raised, your faith is vain; ye are yet in your sins" (I Cor. 15:15-17).

One day a skeptic went to see a friend whom he had not visited in some time. "My friend was not alone," he says. "Since I had last seen him he had found Jesus, and the effect of the discovery was manifest. His whole direction and outlook were altered. There was joy and quiet confidence in his face, and purpose in his life. Jesus was as alive and present to my friend as He had been to the eleven in the upper room. And from that day on He was alive and present to me. I had previously studied the evidence for the resurrection with an unbeliever's critical scrutiny. Now I knew. That event was the turning-point in my life."

How many people have been led to a living union with Jesus Christ who have started by admiring the life of some saint of God. Some would say, "If that's what it takes to make me what he or she is, I want it, too." Can this be said of you and me?

Christianity is a religion of practice and not merely of theory. A person shows he is a Christian, not mainly by what he says but by what he does. Christianity provides a criterion by which to test its validity.

That it is unique among the religions of the world is attested by the fact that the life of the Christian is unique. And this is so because his Lord is alive, indwelling him and living victoriously through him. If it were not for Christ's resurrection, the Christian could not be what he is or do what he does.

As Paul seeks to turn the Corinthians from their misguided speculations concerning the bodily resurrection of the dead, he invites them to examine a tangible evidence of Christ's resurrection. Look at us apostles, he says in effect. Do you think that we are all liars and false witnesses? He knew they did not. The apostles were held in the highest regard by the church people of that day.

Paul often used the blameless reputation of the apostles as a basis of appeal for establishing the trustworthiness of the Gospel. In writing to the Thessalonians he said, "For our gospel came not unto you in word only, but also in power, and in the Holy Ghost, and in much assurance; as ye know what manner of men we were among you for your sake" (I Thess. 1:5). And earlier in his Epistle to the Corinthians he writes, "I beseech you, be ye followers of me . . . . For I would that all men were even as I myself . . . . Be ye followers of me, even as I also am of Christ" (I Cor. 4:16; 7:7; 11:1).

Writing to the Philippians he says, "Brethren, be ye followers together of me, and mark them which walk so as ye have us for an ensample . . . . Those things, which ye have both learned, and received, and heard, and seen in me, do: and the God of peace shall be with you" (Phil. 3:17; 4:9). And again to the Thessalonians he says, "For yourselves know how ye ought to follow us: for we behaved not ourselves disorderly among you" (II Thess. 3:7). Could we preachers write this in clear conscience to every group of people we have ministered to?

Paul sums up the whole matter to the Corinthians by throwing out the challenge: Can you say that I am a false witness of the resurrection of Christ, and that the eighteen months I stayed among you I preached a deliberate lie? He knew that they had a higher regard for his integrity than that.

Paul then goes on to appeal to the Corinthians' knowledge of the work of Christ in their own hearts and lives. "And if Christ be not risen . . . your faith is also vain" (I Cor. 15:14). And again in verse 17, "And if Christ be not raised, your faith is vain." In the Greek text, the word "vain" in verse 14 is *kenee*, meaning "empty, without content, like a bubble," as to emphasis, while in verse 17 it is *mataia*, the meaning of which emphasizes the thought, "without result, fruitless because aimless." Without the resurrection of Christ, faith is without any substance, and such faith will not hold you up. That is why, in verse 17, after saying "Your faith is vain," Paul adds, "Ye are yet in your sins."

But, says someone, why should we concern ourselves in this day and age with what the Corinthians held in regard to the resurrection? I assure you it is of practical contemporary importance. The reality of the resurrection is not a matter of concern merely to those who lived some nineteen centuries ago, but it affects our everyday lives. Men everywhere are seeking relief from the burden of guilt. But they can never know the happiness of sins forgiven unless their assurance is based on fact and not on wishful thinking.

The Corinthians to whom Paul is writing must, for the most part, have been believers. They knew their sins were forgiven through Christ and His work. They could not bear to have anyone cast a doubt on such a vital experience and the radical change it produced in their lives. Paul knew the Corinthians well enough to realize that, once he pointed out the two fallacies into which their denial of the resurrection would lead them, they would disclaim any intention of saying that the apostles were liars and that they themselves were still unregenerate sinners.

A man may not know much theology, but, once he is assured his sins are forgiven through the blood of Christ, the experience is so overwhelming and the relief so great that he is not likely to doubt its reality. If you ask a man if his sins are forgiven and he merely answers, "I guess so," you can be reasonably sure that he has not been regenerated. He whose sins are forgiven resounds with a wholehearted "I know so." Such an experience of salvation is not lightly surrendered. Faith for these Corinthians had been used and approved in the wear and tear of life.

Without His resurrection, we have no proof that the One who suffered on Calvary was more than the feeble victim of an enormous wrong; powerless, as His enemies said, to save Himself, and much more powerless to achieve the salvation of others. But the Corinthians knew full well that they were saved, and therefore the reality of their salvation had to be based on the reality of Christ's resurrection. The cross is the symbol of Christianity, but not Christ on the cross: He is risen. A dead Christ may be the object of a grateful memory, but only a living Christ can be the author of our salvation, the giver of eternal life.

These are the elements of what Paul called his Gospel: "I have nothing to preach if I have not a cross to proclaim that is man's deliverance from sin because on it the Son of God died. And I know that sacrifice is sufficient only because Christ rose from the dead."

A preacher who wore a small gold cross on a watch chain held it up before his congregation and said, "Whenever I am depressed and my work is too much for me and my sky is dark, my hand has found the habit of straying to this symbol and it brings to me this message: The cross is empty; and on the crest of that wave courage comes back to me."

The death of Christ cancels out the guilt of sin, but a living Christ destroys its dominion over us. If God was powerless to help His own Son against the death inflicted upon Him by sin, how can He be expected to help men in their struggles against sin? Only by one means can God reveal Christ's final victory over sin. He must make Christ triumph over the death that sin inflicted upon Him. Otherwise Christ failed in His work, and the power of sin is still supreme in men's lives. The proof of God's power to save men from sin is His power to raise Christ from the dead and thus undo the death into which the sin of man plunged Him.

EMPTY FAITH

"And if Christ be not raised, your faith is vain; ye are yet in your sins" (I Cor. 15:15-17).

People who base their faith on a Christianity that denies the resurrection of Jesus Christ are like children playing tea-party. They gravely pour imaginary tea from an empty pot into an empty cup, or lift imaginary food to their mouths from an empty plate. How can you sustain life without substance? "If Christ did not rise, your faith is empty," Paul told the Corinthians. "It is not resultful." The result of which Paul is speaking here is forgiveness of sins. If Christ did not rise, your sins have not been forgiven. An unforgiven Christian is a contradiction of terms, for one of the conditions of entering upon the Christian life is the acknowledgment of sins, followed by Christ's forgiveness.

But there is more to the content of the Christian faith than forgiveness. The phrase "your faith" (Greek *hee pistis humoon*) in I Corinthians 15:14 and 17 is considered by itself and is not relative to any other word; and this is emphasized in both instances in that the phrase is preceded by the definite article *hee* (the). Paul does not state the object of this faith. He does not say "your faith in Christ" or faith in a particular doctrine. The literal wording is "the faith of yours," whatever it was based on. And what was the basis of their faith? First it was Christ Himself, and then all that He taught as essential.

Undeniably one of the doctrines that Christ taught

is that man continues in some manner to exist after death. The Christian believes that there is a world to come, another life, to which he looks forward. He does not speculate on it as a possibility; he takes it for granted as a demonstrated fact. He looks forward to it as he looks forward to the changes of nature, to the setting of the sun, to the succession of the seasons. He knows that death will come to him as to everybody else; that each day of his life brings it nearer; that it means a momentous and unimaginable change.

But it is not only to a future state of being that a Christian looks forward; he knows what that state will be. Through His resurrection, Christ has changed speculation about the future to certain faith. He has explored that unknown world. He has told the Christian what to expect. The Christian counts on it. He treats this life as a preface to that which is to come. He gives up this life if necessary so that he will not lose the life to come. He looks forward to the time when mortality will be "swallowed up of life" (II Cor. 5:4), and meanwhile he "rejoices in hope of the glory of God" (Rom. 5:2).

Suppose, however, that Christ has not really risen from His grave. What becomes of these bright hopes of the Christian? Is there any real warrant for them? You may say, "There remain the words of Christ, His teachings." But what authority do they have? If Christ never rose from the grave, how do His words about the future life of man differ from the words of Plato? They may be more positive; but do they represent any sources of knowledge altogether distinct in kind from those which Plato had at command? No. If Christ died and did not rise again, if His dust still mingles with the soil of Palestine, then it is trifling with language and with the hopes and anxieties of men to tell us that He has "brought life and immortality (Greek, *aphtharsia*, incorruption) to light through the gospel" (II Tim. 1:10), or that He has given eternal life to all believers. If He is not risen, He has only added a few more assertions on the subject of the future life to the stock of speculations that mankind already possessed. But we do not really know more about the future life than we did before He came. If Christ has not risen from His grave, then our faith as Christians in a future life, so far as it is based on His additions to our natural anticipation, is undoubtedly empty, without content.

Forgiveness of sin and certitude of a joyful life to come are only part of the content of the Christian faith. A third feature is belief in the future moral perfection of man. When we look at ourselves we tend to become discouraged. When we look at the world at large we are distressed. It is only as we look at Christ that we see any valid grounds for hope that we shall be better. Imperfection, morally speaking, is the order of life as we now know it. And we wonder: is sinless perfection at all possible?

A strong faith in man's future sinless perfection by God's miraculous transforming power is a necessary ingredient of all earnest moral effort. If we cannot improve, why try? But as we look at Christ, we are strengthened in faith to believe in God's capacity to give moral perfection to men. Christ's life was unstained by any taint of sin. His was the one absolutely true and unclouded intellect in this present world. His was the one heart whose affections were perfectly pure. His was the one will of which the rectitude and the vigor were never for one instant impaired. He could challenge an envious world to convict Him of sin if it could. In the judgment of those who watched Him most closely, He "did no sin, neither was guile found in his mouth" (I Pet. 2:22). And indeed "such an high priest became us, who is holy, harmless, undefiled, separate from sinners" (Heb. 7:26). We needed Him as our priestly representative in heaven. We needed Him no less as our standard of true human excellence on earth.

But if Christ did not rise, could He still be a perfect character? If the event to which He solemnly referred as the ratification of His mission never occurred at all, can He be acquitted of trifling with the confidence and hopes of His followers, not to say anything of honesty of character? What would be said of a modern teacher or leader who had encouraged men to give up all their prospects in life upon the strength of promises that were never realized, and that he must have known never could be realized—and who had done this with so much solemnity and detail that they could not possibly have misunderstood him? We would severely condemn him. If he could be acquitted of an intention to deceive, it would only be by admitting that he himself was the victim of a delusion so serious as to disqualify him for guiding others. If Christ is not risen, then He was either a deliberate deceiver or mentally deluded, and our faith in Him would be worthless. Since His character would not be perfect, ours could not be either. Any effort for moral betterment, then, because of Christ's influence, would be impossible. Our faith in the perfectability of moral character then falls to pieces.

Forgiveness, immortality, perfectability, all depend upon a risen Christ to make them actual in our lives, as does the fourth basic element of Christian faith: the belief that good will ultimately triumph over evil. If Christ be not risen, a shadow is cast upon any such belief. Isaiah says, "The righteous perisheth, and no man layeth it to heart" (Isa. 57:1). Who cares when a humble, poor Christian dies? The world takes little note of it. Does Jesus care, for whose sake that man may have forsaken all to follow Him? The Psalmist, speaking of the wicked, says, "Their strength is firm. They are not in trouble as other men; neither are they plagued like other men" (Psa. 73:4, 5). This is the face that the world wears from age to age. Here and there we see notable exceptions to the rule. But upon the whole, evil seems to be in possession, and, as far as experience goes, it is likely to hold its own.

When a Christian is haunted by this impression, which strikes at persistent faith in the moral supremacy of God, he turns his thoughts to the resurrection. Never did evil seemingly obtain such a triumph over pure goodness as when it nailed Jesus Christ to the cross. Never was the ultimate victory of goodness so clearly vindicated as on the morning of the resurrection. The greatest proof that ever was given that the world is governed by a moral God was given when Jesus, the sinless victim of evil, was rescued by the resurrection from the clutches of death.

(See H. P. Liddon, *Easter in St. Paul's*, pp. 44-47.)

DON'T ROB THE DEAD!

"Then they also which are fallen asleep in Christ are perished" (I Cor. 15:18).

If two and two equal five, then four and four equal ten: right? "Of course not," you say, "because two and two do not equal five to begin with, and therefore your conclusion is wrong." In logic this sort of thing is called *reductio ad absurdum,* reducing something to absurd terms in order to show the fallacy of your opponent's reasoning.

Paul uses this device to show those Corinthians who denied the resurrection from the dead that, if Christ did not rise, certain preposterous results followed: 1) that the apostles were liars, and 2) that the Corinthians themselves were still unforgiven and unregenerate sinners. Since the Corinthians held the integrity of the apostles in the highest regard, and were fully assured of their salvation and pardon in Christ, Paul knew that they would see at once how absurd it is to reject the fact from which both these conclusions stem: the resurrection of Jesus Christ, which was firmly held and taught by the apostles and which assured their regeneration and forgiveness.

"Look at us," says Paul in effect. "If the resurrection is not true, we apostles are liars. Look at yourselves. If Christ did not rise, you are yet in your sins." And now he points them to a third direction, in I Corinthians 15:18: "Look at those who died as believers in Christ. If Christ did not rise, if there is no resurrection, they have perished. Did they die in the delusion that their sins were forgiven and that they would be raised from the dead? Do you want to rob them of the benefits of Christ's resurrection by your philosophical speculations? You still have an opportunity to re-think your faith, and we apostles can still reconsider the veracity of our message, but the dead cannot do this. Their fate is sealed. If, as some of you say, Christ did not rise, then you must logically conclude that the dead in Christ died still unforgiven, and will never live again. Do you see to what absurdities your assumption leads?"

Anyone has a right to make an assumption, but if practical evidence shows that the conclusion is wrong he must be willing to re-examine his position. This procedure is the basis of the scientific method. You form a theory and then you try it out. If your experiments do not sustain the theory, you do not reject the demonstrable facts but the obviously fallacious theory.

This is what Paul was confident the Corinthian believers would do: they would not reject the honesty and trustworthiness of the apostles; they would not reject the factual knowledge that their sins had been forgiven, and they would not assign the dead to perdition as having died deceived about their faith in Christ, His life, His words, His death, and His resurrection.

To candid minds, this mode of reasoning is most convincing. Show me that my views, if reasoned out or acted upon, lead to consequences as unacceptable to me as they are to you, and I cannot but be moved to reconsider the grounds on which I have adopted them. Paul was pleading with the Corinthians to look at the destructive and totally unacceptable conclusions to which a denial of the resurrection would lead them, and to realize that their speculations about the resurrection were incompatible with the revealed facts.

What did Paul mean when he bluntly stated that, if Christ did not rise, "Then they also which are fallen asleep in Christ are perished"? The Greek word translated "are perished" is *apoolonto* (second aorist indicative middle of the verb *apollumi*). In the New Testament "the lost" (*hoi apollumenoi*) is presented as the opposite of "the saved" (*hoi soozomenoi*). (See I Cor. 1:18, II Cor. 2:15; 4:3, II Thess. 2:10.) This contrast between the saved and the lost is very clearly shown in John 3:16, "For God so loved the world . . . that whosoever believeth [*pas ho pisteuioon*, everyone who believes] on him should not perish [*mee apoleetai*]." Also in John 10:28, "And I give unto them eternal life [the life of God, which is what God is and therefore nonending among other qualities]; and they shall never perish [*apoloontai*]." (See also John 17:12, II Pet. 3:9, and the discussion in Gerhard Kittel's *Theological Dictionary of the New Testament*, pp. 394-6.)

Observe that Paul does not speak of all the dead here, but only of the dead "in Christ," that is, those who died believing in Him. During His earthly sojourn, the Lord repeatedly said that those who believed on Him should not perish. Therefore, if He did not rise as He predicted, He proved Himself untrustworthy. It necessarily follows that any assurance He gave that those who believed on Him should not perish is also untrustworthy. They may have died thinking they were saved, but they were not; they perished forever. You, the living, Paul infers, have a chance to try out new doctrines and ideas, but alas for your friends and loved ones who have gone before. They have risked their all on what now, it seems, turns out to be an error. Therefore our plight—both as living and dead believers —is indeed deplorable.

Christ taught that all who have died continue to exist, but that believers in Him are eternally saved and unbelievers are eternally lost. "He that heareth my word, and believeth on him that sent me, hath everlasting life. . . . For as the Father hath life in himself; so hath he given to the Son to have life in himself; and hath given him authority to execute judgment also. . . . The hour is coming, in the which all that are in the graves shall hear his voice, and shall come forth; they that have done good, unto the resurrection of life; and they that have done evil, unto the resurrection of damnation" (John 5:24, 26-29). By refuting the argument that the dead in Christ have perished, Paul shows that they have not believed in vain. But if Christ did not rise, then their eternal doom is forever sealed.

The word "perished" would not mean that the departed ones had ceased to exist. The very use of the term, "they that have fallen asleep," indicates that Paul believes death is but a passing through from one state of existence to another. The question of man's continued existence is not raised in the argument. What Paul's argument implies is that, if Christ did not rise bodily, then the bodies of those who believed in Him would never be raised either. However, Paul does not imply that the believing dead (or any of the dead, for that matter), would therefore be annihilated. Their continued spiritual existence would not necessarily be denied; only, if Christ did not resume His buried body, they would not consequently resume theirs.

In fact, all the apostle means to imply here about those who have fallen asleep in Christ is not their perishing in the sense of ceasing to exist, either in or out of the body, but their perishing in the sense of not being saved, but being lost. Some of the Corinthians might well have been willing to concede that Christ would have had an unending life, even if His body had not been raised, and that those who died believing in Him would have an unending life in the spirit.

We must understand Paul's statement here, concerning believers who have died, as being immediately connected with that concerning believers who are living. "If Christ be not risen," ye who still live, although you believe in Christ, "are yet in your sins." "If Christ be not risen," your departed brethren, although they fell asleep in Christ, must have died in their sins, and must even now be reaping the fruit of their sins, in condemnation and utter ruin—and that forever. "If Christ be not risen," you now believe in vain; you believe in One who cannot save you from your sins, seeing that He is not Himself saved from the death inflicted by sin. And your friends who have fallen asleep believing in Christ have believed in vain. They died believing in One who could not save them. They are lost; they have perished.

Are you prepared for that consequence inevitably flowing from this speculation of yours about the resurrection? Paul challenges the Corinthians. Are you prepared, not only to invalidate your own faith, which up till now has given you a hope of your salvation from your sins, but also to destroy the faith of mother, father, loved ones, and fellow believers who fell asleep in Christ, depending on His assurance of justification through His resurrection from the dead? Did they walk so fearlessly through the valley of the shadow of death trusting in a lie; and are their eyes now opened to the dreadful truth that for all their faith in Christ they are yet in their sins, eternally lost? And is this because the One in whom they believed, while He indeed died for their sins, was not able to extricate Himself from them and their consequences? Will you awake in eternity to the melancholy complaint of despair, "We trusted that it had been he who should have redeemed us?" Or will you rejoice in the certainty of Christ's promise, "Because I live, ye shall live also"? (John 14:19.)

MISERABLE CHRISTIANS

"If in this life only we have hope in Christ, we are of all men most miserable" (I Cor. 15:19).

The Apostle Paul points out to those who question the resurrection of the body that, if Christ did not rise, no one has ever been saved, either dead or living, even though they believed in Him.

Having looked at living and dead believers in I Corinthians 15:17 and 18, Paul now lifts his eyes toward the future and says in verse 19, "If in this life only we have hope in Christ, we are of all men most miserable." What did he mean by this?

First of all, it must be pointed out that he is not defending the reality of the future life, as some have supposed. Our continuous spiritual existence hereafter does not depend on the resurrection of Christ; it is not a gift of the Redeemer but of the Creator. It is inherent in the nature of man that he shall never cease to exist in spirit, for that is how God made him.

The common notion of the future life did not originate with Christianity. It is as deeply rooted in the human soul as belief in God. In some form or other it is practically universal. Even without any special revelation, man suspects, if he does not certainly know, that he will continue to live after death.

It has been said that in seven years every particle of a human body will have changed. And although the form, the stature, the countenance remain, yet, with time, these also are modified. Man loses the outward semblance of his former self, until we see the final decomposition of his body in death.

But how different it is with the soul. It is always the same in the midst of change. The death of the body cannot be presumed to affect it. There are strong reasons for anticipating its enduring life. In nothing do we more nearly touch the consciousness of a life to come than in our sense of carrying within us much that never attains completion here. We have a hunger for God that can never be satisfied with what we now know of Him. We long for perfection; we want to see justice done; we want to see wrongs righted and entrenched evil routed by the forces of righteousness. All these aspirations are wholly unsatisfied within the limits of our earthly existence, so that we become increasingly certain that there must be a future state in which the demands of justice will be met.

Our knowledge of the future life is older than the Gospel, and our possession of it preceded the work of Jesus Christ on earth. What, then, did Christ add through His death and resurrection? He gave us the hope that our inevitable existence after death will be one, not of uncertainty and fearful speculation, but of joy and fulfillment.

It is true that II Timothy 1:10 tells us that Christ "brought life and immortality [incorruption] to light," but bringing something to light is not the same as bringing it into being. For multitudes before Christ came, the future life was but a vague and dreary anticipation. He has made it a joyous and welcome certainty. He has emphasized the idea that all live unto God; that belief in God as the God of the ancient dead carries with it a belief in their permanent individual existence (Luke 20:37, 38); and He has further taught the future resurrection of the body as completing the life beyond the grave (John 6:40). In fact, He has altogether removed the question of life after death from the region of speculation into that of knowledge founded upon experience. For when He rose from death and presented Himself to the senses of those who saw Him, He was Himself but the firstfruits from the dead (I Cor. 15:20).

Hope in Christ, therefore, is something more than the conviction of life after death; it is the hope of a joyous state of existence of body and soul in which we shall have fellowship with God and be perfected in righteousness. This is what Christ has won for us by His one perfect and sufficient sacrifice on the cross, by which our sins are blotted out. That His cross has this virtue is proved by His resurrection from the dead. That He lives in order that we may live also (John 14:19) is the basis of our hope in Him (Rom. 8:10, 11). Apart from this conviction, Christianity is an empty dream; the efforts and sacrifices of the Christian have no enduring worth; we are the victims of a great delusion; we are of all men most miserable.

Paul's argument in the 19th verse is a continuation of what he has been contending right along—that neither the living nor the dead ever experience the forgiveness of their sins if Christ has not risen. "If in this life only we have hope in Christ, we are of all men most miserable," he proclaims. The very peace of heart and reconciliation with God that make this life at its worst not only tolerable but even desirable to believers in Christ are then merely a delusion. There may be pleasure in having hope in Christ in this life, while this life lasts. But when it is over, and we are faced with a continued state of existence after death, we will find our hope to be utterly hollow and untrue. Why? Because our hope in Christ is the hope of having been saved from our sins. And if Christ has been forever slain by sin, then whatever hope we have in Christ of being saved from our sins rests on a delusion, a fable, an error. At death we shall find, as those who have fallen asleep in Christ before us, that though we based our hope of forgiveness and eternal salvation on Him, our faith is vain and our hope a delusion; that since Christ is not raised we are yet in our sins and must continue in them forever.

Isn't this a truly miserable state? If that is what we have to look forward to, are we not to be deeply pitied?

The "hope in Christ," then, of which Paul speaks is not the hope of the resurrection, nor even the hope of a future life, but the hope of the pardon, the favor, the approval and love of the Most High God. If such a hope is well founded, it is a source of joy and peace to our hearts both for the present and the future.

But how can such a hope be well founded if Christ has not risen from the dead; if your sins and mine are still upon Him, keeping His body in the tomb; if the Great Redeemer has failed to procure, even in His own case, a reversal of the sentence, "dust to dust"?

Any hope we can have in such a Christ must be for this life only. We may try to persuade ourselves that there is pardon for us in Christ. But the pardon, the atonement, what do they avail if our sins are still upon Him—if indeed, under such circumstances, He can be said to have borne them at all? At death we shall discover that our faith that Christ could save us from our sins was a delusion. We have believed in vain; we are yet in our sins after all. We perish, as they who have fallen asleep in Jesus before us have perished, hopelessly and forever—in conscious separation from God for all eternity. No wonder Paul said that if this were so, we were of all men most miserable.

Observe that Paul uses the plural pronoun "we." He is not saying that all men would be miserable if there were no hope of the life to come. Some people never think of another life and are quite happy in their way, enjoying themselves and being comfortable after a fashion. Paul's argument has nothing to do with those who are not Christians.

But we who have fixed our hopes on Christ cannot fall back upon the easy unconcern of worldly security. Our natural peace has been broken, our consciences have been pricked, our hearts have been stirred. Can you imagine the disappointment of a Christian who has been placing all his hopes in Christ, who finds at last that it was all in vain? The Christian is an heir of God and a joint-heir with Christ. His days of heaven begin here on earth. He rejoices because his sins are forgiven. His joy does not depend upon his circumstances. Every Christian will testify that he has often found his sad times to be his glad times, his losses to be his gains, his sicknesses to promote his soul's health, as he accepts them by faith at the hand of God. He can even rejoice in the time of death, believing that his last day will be his best day.

But what a calamity after he comes to it, to discover that his faith was all a delusion! This is what would happen if Christ did not rise.

Who would be more disappointed than the apostles themselves? They were rejected by most of their countrymen; they had lost all the comforts of home; their lives were spent in hardship and privation, and they were daily exposed to violent death. They all suffered a martyr's death, except John, who seems to have been preserved not from martyrdom but in it. They might certainly be regarded as the twelve most miserable of men apart from that hope of the blessedness of the world to come; yet they were of all men the most joyful. This is true not only of persecuted apostles but of all believers. For though God gives us richly all things to enjoy in this life (I Tim. 6:17), the Christian renounces many common and ordinary sources of joy from which other men drink. The Christian's primary joy is in his relationship to the living Christ. He knows that all earthly joys end at death, but the joy of his relationship with Christ is eternal.

OUR HOPE OF HEAVEN

"If in this life only we have hope in Christ, we are of all men most miserable"(I Cor. 15:19).

Pity the poor man who has been promised a fortune by a rich relative, only to find that he has been cut off in his will without a penny. From that moment on, his poverty becomes an intolerable burden, for it is no longer lightened by the hope of better things to come.

It is the same with the Christian who makes sacrifices in this life, counting them as nothing in anticipation of the enjoyment of heaven. If Christ did not rise, then all his expectations are in vain; his hopes are shattered. Will Christ fail us Christians like a rich uncle who made glowing promises and then died without fulfilling them? If the answer is Yes, then all that we have suffered for His sake in upholding holiness and rejecting expediency is pointless. Not that our lives were miserable while we made such sacrifices, for we fully enjoyed our living relationship with Christ here on earth. The joy of the Christian is not in the reward for sacrifice but in his relationship with the living Christ. There is joy in privation and suffering for a loved one, regardless of the final rewards. But what a disappointment it would be to find that our confidence in His promises had been misplaced.

Paul did not mean that we Christians are the most miserable of men if the hopes of the future are taken away from us. He did not mean that the pains and burdens of the Christian life are so much greater than the pains and burdens of non-Christians that only the joys of the other world can compensate for them. He did not mean that we have the worst of it here, and are therefore placed at a terrible disadvantage if there is nothing better hereafter. Paul never felt that he was having the worst of it. He never spoke of his life as wretched and unhappy. He was always bearing witness of its joyfulness. The raptures that he had far exceeded the pangs. The delight that he had in his work always surpassed the suffering it entailed. If the Christian life had brought him many losses, it had brought him still more gains, and, even apart from the future, the balance was on the right side.

We should be able to give the same testimony if we have any deep and true experience of the Christian life. It is a good thing now and always. Its rewards are for the present as well as the future. We are not trusting wholly in promissory notes. We are richer in all things than non-believers, except, perhaps, in material goods. And even then, the Christian is spared substantial sums of money by not indulging in sinful practices that are costly and give no lasting pleasure. We have more inspiring thoughts, more peace of mind, more quiet and happy hours, more freedom from worry, envy, and discontent, from gnawings of conscience and torturing fears. We are unmistakably gainers in this life. However much we give up for Christ, we get a great deal back from Him. It is a great thing to be saved from sin now, for sin brings with it a measure of hell, whether in this world or the next. Right-doing gives a taste of heaven, and if Christ strengthens us to do right we enjoy that taste of heaven before we get there. We have the best of it in this present time, and it is an utterly mistaken view of the Christian life that represents it as a hard, ugly, unwelcome thing, endured for the sake of the bliss which is to follow. It is good all through, good from beginning to end, though far better at the end.

Nevertheless, we cannot divorce the hope of the future from the present. Hope not realized brings misery. And if Christ did not rise, we do not need to wait until after death to experience this, but it is ours here and now, because the very basis of our hope disappears. Paul wants to show that this hope of the Christian for the future is based upon the actuality of the resurrection of Christ.

What does Paul mean here by the expression "most miserable"? The translation is rather unfortunate. In Greek it is *eleeinoteroi*, which literally means "more deserving of compassion or pity." We are more to be pitied than others. Why? Because we have been deceiving ourselves and building airy nothings out of insubstantial dreams. There is nothing that more excites our pity than to see a man building extravagant hopes on a foolish delusion. He may be happy and satisfied, yet we pity him and say, "Poor fellow." We would rather face life in all its grim reality than live in a fool's paradise. The most pitiable beings in this world are those who live in a state of delusion. Now you begin to understand Paul's words. If in this life only we have hope in Christ, we are of all men most to be pitied, because if there is no joyous after-life in the presence of Christ, our confident expectation of such a life is the greatest possible delusion. The man who imagines himself to be Napoleon is no more extravagant and insane than we are. We think ourselves undying spirits when we are only perishing beasts. We think that God has loved us with an undying love, and yet the end of it all is a few handfuls of corrupt dust. We claim a relationship with glorified saints, martyrs, and apostles, and brotherhood with the King in His beauty, and yet we are only heirs with them of six feet of cold earth. We believe that those whom we have loved and lost will greet us beyond the grave, and alas, our love has said its last goodbye in death. We believe that we shall know the answers to all that puzzled us here, that we shall grow and learn the higher wisdom in God's eternal light, but instead we are left naked and disinherited. God could not have dealt with us more cruelly than this. Such a God, if He exists at all, would be a demon who finds His sport in cheating the best of men, some huge liar who pleases Himself by making the noblest souls believe a lie, and laughing at their gullibility.

Some time ago we heard the news that "Father Divine," the self-styled God, was dead. Can you imagine God dying? The Lord Jesus Christ would have been in the same category if His life had ended in the grave. We would have to say of Him, as was said of Father Divine, that "God" had died. It would have been better for the Corinthian believers and for all Christians never to have heard of Christ than to have the One in whom they trusted for the forgiveness of sins die and never rise again. His supposed revelation then becomes the deepest deception and mockery the world has ever known. It is Christ who has deepened in us the hunger for the joy of a future life, and led us to count the world well lost for the joy that is set before us. It is Christ, then, who has done us the greatest wrong imaginable if He has failed us in this.

"If in this life only we have hope in Christ, we are of all men most to be pitied." *Eleeinoteroi*, "more to be pitied," comes from the noun *eleos*, which means "mercy." We thought we had obtained mercy through Christ's death. But if Christ did not rise, neither shall we. If Christ did not rise, no one has been redeemed. And since only the redeemed were promised entrance into a life of future bliss, no one is eligible. There is no escape from the impasse.

Since the thought of heaven is an element in all our present joy, life would be changed for the worse in all respects if anyone were to take out of it the upward and forward look, the great expectations of the hereafter. And above all things, if we who have known Christ—who have learned to love Him and have felt in our hearts that He is the altogether lovely One, who have been saying to ourselves for years, "We shall see Him in His beauty; we shall see Him face to face; and we shall be like Him"—if we were to have that hope taken away from us, and were convinced that we shall never behold Him at all, then indeed we should almost wish we had never heard of Him, and we should be of all men most pitiable.

(See H. P. Liddon, *Easter in St. Paul's*, pp. 1-15.)

Thank God, we can sing with deep conviction the words of that well-known hymn:

He lives, He lives, Christ Jesus lives today!
He walks with me and talks with me
    along life's narrow way.
He lives, He lives, salvation to impart.
You ask me how I know He lives?
    He lives within my heart.

DID CHRIST RAISE HIMSELF FROM THE DEAD?

"But now is Christ risen from the dead, and become the firstfruits of them that slept" (I Cor. 15:20).

When people have fixed ideas based on theory rather than fact, they do not always thank you for pointing out their errors. A "Peanuts" cartoon has Lucy contending that snow comes up from the ground rather than falls from the sky. When Charlie Brown very reasonably asks how it gets up through the pavement, she is taken aback for a moment, then angrily retorts, "Did anyone ever tell you you have a funny face?" Because she could not refute his logic, she resorted to ridicule of him as a person. Paul was not immune to this type of criticism in his day.

Some of the Corinthian Christians of Paul's day still clung to the Greek philosophical idea that the dead could not rise, at least not physically. Because of this, Paul points out, they have placed themselves in the position of seeming to deny an established fact that they actually believed—the physical resurrection of Jesus Christ. He wants to point out how illogical their thinking is.

"Come on," says Paul in effect, "let's face the fact of the resurrection of Christ and go on from there. You have been reasoning backwards. First start with the known and then proceed to the unknown." This is the scientific method, to begin with observation and then go on to form principles based on the facts observed. It starts with the data and ends with the thesis.

It is an inductive rather than a deductive method of reasoning.

As we examine First Corinthians 15:20, we find Paul reasoning from known fact to inescapable conclusion. Notice the logical correspondence of three words in Greek here: the emphatic adverb *nuni* (now), the verb *egeegertai* (is risen), and the participle *kekoimeemenoon* (them that slept). As an adverb of time here, *nuni* refers to the present. The verb *egeegertai* and the participle *kekoimeemenoon*, both in the perfect tense, indicate a historical event in the past whose effects remain and hence are being felt in the present. It is past history that the Lord Jesus arose from the dead, but Paul stresses the fact that He is now alive and the effects of His historical resurrection are with us here and now.

It is also a fact that believers in Christ have died, as indicated by the clause "them that slept," but the important thing according to Paul is that we now regard them as if they were merely asleep, ready to be awakened at any moment. It is therefore the present and living implications of Christ's resurrection that Paul wants to stress. Christ's resurrection is history that very much affects life—including your life and mine.

Paul begins this verse with the words "But now." This expression should not be taken only as an adverb of time, which it is, but is also to be understood in its logical sense as introducing a contrast. We might translate it "but now indeed." It is the "but now indeed" of undeniable evidences. What are these evidences? Christ was seen by many after His death and burial. His tomb was empty. The lives of the disciples were transformed, and they risked their lives to proclaim His resurrection. Other men's lives were transformed as a result, and the Church grew in numbers. (How could the Church possibly have existed for even a week after the crucifixion if Christ did not rise?) Believers died smiling with the confident hope of entering into the presence of the Lord. Former sinners became saintly examples because of their relationship with the living Christ. All this could not have been based on a delusion, reasons Paul. Therefore Christ arose. He is living now.

That is where the Christian Gospel really begins— with the risen Christ. "But now is Christ risen!" Paul says to the Corinthians. Has any other religion ever begun in such a manner? None. Confess it therefore. Admit the fact. When you began to entertain that new opinion about the only possible resurrection being a spiritual one, you did not perceive its bearing upon the resurrection of Christ. Confess that you cannot face the conclusion which forces itself upon you, now that you do perceive the fact. You can never fully or truly believe in Christ unless you believe in the fact of His resurrection. And if He is risen, then the resurrection of the body must be possible. "Christ is risen from the dead, and become the firstfruits of them that slept." His resurrection implies and ensures the resurrection of those that sleep in Him.

To understand the resurrection, it is absolutely essential that we first understand who Christ is. He is truly God, the Apostle John tells us. "And we know that the Son of God is come, and hath given us an understanding, that we may know him that is true, and we are in him that is true, even in his Son Jesus Christ. This is the true God, and eternal life" (I John 5:20).

Though Jesus Christ is truly God, He also became truly man, with a soul (spirit) and body, as John 1:14 declares. "And the Word became flesh, and dwelt among us." Then at death His soul (or spirit) and body were truly separated upon the cross. Again the third day afterward His spirit and body were truly reunited, so that He became the same man as before, except that His body now had added glorious qualities not previously possessed, and had lost the characteristics of mortality.

He was seen and recognized by many eye-witnesses after His resurrection as "this same Jesus" whom they had previously known (Luke 24:13-35, John 20:19, 26, I Cor. 15:6, Luke 24:43-46). Angels also testified to this fact (Luke 24:4-6, John 20:12, Acts 1:11), and it was indisputably confirmed by God His Father (Acts 2:32, Gal. 1:1).

At this point it may be well to consider the question, who raised the body of Christ from the dead? Ephesians 1:19, 20 clearly states that it was God the Father: "According to the working of his mighty power, which he wrought in Christ, when he raised him [*egeiras*, in the active transitive] from the dead, and set him at his own right hand in the heavenly places." Also in Galatians 1:1, "Paul, an apostle, (not of men, neither by man, but by Jesus Christ, and God the Father, who raised him [*egeirantos*, again in the active transitive] from the dead)."

But Scripture also tells us that the Lord Jesus raised Himself from the dead. "Destroy this temple," He said, referring to His body, "and in three days I will raise it up" (John 2:19). Again the verb is future active transitive, *egeroo*, but this time He personally is the subject and His body (the temple) is the object. The Lord spoke of Himself as a personality apart from His earthly body, which leads us to understand that it is not our body that is the real "us," but our spiritual nature.

Again we have confirmation of Christ's having raised Himself in John 2:22, which says, "When therefore He was risen from the dead." The verb here is *eegerthee*, which is in the passive voice as to form but can be understood as intransitive in idea. "When therefore he had raised himself from the dead . . . ." (See Addenda on page 269.)

In view of the context of our Lord's statement that He was going to rebuild the destroyed temple of His body, we would be justified, then, in concluding that the verb *eegerthee*, although passive in form, is used in a middle sense. The Lord raised Himself by His own power as God, co-eternal and co-equal with the Father. His earthly body was not eternal but was subject to death just as your body and mine. But the Lord Jesus Christ was a completely self-existent personality apart from His earthly body, and that eternal personality could do whatever He wanted to do with that body. Whatever God the Father could do, God the Son could also do. Of course, they did not always choose to do the same things, but this was a matter not of incapability but of choice, the choice of omnipotence.

Father and Son are two separate personalities, but both are the same God, eternal and omnipotent. The personality of the Holy Spirit as God is spoken of elsewhere in Scripture (John 14:26; 16:13, 14, Acts 5:3, Eph. 4:30). As the resurrection of the body of Christ and other acts of creation and providence are ascribed to God the Father, so are they ascribed to God the Son. But these are also ascribed to God the Holy Spirit (many times designated as the Spirit of God, even as Christ is designated as the Son of God. See Gen. 1:2, Job 26:13).

Do we need more proof as to the authority asserted by the Lord Jesus concerning the resurrection than His statement in John 10:17, 18? "Therefore doth my Father love me, because I lay down my life, that I might take it again. No man taketh it from me, but I lay it down of myself. I have power to lay it down, and I have power to take it again." Has there ever been another person who could make such a claim and fulfill it? Never. The Lord Jesus Christ is unique. The eternal Son of God could lay down the earthly life of the Son of Man and take it up again, in even more glorious form, at will.

WHAT IT MEANS TO SLEEP IN JESUS

"But now is Christ risen from the dead, and become the firstfruits of them that slept" (I Cor. 15:20).

Sleep is usually regarded as a pleasant state. You lay aside the burdens of the day and give yourself up to the refreshing ministries of those mysterious forces that erase your tensions and restore your energies. It is the awakening that is often so rude.

When you first open your eyes, your mind has been washed blank by sleep. Then the memory of yesterday's troubles and today's problems suddenly stabs you into awareness that another day has dawned, and you must summon up your resolve to meet it with whatever wisdom and fortitude you can. Not all days start like that, of course, but enough of them do to make getting up a reluctant effort of the will.

The Bible tells us that, for the Christian, natural death is only to be regarded as a sleep—a little deeper, it is true, a bit more protracted, but still a sleep. There is no more extinction of our being in one state than in the other. In fact, so far as there is any difference between death and sleep, it is all in favor of death; for our spirits are consciously present with the Lord, and in that state no one can disturb our repose; and when it is over we rise not to the old toil and weariness and tears, but to eternal joy, because soul and body are united in the presence of Christ.

We know sleep better than death, of course, and so we yield ourselves to it as a child to a kind mother in whose arms we lose our sorrows and find peace. If we knew death as well, we would "dread our graves as little as our beds." For those who know Jesus Christ, death in Him is just as little to be feared as closing our eyes in natural slumber.

Jesus did not minimize the sorrow that death brings, nor the fact that it is an object of dread. "The last enemy that shall be destroyed is death," Scripture tells us (I Cor. 15:26). Of course, the reason that we are not to dread it is that Christ has gone through it and come forth in newness of life as "the firstfruits of them that slept."

Notice that adjective "first." This presupposes that there were none prior to this who fell asleep in death and rose to newness of life in the same sense that Christ did. There were raisings from the dead, of course. Christ brought individuals back to life and so did the apostles. We have Old Testament examples of this also. But these individuals were raised only to die again in the natural course of events, when their time came. None was raised on these occasions to live eternally, as Christ did, in body and in spirit.

The adjective "first" also presupposes more to follow. It is interesting to note where this expression "firstfruits" originated. It refers to the old Jewish ceremonies of gathering the harvest and bringing a portion of the very first grain that ripened and formally presenting it to the Lord, waving it before the altar in acknowledgment of His goodness. It was a beautiful regulation. It sanctified their bread before it was harvested.

And so Christ, as the "firstfruits" of those who

slept, consecrated every believer in Him who fell asleep in death. As He was raised, so shall His people be. The fallen bodies of all departed believers are like seeds sown in the ground, from which there will be a future harvest, of which the risen Christ was the first sheaf gathered from a common field.

Perhaps it would be well to note here that though it is not explicitly stated in this verse that it is the dead in Christ who are referred to, we may know that this is so because of verse 18. The resurrection of Christ is the firstfruits, not of the resurrection of all who have died, but of those who have died in Him, as believers.

Now if the firstfruits of a field of grain are wheat, the rest of the harvest will be wheat also. As the firstfruits are, so is the balance of the crop. And as Christ is the firstfruits of them that slept, our waking to newness of life will follow the pattern of His. What His resurrection was, our resurrection is to be. This allows us to know some things about the future state that are of great comfort to us.

First, we know that our bodies will be resurrected. Now, before some literalist asks how a decomposed, or incinerated, or exploded, or devoured body can be reconstituted at the resurrection, let us note what Scripture has to say about this resurrection of the body.

The Apostle Paul says the dead body is like a seed planted in the earth, in that it does not rise in the identical form in which it was planted. Although the seed we plant may be the same identical thing that springs up into a stalk with blossoms and then fruit, there is a wonderful change that is wrought in the process. Much of the seed decays, remains in the earth, and goes back to dust. But the chain of identity that connects the seed with the fruit is never lost.

Remember, if the resurrection of Christ was not a resurrection of the body, it was no resurrection at all, for He was not dead except in body when He lay in the tomb. That is what died, and that alone could be resurrected. The soul sleeps without reverting to unconsciousness or non-existence, and can only be resurrected with the body. This sleep is merely a blessed conscious rest in Christ's presence. There is no ultimate eternal existence for human souls separate and apart from bodies.

We must hold fast, then, to the restoration of the whole man—body, soul, and spirit—in the resurrection of believers, as the distinguishing mark of the Christian faith regarding life after death. "Though after my skin worms destroy this body, yet in *my flesh* shall I see God" (Job 19:26).

And if our resurrection is to be like Christ's, we may rejoice that we shall know our loved ones in the resurrection to come for all believers. Christ knew His friends and loved ones, and was known of them, after His resurrection. What more convincing argument do we need that we, too, shall have a loving and glorious reunion with loved ones who have gone before, or whom we have preceded to heaven?

Much of these earthly natures and constitutions and affections of course must be stripped off in death and left in the grave. But just as surely as we shall carry the identity of our present beings over into the glories of the resurrection, so surely shall knowledge of each other and fellowship of soul go with us, not diminished but amplified in proportion as that life is higher than this present one.

And that glory and blessedness shall be for ever. "Christ being raised from the dead dieth no more; death hath no more dominion over him" (Rom. 6:9). And as the firstfruits of those who fall asleep in Him, He confers a like eternal victory over death upon those who die in the Lord.

(See Joseph A. Seiss, *Lectures on the Epistles*, Vol. I, pp. 459-71.)

IS DEATH OR LIFE THE FINAL WORD?

"But now is Christ risen from the dead, and become the firstfruits of them that slept" (I Cor. 15:20).

Death will very likely touch each one of our lives many times before that final touch when we experience it for ourselves. Yet though we have seen death in the lives of others, and will ultimately experience it personally, we do not understand it fully, just as we experience life without being able to define it precisely.

As Christians, we are prone to make too much of death and its importance in the scheme of things, taking an altogether pagan and un-Biblical view of it, when we fail to rejoice in what happens after death. To dread death as the end of all our hopes and plans is to give the lie to our professed faith in a better life to come, as revealed in God's Word.

How much more God-honoring was the understanding that Victor Hugo had of death when he wrote: "When I go down to the grave I can say, like so many others: I have finished my work, but I cannot say I have finished my life. My day's work will begin the next morning. My tomb is not a blind alley. It is a thoroughfare. It closes in the twilight to open in the dawn."

To many, death is a fearful thought. Yet the death of a Christian can be a beautiful thing. A mother asked a young boy who lay dying, "Is Jesus with you in the dark valley?" "Dark valley?" he whispered. "Why, Mother, it's not dark! It's getting brighter and brighter. Oh, it's so bright now that I have to shut my eyes!"

Physical death is often regarded as the greatest crisis through which a human soul must pass. In looking through my library card index, I was amazed to note how many listings there were under "death," as compared with the much smaller number under "life."

Yet physical death is not given such an important place in our Bibles, or in the economy of redemption. The Bible assigns a subordinate place to our king of terrors. True, the Book of Genesis invests natural death with certain primitive fears, but it does not elevate death to the rank of the supreme and final transaction between man and his Maker. Adam was not commanded by the Lord to live every day as though it were his last, a slave to the fear of death. He was commanded to go and work in the sweat of his brow, but with the promised redemption of God in his heart.

Man is to work out his time here, and to pass through death, as a being not necessarily subject to death, but born under the higher law of the spirit, and with the possibility of eternal life always before him.

And in the New Testament, Jesus Christ reduces death to a metaphor. He calls it a "sleep." (Mark 5:39 and John 11:11). To Him, sin is the ultimate death. If we study the New Testament carefully, we shall find that physical life and death hold a secondary place. The importance of natural death falls into the background, and the new birth by the Spirit comes into the foreground. Physical death does not cease to be regarded as an event appointed by God to all alike;

but it does cease to be a thing of terror, the final word, an utter break in the continuity of man's being.

Physical death is a relative matter, an external event. The Christian doctrine of the resurrection is a stumbling-block to the faith of many because we have allowed ourselves to exalt and to exaggerate death to a degree altogether beyond Scripture and reason. We mourn as though death were the ultimate fact of our experience, and then we have to smuggle in our hope of the resurrection as a miraculous exception to this universal power of death.

But exactly the opposite is true. Life is the law of nature, and death is a natural means to more life and better. Death is the lower fact and life the higher. Or more specifically, the resurrection of Jesus Christ was not the great exception to natural law; it was an exemplification of the higher, universal law of life. To God, the resurrection of His Son was no miracle at all. It was altogether natural.

As I was musing upon this stupendous thought, I went to church and heard that well-known Gospel song that contains the line, "It took a miracle to set the stars in space." Turning to my wife I said, "Did it?" Not for God. For omnipotence there are no miracles; what seems to us a miracle is part and parcel of the natural accomplishment of Him who operates through the law of omnipotence.

When you stop to apply this principle to the resurrection of the Lord Jesus Christ, you will see that that, too, was not really a miracle from the Divine standpoint. His resurrection was the natural outcome of the higher, universal law of life, His law. Death leads to life, not life to death, in the ultimate constitution of this universe which belongs to God. The resurrection of Jesus Christ is the great particular instance of God's general law that life is lord of death.

Twice in First Corinthians 15, the Lord is called "the firstfruits." In verse 20 it is "the firstfruits of them that slept," and in verse 23, "Christ the first-fruits." The Greek word is *aparchee*, meaning the first produced by the earth, or by man, or by God. Christ is called the *aparchee* as the first one recalled to life of them that have fallen asleep. The first fruit of a tree is a guarantee of more to come. Thus, as the first of its kind, Christ's resurrection guarantees the future resurrection of all Christians. The first fruits are a pledge and a promise of the harvest.

The resurrection of the Lord Jesus, in the eyes of the Apostle Paul, was no more out of the divine order of things, no more contrary to the ultimate law of nature, than the first fruits of the summer are exceptions to the general law of life which in the fall will show its universal power in every harvest field.

In saying that the resurrection of Jesus Christ—regarded as the greatest miracle of history—was an instance or exemplification of a general law of life, we are not attempting to deny that it was a miracle as commonly understood. Not at all. But we are saying that the miraculous must be included under God's general law, in its own proper place in His conduct of the world, where we can see some reason in it and for it.

The miraculous nature of Jesus' resurrection was

not that God raised Him from the dead. This is an easy thing for an omnipotent God to do, and it is something that He will do for all of us. No, the miracle lay in the fact that Jesus was raised before the last great day, and that He should be seen by men, and recognized in His transitional or intermediate state between earth and heaven. The visibility on earth of the risen Christ, before He ascended to His Father and ours, was exceptional, out of the common course, or miraculous.

In the natural course of events, at His death, Jesus would have gone to be with His Father. That is what happens to each of us. He made a point of this in His first utterance to Mary Magdalene after His resurrection, when He told her, "I am not yet ascended to my Father" (John 20:17). He made an exception in His case for a good and sufficient reason: that we might believe. Also, in His case, having been made perfect through suffering, He did not have to wait with all the saints for the day of the final redemption of the body, but after a short sojourn on earth He ascended to the throne of God until that day when His enemies should be made His footstool.

The miraculous elements in Jesus' resurrection, then, were those pertaining to the manner and time of it, rather than to the essential fact of it. He was the firstfruits of the resurrection, an exceptional fruit appearing before the harvest, which is the end of the world.

THE RESURRECTION — MIRACLE OR NATURAL EVENT?

"But now is Christ risen from the dead, and become the firstfruits of them that slept" (I Cor. 15:20).

If you were to see a tree break into blossom in the month of June, and the next morning find the fruit already ripe upon the bough, you would hardly dare to believe your eyes. What would astonish you is not that fruit should ripen upon the bough, but that it should ripen in a single day.

That fruit would be a miracle upon that tree. Yet it would not in itself be contrary to the nature of the tree, but only to its ordinary conditions of fruitbearing. The fruit itself would be perfectly natural; only the method of its growth would be extraordinary. And it would not be impossible to conceive a quickening or enhancement of nature's forces that might cause a plant to break into fruitfulness contrary to our experience of its usual times and seasons.

In somewhat the same way we may think of Jesus' resurrection as a firstfruit of the tree of life—not in itself contrary to the law of life, but in its manner and time out of the common order. In the miracle of His resurrection we have only to think of God's quickening or anticipating by His power the course of His law, not as violating any real principle of it.

Why do we believe the miraculous element to have been, not the fact of Jesus' resurrection, but the exceptional time and manner of it with regard to God's general law of resurrection?

First let us examine Jesus' own teaching about the resurrection of the body. He answered the Sadducees of His generation, not merely by asserting His knowledge that the dead shall be raised; but He placed the fact of the resurrection upon the fundamental principle that life, not death, is God's first law. "Now that the dead are raised, even Moses shewed at the bush, when he calleth the Lord the God of Abraham, and the God of Isaac, and the God of Jacob. For he is not a God of the dead, but of the living: for all live unto him" (Luke 20:37, 38).

The fact that the dead are raised, therefore, is no isolated, strange event, no exception to the general nature of things; for life is the rule, and death the apparent exception in the universe of the living God. All men are made to live unto Him; all souls are made capable of existing in some vital relationship to the God of the living. This, according to Jesus' word, is the highest law of human nature, that it should live unto God. If there is to be eternal death, that death must enter as the exception, as the loss of a possible good, as the falling back of a soul from the kind of life for which it was created.

Indeed, it would have been impossible for the Lord not to rise from the dead. Although we call Jesus' resurrection a miracle, that is, contrary to what might have been expected, a great exception to the law of death, that is not the way Scripture puts it. Consider what Peter said in his sermon on the day of Pentecost concerning this. Speaking of Christ he said, "Whom God hath raised up, having loosed the pains of death: because it was not possible that he should be holden

of it" Acts 2:24). And then he goes on to say, "Moreover also my flesh shall rest in hope: because thou wilt
not leave my soul in hell, neither wilt thou suffer thine
Holy One to see corruption" (vv. 26, 27).

It would have been impossible for death to hold
the principle of life, the Lord Jesus. It would be a
violation of all law should the Holy One be given over
to corruption. There is something inherently inconceivable and impossible in such a thought. How can
Holiness see corruption? How can Life itself be given
over to death? Impossible! The real miracle would
have been if Jesus Christ had not risen from the dead.
It would have been a violation of the inmost principle
of the creation had the mere dust of this earth held
Him as its own forever. It would have been a miracle
without reason, a miracle not against the ordinary
course of nature merely, but a miracle against God,
the living God, had He not risen from the dead—the
firstfruits of this power and order of divine life in the
creation.

Consider this 15th chapter of First Corinthians as
a whole. What is Paul trying to prove? First he at-
tests the fact that Jesus was seen after His resurrection. Then Jesus' resurrection is declared to be the
firstfruits of the whole harvest of life which is to follow. And then that great Apostle proceeds to prove
that this process of the resurrection is in the largest
and profoundest sense natural. It is a spiritual out-
growth from this body of death. The nature of the
resurrection is in accordance with law. If there is a
natural body, there is also a spiritual body. The latter
is just as much in the divine order of things as is the

former. The creation is made and constituted for the higher spiritual body as much as for the lower natural body.

The method of the resurrection is also in accordance with law: first the God-given seed, then its quickening in the earth, then its springing up out of its earthbound state into its own element, and its being clothed upon with its own proper form and texture, as God gives "to every seed his own body" (v. 38). The whole process of the resurrection in its successive movements and stages, as we shall later study it in detail, is regarded by Paul as in accordance with law. "Howbeit that was not first which is spiritual, but that which is natural; and afterward that which is spiritual. The first man is of the earth, earthy: the second man is the Lord from heaven" (vv. 46, 47).

As the Apostle wrote this chapter, he was not as one standing dazed before a miracle. He saw no Almighty Power snapping like chains the laws of nature in order that man might be delivered from the bands of death. He did not see nature resistlessly dragging man down to death and destruction, and then, by a sheer act of God's power, the whole downward trend suspended, and the law of death in nature broken, as a life suddenly came forth on the other side of the grave, and ascended and gained the everlasting heights.

No, Paul had caught a glimpse into the first principles of life which go deeper than death. He had looked up and there had been revealed to him something of the larger spiritual environment of earthly things. He had seen what we call nature in its true setting in God's eternal purpose and order. He had followed out into the spiritual realm the ways of God through these natural forces and understood the unseen continuity of the earthly and the spiritual.

Paul had learned, in one word, that the resurrection which he preached is the promised fulfillment of the laws of life which have been in God from before the foundation of the world. That is why he evidenced no surprise, no thought of broken uniformities of nature or miracle of power, in this whole chapter of the resurrection. It is as calm as a chapter of science. It is a lesson from the science of the higher order of the creation.

The stars in the sky are no more miracles than the risen Lord. The sun and the moon are no more exceptions to the ancient order of the heavens than the souls of men raised from the dead are to the divine order and harmony, in the eyes of the Apostle who has seen the risen Lord.

This, then, is clearly and unmistakably the Biblical teaching of the resurrection. It is in accordance with law. It is in the divine order of the creation.

WHAT IS DEATH?

"But now is Christ risen from the dead, and become the firstfruits of them that slept" (I Cor. 15:20).

Why should anyone doubt that God can raise the dead? Is it not partly because of our all too pagan exaggeration of the place and importance of death in the world, and also because we have imagined the resurrection of Jesus Christ to be a violation of natural law?

When we stand upon a law of nature, we feel we are on solid ground. To ask a man to forsake the laws of nature for faith is to ask him to be false to his God-given powers of reason. However, a thoughtful man will concede that we cannot begin to understand or interpret this bit of the universe which we see and call nature, unless we regard it as existing in the midst of a much larger context, and at a thousand points running out into, and continuous with, something not seen as yet just beyond itself. As I cannot think of a star except as being in the sky, so I cannot think of this visible world, or nature, except as existing in some larger context and Presence. The living God is that Presence. And in confirmation of a Scriptural faith in the divine orderliness of the resurrection and eternal life, we must consider the following:

First, death is not the only law of nature; there is also the law of life. Second, of these two laws, life, not death, is the higher and prevailing power, so far as we can see. Even in this sinful world, where death reigns, life has been growing higher, more complex, more capable of larger correspondence with its environment. Plainly, life is something stronger thus far upon this earth than death.

But this is not all. What is death, so far as we can see? Here is a tiny minnow in a bowl of water. You spill the water upon the ground, and that living creature gasps its last. It is no longer moving in an element corresponding to its capacity for vital movements.

What is death then? A living thing is no longer in harmony with its surroundings. It is thrown out of its own proper correspondence with things. Death, then, is a relative thing. It is simply some wrong or imperfect adjustment of life to external conditions. Death may be partial, as when a part of the body is dead. The body, in fact, begins to die long before it is dead. Death is but a relative, negative thing. Life is the principle, the force, the law; death the limitation, the accident, the partial negation of God's great affirmation of life in things.

Now see where this thought leads. It points to two conclusions: Death is the sundering of certain relations of life toward outward things; therefore, when the body finally is wholly dead and buried, when all these physical relations of life are broken off, that much of life is certainly gone. But nothing else in a man is dead. You must prove that there is nothing more to a man than what reacts to oxygen and hydrogen and such things, before you have any scientific right to speak of him as dead.

"You may catch me, if you can find me," said Socrates, as he was about to leave his body. And the

Scripture says, "God is not the God of the dead, but of the living" (Matt. 22:32).

Here is a man walking in a field, thinking of home, perhaps, or musing on the nature of truth. Suddenly a flash of lightning strikes his body down. How much of him is dead? His lungs and his heart have certainly ceased to operate. His body can no longer respond to any vital stimulus in his environment. But did that flash of lightning pierce to the thought of home in his heart? Or did it put out that thinking personal self-conscious entity just then meditating on the nature of truth? The lightning touched the mortal body; who knows that it reached to the spiritual body? Perhaps that is more subtle than electricity.

We know that death is often only in part. Why then should not that force which thinks, that power which loves, in shaking off its imperfect correspondence of this body with things, continue to exist hereafter, clothed upon with still higher and finer powers of contact and correspondence with all nature, and with the living God?

This view of death as having only partial and negative power leads to a further rational possibility of life, which may be stated thus: We have only to suppose a living soul in perfect adjustment to God, and all God's laws of things, to conceive of a being possessing eternal life. "This is life eternal, that they might know thee the only true God, and Jesus Christ, whom thou hast sent" (John 17:3). Eternal life is harmony of being with the true God, and the risen Lord, because of a saving knowledge of both. In such perfect adjustment of being to God and His laws, the finite spirit would exist in its permanent because perfect form, its final spiritual embodiment. Eternal life would be the perfect harmony of the inward and outward conditions—the final union of the spirit of the just made perfect with God and His universe.

Now what is the practical application of all this to your life and mine? So far we have seen that, according to the Scriptures, the resurrection and eternal life are no strange miracle, but the fulfillment of nature in conformity with God's law. And we have seen that the analogies we have drawn of life in nature, combined with all that we really know of death, do not contradict but rather confirm this teaching of the Scriptures, that in the resurrection our life shall be made complete, and the goal of the creation be fully reached. So God's idea of man from before the foundation of the world shall be realized in the kingdom of the risen and ascended Christ.

From this it follows that our true life consists in being in the closest relationship with that which is the real and eternal element of life—with God and His righteousness. We are made to live in perfect harmony with all good, beautiful, and true things, in communion with God. The only thing to be feared is spiritual death. That is non-adjustment of our hearts to God. The wages of sin is death—death piercing further than that flash of lightning could reach; death destroying the heart, intellect, and soul of a man out of harmony with God. It is the soul itself which we stand to gain or to lose. "He that hath the Son hath life; and he that hath not the Son of God hath not life" (I John 5:12). The soul of the man who shuts out God from himself is as dead as that little minnow out of its life-sustaining element, lying shrunken and shriveled upon the bare ground.

A soul can shrink in selfishness, and shrivel in lust, and consume itself in sin, until it becomes at last so dead that it is beyond hope, and will be punished as any person deserves to be who would turn from the full, gracious revelation of God in Christ, "with everlasting destruction from the presence of the Lord, and from the glory of his power; when he shall come to be glorified in his saints, and to be admired in all them that believe" (II Thess. 1:9, 10).

But by the same token, a soul responding to God's grace can expand in self-forgetfulness and love to God and his neighbor, as he is born anew of God's Spirit. "I am come," said Christ, "that they might have life, and that they might have it more abundantly" (John 10:10). And again, "He that heareth my word, and believeth on him that sent me, hath everlasting life, and shall not come into condemnation; but is passed from death unto life" (John 5:24).

In conclusion, then, we see that physical death is but an incident on the pathway of a Christian, leading to fuller and richer life. As Christians, then, let us act as though we believed it. Let us take to heart Paul's advice to the Christians of his day: "I would not have you to be ignorant, brethren, concerning them which are asleep, that ye sorrow not, even as others which have no hope. For if we believe that Jesus died and rose again, even so them also which sleep in Jesus will God bring with him. . . . Wherefore comfort one another with these words" (I Thess. 4:13, 14, 18).

(See *Newman Smyth's Works, The Reality of Faith*, pp. 142-152.)

ADDENDA

Page 247. According to A. T. Robertson, *A Grammar of the Greek New Testament* (pp. 333-4, 814, 816-17), the aorist passive form (such as *eegerthee*) frequently loses its passive meaning for a middle or active force. Robertson says that it is difficult at times to determine whether an aorist passive form really has a passive meaning or a middle meaning. Observe for instance Matthew 27:63, "After three days I will rise again [*egeiromai*, present passive or middle indicative]." This is correctly translated as "I will rise (again)," or "I will raise myself," as being in the middle voice, that is, that Christ told Pilate that He would raise His own body.

It is probable, then, that *eegerthee* sometimes (as in Mark 16:6) is also merely active intransitive (*eegerthee*, "He is risen" of His own power and will), not passive, in idea. The fact that the aorist passive *eegertheen* has at times as a variant reading some non-passive form of *anisteemi*, "rise, stand up, get up," in the aorist tense, or even in the future tense, is a strong indication that *eegertheen* may not be passive in meaning. (See John 2:22, Matt. 16:21; 17:23, Mark 6:14, Luke 9:7.)

IS DEATH A NATURAL PHENOMENON?

"For since by man came death, by man came also the resurrection of the dead" (I Cor. 15:21).

Is death a natural phenomenon? You may think that an unnecessary question, since it is obvious that all living things eventually die. Yet the Bible plainly teaches that death is a disruption of the natural; that man was created for life, not death. Man himself senses this in his instinctive recoil from all dead things. Death is repugnant to his nature.

How, then, did death originate? The Apostle Paul tells us that man brought it upon himself by sin. "By one man's disobedience many were made sinners" (Rom. 5:19). The first man sinned and death came upon all men. And again, in First Corinthians 15:21, Paul says, "By man came death." He is referring to physical death here, of course, since throughout the context he has been speaking of physical resurrection; although it is also true that by man came spiritual death.

Just what is death? We all recognize it, but we really do not know exactly what it is. We may say that it is the cessation of life, but then, what is life? Again we are at a loss for words. We all possess it, and yet it is a mystery.

Death is no less of a mystery in that it is a state of separation of body and soul, which we can't explain, a dissolution of their vital union which results in the beginning in the body of those processes of disintegration by which it returns to dust. It is the act that fixes all other actions of life and gives them their final meaning; and it is the occasion on which the state of the soul is determined for all eternity.

No wonder the natural man regards death with horror and dread. It seems the end of everything to him, the negation of life, the destruction of the flesh that he has so carefully cherished and tended.

The Christian, too, regards the wasting away of the body and its powers with regret, and turns from the grave with sorrow that a loved form is no more. Nevertheless God overrules death for good, because He has a beneficent purpose, as we see in Romans 8:20 and 21: "For the creature was made subject to vanity [Greek, *mataioteeti*, frustration, futility, transitoriness], not willingly, but by reason of him who hath subjected the same in hope, because the creature itself also shall be delivered from the bondage of corruption into the glorious liberty of the children of God."

Though God, because of man's sin, made him "subject to vanity" (frustration, futility, or transitoriness), which results in death, He sent His Son to die on the cross, that by His death "he might destroy him that had the power of death, that is, the devil; and deliver them who through fear of death were all their lifetime subject to bondage" (Heb. 2:14, 15).

Death might indeed seem to be a victory for Satan, were it not for the glorious paradox that in dying the Christian escapes him altogether and is freed from the members of sin of which Paul wrote so feelingly. "I see another law in my members," he said, "warring against the law of my mind, and bringing me into captivity to the law of sin which is in my members. O wretched man that I am!" If he had stopped there, we might well conclude that man was made "subject to vanity," but without the "hope" of which the Scripture speaks. However Paul continues, "Who shall deliver me from the body of this death? I thank God through Jesus Christ our Lord" (Rom. 7:23-25).

Death, then, is unnatural, in that it is a disruption of the original order of creation. It is the result of sin, and it is used against man by Satan, who brought sin into the world. But God causes even this evil to work for good to His children, for, at the very moment when death has the apparent victory over them, our Lord delivers them into eternal fellowship with Himself in that realm from which all sin, sorrow, weeping, and death are abolished forever, and from which Satan and His followers are eternally excluded. Truly, "Death is swallowed up in victory" (I Cor. 15:54). For the believer in Christ it is not the end but a new beginning.

But all that is future for us, though it helps to lift the pall of gloom from the painful realities of the present. In the light of all this, how should we who believe God's Word regard the death of those we love? We might compare it to the feeling that prevails when a member of the family goes abroad to enrich his mind by further study, or to engage in a new and promising career. His friends and relatives may be saddened at the thought of the long parting that lies ahead, and some may even shed tears, but they rejoice nevertheless in the new life that is opening up for him, with all its wonderful possibilities.

In similar fashion, the Christian believer regards death as a time of parting, the pangs of which may be long-lasting and hard to bear. But underlying his deep sorrow at being deprived of the companionship of one he loves is the consolation of knowing that those who "fall asleep" in Christ are happier than they have ever been, and that he will see them again some day.

And when it comes to your own death, if you are truly a believer in Christ, though you may be sorry at leaving your loved ones for awhile, you rejoice at the thought of seeing your Lord face to face and entering into a vastly expanded life of undreamed of dimensions with Him, in companionship with other believers.

Although we do not know exactly what death is, nor how and when it will occur in our particular case, we do know for certain that it will overtake each one of us, with the exception of those who are alive when Christ comes again. Look at the people you meet on the street. Gaze into each face and try to guess what the morrow holds for each individual. You cannot do it. All you know for certain is that each one must eventually die. Rich and poor, young and old, believer or atheist; one thing we know about the future. It holds death at the end of the road, as far as this earthly life is concerned.

We know, too, that once death has occurred, that's it as far as we are concerned. Any future plans we may have had for amending our conduct, or getting right with God and our neighbor, will be unrealized. What we are at the moment of death is the final word.

Although death is the last and most important journey we shall take, it is one to which most of us give the least preparation. We have at most seventy or so years of life on this earth, followed by unending eons thereafter; yet we live as though the seventy outweighed eternity in importance.

Do you think you will have time to be sorry for your neglect of God, and make your peace with Him at the very end of your life? Do you think God will accept the sinner who thinks to make a bargain with Him that says in effect, "I will live as I please, and then ask You to forgive me and let me into heaven at the last moment"?

Although the thief on the cross was pardoned and received into paradise at the last moment, this was not a premeditated act on his part, but a sudden opening of his eyes to the truth regarding Jesus Christ, even in the hour of death.

How do you know you will ever have another chance than this present moment to repent? Death can be sudden, you know. How do you know you will be in full possession of your faculties? The mind often ceases to function rationally, long before the body succumbs to illness, old age, and death.

I would be worse than a coward, I would be a murderer, if I did not warn the sleeping occupants of a burning building of their peril. That is why I am warning you, on the authority of God's Word, of the terrible consequences of unrepented sin in this life and the life to come. For there will be a life to come for each of us. "Marvel not at this," Jesus Christ says, "the hour is coming, in the which all that are in the graves shall hear his voice, and shall come forth; they that have done good, unto the resurrection of life; and they that have done evil, unto the resurrection of damnation" (John 5:28, 29).

HOW TO DIE

"For since by man came death, by man came also the resurrection of the dead" (I Cor. 15:21).

Thousands of books, by various authors, are on the market today telling people how to live. But search the current crop of books as you may, you are not likely to find one that will tell you how to die.

"Who needs it?" you ask. "Death is something that's going to happen to me anyway. I have no say in the matter."

In one sense, that is true. Whether you die of an accident, an illness, or old age, you have little choice. But in the most important area of all, you do have a choice, and you can make it right now. You cannot choose how your body will meet death, but you can choose how your soul or spirit, the real you, will meet it.

In the first place, because of the unforeseeability of the time of death, you should make preparation for it now. A soldier who knows he will be called upon at a moment's notice to go to the front keeps his gear in a state of constant readiness.

"Face reality, don't repress it," is the advice of most psychiatrists. Yet few of them bring their patients face to face with the thought of death. Far better to avoid such a depressing subject. It takes a truly courageous man to face the thought of death without flinching. In a moment of discouragement, a man may exclaim, "I wish I were dead," but let death confront him and he will hurriedly change his mind.

Such an attitude toward death is all wrong. A man

who believes in living well should make every sensible preparation for dying well. We go so far as to accumulate an estate to leave to our dependents. We take out life insurance and make a will. We may even give instructions about our funeral. But these are all outward preparations. What about the inward preparation of the spirit? Can you face death with a rationally based confidence that you will meet it in the right spirit, without fear of what comes afterward?

Here many people will shrug their shoulders and say, "I'll take my chances with the next one. After all, I'm not so bad. I never killed anyone or stole from anyone. I've always tried to live a decent life. We're none of us perfect; but if there is a hereafter, I don't think God will be too hard on me."

Otherwise sensible people talk this way. They would not think of taking up residence in a foreign country without inquiring about the rules of entry and citizenship requirements. They would also make every effort to learn all they could about the country beforehand, even to becoming as proficient as possible in its language. And yet they speak of getting into heaven as though they themselves had set the conditions of entry and were confident that they would be accepted on their own terms.

They have only the vaguest notion of what heaven is like; and they certainly have no notion of the "language" that is spoken there, having never troubled to associate very much here on earth with those who speak it. By language, of course, we do not mean a foreign tongue, but the kind of concord that exists between people who have the same interests and beliefs, and thus "speak the same language." Are your present interests at all in line with "the kingdom of heaven"?

You may speculate as much as you like about who will get to heaven. No one has the answer but God Himself. Now what kind of God would He be who would leave people in the dark on this most important matter? Not a God of love, such as you presume Him to be when you express confidence that He will save you because you've never done anything very bad, and may have done much good.

You are right in believing Him to be a God of love, who is not willing that anyone should perish. He has made it very plain, in word and deed, that He wants you to live with Him as His child throughout eternity. And in order that you may not miss the way, He has given you explicit instructions. They are in the Bible. Anything else is hearsay, man's way of thinking. But an intelligent emigrant lets the ruler of a country tell him the rules of entry and does not try to formulate them to his own satisfaction. Are you intelligent enough to realize that you cannot get to heaven on your own terms, but must seek to discover and comply with God's terms?

Death can be the gateway to life more abundant, or it can be the gateway to eternal separation from God and from all who love Him—an eternity of conscious joy and fulfillment, or an eternity of conscious torment.

Doesn't it make sense to you that you should start to make adequate preparation for life after death now? Though the lowest motive of all for doing this may be fear, do not sneer at it. God may use the fear of eternal punishment to drive you to Himself, so that once you have met Him you will be won by His love. He may instill fear of the consequences of sin in your heart for the same reason that a father threatens a child with punishment to keep him from doing something that would ruin his life. "If you don't stop running with that gang, you'll end up in prison," he warns him. The father may look very stern and forbidding as he says this. But who can doubt that he says it out of love for the son? Let the son reply, "You're right, Dad, and I'll steer clear of that gang from now on," and suddenly the father and son are on entirely different terms.

So it is when fear of death drives you to repentance. God's face then breaks into a smile, and your heart warms to Him in turn. It was fear of death by starvation that brought the prodigal son to his senses and made him realize what a fool he had been. We may presume that he approached his father in some fear and trepidation also; but the father's enthusiastic demonstration of love and forgiveness dispelled that fear forever.

Paul once wrote to the Corinthian Church rebuking them for allowing one of their number to engage in immorality and still have fellowship with them as though he were a member in good standing. His words had the desired effect. They repented, and Paul once more spoke approvingly of them. "Now I rejoice, not that ye were made sorry," he told them, "but that ye sorrowed to repentance. . . . For godly sorrow worketh repentance to salvation that brings no regret, but the sorrow of the world brings death" (II Cor. 7:9, 10).

And again Paul says in Romans 2:4 that "the goodness of God leadeth thee to repentance." And this final word from Peter: "The Lord . . . is longsuffering toward us, not willing that any should perish, but that all should come to repentance" (II Pet. 3:9).

But after godly fear has inspired repentance, we are like those of whom Luke speaks when he says that God "would grant unto us, that we being delivered out of the hand of our enemies might serve him without fear" (Luke 1:74). That man who regards death as an enemy, and runs to God in repentance that he may be delivered from the consequences of sin in the life to come, will find to his amazement that, as he continues in a state of sincere penitence before God, as he reads His Word, learns to pray, and enters into Christian fellowship in the life of the Church, his fear will be replaced by love. "Perfect love casteth out fear" (I John 4:18).

So though fear may be the whip that drives us to God, love takes over and drives out fear. God is not too proud to take in a sinner who comes to him motivated by fear; it is always man who is too proud to accept God's pardon without deserving it.

"By man came death," for it was man's sin that brought death into the world in the first place. But "by man came also the resurrection of the dead," and that man was the God-man, Jesus Christ, God incarnate. Who can doubt the love of a God who cared so much for us that He came to earth to die for our sins, that we, believing in Him, might not perish eternally but have everlasting life?

WHAT HAPPENS IMMEDIATELY AFTER DEATH?

"For since by man came death, by man came also the resurrection of the dead" (I Cor. 15:21).

In all the discussions about whether it is right or advisable to tell a person who has an incurable illness that he is going to die, no one seems to have given much thought to anything but the temporary aspects of the situation. People seem concerned to make the dying person comfortable and keep him untroubled in mind for the little time he has left, but no one seems concerned about what the effect of such treatment will be on the person's eternal welfare.

What if he is not a believer in Christ? What if he has not in faith repented of his sins and cast himself upon the mercy of God for forgiveness? May not the knowledge that death is near be God's salutary means of awakening him to his lost estate and leading him to seek His mercy before it is too late? Since the man is going to die anyway, who are you to decide that he shall not know it and make his peace with God if he so desires? Who are you to allow a soul to slip into eternity all unawares and perhaps all unprepared? Let the qualified man of God break the news to him as gently as possible, and hold out before him the glorious hope of eternal happiness with God. Let him deal tenderly but firmly with his sins, and seek to lead him to repentance and faith in Christ.

Of course, this takes courage and love of a high order. Your motives must be of the purest: not the selfish ones of absolving yourself of guilt and responsibility, but of faithful obedience to God and concern for the eternal welfare of the dying man or woman.

And you yourself, if you are a believer, should be clear in your own mind about the necessity of being told, if possible, that you are about to die. For you, too, these should be precious moments of communion with God and of supplication for those left behind, as far as your condition allows. Let not an un-Christian fear of death rob you of the joyous anticipation of going to be with the Lord and of being reunited with loved ones who have gone before. Let your strong faith in Christ in the valley of the shadow be a testimony to His saving and keeping power.

But having closed your eyes for the last time on the sights of earth, what then? What happens to you immediately after death? The Apostle Paul asserts that to be "absent from the body" is to be "present with the Lord." In the moment after death, the Christian soul confronts its Saviour. And may it not be that the unbelieving soul also confronts Christ for immediate judgment and consignment to "his own place" (Acts 1:25)? In fact, for both believer and unbeliever we might call this an instantaneous judgment as to the place in which each shall spend eternity. Since the soul never becomes unconscious, after death it must pass into a state either of conscious joy or conscious torment until the time of the resurrection of the body.

The question we have to answer, then, is how do we attain to a state of happiness hereafter rather than to one of anguish? Again we go back to the verse we have under consideration, First Corinthians 15:21. Here Paul declares that this thing called "death" came about through a man, and our salvation—the antidote for death—comes through another man. The first man is Adam, the second the Lord Jesus Christ. Our present state of sinfulness is due to Adam, and the possibility of our being in a state of salvation is due to Jesus Christ.

This is on the principle of representation. It was through a representative of the human race, Adam, that death came upon all men; it is through a representative man, the God-Man Jesus Christ, that the resurrection life can be yours. Christ, in His resurrection, represents you, even as Adam, in sinning and bringing death upon mankind, represented you.

Adam did not sin merely as an individual but as our federal head, the representative of the whole human race. Otherwise the Bible would not state, "In Adam all die," but would lay the blame on Eve, who was actually the first to sin. In Genesis 5:1 and 2 we read that God gave the name "Adam" to both members of the created pair as parents of the human family. "Male and female created he them; and blessed them, and called their name Adam, in the day when they were created." Thus collectively they are called Adam and share in the guilt. Then again, the man, as the head of the family, and concurring in the sin, bore the responsibility for that sin in the eyes of God.

God had made a covenant with Adam, the terms of which, reduced to their essentials, were, "Disobey me and die" (with the implied corollary, "Obey me and live"). Adam disobeyed and incurred the penalty of mortality.

Since all men from that time on have suffered the

penalty of death, we may reason that they are all regarded as having broken God's law. The infliction of a penalty implies the transgression of a law, since an act is not considered sinful if there is no law against it. Reasoning backwards, we see that this law could not have been the law of Moses, because men died long before that time. Since even infants have died since Adam's sin, we must conclude that all men are subject to death on account of Adam—that is, for the offense of one, all die. Not on account of Adam's sin as an individual, let me repeat, but on account of his sin as representative head of the race.

Now since the New Testament clearly states a parallelism between Adam and Christ in this connection, it is important to understand just how far this parallelism extends. I believe it begins and ends right here: that both are representative heads, and the influence of their acts is communicated to those whom they represent. Adam sinned, and death came upon all human beings, for he represented the race. Christ paid the penalty for sin for all men, Jew and Gentile alike, and became their representative before God in this respect; so that any who would come to God on the merits of Christ and His act of atonement would do so in their representative Head, the Lord Jesus Christ.

As Christ rose from the dead, and extended the offer of resurrection to eternal blessedness to all men, we find a further evidence of parallelism here. What Adam did, Christ undoes, if we may put it that way.

But though there was some sort of analogy between the results of Adam's act and the results of the work of Christ, the parallelism is not perfect. The effects of the work of Christ were far more than simply to counteract the evil introduced by the sin of Adam. The differences between the effect of his act and the work of Christ are twofold:

1) The evil brought about by Adam's sin brought death, but the blessing brought about by Christ not only recovered from ruin but abounded to unimaginable happiness. It not only recovered that which was lost but conferred much more than was lost.

2) Whereas condemnation came by one sin on the part of Adam, the gift of God in Christ brings to the one who receives it not only the pardon of that one offense but it also brings to him the pardon of his many personal offenses.

As men were one with Adam in his fall, so shall all who believe in Christ be one with Him in His resurrection, in His final victory over the forces of evil, and in His triumphant and eternal reign.

REWARDS AND PUNISHMENTS AFTER DEATH

"For since by man came death, by man came also the resurrection of the dead" (I Cor. 15:21).

Have you ever thought what would have happened if Adam, the representative of the human race, had never sinned? Logically, it would seem, one result would be that no one would ever die. Man would be immortal on earth, or would be translated to heaven as were Enoch and Elijah, without seeing death. Although we might envision an overpopulation problem of unimaginable magnitude, there would be no need to worry. God the Creator can sustain all that He creates.

But Adam did sin, and First Corinthians 15:21 clearly indicates the reason for the necessity of the incarnation. "For since by man came death, by man came also the resurrection of the dead." Why didn't God save man by sending His Son from heaven without the intermediary step of being born of the Virgin Mary? Why was it necessary for Him to be born a man among men, rather than to descend directly from heaven in a superhuman or other-than-human form? Let's look at this verse again and see what light the Greek text sheds on it.

It begins with the words "for since," *epeidee* in Greek, meaning "because." This conjunction is causal, showing necessity: "Therefore because through a man came death" is the argument here. Adam was a man; therefore the Redeemer had to be a man also. Of course, Adam brought sin, but Christ took away sin. Because of the first man, Adam, we die physically;

because of the second man, Jesus Christ, the way is open for us to experience bodily resurrection, just as He did.

Actually the verb "came" is not in the Greek text. It is understood. "Therefore because death through a man [or by means of a man], also through a man the resurrection of the dead," is the literal translation. Also, it would be more correct to suppose the understood verb to be in the present perfect, "has come," than in the aorist or past tense. Death is very much with us. "Therefore because death has come through a man." Paul is concerned with the effect of that act of disobedience upon us now. That this should be the tense of the supposed verb is indicated by the participle *kekoimeemenoon*, "the slept ones," in the previous verse. "Them that slept" is a defective if not actually an incorrect translation. The Greek word is a participle in the perfect passive and might better be translated "those slept ones," that is, "those who have been caused to sleep [by God]," if we may be permitted such an awkward construction in English. It refers to "those who are now asleep." The fact of their being asleep or dead now is what Paul stresses here, and not so much the time and occurrence of their death.

Again we may ask, what is it that is asleep, their souls or their bodies? Obviously, it is their bodies, since it is of the resurrection of the body that Paul has been speaking in this passage. Scripture abounds with evidence that the soul of man continues to live on after death occurs. Remember, death is the separation of the material body from the immaterial soul. Since Paul represents resurrection as the victor over physical death, resurrection cannot be other than the joining together again of the body delivered to the earth in death with the soul that, until the day of resurrection, awaits its re-embodiment.

There is therefore only one resurrection, as there is only one death, and this is the rejoining of a transformed body to a soul or spirit. While the body of Jesus was in the grave, His soul was in existence in hades, the place of departed spirits. David predicted it in Psalm 16:10, and Peter confirmed it in Acts 2:27 and 31. "Because thou wilt not leave my soul in hades, neither wilt thou suffer thine Holy One to see corruption. . . . He seeing this before spake of the resurrection of Christ, that his soul was not left in hell [hades], neither his flesh did see corruption."

From this we understand that the resurrection of Christ was the joining of His body with His soul, His material self acquired at conception and birth through the Virgin Mary, and His soul or self, which, because He was God, was self-existent and self-generated. When a human being dies, then, that which sleeps is his body and not his soul. And it is the Christian's body that will be resurrected, glorious, transformed, to complete his bodiless personality now in the presence of the Lord. Of course, the unbeliever's soul waits in hades, the place of torment, for this reunion with his body.

The joys of heaven are the joys of disembodied souls now, but after the resurrection they will be the joys of the complete man. Similarly the sorrows and torments of dead unbelievers are now those of the soul only, until they receive their bodies at the resurrection.

"Marvel not at this," our Lord said, "for the hour is coming, in the which all that are in the graves shall hear his voice" (John 5:28). Notice that in this verse the Lord speaks of those who are in their "graves" here, and not those who are in "hades" if they are unbelievers, or in Paradise in God's presence if they are believers. It is bodies only that are in graves; souls or spirits are in hades. Therefore it is bodies that will come out of graves in the resurrection. Nowhere in Scripture does it say that a soul goes to a grave (*mneemeion*). The soul is either in heaven or hades after leaving the body at death. And when the Lord says that those in the graves shall hear His voice, the word "hear" means obey, for a dead body cannot hear.

The revivifying of the body is a re-creative act of God, comparable to His creative act when He first made our bodies. Enabling dead bodies to "hear his voice" does not refer to their voluntary obedience but to involuntary compliance on their part, at least as far as unbelievers are concerned, for what awaits them is not something to look forward to.

This is a sovereign act of God. "And [they] shall come forth; they that have done good, unto the resurrection of life; and they that have done evil, unto the resurrection of damnation" (John 5:29). True, the rich man in hades, mentioned in Luke 16, was suffering; but since his body was in the grave, and this was prior to the general resurrection of the dead, he must have been suffering in a disembodied state, which could be equated with physical suffering or worse. If that were so, how much greater his suffering would be when body and soul were permanently reunited at the resurrection.

Thus we conclude that the joys or sorrows experienced by those now dead are experienced only by disembodied souls, or at least by their personalities minus their natural bodies or their resurrection bodies.

"Therefore because by a man death. . . ." This man Paul later identifies as Adam. But here he simply uses the generic term *anthroopoo*, "man." Actually, it was a woman who first disobeyed, but a woman is a human being, and that is actually what the word "man" indicates here. Paul absolves God of all responsibility as being the author of death as the consequence of sin. Was God the author of sin? No, but in order to make a being capable of doing good, He had to permit the possibility of his doing evil; He had to create man a free moral agent. God could not command an obedience that was of any moral value unless it were an obedience of choice. And God would not be God if He gave man a choice without fixed consequences of that choice, whether obedience or disobedience. What kind of legislator would make a law without consequences? Obedience results in blessing and liberty; disobedience involves punishment and restriction. No one blames the legislator when a man breaks a law. No one blames the judge who applies the punishment. The criminal, and he alone, is morally responsible for his suffering. If he had not disobeyed, he would not have been punished.

Had God neglected to institute rewards and punishments for obedience and disobedience to His laws, the result would be utter chaos and confusion.

Thus Paul declares truly that through a human being we all taste of death. Let's blame ourselves and not God. We now as fallen men die by our own depraved choice of sin, which caused and still causes death.

CAN THE DEAD BE RAISED TO LIFE?

"For since by man came death, by man came also the resurrection of the dead" (I Cor. 15:21).

All men want money. But they take many different ways of acquiring it. Most men engage in honest work that produces financial rewards. Others, out of necessity or laziness, look to others to support them. And still others prefer to steal.

Yes, all men want money, but not all men are willing to acquire it legitimately. Similarly, given a choice, most men would express a preference to go to heaven when they die. However, the difference between securing heaven and securing money is that no man can earn his way into heaven; he cannot look to other men to get him in; and he cannot steal his way in. In fact, no one can get into heaven who is guilty of sin—not only the sins he has committed in his lifetime, but the original sin passed on to the human race by Adam. "In Adam all die," says Paul in First Corinthians 15:22.

And yet God does hold out the hope of heaven to those who are willing to enter on His terms. He had such compassion on men who were under the condemnation of sin, that in His love He sent Christ to pay the penalty of their sin. He offers them peace and pardon, which they may have by receiving Christ as their Saviour and coming to Him in true repentance. But if man is so ungracious as to refuse Christ's sacrifice on his behalf, he has only himself to blame if he misses out on the joys of heaven.

We must not conclude that because death, physical

and spiritual, automatically passed on to the entire human race because of Adam's sin, the life of Christ or the work of Christ is automatically effective for all men. Everyone dies physically and is therefore under the condemnation of the sin of Adam. But not everyone is alive spiritually because of the work of Christ. A choice is involved here. Not everyone's death will be a "falling asleep in Christ," and therefore not everyone will be among those who take part in the resurrection of which Paul speaks in First Corinthians 15. This is not the resurrection of all people, but only the resurrection of believers, those who "are fallen asleep in Christ" (v. 18). Sinners who have not yet believed are still "in Adam." They are not only represented by Adam but are also one with him, partakers of his nature, heirs of the loss and damage which his nature sustained when he sinned and fell.

All men are likewise in Christ in the sense that He is their representative as having paid the penalty for their sin, if by faith they will avail themselves of His sacrifice; and they are one with Him in being human beings. But not all men are Christians, for as we have said, voluntary choice is involved. They must accept His representative work, as John 1:12 clearly indicates: "But as many as received him, to them gave he power to become the sons of God, even to them that believe on his name."

This, therefore, is the basic difference between the representative work of Adam and that of Christ. Adam brought death to us, and it is ours without any choice on our part. Christ brought life for us, and it is ours by choice. It is a real union in either case. It is by necessity of nature in the one case; it is by the election of God's grace and our own choice in the other. It is hereditary in the one case; it is personal in the other. It is involuntary, without consent, in the one case; it is with our own full and free concurrence in the other.

You are, or can be, in Christ only by a special act of God's grace toward you, and a special work of grace in you. You are in Him, not by your natural birth, but by your new spiritual birth; not by any rite or ceremony, which may be performed without intelligence or consent on your part, but by the work of the Holy Spirit making you the Lord's willing child.

Couldn't God have provided salvation for the human race in some other way than through His Son becoming man? He could have, but He didn't choose to do so. We are not saved through God's eternal Son acting purely as deity. Neither are we saved through the ministry of angels; for although there are fallen angels (Isa. 14:12-14, Jude 6), man did not fall through the representative fall of an angel but through the fall of a representative man, Adam. God, therefore, chose that salvation should come through deity acting also as man. This is why the eternal Son became flesh (John 1:14), so that He could die as man and be resurrected bodily, as indubitable proof of all that He claimed He was and would do for mankind.

In the Greek text of First Corinthians 15:21, there are no verbs at all. This means that each noun is stressed even more as to its quality, and that the quality of meaning lies wholly in the nouns. One of the most important nouns in this verse is "man." "For since by man death, by man also resurrection from dead" is the literal translation. By leaving out the verbs here, Paul stresses nothing more than the exact parallel: man the death medium, man also the resurrection medium. The preposition *dia* (by) in Greek definitely denotes the medium by which death and resurrection came into being.

And what are we to understand by "resurrection from dead"? First, "dead" (*toon nekroon* in Greek) is in the plural number and could be translated "the dead ones." However, these dead ones are they "which are fallen asleep in Christ," as indicated previously. There would have been a resurrection of all the dead whether Christ rose or not. His resurrection affects only the believing dead, the righteous in Him. Their resurrection will be like His, a blessed resurrection to eternal life and fellowship with Him, and not a resurrection of damnation, as in the case of the unbelieving and unrighteous (John 5:28, 29).

In Philippians 3:21 we have not only the fact stated as regards the resurrection of the body, but also the nature and result of this transformation. It is the Lord Jesus Christ Himself "who shall fashion anew [transform, change the form of, *metascheematisei*] the body of our humiliation [that is, our present body], that it may be conformed [*summorphon*] to the body of his glory [that is, have the same form as the glorified body of the very Lord Himself]." It is inconceivable that unbelievers will have the privilege of such a resurrection into life and glory. They will be called forth from the graves to be further condemned.

Having determined that the word "dead" in I Corinthians 15:21 means "believers who slept in Christ," what more are we to understand by the term, "resurrection of the dead"? Man is both spiritual and material, and so long as these two parts of his nature are united the man is said to live. When one is separated from the other, the man is said to die, to cease to be what he is in this life. If, after separation, these two parts be reunited, then the man that was dead may properly be said to rise again, as in Christ's resurrection (John 20:20, 27).

Can this be done? Paul says it has been done by God. And since God has not changed, if He did it in the case of the Lord Jesus He can do it in our case, too. If you think that the God who made your body cannot remake one with identical characteristics, although transformed and glorious, you are certainly limiting omnipotence.

"I will praise thee," the Psalmist writes, "for I am fearfully and wonderfully made: marvellous are thy works. . . . . My substance was not hid from thee, when I was made in secret, and curiously wrought in the lowest parts of the earth" (Ps. 139:14, 15). Now listen to the Lord Jesus speak: "Are not two sparrows sold for a farthing and one of them shall not fall on the ground without your Father. But the very hairs of your head are all numbered. Fear ye not therefore, ye are of more value than many sparrows" (Matt. 10: 29-31). Nothing is impossible with omnipotence. "With God all things are possible" (Matt. 19:26). "Whatsoever the Lord pleased, that did he in heaven, and in earth, in the seas, and all deep places" (Ps. 135:6).

But we cannot be satisfied merely that the resurrection is possible. We need to be assured that God who can do it will certainly do it. Christ is our authority, for He is entitled to speak by virtue of His having risen from the dead. He cited certain resurrection references from the Old Testament that confirm the fact of the resurrection for God's people.

In Matthew 22:32, the Lord said, "I am the God of Abraham, and the God of Isaac, and the God of Jacob. God is not the God of the dead, but of the living." (See also Exod. 3:6, Job 19:25, Dan. 12:2, Acts 23:6 and 24:21.)

The New Testament states that during His earthly ministry Christ did raise some dead persons, though not permanently; they died again (Mark 5:41, 42; Luke 7:12-15, John 11:39-44). And then He rose Himself, but permanently, never to die again (I Cor. 15:12, 20). The resurrection is a certainty because it is so asserted expressly in the Word of God (Acts 4:2, I Cor. 15:52, I Thess. 4:16).

Our reason also forces us to admit the certainty of the resurrection. Since we are capable of doing good or evil, we must also be capable of receiving a final reckoning of everlasting rewards and punishments as men, and so as having bodies in the life to come, as well as souls.

A visitor was walking on the campus of a great university and fell into conversation with a young law student. The visitor asked, "When you have completed your studies, what do you intend to do?" "I shall take my doctor's degree." "And then?" "Then I shall have a number of difficult cases to deal with and shall call attention to myself by my eloquence and my learning, and gain a great reputation." "And then?" "And then I shall be promoted to some high office and make money and grow rich." "And then?" "Then I shall live comfortably in wealth and dignity." "And then?" "Then I suppose I shall die." "And then?" The young man made no answer. Hanging his head, he went thoughtfully away. That last question struck home, and he came to realize the utter futility of living for this world alone.

Death is the one future fact of which we are all certain, and it is wise for us to come to terms with it now—God's terms. When we commit ourselves into God's care and keeping by accepting His provision for our salvation in Christ, death is robbed of its terrors. Then eternal life becomes a present possession and a future certainty, as we are able to say with Paul, "I know whom I have believed, and am persuaded that he is able to keep that which I have committed unto him against that day" (II Tim. 1:12).

WHERE DO YOU STAND?

"For as in Adam all die, even so in Christ shall all be made alive" (I Cor. 15:22).

Back in the third century B.C., when King Antiochus was asked by the Roman ambassador whether he was for peace or war, he said he must have time to consider. Quick as a flash the ambassador drew his sword, inscribed a circle around the king in the sand, and said, "Give an answer before you move out of that circle, or if you step out of it your answer is war."

Some people think they can go through life without taking a stand for or against Christ, thus declaring allegiance neither to God nor to the devil. They remind us of that burying ground where some of the tombstones have no names on them. When a tourist asked the reason, he was told that those who were buried in this way believed that the angel of the resurrection would point to each grave that had a name on it and declare instantly whether its occupant should go to heaven or hell, but would overlook the nameless graves when he came to awaken men to their everlasting destiny.

But there is no middle ground in this world or the next in regard to man's salvation. First Corinthians 15:22 makes this very plain. "For as in Adam all die," it says, "even so in Christ shall all be made alive."

Some persons take this verse to mean that everyone, regardless of what he has done, or whether he has believed in Christ or not, will be restored to eventual fellowship with God. Because this interpretation has such tremendous significance, and because it runs counter to other teachings of the Bible, we need to examine this verse carefully to see what it really does teach.

Obviously Paul is explaining here who these two representatives of the human race are, of whom he has spoken briefly in the previous verse: "For since by man came death, by man came also the resurrection of the dead" (I Cor. 15:21). We judge from these verses that the one who brought death is Adam and the One who brought life is Christ. In the original Greek text the definite article appears before the two names in verse 22, as if to stress how well-known they are: "the Adam . . . the Christ."

Literally translated the verse would read: "For as in Adam all keep on dying, thus also in Christ all shall be made alive."

So that there can be no mistaking the identity of the two, Paul does not use the same prepositions in verse 22 as he does in verse 21. In verse 21 the preposition is *dia*, which occurs twice and is commonly translated "by, through, by means of," and denotes the means by which something is accomplished. Adam is the *cause* of death and Christ is the *cause* of the resurrection of the dead in Him.

The preposition used in verse 22 is *en*, which also occurs twice, both in regard to Adam and in regard to Christ. Fundamentally it means "in," and is correctly translated so some 2,698 times in the New Testament. Although of all prepositions this is the one most commonly used, determining just what it means in each instance is not an easy task. We cannot generalize on its meaning, but must always take into consideration the context of words and thought.

What does it mean, then, to be "in Adam" or to be "in Christ"? Simply stated, this preposition *en*, translated "in" in I Corinthians 15:22, places a circle around Adam and another circle around Christ. They are opposites. One signifies death and the other life. Everyone who is born into the world comes into the circle or sphere of Adam both physically and spiritually. Consequently, everyone must die physically, whether he wants to or not. He has no choice. Adam's original choice as the representative of our race spoiled it for us all. However, spiritually, the "all" in Adam does not refer to inevitable death for all humanity, nor does the "all" in Christ refer to automatic resurrection to eternal blessedness for all humanity. It is when both "all's" are added together that we come to a totality of the human race as regards their final destiny—both physical and spiritual.

In Adam all are lost until, and unless, they cross over from the sphere of death into the sphere of life. On the other hand, though Christ died for all, that death is only made effective for individual ones who by exercising faith in Him are delivered and brought from the sphere of death into the sphere of life.

That is the meaning of I Timothy 4:10, "God is the Saviour of all men [potentially], specially of those that believe [in which case the potential becomes actual]." And Jesus Christ in His high-priestly prayer (John 17:2) said, "that he [the Son] should give eternal life to as many as thou [the Father] hast given him."

So we gather that the word translated "all" (*pantes*) does not mean a totality in the absolute sense, but a totality within absolute totality.

With this as a base, let us paraphrase these two phrases in I Corinthians 15:22, "Everyone who is in the sphere of Adam will go on dying spiritually; thus also everyone who is within the circle or sphere of Christ will be made alive." It is to be noted here that all men incur physical death as a result of Adam's sin (with the exception of those who will be living on this earth at the time of Christ's return). But the one who remains in the sphere of Adam spiritually will go on dying spiritually; while the one who has stepped over into the sphere of Christ is alive spiritually *now and forever*. The only thing left to be redeemed for the believer in Christ is the body, and that will occur at the resurrection, when he receives a glorious transformed body like that of his Lord. The unbeliever on the other hand, unredeemed in soul, will nevertheless be resurrected, but in a body capable of suffering endless torment. These distinctions must be plainly understood as we proceed with this verse.

Now we can see that in these two collective pronouns—"all" referring to those in Adam and "all" referring to those in Christ—we do not have collectivity, but individuality *within* collectivity. How does everyone die? Individually. How is one made alive in Christ? Individually. So there is neither collective perdition nor collective salvation. Everyone *as an individual* dies in his own sins, and everyone who is saved is saved because of his own personal belief in Christ.

A party of climbers, roped together, were making

their way along a snow ridge high up in the Alps, when the leader slipped and fell over the edge of a precipice. The rope attached to him jerked the next man off his feet, and each of the party except the last was in turn dragged over. The last man, an experienced climber, had time between the first slip until the rope tightened around his own body to plunge his ice-axe deeply into the snow, dig his heels into the snow, and brace himself for the coming strain; and when it reached him he held firm. For a short time all hung out in space, with a terrible death threatening them thousands of feet beneath. Then the first man swarmed up the rope, and over the body of the next who followed after him, and all managed to climb to safety.

The first Adam slipped and fell over the precipice of eternal death, and in his fall he dragged all mankind after him. But at length one man, the God-man who came to this earth for the purpose of saving fallen humanity, held firm, the last Adam, Jesus Christ, and through Him all mankind is enabled to climb to safety. Had the climbers not availed themselves of the rope, they could not have been saved. A decision had to be made. Confronted with the decision whether to remain "in Adam" or "in Christ," which will you choose?

HOW TO LIVE FOREVER

"For as in Adam all die, even so in Christ shall all be made alive" (I Cor. 15:22).

Every once in awhile you read in the papers of some child who has but a short while to live. Doctors, relatives, interested persons do all they can to reverse this sentence—sometimes successfully, sometimes not.

But in a general sense we have all but a relatively short while to live, and we die a little each day. We accept this as our common fate, irreversible and inevitable. But is the body all that is involved in death?

The Bible tells us, "In Adam all die," or more literally, "In Adam all keep on dying." The verb here (*apothneeskousin*) is in the frequentative or iterative present. (A. T. Robertson, *A Grammar of the Greek New Testament*, p. 880.) This verb does not refer to the instantaneous act of dying, but to the continuous act of dying every moment. In other words, those who are within the sphere of Adam are in the continuous process of dying. And Paul is speaking here of what is going on in the lives of all who are within this circle of Adam, who are there because of Adam's original sin. (See Rom. 5:12.)

But here in First Corinthians 15:22 Paul is not speaking of men's entrance into the circle of Adam's influence, but of what is going on while they are there —*they keep on dying*. Every moment of their stay in that circle brings them closer to the final death—not to the physical death of the believer in Christ, which spells the hope of a brighter day, but the death of the unbelieving and unrepentant, which brings doom and eternal loss.

How terrible it must be while one is living to feel that he is moving inevitably toward death. Two boys were enjoying a last-minute skate on the lake after everyone had gone home, when the ice broke and began carrying them out to deep water. One of them, the one nearest shore, saw their danger and leaped across the narrow gap, at the same time calling a warning to his companion. The other boy came to the gap where the dark water was swirling, concluded it would be safer to stay where he was, and told his companion to go for help. But though he came back with men and a boat, and they searched and called far into the night, no trace of the boy was found. What must have been his thoughts as he slowly and inevitably moved toward death?

Do you ever have moments of self-realization in which you feel that you are moving inevitably toward spiritual death? The prospect of ultimate and eternal separation from God is inescapable as long as one stays within the circle of Adam. There is only one way not to "keep on dying" and that is to move on to the circle of Christ and keep on living in Him.

In speaking of the resurrection of the bodies of believers, Paul does not exclude a resurrection of the bodies of those who die in their sins. In this passage he is simply stressing the resurrection of believers without attempting to exhaust the subject of resurrection. Briefly stated, the resurrection of believers is a resurrection unto life, and the resurrection of unbelievers is a resurrection unto condemnation. (See John 5:28, 29.)

Of what death is Paul speaking when he says, "In Adam all keep on dying"? He refers primarily to those who died without accepting Jesus Christ as their Saviour. There they are in their graves. There is not now nor will there ever be any hope for their salvation. What they sowed in life they will reap in death. They keep on dying even when they have closed their eyes and their hearts have stopped beating. Their souls are now separated from God in conscious torment, as was the soul of the rich man of Luke 16:19-31. In other words, those who once died in Adam spiritually and then died physically will continue in spiritual death.

For unbelievers, nevertheless, there will be a physical resurrection, as Christ foretold in John 5:28, 29. "Marvel not at this: for the hour is coming, in the which all that are in the graves shall hear his voice, and shall come forth; they that have done good, unto the resurrection of life; and they that have done evil, unto the resurrection of damnation."

But after physical death, according to the Scripture, there can be no transfer from the circle of Adam to the circle of Christ. It is finished. What is done is done and sealed. That is why we stress the necessity of salvation and acceptance of Christ in this life. When physical death strikes, there is no hope of bridging the gap between man and God. That gulf is fixed forever. For those who die in Adam there will be a bodily resurrection, but the separation between them and God will never cease. That is what Paul means by the words "keep on dying."

What does the phrase "in Christ all shall be made alive" mean? What part of the believer's personality needs life? The body, naturally, for that is what lies in the grave. His soul, of course, already has life. Giving life to the body means joining it with that which was separated from it at the time of physical death—the spirit. That rejoining, Paul says, takes place in an instant of time. And that is why the verb used here is not in the present indicative tense, as in the case of those in Adam, but is in the punctiliar future tense. That is, it is an instantaneous act, not a progressive one. In an instant of time the spirits of those who are in Christ will be joined to their bodies, glorified, as Paul explains later in this chapter.

The verb translated "shall be made alive" must not be understood to mean the spiritual life given to a person who during his earthly lifetime left the circle of Adam to enter the circle of Christ. The believer in Christ who has died does not need such spiritual life, because he does not lose it—even in physical death. Spiritual life means the communion of the spirit of man with the Spirit of God, and those who are in Christ have this both in life and in death. Resurrection unto life, as we have said, means the joining of the spirit of man to his body. This is what Paul is trying to prove to the Corinthians and to us throughout First Corinthians 15.

Finally let us note the voice of the two Greek verbs found in this verse: the one, "keep on dying" (*apothneeskousin*), and the other, "shall be made alive" (*zoo-opoieetheesontai*).

The first verb is in the active voice, signifying that man is responsible for his own death. He cannot blame God. Adam sinned, man fell, and man of his own choice continues to fall. He keeps on dying of his own volition. Therefore he is responsible for his own destiny.

The voice of the second verb, "shall be made alive," is passive. This indicates that only through the power of someone outside ourselves can the act be accomplished. That is, we cannot make ourselves alive; we must be made alive by someone else, in this instance by Christ.

Faith that is not placed in the right person is a vain and empty faith. Our decision to leave the circle of Adam and enter the circle of Christ would be of no avail were it not for the attraction of Christ and His keeping us within the circle of His sacred influence and life.

When asked how he had found Christ, a young man replied, "I did not find Christ, Christ found me." And he might have added, "Once He found me, I gladly went along with Him," for his changed life gave evidence that he had stepped from the circle of death into the circle of life, and was rejoicing in fellowship with the One who had saved him.

WILL ALL MEN EVENTUALLY BE SAVED?

"But every man in his own order: Christ the first-fruits; afterward they that are Christ's at his coming" (I Cor. 15:23).

"If I didn't think that there was any future life," said a business executive to his staff, "I wouldn't care how I ran my business, or my personal life either. I'd just go all out for everything I could get."

Our belief or disbelief in a life to come determines to a great extent the way in which we live. Those men who believe they are destined to die like animals will be tempted to live like animals. But those who believe in the resurrection of the dead, because they have believed in Jesus Christ, know they cannot find true happiness in this life except through the knowledge of God, and conformity to the life and death of the Lord Jesus Christ.

In First Corinthians 15:23, we learn more about this resurrection as it affects each man personally. "But every man in his own order: Christ the firstfruits; afterward they that are Christ's at his coming." First we see that Christ is already risen from the dead; second, that His resurrection is the guarantee that we also shall rise *in God's time* and *in our own order.*

Although at first glance we might think that this verse speaks only of the resurrection of those that belong to Christ, as we examine it more carefully we see that Paul says there shall be an order of resurrection for "every man," which implies the more universal resurrection to judgment. The resurrection of the unjust will be the last in the sequence of events at the final resurrection, suggesting that God is more eager to glorify His servants than to condemn the wicked. But at last they too shall rise to their condemnation, for that must be done also; every man in his own order: first Christ, then Christ's servants, and finally Christ's enemies.

That Christ rose from the dead is the great ground of our faith—the foundation of God that stands sure.

That we believers shall rise is the great consummation of all our hopes—the superstructure that shall never perish.

That unbelievers shall rise to receive their punishment is the necessary corollary to the reward of the righteous—the demonstration of God's justice.

Paul has previously discussed the resurrection of Christ and proven it to be true. Now he proceeds to demonstrate the second truth in First Corinthians 15:23, "But every man in his own order." A better translation is, "But each one in his own order." This verse further explains verse 22, in which we learned that there are two circles, that of Adam and that of Christ. The number of people in one plus the number of people in the other make up the aggregate of all mankind. Unbelievers plus believers equal all. The "all" in Adam plus the "all" in Christ equal all.

Those in Adam's circle keep on dying. They are spiritually dead in their trespasses and sins. They are separated from God and they will keep on being separated as long as they remain in Adam's circle. Their physical resurrection will not deliver them from spiritual death (that is, their separation from God), for they will keep on dying or being separated from Him. Their physical resurrection leads not to the hope of a better life but to eternal doom. This will happen to "all" (*pantes*), to each one in this group.

This is the significance of the word "all" (*pantes*) in verse 22; it refers to each one in a group—each one in Adam's circle and each one in Christ's circle. The Apostle thus indicates that men condemn themselves as individuals and are saved as individuals. Christianity is not a religion of group faith but of individual faith. John 3:18 makes this very clear. "He [singular number, referring to an individual] that believeth on him is not condemned: but he that believeth not is condemned already, because he [again as an individual] hath not believed in the name of the only begotten Son of God."

That the Greek word *pantes*, "all," of verse 22 refers to all the individuals within a group is further borne out by the word *hekastos*, "each one," with which verse 23 begins. Observe that it is preceded by "but" (*de* in Greek), "but each one in his own order": those in the circle of Adam will be raised each in his own order, and those in the circle of Christ will be raised each in his own order.

The word translated "order" in Greek is *tagmati* (nominative, *tagma*), a substantive derived from the verb *tassoo*, which means to place or station a person or thing in a fixed spot. *Tagma* is that which is ordered and fixed. Here it refers to a number of persons who belong together and are therefore arranged together, a division or group. The idea in verse 23 is that there are three fixed groups or divisions: first Christ; then those who belong to Christ through having received Him and been redeemed by Him; and finally those who are still in Adam, the unbelievers, those who have rejected Christ, either as the coming Messiah in Old Testament times, or after He had come into the world as the incarnate Son of God. When the final resurrection takes place, the position of each group is fixed forever. Nothing can change it; no prayer or pleading can alter this state of being.

But *tagma* (order) not only conveys the meaning of fixed position but also the implication of fixed time. The resurrection of these groups will take place at the time God has ordained for each. For Christ, the resurrection is an accomplished fact. For Christians, it will be next, at a time ordered by God and known to Him alone. For unbelievers, it will be last, again at a time fixed and known by God.

To strengthen the idea of fixed position and time for each group, Paul uses the word *idioo*, "in his own" —"but every man in his own order." There will be no mixing of the groups or of the time of their resurrection. Also observe the contrast provided by that word "but." "Don't think that because every human being is to be resurrected in his body," Paul seems to be saying here, "they will all be in one group and will be raised at one and the same time." This is a definite argument against the erroneous doctrine of universal salvation, which teaches that all will be well at the end for all men. It is just not so. If it is not well with your soul in this life, then once you have closed your eyes in death it never will be.

To eliminate all possible misunderstanding of any mixing of the two groups in the resurrection and what is to follow, Paul uses a more emphatic pronoun than would normally have been necessary. He could have said *en too tagmati autou*, "in his (own) order." But instead of *autoo* he used *idioo*, making the phrase mean "in his very own order." There can be no mixing up of the order in which these events are to take place. "But each one in his very own order, his very own battalion." Those who are in Adam, and die physically while still in him, shall rise each in his own circle and order; those who are in Christ, each in his own order.

Paul stated this truth in no uncertain terms when he gave his defense before the Roman governor Felix. "There shall be a resurrection of the dead, both of the just and unjust" (Acts 24:15). Again in First Thessalonians 4:16 he says, "And the dead in Christ shall rise first," that is, before the dead in Adam—each group in its own order.

Thus we see that Paul consistently teaches that each one, believer and unbeliever, shall be raised physically from the dead, but that the two groups will be kept separate and that the time of their resurrection will not be simultaneous but will follow God's prescribed sequence.

That each one of us in the resurrection will have our bodies transformed yet individually identifiable, reunited with our spirits or souls, may be beyond our understanding, but what of that? Just because we do not understand something does not mean that it is not so, or that it is impossible. We cannot fully understand the changes of nature, yet we have to admit that they do take place.

One poet who had made a strong statement of his faith in Christ ended his poem thus:

> Ask me not how I am oracular,
> Nor whence this arrogant assurance springs.
> Ask rather Faith, the canny conjurer,
> Who, while your reason mocks him, mystifies,
> Winning the grudging plaudits of your eyes—
> How suddenly the supine egg has wings.
>   —Countee Cullen

Is it impossible for Him who originally made us to re-make us? Is our opinion of the power of God so low that we believe He can do no more than we can understand? Paul shows how ridiculous the conclusions of unbelief are by appealing to nature. If a grain of corn dies and lives again, he argues, why should we shame our understanding or faith by thinking that corn can be restored to life but man cannot? Every creature, including you and me, can be anything God decrees in His infinite wisdom and power.

THE RESURRECTION AND THE SECOND COMING
OF CHRIST

". . . Afterward they that are Christ's at his coming" (I Cor. 15:23b).

Unidentified flying objects have been very much in the news in recent times. People's attitudes toward these reported phenomena have varied all the way from sober and scientific investigation to the wildest flights of fancy. It has even been suggested, without any concrete evidence, that they are craft manned by intelligent beings from another planet, who are sizing up our earth preliminary to an invasion.

Most people, however, are suspending judgment as to what these UFO's are and what they may portend. Scripture certainly sheds no light on the subject.

However, Scripture does speak of a time when our planet will be invaded from without, and gives very specific details of what will take place at that time (none of which includes flying saucers!).

First Corinthians 15:23 definitely links the resurrection of the dead with this invasion. We have previously seen in verse 20 that Christ is the "firstfruits" of those that are raised from the dead, who have "fallen asleep" in Him. Now, in verse 23, we find this word "firstfruits" again applied to Him, with further elucidation of the order in which the resurrection takes place.

Christ was the first in point of time; believers will be second; and unbelievers will be last. The Scriptures teach us that there will be two resurrections besides Christ's: "Blessed and holy is he that hath part in the first resurrection: on such the second death hath no power" (Rev. 20:6). And in I Thessalonians 4:16 Paul tells us that "the dead in Christ shall rise first," which of course presupposes that the wicked shall rise after that.

Let us look a little more closely at the second half of First Corinthians 15:23, which reads, "afterward they that are Christ's at his coming." It refers to the time of the resurrection of believers who have fallen asleep in Him. Paul tells us they will be raised "at his coming." The preposition *en*, translated "at" in this phrase, signifies "at the time of this event." Therefore the resurrection of the believers will occur at the same time as the *parousia*, the appearance or coming of the Lord. This cannot mean Christ's first coming as the Babe of Bethlehem. The word *parousia*, which is here translated "coming," is never used in the New Testament to refer to the first coming of the Lord Jesus to this earth. That is referred to by Stephen just before he was martyred as the *eleusis* (nominative), "the coming of the Just One" (Acts 7:52).

The word *parousia* in the New Testament, when used in reference to the Lord Jesus, always means the second coming of Christ. In ecclesiastical writing this is called "the second coming" (*hee deutera parousia*). (See Matt. 24:3, 27, 37, 39; I Cor. 15:23; I Thess. 2:19; 3:13; 4:15; 5:23; II Thess. 2:1, 8, 9; James 5:7, 8; II Pet. 1:16; 3:4, 12; I John 2:28.)

In some instances the word *parousia*, "coming," is connected with the resurrection of believers. The first instance is in First Corinthians 15:23, where we are told that they that are Christ's shall be raised at His coming. The second instance is in First Thessalonians 4:15, "For this we say unto you by the word of the Lord, that we which are alive and remain unto the coming of the Lord shall not prevent them which are asleep." Actually, the Greek word translated "prevent" here is *phthasoomen*, which means "precede, come before." What Paul is saying is that the dead in Christ shall rise before the living in Christ are caught up to be with the Lord.

The word *parousia* is the antonym of the Greek word *apousia*. It means "presence" as opposed to "absence." It comes from the preposition *para*, indicating close proximity, meaning in composition "near, beside, by," and the verb *eimi*, meaning "I am." The adjective *paroon* is used even in Modern Greek to mean "present." The teacher calls out the names of his pupils, and each one answers "Present."

Why is this word so distinctively used to indicate the second coming of Christ? First of all, it implies that His long physical absence will be broken—the absence between His ascension and His returning again to earth. Some people do not believe this will be a physical coming, for they say that the presence of the Lord is always with the believer.

It is true that He has never ceased to be with His redeemed people, as He promised in Matthew 28:20, "Lo, I am with you alway, even unto the end of the world." Who of His redeemed people does not feel the presence of the Lord Jesus? And yet, when He walked the streets of Palestine, His presence was of a different nature—it was a physically tangible presence. The nature of His *parousia*, or presence, must correspond to the nature of His present absence. And who can claim that the absence of Jesus now is not purely physical? As His absence is physical, so must His presence, His *parousia*, be. We have the word of angels for this, for at the ascension of Christ, when He was taken up "out of their sight," and men stood gazing after Him, "Behold, two men stood by them in white apparel; which also said, Ye men of Galilee, why stand ye gazing up into heaven? this same Jesus, which is taken up from you into heaven, shall so come in like manner as ye have seen him go into heaven" (Acts 1:10, 11).

The word *parousia* implies more than the word *eleusis*. The latter word stresses more the act of arrival and coming—as when Christ was born in Bethlehem—while the *parousia* of Christ stresses more the continuity of His staying. The Lord in His *parousia* is not coming merely temporarily, as He did the first time in His incarnation, when He remained for a relatively short period of time. We never find His incarnation, or first coming, referred to as His first *parousia*. Only His second coming is referred to as a "presence." And that is because He will always be present. The time of His absence will have passed forever. His presence will then be so different from the way we experience it now that the change from one to the other will be no less than a "coming again."

In Ancient Greek, *parousia* was sometimes used of the "invasion" of a province by a general. It is thus used in referring to the invasion of Asia by Mithradates. It describes the entrance on the scene of a new and conquering power. Isn't this what First Corinthians 15 tells us? Here is what will take place at Christ's *parousia:* They that are Christ's shall rise. Then He will put an end to all power and authority. He will reign. He will put His enemies under His feet. Death will be conquered. All things will be subjugated to Christ. What is all this but an invasion of our world, as we know it, by a new and conquering power? That is, it will be new as far as those who do not recognize Christ are concerned, but not as far as His followers are concerned.

Believers in Christ look forward to His return as the time of their completed salvation, when their redeemed souls shall be reunited to their resurrected bodies. Their attitude is one of confident waiting.

It is said that when Shackleton was on one of his Arctic explorations, he once left some of his men camped on a bay and went overland to bring his ship for them, promising to return within a few days. However, dense fog at first and then an ice pack prevented him, and it was weeks before he could get back to learn how his men had fared.

When the wind finally blew enough to lift the fog and move the ice so that his ship could make it back into the bay, to Shackleton's surprise and joy he found the men packed and ready to step into a boat and be rowed out to the ship. None too soon, for already the ice was moving back in to close it up again. When the explorer asked the men how it happened that they were all ready to go, after a wait of weeks, one of them said, "It was this way—Captain Wild, whom you left in charge, would not give up hope of your coming. Every morning he would say, 'Roll up your sleeping bags, boys; the boss may come today.' So we were always ready, expecting you every day." That should be the attitude of all who truly trust in Christ, who said, "Therefore be ye also ready: for in such an hour as ye think not the Son of man cometh" (Matt. 24:44).

WHAT WILL CHRIST'S COMING MEAN TO YOU?

"... *Afterward they that are Christ's at his coming*" (I Cor. 15:23b).

In the Jewish temple service, when the high priest beyond the veil had accomplished his priestly office, the people stood in the outer court awaiting his return. And so it is with the High Priest Jesus; His coming to the outer court of the temple of the natural world is the blessed hope of the waiting Church.

He will "appear the second time without sin unto salvation," as Hebrews 9:28 tells us. He will not come as Redeemer, to atone for the sin that He will still find, as was His purpose in His first coming. But His coming will be for the bodily salvation of those whom He has already saved in spirit.

This is precisely why the resurrection of the believers in First Corinthians 15:23 is mentioned in connection with the *parousia*, the "coming," of the Lord. The resurrection spoken of in this chapter is never referred to as that of the soul, but always that of the body. This physical resurrection, the receiving of a new "spiritual body" like that of the risen Christ, will spell the salvation of our present bodies full of sickness, tears, and afflictions.

In the Greek text of Hebrews 9:28 we are told, "The second time he shall physically appear (*ophtheesetai*) unto them expecting him unto salvation." This word *ophtheesetai* in this context refers to the most visible exhibition of Himself as King, in the judicial form of His kingly office. He vindicates His atonement as against all who have despised it. In First Corinthians 15:23 and what follows, we have the *parousia* of the Lord connected with the subjugation and punishment of the unbelievers. This is made clear also in First Thessalonians 2:7, 8: "The Lord Jesus shall be revealed from heaven with his mighty angels, in flaming fire taking vengeance on them that know not God, and that obey not the gospel of our Lord Jesus Christ." We see then that the *parousia* is the object of joyous expectation only to the Church as such.

Parousia occurs in all twenty-five times in the New Testament. When applied to others than the Saviour (I Cor. 16:17, II Cor. 7:6; 10:10, Phil. 2:12, etc.), it is admitted to mean nothing short of a personal coming. In the seventeen times that it is applied to the Saviour, its meaning can be no different. His second coming will be nothing short of a personal reappearance.

In the papyri and in hellenistic Greek (used in New Testament times), *parousia* is the technical word for the arrival of an emperor, a king, a governor, or other famous person, into a town or province. For such a visit, preparations had to be made. Taxes were imposed, for instance, to present the king with a golden crown. This gives us an idea of why the Word of God instructs believers to be ready for the coming of the Lord. "And now, little children," says John the beloved apostle, "abide in him; that, when he shall appear, we may have confidence, and not be ashamed before him at his coming" (I John 2:28). (See also I Thess. 3:13; 5:23.)

A common practice in those days was for a province to date a new era from the *parousia* or coming of the emperor. The island of Cos dated a new era from the *parousia* of Gaius Caesar in A.D. 4, as did Greece from the *parousia* of Hadrian in A.D. 124. Similarly an entirely new era will emerge for the Christian and the world as a result of the coming of King Jesus back to this earth, physically and personally.

We have previously noted that *parousia* is sometimes used of the invasion of a province by a general. It is also used of the visitation of a god. It is used, for instance, of the mythological visit of the god Aesculapius to a sufferer who was healed in his temple. The *parousia*, the second coming of Christ, will certainly be the visitation of God Almighty to our world of suffering. At present the body of the believer is subject to the same influences as the body of the unbeliever. There are sick Christians and sick unbelievers. Of course, the Lord is gracious to His own, often healing in answer to prayer; but above all He gives grace to bear and use whatever suffering befalls our frail and mortal bodies.

Coincidentally, these lines were penned in the waiting room of a clinical laboratory. I was there forcibly reminded of the fact that, though our present body is one of humiliation, the day is coming when our Lord will once again descend from heaven, this time to give us our new and glorified resurrection bodies. That will spell the end of physical suffering as far as believers in Christ are concerned.

On the political side, the *parousia* of a king, a governor, or an emperor was often an occasion when petitions were presented and wrongs were righted. This is what the *parousia* of Christ will do. It will crush the enemies of righteousness who today are having their full say and sway. The day is coming when the order will be reversed. This is what First Corinthians 15 tells us.

In the book of the Revelation, which is the fullest account of the *parousia* of the Lord, the key thought may be paraphrased, "I come quickly. The world seems to have all things its own way, to destroy my servants; but I come quickly." (See Rev. 1:7; 2:5, 16; 3:11; 6:17; 11:18; 14:7; 16:15; 18:20; 22:7, 12, 20.) This keynote is Christ's word of comfort, or, where needed, His word of warning to His friends.

During the dark days of the struggle for Italian liberty in the mid-nineteenth century, the people generally looked upon Garibaldi as their invincible deliverer. Prisoners, hurried away to loathsome dungeons, would be cheered as they passed along the streets by friends whispering in their ears, "Courage, Garibaldi is coming!" Men would steal out at night and chalk on the walls and pavements, "Garibaldi is coming!" And when the news of his approach near to a city was announced, the people broke out into the joyful shout, "Garibaldi is coming!" He came, and Italy broke her political and religious fetters, never to be so enslaved again. A greater than Garibaldi is coming to God's people. The Desire of all nations is on the way—to right all wrongs, to deliver His servants, and to reign in righteousness.

But the message of Christ's second coming is a word of terror to His foes. The prospect of Christ's victory over His enemies in His *parousia* is what James gives as the reason for believers to exercise patience (James 5:7, 8). "Be patient therefore, brethren, unto the coming of the Lord," he says. "Behold, the husbandman waiteth for the precious fruit of the earth, and hath long patience for it, until he receive the early and latter rain. Be ye also patient; stablish your hearts: for the coming of the Lord draweth nigh."

Is your heart established in Christ, so that you are patiently and joyfully anticipating His coming? Or are you like one who is fearfully waiting for the approaching storm to break over your head?

A tourist while crossing the Bay of Biscay became alarmed and anxious as he beheld what he thought was an approaching hurricane or tornado. He grabbed the arm of an experienced seaman and asked, "Do you think she'll be able to live through it?" "Through what?" inquired the sailor. "Through that fast approaching storm!" The seaman smiled and said, "Sir, you needn't be alarmed; that storm will never touch us; it has passed already."

So it is with regard to the believer in Christ. Judgment, as far as sin is concerned, is past already. Christ has been tried, condemned, and executed in his stead for his sins. Whether he goes to meet his Lord in death, or is still living when Christ returns to this earth, he "fears no evil," but can say, "Even so come, Lord Jesus."

WILL THERE BE A FINAL ANNIHILATION OF ALL THINGS?

"Then cometh the end, when he shall have delivered up the kingdom to God, even the Father; when he shall have put down all rule and all authority and power" (I Cor. 15:24).

"What's this world coming to?" is a question you often hear asked with a great deal of foreboding. History can tell us only what has already taken place in the world. It cannot tell us about the future except on the basis of probability.

But man desperately longs to know more about the future, and with a greater degree of certainty, than he can learn from the experiences of the past. Especially does he want reassurance about the times in which he lives, and his own personal history. "What is going to become of *me?*" is the anxiety that haunts modern man, either consciously or unconsciously. "Will I live out my days in health, prosperity, and peace of mind? Or will disaster overtake me, as it has so many others? Will the world be any different for my having lived in it? Will I ever find the answer to all the questions that trouble me now? Will my life end in the grave, or will my personality persist after death? If death does not end all, what will become of me?" And there he is, right back where he started.

Such anxieties may drive the superstitious to fortune tellers, the intellectual to philosophy, and many over-emotional persons to drink, or drugs, or to strange religious cults. It may drive the more optimistic to a philosophy of "eat, drink, and be merry"; or the pessimistic to insanity or suicide.

If the troubled person propounds these questions to an equally perplexed fellow mortal, he is likely to be answered with a shrug of the shoulders and the offhand remark, "God knows." This profession of ignorance is actually the wisest answer that can be given. For God does know, and He has made this knowledge readily available. The Bible, the divinely inspired Word of God, holds the only authentic answer to man's questions about his ultimate destiny. God Himself tells each man what the end of all things—and his own personal end—will be.

As a starting point, let us turn to I Corinthians 15:24-28. This passage is unique, for it is the only place in Scripture where we are told that one day Jesus Christ, the Son of God, will deliver up His present kingdom to God the Father. Verse 24 reads: "Then cometh the end, when he shall have delivered up the kingdom to God, even the Father; when he shall have put down all rule and all authority and power."

In order to understand the significance of this, and its relation to you personally, you must first understand Christ's office in this present age. This is the age of Christ as Mediator. He stands between God the Father and us human beings, to mediate salvation to all who will come to God by Him. "For there is one God, and one mediator between God and men, the man Christ Jesus" (I Tim. 2:5). A mediator is one who interposes between parties as the equal friend of each, to effect a reconciliation. Now you have the opportunity to become reconciled to God because Christ, as mediator, has paid the penalty for your sins on the cross, and God stands ready to forgive you for His sake.

But the era of Christ as Mediator will one day come to a close, and a new era will be ushered in. Scripture tells us that this will take place when Christ comes back to earth again, and after the general resurrection of the dead. The events listed in I Corinthians 15:23 and 24 are as follows: First the resurrection of Christ; then the resurrection of believers at the coming of Christ; and "then the end."

How long a time may we assume will elapse between one event and the other? Christ's resurrection took place nearly 2,000 years ago. When will the resurrection of those who believe in Him take place? When will Christ return to raise the bodies of those who sleep in death? When will the new era of righteousness be ushered in? We cannot make any definite assumptions; the time element is indeterminate in this passage. Nor can we assume that the resurrection of the believers and "the end" will follow one upon another with no intervening events. We are given the order of events in relation to each other, but not in relation to other events that may occur in between.

What is this "end" to which the Apostle Paul refers? The Greek is *to telos*, translated "the end," in the clause "then [cometh] the end." Does this refer to the end of the world, the termination of all things? It does not seem so. Cremer, in his *Biblico-Theological Lexicon of New Testament Greek* (p. 541), says that *to telos*, "the end," does not primarily refer to the end or termination of time but denotes the goal reached, the completion or conclusion at which anything arrives, either as issue or ending. We use this word in similar fashion today when we say, "I have a definite end in view." *Telos* may also mean the result, acme, or consummation, as for instance *polemou telos*, "the end of war," which means victory, measuring not time but object; or *telos andros*, "the end of man," which does not refer merely to the death of man but may mean "the full age of man."

"Further," Cremer says, "*to telos*, the end, which in Mt. 24:14, 'and then shall the end come,' Mk. 13:7, Lk. 21:9, means the termination of the present course and condition of the world; in I Cor. 15:24 on the contrary it means at the same time, the goal reached. and the beginning of a new order of things—Heb. 7:3."

When Paul wrote the words of I Corinthians 15:24, "Then [cometh] the end," what goal was he referring to? What is the object of resurrection for man? Does it not take him back into the place intended for him in God's purpose, for which sin and death had for a while rendered him unfit? The resurrection is the consummation of our deliverance from the consequence of sin which came upon all people, believers and unbelievers. The divine purpose is not fully accomplished here on earth even for the believer during his earthly life. The last enemy to be destroyed on earth is death. We all die. That is the end, the consequence of sin. Therefore the end or consequence of the resurrection must be the exact opposite of the end or object of sin. Sin produced death; the resurrection cancels out death. It puts an end to the present course and condition of the world, and spells the beginning of a new order of things.

For God to accomplish His ultimate purpose and object for all mankind, He has to raise them from the dead. When we believe on Christ, He cancels our sin; and when we are risen, He cancels the penalty of our sin, death. Our deliverance from sin actually comes in three stages. By Christ's atoning death, He delivers the believer from the guilt of past sin. Through His intercessory life in heaven for us now, He delivers us from the power of sin. And when He comes for us at the resurrection, He will deliver us from the presence of sin, within us and around us.

Although as believers we now possess eternal life, our present experience, in a body doomed to death, is little to be compared to the experience of eternal life in our resurrected body, which will be like Christ's. So embedded in the very structure of our present existence is the sin nature, with all its unholy demands and its contrariness to God's indwelling Spirit, that it is difficult to imagine what it will be like in the hour of our release. To be like Christ—with the motions of sin no longer striving within us; our human nature completely transformed into the likeness of Christ's human nature, so that we shall forever serve, and love, and worship God with an undivided heart—this will truly be heaven and eternal life.

To go back to the question with which we started, "What will become of me?" The man who rejects God's proffered salvation in Christ has no ultimate hope, "but a certain fearful looking for of judgment and fiery indignation" (Heb. 10:27). But the believer in Christ can say with utmost confidence, "Whether we live . . . or die, we are the Lord's" (Rom. 14:8).

WILL THE WICKED DEAD ALSO BE RESURRECTED?

"Then cometh the end, when he shall have delivered up the kingdom to God, even the Father; when he shall have put down all rule and all authority and power" (I Cor. 15:24).

The Bible states that God takes no pleasure in the punishment of the wicked. And in the 15th chapter of First Corinthians we find the Apostle Paul more concerned about the divine purpose to be accomplished in the believers than in what God's ultimate purpose is with regard to unbelievers. That, no doubt, is why he makes no direct mention of the resurrection of unbelievers. Paul makes no diversion from his theme. This, however, should not be construed as meaning that God will not deal with unbelievers.

Throughout this chapter Paul discusses the resurrection of Jesus Christ as being directly responsible, in time and cause, for the resurrection of the believers. He is writing to believers, and therefore he discusses the logical relationship of the bodily resurrection of Christ with the faith of the Christian believers.

He says not a word about the fate of the unbelievers as a consequence of the resurrection of Christ. This was not the direct object of Christ's resurrection; He did not rise that unbelievers might be punished but that believers might be glorified. The unbelievers continue to reap the consequence of their sin inherited from Adam; that is, they "keep on dying"; they continue in their state of separation from God. Christ is not responsible for the death, sin, and punishment of man;

it is Adam who is basically to blame for that. Christ in His office of mediator does not condemn anyone. Unbelievers have been condemned by Adam's sin and continue to condemn themselves through rejecting Him who atoned for their sin, the Lord Jesus Christ. One of the most sublime declarations of Scripture is found in John 3:17, 18: "For God sent not his Son into the world to condemn the world; but that the world through him might be saved. He that believeth on him is not condemned: but he that believeth not is condemned already, because he hath not believed in the name of the only begotten Son of God."

We see, then, that there is no reason for Paul to discuss here either the fact or the time of the resurrection of the unbelievers, since the resurrection of Christ is only indirectly related to their resurrection. They will be raised to continue dying spiritually, to continue in their state of separation from God, and to suffer torment in their resurrected bodies.

The object or end of Christ's resurrection, then, is not punitive and revengeful. The object is positive— the reward and glorification of believers. And even the subjugation of God's enemies will be brought about for the sake of the resurrected believers, so that sin and the perpetrators thereof may not have the upper hand any more. Wicked people and systems are having their day now, but this will no longer be true after the resurrection of the believers. Since this event is the result of Christ's resurrection, the object of resurrecting the believers would be defeated if the wicked were permitted to continue in power. There will most certainly be a basic difference in the conditions that prevail in the period of time that follows the resurrection of the believers.

While it is true that the resurrection of the wicked does not stand out prominently in Scripture, as does the resurrection of the believers, we do have some definite statements about it. That it will be a resurrection unto eternal separation from God, which is eternal death, is apparent from the following Scriptures:

"Marvel not at this," Christ said, "for the hour is coming, in the which all that are in the graves shall hear his voice, and shall come forth; they that have done good, unto the resurrection of life; and they that have done evil, unto the resurrection of damnation" (John 5:28, 29). "There shall be a resurrection of the dead, both of the just and unjust" (Acts 24:15). "And the sea gave up the dead which were in them: and they were judged every man according to their works. And death and hell were cast into the lake of fire. This is the second death. And whosoever was not found written in the book of life was cast into the lake of fire" (Rev. 20:13-15).

The resurrection of the unbelievers unto eternal death actually has no direct relationship with the mediatorial work of Christ, His death and resurrection. But it is indirectly connected with it, as a by-product of what Christ's object is for the believers. What sense is there in rewarding the believers if the unbelievers are also redeemed from the consequences of their unbelief? The Lord can redeem us from the consequences of sin only if by faith we accept His redemption from sin itself.

If you do not commit a crime, the law has no power to punish you. But if you do, it would be most unfair to the law-abiding citizens if you were to go unpunished. The law is not unfair. It follows the only course logically possible. The punishment of sin is the necessary corollary of God's love and justice. If He lets the wicked be annihilated at death, and permits the believers to be resurrected to eternal fellowship with Himself, He is being unfair. He would be giving men a choice to which no penalty is attached, thus discriminating in favor of the law-breaker. For the believer, the just demands of the law have been met in Christ. For the finally impenitent, these have never been met; hence they must continue in a state of punishment.

The justice of God may be illustrated in history by the example of Brutus the Elder, who passed sentence of death upon his own sons for conspiring against their country. While they stood trembling and weeping before him, the father had to consider the greater good— the public welfare and the honor and security of the government. Thus the father was lost in the judge, and the love of justice had to override the natural inclination of a parent to condone the misdeeds of his children. He condemned them to death for the good of the larger number.

Yet this is but a feeble illustration of the justice of God. Though these young Roman traitors died a cruel death, their sufferings were trifling compared to those of the Son of God. They were criminals and deserved to die; He was holy and free from sin. The law and government for which they suffered were insignificant in comparison with God's law and government. And how small was the good of the public in the one case when measured against that of the other.

Then again, as Chrysostom reminds us, many sinners have departed this earthly life without punishment; and many righteous men have died after a lifetime of suffering. If God, therefore, be just, when will He reward the one class and punish the other, if not after death? Scripture teaches that both believers and unbelievers will be raised bodily from the dead for this express purpose.

True, God, being a God of love, does not want to harp on the resurrection of the unbeliever to everlasting punishment. It is not His will that any should perish, but He permits it as a necessary counterpart of the resurrection of the believers. He prefers to emphasize the positive aspect, however. If Christ is lifted up, He says, He will draw all men unto Himself. The "all" in this case refers to all men without discrimination, but not to all men without exception.

This attraction to Christ implies alienation from sin. It is harder to quit sin and to hate evil if you don't have the Lord Jesus Christ to attract you to Himself. The abandonment of sin becomes relatively easy when the Lord Jesus becomes all in all to you.

This is the principle followed by the Apostle Paul. He extols the wonderful privilege of the resurrection of those in Christ so that those in Adam, seeing this, may be motivated to follow Christ, who assures us of a glorious eternal fellowship with Himself.

The resurrection of the wicked, then, is not an act of redemption, as in the case of the believers, but of sovereign justice on the part of God. The resurrection of the just and the unjust has this in common, that in both cases their bodies and souls are reunited. But for the believers this results in perfect life, while for the unbelievers it issues in continued conscious separation from God, which is eternal death.

We recognize that opinions differ as to the time when these resurrections of believers and unbelievers take place, especially in connection with Revelation 20:4 and 5. But since Paul does not refer to the time element here in I Corinthians 15, or even directly refer to the resurrection of unbelievers, we do not feel that we should take up this matter of timing here. What is unmistakably evident from this passage is that the resurrection of the believers and unbelievers will take place at the *parousia*, the "coming" or "presence" of the Lord. Then the object of the resurrection will be accomplished—the triumph of justice and the subjugation of evil, which must necessarily involve the punishment of evil-doers. This must include all evil-doers, dead and alive, the dead necessarily having been raised for the purpose of judgment. In all honesty, this is all that we find in I Corinthians 15:23, 24. We find events described but their timing unspecified.

After all, it is not so very important to know the exact time when these events will take place. The really important question for each of us is, "In which resurrection will I have part—'the resurrection of life' or 'the resurrection of damnation'?" Settle this question now, while by God's grace you still have a voice in the matter.

AFTER THE RESURRECTION, WHAT?

"Then cometh the end, when he shall have deliv-ered up the kingdom to God, even the Father; when he shall have put down all rule and all authority and power" (I Cor. 15:24).

When the Lord Jesus Christ came to earth the first time, over 1900 years ago, He conquered evil in the hearts and lives of those who believed in Him. He still does today. That is why the Christian life is spoken of in Scripture as one of victory. But victory implies the possibility of defeat, of an enemy to be fought. Evil in society at large still continued to make its presence and activity felt, and it still does.

At the second coming of Christ, however, after the believers are resurrected, the final object of God's redemptive work will be accomplished. "Then the end," of which Paul speaks in I Corinthians 15:24, will be seen as the culmination and fulfillment of God's redemption in and through Christ.

In this verse, and continuing on through verse 28, Paul gives a series of accomplishments that will characterize the end or goal of God's redemption in and through Christ. The expression "then the end" is the same as saying, "Then this is what is finally going to take place." Here is the list:

1) "Then cometh the end, when he shall have delivered up the kingdom to God, even the Father;" (v. 24a)

2) "When he shall have put down all rule and all authority and power." (v. 24b)

3) "For he must reign, till he hath put all enemies under his feet." (v. 25)

4) "The last enemy that shall be destroyed is death." (v. 25)

5) "For he hath put all things under his feet." (v. 27a)

6) "Then shall the Son also himself be subject unto him that put all things under him, that God may be all in all." (v. 28b)

In our study of this passage, it is important for us to find out what each of these declarations means and involves.

After the resurrection of believers at the coming of the Lord, the first thing listed here as taking place is the delivering up of the kingdom to God the Father. How soon after the resurrection of believers this will take place, Paul does not tell us. The adverb of time *eita*, "then" or "after, next, thereupon," with which verse 24 begins, places it after the coming of the Lord. Sometimes *eita* denotes consequence and means "and so," "therefore," "accordingly" (Liddell and Scott, p. 498). It is not only chronologically after the resurrection that the kingdom will be delivered to the Father, but the resurrection having been accomplished as the final goal of Christ's redemptive program. If these two events were simultaneous, another Greek adverb would have been used, *tote*, meaning "at that time," which would emphasize the simultaneity to a greater degree.

In order to avoid any possible misunderstanding of this verse, we should translate *eita* as "afterwards" or "thereafter, next." Those events, therefore, that

Paul describes in this passage must not be understood as taking place simultaneously with the *parousia*, the coming of the Lord, and the resurrection of the believers, but after them.

Afterwards comes the end or object that God had in view. The end or object of what? Of Christ's resurrection, no doubt. It does not state this directly, but we may assume it indirectly from verses 24-28. We could summarize their contents in two statements: the subjugation of evil and the delivering up of the Kingdom by the Son to the Father. These are the objectives of the second coming of Christ.

Observe that the word "when" occurs twice in verse 24: "Afterward the end [or object], *when* he shall have delivered up the kingdom to God, even the Father; *when* he shall have put down all rule and all authority and power." Verses 25 through 28 are a further explanation of the two main statements of verse 24.

We must assume that the word *telos*, "end," here has a qualified meaning. One thing is certain—it cannot refer to the termination or annihilation of the world. It is quite evident from these verses that after the second coming of Christ there will still be activity in the world, though under divine control. How could the enemies of Christ, or the world, be annihilated and at the same time have all their rule, authority, and power finally put down? Such a future state indicates a reversal of the state that exists in this present interval of time, prior to the second coming of Christ and the consequent resurrection of believers. In our day unbelievers have the upper hand, permitted to do so by God in His sovereign will and purpose.

Observe how this entire section ends with the statement in verse 28, "That God may be all in all." If everything were to be annihilated or destroyed at this time, as some teach, there would be nothing but void and vacuum. Is it any victory to be king over nothing? How nonsensical to believe that God's ultimate objective is the annihilation of everything, resulting in His rule over nothing!

No, God's victory, the end He has in view, is rather the resurrection of the believers and their reign with Christ, and not merely the reign of Christ in them, as is the case in this age of grace. This was accomplished potentially through Christ's resurrection, but will be made actual and complete after His second coming.

Yes, it is the object of Christ's resurrection that Paul is speaking of in this passage—its ultimate consequences. In this life it gives us a sure and steadfast faith and a hope of our own resurrection to come. His resurrection gives us the certainty that He will come again. And it gives us the expectation of the completion of Christ's mediatorial work and His victory and ours over this evil world and its present authority. This is the many-faceted object of Christ's resurrection, the ultimate fulfillment of His eternal plan of redemption.

Although Christ will come again primarily for the glorification of the believers, His dealings with them necessarily involve a reckoning with the world. Of what use would it be to raise believers to a state of continued subjugation to the world and constant harassment by the forces of evil? The checking of these forces is part and parcel of the blessings of resurrected believers. Just be patient. Evil-doers will not always have the upper hand.

It is said that when the Emperor Julian, who apostatized from a profession of the Christian faith and sought to restore pagan worship, was on the march with his army in the campaign against Persia in the year 363, one of his soldiers who was abusing a Christian said, "Where is your Carpenter now?"

"He is making a coffin for your emperor," was the reply of the Christian.

A few months afterward, Julian received a mortal wound in battle. The rumor spread through the army that the wound had been inflicted by a Christian soldier in the ranks of the Roman army. According to one story, Julian, realizing that his death was near, dipped his hand in the blood of his wound and threw the blood toward heaven, exclaiming as he did so, "Thou hast conquered, O Galilean!"

Yes, the Carpenter of Nazareth, exalted to the right hand of God, is making a coffin for all the kings and kingdoms of this world. One by one they flourish and are gone. But Christ's is an everlasting Kingdom. All that is not obedient to Him will one day be subdued and brought under subjection to Him. They alone shall reign who belong to Him.

THE KINGDOM OF CHRIST—WILL THERE BE AN END TO IT?

"Then cometh the end, when he shall have delivered up the kingdom to God, even the Father; when he shall have put down all rule and all authority and power" (I Cor. 15:24).

Think for a moment of what will happen to you as a believer in Christ, when your life on earth is over. Your soul will go immediately into the presence of the Lord, and your body will "sleep" as it were in the grave until Christ's second coming. It will then be resurrected, and your soul and body will be reunited to dwell in joyous fellowship with the Lord for eternity.

The resurrection of the believers, when Christ comes to earth again, will complete the work for which He became flesh. The only reason for the eternal Christ being born into the world was that He might redeem the world for God the Father. He came to act as the only Mediator between God and man (I Tim. 2:5). In order for Him to do this, He had to be both God and man: God, in order to reconcile the Father with humanity; and man, in order to reconcile humanity with God.

That is exactly what He became, the God-man. As a mere human being, He could not have become the man-God, but as God he could very easily become the God-man. Infinity can at will, and by its own power, take finite form; but finite beings cannot become infinite. The mystery of the incarnation, however, is that Christ became finite without ever ceasing to be the Infinite God, the Son. To accomplish the work of human redemption He had to assume a position of subordination in time and space, but not in eternity and infinity.

After the resurrection of the believers, Scripture states that the Lord will deliver up the "Kingdom" to God the Father. The Kingdom speaks of a task and not of the nature or character of the individual at its head. A king is a human being just like you and me. There are good and bad kings, weak and strong; but they are all rulers, men who have the responsibility of kingship over a group of people.

This is exactly the responsibility our Lord assumed from the moment He came to earth as the Babe of Bethlehem. He was only a helpless infant born in a stable, and yet He defied a king with his armies who tried to kill Him. The object of Christ's earthly kingship will have been accomplished when the believers rise from the dead at His second coming. His distinctive subordinate ministry as Mediator will then come to an end. His resurrection is an omen of ours, "When he shall have delivered up the kingdom to God, even the Father."

What a privilege Paul gives us here of entering upon the holy and mysterious ground of the interrelation of God the Father and God the Son. Each has His own particular task to accomplish in the redemption of man; and yet since Father, Son, and Holy Spirit are one Godhead, their operations cannot be conceived of except as being part and parcel of the task of each.

Here in I Corinthians 15:24 we have a transaction between the Son and the Father. "Then the end" refers to the end or goal of this present age, of this present state of affairs, accomplished as the result of Christ's resurrection followed by the resurrection of the believers. Paul is not so much concerned about the time of the end goal as he is about these two tremendous events that will take place and that will mark the transition from the pre-resurrection to the post-resurrection period.

What is this Kingdom of which Paul speaks? It is not a physical kingdom, as we understand it. Paul completely rejects the physical nature of the Kingdom when he states in verse 50, "Now this I say, brethren, that flesh and blood cannot inherit the kingdom of God; neither doth corruption inherit incorruption." The Kingdom in verse 24 does not refer to territories over which kingly authority is to be exercised, but to *the kingly authority itself.* When we speak of the Kingdom of Great Britain, we immediately think of territories, but not when we speak of the Kingdom over which God the Father or God the Son are the Kings. Christ is not going to deliver up certain dominions to the Father, but He will yield *the right of dominion—* His mediatorial sovereignty. He has rule now over those He has redeemed, the rule not of force but of love. There will come a time, after the resurrection of believers, when He will not need to stand between God the Father and man as the Mediator. The resurrection of the believers will mark the end of His mediatorial responsibility.

How will the Lord Jesus deliver this Kingdom to God the Father? Our verse speaks of a *voluntary termination* of His office as King. And yet the Scriptures declare that the Messiah is to reign for ever and ever.

How else are we to understand Isaiah 9:7, which says, "Of the increase of his government and peace there shall be no end, upon the throne of David, and upon his kingdom, to order it, and to establish it with judgment and with justice from henceforth even for ever"? Daniel also speaks of Messiah's Kingdom when he says, "And in the days of these kings shall the God of heaven set up a kingdom, which shall never be destroyed: and the kingdom shall not be left to other people, but it shall break in pieces and consume all these kingdoms, and it shall stand for ever" (Dan. 2:44). The Angel also clearly announced this to Mary: "Of his kingdom there shall be no end" (Luke 1:33).

Now since the Scriptures speak so consistently of the everlasting nature of Christ's Kingdom, in what sense can He be said to deliver up His Kingdom? Hodge says: "The Scriptures speak of a threefold kingdom as belonging to Christ. 1) That which necessarily belongs to Him as a Divine person, extending over all creatures . . . . 2) That which belongs to Him as the incarnate Son of God, extending over His own people . . . . 3) That dominion to which He was exalted after His resurrection, when all power in heaven and earth was committed to His hands." (See A. A. Hodge's *Systematic Theology*, Vol. II, pp. 594 ff.; 630 ff. Also his *Outlines of Theology*, p. 428.) The first two kingdoms belong to Him eternally. It is this latter kingdom which He now rules as the God-man, which He will voluntarily relinquish when the work of redemption is completed. Headship over this Kingdom was conferred upon Him so that He might mediate salvation to all men until the close of this age of grace. Then, when

He has finally subdued all His enemies, He will no longer reign as Mediator but only as God.

The verb "delivered up" in verse 24 is *paradidoi* in Greek (some readings have *paradidoo*). This is a present subjunctive that is punctiliar in sense, that is, it relates to the element of time. This sense is necessary because of the nature of the act. This delivery of the Kingdom can take place only once, at a time prescribed by God and known only to Him. That is, the act of delivering up the Kingdom will happen at a prescribed time in history. And Christ will do it in His own power and of His own volition.

Again let us emphasize that, as He delivers up His mediatorial authority to the Father, it must be remembered that there was a time when He received it. (See Matt. 28:18.) This has nothing to do with His character but only with His work. No reference is made here to His essential unity with the Father and the Holy Spirit. His mediatorial sovereignty is not from everlasting to everlasting. It had its beginning in time, while He Himself has no beginning and no end, nor does the benevolence of His character. On the cross the Lord cried out to His Father, "It is finished." The same words would seem to be appropriate when He presents the resurrected saints to His Father, as if saying, "The task of redemption, not only of the soul but also of the body, is finally accomplished."

Is Christ King of your life now? Not merely, do you believe in Him as your Saviour from sin? That is the minimal and initial requirement for entrance into His Kingdom. But does He have dominion over your complete personality, so that you have no wish to escape His rule, but cry out, "O Jesus, subdue me more completely! Drive out all my old enemies! Root out my sins! In the entire kingdom of my nature, over my whole spirit, soul, and body, be Thou the supreme and only Lord, and let no rebellion be so much as thought of." But it is only the grace of God — the mighty love of God in Christ Jesus—that can subdue your spirit to the dominion of Christ. For what He has done so far in our lives, let us praise Him; and in any respect that His will in us is not fully accomplished, let us cry to Him to complete it.

(See *The Treasury of the Old Testament*, by C. H. Spurgeon, p. 52.)

THE TIME WHEN CHRIST WILL NO LONGER BE MEDIATOR

"Then cometh the end, when he shall have delivered up the kingdom to God, even the Father; when he shall have put down all rule and all authority and power" (I Cor. 15:24).

"Christ was once offered to bear the sins of many," the Scriptures tell us; "and unto them that look for him shall he appear the second time without sin unto salvation" (Heb. 9:28). What salvation is this? Not that of the soul, for when Christ appears a second time it will be too late for anyone to receive Him as Saviour from sin and its consequences. No, the Bible is referring here to the salvation of the body, as well as salvation from the oppression of evil to which we are now subject, even as believers.

After this, Jesus Christ will deliver up His Kingdom to God the Father. This can take place only once, at a time prescribed by Him and known by Him alone. Matthew 11:27 and Luke 10:22 throw light on this, indicating that the Son was given a task to perform by the Father that is now formally accomplished. The Lord said, "All things are delivered [*paredothee*—the same Greek verb as in I Cor. 15:24, but in the second aorist, which indicates punctiliar action in time and space] unto me of my Father: and no man knoweth the Son, but the Father; neither knoweth any man the Father, save the Son, and he to whomsoever the Son will reveal him." The Lord then delivers up that which He received, and that was the work of revealing the

Father. That task will be completed when believers are ushered into the very presence of the Father God, after their resurrection. Is it not true that the revelation we have of God now is partial because of the limitations of our sinful bodies? This limitation the resurrection will eliminate.

That this delivery is punctiliar and not progressive is also supported by the tense of the next verb, *katargeesee*, which is in the aorist, *"When he shall have put down* [or rendered idle] *all rule and all authority and power."* This is to happen at an instant of time and will be consequent to the coming of the Lord.

Christ is still King of His own throughout eternity, but in a different way than He was prior to their resurrection. During their earthly lives, the redeemed of the Lord were told that the only approach to the Father was through the High Priest, the Lord Jesus Christ. His kingship was that of protection, of shielding from the overpowering of the enemy. But this enemy is now subdued, and therefore the protection of Christ as King is not needed any more. Observe that these two events referred to are related. "When he shall have delivered up the kingdom to God, even the Father; when he shall have put down all rule and all authority and power." The second event explains why the first is possible. If the enemies of the believers were permitted to exercise their authority, the Lord Jesus would have continued His kingship of protection against them.

The Authorized Version correctly translates the aorist *katargeesee*, "shall put down," with the sense of an English future-perfect tense, "When he shall have put down." The first is possible because of the second.

The Kingdom would not have been delivered to God the Father if the enemies of God and the unbelievers had not been utterly subdued. When evil is completely overruled, Christ is not needed to play the role of Mediator any longer.

This is a wonderful declaration of the essential difference in our present bodies, so vulnerable to sin, and our future post-resurrection bodies, which will not be subject to sin or evil. Christ needs to be King now to give us victory, but then victory will be inherent in our glorified bodies and characters. This spells the end of the struggle against sin and evil. They shall no more dwell in our mortal bodies. This is one of the main differences between our mortal and our immortal bodies. Evil will be conquered within us and outside of us.

Christ in His mediatorial state is presented as having a Kingdom of His very own here, which we could call the Kingdom of the Son. As G. Campbell Morgan says, "There is a distinction . . . between the Kingdom of God and the Kingdom of the Son of His love. When we speak of 'the Kingdom of God' we speak of the fundamental fact of His kingship and of that kingship exercised. When we speak of 'the Kingdom of the Son' we think of that within the Kingdom of God which needed redemption and which the Son redeems. The Kingdom of the Son is always the redeemed Kingdom. It is in that sense that the apostle declares that He must reign till He hath put all His enemies under His feet. . . . Christ reigns in order to put an end to Sin and in order to put an end to Death." ("The Christian Empire," in *The Christian World Pulpit*, Vol. 90, pp. 290-3.)

What amazes us as we read the New Testament is the unique intimate relationship existing in eternity between the Three Persons of the Triune God. To whom does the Lord Jesus deliver the Kingdom? To God the Father. This task of redemption of the human race was not one which the Lord Jesus one day found Himself worthy of handling and to which He was thereafter assigned the responsibility. That's what usually happens with us. Who of us can say the very moment that our son is born, "Here is a boy who is going to be President, who is going to lead a certain kind of life, and accomplish certain specific tasks"? The suitability of the personality to the task is something that cannot be foretold. Experience brings the two together. After a person proves himself to possess certain abilities, he is assigned a task.

Nor can it be said of any one of us that our knowledge of our son or of our father is thus perfect and intimate. This is a relationship unique to deity. Jesus demonstrated such self-consciousness and intimacy with His Father that it carries great conviction with it. He knew well what He was saying; it all comes with ready spontaneity. He had a deep personal knowledge of the Father and was aware that the Father had the same intimate knowledge of Him. It was not a knowledge that He had acquired in this life by a certain course of moral and spiritual discipline, a knowledge, therefore, to which others might attain. It was a knowledge that He had brought with Him into the world, a knowledge, therefore, that no human being could obtain except through Him.

It was a unique relation between Him and the Father; as Father and Son they were so related that no human being could lay claim to share the intimacy. Here we are face to face with a fact that, revealed in time, yet lies in eternity. God is Father and Son. The Divine Being involves also a relation between Father and Son. The Son did not begin to be, but always was. Before all worlds, before any creature was made, God in His absolute self-completeness was Father and Son, and, as we see in other Scripture, Holy Spirit.

Although no one can predict what human babies will grow up to be, with the Lord Jesus it was uniquely different. At the very time He was announced as coming into the world, we were told by God what He was going to be—a Saviour, a King, the Redeemer. There was a uniquely intimate knowledge of the humanly unpredictable between God the Father and God the Son. So that there would be no misunderstanding about this eternal relationship between the Father and the Son, Paul does not merely say, "When he shall have delivered up the kingdom to God, *even* the Father." The word "even" in Greek is *kai*, the primary meaning of which is "and." "Remember," Paul seems to say to us, "that the eternal relationship between these two persons of the Trinity is that of Father and Son. He is not only God but also Father, the Father of the Lord Jesus Christ, in the assignment and prediction of His ability to carry on the task of human redemption."

Listen to the Lord Jesus Himself speak of this eternal unique relationship of Son-Father: "I thank thee, O Father, Lord of heaven and earth, because thou hast hid these things from the wise and prudent, and hast revealed them unto babes. Even so, Father: for so it seemed good in thy sight. All things are delivered unto me of my Father: and no man knoweth the Son, but the Father; neither knoweth any man the Father, save the Son, and he to whomsoever the Son will reveal him" (Matt. 11:25-27. See also Luke 10:21, 22). But observe that the invitation to the weary sons of men comes immediately after this assertion of the Son-Father relationship. "Come unto me, all ye that labour and are heavy laden, and I will give you rest" (Matt. 11:28). This indicates the distinct responsibility and ability of the Son of God to give rest to weary man, to redeem his soul. The mutual knowledge of the Father and the Son, and the common and yet separate responsibilities in the redemption of man, are of such kind that no creature can meddle with them. If any man comes to know the Father, it is only by the will of the Son who makes the revelation.

Could any man make such a claim? If the best and the greatest man that ever lived had maintained that he had an exclusive knowledge of the Father, and that no man could know the Father except by him, we should still consider him a religious maniac. That is the dilemma in which Jesus has always placed us by His language—between His being God or a monomaniac. If that dilemma is rightly stated, no sane person can hesitate between the alternatives. No matter how great a skeptic you are, it is easier and more reasonable to accept Him as God than as a deluded megalomaniac.

(See R. F. Horton, *The Trinity*, Horace Marshall & Son, London, 1901, pp. 39-54.)

CAN MEN MAKE THIS A GOOD WORLD?

"Then cometh the end, when he shall have delivered up the kingdom to God, even the Father; when he shall have put down all rule and all authority and power" (I Cor. 15:24).

How would you like to rule the world? Most of us would throw up our hands in horror at the idea. We may be only too eager to criticize the powers that be, but don't ask us to take on any of the responsibility of government.

Yet we know that there are some men in our own day—as there have been in every age—whose ambition to rule the world is evident in all they say and do. However, up till now, no ruler, king, or despot has ever succeeded in gaining control of the whole earth. Some, like Alexander the Great, did succeed for a time in extending their rule to most of the civilized world as they knew it; but the greater portion of the globe still eluded them.

As for controlling nature, they had to own defeat. Even today, though man has harnessed the elements in many ways, such a simple, soft, and silent thing as snow can cripple transportation and slow down the wheels of industry.

Then again, the power of these rulers could not extend beyond the limits of one lifetime, for death finally became king and robbed them of their rule and authority. Nor was it ever heard that a conquering king or dictator voluntarily relinquished his empire to a successor while he could still keep his hands on the reins.

Is it not a further evidence of the deity of Christ, then, that at His second coming, after He has raised the dead, and subdued all earthly powers and the evil that is in the world, He will voluntarily deliver up His Kingdom to the Father? Jesus Christ is both human and divine. As a human being, He is not power-hungry, because He has always been Almighty God, who has no need to make Himself greater than He is. His mediatorial Kingdom, over which He began to reign during His earthly lifetime, and over which He still reigns, is merely an assignment in time and space; and once He has accomplished the purpose of this assignment He will quit it, having no wish to continue in the glory of its accomplishment.

This Kingdom is like a gift which the Son will deliver to the Father. In fact, the verb *paradidoomi*, translated "deliver up" in I Corinthians 15:24, comes from the root verb *didoomi*, meaning "to give." It is from this verb that the substantives *dooron* and *dosis*, "gift," are derived. What a wonderful thought—that Christ, who is called God's gift to us in John 3:16, should redeem us by His blood and then return us to God the Father as a gift, pure and cleansed from all unrighteousness.

When the Lord comes again, He will not only deliver the Kingdom to God the Father, but He will also put an end to "all rule and all authority and power." The grammatical structure of the two main verbs in this verse (*paradidoi*, "deliver," and *katargeesee*, "put down") indicates that the second event precedes the first. The Lord Jesus will not deliver the Kingdom to the Father until He has "put down all rule and all authority and power."

Although *katargeesee* is translated "put down" in the Authorized Version, the literal meaning of the verb is "abolish, render inactive or idle." It is made up of the preposition *kata*, "down," and *argos*, "inactive."

The evil powers of the world have been active since the time of Adam and his sin. They do not have the upper hand and ultimate victory in the lives of born-again believers in Christ, but they are constantly battling for the supremacy. In this stage of our history, before our resurrection, we are constantly experiencing the activity of evil and, by God's grace, achieving victory over it. But after our resurrection, evil will have been rendered inactive. We will not yield to temptation, for temptation will no longer assail us. That will be a glorified state of the supremacy of good, of the Lord, of holiness and righteousness.

Now no man or federation of men can bring about such a state of perfection. Only Christ can do it. The verb *katargeesee*, "put down" or "abolish," is in the active voice. Paul does not say, "when all rule and all authority and power shall be abolished," but "when he shall abolish all rule and all authority and power." This is Christ's work, His accomplishment. Your efforts and mine in this world, commendable and necessary as they are, would never usher in the great day when evil is abolished. No matter how great we may manage to make our society, we can never purify it from the defilement of evil. Some men may even call a society "great," when the greatness is that of uncontrollable evil rather than of all-pervasive good.

The United States will remain a great nation only as long as it continues to assure all men of their rights under God. When it begins to give license to evil, to set the purveyors of evil and crime free to prey on the innocent and law-abiding, and assure all men of their rights under the devil, it will no longer be a great power for good but a power for corruption.

As believers in Christ we fight evil now; we resist it; but we cannot abolish it. Only Christ can subdue the power of evil now, especially in the lives of those who receive Him as Saviour and Redeemer. Paul sounds this triumphant note of victory in Romans 8:33-37, when he says, "Who shall bring any charge against God's elect? It is God who justifies; who is to condemn? It is Christ Jesus, who died, yes, who was raised from the dead, who is at the right hand of God, who indeed intercedes for us. Who shall separate us from the love of Christ? Shall tribulation, or distress, or persecution, or famine, or nakedness, or peril, or sword? . . . No, in all these things we are more than conquerors through him who loved us."

Yes, Christ rules in a very real sense, and the rule of evil in this unbelieving world is not ordained by Him but only tolerated in this dispensation of grace. Read Ephesians 1:19-23 and take heart in your struggle against evil. "That ye may know . . . what is the exceeding greatness of his power to us-ward who believe, according to the working of his mighty power, which he wrought in Christ, when he raised him from the dead, and set him at his own right hand in the heavenly places, far above all principality, and power, and might, and dominion, and every name that is named, not only in this world, but also in that which is to come: and hath put all things under his feet, and gave him to be the head over all things to the church, which is his body, the fulness of him that filleth all in all." This is the present rule of the risen Christ in the lives of the believers. He has His foot upon evil and evil-doers.

Observe that Paul states the ultimate abolition of evil *after* he has argued about the certainty of the resurrection of the Lord Jesus. The resurrection of Jesus Christ is the keystone in that arch of truth over which the souls of redeemed men pass to the possession of joy, honor, incorruption, and eternal life. Remove the keystone and the whole arch crumbles to the dust, and the dark valley of the shadow of death remains an impassible gulf between heaven and earth.

The resurrection of Christ's dead body is one of the most striking evidences and displays of power that we can imagine. What power did all our scientific know-how have over the assassinated body of a recent President of the United States? Crush the smallest insect that crawls in the dust; put out that tiny spark of vitality; and you have caused irreparable damage. Not all the universe, apart from the Divine Creator, can undo it. No wonder, then, that Paul refers to the resurrection of Jesus Christ as a grand display of omnipotence in executing God's final designs and purposes.

Take heart then; evil will not always triumph. The end is not yet. ". . . at his coming. Then cometh the end . . . when he shall have put down all rule and all authority and power."

CAN MAN PREDICT THE FUTURE COURSE OF HISTORY?

"Then cometh the end, when he shall have delivered up the kingdom to God, even the Father; when he shall have put down all rule and all authority and power" (I Cor. 15:24).

Where is Christ now? "Dead as a doornail," says the atheist. "His soul is in heaven, but we do not know what has become of His body," answers the member of a certain sect. But what does God's Word say? In Ephesians 1:19-21, the Apostle Paul speaks of "the working of his [God's] mighty power, which he wrought in Christ, when he raised him from the dead, and set him at his own right hand in the heavenly places, far above all principality, and power, and might, and dominion, and every name that is named, not only in this world, but also in that which is to come."

Here the Apostle advances another step. He speaks of the power of God as displayed in the exaltation of Christ. Now, we must be careful, when the Scriptures speak of something done by or for Christ, to find out to which of His two complex natures they refer, His humanity or His deity. The honor here mentioned as being conferred upon Christ cannot refer to His divine nature, which is incapable of further exaltation. No additional honor can be put upon God. Paul is not speaking of Christ's deity here, but of His humanity, and especially as it stands connected with the event constituting His complex role of God-man Mediator.

We must at all times bear in mind the three states of existence of our Lord Jesus Christ, as revealed in Philippians 2:6-11.

1) "Who, being in the form of God, thought it not robbery to be equal with God." This refers to Christ's antecedent and eternal existence as God.

2) "But made himself of no reputation, and took upon him the form of a servant, and was made in the likeness of men: and being found in fashion as a man, he humbled himself, and became obedient unto death, even the death of the cross." This speaks of His subsequent state of existence in His humiliation as "a man of sorrows, and acquainted with grief" (Isa. 53:3).

3) "Wherefore God also hath highly exalted him, and given him a name which is above every name: that at the name of Jesus every knee should bow." This tells of the state arising out of His humiliation, in which He is exalted as God-man, Mediator, Governor of the world. This text in Ephesians refers precisely to this subsequent state of exaltation of our Lord Jesus Christ, consequent on His humiliation, and as the reward of His sufferings: "which he [God] wrought in Christ, when he raised him from the dead, and set him at his own right hand in heavenly places" (Eph. 1:20).

Of course, this language is partly figurative, since God is a Spirit and has neither a right hand nor a left. His "right hand" here simply means the place of honor. Scripture refers to Christ's position of honor at God's right hand in numerous passages.

Let us look for a moment at the reference in Hebrews 1:3, which speaks of Christ as being "the brightness of his [God's] glory, and the express image of his person, and upholding all things by the word of his power," who, "when he had by himself purged our sins, sat down on the right hand of the Majesty on high." Christ as our great High Priest sprinkled His own blood on the mercy seat as the ground of our reconciliation with God. But no earthly high priest offering animal sacrifices would have dared or presumed to sit upon the mercy seat within the holy of holies. Only Jesus Christ could rightfully take His seat there, as it were, and be enthroned as the universal Lord and Intercessor on behalf of His people.

There, at God's right hand, Christ now mediates salvation to all who will come to the Father by Him. There He now rules and overrules, "far above all principality, and power, and might, and dominion, and every name that is named, not only in this world, but also in that which is to come," for God "hath put all things under his feet, and gave him to be the head over all things to the church" (Eph. 1:21, 22).

Yes, even now Christ is Lord of all. Where good triumphs, it is He who has brought it to pass; and where evil designs flourish, He makes even these serve to further His ultimate purposes. As Head over all things to the Church, He has made it the end, the object, the purpose of His sitting upon the mediatorial throne. Its preservation is His dearest care. In this world of sin and death, only His omnipotent strength can keep the Church alive. Despite persecution, martyrdoms, ridicule, and slander, the Church has risen from the ashes of each fresh holocaust, strengthened and invigorated by the Head of which she is the body. The life of the Church is one of increase; and it will continue to increase through the outpouring of Christ's Spirit in and through it.

Yes, Christ is now upon the throne, and "he must reign, till he hath put all enemies under his feet" (I Cor. 15:25). God in the Scriptures has laid open the secrets of the future world to us. He has told us that Christ is Head over all things to His Church, and therefore the Church must ultimately triumph in Him.

Apart from the Bible, who can tell us what the future course of history will be? No one denies that society is progressing intellectually; but was not Greece intellectual—and Rome? And did not their moral laxity sap their vitality and do much to plunge them into the Dark Ages, never fully to regain their greatness? There is no necessary connection between science and virtue, as witness the destructive uses to which man puts some of his inventions. There is no necessary connection between the arts and moral improvement, as witness the hopeless anarchy that has virtually taken over all forms of artistic expression today. Where does it all end? Apart from the Bible, who can say? But we know that Christ is "Head over all things to the church," and therefore all this will one day end in the glories of the millennium and the universal reign of our Saviour.

This world is not ruled by blind chance, or by the counsels of men, but by the eternal hand of God, guiding all things to the fulfillment of His eternal and benevolent purposes. However dark and contrary your circumstances, never doubt that, if you are a member of the body of Christ through faith in Him as your

Saviour and Redeemer, He is ruling and overruling for your ultimate good.

"But now we see not yet all things put under him" the author of Hebrews tells us (2:8). This is the time of our testing, when we endure "as seeing him who is invisible" (Heb. 11:27). This is that period of which Peter speaks when he says, "Now for a season, if need be, ye are in heaviness through manifold temptations: that the trial of your faith, being much more precious than of gold that perisheth, though it be tried with fire, might be found unto praise and honour and glory at the appearing of Jesus Christ" (I Pet. 1:6, 7).

All this sheds light on Paul's affirmation in I Corinthians 15:24 and 25 that there will be an "end"—a goal or object to which all Christians look forward—when Christ "shall have delivered up the kingdom [i.e., His mediatorial reign] to God, even the Father; when he shall have put down all rule and all authority and power. For he must reign [as Mediator, as God-man] till he hath put all enemies under his feet."

"Wherefore lift up the hands which hang down, and the feeble knees" (Heb. 12:12). Take courage, for there shall be a "removing of those things that are shaken, as of things that are made, that those things which cannot be shaken may remain. Wherefore we receiving a kingdom which cannot be moved, let us have grace whereby we may serve God acceptably with reverence and godly fear" (Heb. 12:27, 28).

(See "Our Risen Lord," by John Angell James, in *The Pulpit*, Vol. LXIX, pp. 365-71.)

WILL EVIL EVER BE FINALLY DEFEATED?

"Then cometh the end, when he shall have deliv-ered up the kingdom to God, even the Father; when he shall have put down all rule and all authority and power" (I Cor. 15:24).

A favorite theme of the so-called comic books is that of some sinister super-power that seeks to en-slave the world, and its defeat by some superman who foils its evil designs and rescues its innocent victims. This same plot, in more sophisticated form, is the basis for much adult reading and television viewing also.

The public appetite for this sort of fare reflects an underlying feeling that much of life is indeed threatened by forces that would destroy us. It also reflects the longing for a champion and deliverer with whom good men can identify.

The sad part of it is that people will get a vicarious satisfaction out of these fictitious episodes of goodness overcoming evil, yet reject the only valid Champion of righteousness who can conquer the forces of evil in the real world.

When Scripture tells us that Christ "must reign, till he hath put all enemies under his feet," it is offer-ing us the assurance that Christ will spare none of the empire of evil. The writers of the New Testament knew how highly organized it was then, and we know how it is still trying to get the upper hand. The Apostle Paul lived under the most appalling conditions of hu-man government. Think of Rome, Corinth, and Athens. They were centers of such unnameable corruptions as are not to be matched today in any city of the world. The Apostle clearly saw behind the material manifestations the dark spiritual forces. "We wrestle not against flesh and blood," he wrote (Eph. 6:12). We have to deal with the dark and sinister system of evil that lies at the back of this material corruption; with the principalities and the powers, under the inspiration and domination of which these evil things of the flesh result. That was the apostolic outlook, and here Paul gives us a most accurate description of the whole organized empire of evil in the words "rule, authority, power." This is not a case of using three words where one would suffice. The three are necessary if we are to understand the conditions that exist in this world. Let us take them in order:

The first is "rule," *archee* in Greek. This has reference to the central mind and will and hate governing all the forces of evil. The verb *archoo* means "to be first," and *archoon* denotes a ruler. You can see from this how there also arose the idea of a beginning, the origin, the active cause, whether a person or thing. (See Col. 1:18 and John 1:1.) In the sense of "dominion" or "force," *archee* is always coupled with *exousia*, "authority," in the New Testament. (The single exception is Jude 6.) In Luke 12:11 and Titus 3:1 it denotes the secular or spiritual authorities, and in Luke 20:20 it denotes the official power of the Roman procurator.

According to Kittel (*Theological Dictionary of the New Testament*, pp. 483-4) the reference of *archai* (rulers) is perhaps to supraterrestrial and demonic powers which are subdued by the Messiah, and which cannot therefore hurt the people of God any more. They are spiritual beings (Eph. 6:12), related to angels (Rom. 8:38). In the plan of creation they were originally meant to be good spirits and were created as such (Col. 1:16). Their abode is now in the lowest of the heavenly spheres, from which darkness comes into this world.

These powers of the air have separated God and man until the coming of Christ. They believed that with the rejection of the human race by God they would become unconditional governors of the world, until God's original plan of salvation was disclosed in and with the resurrection of Christ. But this government of the world never became absolutely theirs. By the crucifixion of Christ they have been deprived of what power they had. The wall of partition, which their limited power over the world implied, has been broken down. Christ has completely subjected them to Himself. He has now been revealed as their Lord, as He has been from the very first as their Creator.

This does not mean, Kittel's Dictionary goes on to say, that their active power is completely destroyed as yet. Man is still engaged in continuing conflict with them, practically speaking. They are not merely behind those who threaten Christians for their faith; they are also behind all moral temptations. Yet they cannot decisively affect the relationship between the Christian and God, and in the end they will be stripped of all their influence.

To Paul this was not merely an abstract idea. He was not foolish enough to imagine that thought can operate without personality. This was the devil, or

Satan, that first deceiver, and all his demons, operating in the world today. He was the cause of man's fall that necessitated the incarnation of the Word (*Logos*) for the ultimate redemption of man. He is a spiritual being establishing his rule wherever he can, through influencing man's intelligence, mind, and will, though his activities are constantly being frustrated by God. He is active but providentially held in check by God.

The second word of this trilogy of "rule, authority, power" is *exousia* in Greek, meaning "authority." It comes from the impersonal verb *exesti*, "it is lawful." From the meaning of permission or liberty to do as one pleases, it passed to that of the ability or strength with which one is endued, then to that of the power of authority, *the right to exercise power*. In other words, the word "authority" in this context describes those to whom is committed the executive application of the rule, the higher command, those who carry out the purpose of the central mind, will, and hate in the spiritual world.

In the New Testament the word *exousia* denotes the power of God in nature and the spiritual world. This is the word that is used in I Corinthians 15:24. Since all *exousia* or power over nature and the spiritual world belongs to God and is given to others by God, it follows that any power that Satan may have is only by God's sufferance. The great wonder here is that the power of evil, which is radically hostile to God, may be exercised as such and yet be encompassed by the divine overruling. "Ye thought evil against me," said Joseph to his brethren, "but God meant it unto good" (Gen. 50:20). And although it is said of Antichrist that the dragon has given him his power, nevertheless further statements of Scripture imply that the time when Antichrist is given a free hand is decided by God, so that even the rule of the Antichrist does not take place apart from the will of God. (See Kittel, Vol. II, pp. 566-74.)

The last word, *dunamin*, "power," means ability, physical or moral, as residing in a person or thing. It may also then come to signify *power in action*, which is the meaning in this context. It covers in this verse the whole of the rank and file that constitute the means by which that authority is executed.

Rule, Authority, Power! In these words the sinister organization of the underworld of evil is in view, both in the spiritual and material realms. Paul says that Christ must reign as King till He has abolished all these evil things.

Of course, all three words may have a good as well as a bad meaning. Here we see them used to signify evil rule, evil authority, evil power, since immediately in the next verse they are called Christ's enemies.

The word "all" (*pasan*), although used before "rule" and "authority" only, is to be understood as applying to the word "power" also. *Pasan*, when used of a number, means "all," and when used of several persons or items in a number means "every," like the Greek *hekastos*. (*Greek-English Lexicon*, Liddell-Scott, p. 1160.) Paul wants to impress upon us here that every one of these evil rules, authorities, and powers will be completely abolished as to doing any more evil as a result of Christ's returning to earth. Your mind may focus upon some evil that seems irremovable, but it will go, it will be rendered inactive, no matter what it is. This means not only each one individually, but all of them together. No evil is great enough to stand in His presence and exercise its power; and all of them collectively will not avail before the Lord of Hosts.

Where is all this to take place, in heaven or on earth? The answer is obvious. It must be on earth, for in heaven there are no evil rules, authorities, or powers to abolish, no enemies of Christ to subdue. We have indicated previously that the grammatical construction of the verbs in Greek places this abolishing of evil before the time when Christ delivers up the Kingdom to the Father. Could it be that the abolition of evil pertains to earth, and the delivery of the Kingdom to heaven?

Although Paul does not concern himself with the place or time of these events, Revelation 20:4-6 points to a prescribed period of a thousand years during which Christ and His resurrected saints, along with those caught up in the air with Him at His coming, shall reign with Him on earth. Such a reign involves the abolition of evil and the subjugation of Christ's enemies. This can take place only where they exist — on earth.

You who yearn for justice now, who hunger and thirst after a world in which righteousness reigns, lift up your heads, for the coming of the Lord draws ever nearer. The wrongs you are helpless to right, He will redress.

Though the cause of evil prosper,
Yet 'tis truth alone is strong;
Though her portion be the scaffold,

And upon the throne be wrong,
Yet that scaffold sways the future,
And, behind the dim unknown,
Standeth God within the shadow
Keeping watch above His own.

IS CHRIST REALLY REIGNING NOW?

"For he must reign, till he hath put all enemies under his feet" (I Cor. 15:25).

A father who had to go on a long journey was concerned lest his two small children forget him. His wife suggested that they hang a large portrait of him in the living room, where the children could see it every day. En route, he sent home picture postcards with loving messages, as well as occasional small gifts. In all his notes he would say, "When Daddy comes home, he will tell you more about this," and also hinted at a wonderful surprise he would be bringing them. Needless to say, the children looked forward with anticipation to his coming.

On the day of his return, the children looked from him to the picture and back again. Then they ran into his open arms with unaffected joy, crying out, "Daddy's home!" He had been an important factor in their lives all the time he was gone; his headship over the home and his love for them had been emphasized by his letters and gifts; and they had looked forward to his return for the fulfillment of his promises. His "surprise" gift brought forth cries of delight. Now that he was with them, their fullest hopes were realized.

This is just an imperfect illustration from life of the present and future state of the Christian. We, too, as children of the Heavenly Father, look forward to the day when Christ will return to keep His promise to redeem our bodies from the grave and to abolish all evil, both visible and invisible.

But how can we tolerate the activity of the forces of evil now? If the power that is going to act in the future is not fully in control here and now, how can we be certain of our hope of that future? Is Christ reigning here and now? The unequivocal answer of the Apostle Paul is given in I Corinthians 15:25. "For he must reign, till he hath put all enemies under his feet." What does he mean by this triumphant declaration, as exuberant and certain as his proclamation concerning the resurrection, "But now is Christ risen from the dead"?

"For he must reign!" According to Jelf (*A Grammar of the Greek Language*, p. 490), the conjunction *gar*, translated "for" in English, that connects verse 24 with verse 25, suggests a sort of reason or ground for that which precedes. In other words, Christ must reign now, if He is ultimately to reign so triumphantly as for evil to be rendered completely inactive. He is not now in retreat as one who has been temporarily defeated but who will at some future date recover from His weakness and manage to gain the upper hand. If He is to triumph at His coming, after the resurrection of the believers, He must be triumphant now.

He has always been triumphant in ways that He chooses to be. Any seeming defeat is not due to impotence but to His permissiveness in His omnipotence. The triumphs of Christ, present and future, as Mediator and coming King, are not triumphs of effort but of choice. The type of absolute rule that He will impose at His coming He could impose here and now if He wanted to; but He chooses to be triumphant in a different way now. He allows the activity of evil, along with the triumph of individual believers over evil influences through His enabling power. Every truly redeemed child of God knows that Christ can here and now enable him to triumph over evil, for greater is He that is in us than he who is in the world (I John 4:4).

As an example of this, out of the thousands of letters from readers of the Gospel messages published in Greek newspapers by American Mission to Greeks, a few are selected for personal contacts. "There was nothing particular in one letter to urge me to go," commented one of the missionaries, "but I felt a prompting of the Holy Spirit. The man who had written the letter was not at home, but I met his sister-in-law.

"This woman listened to me with such absorption that her cigarette lay forgotten in the ash tray. Finally she burst out, 'It was God who sent you here today to prevent me from taking a tragic step! I was about to go to my husband's office to shoot him and then myself, but the message of Christ's love and grace has softened my heart. Yes, it was God who sent you here at the right moment. Oh, thank you so much!' "

Satan had entered into this woman's heart, but the Word of God defeated him and delivered another soul from darkness to light. Yes, Christ who will triumph over all rule, authority, and power at His second coming is triumphant now; but this triumph, by His own choice, is of a different kind.

Secondly, as the Christian looks in and around him, at the victories of Christ in his own experience and in history, he is able to conclude that the One who is victorious now cannot but score an ultimate victory over His enemies and evil in general. This is the hope of all Christians. Evil and Satan do not now have the upper hand in the life of the Christian. They are defeated enemies here and now. And this assures us that their defeat will eventually be complete.

The Christian may know failure, but he also knows that, because of the interceding and indwelling Christ, no failure is final. As he sinks to his knees and cries out, "Who shall deliver me?" he can add with Paul, "Thanks be to God, which giveth us the victory" (I Cor. 15:57). As J. Hudson Taylor eloquently expressed it, "We are a supernatural people, born again by a supernatural birth; we wage a supernatural fight and are taught by a supernatural teacher, led by a supernatural captain to assured victory."

> I cannot do it alone;
>   The waves run fast and high,
> And the fogs close all around,
>   The light goes out in the sky;
> But I know that we two
>   Shall win in the end,
>   Jesus and I.
>
> I could not guide it myself,
>   My boat on life's wild sea;
> There's one who sits by my side,
>   Who pulls and steers with me.
> And I know that we two
>   Shall safe enter port,
>   Jesus and I.

How do we know that Christ has been reigning all through history? What evidence do we have? The first evidence is that of changed lives. If the forces of evil now really have the upper hand, how do you explain the lives defiled by sin that have been snatched from the enemy's hand and transformed into living miracles? How explain the "about-face" of drunkards, murderers, drug addicts, the morally impure, persecutors of the Church, atheists, and slaves to every sin you can name, because of their confrontation with Jesus Christ? When philosophy has succeeded in making a reputable or admirable moral character, it has always started with a respectable subject. The power of Christ, on the other hand, has succeeded in the case of the lowest and most debased of mankind. He is able to save to the uttermost all who come to God by Him.

What a glorious roll of apostles, saints, and martyrs have testified to Christ's power down through the ages—a great multitude that no man can number, out of all tribes and peoples and nations and tongues, who have come up out of the stained and broken lives of earth, and have washed their robes white in the blood of the Lamb. What a contrast Christ's multitude of transformed lives presents to the meager scroll of the upright men of pagan philosophy. Marcus Aurelius, Seneca, and Socrates have been worn out with having to do duty as the shining examples of the power of philosophy. There is almost no stock on the shelves behind the samples in the pagan show-case of virtue.

AN UNCHANGING REMEDY FOR THE ILLS OF A CHANGING WORLD

◄▬►

"For he must reign, till he hath put all enemies under his feet" (I Cor. 15:25).

Not too long ago, the accepted treatment for a child with a fever was to put him to bed, dose him with aspirin, and give him plenty of liquids. A grandmother of my acquaintance was horrified the other day when the pediatrician ordered her little grandson, who had a temperature of 104, to be placed in a tub of cold water at intervals until his fever broke; and meanwhile not to confine him to bed, but to let him run around clad only in his underclothes. She was sure such treatment would induce pneumonia.

Whether this is a good method for treating fever or not, I am not qualified to say. But I think I can safely predict that in a few years something new will be tried out, and the old methods discarded.

In the last two thousand years of the world's history, human theories of all kinds have undergone tremendous changes. Science has reversed its dogmas time and again, and is still in the process of rejection and change. Philosophies have come and gone; social and political ideas have altered with the times. But in the midst of this great change, the message of the Gospel of Christ remains substantially unchanged. It is the same message today as when it was first proclaimed to the world.

How do we know that Christ has been reigning down through the ages? Because His power and message have remained triumphantly unchanged and effective throughout nearly 2,000 years. Of course, many men have tried to change that message, and some are proclaiming a new Gospel under the old name of Christianity. But like the changing styles in fashion, these false Gospels are discarded along with the changing fancies of men. Every attempt to change the message of Christ has met with the same fate. Centuries ago the Gospel was declared obsolete, yet here am I—in company with countless other Christian believers— proclaiming it still. And if our world should exist for thousands of years to come, I believe that the messengers of Christ will then be preaching this very Gospel of the resurrected Christ that I am preaching today. "Heaven and earth shall pass away," said the Lord Jesus, "but my words shall not pass away" (Matt. 24:35).

Yes, Christ has been reigning in the world for all these centuries, and He will continue to reign in the days to be. How do we know?

First, because His message alone has power to redeem the moral failure of this world. Man is in need of salvation to the very core of his being. He is guilty and needs an all-sufficient atonement for his sin. He is separated from God, and needs a Mediator to bring him to the Father. He is dead in trespasses and sin, and needs to be born again by receiving the life of Christ in his soul.

Jesus must and will continue to reign because His message appeals to that which is deepest in the heart of man. Paradoxically, the very depth of His appeal is what causes many to turn away from Him. But Jesus is at grips with man in his deepest nature, and this grip must ultimately win.

It is true that we see the superficial appeal apparently winning for a time. The world responds only too readily to those who appeal to its lusts and passions and self-love and self-interest, and closes its ears to those who call it to saving faith in Christ, and to consecration, love, and self-sacrifice through following Him. That is why the prodigal son deserted the Father's house for the land of riotous living. That is why many professed followers forsook Jesus and His Words of eternal life for the grosser voices of the world. But the Divine Voice will win in the long run. The redemptive union of Christ with our race assures the ultimate and certain victory. It is this assurance that makes us calm in the midst of the scorn of the Christ-rejecting world.

Jesus must and will continue to reign to the end, because He Himself is coming in visible presence and power to take possession of His Kingdom. He first established this Kingdom by His incarnate presence on earth. Now He continues it by His invisible presence with His people. At last He will complete it by His visible presence in manifested glory.

But what difference can there be between His invisible and visible presence? If He is here, and reigning now, why should He come again? We may compare His invisible presence with the unseen vapor that is present in the atmosphere on a clear and cloudless day. At nightfall it suddenly materializes as clouds in the sky. It was present all along, but only at the close of day did it become apparent to the eye. Even so, in the evening of the world Christ will clothe Himself with the robes of His visible glory, and all the world shall see the Son of Man coming in the clouds with power and great glory. This is not less certain than His first coming in the flesh, or His presence among us now.

This final manifestation of the Lord will make still another contribution to the sum of His final rule. It will be the last great act of His power of redemption and judgment in affirming and developing His Kingdom. It will complete the triumph of His reign. His promised coming assures us that He will not leave His Kingdom incomplete or His sovereignty doubtful. "For he must reign, till he hath put all enemies under his feet."

The kingdoms of this world shall become the Kingdom of our God, and of His Christ, and the followers of the Lamb shall become an everlasting priesthood and kingdom unto God. Without shall be weeping and gnashing of teeth; but in the courts of our God shall be heard the glad cry, "Blessing, and honour, and glory, and power, be unto him that sitteth upon the throne, and unto the Lamb for ever and ever" (Rev. 5:13).

(See John Thomas, *The Mysteries of Grace*, pp. 318-28.)

In view of all this, "What manner of persons ought you to be?" the Apostle Peter asks (II Pet. 3:11). Jesus Christ is coming back to earth again, this time not to be judged but to judge. He will separate men into two categories, some of whom will be in for tremendous surprises.

For whom will the happy surprises be? For those

who, knowing Christ as their Saviour, were so filled with love for Him that their love overflowed into helpfulness for others. Christ will say to them, "Come, you blessed of my Father, inherit the kingdom prepared for you. . . . For I was hungry and you gave me food, I was thirsty and you gave me drink, I was a stranger, and you welcomed me" (Matt. 25:34, 35). Every good deed done in His name, Christ considers as done unto Him.

But many in the second group will be shocked to hear Him say, "Depart from me . . . into the eternal fire . . . for I was hungry and you gave me no food, I was thirsty and you gave me no drink, I was a stranger and you did not welcome me" (Matt. 25:41-43). They will protest that they never treated Christ in such a way, but He will reply, "Truly, I say to you, as you did it not to one of the least of these, you did it not to me" (v. 45). The absence of good works is simply a proof of your unbelief in Christ. It is faith in Christ that saves; it is good works that proves that faith to be real.

If Christ were to return today, in which category would He find you? God give you grace to settle that matter now, before it is too late.

WHO IS YOUR BOSS?

"For he must reign, till he hath put all enemies under his feet" (I Cor.15:25).

If you want to start a lively discussion, just ask some of your married friends, "Who's the boss in your house?" One couple who had a very happy marriage laughed when this question was put to them. Then the husband said, "There's no need of a boss when each of you wants to please the other." For such people, the word "obey" really doesn't need to be included in the marriage ceremony, for the question of compulsion never arises.

In the beginning, when God created man, His relationship to him was not so much that of a ruler but of a loving Father. But when the desire to obey God out of love was weakened in man by Satan's first temptation to self-gratification, that relationship of necessity changed. Then God had to impose His will upon men, for their wills were no longer one with Him, but were often in opposition to Him.

Again, when the Lord Jesus Christ came to earth, He came not as a ruler, although as God He had every right to impose His righteous reign, but as a servant, as a Mediator between God and men, to reconcile them to God. To serve is Christ's nature; but to reign has become His necessity. It is not natural to Christ that He should be a king. He feels more humiliation in having to assume that office than He did in being a servant.

Remember, the intrinsic nature of God is love. Love never finds pleasure in reigning. It can do it; it is often compelled to do it; but it does not like to do it. As a father, I would much prefer not to have to use compulsion to secure obedience from my children. I would much rather they did what they should of their own accord. But because it is in the nature of children to become unruly and endanger their own safety and that of others at times, I must at times exercise firm control over them.

Why does the Apostle Paul say in I Corinthians 15:25 that Christ *must* reign until He has put all enemies under His feet? The Greek word translated "must" is *dei*, which in the New Testament is expressive of the character of necessity or compulsion, especially in relation to events yet to come.

As Kittel's *Theological Dictionary of the New Testament* says (Vol. II, pp. 23-4), the word *dei*, "must," is well adapted to express the necessity of future events, since that which is to come is hidden from man, can be known only by special revelation, and leads man to realize the necessity of its historical occurrence because it is grounded in the divine will. The word *dei*, "must," is so strong that it denotes that God is in Himself committed to these plans, and will definitely keep His promise as to their fulfillment. This "must" relates both to judgment and salvation; and under this categorical imperative stand all the events of the Messianic time, beginning with the return of Elias (identified by Christ as John the Baptist), on through the suffering, death, and resurrection of the Lord, and including the judgment and the changes that will take place at our bodily resurrection.

Therefore, when Paul says that Christ "must" reign until He has put all enemies under His feet, he is stressing an imperative to which God is committed, and which involves the very reason why Christ must fulfill this prophecy. The stress of the word "must" is not merely on the fact, but extends to the reason for the fact.

And what is this reason? It is just this — that if Christ is going to be absolute King of all persons and over all things in the future, He must be absolute Ruler here and now. Paul could merely have stated that Christ is going to reign, not that this constitutes a necessity consistent with His character. But Christ, the Sovereign One to be, must be sovereign now. To some, it would seem that He is being trampled on now, but this is a mere delusion of His enemies, who believe that they are now ruling the universe. Christ is Lord and King now. We Christians would have no hope for the future if He were not now in full control, if we were not fully persuaded of His present sovereignty.

Yet it bears repeating that God is love, and love never finds pleasure in reigning, especially by force. None of the crowns of the Son of God is as thorny as the crown of His power. It grieves Him to have to impose His will upon you and the universe. He would rather give no commands, but would prefer that obedience be instinctive, part of our redeemed nature. Kings are often lonely. They would rather be on terms of affectionate intimacy with their subjects than enthroned above them. Christ wants to be one with us, if only we will be one with Him. It is precisely because we do not feel with Him, think with Him, and become one with Him, as He and the Father are one, that He must rule. He must reign now because of the imperfections of His own children. But His basic reign even now is that of love, wooing beloved but undeserving sinners to Himself.

But the day will come when He will no longer reign. He will deliver up the Kingdom to God the Father, resigning His rule as Mediator, because we, His redeemed children, will have no will opposed to His, as we often do now. He must overpower us now because of the inadequacy of our obedience to Him. The necessity for Christ's rule over us will cease when evil no longer exists to tempt us, to exercise its power of attraction over us. Christ will cease to rule only when He shall have rendered inactive every rule, authority, and power.

In I Corinthians 15:24 Paul has stated that Christ will deliver up the Kingdom to the Father after He has put down all rule, authority, and power. He restates this in verse 25, giving the necessity for putting down His enemies as the reason for this rule. Because His enemies are now active, "He must reign, till he hath put all enemies under his feet." He must rule now because of the imperfections of our obedience. This imperfection will cease when evil is no more, at which time Christ will no longer need to reign.

(See George Matheson, *Searchings in the Silence*, pp. 187-9.)

Of course, for the Christian who is growing in grace, the maturing of His love for God brings him more and more into the relationship of a friend with Christ even in this life. As he yields himself more and more to Christ in loving obedience, as ever larger areas of his life and thought come into captivity to Christ, he experiences the joy the disciples must have known when Christ told them, "Ye are my friends, if ye do whatsoever I command you. Henceforth I call you not servants . . . but I have called you friends" (John 15:14, 15).

God is love, absolute love, and it is the nature of love to give. God does not reap where He has not sowed. He does not ask if He has not first given. He gave you the life you now have, but, because you cannot keep it and give it meaning, He asks you to put it back into His hands. Then, instead of a restricted and burdened life, it will become one of abundance and enjoyment. Instead of obeying Him by constraint, you will obey Him because your one desire is to please Him. If you come to Him believing in His love and accepting His gift of love, the Lord Jesus Christ, you will find Him not a hard Taskmaster, an autocratic Ruler, but a loving Father.

SOME DAY YOU MAY HELP RULE THE EARTH

"For he must reign, till he hath put all enemies under his feet" (I Cor. 15:25).

One of the best known of Aesop's Fables concerns the frogs who desired a king. These creatures lived a free and easy sort of life, but they became dissatisfied and decided to pray Jupiter to send them a king. At first he threw them a log, but they soon tired of this lifeless ruler, and asked Jupiter to send them something more like a king. This time he sent them a stork, who gobbled many of them up without mercy. They lost no time in beseeching Jupiter to restore them to their former state. But he told them this was not possible; they had not been contented with a king that did no harm, and now they must content themselves with the one they had.

Since Aesop's Fables are always told with an eye to human frailties, we may take it that this is no exception. However, may we not go even further than Aesop and interpret it in the light of a Christian understanding of man's present plight in this world? Not content with the life of fellowship in voluntary obedience to God to which he was first called, man chose under Satan to be governed by human rule — first his own, and then that of others. But his choice of rulers has not always been wise, and he has suffered much in consequence.

If you had to choose someone to rule the world, whom would you choose? Would you look for a stranger whose ways and intentions have not been tried, or would you go to someone of tried and proven character and ability?

Since it is evident that man needs to be ruled over if he is not to bring about his own destruction, whom among men would you choose as the most unselfish, the most compassionate, the most loving, wise, and capable person to rule over this world? Is there anyone other than Jesus Christ who could meet all these qualifications? Study the life of the Lord Jesus, His sacrifice on the cross, His love for you, and then compare it with the life of anyone else. This thought came to me as I mused on the implications of the third word in I Corinthians 15:25, the Greek pronoun *auton*, "him, himself." "For he must reign" is the English translation of the Authorized Version. But the personal pronoun "he" in Greek could have been understood without the added demonstrative pronoun *auton*, "himself." It was put there for emphasis, "He, himself, must reign." This active rule must remain in His hands now. It is so difficult to find men with great power who use it wisely, with no thought but the highest welfare of those they serve. But Christ the King not only has the power; He also has love in proportion to His power. This is just another proof that He is God.

He had power to burn Jerusalem in its disobedience, but instead He wept over it. He had power to smite Judas and those who came to arrest Him, but He permitted them to carry through their evil work. He could have descended from the cross and brought death upon those who were putting Him to death, but instead He prayed God to forgive them, thus reigning even from the cross in procuring our salvation. He did none of these things, not because He could not, not because of fear of punishment, which so often serves as a deterrent to the exercise of human power, but because the motive behind the exercise of divine power in this age of grace is love.

With Christ, power and love are not acquired but are inherent in His nature and character. He Himself must reign — no one else. Earthly monarchs *may* reign, but Christ *must* reign — over and above them. Theirs is a reign by the permission and toleration of God. Christ's is a reign of necessity for the sake of redeemed believers.

As John the Baptist said of Christ the Messiah that He must reign, so Paul says of Christ the Risen Lord that He must reign. If He had remained in the grave, this statement could never have been made.

He must reign not only over all earthly rulers, but He must also reign over creation. This is His world, not ours nor Satan's. He made it, and He alone knows how to maintain it. When a machine goes wrong, our ultimate resort is to the manufacturer who produced it. If our cosmos is not to collapse, this same Christ who made it must reign over it. As the Apostle John says, "All things were made by him, and without him was not any thing made that was made" (John 1:3). The mountains and lakes, the sea and clouds, the stars and the whole wide universe — who keeps them in space and functioning? Not you and I. If they are not disintegrating, it is because Christ is reigning. He holds the whole world in His hand. Paul says of Him, "For by him were all things created [*ektisthee*, used in the Greek Bible only of God's creation, which refers to making the world out of nothing, not merely manufacturing things out of raw materials, as men do], that are in heaven, and that are in earth, visible and invisible, whether they be thrones, or dominions, or principalities, or powers: all things were created by him and for him: and he is before all things, and by him all things consist [*sunesteeken*, 'stand together']" Col. 1:16, 17). Christ is the Creator and Sustainer of life. If He ceases to reign, you and I and all things cease to exist.

Christ must reign over all earthly rulers; He must reign over nature; and He must reign also in the Christian. Because they are human, even Christians may become puffed up at times with a sense of their own importance. To guard against this in His disciples, Jesus performed the lowly task of washing their feet at the last supper, telling them that if He, their Master and Lord, did not feel it beneath Him to perform such humble service, they should also humble themselves in service to others. "The servant is not greater than his lord," He reminded them. "If ye know these things, happy are ye if ye do them" John 12:16, 17).

In desiring to lord it over others, we are usurping Christ's unique prerogative of rule. You and I, redeemed by the grace of God, must not arrogate to ourselves the right to rule supreme even in our own affairs. We shall do a miserable job of it, and an even more miserable one if we seek to lord it over our fellow Christians. Let Christ be King in your own life and in the lives of others also.

It is true that Revelation 1:6 says that the Lord has made us "kings and priests." However, the Nestle's Greek text gives the first reading as *basileian*, "kingdom," and only as an alternate reading gives *basileis*, "kings." The sense here would seem to be that we are Christ's "kingdom" over whom He rules.

In fact, nowhere in Scripture do we find that we are supposed to possess co-rulership over the world with Christ in this dispensation of grace. This is reserved for a future state. Now we are made kings over sin and evil through the indwelling Christ (Rom. 5:17, 21). But in the future, Revelation 5:10 tells us, "we shall reign on the earth." Revelation 20:4 continues, "And they [the souls of the redeemed martyrs] lived and reigned with Christ a thousand years." And again in verse 6, "he that hath part in the first resurrection . . . shall reign with him a thousand years." And lastly, Revelation 22:3, 5, "And his servants shall serve him . . . and they shall reign for ever and ever." This is clearly a co-reign with Christ on earth, subsequent to His second coming, not merely in the form of victory over sin and evil, but in a more specific temporal exercise of power. (See G. Kittel's *Theological Dictionary of the New Testament*, Vol. I, p. 590.)

Now we reign *through* Christ. Then, in the millennial Kingdom, we shall reign *with* Christ. Now we are not to usurp authority over others, for we ourselves are imperfect. We would misuse such power; for though we are indwelt by God, we are still human. But when our present body of imperfection is changed at the resurrection, and our wills are made perfect also, we shall have this blessed and unexcelled privilege of reigning with Christ over the world.

Sounds incredible, doesn't it? But the unique Ruler of all things has promised it, and He can bring it to pass. In fact, in this 15th chapter of I Corinthians, Paul injects verses 24 to 28 in his argument about the resurrection to show that the past, the glorious fact of the resurrection of Christ, is a guarantee that the promises of the future will be fulfilled. Stand on history and you will believe prophecy.

Now, lest anyone misunderstand me, I am not saying that those who occupy positions of authority are not to exercise that authority as their office requires. What I am saying is that they are to do it as those who serve, recognizing their responsibility under God to rule for the benefit of those under them, rather than in a proud, arrogant, and selfish spirit. This really takes the grace of God in a man's heart; and that is why we should pray for our heads of government and all in authority, that they may realize their accountability to God.

Is it really possible for evil to be suppressed and for Jesus Christ to reign supreme, imposing His will to a degree that we have not seen in the past and that we do not see now? The resurrection assures us that it is; and even more wonderful (considering our present imperfections) is the fact that, if you have received Christ as your Saviour and Lord, you will one day reign with Him. For as He Himself must reign — and this is guaranteed by His resurrection — so must we reign with Him — and this in consequence of our own resurrection.

HOW TO BECOME POWERFUL THROUGH SUBMISSION

"For he must reign, till he hath put all enemies under his feet" (I Cor. 15:25).

A king is not elected; he rules by right of birth. He knows from his earliest days that he is destined to take the throne. Though most kings nowadays have limited power, in the past they were absolute monarchs over all their subjects.

From the beginning of Christ's public ministry to the end, there was never the shadow of a doubt in His mind that He had come to rule. The words "king" and "kingdom" in reference to Himself were often on His lips. If you study His life and words, you will find throughout a note of entreaty. But do not miss the sovereignty behind the entreaty. He entreats men, not as an impotent beggar, but as a loving King.

Yet He turned a deaf ear to any suggestion that He aspire to a local or provincial kingdom in Jerusalem; because for that He would have had to abdicate His universal throne. For the sake of one petty kingdom He would not sacrifice His blood-bought world-wide empire.

"He must reign," Scripture tells us. The verb "reign" in Greek *(basileuein)* is in the durative present active infinitive. This indicates that this is not a new reign, which begins here, but is a continuation of the reign of Christ as it now exists. It is equivalent to "for he himself must continue to reign." He has always been King over His universe, and this Kingship He will never abdicate. As King He chooses to act in a variety of ways, according to the purposes He desires to fulfill. Because He chose to save man from sin, He voluntarily laid down His life for all mankind. "No man taketh it from me, but I lay it down of myself," He said. "I have power to lay it down, and I have power to take it again" (John 10:18). What mere human could make this claim? Yet even on the cross, Jesus Christ was at the height of His reign. He never ceased for one moment to be King; and the only Kingdom He will ever relinquish is His mediatorial throne, when His work as Redeemer of sinful men is at an end. This redemption is not limited to our souls only, but also includes our bodies. Christ's particular work in the eternal plan for man's salvation is that of a Redeemer of the total man.

You cannot be a believer in Jesus Christ without a true consciousness of the reign of Christ. This is a spiritual reign now, but when He comes again His reign will extend to the elements which now seem to make it partial. "He himself must keep on reigning till he hath put all enemies under his feet" is the literal translation of I Corinthians 15:25.

Christ is Lord in the region of conduct. Consider the disciples. They were men like you and me, inclined to be prejudiced and self-opinionated. Yet when they heard the kingly command of Christ, "Follow me," they offered no resistance. They did not know Him, yet they were attracted to Him. Accustomed to having their own way, they laid down their way and will without opposition or delay. For they had heard their

Master, they had found their Lord — or rather their Lord had found them. The Lord Jesus never appears to have reasoned with them, or attempted to persuade them. He simply told them to come, and they came.

When he confronted the multitude on the Mount, He declared with amazing confidence and fearlessness, "Ye have heard that it was said by them of old time . . . but I say unto you" (Matt. 5:21, 22). What would have sounded boastful and profane on other men's lips on His sounded truthful and sacred. Why? Because, when men saw and heard Him, their minds accepted Him as one who taught with authority, and not as the scribes. Christ was Lord in the region of thought, even as He was in the region of conduct.

As you study the actions and words of Christ, you are convinced that from the very beginning His object was to master the world. He came to this earth to reign. All the means and methods that He employed were designed to master the hearts of men. Just as a wise parent seeks to win a difficult, wayward child to better ways by mingled tenderness and firmness, so Jesus Christ set Himself to master the world. And from the very outset of His public ministry He never allowed His hearers to be under any delusion about His purpose and claim.

He had come to be Master — in the realm of thought and conduct — but He never defended His right to do so. He never argued, or sought to conciliate men. If they went away because His sayings were too hard, He let them go, knowing that at last truth always finds its home in the hearts of those for whom it is intended. The inference of such conduct was that what He spoke was not something men were permitted to accept or reject as they pleased, or from which they could select what they liked best. No, Christ was out to master them, to become the dominant, ruling authority and spirit of all their lives. He came to earth to offer them God's truth.

Christ still makes this claim on men's lives today. He is in the world still, and His Spirit is the one argument men cannot and dare not refute. They still have to reckon with Him. Despised and rejected, He still sets the standard to which they conform, or from which they flee.

It is a deep if often unconfessed need of the human heart to have a Master. Life must have its Lord. Even the novelist and dramatist recognize this need when they portray love in woman seeking its master, and love in man seeking its mistress. But this universal need to be ruled over can never be satisfactorily filled in its entirety by a merely human being. Only an infinite love can meet the need of the human heart to be mastered by love.

It may seem paradoxical, but the secret of strength and power in life is to be mastered, conquered, dominated. There are two classes of people in this world — those who hold certain truths, and those of whom we say that the truth holds them. This latter attitude we call "conviction," which is only another way of saying that the truth has made a "conquest." These men have been conquered, convicted by the truth. It has fought its way past mere intellectual assent to the inner citadel of their hearts, where it sits enthroned and dominates all their thoughts and actions. Men thus dominated are the strong and powerful forces for good in this world.

What is the difference between a politician and a statesman, as those terms are commonly used to describe men in government? Is it not that one seeks to make all things serve his own ends, while the other is possessed by a desire to serve his fellow men?

The strong and irresistible men of the world are those who are mastered and dominated by divine ideas. Let Jesus Christ be Lord and Master of your life, and He can make you a power for untold good. I know perfectly well that what keeps many people away from Him is just this fact — that they know in their hearts that they must take Him altogether or not at all; that if they come to Him He will lay hold of them, He will take them firmly in His hand, and make them what He wants them to be. And they are not prepared to go that far. This claim to the mastery offends the modern spirit. Men resent the Lordship of Jesus Christ. They are willing to bear the name of Christian without committing themselves to the idea behind it. But if we are to learn the secret of power, if we are to be effectual in any way that counts, Jesus Christ must master us. God grant each of us the grace to rise up and follow Him, without question or delay.

(See "The Kingship of Christ," by C. Silvester Horne, in *The Christian World Pulpit*, Vol. 32, pp. 245-7.)

YOU OUGHT TO HAVE ENEMIES

"For he must reign, till he hath put all enemies under his feet" (I Cor. 15:25).

When you and I came into this world, we were completely self-centered human beings. We recognized no will but our own. We cried as loudly as we pleased, whenever we pleased, until someone came to see what was the matter. We very early sensed the relation between cause and effect: If I cry, someone will answer.

If this pattern had been allowed to continue indefinitely, we would have begun to conclude we ruled our parents. A day had to come when our parents let us know who was in control. We had to learn that we could no longer assert our wills independently of parental restriction, but must henceforth submit our wills to theirs.

This same lesson will one day be brought home forcibly to those who now think they have the upper hand in this world — the powers of evil who are seeking to control the lives of men. If they only realized that they are functioning not by personal conquest but by divine tolerance and permission, they might be less arrogant. The day will come when these self-willed enemies of Christ will be brought up short and made to realize that He is the real Ruler of the universe. "For he himself must reign, till he hath put all enemies under his feet," says the Apostle Paul.

The Lord Jesus has always been King, though at this stage of His rule He has many enemies. They are now allowed to be active and to think that they have the upper hand. This is the fundamental difference between the present reign of Christ and His future reign. It allows the existence and activity of evil, although under Christ's restraint and restriction.

All that is evil is an enemy of God — Satan, demons, evil men, or evil influences of any kind. The term "enemy" *(echthros* in Greek) is particularly used in the New Testament for that which is hostile to God and His Christ, as in Luke 19:27, Acts 13:10, and Philippians 3:18. Why God permits the co-existence of evil and good in this present age has not been revealed to us. It may be that in the context of eternity, when we are in our resurrection bodies, we shall be told the reason. We cannot now conceive of what our world would be like without any resistance to God, His will and plan. Like the state after death, of which we have been given so little specific revelation, God knows we could not possibly conceive of it in our present limited frame of being. All we are told on that subject is that we shall continue to exist, and that we shall be with Christ in a state of blessedness throughout eternity, and very little more. As to why evil is allowed a relatively free hand now, all we know is that it exists, but that it will ultimately be defeated and its influence completely suppressed. This will take place after the second coming of Christ.

Nevertheless, till then the Lord Jesus Christ does reign. And He will continue to reign as Mediator-Redeemer "till he hath put all enemies under his feet." If we rejoice in Christ's sovereignty now, how much greater will be our joy then. But for this we must wait until He appears the second time.

The expression *achri hou* is actually a shortened form of the Greek *achri chronou hou*, "until such time when." The word "time" is therefore understood here. In the foreknowledge of God there is a definite time when this will take place, though He has not revealed it to us. Christ will come suddenly, when evil has become almost uncontrollable and seems completely to have gained the upper hand. Read Matthew 24 to see some of the signs of His coming. There will be "wars and rumours of wars" (vs. 6). "Nation shall rise against nation, and kingdom against kingdom; and there shall be famines, and pestilences, and earthquakes" (vs. 7). It is going to be a time when "iniquity shall abound" (vs. 12).

It is then, when the believers are disheartened over the seeming triumph of evil, that the Lord shall appear to put His enemies under His feet. The day and hour are settled; He is just biding His time now. This time can hardly come too soon for the believer. But it will be a terrible day for His enemies.

Christ will first subdue His enemies and then deliver up His mediatorial Kingdom to the Father. The verb "he shall put" is in the aorist subjunctive in Greek *(thee)*. Therefore the whole phrase, *achri hou thee*, is more literally translated "until such time when he shall have put." The tense of this verb is further confirmation that the second event mentioned in I Corinthians 15:24, the putting down of "all rule and all authority and power," will precede the first event, the delivering up of "the kingdom to God, even the Father."

Does it seem strange to you that the One who said "Love your enemies" will one day put His own enemies "under his feet"? He can do this without violating the principle of His love. These will be the enemies whose wills have forever rejected His grace and salvation. When all the elect are in — and only He knows when that will take place — there will be no point in allowing evil to continue, for the wicked will have no further opportunity of salvation. Christ's office of Saviour-Lord will give place to that of Judge-Lord.

This is the great and final victory, when no enemy is left, and Satan himself, the arch-foe, is conquered. All rebellious powers in heavenly places are completely subjugated. Every trace of human resistance is abolished. Even death itself "is swallowed up in victory" (I Cor. 15:54). "The end" has come: the end of sin, the end of the curse, the end of pain, the end for which the saints of all ages have waited in long patience, the end that was envisaged by Christ when He hung upon the cross. At last "He shall see of the travail of his soul, and shall be satisfied" (Isa. 53:11). The end for which believers have prayed all down the ages when they have said, "Thy kingdom come; thy will be done, on earth as it is in heaven" will finally be realized.

Paul no doubt had in mind the prophecy of this event in Psalm 110:1, which reads, "The Lord said unto my Lord, Sit thou at my right hand, until I make thine enemies thy footstool." He added the word *pantas*, "all," to show that not one enemy of Christ shall be left undealt with. This is something Paul wanted to impress upon the Corinthians and upon us. They were questioning the resurrection. But it takes belief in the resurrection of Christ to believe Him capable of subduing all evil powers — past, present, and future. His victory is limitless as far as time is concerned. None who have died seemingly triumphant over Him, or who are now defying His grace, or whose evil ways will prosper in days to come, will be ultimately victorious over Him. Every one of them, and all of them put together, in full consciousness of their defeat, will stand before the Lord and declare His victory over them. What a great day of vindication of all that is pure and honest and true that will be!

Paul did not wish to intimate that the forces of evil were simply Christ's enemies. This may be why he did not use the emphatic pronoun *autou*, "his." He simply says "all the enemies," not "all the enemies of his." They are also enemies of God the Father and God the Holy Spirit, as well as of every Christian believer. The future victory, therefore, is not only Christ's victory but also every believer's victory. Every enemy of Christ now is our enemy; every victory of Christ is one in which we share. God help us if we take the devil and his followers for our friends. The Christian has enemies, even as His Lord has. If he doesn't, he is surely compromising with evil.

This does not mean that we are to hate our enemies. Christ does not hate men, but He abhors their evil works. He hates their rebellion against Him and their rejection of His salvation. The fact that God has enemies is not found in His attitude toward evildoers but in their attitude toward Him. God loves them; it is they who have set themselves at enmity with Him.

We, too, must love our enemies and seek to reconcile them to God through our Christian testimony and attitude toward them. We are to return good for evil. Yet we, too, will be rejected and hated by many. Remember, however, that no fellow-believer is to be regarded as an enemy. Only Christ's enemies can be our enemies. Over such enemies, who have had love shown to them and have rejected it, Christ will one day declare His complete and unyielding victory. Thus it is not only His enemies, but ours as well, over whom He will triumph.

Another thing we must remember is that we are not the ones who will do the triumphing, if I may put it that way. He will put them under His feet, not ours. If you think about it, you will see why this should be so. All that we are or ever shall be is because of Christ's indwelling power. We have no righteousness of our own. Any victory we seem to have achieved must rightfully be ascribed to Him. Let's never lose sight of this, and then all the pride will be knocked out of us, and any spirit of vindictiveness will disappear. Even as we are going to rise because Christ rose, as Paul declares in this chapter, so we are going to be victorious over our enemies because He is the Victor.

THERE'S A GREAT DAY COMING!

"For he must reign, till he hath put all enemies under his feet" (I Cor. 15:25).

Have you ever had an impulse to stroll through a city park on a beautiful spring night, or to walk along a lonely country road — and then regretfully gave up the idea because of the dangers involved? At such moments you probably reflect, "What a wonderful world this would be, if men were only good." Think how pleasant it would be to go anywhere without fear of molestation, to leave your doors unlocked and your possessions unguarded. How relaxing it would be not to have to keep your guard up against people, because no one was envious of you, or misconstrued your motives, or tried to rise above you by pushing you down and stepping on your prostrate form.

Yet Christ tells us that we are not to become hardened because of the evil in the world, so that we ourselves render evil for evil. Instead we are to love our enemies. This love is not a sentimental emotion but involves an active ministry of prayer for them and of rendering good for evil. Again this does not mean that we are to permit them to continue unchecked in their harmful activities, but we are always to be motivated by love, even in restraining them. Our motive in dealing with them must be to win them to Christ rather than to avenge ourselves.

We are to take this attitude out of a sincere desire that all men should be given the opportunity to come into a saving relationship with Christ, before it is too late. For a day is coming when those who remain stubbornly opposed to God's offer of salvation in Christ will find the offer withdrawn and their freedom of choice taken from them. That will be a day of reckoning, when those who have trampled underfoot the Son of God will themselves become His footstool.

There is little difference between the prophetic utterances of this event in the Old Testament and in the New. In Psalm 110:1 David said, "The Lord said unto my Lord, Sit thou at my right hand, until I make thine enemies thy footstool." In I Corinthians 15:25 Paul says, "For he [Christ] must reign, till he hath put all enemies under his feet." He omits the word "footstool" in this verse. In the Greek translation of the Hebrew Old Testament, the LXX, the word "footstool" is *hupopodion*, which is also used in identical form in Matthew 22:44, Luke 20:43, and Acts 2:35, which are New Testament quotations of Psalm 110:1. It is derived from the preposition *hupo*, meaning "under," and the noun *podion*, a diminutive of *pous*, "foot."

Thus we see that the enemies of Christ will one day, after His second coming and the resurrection of the dead, be placed as a stool under His little foot. This, of course, is figurative language, expressive of the ease with which our Lord will obtain the victory over them, so that there need be no fear of a revolt against Him that will enable them again to gain the upper hand, especially over His people. Christ will have each and all of the enemies of righteousness as a stool under His little foot. They who once thought they had overcome Him on the cross, and who throughout history have wielded their earthly power in defiance of His supreme authority, will find themselves unable to move even His little foot one inch. What a glorious day of vindication that will be!

At a dinner party one night over in Scotland, the host said, "Suppose each of us tells in what part of the body of our Lord we would like to be." Someone said he would like to be in His head to help rule over all. Another replied that he would like to be next to His great loving heart. But when it came Janet's turn she said, "His heel." No one understood what she meant, but when they questioned her she said, "I'd like to be His heel when He's doing the bruising!"

Very interestingly, *hupopodion*, translated "footstool," means a stool placed under the foot of someone in a sitting rather than a standing position. We employ it in the same sense today. (See D. Demetrakou, *Lexicon of the Greek Language*, Athens, 1951, Vol. 9, p. 7497.) This is indeed most suggestive. When the Lord comes to reign as victor over the entire cosmos, He will not have to fight and keep on fighting to maintain His status, as is so often the case with human conquerors, but He will, figuratively speaking, be able to do it in a sitting position with His little but mighty foot upon all the enemies of truth, who will serve as His footstool.

The finality of this victory is also inherent in the aorist subjunctive tense of the verb *thee*, "put," which means here "until such time when he shall have put" once and for all, finally, conclusively, with no chance of the enemies of truth and righteousness ever rising again. This final victory of Christ, then, must follow the millennium and the time when Satan will be loosed for a little season (Rev. 20:3, 7). The final doom of Satan and all the evils of which he is the author is described in Revelation 20:10, "And the devil which deceived them was cast into the lake of fire and brimstone, where the beast and the false prophet are, and shall be tormented day and night for ever and ever."

And here is our blessed Lord, who on the cross cried out, "My God, my God, why hast thou forsaken me?" (Matt. 27:46), sitting victorious over His enemies, and staying victorious over them without effort. "Standing" in Scripture denotes ministry, and "sitting" denotes rest. There is no posture so restful as to sit with a stool under one's foot. Until Christ's enemies are all under His feet, He will not have fully entered into His rest.

In this present age, we as believers are struggling and Christ is ministering, for in His own words He "came not to be ministered unto, but to minister" (Matt. 20:28). But when His enemies are finally put under His feet, He will rest from His labor and so shall we. Let us live in anticipation of that great day.

All down through the ages we have seen how evil has seemingly prevailed and exalted itself in this world. Even before the first man transgressed, however, Satan had exalted himself against God and drawn many of the angels of heaven into rebellion with him. He prevailed over Adam and Eve, our first parents, and has infected the world with his spirit of disobedience ever since. He prevailed against Christ in inducing men to hate Him and treat Him despitefully. He prevailed against a disciple of Christ, Judas, to betray the sinless Son of God.

Individual men have continued to exalt themselves against God, flaunting their corruption and wickedness, so that good has been regarded as evil, and evil as good, in every realm of life.

Nations have exalted themselves against God, shedding the blood of martyrs and persecuting the Church. Suffering and misery have flourished, even among the believers, and especially is this true in the supreme sufferings of Christ.

And the final seeming victory of the "enemy" over Christ in this world is death itself, which claims every man.

Nevertheless, even now Christ has triumphed over all these enemies.

He triumphed over Satan, who thought he had secured the victory when he procured the death of Christ on the cross. The truth is that Christ, through His sufferings, death, and resurrection, triumphed over Satan by laying the foundation for the utter overthrow of his kingdom.

Again, Christ has prevailed over the corruption and guilt of men, in that through His redemptive sacrifice He purchased holiness for even the chief of sinners. Though their guilt may appear to them as high as the Alps, His dying love and His merits are like a mighty deluge that overflows the highest peaks. His sacrifice was sufficient to do way with all the guilt of the whole world.

And Christ even now has prevailed over all misery, for in undergoing the extreme affliction of the cross He laid the foundation for the final abolishment of all affliction for believers in the life to come.

(See "Christ Exalted," in *The Select Works of Jonathan Edwards*, London: The Banner of Truth Trust, Vol. 1, pp. 152-62.)

Yes, Christ is victorious here and now; the apparent contradictions in this topsy-turvy world are just that — apparent and not real. All His purposes are being worked out, not only through His avowed followers, but even through His enemies; and one day we will see the pattern whole, and rejoice in the manifestation of His power in the final subduing of all opposition.

Until then we walk by faith. "Whom having not seen, ye love; in whom, though now ye see him not, yet believing, ye rejoice with joy unspeakable and full of glory" (I Pet. 1:8).

A soldier who had been blinded in war was playing the piano in the convalescent ward of a London hospital when he felt a hand upon his shoulder, and a voice said, "Well done, my friend!" Thinking it was one of his comrades, the soldier turned around smilingly and said, "And who are you?" Quick as a flash, and as startling, came the reply, "Your king!"

Even so, you and I will one day be surprised by the return of the King of Kings to set up His rule on this earth. Will we hear Him say, "Well done"? Let us voluntarily submit our wills to Him now, that we may not be forced to submit as an enemy when He comes again.

HOW MANY TIMES WILL YOU DIE?

"The last enemy that shall be destroyed is death"
(I Cor. 15:26).

If you were asked, "What is the opposite of death?" what would you reply? "Life"? "Birth"? The Apostle Paul gives a different answer in I Corinthians 15. He says that it is "resurrection." And the reason that it is death's opposite is that it cancels out death. No one reading this chapter could possibly conclude that Paul was speaking only of a spiritual resurrection. Spirits do not die in the sense that bodies die. They cannot undergo decay and return to dust. We know that Christ's resurrection was physical, because it was His body only that died on the cross and was buried in Joseph's tomb.

Paul speaks of death as "the last enemy" to be destroyed. What does he mean by "death" here?

When God made man, He gave Him tangible substance, a body. He also gave him a spiritual or immaterial nature. That these are diverse is evident from Scripture. Job 32:8 tells us, "There is a spirit in man: and the inspiration of the Almighty giveth them understanding." And in Zechariah 12:1 we read that the Lord "stretcheth forth the heavens, and layeth the foundation of the earth, and formeth the spirit of man within him." I Corinthians 2:11 also speaks of "the spirit of man which is in him." The "spirit in man" and the "man" are as distinct as a house and a tenant within the house.

That man comprises both spirit and body is clearly

brought out in Job 14:22, "But his flesh upon him shall have pain, and his soul within him shall mourn." And in I Corinthians 6:20 Paul says, "For ye are bought with a price: therefore glorify God in your body, and in your spirit, which are God's."

Our Lord definitely differentiated between the material and spiritual aspects of man when He said in Matthew 10:28, "And fear not them which kill the body, but are not able to kill the soul."

Genesis 2:7 tells us how God first brought human life into being: "And the Lord God formed man of the dust of the ground, and breathed into his nostrils the breath of life; and man became a living soul." Thus man's life, as we know it to this day, began with the union of his material and spiritual natures.

But sin entered into the world, and in Genesis 3:19 God pronounced the decree of death: "In the sweat of thy face shalt thou eat bread, till thou return unto the ground; for out of it wast thou taken: for dust thou art, and unto dust shalt thou return." We may infer from this verse that only so much of man as was "dust," and taken out of "the ground," was doomed to return to dust again. But the "breath of life," the spirit breathed into Adam by his Creator, was not "dust" nor taken out of "the ground." It was therefore not doomed to return to dust with the body at death.

Death, then, is the separating of the spiritual nature, the spirit or soul of man, from his body. Ecclesiastes 12:7 tells us what becomes of each at death: "Then shall the dust return to the earth as it was: and the spirit shall return unto God who gave it." There are any number of Scriptures that speak of giving up the ghost or the spirit at death, as Job 14:10, where we read, "But man dieth, and wasteth away: yea, man giveth up the ghost."

However, there are two kinds of death mentioned in Scripture. As death when it relates to the material and spiritual natures of man means their separation, so death when it relates to the spirit of man and the Spirit of God means their separation also. It is in this sense, as spiritual separation from God, that the word is used in Genesis 2:17, where God said to Adam, "But of the tree of the knowledge of good and evil, thou shalt not eat of it: for in the day that thou eatest thereof thou shalt surely die." But the day that Adam and Eve ate of the fruit they did not die physically. They died spiritually. Physical death came years later. Spiritual death came upon them immediately. This was manifested by the fact that they no longer sought communion with God, but tried to hide from His presence.

In Proverbs 8:36 we have another allusion to spiritual death: "But he that sinneth against me wrongeth his own soul: all they that hate me love death." And Ezekiel 18:20 says, "The soul that sinneth, it shall die." Paul tells us in Romans 6:23, "The wages of sin is death; but the gift of God is eternal life through Jesus Christ our Lord." Eternal life is not the opposite of physical death; because all who have by faith received Jesus Christ as their Saviour have already received eternal life; and yet their bodies die physically. Eternal life is the spiritual life of God in man, which stands in contradistinction to spiritual death, which is the immediate result of sin. Physical death has been the ultimate lot of all men—believers and unbelievers alike. It is the resurrection that stands in contradistinction to this death of the body. Just as eternal life defeats spiritual death, the resurrection of the body defeats physical death. The first is immediate, upon receiving the Lord Jesus Christ as Saviour; the other is ultimate, at the second coming of the Lord.

Paul speaks of the believers' spiritual death and spiritual resurrection in Ephesians 2:1, when he says, "And you hath he quickened [made alive], who were dead in trespasses and sins." (Other verses referring to spiritual death are Rom. 8:6, James 1:15; 5:20, Rev. 21:8.)

Spiritual death has already been conquered by the Lord Jesus Christ on the cross of Calvary. The same cross and the glorious resurrection of the Lord Jesus have also removed the sting of physical death for the believer; but physical death itself has not yet been abolished. This event, Paul says, will take place in the future, at some time after the second coming of Christ. "The last enemy that shall be destroyed is death."

But is all death God's enemy and ours? Is the death of plants and animals, for instance, at enmity with God's original purpose for this world, or merely His arrangement to suit a temporary purpose during an imperfect state of things? We can scarcely include the death of plants and animals in the "last enemy" that has to be destroyed. It must be the death of some creature that was never meant to die at all—some death that has come across the original purpose of God, and set itself in opposition to His will. He may bring a higher good out of the opposition. He may gain a higher triumph, and reap more abundant spoils, by overcoming and destroying the enemy than He could have done if the enemy had never appeared. But the death here spoken of must *be* an enemy, and not merely an ordained state of things.

It is of the death of man, and of man only, that Paul is speaking. Man was made for immortality, but sin drove him away from the tree of life, and he became subject to death. If it had been the purpose of God that he should perish, death would have been no enemy but simply the execution of the divine sentence, "In the day thou eatest thereof thou shalt surely die" (Gen. 2:17). A penalty inflicted by God cannot be called an enemy of God as such, and it is with reference to Him that death is called the "last enemy."

This statement, then, cannot include "the second death"—the everlasting punishment, body and soul, of the finally impenitent; neither can it include the final destruction of the rebel angels: for both of these are God's own act. The "last enemy" is the natural death that sin has introduced into the human race, and that is regarded as the enemy of God, because He does *not* mean to let man perish, but means to rescue him *from* death to various degrees of blessedness and conditions of life. (See "The Last Enemy," by Samuel Minton, in *The Christian World Pulpit*, Vol. V, pp. 305-6.)

The physical death of man, as we know it, will be destroyed. The Greek word here is *katargeitai*, from *katarge-oo*, "make ineffective or powerless." But since physical death in man has a moral cause, its elimination must also have a moral cause. This is provided through the death of Christ, who "through death" destroyed "him that had the power of death, that is, the devil" (Heb. 2:14). Our Lord is said to have already "abolished death, and hath brought life and immortality to light through the gospel" (II Tim. 1:10).

The first visible result of this moral victory was Christ's own resurrection. The next will be that of His people at His coming. Lastly there will be the cessation of death in the race altogether, when man shall no more be subject to physical death or pain.

Yes, death is the last enemy that shall be destroyed. It is an enemy because it is the result of sin. And he who introduced man to sin is the arch-enemy of God and man, Satan himself. He tempted man to disregard the consequences of disobedience to God. It is his prime tactic still.

Men are often so shortsighted where their eternal destiny is concerned. They will lay long-range plans, and make all sorts of sacrifices, to secure an education and further their careers for the few brief years they are here on earth; but for the eternity of conscious existence that will be theirs hereafter, most of them make no adequate provision at all.

God gives you a choice: will you live only once and die twice, or will you die only once and live twice? Receive Jesus Christ by faith as your Saviour from sin and its consequences, and death will touch you only once, while a life of joyous fellowship with Christ and your fellow believers will be yours forever.

WILL MEN EVER BE RESTORED TO GOD'S ORIGINAL PLAN FOR THEM?

———◄———

"For he hath put all things under his feet"
(I Cor.15:27a)

A general may defeat all his enemies on the battle-field yet be unable to defeat his critics at home. He may be able to control the men under him and yet be unable to control himself. He may be victor in the eyes of men yet defeated in the estimation of God. And he may congratulate himself that no one has been able to stand up against him, yet go down at last before man's final enemy, death.

Thus, all men's victories are partial in this life. Even the victory of regenerated believers in Christ over sin and evil is at best incomplete. Only one man has ever conquered sin and death completely and defeated all His enemies.

In I Corinthians 15:24 Paul speaks of the God-man, the Lord Jesus Christ, as abolishing all rule, authority, and power. In verse 25, he speaks of even more personal enemies, for the word there is in the masculine gender. Thus, impersonal powers and personal enemies are brought into subjection to Christ at His appearance. Then, in verse 26, the last enemy, death, is abolished. And that, Paul wants to assure us, spells the victory over absolutely all.

In English, verse 27 begins, "For he hath put all things under his feet." But in the Greek text the first word is *panta*, "all," in the neuter gender, meaning "all things." It includes the whole created world, not only things animate and inanimate, but also people, angels, devils, everything. This is the same word with which John 1:3 begins: "All things were made by him," that is, by the eternal Word, the pre-incarnate Christ.

The declaration, "For he hath put all things under his feet," is taken from Psalm 8:6. It is also quoted in Hebrews 2:8. This is a Psalm of David, in which he thanks God for the exalted position given man over creation. "Thou madest him to have dominion over the works of thy hands; thou hast put all things under his feet" (v. 6).

In the creative purpose of God, the entire universe was put under man's power. But because of man's sin, this position has been reversed to some degree, and man is now more or less at the mercy of forces over which he was originally destined to rule. But the purpose of the Creator cannot ultimately be set aside. It will be accomplished through Christ, who became man that He might recover for Himself and for His brethren their lost rule over the universe. Until all things are finally put under the feet of Christ and of His people, His work will not be complete.

Now, of all forces in the world, material and spiritual, the least under man's control is death. Before that dread conqueror all men bow. Therefore the original creative purpose of God, which Christ came to accomplish, implies the overthrow of death.

What Paul is pointing out here is man's failure in attaining God's eternally intended purpose for him, and its accomplishment in and through Christ. That is why the New Testament refers to Psalm 8 as a Messianic fulfillment. In the Messiah, God fulfilled His purpose for man. Christ became the bridge that brought man to God and God to man.

When a man has Christ within him, he has victory and control over the spiritual evils in the world that would separate him from God. Even though a believer may lose a battle, he always wins the war by God's grace. Paul says that the complete victory of Christ and His followers over all spiritual and material forces, including death, will be realized at His second coming. Paul's stress throughout this 15th chapter of I Corinthians, and in all his writings, is that Christ's victory is not an accomplishment intended primarily for Himself, but for our sakes, that we might reign with Him for ever and ever.

Before man was ever created, this was Christ's announced purpose, in concert with the Father and the Holy Spirit: "And God said, Let us [note the plural pronouns throughout, indicating a plurality in deity] make man in our image, after our likeness: and let them have dominion over the fish of the sea, and over the fowl of the air, and over the cattle, and over all the earth, and over every creeping thing that creepeth upon the earth" (Gen. 1:26). Christ's resurrection was in a sense not a victory for Him, for it was an effortless accomplishment. But it was a vindication of His original purpose for man, accomplished partly on this side of the grave and more fully after our resurrection.

The word *gar*, translated "for" in verse 27, introduces in this context words that have the meaning of absolute finality in relation to Christ's conquest. With the abolition of death, all that needed subjugation has been conquered. Death was the final enemy, and this completes the round of enemies to be defeated.

That this subduing of His enemies will be an orderly process is indicated by Paul's use of the verb *hupotassoo*, which is made up of the preposition *hupo*, "under," and the verb *tassoo*, "to arrange." Christ will literally arrange His enemies under His feet. Actually this verb and the substantive *tagma*, "order," in verse 23 are related; they come from the same root verb. This applies to the orderly subjugation of Christ's enemies, and suggests the ease with which He puts them down. Usually victory is the result of a long and painful battle. But not in this case, for, although the enemies of our Lord have been free to act, it has only been by His permission. And when His timetable calls for an end to the exercise of their evil power, it will be accomplished with a mere word. With His word the universe was created (Gen. 1) and with His word the world will be subjected to Him. There will be no scattering of His enemies, but absolute order.

Of course, the reign of the Lord spoken of in this passage involves His judgment upon the wicked. This will be an orderly judgment, with punishment set in degrees according to the evil nature and work of each individual. God will open His books in which He keeps a record of men's lives and judge them accordingly. "For we must all appear before the judgment seat of Christ; that *every one* may receive the things done in his body, according to that he hath done, whether it be good or bad" (II Cor. 5:10). "And I saw the dead, small and great, stand before God; and the books were opened: and another book was opened, which is the book of life: and the dead were judged out of those things which were written in the books, according to their works" (Rev. 20:12).

Men will be judged not only according to their works but also according to their attitude toward the Lord Jesus Christ. If they are His enemies they will be put under His feet. John 3:18 says, "He that believeth on him is not condemned: but he that believeth not is condemned already, because he hath not believed in the name of the only begotten Son of God." (See also John 5:24.)

And the Lord Himself said, "He that rejecteth me, and receiveth not my words, hath one that judgeth him: the word that I have spoken, the same shall judge him in the last day" (John 12:48). Any number of Scriptures indicate that this judgment of the enemies of Christ will be orderly and without any special effort on His part.

The tense of the verb *hupetaxen*, "he did put under," in verse 27, is in the first aorist active indicative, indicating that there is a definite time when this is accomplished, and that this subjugation is final. The day of judgment is appointed, and the fate of Christ's enemies will then be final and irrevocable. One life, one death, one judgment. This is Satan's final overthrow after the millennial reign of Christ on earth spoken of in Revelation 20:1-6.

ANOTHER STRIKING PROOF OF CHRIST'S DEITY

"For he hath put all enemies under his feet"
                                    (I Cor. 15:27).

Do you have a few favorite books that you read over every now and then? If you like to read at all, I am sure you do. But you wouldn't want to read them every day, for you would soon tire of them.

There is only one book that I have found of which I never tire. It is fresh every time I come to it. The more I study it, the more I learn—and yet, paradoxically, the more I find that I still have to learn about its contents. This book is the Bible, the Word of God. It is full of much that seems mysterious; yet when you patiently apply yourself to understanding it, you find that even apparent contradictions lead to the most profound unfoldings of truth.

We have such a mystery to unravel here in the 15th chapter of I Corinthians. Verses 25 and 27, at first glance, look as though Paul were simply repeating himself. But when we examine them a bit more closely we shall see that in verse 25 Paul says that Christ will put all enemies under His feet, while in verse 27 he says that God the Father will do this. Is there a contradiction here? It seems a minor mystery, perhaps, yet it opens up the whole field of the nature of God— who He is and how He operates.

The interaction of the work of the three persons of the Trinity is indeed a mystery to our finite minds. Yet Scripture tells us in many places that whatever one person of the Trinity does the others participate in, at least to a degree. This does not contradict the fact that each person of the Trinity has His own particular offices or functions. However, these all operate for the same general purpose of God, that is, God creates, the Son redeems, the Spirit calls, but all for one purpose. Though their personalities are separate, their purposes are identical. Each person of the Godhead has a specific work to accomplish, but not without the concurrence and interaction of the other persons of the Trinity.

God the Father fully concurs with what God the Son does. "I and my Father are one," said Jesus (John 10:30). The word "one" in Greek is not *heis*, which would indicate identity of personality, but the neuter *hen*, which indicates or emphasizes oneness of purpose, nature, and attributes.

This same principle is seen in the testimony regarding Christ's resurrection. God the Father is said to have raised the Son from the dead (Eph. 1:20); yet in John 2:19 Christ says, "Destroy this temple [referring to His body, v. 21], and in three days I will raise it up." He also said that He had power to lay down His life and power to take it up again (John 10:18).

Thus also in the matter of subjugating evil, it is done by the mutual power and cooperation of God the Father and God the Son. Each one is said to do it. This is a definite proof of the deity of Christ, for if He can do what God can do He must be God.

Now let us look again at verse 27, paraphrasing it thus: "For he, God the Father, did put all under Christ's feet." Since Christ is the active agent in creation and redemption, those who did not receive His work in their behalf are subjugated under Him. "His feet" (*tous podas autou*) of course refers to Christ's dominion. Ephesians 1:22 states it even more explicitly: "And [God] hath put all things under his feet, and gave him to be the head over all things to the church," that is, for the advantage of the Church.

The rest of verse 27 confirms the fact that God the Father is the subject of "did put under," and that Christ is referred to in the term "his feet." It says by way of amplification and explanation, "But when he saith all things are put under him, it is manifest that he is excepted, which did put all things under him."

God the Father is the single exception to the "all" that have been subjected to the Lord Jesus. He will not be subject to Him, nor was there ever a time when He was. This form of absolute exclusion and single inclusion is found elsewhere in the New Testament. For instance, the first statement of John 1:18, "No one has seen God at any time," speaks of absolute exclusion; but the second statement in the verse gives the solitary inclusion. "The only begotten Son, which is in the bosom of the Father, he hath declared him." So it is in I Corinthians 15:27. God has put all things under Christ's feet with the single exception of Himself.

Paul presents God as an independent personality from the Lord Jesus Christ even in their eternal state. They are not to be confused as one and the same person. They are both capable of subjecting all things, and therefore they are both God. But they have different tasks to perform on behalf of humanity, and particularly among the redeemed.

The second sentence in verse 27 begins, "But when he saith. . . ." When who says? Since the subject of "did put under" in the first sentence is God, the subject of "saith" in the same context must by grammatical necessity be God also. The literal rendering of *eipee*, "saith," implies the future: "when he shall say." This takes us forward in time, after the second coming of the Lord, after the final judgment and subjugation of God's enemies including death, to God's declaration of victory: "But when he will say that all things have been put in subjection." What is it that God will say in this declaration of victory? That all things have been "put under him" (Christ).

In the first part of the verse the verb "hath put under" is in the aorist or past tense (*hupetaxen*), but in the second part, when God speaks, saying "all things are put under him," the verb is in the perfect tense (*hupotetaktai*). This latter statement refers not so much to God's act in subjecting these enemies as to the fact that they are now subjected and will continue to be in subjection. It refers to the effectiveness of God's action.

God the Father spoke at the beginning of Jesus' public mediatorial ministry, when He was baptized, saying, "This is my beloved Son, in whom I am well pleased" (Matt. 3:17). Now, at the end, when the task is finally completed, with all the elect gathered in and all the enemies subjugated, God the Father speaks again, saying, "All things have been put in subjection."

Paul concludes this verse by making the single exception very clear: "It is manifest that he [God the Father] is excepted, which did put all things under him [Christ]." God the Father, who subjected everything to Christ, is Himself excepted from subjection to Christ.

Since Scripture teaches that Christ is God, and since God cannot be subjected to Himself, how is it that in verse 28 we find that the Son will finally Himself be subject to the Father? This is another mystery, whose unraveling leads to still further revelations of the nature of Christ and His work. We shall take this up in our next study.

WILL CHRIST EVER CEASE TO BE EQUAL WITH THE FATHER?

"And when all things shall be subdued unto him, then shall the Son also himself be subject unto him that put all things under him, that God may be all in all"
(I Cor. 15:28).

In studying any passage of Scripture, we must never take it out of context. The verse we are about to study, I Corinthians 15:28, is a case in point. In the King James Version, it reads as we see it above. But unless we refer to the context, how can we know to whom the personal pronouns "him" and "himself" apply? Let me quote it by substituting the proper referents for the pronouns, as follows: "And when all things shall be subdued unto Christ, then shall the Son also himself be subject unto God the Father that put all things under the Son, that God may be all in all."

Even when we have determined to whom the pronouns refer, this is a difficult verse to understand. We do not find this teaching anywhere else in Scripture—that when everything shall be subdued unto Christ, the Son will voluntarily subject Himself to the Father. We must not look at this verse in isolation, but in relation to the rest of Scripture. For instance, it cannot possibly mean that a time is coming when Christ as a distinct personality will cease to exist. This would be contrary to the rest of the teaching of the Apostle Paul and the other New Testament Scriptures.

The Bible plainly teaches that Christ had no beginning and consequently He will have no end. He is and always has been God. John 1:1 states, "In the beginning [*en archee* in the absolute sense] was the Word, and the Word was with God, and the Word was God." (For a fuller discussion of this, see the author's book, *Was Christ God?*, Grand Rapids: Eerdmans Publishing House, pp. 47-52.)

In John 20:28 Thomas expressed his belief in the resurrection of Christ by addressing Him as "My Lord and my God." Jesus not only did not contradict him, but said the same thing of Himself when He claimed equality with the Father (John 14:9).

In Romans 9:5, Paul, speaking of Christ, calls Him "God blessed for ever."

In Titus 2:13, Paul calls Christ "the great God and our Saviour."

Thus we conclude that the subjection of Christ to God cannot possibly mean that Christ will be God up until that point and then cease to be God thereafter. Scripture tells us that Jesus Christ is "the same yesterday, and to day, and for ever" (Heb. 13:8).

The second thing that this verse cannot mean is that there will be such a merging of the personalities of Father and Son that they will become identical. This is not a forced subjection of the Son to the Father here but a voluntary one. This is not made very clear in the King James Version. A far better translation would be, "Then also the Son himself shall subject himself to him who did subject all things to him." The verb *hupotageesetai*, "shall subject himself," or "shall be subjected," can be considered either as future passive or in the middle voice as to its actual meaning, depending on the context, for, in first-century Greek, aorist passives and future passives are sometimes used as aorist middle and future middle. In form, of course, it is a second future passive, third person singular. If it is passive in use, it means that coercion was brought to bear by the Father in subjecting the Son, even as it was brought to bear in subjecting all things to Christ. If it is in the middle voice in usage, it means that the Son voluntarily offered Himself to the Father. Why do we believe this to be in the middle voice instead of the passive? Because of verse 24, which speaks of Christ voluntarily delivering the Kingdom to the Father: "Then cometh the end, when he shall have delivered up the kingdom to God, even the Father."

This voluntary subjection of Son to Father is not the subjection of one person of the Trinity to another. It is Jesus Christ's subjection of His role in the divine plan as the God-man. Scripture nowhere infers that the Lord Jesus Christ will lose His identity in eternity. He will not be merged in God, so as to be no longer discoverable. He told His disciples, "And if I go and prepare a place for you, I will come again, and receive you unto myself: that where I am, there ye may be also" (John 14:3). Nowhere in Scripture do we find Christ disappearing from the eternal fellowship of believers. I Thessalonians 4:17 makes this very clear, when it tells us that at Christ's second coming, after the dead in Christ have risen, "then we which are alive and remain shall be caught up together with them in the clouds, to meet the Lord in the air: and so shall we ever be with the Lord."

We shall never be separated from Christ in eternity. Therefore His subjection to the Father cannot mean the end of His existence as a distinct personality, even as the subjection of everything under Him cannot mean the end of their existence. Subjection, whether forced or voluntary, necessitates the continued existence of that which is subjected; otherwise it would be spoken of as annihilation.

And the third thing this verse cannot mean is that the Son in His eternity is or will be in any way inferior to God the Father. What was it that most outraged the contemporary religious leaders who persecuted Christ during His earthly lifetime? In addition to His so-called Sabbath-breaking, was it not that He said that "God was his Father, making himself equal with God" (John 5:18)?

Philippians 2:6 tells us that Christ's equality with God was not something that had to be attained. It was natural and not acquired. "Who, being in the form of God, thought it not robbery to be equal with God." Being equal with God from the beginning, He voluntarily "made himself of no reputation, and took upon him the form of a servant, and was made in the likeness of man" (v. 7). Christ gave His contemporaries the impression that He claimed to be God. If He is not God, He was a deceiver or was self-deceived, and in either case would be completely discredited.

There is overwhelming Scriptural evidence of the deity of Christ. When He called Himself the "Son of God," He never applied this designation in such a way as to suggest a merely religious and ethical relationship to God, such as that which might be possessed by others. While there were and are many "sons of God," there is but one "only begotten Son," the only One of the same family as God. (See the discussion of *monogenees* on pp. 23-27 of the book, *Was Christ God?*)

Here are other Scriptures that attest the deity of the Lord Jesus Christ. When Pilate said to Him, "I adjure thee by the living God, that thou tell us whether thou be the Christ the Son of God," Jesus replied, "Thou hast said." (Matt. 26:63, 64.) It was for this testimony that Jesus was put to death.

Colossians 1:15 calls Him "the image of the invisible God," and Hebrews 1:3 speaks of Him as "the brightness of his [the Father's] glory, and the express image of his person."

Christ Himself said, "I and my Father are one" (John 10:30). Again, in John 16:15, He said, "All things that the Father hath are mine"; and in John 17:10, "All mine are thine, and thine are mine." And in reply to Philip's request to show them the Father, Jesus replied, "He that hath seen me hath seen the Father" (John 14:9).

Colossians 2:9 declares, "In him dwelleth all the fulness of the Godhead bodily"; and in Colossians 1:19 we read, "For it pleased the Father that in him should all fulness dwell."

The doctrine of the Trinity is nowhere explained in Scripture; it is taken for granted. And we are not so much to seek to understand it—something that is impossible to our finite minds—as to accept the demonstration of it in Scripture. As John Wesley said to someone who professed himself puzzled by the doctrine of the Trinity, "Tell me how it is that in this room there are three candles and but one light, and I will explain to you the mode of the divine existence."

ONE GOD IN THREE PERSONS

"And when all things shall be subdued unto him, then shall the Son also himself be subject unto him that put all things under him, that God may be all in all"
(I Cor. 15:28).

We have discovered what Paul did *not* mean by saying that, when all things shall be subdued under Christ, then shall the Son also be subject to God the Father, "that God may be all in all" (I Cor. 15:28). He did not mean that the day is coming when Christ will no longer exist as a distinct person. He did not mean that Christ's personality will be swallowed up in the personality of God the Father, thus resulting in a unitarian type God. He did not mean that Christ will ever cease to be God, as He proclaimed Himself to be, and as He was believed to be, and for which claim He was crucified.

But before we can discuss what Paul actually did mean when he said that the Son would ultimately subject Himself to the Father, we must have a clear understanding of the nature of God and the personalities in the Godhead—Father, Son, and Holy Spirit.

Scripture teaches that all three persons are God. The deity of the Father is self-evident in Scripture; and we have already demonstrated the deity of Christ. Just a few verses will suffice to indicate the deity of the Holy Spirit and His existence as a separate personality.

When Ananias gave a false account of the money he and his wife had donated to the Church, Peter told him that he had lied to the Holy Ghost, and in doing so had lied to God (Acts 5:3, 4).

I Corinthians 3:16 tells us that we are "the temple of God," that "the Spirit of God dwelleth" in us. And I Corinthians 12:4-6 says, "There are diversities of gifts, but *the same Spirit*. And there are differences of administrations, but *the same Lord*. And there are diversities of operations, but it is *the same God* which worketh all in all."

Scripture ascribes to the Holy Spirit the attributes of God, such as life, truth, love, holiness, eternity, omnipresence, omniscience, and omnipotence. He is said to do the works of God such as creation, regeneration, resurrection. He receives honor due only to God. He is associated with God on a footing of equality, both in the formula of baptism and in the apostolic benedictions.

Here are three persons, then, each one separately spoken of as God. That He is a personal God is demonstrated in Scripture by His attributes of rationality, love, and moral consciousness, which permit our dependence upon Him and a sense of personal relation.

And yet God is not characterized by personality in the limited sense that you and I understand the term, but is an infinite spiritual being, made apparent to our spiritual intelligence and feeling in such qualities as belong to personality, notably self-consciousness. We tend, of course, to think of Him in human terms, as having a shape like ours, with eyes, ears, hands, feet, and so on. But in reality He is not like us, particularly in this respect, being pure spirit, and not being physical or material at all, although in certain ways we are spiritually like Him, because although He is an uncreated being, we are created in His image spiritually.

It is we who call Him "person," but He has never called Himself directly or precisely that, although Scripture uses terms concerning Him that definitely indicate what we would call personality. However, God's personality is accurately expressed only when He is represented as three persons or self-consciousnesses, as Scripture presents Him. If we represent Him as one person, in contradiction to Scripture, we stand in danger of imagining Him to be an extension of our own concept of a person, only infinite from our point of view. But the adjective "infinite" has little meaning to us, whereas the noun "person" is concrete. Frankly, we are inherently as ignorant of true infinity as we are of God Himself, because this infinity is found only in God.

One God in three persons, then, is the only way inspired human language can express the fact that He is a God not limited to our own inherent concept of what a person is, but surpasses our understanding of personality by being One in Three and Three in One. This is not only the best way to express God; it is the only accurate way. Thus the Holy Spirit helps us to comprehend a little bit of His "infiniteness."

Although I do not go along with everything Horace Bushnell says about the Trinity, I find his illustration of how men attempt to conceive of the Triune God most illuminating. He says we do it in somewhat the same way as we attempt to conceive of infinite space. (Actually, of course, there is no such thing, for space is in the realm of creation and is therefore finite. It is only because space is so vast that man has not been able to discover its outer limits that he calls it "infinite.")

We conceive of space by laying out three lines, which we designate as length, breadth, and height— and we run them out until we are obliged to stop because neither our minds nor our pencils can go any farther. We then give these lines as our notions of infinite space, although actually we do not even know what the word "infinite" means in relation to anything. The lines themselves are certainly not space, but are only devices by which we try to conceive of it.

In somewhat the same way the Holy Spirit teaches us to conceive of the infinite Deity of One God in Three Persons, by a grammatical device He suits to our finite minds. Of course, without words, without grammar, we could not conceive of God at all. They are just as necessary for an understanding of a due concept of God as the three lines are for conceiving of space. Our ability to comprehend what God's Spirit teaches us in this respect is not perfect, but this concept of Scripture is as adequate as any human thought could allow. Of course, this implies that words of Scripture accurately represent the concept of the Triune God, but we, on the other hand, are too finite and sinful to perceive their full meaning.

By thinking of the persons of the Godhead as Triune, as one that is three and three that are one, we accept what God Himself has revealed. This is what enables us to hold the nature of the deity of God without reducing Him to our own measure, as we would be inclined to do if we thought of Him always as a single person. Apart from the revelation of God in Scripture, we would be tempted to think of God as just a bigger and better human being, a projection of our ideal selves.

God always has been, is, and always will be Triune. Therefore when I Corinthians 15:28 speaks of the Son as finally subjecting Himself to the Father, or being so far discontinued as to let God be all in all, it cannot mean that the Son as the God-man is to be taken away, or will disappear, in any sense that would modify the fact of Trinity or that would modify the fact of our Lord's humanity, for that matter. If God is to be all in all, it must be as Trinity and not otherwise.

There is only one possible sense in which the Son can subject Himself to the Father, then, and that is in those aspects of His office that are of a temporary nature. The reign of Christ as Redeemer and Mediator will one day cease, and He will yield His mediatorial Kingdom back to the Father. Our relationship to Christ in eternity will not be to the Son of man but to His eternal Sonship—not to Jesus the man as King, but to Christ as God. However, Christ's humanity, let us repeat, will not be modified or cease to exist. What would be the sense of our bodily resurrection, if Christ should cease to have a human body or other human characteristics? Our relationship to Christ in eternity will center in the Trinity, and especially in the Eternal Word or Son, who is represented only for a time in the person of Jesus as King.

To summarize what has been discussed so far: At the end of the age, when all of God's enemies, death, and Satan have been defeated and subjugated (Rev. 20: 10-15), and are placed by God the Father under the feet of the Lord Jesus, then the work of Christ as the Redeemer and Mediator will be completed. Then (*tote*, "at that very time") even He, Himself, Jesus as King,

Mediator, Son of man, will voluntarily subject Himself to God, who had subjected all to the Son.

When the Lord Jesus was dying on the cross, He said, "It is finished." This applied to the completion of His work of redemption as far as man was concerned. He had accomplished all that was necessary to redeem man from sin and to bring him into a right relationship with his Creator God.

But the whole creation still groans and travails in pain (Rom. 8:22). This was only part of the work of the Lord Jesus as the Servant of man, the Son of man. After His ascension He is still the Mediator-Intercessor on our behalf (Rom. 8:34). The Lord maintains this mediatorial state because He is coming back as He was seen ascending into heaven. "This same Jesus, which is taken up from you into heaven, shall so come in like manner as ye have seen him go into heaven" (Acts 1:11b).

However, one day there will be an end to this relationship of Christ as the Mediator between God and man. At that time the fate of all will have been sealed. There will be no more work for Christ to do in the redemption of man. He will then restore Himself to the position He had with the Eternal Father God before the world began.

WILL EVERYONE WHO GOES TO HEAVEN ENJOY IT EQUALLY?

"And when all things shall be subdued unto him, then shall the Son also himself be subject unto him that put all things under him, that God may be all in all"
(I Cor. 15:28).

Do you know what God is doing right now? I'm not asking this question just for the sake of propounding a riddle. Of course you and I can't know the exact activity that God is engaged in at any given moment. What I am trying to bring home to you is that God is alive and active in the world today.

Sometimes people have an over-simplified notion of God. They seem to think that all His acts are confined between the two covers of the Bible. They reduce these actions to the bare essentials: He created man, punished him when he disobeyed in the Garden of Eden, gave him the Ten Commandments through Moses, sent Christ into the world to die and rise again for man's redemption, promised He would return for the final reward of the righteous and the judgment of the wicked, and that's it. But what do you think He has been doing for the past 2,000 years?

Scripture teaches that the Lord Jesus Christ is still active on our behalf—still interceding for us, still mediating between a holy God and sinful man. The Holy Spirit is still convicting men of their sins and wooing them to the Saviour. God the Father is still saving all who come to Him through Christ, still answering the prayers of those who look to Him in faith, still overseeing, over-ruling, and achieving His purposes for this present age.

And in the future? Some people think that I Corinthians 15:24-28 teaches that, at the end of this age, Jesus Christ will give up His powers, take a back seat, and thus let God be "all in all." But we must interpret this passage in conjunction with the total teaching of Scripture regarding the end times.

This present age of grace will come to a close with the return of Jesus Christ. The dead in Christ will be raised at that time. All God's enemies will be subjugated to Christ. Then His redemptive work for man will be finished, and He will finally subject Himself to the Father. This, however, will merely be in His role as Mediator-King, as God-man, so that He may revert to His role of the Eternal Son, which antedated His temporary role of Jesus the Redeemer, with this important difference, that He will continue to be the God-man, He will not lose His humanity in thus finally subjecting Himself to the Father.

What is the purpose for the subjugation of all things to Christ, and His restoration to His position as the Son of God who no longer acts as the Mediator? It is "that God may be all in all."

The word translated "that" is actually the Greek conjunction *hina*, meaning "in order that." It denotes purpose, aim, a goal. It is the purpose of an act that is spoken of in this verse. Therefore the conjunction must refer to a verb denoting a specific act, which in this case is *hupotageesetai*, "He [Christ] shall subject Himself." And the purpose stated in the text is "that God may be all in all."

You see, the eternal plan of God is not centered around man but around Himself. God is the center of the universe and not man. It is His purpose and plan that must ultimately prevail, not man's. We are just the outer rim of the wheel; He is the hub. Man's rebellion since the fall has had under Satan but one aim: to thwart the will of God. Man wants his own way; he would like to displace God from the center and enthrone himself there. The apostasy of many of the past and present religious systems stems from just this, that they are man-centered rather than God-centered. This is an abomination to God. The restoration of all things will have as its primary purpose the giving to God in man's reckoning of the central place that eternally belonged to Him.

If you want God's eternal purpose to be realized in your life, beginning right now, take one important step: put God at the center of all things in your thinking. Let Him be your first and most important consideration. Nothing—and no one—should be allowed to come before Him.

When Mark Twain was in Berlin he received an invitation asking him to call upon the Kaiser. "Why, Papa," exclaimed his little daughter, after contemplating the letter for a moment in speechless awe, "if it keeps on this way there won't be anybody left for you to get acquainted with but God!" An amusing remark, but how it strikes to the root of man's pride in desiring to become great by associating with the so-called great of this earth. Greatness in the eternal sense in the sight of God is when God becomes "all in all" in a man's life.

This eternal state of things, which will be the norm after the final judgment and ultimate subjection of evil, really begins in a spiritual sense here on earth with the believer. Thus we have a beautiful analogy between that which now is and that which must one day be. Now the enthroning of God in our hearts and lives is voluntary though not perfect; then it will be complete, perfect, and changeless—still with our most joyful consent. When you voluntarily yield yourself completely to God, joy must follow. But not every believer finds in God his "all in all." To those who do, the future joy of heaven is realized in some degree here and now. How wonderful to have such a foretaste of heaven on earth!

I honestly believe that those who have voluntarily sought to make God their "all in all" on earth, as far as possible, will enjoy Him the most in heaven. For them heaven will be a continuation of a state they chose on their own, instead of a mere state of conforming to standards they avoided while on earth. I do not believe that all born-again believers will enjoy God equally or in the same manner in heaven. Of course, they will experience that basic joy that results from redemption in and through Christ, but surely the rewards for works of faith and an earthly state of yieldedness will play a significant part in determining how much or in what manner they enjoy God's presence. Isn't it true that what you choose to do you love and enjoy, while what you have to do against your natural inclinations you usually grumble about? You may find little heavenly joy in doing what you never did voluntarily and cheerfully on earth, out of sheer love for the Lord.

Spurgeon recognized this when he said, "After Christ has been received into the heart, everything else will have to be done cheerfully and voluntarily. He did not command Zaccheus to give the half of his goods to the poor; but spontaneously, as soon as Christ came in, Zaccheus said of his own accord, 'Behold, Lord, the half of my goods I give to the poor' (Luke 19:8). No ordinance to this effect had proceeded from the Saviour's lips: 'Zaccheus, you must restore fourfold to all whom you have wronged.' No; but gladly, out of the fullness of his renewed heart, he freely said, 'If I have taken any thing from any man by false accusation, I restore him fourfold.'

"This is the very essence of true religion; it is cheerful voluntariness. When a man who professes to be a Christian begins to ask, 'Must I do this?' or 'Must I do that?' he makes us stand in doubt concerning him. Believers in Christ are not under the law, but under grace. The principle that rules us is not 'Must I?' but 'May I?' It becomes to the believer a joy and a delight to serve Christ; he is not flogged to his duty. . . . Such a man works not to obtain heaven; why should he? Heaven is his already; in Christ Jesus, it is given to him by a covenant which cannot be broken. And this blessed voluntariness, this joyous freedom of the will, conferred by sovereign grace, becomes the very life and soul to vital godliness." (See "Cheerful Voluntariness," by C. H. Spurgeon, in *The Christian World Pulpit*, Vol. 58, p. 398.)

HAVE GOD'S PLANS FOR THE WORLD BEEN FRUSTRATED?

"And when all things shall be subdued unto him, then shall the Son also himself be subject unto him that put all things under him, that God may be all in all"
(I Cor. 15:28).

God loves the whole world, but does He love each person in the world equally and indiscriminately? Yes and no. Yes, as far as extending His offer of salvation to them and providing them with life's common mercies. No, in the sense that He has a special and tender love for "His own"—those who believe in Him, trust Him, obey and serve Him with cheerfulness. It is for them that Jesus Christ went back to heaven to "prepare a place," that they might enjoy fellowship with Him throughout eternity. It is for them that He reserves His special blessings and rewards — some here and many more hereafter.

In our study of I Corinthians 15, we see that this chapter mainly concerns the believers. It is only as a natural consequence of God's concern for believers that we are told what will happen to Satan, unbelievers and evil in general. It is for the establishment of God's final plan and purpose, which includes the vindication of the believers, that unbelievers will be eternally judged and rendered powerless to continue to spoil God's world.

Because the general theme of this chapter is the resurrection of the believer and what will follow, I believe that it is in the life of the believer in heaven that God will be "all in all." Then there will be no more half-hearted dedication but unreserved obedience. Man's option to sin will happily cease at this stage of his history, for He will be conformed to God's will. God will be "all in all" first in the believers' lives. The very purpose of God is that redeemed men shall give Him complete and unreserved obedience. That's what He longs to receive from us now, and He will finally accomplish this even by conforming our nature to full obedience hereafter. This is the ultimate reason why the second person of the Trinity, the Son of God, became the Son of man. This is the ultimate purpose of the incarnation. The Lord Jesus as the God-Man cannot deliver the Kingdom to God the Father unless redeemed man is brought into full obedience. God must be made "all in all," and the first group included in that second word "all" is the redeemed believers.

Again, the phrase, "in order that God may be all in all," implies that God at this particular time will be in a sense what He has not been right along. As a result of the fall of Adam and consequently of all humanity, God has not been given His rightful place in the world He created. People and things are not functioning as He desires. If the redeemed believer cannot fully conform to God's will on earth, because of the remnant of sin which is in him, how much less can the rest of creation do God's will? It is true God is sovereign now in this age of disobedience and grace, but His sovereignty is not fully imposed. This is not because He cannot enforce it, but because He chooses not to. In line with His present purposes, He permits certain things to happen in the world, in the lives of believers and unbelievers, which He is not directly responsible for. He allows sin and Satan a certain latitude. It is to counteract their activity, and to bring ultimate good as God sees it out of this evil, that the Lord Jesus now acts as our Mediator. But all this is the consequence of man's sinfulness.

Though God gave man free will, He is not morally responsible for man's choice of sin. He provided a Redeemer in the person of the Lord Jesus. But sin and Satan have not been bound. They are active and responsible for the suffering that God permits for the present. But they will not always be active. Scripture teaches that Satan will be bound during the millennium, after which he will be released for a season. He will deceive the nations. But the time will come when, as Revelation 20:10 tells us, Satan will be "cast into the lake of fire and brimstone." However, until that overthrow, he is active in and around everybody. In unbelievers he may be "all in all," but in believers he is an unwelcome annoyance. This same Apostle Paul who said, "Christ liveth in me," also frankly confessed in Romans 7:15-17, "For that which I do I allow not: for what I would, that do I not; but what I hate, that do I. If then I do that which I would not, I consent unto the law that it is good. Now then it is no more I that do it, but sin that dwelleth in me."

God is not in the believer to the complete exclusion of the activity of Satan and sin. Neither is He in the world to the exclusion of the natural consequences of sin. War, natural calamities, pestilences, sickness, and suffering—these are natural to us, but they are foreign to the character of God and His original desire for us His creatures. They are also alien to His ultimate purpose for the world. It is when this new state of being is ushered in that what Revelation 21:4 speaks of shall come to pass: "And God shall wipe away all tears from their eyes; and there shall be no more death, neither sorrow, nor crying, neither shall there be any more pain: for the former things are passed away." Remember that this state is described in Revelation after we have been told of the eternal casting of the devil into the lake of fire. What God intended for man and His creation at the beginning will ultimately come to pass at the end.

"That God may be all in all." The Bible translators used the expression "may be," but there is actually no "may be" about it. It is surely going to be so. The literal Greek here is "In order that God *be* (*hina ee*)." This refers to a definite state in the future. He will be in this sense what He is not now.

Of course, this doesn't imply a change in the nature or character of God, for this can never change. "With whom [God]," James states, "is no variableness, neither shadow of turning" (James 1:17). This is the doctrine of the immutability of God. "But thou art the same, and thy years shall have no end" (Ps. 102:27). "For I am the Lord, I change not" (Mal. 3:6). "But thou art the same, and thy years shall not fail" (Heb. 1:12). And confirming the divine nature of the Lord Jesus, the Apostle in Hebrews 13:8 says concerning Him what is said of God the Father, "Jesus Christ the same yesterday, and to day, and for ever."

But God takes different attitudes toward His creation at various periods of history. Read the Bible carefully and you will notice this throughout its pages. His dealings with Israel are different today from what they were in times past and what they are prophesied to be in the future. His attitude toward man varies with the opportunity and favor He affords man. Man's responsibility is conditioned by the laws and attitudes of God. When there is no law there is no sin. "Because the law worketh wrath: for where no law is, there is no transgression" (Rom. 4:15).

God's present attitude in this period of grace is that of a Saviour pleading for the acceptance of His salvation through Christ. But He will not forever strive with man (Gen. 6:3). The Scriptures tell us that the time will come when He will no longer fill the role of a Father awaiting the prodigal's return home with outstretched hands. This age of grace will close. God will no longer be frustrated in His purposes for His own redeemed people, or defied by the rest of His creation who have rejected His offer of grace. In that day He will become the Rewarder of the faithful and the Judge of the unbeliever.

WHEN GOD BECOMES "ALL IN ALL," WILL WE BE NOTHING?

———◆———

"And when all things shall be subdued unto him, then shall the Son also himself be subject unto him that put all things under him, that God may be all in all"
(I Cor. 15:28).

If God is to be "all in all" in our lives when we get to heaven, will we then be lost in God? Will our whole personal life be absorbed and overshadowed in His life? Will we have no more separate being than so many drops of water in the ocean? If so, then eternal "life" is a misnomer, for to lose our identity is death indeed.

However, that is definitely not what I Corinthians 15:28 means when it says that God will be "all in all." You will find similar expressions in Ephesians 1:23, Colossians 3:11, and I Corinthians 12:6. The Greek is *panta en pasin*. *Panta*, "all," is used repeatedly here in I Corinthians 15:24-28. Sometimes it is preceded by the definite article *ta*, "the," and sometimes not—with no real change in meaning.

In I Corinthians 12:6, of course, it refers to all the spiritual gifts that believers may possess. In Colossians 3:11, where Paul says that "Christ is all, and in all," he is speaking about the new man in Christ. He transcends nationality and to him everything is Christ. He is above national feeling and human ancestry. To him Christ is supreme.

Similarly in I Corinthians 15:28 Paul declares that God *will be* everything that He *must be* in all His creation. He must be everything *first* to the believers, who are the subject of this entire 15th chapter. This is expressed in Ephesians 1:22, 23, "And [God] hath put all things under his feet, and gave him to be the head over all things to the church, which is his body, the fulness of him that filleth all in all." Here as in I Corinthians 15 we have the subjugation of evil for the sake of the Church of Jesus Christ. This is the only way God can be all in all, that is, the only way He can be everything He *wants to be* in the believer. It is the presence of evil in the world now that hinders God from being everything He wants to be in you.

What will God be to the unbeliever? Everything God *needs to be* in him. Not an unwilling Saviour, for God never saves anyone without his consent. He will put the unbeliever under His feet, we are told.

Here is where an adequate understanding of *en pasin*, "in all," is necessary. It means "in every way" or "in all possible ways." (See Lenski on I Cor. 15:28 and Eph. 1:23.) Actually this adverbial phrase does not denote the whole universe as such, but the individual elements of God's creation. In each one God *will be* everything that He *must be* in order to be God supreme. (See Liddell - Scott, Oxford, 1958, p. 1345.) This does not mean the elimination of the distinctive character of God's created beings, animate and inanimate. It is not that all will be God and not their own selves, but that each one will be what *must be* under God, so that He will be supreme and so that none of His laws and interests will be violated as they are now.

Note that the statement is not that God is to be "all," but that He is to be all "in all." His universal life is not to destroy the old varieties of being, as that blind preacher George Matheson so beautifully points out, but it is to pulsate through these varieties. His music is to fill the world, but it is to sound through all the varied instruments of the world. His sunshine is to flood the universe, but it is to be mirrored in a thousand various forms. His love is to penetrate creation, but it is to be reflected in the infinite diversities of the hearts and souls of men.

We speak of losing ourselves in the ocean of His love, but this is only poetically true. God's love is an ocean where no man permanently loses himself; he is submerged therein only to regain himself in richer, nobler form. The only ocean in which a man loses himself is self-love; God's love gives him back his life that he may keep it to eternal life.

Man is not truly himself until he has found God. He will never become a power to himself until God has become all in him; he will never really live until he has lived in God. Forget yourself. Forget your pride and selfishness, your cares and crosses, that inner world that centers on yourself. Unbar the doors of your being to God, who stands without, waiting to get in. And truly your forgetfulness will make you strong, your surrender will make you mighty, your dying to self will make you alive for evermore. (See *Moments on the Mount*, by George Matheson, London, pp. 182-4.)

God cannot be all that He intrinsically is, in each one of us or in each subject of His creation. This would result in a multiplicity of gods, which would be pantheism. "That God be all in all" really means "that God be everything in each one individually," that God's plan be fulfilled in each man as an individual. In the eternal state of all persons and things, there will be a fulfillment of God's purpose and eternal intent for each one, without the loss of individual distinctives and capacities. God will be everything to each in all possible ways.

As Lenski says, "Christ fills some things in one, some in another way, for all are by no means alike, some being inanimate, some only animate, some rational, some spiritual (the church), some angelic." (*Interpretations of Ephesians*, p. 404.)

God will be one thing to the believer—a rewarder of his faith according to his work; and another to the unbeliever — a judge of his unbelief and his works of unbelief. He will not make a believer out of an unbeliever. God fulfills His purpose for each part of His creation, for each being at the consummation of the age, but He does not ignore the nature and the capacity of each being. After all, isn't He the One who created that nature? He is the only One who really knows its capacities in full. Therefore God will be everything to each one according to his nature and capacity, not in spite of it.

This is like the attitude of a wise and understanding parent to his child. You do not force your child to become what you want him to be, regardless of his capacities and capabilities. You take these things into consideration. You neither push your child beyond his capacity nor neglect to develop his capabilities to the utmost. That is what God as our Heavenly Father will ultimately do. He will fill our cup with everything that it can hold. No one will be able to act contrary to His eternal will and purpose. This state of things actually does exist now, with the exception of the limited function of Satan and evil that God now permits.

Note that the subjugation of evil and those who perpetrate it is the main theme of I Corinthians 15:24-28. Evil and death as they have been operating in our world are the results of man's original disobedience to God. Those consequences and their cause—sin—must be dealt with decisively, primarily for the believers so that they may be everything God meant them to be—each one individually.

Only as a necessary consequence of the blessing of believers will God put all His enemies under His feet, so that He may be supreme in a fuller sense than He now chooses to express His sovereignty. Now He is sovereign with the single exception that evil operates under His permission. But then evil will no longer be permitted free course, and will receive all that it has earned—its just punishment for the rejection of God's redemptive grace.

Man cannot forever reject God and hope to escape the consequences. The day is coming when God will be everything to each one as He deems necessary, according to the standing of each one with Him.

HOW CAN A GOD OF LOVE PUNISH ANYONE ETERNALLY?

".... that God may be all in all" (I Cor. 15:28c).

If you had made the world, would you have done certain things differently? Most of us at one time or another have spoken, either jokingly or seriously, of some change we would like to make. But this is to say that God does not know His business; or to fail to recognize that sin has marred His original creation.

However, when men presume to tell God that He cannot be a God of love and do thus and so, they are treading on dangerous ground. Some people are unwilling to accept the plain teaching of Scripture, that not only will the righteous in Christ be eternally rewarded but also that the unrighteous will be eternally punished. They say that eternal punishment is incompatible with God's nature. But since Scripture definitely teaches it, they must either twist Scripture to suit their purposes, or be placed in the position of telling God what He can and cannot do.

In I Corinthians 15:22-28, some people profess to find ground for believing that God's attitude toward unbelieving mankind will not be that of a judge, but that He will eventually restore everyone to His favor. This is called the doctrine of universal restoration, or universalism. There is even a Universalist denomination, whose members believe that God will ultimately save everybody, whether they die believing or unbelieving.

Unfortunately, you find individuals who hold to

this belief in most denominations today. God is love, their argument goes, and by virtue of His nature cannot ultimately consign anyone to eternal punishment. Everybody, the universalists say, will be in heaven. There is no hell.

It may sound desirable, superficially, to wish that there were no hell and no punishment for anyone in the future. But the man of profounder insight, who places his faith in God's wisdom rather than his own, realizes that this would not be for ultimate good. We must want to find out the truth about what awaits men hereafter, and we can discover this only in God's revelation of His purposes in Scripture. You cannot risk your eternal future on the unfounded hope that all will be well for all men at the end. You must take steps to make sure, as far as you individually are concerned. Hope must be based on knowledge of God's spiritual laws of cause and effect.

Right along in I Corinthians 15 Paul has been stressing the historical proofs of the resurrection of Christ. He bases his theological arguments on this incontrovertible fact. Because Christ rose, He is unique. Therefore we may have confidence that His revelation about the future of the world is unique and true. He told us that we shall all rise, both believers and unbelievers. Had He not risen Himself, we might reject His statements about our resurrection, and our ultimate fate with regard to reward and punishment, as fanciful conjecture. But if we believe in the resurrection of the Lord Jesus Christ, we cannot logically reject His teachings about the future life or anything else.

Of course, if you do not believe Christ rose from

the dead, you are at liberty to disregard His teachings and formulate your own beliefs. Only do not call them Christian, for that would be a misnomer.

The Lord Jesus made a clear and unequivocal statement about the future of the human race. "Marvel not at this," He said, "for the hour is coming, in the which all that are in the graves shall hear his voice, and shall come forth; they that have done good, unto the resurrection of life; and they that have done evil, unto the resurrection of damnation" (John 5:28, 29).

The universalists disregard this plain statement and offer instead their interpretation of I Corinthians 15:22, "For as in Adam all die, even so in Christ shall all be made alive." We have already given a full explanation of this verse, showing that the Greek text indicates that two groups of people are spoken of here. It is as though there were two circles: one that includes all who are in Adam, which means all of mankind; the other, all who are in Christ, which includes all believers. Everyone starts out in Adam's circle at birth; and all who remain there are dead in their trespasses and sins and "keep on dying" (*apothneeskousin*). That is the literal translation of the original Greek.

Who keep on dying? Only those who remain in Adam's circle, who have not by faith stepped over into the circle of those who receive Christ's offer of salvation. Once a person becomes a believer in Christ, he is in the circle of Christ and no longer "keeps on dying," for "in Christ all shall be made alive." This refers to the physical resurrection of the already spiritually alive believers.

The verb translated "shall be made alive" in Greek

is *zoo-opoieetheesontai,* in the future passive indicative, used here aoristically, thus referring to a definite act of God at a particular time. Here it refers to the physical resurrection of believers and not to spiritual life to be conferred on all people. Since believers already have spiritual life, the latter teaching would not make sense. Thus we see that I Corinthians 15:22 does not teach ultimate universal salvation.

This entire passage in verses 22-28 speaks of the ultimate subjugation of evil, not its forced reconciliation to a holy God. It says that God the Father "hath put all things under his [the Son's] feet." You do not put your friends under your feet, do you? You put them at your side in a place of honor.

The last statement of the passage, "that God may be all in all," is a continuation of the process of subjugation of all things, not of their reconciliation. God has never made unwilling friends and followers. Man's consent is necessary. If that has always been so, what reason do we have to believe that God's character and disposition will change, since man will continue as he is?

Another reason why we must logically reject the theory of universalism, that all men will ultimately be saved despite their unbelief and wickedness, is that it is contrary to what we humans—including the universalists—believe to be proper and just for the normal operation of our society. When we punish the offender, we do not sin against love. We would not want people to think that of us, nor do we think it of ourselves. Punishment rightly administered is both just and loving. It is just because it equally considers the keepers of the law and the offenders against the law. If you do not restrain and punish the offender, you are unjust toward the law-abiding citizens who may suffer from his unrestrained acts. You are also unjust toward the morally weaker element of society, who would feel encouraged to engage in unlawful behavior with impunity.

Punishment is loving, because love considers all people. If you let a child-murderer go free, you may feel you are being loving toward him; but then you would not be loving to all the other children in our society, would you? Punishment is loving in this life because it affords protection of the innocent and an opportunity for the guilty to recognize and repent of their evil.

When it comes to God's dealings with men, by what logical consideration do we expect Him to act differently? Our punishment of the evil doer is just and loving, but when God warns that He will punish the unbelieving and wicked, we inconsistently declaim, "Such a God would be guilty of hatred. We cannot believe in a God like that!"

"That God may be all in all" means that He will fully recompense and reward the believer and accomplish His eternal purposes in him by conforming him fully to His will. In order to do this, He must punish evil and restrict it fully.

Of course, where the difficulty lies, I think, is that most people might be willing to concede—and even be happy about it—that a ruthless tyrant with thousands of innocent victims on his conscience might very well be tormented forever in hell. Few would feel sympathy for such a man as Hitler, for instance.

But what causes them to shudder and doubt that a God of love could allow it, is that some whom they regard with strong feelings of affection or respect may be condemned to an eternity of endless torment, simply because they do not believe correctly. "These are good people," they say, "good neighbors, good friends, good citizens. What have they ever done that merits such an awful punishment as eternal fire? Why must the sins of one lifetime be punished forever and ever? I couldn't do this to them. How can God?"

What they fail to realize is that, just as God was not responsible for man's sin in the first place, He is not responsible for man's ultimate condemnation. God gave man every opportunity to enjoy life to the fullest in obedience to Him, and man rejected it. Ever since, God has been holding out His hands pleading with the whole world to come to Him. He became incarnate, that He might even die in their place, to atone for their sins and reconcile them to Himself in the person of Jesus Christ. If they turn away from Him, after all His sacrifice and warnings, it is they who condemn themselves to eternal separation from Him. That is what constitutes hell. Whether the fires of hell are literal, as some consider them, is open to question. But the fires of regret and remorse will burn forever. Men will want to be rescued then only that they may not suffer. But they will not desire to love and obey God any more because of the punishment of hell than they did while He pleaded with them and gave them every opportunity to know Him on earth. God saves all who willingly turn to Him in repentance and faith, of that I am sure. He condemns no one to hell who is innocent of rejecting Him—either openly, or through lack of desire to know Him and follow His will.

"O Jerusalem, Jerusalem," mourned Christ, "how often would I have gathered thy children together, even as a hen gathereth her chickens under her wings, and ye would not!" Is that true of you? Remember, the loving invitation of the Saviour is still open to you: "Come unto me, all ye that labour and are heavy laden, and I will give you rest. Take my yoke upon you and learn of me . . . and ye shall find rest unto your souls." (See Matt. 23:37 and 11:28.)

WILL ANYONE GET A SECOND CHANCE
AFTER DEATH?

"And when all things shall be subdued unto him, then shall the Son also himself be subject unto him that put all things under him, that God may be all in all"
(I Cor. 15:28).

If I were to tell you not to put your hand into the fire because it would burn, you'd think I was insulting your intelligence. If I were to tell you to be sure to eat and drink if you wanted to go on living, you'd think I was a fool—or that I took you for one. Everybody knows that fire burns; that you have to eat and drink in order to live. These are natural laws; and if we disobey them, we expect to pay the penalty. We cannot escape from the consequences of disobedience to God's physical laws. Yet no one resents this or calls it unjust. Why, then, should we expect His spiritual laws to be different?

When God said, "The soul that sinneth, it shall die" (Ezek. 18:4), He was stating as incontrovertible a fact as if He had said, "The body that goes without food shall die." Why should we believe the one and not the other? God is the Author of natural law and of spiritual law. Disobey either and you pay the penalty.

The spiritual law that decrees death as the result of sin runs right through the Bible, from Genesis to Revelation. The Apostle Paul tells us, "The wages of sin is death; but the gift of God is eternal life through Jesus Christ our Lord" (Rom. 6:23). It is also a spiritual law that this eternal life becomes the possession only of those who believe. John 1:12 says, "As many as received him [Christ], to them gave he power to become the sons of God, even to them that believe on his name." And "Except ye be converted, and become as little children, ye shall not enter into the kingdom of heaven" (Matt. 18:3).

Wishful thinking will never change God's laws, whether they be physical or spiritual. The Bible verses just quoted tell us clearly just who are God's children and who will enter His Kingdom. They are the believers in Jesus Christ, who have been born of His spirit, and have been converted from their old sinful ways to Christ's way. In fact, in the days of the early Church, Christians were often called "followers of the Way."

Man's life on earth is a probationary period in which God gives him the choice of receiving Him or rejecting Him. Is it logical to believe that God will reward receivers and rejecters alike? Would this not be unfair to those who accepted His offer of pardon and salvation in Christ? When you say that a God of love would not punish the unbelieving and wicked, remember that a human father who did not reward obedience and punish disobedience could scarcely be called loving at all. He would be encouraging anarchy. God must be fair to the believer by being impartial to all.

The only way in which the law of life for the believer and death for the unbeliever could be set aside or modified is if the unbeliever were given another chance, after death. Is there such a possibility? If there is, why do we find such constant urgency in the Scriptures for man to believe? Why do we find such warnings as "Except ye repent, ye shall all likewise perish" (Luke 13:3)? Why does Paul say, "Behold, now is the accepted time; behold, now is the day of salvation" (II Cor. 6:2)? Why bother your head about being saved now, if you are going to be given another chance hereafter? This is a most un-Scriptural notion. You will not find one instance in the entire Bible of anyone repenting after death and being saved.

Those who feel that a loving God could not condemn anyone to eternal separation from Himself, thus rejecting the most explicit statements of His Word, seek to find comfort and support for their view in certain passages of Scripture, among them I Corinthians 15:28. This verse declares that, in the end, all things will be subdued under Christ; that then Christ will also subject Himself to the Father; and that God will be "all in all." To claim that the expression, "that God may be all in all," means that God will confer salvation, apart from responsible voluntary choice, on those who rejected their God-given opportunities on earth, is most illogical and contrary to Scripture. Here on earth God forces salvation on no man, saves no one against his will. He freely offers the gift of eternal life in Christ, leaving it up to man to accept or reject it.

Another verse often quoted in support of the universal salvation of men is I Timothy 2:4. But when Paul says that God "will have all men to be saved, and to come unto the knowledge of the truth," he is speaking of God's willingness and not of coercion. This is God's attitude toward all men now. Is it logical to assume that He will so radically change toward those who died unrepentant as to save them against their will in the world to come?

The absurdity of this will at once be seen if we give a concrete example. Suppose a man to have heard the Gospel in his youth and to have rejected God's offer of pardon and salvation. Suppose him to have chosen a life of lying, stealing, murdering, and persecuting all who professed to believe in God. At last he comes to die, and with his last breath he curses God.

Do you mean to tell me that, when he is raised from the dead, God is going to say to him, "I freely forgive you, and you may now enter heaven"? Just because this man is on the other side of the grave, will his attitude toward God be any more loving, accepting, and obedient? He may now believe that God exists— how can he help it? But will he be changed in any respect from the rascal he always was? He may want to escape hell, but would he feel at home in heaven? Does he belong there? If the love of God could not move him while on earth, will it suddenly change him from a vile sinner to a purified saint on the other side of the grave?

If God is going to bestow salvation on all hereafter, why not do it now and hasten the blessedness of all people? How awful if God were so unpredictable that He told us in one place that the wicked and unbelieving would suffer eternal punishment, and in another that some day He would confer salvation on everyone. If He is going to change His attitude toward unbelievers, what guarantee do we have that He will not change His attitude toward believers and fail to keep His promises to them? We need a God whose word we can trust and believe; and Hebrews 13:8 assures us that we have such a God: "Jesus Christ the same yesterday, and to day, and for ever."

Universalists would certainly not agree to anything that would deprive them of their power of choice. When it comes to the hereafter, then, how can they logically sustain their position that God will save even those whose wills are opposed to Him? Will He wave a magic wand and suddenly turn black sheep into white? What happens to free will, if God's being "all in all" means salvation for all in the world to come, whether they have shown any inclination for it or not? God will subjugate evil men and unbelievers as His enemies, even against their will; but Scripture gives us no ground for supposing that He will save them in spite of their will.

"Hold on," someone may say. "These unbelievers may not be saved in spite of themselves, but they will repent when they confront God and recognize their sinfulness." This, too, is inconsistent with man's behavior, as recorded in Scripture. Despite God's prolonged dealings with Pharaoh, and the many opportunities He gave him to do an about face, and the many punishments He inflicted on him, Pharaoh's heart became harder yet.

And what about Satan? He, too, should be included among those who are to be saved, if God's being made "all in all" means that God will ultimately save all. Yet God's Word declares unequivocally that Satan is the father of lies, a murderer from the beginning, and there is no indication that he will ever change (John 8:44). In fact, right down to the end he is depicted as doing battle with God and the forces of righteousness. If he were to be saved, either by force or by his own desire if given a second chance, how can we explain what is said of his ultimate end and that of his followers? "And fire came down from God out of heaven, and devoured them. And the devil that deceived them was cast into the lake of fire and brimstone, where the beast and the false prophet are, and shall be tormented day and night for ever and ever" (Rev. 20:9, 10).

But this need not be the fate of anyone who will take God at His word. "I have no pleasure in the death of him that dieth, saith the Lord God: wherefore turn yourselves, and live ye" (Ezek. 18:32). "For God so loved the world, that he gave his only begotten Son, that whosoever believeth in him should not perish, but have everlasting life" (John 3:16). But "How shall we escape, if we neglect so great salvation?" (Heb. 2:3).

WHY PREACH ON ETERNAL PUNISHMENT?

"And when all things shall be subdued unto him, then shall the Son also himself be subject unto him that put all things under him, that God may be all in all"
(I Cor. 15:28).

What kind of child were you? Were you so eager to please your parents, and so quick to obey them, that they never needed to warn you of the dire consequences of disobedience? If so, you were not like me. My parents often had to employ the threat of punishment to make me toe the line, and to keep me from getting into trouble. But there's one thing about punishment, and that is, unless it's strong enough to inspire wholesome fear, and is carried out when disobedience occurs, it will accomplish nothing.

As a father, I would prefer to speak only kind words to my children, to shower gifts upon them, to see only the good in them. But love cannot escape the responsibility to discipline, to curb wrong tendencies, and to impress on a child that he is responsible for the consequences of his actions.

If a child does not know his lessons, and his father or mother covers up for him by doing most of his homework, they may think they are doing the child a kindness, when actually they are teaching him that someone will always come to the rescue when he has failed to fulfill his responsibilities. It's a hard lesson for both parents and children to learn, but our juvenile courts are filled with teen-agers who never learned through home discipline that they must be held accountable for their own wrongdoing.

God is a Father on a much higher scale than we human parents. And yet, in our own experience, we can dimly trace the feelings that must be His as He looks down on His human creation, not only with love, but with the unimaginable responsibility of disciplining and teaching these self-willed and disobedient children of earth. He first of all appeals to love; and those who will come to Him in response to this appeal are indeed blessed. But not all children will respond to such an appeal; and so sorrowfully He must resort to the warning of dire consequences if men turn from His way of life and choose instead the way that leads to eternal death.

Strangely enough, many people reject the thought of eternal consequences for disobeying God's spiritual laws. When they suffer for violating the laws of healthful living, abusing their bodies with alcohol, drugs, and other excesses, they do not think it a harsh punishment that they should become ill and even die. Such results they call the inevitable consequences of ignoring the laws of cause and effect.

But when men and women turn a deaf ear to all the pleas of God to turn to Him and live; when they are earnestly and lovingly warned that the wages of sin is death, but the gift of God is eternal life, through Jesus Christ, and yet continue to harden their hearts against Him; why do they protest that God cannot allow them to perish, to reap as they have sowed? Why do they seem to think He must save them even against their natural bent and will?

Can you save the alcoholic against his will? Can you force food into a stubborn child's mouth and make him swallow? If a person's will is set against you, and all persuasions and pleas of love fail, you must let him suffer the natural consequences, though your heart breaks.

In order to justify their reluctance to believe that a God of love really means it when He says that the unrepentant sinner must suffer the eternal consequences of his rejection of Christ as the way of salvation, those who teach universal salvation quote various Scripture passages. One of these is I Corinthians 15:28, which declares that in the end God will be "all in all." We have already shown that this means He will be all to the believer that He *desires* to be—He will be his entire life, motivating power, and joy. But He will be all to the unbeliever that He *must* be—His judge and conqueror, who subdues him as an enemy under His feet, so that he is forever restricted from perpetrating further evil, along with the devil and fallen angels.

In fact, the doctrine of future punishment is so clearly taught in God's Word that no one can escape it. It is not that God wants to threaten or scare people into being good. As Dr. S. M. Merrill says, "It is the last resort of God's wisdom and holiness. . . . In it God takes no delight. Yet the necessities of good government, the maintenance of order under rightful authority, and the highest regard for the welfare of the good, require this ultimate vindication of righteousness at the expense of the incorrigibly wicked." (See *The New Testament Idea of Hell*, pp. 17, 18.)

The Lord Jesus Christ, who preached the love of God so movingly in the Parable of the Prodigal Son, nevertheless very definitely taught eternal punishment as well as eternal rewards, in Matthew 25:31-46. "Come, ye blessed of my Father, inherit the kingdom prepared for you from the foundation of the world. . . . Depart from me, ye cursed, into everlasting fire, prepared for the devil and his angels. . . . And these shall go away into everlasting punishment: but the righteous into life eternal" (vv. 34, 41, 46).

In Matthew 13 we have several parables that teach eternal punishment. In the Parable of the Tares, Jesus said, "As therefore the tares are gathered and burned in the fire; so shall it be in the end of this world. The Son of man shall send forth his angels, and they shall gather out of his kingdom all things that offend, and them which do iniquity, and shall cast them into a furnace of fire: there shall be wailing and gnashing of teeth. Then shall the righteous shine forth as the sun in the kingdom of their Father" (vv. 40-43).

A little farther on we have the Parable of the Dragnet that was cast into the sea. The good and bad fish were drawn to land, the good kept and the bad discarded. Concerning this our Lord says, "So shall it be at the end of the world: the angels shall come forth, and sever the wicked from among the just, and shall cast them into the furnace of fire: there shall be wailing and gnashing of teeth" (vv. 49, 50).

And in Mark 9 Jesus clearly teaches the sure and

everlasting nature of future punishment. "And if thy hand offend thee, cut it off: it is better for thee to enter into life maimed, than having two hands to go into hell, into the fire that never shall be quenched: where their worm dieth not, and the fire is not quenched" (vv. 43, 44). Our Lord repeats this warning two more times in verses 45-48.

Again, we have Christ's account of the rich man and Lazarus in Luke 16:19-31, depicting their destiny after death. One suffers and the other is comforted. There isn't a ray of hope for the rich man who died unrepentant and is suffering in hades.

Instead of turning away in disbelief from a God who permits such suffering as a necessary part of His program for the proper government of His creatures, why not remove yourself entirely from the category of those who will suffer such punishment? Why not in faith accept God's love revealed in the sacrifice of Jesus Christ for you on the cross? God no more wants to punish you—or anyone else—than you want to punish those you love. He wants to shower all His best gifts upon you, both here and hereafter. Necessarily and regretfully He must enforce His law that "the wages of sin is death," but His Word still proclaims the joyous news to everyone who will listen, that "the gift of God is eternal life through Jesus Christ our Lord" (Rom. 6:23).

WILL A GOD OF LOVE PUNISH
ANYONE ETERNALLY?

A young man speeding along a highway crashed into an oncoming car, and the resultant chain reaction caused the death and crippling of several innocent victims. Yet the judges, after only five minutes deliberation, let him go free. The resultant public uproar caused a re-opening of the case and a conviction—although ultimately the sentence was suspended.

The public outrage in this case, and in similar instances where justice is flouted, shows that men have a built-in recognition of the fact that, where wrongdoing goes unpunished, the law-abiding are threatened and the innocent victimized.

We have said that parental love cannot allow disobedience to go unchecked, nor let continued rejection of authority go unpunished. To do so would be to encourage anarchy and to discourage those who are trying to do what is right. The doctrine of love that the Lord Jesus Christ preached was no wishy-washy affair of permissiveness, of "anything goes," but was balanced by stern warnings about sinning against God and man.

All four Gospels depict the Lord Jesus as teaching eternal punishment for unbelievers as the other side of the coin of eternal reward for believers. John the Evangelist records these words of Christ: "He that believeth on the Son hath everlasting life: and he that believeth not the Son shall not see life; but the wrath of

God abideth on him" (John 3:36). This does not refer simply to the present life but more especially to the life to come. It gives no hope that a time will come when the wrath of God will be lifted from the unbeliever. Of course, unbelievers may reap some of the consequences of their sin down here on earth, but not fully. We see many unbelievers prospering in spite of their sinfulness. But the day of final reckoning will come.

In John 8:21 the Lord answered scoffers by saying, "I go my way, and ye shall seek me, and shall die in your sins." The consequence of this would be, He added, that "whither I go, ye cannot come." Thus we see that those who die unrepentant can never go to heaven to be with the Lord.

Many other verses confirm this doctrine of everlasting punishment for the unbeliever, such as Luke 13:24, John 6:37, Hebrews 2:3. In Matthew 16:26 our Lord said, "For what is a man profited, if he shall gain the whole world, and lose his own soul? or what shall a man give in exchange for his soul?" Why did Christ speak of the possibility of losing one's soul, if every soul is finally going to be reconciled to God?

If universalism is true, no sin is unforgivable. Yet our Lord said, "Whosoever speaketh against the Holy Ghost, it shall not be forgiven him, neither in this world, neither in the world to come" (Matt. 12:32). No opportunity for a second chance there. See also I John 5:16.

Will Judas Iscariot one day be reconciled to the same Christ that he betrayed? If so, why did Christ say of him in Matthew 26:24, "The Son of man goeth as it is written of him: but woe unto that man by whom the Son of man is betrayed! It had been good for that man if he had not been born." Is it possible, even by the wildest stretch of the imagination, to think that Judas will ultimately enjoy the same eternal bliss as those disciples who gave their lives for Jesus Christ in martyrdom?

What does the Apostle Paul have to say about this doctrine? In Philippians 3:18, 19 we read, "For many walk, of whom I have told you often, and now tell you even weeping, that they are the enemies of the cross of Christ: whose end is destruction." The Greek word for "destruction" here is *apooleia*. It does not refer to physical death, because that is common to believers and unbelievers alike. It must therefore refer to something that especially affects the unbelievers, and that is their punishment, or the second death—as confirmed by other verses of Scripture.

In Romans 2:3-12, Paul gives the basic principles governing this final judgment of the whole world. There can be no doubt that this passage teaches the future punishment of unbelievers. It says in part, "And thinkest thou this, O man, that judgest them which do such things and doest the same, that thou shalt escape the judgment of God? . . . But after thy hardness and impenitent heart treasurest up unto thyself wrath against the day of wrath and revelation of the righteous judgment of God; who will render to every man according to his deed: to them who by patient continuance in well doing seek for glory and honour and immortality, eternal life: but unto them that are contentious, and do not obey the truth, but obey unrighteousness, indignation and wrath, tribulation and anguish, upon every soul of man that doeth evil. . . . For there is no respect of persons with God. For as many as have sinned without law shall also perish without law: and as many as have sinned in the law shall be judged by the law."

And in writing to the persecuted Thessalonians, Paul says, "It is a righteous thing with God to recompense tribulation to them that trouble you; and to you who are troubled rest with us, when the Lord Jesus shall be revealed from heaven with his mighty angels, in flaming fire taking vengeance on them that know not God, and that obey not the gospel of our Lord Jesus Christ: who shall be punished with everlasting destruction from the presence of the Lord, and from the glory of his power; when he shall come to be glorified in his saints, and to be admired in all them that believe (because our testimony among you was believed) in that day" (II Thess. 1:6-10).

We could parade a multitude of other Scriptures to prove beyond doubt that, just as surely as there is an eternal life of bliss for believers there is eternal punishment for unbelievers. The references quoted, however, are sufficient to persuade any objective inquirer that this truth is taught in the Word of God.

But the universalists claim to have Scripture on their side also, and in all fairness we must examine their claims. Again we cannot be exhaustive, but a fair sampling should show us whether or not they have rightly interpreted Scripture. One of their proof texts is Psalm 22:27, "All the ends of the world shall remember and turn unto the Lord: and all the kindreds of the nations shall worship before thee." A similar verse is Psalm 86:9, "All nations whom thou hast made shall come and worship before thee, O Lord; and shall glorify thy name."

But there is nothing to indicate that these verses refer to the ultimate reconciliation of unbelievers to God. Comparing Scripture with Scripture, we find that they refer to the universal spreading of the Gospel during the end times, and particularly during the millennial reign of Christ. During this particular period, Satan will be bound. This is clearly prophesied in Revelation 20.

Another verse claimed by the universalists is Proverbs 11:31, "Behold, the righteous shall be recompensed in the earth: much more the wicked and the sinner." The consistent universalists say that this indicates that the punishment of the righteous takes place here on earth, and not after death. This, however, is an unwarranted assumption, for on the basis of such logic this verse would then also be teaching that the righteous will be excluded from their future reward. All this verse declares is that, since the righteous suffer on earth, it must certainly follow that the unrighteous will suffer even more. It agrees with all other Scripture on this subject in teaching that the suffering of the unbeliever begins here on earth but does not end here. Even so, the eternal life of the believer begins here with the peace of God in his heart, but the fullness of his life of full joy and glory is in heaven.

To show how inconsistent such teaching is, take another verse the universalists quote, Psalm 145:9. "The Lord is good to all: and his tender mercies are over all his works." "Here you are," they say. "God is not going to punish anybody." Since in the previous verse referred to they have said that unbelievers receive their punishment on earth, they must believe that this verse refers to the future life. Then, logically, God is good and merciful only in the hereafter and not now, or He would not punish anyone at any time. How mixed up can you get?

Yes, God is a loving Father, but what father worthy of the name does not punish his disobedient child and limit the evil that child can do to others? Exodus 34:6 and 7 presents a far more balanced picture when it states, "The Lord God, merciful and gracious, longsuffering, and abundant in goodness and truth, keeping mercy for thousands, forgiving iniquity and transgression and sin, and that will by no means clear the guilty."

Thus we see that the punishment of the guilty does not nullify the mercy and goodness of God. In order for us to experience His goodness and mercy, however, we must accept it on His terms. Christ died for the salvation of all, but only those who receive Him by faith as their Saviour are forgiven, and will go to be with Him in a fellowship of eternal joy.

DOES THE RESURRECTION OF ALL MEAN THE SALVATION OF ALL?

Have you ever asked someone for information, only to have him respond, "You mean to say you don't know that? Why I thought *everybody* knew that!" Now obviously he didn't really think everybody in the world knew that particular fact. What he really meant to imply was that "everybody who is anybody" knew it, anyone of intelligence was aware of it. That leaves out quite a number of people. He was merely playing the game of "one-upmanship," putting you in your place by flaunting his superior knowledge.

We quite often use such expressions as "everybody knows," or "everything has gone wrong today," when both we and our listeners know we mean that "a great many" people or things are involved.

It is the same when we come to verses of Scripture that employ such expressions as "all," "the whole world," "every creature which is under heaven," and so on. It is necessary to understand the basic principle involved with regard to their limited meaning or all-inclusiveness.

In the first chapter of his Epistle to the Colossians, for instance, Paul speaks of Christ as the Creator of all things: "All things were created by him, and for him" (v. 16). He also states that Christ existed before all things: "And he is before all things, and by him all things consist" (v. 17). These expressions are absolute and all-inclusive, declaring the complete sovereignty of the Lord Jesus in creating and sustaining the world.

But the words "all" or "every," and such expressions as "the whole world," are not always used with the meaning of every man or every thing. The meaning depends on what is referred to or what truth is set forth. "All" or "every" may be used with certain restrictions and definitions. Here are some examples:

In I John 5:19 we read, "And we know that we are of God, and the whole world lieth in wickedness." Taken superficially, the first half of the verse would contradict the second half. If believers are "of God," how can it be said that "the whole world" is wicked? It is obvious, then, that the expression "the whole world" here means the greater portion of the world, most of the people, and that believers are excepted.

Again, in Colossians 1:23, Paul speaks of "the gospel, which ye have heard, and which was preached to every creature which is under heaven." Now was Paul falsifying the facts when he declared that the Gospel had been preached to all people then living, or was he merely using the expression "to every creature which is under heaven" to express the wide scope of Gospel preaching? Commentators are agreed that this is hyperbole, a heightening of the facts for effect.

Another example of the restriction that must be placed upon such absolute expressions as "all, all men, all things, the whole creation," is Paul's statement in I Corinthians 10:23: "All things are lawful for me, but all things are not expedient: all things are lawful for me, but all things edify not." What does Paul mean here by the expression "all things"? That he was free to disobey all the moral law of God? Of course not. He obviously meant "all things" in the limited sense of the things that are permitted by the moral law but that do not always set a good example. We must place the same type of restriction on the meaning of "all" in I Corinthians 13:7, "Love . . . believeth all things." Obviously love does not believe even falsehood and deceit.

The universalists quote Colossians 1:20 as proof that God will eventually save every human being. "And, having made peace through the blood of his cross, by him to reconcile all things unto himself." Paul says something similar in Ephesians 1:10, "That in the dispensation of the fulness of times he might gather together in one all things in Christ, both which are in heaven, and which are on earth; even in him."

In Colossians 1:18 Paul has been speaking concerning Christ as the Head of the body of the Church. The reconciliation of all things unto Him is the completion of the Church of Christ by those who live on earth and by those who are in heaven. Nowhere does Scripture state that He will reconcile Hades and all its inhabitants to Himself. Nor does Ephesians 1:10 mean that all men will repent after death, but rather that the Lord will subjugate all people, and the whole of creation, when He shall come in His glory. Today the world in every phase of its manifestation, whether natural, material, or spiritual, is in general apostasy against God. The whole creation is not in harmony with its Creator. This is why we suffer.

In our examination of I Corinthians 15:25 and 26, "For he must reign, till he hath put all enemies under his feet. The last enemy that shall be destroyed is death," we pointed out that these verses have absolutely nothing to do with unbelievers being reconciled to God after death. You would never speak of putting your friends under your feet, but only your enemies; and nobody would be happy, either in this life or the next, being under the feet of somebody else. These verses refer to the elimination of the activity and existence of evil after the second coming of the Lord Jesus Christ. Furthermore, let us not forget the context of these verses. Paul is speaking in the 15th chapter of I Corinthians specifically of the resurrection of the bodies of believers and their putting on immortality and glory. He is not primarily dealing with unbelievers and the unrighteous.

We also saw that the 22nd verse of this great chapter refers only to the making alive of the bodies of believers, and in no way implies that spiritual life will ultimately be given to all. Let us never make the mistake of thinking that, because the bodies of all men, both believers and unbelievers, shall rise from the dead, this necessarily presupposes that unbelievers shall also receive spiritual life from Christ.

Two questions often arise in connection with future punishment: Will all unbelievers be punished equally? And what about those who have never heard the Gospel? From the words of our Lord in Luke 12:47, 48, we understand that the unrighteous will all be punished, though not all with the same degree of punishment. "And that servant, which knew his lord's will, and prepared not himself, neither did according to his will, shall be beaten with many stripes. But he that knew not, and did commit things worthy of stripes, shall be beaten with few stripes. For unto whomsoever [and this must include believer and unbeliever] much is given, of him shall be much required: and to whom men have committed much, of him they will ask the more."

The fact that all shall be raised does not mean that all shall be raised to a life of bliss. The words of Christ stand true: "The hour is coming, in the which all that are in the graves shall hear his voice, and shall come forth; they that have done good, unto the resurrection of life; and they that have done evil, unto the resurrection of damnation" (John 5:28, 29). Does this verse include those who have never heard the Gospel?

Yes, for in Romans 1:18 Paul says, "For the wrath of God is revealed from heaven against all ungodliness and unrighteousness of men, who hold the truth in unrighteousness; because that which may be known of God is manifest in them; for God hath shewed it unto them. For the invisible things of him from the creation of the world are clearly seen, being understood by the things that are made, even his eternal power and Godhead; so that they are without excuse."

As Joseph Angus says in his little book on *Future Punishment* regarding the heathen, "Even in their case God has not left Himself without witness; nor need we scruple to say that if men are finally punished it will not be because they have sinned, but because they have *persisted* in sin against such light as they have; not because they have failed in goodness, but because they have failed even to desire it."

He goes on to say, "We frame excuses for men, and often speak of sin in slighting terms. . . . It seems so natural. But this tendency of ours Scripture never sanctions. It shows indeed the utmost tenderness to the errors of the man who is, on the whole, struggling after holiness; but men who sin 'with a will,' who 'take pleasure in iniquity,' who yield . . . to disbelief and gross sin, are spoken of by our Lord and by His apostles in language that ought to ring in the ears of us all. . . .

"Every form of expression used in Scripture to describe the *everlastingness* of the blessedness of the righteous is applied to the condition of the lost; and the 'destruction' to which men are doomed is set forth in terms that describe moral disorder and misery, not annihilation." And when we see things more clearly on the other side of the grave, "our exclamation will be, in the language of the Book that contains the most vivid descriptions of the coming wrath and of the coming glory, 'Thou hast done all things well!' 'Just and true are Thy ways, Thou King of Saints!' "

THE FOLLY OF BELIEVING IN
UNIVERSAL SALVATION

Getting children to eat what is good for them can be quite a problem. Convincing them that you mean business takes more strength of character than some parents possess. Yet the mother who lets her child indulge his preference for sweets, at the expense of such body-building foods as milk, meat, and vegetables, does not really love him as much as the mother who does her best to see that he gets a balanced diet. The parent who gives in to a child on matters that affect his future health and character is merely encouraging him to go on getting his way in all future contests of will— and laying the foundation for trouble for the rest of his life.

So it is with God. Unless people believe that He means what He says, they will run to all kinds of excesses, and ruin their lives for time and eternity. Although the Bible everywhere proclaims that unbelief and sin, if unrepented of in this life, will result in eternal loss, too many people refuse to take God at His Word. They choose to believe He is too soft-hearted ever to condemn anyone to eternal punishment.

What would be the consequences if God provided an opportunity for unbelievers to be reconciled to Himself after death? Wouldn't this encourage people to continue in their unbelief with no fear of God or the consequence of their sin?

The Word of God plainly sets forth the only way

that men can be reconciled to God, and that is through receiving Christ as their Saviour in this life. Hebrews 2:3 pointedly asks, "How shall we escape, if we neglect so great salvation?" Belief in a second chance after death may cost you more than you can imagine. And how much greater will the punishment be for those who preach such a dangerous doctrine and thus encourage people to continue in their way of sin? If we reject the doctrine of punishment after death that the Bible so clearly teaches, we might as well throw the Bible away and not profess to accept its authority on anything.

If there is no future punishment, then God is not concerned with justice. What about the many unrighteous people who are now prospering, and the many righteous who are now suffering? Will there be no final accounting? If not, the distinction between good and evil collapses. In fact, our society would completely fall apart if the instinct were erased from human consciousness that sooner or later sin must be punished. Law without punishment for the lawbreaker is a mockery. How many would obey the laws of this nation if they recognized that disobedience would incur no penalty? How many would tell the truth in a courtroom if they were not afraid of the consequences of perjury? Those who preach that, no matter what people believe or do, they will finally be saved, must take account of the chaos into which the human race would be plunged if their doctrine became acceptable even upon this earth during this life.

If no one is to be punished after death, then unbelievers who die in their unbelief and unrighteousness are really much better off than the righteous ones still living on earth who are suffering because of their righteousness. Those who were unrighteous in Noah's day, and perished before the flood, actually fared far better than Noah, because they escaped all the difficulties and sufferings of life. What did they lose, after all, if in the end they are going to heaven?

If this doctrine is true, then Judas did not do badly by taking his life. He put an end to his own suffering, while the sufferings of the other disciples continued, and he will end up in the same heaven as they. The belief in universal salvation after death would justify even suicide and murder. You might rationalize that you are putting an end to the sufferings of another person by killing him, and you would be doing no harm to yourself. These are the absurd yet logical consequences of such a belief.

Furthermore, this doctrine makes repentance and a holy life unnecessary. The sinner would have every right to enjoy heaven on an equal footing with the righteous, in spite of the fact that he is in no sense prepared for heaven. Just imagine murderers, adulterers, thieves, and liars in heaven, along with the purest and godliest of men, without any preparation for it. How ill at ease they would be! Their only joy might be that they had escaped hell. Why should anyone, then, go to the trouble of being content with God's will, of leading a sober and holy life, for all of which there is a price to pay in this world? You might as well sow your wild oats; eat, drink, and be merry, because tomorrow you die, and heaven is assured you in spite of your sins.

A doctrine of universal salvation would actually eliminate the need for any religion whatever. Why bother, since we are all going to end up in heaven? Atheism would be just as acceptable as godliness. Idolatry would have the same value as spiritual worship. We need believe or do nothing to gain heaven. We need fear nothing, since no one will ever perish and all will ultimately be saved. In fact, why preach at all?

What is the difference, then, between atheism and this doctrine of universal salvation? Hardly any at all, since the atheist, in spite of himself, will one day be restored to a relationship with a God whom he rejected on earth, and in whom he did not even believe. In fact, the doctrine of universal salvation is far worse than atheism in that it promises not only deliverance from future punishment but also the prospect of eternal bliss for the unrepentant sinner. Such a doctrine would say to the most viciously depraved, "Even if you die committing the most atrocious murder, do not be afraid. Heaven with all its glory and happiness will be your reward." There could be no greater encouragement to sin than that.

Besides, for a person to enjoy a particular state of existence, he must be conditioned for it. A person in mourning cannot enjoy a party. His inner spirit is at variance with the revelers around him. So it would be with the unrepentant sinner suddenly transported to heaven. He is by nature incapable of enjoying its holy atmosphere. What magic is there in death that could possibly change him so radically that he would be fitted for heaven or find it congenial?

Nothing in the Word of God indicates that this will ever happen. Nor is there any Scriptural warrant for believing that temporary and limited punishment after death would lead him to voluntary repentance. Consider how God scourged the Egyptians, yet Pharaoh's heart became harder and harder rather than being softened.

Or consider the unrighteous people mentioned in the Book of the Revelation, of whom it is prophesied that, when the vials of God's wrath are being poured out upon them, rather than repenting and turning to Him, they will implore the rocks and mountains to fall upon them to hide them from His presence (Rev. 6:16, 17). And when the scourge of hail comes upon them, instead of repenting they will blaspheme (Rev. 16:21). As for Satan himself, the Bible prophesies that after suffering for a thousand years in the pit he will come out as evil as when he went in (Rev. 20:7, 8).

We conclude therefore that the verses offered in proof of universal salvation, and which speak of the subjugation of all things to Christ, do not speak of a future change of heart on the part of unbelievers toward the Lord Jesus Christ at His second coming, but of a mere recognition of His power, glory, and majesty in being able to impose His will and abolish the power of evil. In a limited sense this is actually what happened in the lives of the demoniacs when Jesus was here on earth. The Word of God tells us that even the demons believed and trembled (James 2:19). Did

— 484 —

they not shout and say, "What have we to do with thee, Jesus, thou Son of God?" (Matt. 8:29). Did this mean that the demons had received Christ as their Saviour and had repented? Not at all. (See also Mark 1:24; 3:11; Luke 4:41; Acts 19:15.)

As regards Satan, the Word of God informs us that he will be punished in the lake of fire (Rev. 20:10). How, therefore, can anyone even conceive that some day he and his followers are going to be restored to the favor of God?

Could Scripture make it any plainer than this: "He that believeth on the Son hath everlasting life: and he that believeth not the Son shall not see life; but the wrath of God abideth on him" (John 3:36).

A NEW STATE OF AFFAIRS

"And when all things shall be subdued unto him, then shall the Son also himself be subject unto him that put all things under him, that God may be all in all"
(I Cor. 15:28).

Look at the latest crime statistics. Frightening, aren't they? Glance over your morning paper. Turn on the news reports on T.V. or radio. Wars, riots, violence, hatred, charges and counter-charges; that's all you hear. The Republicans blame the Democrats and vice versa.

But whom does the Bible consider as the real instigator of the evil and unrest in the world today, who misleads our universe? The Apostle Paul speaks of him as "the prince of the power of the air, the spirit that now worketh in the children of disobedience" (Eph. 2:2). He is the devil or Satan. And anyone who believes in the doctrine of universal salvation must logically include Satan and his followers in its benefits.

But Scripture teaches that the Lord Jesus has no intention of saving Satan, or the sons of disobedience after they die, but will subjugate their power so that He may be "all in all." Christ will impose His peace and harmony in two ways: voluntarily in those who accept it through Christ Himself, and forcibly upon those who reject it. The former are thus enabled to live eternally because they accepted His peace through faith. They will not be disturbed in eternity. Christ will put down all rule and all authority and power (I Cor.

15:24). This does not mean the redemption of those who disobeyed Him, but rather their subjugation by putting an end to the evil in which they now engage, and to the activity of those who engage in it.

In the entire Bible, Christ is presented as redeeming all those who believe, and as finally subjugating all those who do not believe, so that His purpose may be accomplished and His absolute sovereignty may be established. For the believers it is voluntary subjection, which produces great joy; but for the wicked and unbelieving it is forcible subjugation, which produces great grief and punishment.

This new state of affairs is called "regeneration" in Matthew 19:28 (*palingenesia* in Greek). "And Jesus said unto them, Verily I say unto you, that ye which have followed me, in the regeneration when the Son of man shall sit in the throne of his glory, ye also shall sit upon twelve thrones, judging the twelve tribes of Israel."

The word "regeneration" in this context does not mean the new birth, the entrance of the believer into the spiritual Kingdom, as in Titus 3:5, James 1:18, and I Peter 1:23, but refers rather to the establishment of a new state of affairs in the world, even as the spiritual new birth is the establishment of a new state. This state of affairs, among other things, is for the purpose of judging the unbelieving Israelites. The apostles and the believers in general shall act as co-judges with Christ in the judgment spoken of in Matthew 16:27. "For the Son of man shall come in the glory of his Father with his angels; and then he shall reward every man according to his works." (See also Matt. 25:31, 32; I Cor. 4:5; II Tim. 4:1; Jude 14, 15.) Note that in Matthew 19:28 Christ is presented as sitting on the throne of His glory. He is not usually represented as sitting on such a throne when He acts as Saviour, but only when He acts as Judge. In I Corinthians 6:2, the Apostle Paul asks, "Do ye not know that the saints shall judge the world?" (See also Ps. 91:14, Isa. 58:14, Dan. 12:3, Hab. 3:19, Luke 19:17.) "To him that over-cometh will I grant to sit with me in my throne, even as I also overcame, and am set down with my Father in his throne" (Rev. 3:21).

This judgment of Christ, participated in by His saints, brings about a new state of affairs in the world. The devil is dethroned and Christ is enthroned. The Apostle Peter declared this to the Israelites of his time in Acts 3:19-22. "Repent ye therefore, and be con-verted, that your sins may be blotted out, when the times of refreshing shall come from the presence of the Lord; and he shall send Jesus Christ, which before was preached unto you: whom the heaven must receive until the times of restitution of all things, which God hath spoken by the mouth of all his holy prophets since the world began."

Christ is now in heaven. He shall appear again to fulfill all that has been prophesied concerning the fu-ture. Israel will be restored to a recognition of Christ as its Messiah. Concerning this restoration the Word of God speaks clearly in Isaiah 1:26; 11:12; 33:20; 40:2; 49:22; 60:10; Ezekiel 20:40; 36:8; Zechariah 1:17; 10:6; 14:11; and Malachi 3:4.

That which God has promised in His Word He must do. But it is completely nonsensical to make "the restitution of all things" spoken of in Acts 3:21 refer to the restitution of unbelievers to the favor of God. What it does declare is that the prophecies that God has made concerning the final state of affairs will be fulfilled. "Until the times of restitution of all things"—and note what follows—"which God hath spoken by the mouth of all his holy prophets since the world began."

The Word of God tells us that under the freedom now allowed Satan and his followers, in this fallen state of affairs in which the world exists, "The whole creation groaneth and travaileth in pain together until now" (Rom. 8:22). Not even the believers are exempt from this suffering, because they are under the influence of evil, although they are governed by the indwelling Christ.

Paul continues in Romans 8:23, "And not only they [that is to say the world, the unbelievers] but ourselves [that is to say, we believers] also, which have the first-fruits of the Spirit, even we ourselves groan within ourselves, waiting for the adoption, to wit, the redemption of our body." This is what Paul calls the restoration or the gathering together of all things.

"Nevertheless we, according to his promise, look for new heavens and a new earth, wherein dwelleth righteousness" (II Pet. 3:13). "And I saw a new heaven and a new earth: for the first heaven and the first earth were passed away; and there was no more sea" (Rev. 21:1). Such a heaven and such an earth are anticipated only by believers. May you be counted among them. Do not take your eternal destiny in your hands with the conjecture that when you die you may have a second chance to be saved. The Word of God declares unequivocally that such a chance does not exist.

In our Lord's parable of the ten virgins, He speaks of five who were ready for the bridegroom's coming, and so were admitted to the marriage feast. But those who were unprepared for his coming and arrived too late were not admitted (Matt. 25:1-13). Thus it will be when the Heavenly Bridegroom, Jesus Christ, comes for His Church at the end of this age of grace. Those who are not prepared to meet Him by then will have no second chance to get ready.

When Scripture asks the fearful question, "How shall we escape if we neglect so great salvation?", it also tells us there is yet hope, if we act now. "The Holy Ghost saith, To day if ye will hear his voice, harden not your hearts . . . behold, now is the accepted time; behold, now is the day of salvation." (Heb. 2:3; 3:7, 8; II Cor. 6:2.)

WHAT BAPTISM FOR THE DEAD DOES NOT MEAN

"Else what shall they do which are baptized for the dead, if the dead rise not at all? why are they then baptized for the dead?" (I Cor. 15:29).

This is a very strange verse, of which there are many different interpretations and explanations among Bible scholars. Nowhere else in the New Testament do we find any reference to baptism for the dead. We must fit this verse into the context of Paul's whole argument about the resurrection in I Corinthians 15. It connects up with his contention that "if so be that the dead rise not . . . your faith is vain" (vv. 16, 17). In other words, Paul argues, if there is no resurrection, why be baptized for the dead?

What does this expression mean? Who were those "baptized for the dead"? We shall understand this better if we first consider what it cannot mean, in the clear light of the rest of the Scriptures.

First of all, it cannot mean that, because baptism was thought to be essential for salvation, it was administered to living believers as proxies for those who died unbaptized. We have no record in Scripture that proxy baptisms actually took place in apostolic times. In their ministry to the dying, the Apostles' message was one: that of repentance and faith, never an assumption that submitting anyone to involuntary baptism would assure his eternal salvation.

Throughout the New Testament we find that baptism is an act of obedience on the part of the baptized.

It is never an involuntary matter, never arbitrarily performed without the intelligent consent of the person baptized. It is a choice by the individual, even as faith and discipleship are voluntary. To baptize any who do not believe and consent to the act accomplishes nothing for their souls. As we cannot believe for another, so we cannot be baptized for another. You or I cannot be baptized in lieu of any living or dead person.

Will any believer who has died without baptism be eternally lost? The answer of Scripture is No. In John 3:18 we read, "He that believeth on him [Christ] is not condemned: but he that believeth not is condemned already, because he hath not believed in the name of the only begotten Son of God." Nowhere does God's Word teach that he who is not baptized is condemned. Nor did Christ command, "Be ye baptized, or ye shall perish," but rather, "I tell you, Nay: but, except ye repent, ye shall all likewise perish" (Luke 13:3).

In the New Testament, baptism is always presented as the step following faith in Christ. "He that believeth and is baptized shall be saved; but he that believeth not shall be damned" (Mark 16:16). These words of our Lord contain both an affirmative and a negative statement. Observe that the affirmative declares, "He that believeth and is baptized shall be saved." But, in order to show that the essential element in salvation is belief and not baptism, the negative statement is "he that believeth not shall be damned." Nowhere does Scripture make a similar statement about baptism to the effect that he who is not baptized shall be damned. If it did, then and only then could baptism be considered essential to salvation.

Whenever baptism is mentioned alone as being the means of salvation, it must be presupposed as having been preceded by faith and repentance, which in Scripture are basic to salvation. If a person has entered upon the second step, baptism, the Scriptural presupposition is that he has already taken the first. If I say I have ascended to the second floor of a building, without making any mention of the first, this does not mean that I somehow eliminated the necessity of passing through the first floor to reach the second.

There are only two or three instances in Scripture in which baptism is linked verbally with the concept of salvation. Mark 16:16, "He that believeth and is baptized shall be saved; but he that believeth not shall be damned." First Peter 3:20, 21, which speaks of the "eight souls" in Noah's ark who "were saved by water. The like figure whereunto even baptism doth also now save us." And some have construed the words of Titus 3:5 to refer to baptism, ". . . according to his mercy he saved us, by the washing of regeneration. . . ." Yet it is obvious in all these instances that faith preceded baptism, and that the linkage of baptism with salvation is one of association, and not of cause and effect.

In contrast to these few instances where baptism is mentioned in connection with salvation, Scripture gives dozens of instances in which faith alone is mentioned as the essential ingredient of salvation. When the Philippian jailer asked Paul what he must do to be saved, the Apostle gave him the essential requirement in a nutshell, "Believe on the Lord Jesus Christ, and thou shalt be saved" (Acts 16:31). No mention was made of baptism or confession by mouth as procuring salvation. This is the predominant note of Scripture.

Very interestingly the word "confession" is used in the same way as the word "baptism" as leading to salvation, but by no stretch of the imagination can this be said not to include belief of the heart, even as baptism does. "Hereby know ye the Spirit of God: Every spirit that confesseth that Jesus Christ is come in the flesh is of God: and every spirit that confesseth not that Jesus Christ is come in the flesh is not of God" (I John 4:2, 3). Romans 10:9 and 10 tells us, "If thou shalt confess with thy mouth the Lord Jesus, and shalt believe in thine heart that God hath raised him from the dead, thou shalt be saved. For with the heart man believeth unto righteousness; and with the mouth confession is made unto salvation."

Why is confessing coupled with faith? Because like baptism it is the expression of an inner experience. But in verse 13 we read, "For whosoever shall call upon the name of the Lord shall be saved." Acts 2:21 says the same thing. A person who may not confess, but believes, is nevertheless saved, though he will never experience the same joy as the one who does both. A witnessing Christian will be a rewarded Christian, but a non-witnessing Christian will get into the Kingdom, though perhaps "by the skin of his teeth."

The same may be said of baptism. A man can be saved without it. But Christ will surely reward believers who were baptized in obedience to Christ's command and example, even in the face of persecution and death. "Whosoever therefore shall confess me before men, him will I confess also before my Father which is in heaven" (Matt. 10:32; see also Luke 12:8).

When the Holy Spirit falls upon a man, we may surely believe that he is saved. Thus, in the account of the conversion of Cornelius and his household, in the 10th chapter of Acts, we read that, when Peter preached the Gospel to these Gentiles who were seeking to know the truth about God, the Holy Spirit fell upon them *before they were baptized*, thus demonstrating that as soon as they believed the Gospel they were saved.

An outstanding example in the New Testament of one who believed, was not baptized, and yet was eternally saved, is one of the two thieves crucified with Christ. The Lord Jesus assured him, "Verily I say unto thee, To day shalt thou be with me in paradise" (Luke 23:43). His salvation was based on his faith in the finished work of Christ on the cross, not on baptism. If he had lived, no doubt he would have followed Christ's example and precept in the matter of baptism. But since he had no opportunity to do so, he could not be charged with an act of disobedience, since there was no opportunity for him to be baptized after he believed. Wherever there is lack of opportunity for obedience, there can be no charge of disobedience.

Even later we do not find that any one of the surviving believers was baptized on behalf of this thief, thus making up for what he lacked the opportunity to do. Speaking of the dead generally, the Bible nowhere teaches that the living can compensate in any way for that in which they fell short. If they died in unbelief, they will be judged as unbelievers. Their death seals their fate, and the living can do nothing to change it. Christian ministers have witnessed many deathbed scenes in which those who neglected to make their peace with God earlier have realized their lost condition and been unable to face death with anything except terror and despair. Although genuine deathbed repentances do occur, they are rare, and certainly should not be depended upon by anyone who thinks he can wait until the last minute. The two thieves on either side of Christ had the same opportunity to believe, but one died unrepentant and went to hell; the other died repentant and believing, and went to Paradise. Don't count on being in this latter category. The thief who was saved did not deliberately put off repentance until the last moment. He had a sudden confrontation with the Son of God in his dying hours and met it with saving faith. You are not likely to have that opportunity on your deathbed.

Yes, death seals our fate, and no living persons can change it for us. How carefully that ought to cause us to live. There is no record in the history of the apostolic church that anyone was ever baptized on behalf of or for the sake of the dead, or believed or did anything that could benefit the departed ones. Even as late as the second century, Tertullian, the Latin Church Father, knew nothing of the existence of any such usage even among the heretical Marcionites, against whom he wrote. He condemns such a possible interpretation of this passage (Cont. Marcion V., 10). Chrysostom and Epiphanius, the Greek Church Fathers who wrote fully three hundred years after this Corinthian epistle was written, are our earliest vouchers for the existence of a practice of baptizing the living for those who died unbaptized. The sum of historical testimony is that nearly three hundred years after the Apostles, in an age when the most exaggerated notions regarding the efficacy of baptism prevailed, such a custom existed among one or two small, heretical, ignorant sects; yet not even then in the church generally, and not even among these at an early period. How great, then, is the improbability that it should have already sprung up among the Corinthians, and gained a footing sufficient to secure its canonization in an apostolical epistle!

The belief that baptism is essential to salvation, which could have given rise to such a superstitious practice as proxy baptisms, may have carried over even into our day. Some denominational groups are so fearful that a child or adult may die unbaptized, and so be lost, that their religious leaders, and even medical doctors, will sprinkle a dying person. But such an interpretation of this verse must be rejected on the basis of the teaching of the New Testament as a whole. It would be an ignorant person indeed who would suppose that he could make a sick person well by taking his medicine for him. The Apostle Paul was far from ignorant. That he could suppose for one instant that baptism—which in the New Testament is everywhere regarded as an act of obedience to Christ—could be administered to a living believer and benefit a dead unbeliever, or even a dead believer—is unthinkable. And if such a superstitious practice actually did exist in the Corinthian church, it is equally unthinkable that Paul would have sanctioned it.

However, the Corinthian believers were anything but superstitious. Superstition is the twin sister of ignorance. Remember, the Corinthians had been rejecting the possibility of the resurrection of the dead on philosophical grounds. To them, their proposition was self-evident: the resurrection is impossible because our minds can't conceive of it. This is how a philosopher thinks, not how an ignorant, superstitious person would reason. Of course, Paul proves such a philosophical conclusion wrong through the historical proofs of the resurrection of Christ.

In Corinth, the intellectual climate would have been completely unfavorable to the springing up of such an abuse as the baptism of the living for the dead. Men of a philosophical turn of mind could hardly embrace a custom that would imply that the mere physical act of baptism was the one thing necessary to salvation. For if the dead died believing in Christ, to be baptized for them would imply that belief was not sufficient for salvation. And if the dead died not knowing Christ or believing in Him, to be baptized for them would imply that baptism without personal faith can save.

The disorders in the Corinthian church were rather the result of lax morality, lax discipline, spiritual and intellectual pride, than of a superstitious and slavish ritualism. The Corinthians turned from Paul to the more eloquent and philosophical Apollos; they suffered a man to live incestuously with his father's wife; they displayed their superiority to over-scrupulous conscientiousness by sitting in temples dedicated to idols and partaking of their sacrifices; they desecrated the Lord's Supper by turning it into a common meal; they used their spiritual gifts to show off; and finally they speculated with philosophical license on the impossibility and absurdity of the resurrection.

All of these tendencies were in the direction of an idealistic exaltation over and contempt of ceremonies rather than of a superstitious enslavement to them. The persons who would deny the resurrection for idealistic reasons could hardly become victims of such a gross and materialistic superstition as baptizing the living in lieu of the dead.

Settle it once for all with yourself, on the authority of Scripture, that it is only a genuine faith in the merits of Christ's atoning work on the cross that can procure your salvation.

WHAT BAPTISM FOR THE DEAD MEANS

"Else what shall they do which are baptized for the dead, if the dead rise not at all? why are they then bap_tized for the dead?" (I Cor. 15:29).

We have seen that this verse does not mean that living believers could be baptized for those who had died without baptism. But why does Paul connect baptism with death and resurrection in the 15th chapter of First Corinthians? Because baptism in Scripture is presented as a symbol of the death and resurrection of Christ. The same Apostle says in Romans 6:3, "Know ye not, that so many of us as were baptized into Jesus Christ were baptized into his death?" In view of His suffering on the cross, our Lord said to His disciples, "Can ye drink of the cup that I drink of? and be baptized with the baptism that I am baptized with?" (Mark 10:38). This is the baptism of suffering.

The word *baptizoo* in Greek, in its general sense, means "to envelop, to surround completely," whether this be by water, a cloud, or whatever physical or spiritual medium is referred to. Sometimes by implication it refers to identification with the surrounding element, as in Romans 6:3. To be baptized into the death of Christ means to be completely identified with the death of Christ.

I believe the word "baptized" in I Corinthians 15:29 has a dual meaning. It not only refers to believers who were baptized in water even as our Lord was, but indicates that this water baptism was also a declaration of their identification with the believers who had died, many of them as martyrs. Observe how Paul expresses it: "Else what shall they do which are baptized for the dead?" In Greek it is *hoi baptizomenoi*. This is a present participle preceded by the definite article, indicating that a definite class of people is referred to—not all the baptized, but just those who are "baptized for the dead." (See A. T. Robertson's *A Grammar of the Greek New Testament in the Light of Historical Research*, p. 757.)

We see an example of this use of the definite article in the Beatitudes. "Blessed are the poor in spirit . . . they that mourn . . . the meek," and so on (Matt. 5:3-10), and also in Luke 6:20, 21: "Blessed are ye poor . . . . ye that hunger . . . . ye that weep." Our Lord here is not pronouncing blessedness on all the poor, hungry, and mournful, but only on a certain class of these people—those who voluntarily undergo these privations for the sake of Jesus Christ. (See author's book, *The Pursuit of Happiness*, Grand Rapids: Eerdmans, 1966.)

So it is with those "who are baptized for the dead." Among the baptized is a special class of believers who are facing death and are baptized despite this threat to their lives. We conclude, then, that the term *hoi baptizomenoi*, "those who are baptized," indicates not the whole body of Christians but only a part. All Christians are saved, but not all have the same degree of dedication. Those who obey the command of Christ by taking up the cross and allying themselves with the dead are unfortunately all too few. This verse, then, does not denote the necessity of baptism if the dead are to be saved, but refers to the baptism of those whom their Christian profession subjected to actual suffering, peril, and perhaps martyrdom. Of these, especially of such as underwent death for Christ's sake, it would surely be no harsh language to say that they were "baptized for the dead"; that they underwent a baptism that destined them for and allied them with the dead.

As to the *thought*, look at the Apostle's frequent language elsewhere: "God hath set forth us the apostles last, as it were appointed unto death"; "I die daily"; "In death oft." And take the entire passage of II Corinthians 11:23-28 as an emphatic commentary on the idea of being baptized for the dead, and the whole following portion of the passage.

As to the *expression*, it is determined by the subject about which the apostle is writing. His mind is here on the dead with reference to their resurrection, and nothing would be more natural for him than to assimilate the phraseology in which he describes deadly suffering to the language of the context, and thus to set over against the resurrection of the dead a "baptism for the dead" as emphatically and justly descriptive of their earthly life, at least of that of himself and his fellow-preachers and propagators of the Gospel, who, wherever they went, went in the very face of martyrdom.

This expression also has the iterative sense as well as a kind of timelessness. It refers to the believers who were baptized in the past, in the present, and in the future. It is the act of baptism that is stressed, rather than the time. Those who were baptized in the past would do it again if necessary, unafraid of the death of martyrdom. Those who are now baptized are submitting to it with the full knowledge of what it has cost believers in the past. And those to be baptized in the future will submit with the full knowledge of the present cost of baptism to suffering believers.

What Paul is actually declaring here is that the ordinance of believers' baptism will be repeated in all ages in this era of grace, no matter what the cost and consequences implied in its testimony. He is speaking of baptism as a believer's declaration of identification with the dead, with Christ and with His followers who died for His sake.

Paul's statements always contained an encouraging note for the present. He did not engage in merely academic discussions concerning the past or the future without relating these to the present. That is why his statement is not "Else what shall they do (future) who were baptized (past) for the dead?" but "What shall they do who are baptized?" (present tense, meaning "now"). In other words, the atrocities and martyrdom that believers of the past have suffered, in no way deter believers now from being baptized and suffering the known consequences of persecution and death. It is as if Paul were triumphantly saying, "Christians in the past were baptized and died a martyr's death as a result. But Christians today are doing the same thing."

It cost something to be a Christian during the first three hundred years of the Christian era. During that time there were ten serious persecutions, from the first under Nero, thirty-one years after our Lord's ascension, to the tenth, which began in the 19th year of Diocletian, in 303. In this dreadful persecution, which lasted for ten years, houses filled with Christians were set on fire, and whole droves of people were twisted together with ropes and cast into the sea. It is related that 17,000 were slain in one month. In this fiery persecution it is believed that not less than 144,000 Christians died by violence, besides 700,000 that died as a result of banishment or the public works to which they were condemned.

But then came the period of Constantine the Great, when persecution against the Christians stopped, and the compromise of the Christian Church with heathenism and the world began. The Church, no longer persecuted, began persecuting others—thus completely betraying the spirit and teaching of Christ. The Lord Jesus never used anything resembling force or violence except once, and that was to drive evil men out of the temple, certainly not to drive unbelievers in and compel them to worship according to His dictates.

Unfortunately, Christianity has so degenerated in some areas of the Church that we usher people into it by the most sacred outward declaration of baptism without the inner conviction of the person being baptized that it is a witness of faith unto death. Oh, for the Christian Church to restore to the ordinance of baptism its original value of readiness to die for Christ, having been buried in sinfulness with Christ in His death and risen in His might victorious.

WHY BE BAPTIZED IF THERE IS NO RESURRECTION?

"Else what shall they do which are baptized for the dead, if the dead rise not at all?" (I Cor. 15:29).

So far we have seen that the phrase "baptized for the dead" does not mean that living believers could be baptized in place of those who had died unbaptized. What Paul was actually seeking to convey here is that only those who were willing to be identified with the dead in martyrdom for Christ's sake, as well as with Christ in His death and resurrection, could be described as "those baptized for the dead."

But why does Paul use the words "for the dead"? Let us examine this phrase carefully. The first word, "for," is *huper* in Greek, which basically means "over" or "above." The literal translation of this phrase would be "baptized over the dead"; that is to say, solemnly admitted publicly into the visible Church of Christ, as if the dead bodies of those who were similarly admitted into the Church before them were lying beneath their feet. Metaphorically it means in the prospect of death and as a continuance of the testimony of those who have heroically died for the faith.

This may be illustrated by comparing what happens on a battle-field. It is strewed with the bodies of those who fought and perished nobly; but the contest is still raging, and fresh combatants are continually pressing into the action. These, as they come up, may be said to be initiated into the soldiers' work over the bodies of those who have bled and died before them. Now this world is a spiritual battle-field. The contest between sin and righteousness, which commenced so soon after the fall, has been waging from generation to generation; it is waging still; and it will continue to do so till sin and Satan are overpowered, and death is swallowed up in victory. All who in bygone ages have been engaged in this warfare have fallen on the battle-field, fighting the good fight of faith. Fresh combatants, however, at the summons of the great Captain of our salvation, are continually pressing forward to occupy the places of the slain and bravely maintain the contest. These by the rite of baptism were admitted to the position they now occupy, or were constituted Christian soldiers. With reference either to the past or to the future—the deaths which have already occurred or their own death most certainly to occur—it may be said that they are either "baptized over the dead" or "baptized in the prospect of death." In this way the meaning of the expression becomes clear.

The ancients looked upon death as a deep, dark pit, into which all who preceded them had descended, and into which they must inevitably follow. If, therefore, Christians in days of persecution did not shrink from a public profession of the Gospel, although it exposed them to death, they might figuratively be said to have been "baptized over the dead"—over, that is to say, the place of the departed, into which place they too, as a result of their confession of faith, might momentarily be precipitated.

Even today, when martyrdom is rare, the same figure of speech may be used to illustrate our constant liability to natural death. We are dying; there is no escaping the fact that the dark, pit-like grave yawns ever at our feet. Scripture continually reminds us of this fact, and in allusion to this striking and solemn event Paul reminds Christian believers that we are "baptized over the dead."

The expression "baptized for the dead" indicates by implication that those who are now being baptized are also dying and will presently join the company of those who died before them. It is even possible that their death may be hastened by taking a public stand for Christ in baptism. Where is the meaning or benefit of all this, if there is no resurrection? It would be just as well not to be baptized at all.

This explanation of the text fits in very well with Paul's whole argument. The resurrection of the body is his great theme in I Corinthians 15, and this 29th verse must be consistent with that great doctrine. What Paul says here is that it is a strong proof of our bodily resurrection that God has commanded the waters of baptism to be applied to the body, even in the near prospect of death. In other words, why baptize a dying man if there is no resurrection? Why apply the waters of that holy ordinance to something that is no better than a handful of earth, a tabernacle of clay—destined to fall in pieces, never to be inhabited again? There is no meaning in such a service. But grant a resurrection, and the purpose of baptism is manifest. God thereby recognizes not merely the souls, but the bodies of His saints; puts His mark upon them in token that they are His; and pledges His almighty power that death, however near it may be, shall not hold them in everlasting constraint. If baptism is the forerunner and token of their death, it is also the pledge of their resurrection. (See *Discourses on Some of the Most Difficult Texts of Scripture*, by James Cochrane, pp. 104-122.)

In the Greek text, the definite article appears before "dead" the first time it is used in this sentence, but not the second. This is not apparent from the English translation. Literally this verse should read, "Thereupon what will they do who are baptized over the dead, if dead are not raised at all?" The definite article before the first use of the word "dead" is significant. It makes the phrase "baptized over the dead" refer, not to all the dead, but only to a certain class among the dead, even as we saw in our previous study that the definite article before *baptizomenoi* meant only a certain class among the baptized. The dead here are those Christians who suffered martyrdom for the sake of or on account of baptism. The inference is that they, too, were baptized believers.

Under no circumstances could this phrase be construed to mean that the baptism of any living person can benefit anyone who has died. The definite article before the word "dead" would have had to be omitted, making the phrase read *hoi baptizomenoi huper nekroon*, "the ones baptized over dead people," instead of "over the dead." If the word "dead" had been used without the article, there would be some possibility that what Paul was talking about here was vicarious baptism of the living for dead people who for some reason died unbaptized. But the use of the definite article totally eliminates this remote possibility, so foreign to the total spirit and precept of the Scriptures.

God's Word nowhere states that the unbaptized will be eternally lost. It does state this with reference to the unbeliever, however. Now if faith cannot be vicariously attributed to an unbeliever by a believer, certainly the merits of baptism cannot be transferred from a living person to one who has died without baptism. You, a living person, cannot believe or be baptized for the sake of someone who has died without faith or baptism.

The Authorized Version translates the Greek preposition *huper* as "for," in the phrase "baptized for the dead." Although *huper* most commonly means "in behalf of, for one's benefit," we have seen that it cannot refer to the unbaptized dead here. We must seek its meaning in the two classes of people presented in this verse: the living Christians who demonstrate enough courage to be baptized, and dead Christians who died a martyr's death as a result of their witness for the Lord. It is the courage of example that the Apostle Paul is pointing out here. And this courage is derived from the fact of the resurrection of Christ and the assurance it gives us of our own resurrection as believers in Him. We should never be afraid to obey God, even in the face of death, for our resurrection is as certain as the resurrection of our Lord.

LIVING IN THE HOPE OF THE RESURRECTION

"Else what shall they do which are baptized for the dead, if the dead rise not at all? why are they then baptized for the dead?" (I Cor. 15:29).

"If the dead rise not," said the Apostle Paul in I Corinthians 15:16 and 17, "then is not Christ raised: and if Christ be not raised, your faith is vain; ye are yet in your sins."

This clause, "If the dead rise not," is the basis of all Paul's argument in this chapter concerning the resurrection. He repeats it in the second part of verse 29. This might be better punctuated to read: "If the dead rise not at all, why are they then baptized for the dead?" Remember, there were no punctuation marks used when the New Testament was written. These are later additions. The punctuation marks were placed in the text by the editors, to give the sense as they understood it. Actually, I believe that the suppositional phrase, "if the dead rise not at all," fits into the clause that precedes it as well as into the clause that follows it. Neither of them would be complete without this fundamental supposition. If the dead do not rise at all, why are Christians baptized now, in view of the fact that so many who were baptized in the past died as a result of that testimony? Faith in the resurrection is a source of courage even in the face of death.

Paul adds something to this phrase not found in his previous use of it in verse 16. It is the adverb "at all" (*holoos* in Greek). This adverb might better be translated "actually" or "really." If the resurrection of the dead is not an actuality, not an absolute fact, why be baptized and thus run the risk of suffering martyrdom for Christ's sake?

Paul wants to stress that, to the believer who enters the waters of baptism, is buried with Christ, and raised with Him, the resurrection is an absolute fact. Of course, it is a fact of the future as far as the Christian is concerned, and this may seem presumptuous; but our present is connected with the past, and our future is as sure as the acts and promises of God. If it were not for the resurrection of the Lord Jesus, we would not be baptized now and we would not look forward with such assurance to the day of our own resurrection.

Paul here is living an event of the future in the present. Observe that he does not say, "if the dead will rise not," but "if the dead rise not [now]." This is a futuristic present tense. To Paul and all those who were then baptized and suffered in consequence, the resurrection was a present actuality.

The resurrection of Jesus Christ, a proven historical fact, is our anchor for steadfastness and the assurance of our own future resurrection. We live as if it were a present fact. "If the dead absolutely do not rise, then why are they [the living] baptized for the dead?" The hope of the resurrection has present value. As C. S. Lewis says, "Hope is one of the Theological virtues. This means that a continual looking forward to the eternal world is not (as some modern people think) a form of escapism or wishful thinking, but one of the things a Christian is meant to do. It does not mean that we are to leave the present world as it is. If you read history you will find that the Christians who did most for the present world were just those who thought most of the next. The Apostles themselves, who set on foot the conversion of the Roman Empire, the great men who built up the Middle Ages, the English Evangelicals who abolished the Slave Trade, all left their mark on Earth, precisely because their minds were occupied with Heaven. It is since Christians have largely ceased to think of the other world that they have become so ineffective in this. Aim at Heaven and you will get earth 'thrown in': aim at earth and you will get neither." (From *A Reader's Notebook*, Harper and Brothers: pp. 126-7.) Lose your grasp of the future resurrection as a present fact and you will be tempted to prove cowardly in the face of persecution.

A Chinese boy in Singapore found Christ as his Saviour and arranged to be baptized shortly after his graduation. But to his surprise he won a scholarship of $500 a year for four years in the Hongkong University. One of the conditions was, "The winner must be a Confucianist." To a poor student the temptation to defer baptism was great, but he resisted and presented himself for baptism at the appointed time. A friend, a Confucianist, stood next in line for the scholarship, but was so impressed that he refused it, saying, "If Christianity is worth so much to my classmate, it can be worth no less to me. I will be a Christian." He also was baptized. This exactly illustrates what Paul meant in I Corinthians 15:29.

As we saw previously, the definite article before the word "dead" in the first clause of verse 29, "Else what shall they do which are baptized for the dead," makes it refer to a definite class of the dead, the dead Christians who suffered persecution and martyrdom as a result of their open confession of Christ in baptism. But in the second clause, "if the dead rise not at all," there is no definite article before "dead" in the Greek text. The literal translation is "if dead ones rise not." There is no limitation on the dead here as there is in the previous clause. Paul does not want to make it appear as if the resurrection is limited only to those who have died for the faith. Therefore he does not say "if *the* dead [*hoi nekroi*] rise not," but "if dead ones rise not"—all the dead, believers and unbelievers. He refers here to that fact of the resurrection which intrinsically will affect the entire human race. "Why are the living baptized in the prospect of death," he asks in effect, "if the resurrection of humanity is not a fact of the future?"

In closing, Paul again asks a question, actually the same question that he had asked at the opening of the verse and the entire passage concerning Christian martyrdom inspired by faith in the resurrection: "Why are they then baptized for the dead?" In fact, some manuscripts, and the main reading in the Nestle's text, render the phrase "for the dead" as "for them," the "them" of course referring to the same dead ones Paul spoke of at the beginning of the verse, those who had suffered martyrdom for the sake of Christ in consequence of their baptism.

It is noteworthy that Paul uses the present tense of the verb "baptize." "Why *are* they baptized," not "Why *were* they baptized." Why are they baptized here and now? The examples of Christians submitting to the waters of baptism at the risk of their lives were fresh and current. Paul was not resting on the laurels of history but on present examples of Christians. These "baptisms unto death," so to speak, were not heroic deeds of the past but pertained to the present. Would to God that we could say today, "Why then are they baptized for the dead?" It is a sad commentary on the state of our faith that Christian baptism has become relatively inconsequential in comparison with the early days of the Church.

BAPTISM AND THE RESURRECTION

"Else what shall they do which are baptized for the dead, if the dead rise not at all? why are they then baptized for the dead?" (I Cor. 15:29).

Baptism today is often taken lightly by many churches and individuals. It is often entered upon without the understanding or consent of the one baptized, instead of being an act of individual obedience to Christ's example and command. In the New Testament, baptism was entered upon as the result of individual faith, as an external witness to the world. It often meant persecution. Secret disciples might escape this persecution, but not those who outwardly proclaimed their faith by baptism. The baptized were marked people, so to speak. No one would risk baptism who did not love the Lord enough to be willing to suffer for His sake. Would to God that this sacred ordinance had kept its original meaning.

A converted native was to be baptized in a river. The missionary took a long spear with him into the swift current to steady himself. Inadvertently he stabbed the foot of the convert beneath the water. The man neither spoke nor moved. After the ceremony, when the accident was discovered, the convert was asked why he had kept silent. "I thought it was part of the ceremony," he replied. In a way he was right. Baptism should be an external expression of willingness to suffer for the Lord Jesus Christ, in whose name the believer is baptized.

Baptism in the New Testament, an ordinance involving believers and water, was a physical act. But no physical act can of itself accomplish a spiritual work in the human heart. Faith is the spiritual exercise by which a man appropriates God's grace made available through the shed blood of Jesus Christ. We never find any indication in the New Testament that a believer who is not baptized is condemned and will perish—only that those who do not believe will perish. In most Scriptures, water baptism is mentioned as the resulting accompaniment of faith. Whenever it is mentioned by itself as producing salvation, the fact of regenerating faith is presupposed. When you speak of a second step, you naturally presuppose a first step. Every baptized person in the New Testament was a believer, but not every believer necessarily submitted to baptism, as in the case of the thief on the cross who repented just before dying. In those days there were both baptized and unbaptized believers, but today we find many baptized unbelievers. If you are one of these, do not think your baptism will save you. You need to believe in Christ as your Saviour from sin, and be born again.

Baptism in I Corinthians 15:29 must be equated with a public profession of faith exposing baptized believers to suffering and peril. Verse 30 throws further light upon the somewhat enigmatic 29th verse, when it says, "And why stand we in jeopardy every hour?" Again, in verse 31, the Apostle Paul says, "I die daily." What a struggle Paul must have had in the heathen city of Ephesus, from which he wrote this epistle to the Corinthians. Why all this exposure to danger and death if there is no resurrection of the dead? "Let us eat and drink: for to morrow we die" (v. 32).

In this passage, Paul equates baptism with willingness to suffer for Christ. It presupposes belief in Christ and a life of faith and Christlikeness. "All that will live godly in Christ Jesus shall suffer persecution," he wrote to Timothy (II Tim. 3:12).

What else can we learn from this 29th verse, which says, "Else what shall they do which are baptized for the dead, if the dead rise not at all? why are they then baptized for the dead?" Let us look at the very first word of this verse. The conjunction "else" in Greek is *epei*, a compound of *epi*, meaning "on," and the suppositional preposition *ei*, "if," which Paul used constantly in his hypothetical propositions from verse 12 on. It means "thereupon" or "otherwise." With this conjunction Paul resumes the argument where he left off in verse 19. From verses 16 through 19 he stated the consequences of a denial of the resurrection. Such a denial made the apostles' preaching and the believers' faith vain; it branded the apostles as false witnesses and left the Corinthians still in their sins; it meant that those who died perished, and that living believers were to be pitied who suffer for Christ.

Here in verse 29 he takes up the argument again. If there is no resurrection, he says, even our baptism as believers has been in vain. All along Paul has been speaking of the disastrous consequences of a denial of the resurrection, not upon unbelievers or infants, but upon believers. If you do not want to go astray in the interpretation of verse 29, be sure to keep it in its total context—the effect of a denial of the resurrection on believers.

Furthermore, reasons Paul, if there is no resurrection of the dead, "What shall they do which are baptized for the dead?" What does Paul mean by the expression, "what shall they do"? Observe that the verb is in the future tense. In Greek it is *poieoo*, "to do" or "to accomplish." What will they gain or accomplish if there is no resurrection of the dead? What will they have really accomplished when they discover that they have suffered in vain? Their hope of reward for enduring persecution is dashed. Christ will be proven a liar, because He said, "Blessed are ye, when men shall revile you, and persecute you and shall say all manner of evil against you falsely, for my sake. Rejoice, and be exceeding glad: for great is your reward in heaven: for so persecuted they the prophets which were before you" (Matt. 5:11, 12. See also Luke 6:22, 23). That day of heavenly rewards presupposes the resurrection. If the resurrection is not a reality, what will they do who believed that Christ is the rewarder of them that believe? They will be sorely perplexed and crushed, and will discover that in the end they accomplished nothing worthwhile or lasting.

It might be good for you to ask yourself some questions similar to Paul's. For instance, what will you have accomplished if you finally discover you are not saved by the mere physical act of baptism, that is, contact with water administered in a rite of the church? What will you have accomplished if you find that good works do not avail for your salvation? What will you

—518—

do when you discover that there is an eternal hell in which you did not believe? What will you do when you discover that there is indeed a reward for sacrifices made for Christ's sake?

Hopes are based on beliefs, but beliefs must be examined to determine whether they can be intelligently held. Christian beliefs are trustworthy because of one historically attested fact, that Christ rose from the dead. No other religious leader or being can validly claim this distinction. Hence the uniqueness of Christ and His utterances. If it were not for His resurrection and His assurance of our resurrection, all our hopes would be found to be the most disappointing self-deceptions.

Paul wants us to beware of false hope just as much as he wants us to rely on the hope of the resurrection. False hope puts us to sleep and sets us to dreaming. But what shall we do when we wake up and find out it was all a dream? False hope makes us dream of riches, then suddenly plunges us into poverty.

The resurrection of Christ and the resulting assurance of the believer's resurrection is like that white bird that suddenly descended on the mast of a vessel in a hurricane. As soon as the crew saw it, hope dawned. To the believer who confesses his faith to the outside world through his obedience in entering upon the ordinance of baptism, the storm is sure, but the resurrection is just as sure, with its coming rewards for fidelity.

EXPOSURE TO DANGER, AND THE RESURRECTION

"And why stand we in jeopardy every hour?"

(I Cor. 15:30).

In many of our big cities, people are afraid to go out alone on the streets at night. Man constitutes the greatest danger to man. But the world is full of natural dangers also: storms, floods, earthquakes, wild animals —whatever leads to suffering and ultimate death for man in this world.

However, God did not create the world to be evil, but, because man chose to disobey Him, he has been reaping the consequences of his disobedience ever since. Foremost among these evils is death, and all the perils that lead to it. Danger is but a foreshadowing of death.

There are certain dangers we cannot help encountering, because we cannot choose all the circumstances of our lives. We may travel in a plane or car that meets with an accident. None of us can escape the inevitable consequences of such events. The Christian is not exempt from them either. Yet there is a fundamental difference between the attitude of the believer and the unbeliever in such matters, as well as in the eternal consequences to each. The believer considers even accidents as God's providences. He regards his life as consisting not merely of his brief sojourn on earth but as an unending life, begun here and continued in the heavenly Kingdom hereafter. Whenever God wishes to transfer him from one world to the other, the consistent believer thanks Him for having timed all things well. But the unbeliever regards accidents and death as calamities of unmitigated woe. The believer regards his life as ruled by a governor, the unbeliever does not. One believes in design and the other in chance. That's the basic difference.

However, the believer must face certain other dangers that are a consequence of his own choice. These are the dangers of persecution, ridicule, and possible martyrdom that he exposes himself to because of his public stand for Jesus Christ. Such dangers have been inherent at certain times in baptism, for instance. This is what the Apostle Paul says in I Corinthians 15:29, when he declares that those who openly profess their faith in baptism are doing so over the dead ones who were martyred for the faith. If you enter into baptism with the determination to be identified with Christ in all things, the unbelieving world stands ready to oppose you to just that degree that your presence acts as a check upon the evil they perpetrate.

But these voluntarily accepted dangers are all worthwhile to the baptized Christian in view of the resurrection. If the resurrection of the believer were not a reality, what would motivate him to expose himself to such dangers of holy living and witness? "And why stand we in jeopardy every hour?" Paul asks in I Corinthians 15:30. Again we understand that this is preceded by the suppositional phrase, "if the dead rise not," which underlies his whole argument in this passage. In fact, the connective phrase *ti kai*, "and why," with which verse 30 begins, joins it with the argument that begins with verse 29. It has the implied meaning of "why at all?"

The expression "stand we in jeopardy" is *kinduneuomen* in Greek, from the noun *kindunos*, meaning "danger." Paul refers to the risk of life that he and other believers incurred daily as a result of their open testimony for Christ. "Every hour" means "all the time," of course. Paul and other Christians who had a strong faith in the resurrection were willing to accept any risk as they lived and witnessed daily for Christ. The resurrection, Paul declares, makes fearless Christians. History fully bears this out.

A pagan sneeringly asked a missionary, "Where are your converts?" Pointing to a nearby graveyard the missionary answered, "There!" In faithfully standing for their Lord, they had been cruelly murdered. "They loved not their lives unto the death" (Rev. 12:11).

A Christian about to be executed shifted his position somewhat after he had laid his head upon the block. The executioner noticing this asked if he wished to rise again and escape death by renouncing Christianity. He calmly replied, "Not till the general resurrection. Strike on."

Paul gives an account of the sufferings and dangers that he himself lived through, in II Corinthians 11:23-30. "In labours more abundant, in stripes above measure, in prisons more frequent, in deaths oft. Of the Jews five times received I forty stripes save one. Thrice was I beaten with rods, once was I stoned, thrice I suffered shipwreck, a night and a day I have been in the deep; in journeyings often, in perils of waters, in perils of robbers, in perils by mine own countrymen, in perils by the heathen, in perils in the city, in perils in the wilderness, in perils in the sea, in perils among false brethren; in weariness and painfulness, in watchings often, in hunger and thirst, in fastings often, in cold and nakedness. Beside those things that are without, that which cometh upon me daily, the care of all the churches. Who is weak, and I am not weak? who is offended, and I burn not? If I must needs glory, I will glory of the things which concern mine infirmities."

Even today, in this so-called advanced state of civilization, we hear of brave soldiers of the cross who lay their lives on the line when they bear a fearless testimony for Christ. Dear personal friends of mine, Costas Makris and his wife Alki, are Greek missionaries to Indonesia. As Costas labored in the jungles there, more and more natives were converted and then baptized. The chief became so disturbed about his people turning to Christ, especially the young people, that he decided to do away with Costas. He lined up his spearmen in front of this dedicated young missionary. In the distance Costas' wife and three small sons stood watching their husband and father about to be executed for the cause of Christ. How would you feel in their place?

But the face of this missionary shone with a heavenly glory that puzzled these savage people. How could a man face death with a smile? Of course, his wife and many others must have been praying. As the men lifted their spears for the kill, the chief called out

"Stop!" He walked up to Costas, embraced him, and told him that a man who could face death with such courage and with such a smile on his face had something that they themselves needed.

Can you imagine the reunion with his wife and three boys? What an exemplification of I Corinthians 15:30, "in jeopardy every hour"! How many of us can truly say, "Because I believe in the resurrection of the dead, I am ready to die at any time for the sake of Jesus Christ"? If we had more Christians with that faith and determination, the world would be turned upside down. Does the resurrection impel us to such self-sacrifice that our lives are daily laid on the line for our Lord?

A missionary society was deeply impressed by the courageous devotion of David Livingstone, who worked single-handedly for God in Africa. The society wrote to Livingstone: "Have you found a good road to where you are? If so, we want to send other men to join you." Livingstone replied, "If you have men who will come only if there is a good road, I don't want them. I want men who will come if there is no road at all."

Are you willing to expose yourself to danger because of your passionate belief in the resurrection? The greatest of Christian doctrines has the most practical involvement: courage unto death. What have been the testimonies withheld because of the fear of ridicule or even harm? Without being offensive we can be effective and fearless witnesses. Let us never count our lives more precious than the salvation of others. For us the resurrection will mean eternal joy, but to the unsaved it will mean eternal separation from God.

A CALL TO HEROIC LIVING AND DYING

"I protest by your rejoicing which I have in Christ Jesus our Lord, I die daily" (I Cor. 15:31).

Some people think of Christianity as a passive religion, whose followers let themselves be crucified like their Master, without uttering a word. Peace is said to be the key word of Christians, even if it means complete submissiveness to the forces of evil and to men of evil intentions. This is a complete misunderstanding of what Jesus Christ taught. The Christian religion is not one that gives in to all things and all people under all circumstances, but one that aggressively seeks to win all people, even at the cost of sacrificing all things and self itself.

When the Apostle Paul says, "I die daily," is he taking a fatalistic attitude toward death? Is he saying, "Since I am going to die, and am each day one step nearer the grave, why should I bother to accomplish anything that would hasten my end?" Does the daily dying of which he speaks rob life of its vitality, of the vigor of service? Far from it.

I doubt whether Paul was in a passive mood when he wrote these words. They do not sound like the whimperings of a weak old man but rather like the strong language employed by one whose blood is fired by the inspiration of a living Saviour. "I protest," he says, using a particle of strong affirmation in Greek (*nee*) to show that he was indeed stirred up. This particle is used nowhere else in the New Testament. The ancient

Greeks used it when they wanted to affirm something in the name of their gods. It is similar to the preposition "by," in the expression "By Zeus," or in modern parlance "By God." The Authorized Version translation, "I protest," is a pretty good rendering of the meaning of the Greek word. Of course, Paul is not swearing here. He does not call upon God to affirm what he is saying, but he calls upon the work he has done among the Corinthians to witness to the truth of his willingness to die for the cause of Christ. He does not want to die sleeping his days away in passive waiting, but in fighting the good fight of faith.

"I protest," says Paul. People don't usually protest sitting down, do they? Unfortunately too many who call themselves Protestants are doing no protesting whatever. They are dying of inactivity rather than dying on the battlefield for the Lord. It is no sin to protest and to die fighting for the cause of Christ. Paul did it, and we must be willing to do it, too. Let's say to the world, "I'm willing to die in the defense and propagation of the Gospel of Christ."

As proof of his heroic stand, Paul called upon his work among the Corinthians. "I protest by your rejoicing which I have in Christ Jesus our Lord." The translation of the Greek text is rather ambiguous here. A better rendering is, "I protest, brethren, by my pride in you which I have in Christ Jesus our Lord." The word "rejoicing" in Greek is *kaucheesin*, which basically means "boasting." Paul is referring to his boasting about the Corinthians. He was proud of what the Gospel he preached had accomplished among them.

He had not found his work among them easy. He had been greatly persecuted in Corinth, as we learn from the 18th chapter of the Acts. Yet despite this, he had been instrumental in leading two chief rulers of the synagogue, Crispus and Sosthenes, to Christ, and in founding a vigorous church in that debauched city. Persecution did not drive Paul into a life of retirement. He continued preaching the Word for a year and a half in Corinth. He preferred to risk death rather than give up preaching. Many souls were won to Christ simply because Paul was willing to die at any time by remaining in Corinth. Paul had every reason to be proud of the work of Christ in these converts. They were his cause for rejoicing in the midst of suffering for Christ.

Thank God there are still servants of the Lord who can say with Paul, "I die daily." Paul was not interested in saints like Simeon Stylites who rotted away on the top of a pillar. It is not in cell or monastery that we search for heroism but on the battlefield. The Christian doctor who will endanger his life to save the lives of others is a man who dies daily. The Christian student who will hold fast to the truth though a score of voices denounce him as heretical and behind the times; the Christian worker who goes down to the slums and toils there, when all the novelty is gone, for the poor and fallen for whom Jesus died; the Christian girl, trained in a quiet home, who volunteers for mission work— these are types of the heroic who can say with Paul, "I die daily."

As I write these lines I have before me a prayer

letter from Gordon Magney, whose heart the Lord burdened for missionary work among the Turks. He writes from Idil Prison in Turkey: "On November 19th three fellows and I were visiting a Syrian Christian village in S. E. Turkey about 30 miles north of Syria. We were arrested while selling Gospel portions and have been in jail since then. Praise the Lord."

And then on Christmas day he wrote: "Christmas greetings from Cell #1. A week ago we moved here from Idil Prison and are praising God for all His blessings during our five weeks in confinement. We have sensed that many have been praying for us. Before we left Idil Prison, the Lord wonderfully brought a young Syrian boy, Behnan, to Himself. Behnan was like an angel of light to us, daily tending to our needs and bringing many kind gifts from the Christian community. Pray for him as he probably is the only born-again person in his town. Jeff Cobb, George Jaquith and myself have been given a separate wing of the jail all to ourselves. We have been allowed only one visit to the Turkish brother, Adip, who was arrested with us. Pray that God will use his witness as he lives with 17 Curds in his cell." Sounds like the book of the Acts, doesn't it?

Why are these men in prison? Certainly not for their passivity but because of their active witness for Christ. So it was with Paul. "By my boasting of you brethren," Paul writes, "I die daily." He calls them to witness that to win them to Christ he endangered his life every day. He might almost be saying that, had it not been for his determination to work for them even in the face of death, they might not have been his brethren in Christ now.

Paul is careful, however, never to take any credit to himself. That is why he adds concerning this boasting or rejoicing that it is "in Christ Jesus our Lord." He recognizes that he was only Christ's instrument; that it was Christ who did all the work of conviction and conversion. Paul preached and Christ saved. That is how God has ordained it. Let us be faithful in doing our part, and trust Christ to do His. God have mercy on the world if we fail to speak out for Christ because we count our lives precious.

What Paul is pointing out in verses 29-31 is that the resurrection of the Lord Jesus Christ makes heroes, not cowards, out of those who believe in it. The heroic in Christianity, of course, must not be confused with the foolhardy. Endangering one's life out of egotistical bravado, or for any other reason than fidelity to the Lord Jesus and the love of those for whom He died, is absolute foolishness.

It was heroism that made the Christian Church. It is cowardice that silences the witness for Christ. Are you an active or a passive Christian? Are you ready to die on the battlefield any day, or are you rotting away in your secluded and undisturbed worship? It is far better to die young fighting and accomplishing for the cause of Christ, than to die old having done nothing of eternal value.

(See G. H. Morrison, *Sun-Rise: Addresses from a City Pulpit*, pp. 300-10; and C. H. Spurgeon, *The Treasury of the New Testament*, pp. 211-17.)

IS THE CHRISTIAN'S DAILY STRUGGLE
WORTH WHILE?

"I die daily. If after the manner of men I have fought with beasts at Ephesus...." (I Cor. 15:31b, 32a).

How many times will you die? The question seems nonsensical on the face of it. But the Apostle Paul had an answer other than the obvious. He said, "I die daily." Men expect to die only once. But if you fail to die daily like the Apostle Paul, the anticipation of that one death may frighten you all your life. To achieve inner serenity and to be able to get the most out of life, you must learn to say with the Apostle Paul, "I die daily."

Paul was not afraid to die, because he believed in the resurrection of his body. His faith in his own future resurrection was based on the historical fact of Christ's resurrection. For the Christian who believes in the resurrection, it is not death to die. Paradoxical as it may seem, the Christian dies to live. And because of this he does not fear the prospect of death. He is ready to lay down his life at any moment without counting this as loss.

A family lost three children in less than a week in a terrible epidemic. Only a three-year-old escaped. The following Sunday was Easter, and the parents and child went to church as usual. The mother taught her Sunday school class and the father took his place at the superintendent's desk, where he read the Easter story from the Gospels and led the school in worship, with only now and then a break in his voice.

"How could they do it?" the people said to each other as they left the church. One fifteen-year-old boy said to his father, "Dad, I guess they really believe it, don't they?" "Believe what?" asked the father. "The whole big thing, all of it, Easter you know," replied the boy. Paul did, too. That's why he could say, "I die daily." Can you say that? Do you believe the whole big thing? There can be nothing bigger than this glorious doctrine of the resurrection based on fact.

Being a Christian means standing for godly principles. The world may demand of us the sacrifice of these principles or else the sacrifice of our life. We do not find this so much in the more enlightened parts of the world, but under totalitarian governments or among primitive cultures such a choice often confronts the dedicated Christian.

If you prefer compromise to sacrifice or even death, that means that you value this world more than the life to come. You show your doubt that departing to be with Christ is far better (Phil. 1:23). Why should you fear that which is far better for you, which will rid you of all your ills, admit you into unlimited blessedness, take you away from all fear and care, and conduct you to the fullness of the glory which is laid up in Christ?

Note that Paul makes a shift in pronouns from verse 30 to verse 31. In the former verse he says, "And why stand we in jeopardy every hour?" He meant himself in company with other believers. All believers face common dangers that may lead to physical death. But in verse 31 he changes to the first person singular, "I die daily." Death is experienced by each person separately. There is companionship in life in facing danger together, but not in death. We come into the world alone, and we must leave it alone. Death, like salvation, can never be experienced vicariously. Paul may have had in mind those who gave up or kept silent rather than face persecution. But Paul was willing to die at any moment for the sake of the Lord Jesus. He was not a man to follow the crowd, to do that which was expedient, but was concerned only with pleasing the Lord.

Never do what others are doing simply because the course is followed by some or many. Be willing to die alone, if need be, for the sake of the Lord Jesus Christ. Never be dissuaded by the compromising example of others. When you stand before the judgment seat of Christ, you cannot excuse yourself by saying that you did wrong because everybody else did it. Rise up and declare that you are willing to stand alone for the truth, and to die for it alone, if necessary.

A poor but devout Frenchman once came to his spiritual advisor and said with a sorrowing heart: "I am a sinner; I feel that it is so, but it is against my will. Every hour I ask for light, and humbly pray for faith; but still I am overwhelmed with doubts. Surely, if I was not despised of God, He would not leave me to struggle thus." The clergyman answered with much kindness, "The King of France has two castles, in different situations, and sends a commander to each of them. The castle of Mantleberry stands in a place remote from danger, far inland; but the castle of La Rochelle is on the coast, where it is liable to continued sieges. Now which of the two commanders, do you think, stands highest in the estimate of the King—the commander of La Rochelle, or he of Mantleberry?" "Doubtless," said the poor man, "the King values him the most who has the hardest task, and braves the greatest dangers." "You are right," replied his advisor. "And now apply this matter to your case and mine."

Does that shed some light on why God may have placed you in circumstances where life is a real struggle? Fellow minister, do you wonder why God sent you to work in an area where there is so much resistance to the Gospel? There is a reason. It is because God has a high estimate of you. Live up to it.

The Apostle Paul seems to have had a hard time everywhere he went to preach the Gospel. God needed a man like him for the hard places. He did not shrink but accepted the challenge. Strong characters like to face strong opposition. My wife, on hearing me remark the other day that I sometimes grew weary of the constant problems I faced in connection with the work the Lord had given me, said, "If you had an eight-hour-a-day job with nothing but routine duties you would die of boredom." She was right. It is in the struggle that we gain more strength, and it is hardship that tests our mettle. You can tell what you are made of by how you feel toward the challenges of life.

For a year and a half Paul had preached the Gospel in Corinth under all kinds of difficulties. When he left there, he came to a city equally as sinful—Ephesus. In Corinth they deified prostitution, and in Ephesus they worshiped the Goddess Artemis, who represented the reproductive powers of men, animals, and all living things. Paul's struggles in these two cities were by divine appointment. That is why, when he wrote from Ephesus to the Corinthians, among whom there was a lively discussion as to the reality of the resurrection, he said, "If, after the manner of men I have fought with beasts at Ephesus, what advantageth it me, if the dead rise not? let us eat and drink; for to morrow we die" (v. 32).

For the sixth time in this chapter the Apostle uses the principle of *reductio ad absurdum* by employing the phrase, "if the dead rise not." Paul tells the Corinthians that not only is the whole Christian faith a farce if the dead do not rise, but also that any exposure to danger in Ephesus and elsewhere for preaching the Gospel is senseless. "Do you think that an intelligent man like me would have suffered in Ephesus for a belief that is not based on fact?" he seems to be asking. "If it were not for the certainty of the resurrection, I would never consent to suffer for Christ in this way."

It is doubtful whether Paul fought with literal beasts at Ephesus. He was a Roman citizen and therefore could not be thrown into the arena with wild beasts, as was often the practice in this sinful city. It is more likely that Paul was referring here to human beings, to the fierce attacks of the Ephesians who persecuted him as far as the law allowed. Heraclitus the Greek philosopher who flourished about 513 B.C. is said to have called the Ephesians *theeria*, "wild beasts," and this designation may have persisted even to Paul's day.

If you will read the 19th chapter of the Acts, you will begin to appreciate some of the struggles Paul had at Ephesus. These must have been struggles with unbelievers, more especially with those who earned much revenue from the superstitions of the pagans. Paul had quite a time with these followers of the goddess Artemis, who were so uninformed in the doctrine of Christ.

It is probably because of these struggles in Ephesus that Paul refers to them in this resurrection chapter immediately after he mentions the implications of Christian baptism. The believer who is baptized declares to all the world that he is willing to die for Jesus Christ, and that he is not afraid of death in view of the certainty of the resurrection. In spite of his struggles with the "wild beasts" of Ephesus, Paul was eminently successful. How wonderful to read, "So mightily grew the word of God, and prevailed" (Acts 19:20).

THE SINS OF THE BODY

"If the dead rise not . . . let us eat and drink; for to morrow we die" (I Cor. 15:32b).

What you believe shows in the way you live. As a man "thinketh in his heart, so is he" (Prov. 23:7). And the way you choose to live affects what you choose to believe. This is what Paul meant when he said to the Corinthians, "If the dead rise not . . . let us eat and drink; for to morrow we die." The phrase, "if the dead rise not," should be taken as referring not only to the first part of the verse, in which Paul questions the worth of having suffered for the cause of Christ in Ephesus, but to the second half also, which suggests that unless we believe in the resurrection of the body we might as well give free rein to our appetites, since life is so short.

It was no idle reproof that Paul gave concerning gluttony, for men of that day, especially among the Romans, indulged in it to the extent that they were worse than beasts. They would eat all they could hold, take an emetic, and then eat more. "They vomit to eat, and eat to vomit," said Seneca.

But in the expression, "let us eat and drink," is Paul suggesting that there is something inherently evil about satisfying such bodily appetites? Hardly, for eating and drinking are necessary to the preservation of life. While the Lord Jesus Christ was here on earth in a natural body, He maintained it by eating and drinking. God created us with bodily appetites, and constituted the earth in such a way as to provide the food and drink necessary to satisfy them and maintain us in health. No one should feel guilty over the healthy satisfaction of his God-given appetites for food and drink.

But because of man's sinful nature, he tends to be unbalanced in the expression of his appetites. He allows his body to have ascendancy over his soul. His God-given constituent parts are at war with each other because man is at war with his Maker. Only as we allow our Creator to direct our appetites and functions will we achieve proper balance among them. Each one will then perform as it was originally intended to do.

That man is wrong who despises his body; even as that man is wrong who despises his spiritual nature. It is just as wrong for the ascetic to refuse to eat as for the glutton to refuse to nourish his spiritual nature. The harmonious person is the balanced person. He is the one who balances all his functions to perform as they were divinely and originally intended to do.

Now the Corinthians, following the philosophy of the early pagan Gnostics, felt that in the after life only the soul was important. They therefore rejected the possibility of man's physical resurrection, despite the proven fact of Christ's bodily resurrection. They attached more importance to a philosophical speculation than to a historical event. That sort of thinking persists to this day. Paul demonstrates by his masterful and logical arguments how absurd it is.

In spite of the little importance the Gnostics of every description attached to the body, declaring that it could not possibly live after death, certain Gnostic sects attached an altogether undue importance to its gratification in this life. They reduced life to little more than over-indulgence in food and drink. In a land like ours, where food and drink are plentiful, we are prone to be given to the same excess. Someone has said that one-third of what a man eats is usually all he needs in order to live. A smart reporter commented, "In that case, what becomes of the other two thirds?" "Oh, that enables the doctor to live," was the retort.

The sum total of Paul's argument against those Corinthians who rejected the possibility of a physical resurrection is, if our bodies are so unimportant as to have no future existence after death, why assign such importance to them now that we say to them, "Eat and drink; for to morrow we die"? Can there be such a radical change of values between this world and the next? No indeed, argues Paul. If your body is so important to God that He intends to raise it from the dead, then you must be careful what it does in this life. You cannot let it run to excess or indulge in gluttony. Death does not end your accountability for the deeds done in the body here on earth.

Paul implies here that belief in a physical resurrection has a sanctifying effect on our bodies, and that disbelief in it can lead to debauchery. Truly our bodies are temples of the Holy Spirit (I Cor. 6:19). But also think of it this way. How dare we stigmatize and scar the body with sin when we know that this self-same body in its metaphysical state will rise or be re-constituted to rejoin the soul which parted from it at death? I have no doubt that our resurrected bodies will be capable of enjoyments in heaven in a manner somewhat comparable to their capabilities on earth. That is, the more the body of the Christian has been given over to harmful excesses on earth, the less its enjoyment will be of the pleasures of heaven. Remember, the body you now mar with sin will be with you after the resurrection.

Is this true of unbelievers also? I believe it is. Although this 15th chapter of I Corinthians deals primarily with the bodily resurrection of believers, we know that the bodies of unbelievers will also be resurrected. (See Dan. 12:2, John 5:28, 29, Acts 24:15, Rev. 20:13.) For believers and unbelievers, both soul and body will share in the rewards or punishments of the life to come. When the Lord Jesus spoke about those who committed adultery—a sin of the body—He said, "and not that thy whole body should be cast into hell [Gehenna]" (Matt. 5:29, 30). This refers to man's resurrection body, of course, and not his earthly body. The conclusion we reach, then, is that what the body sows it reaps, not only here on earth but also in its resurrected form.

Christians may and do fall into sins of the body on occasion. In the Corinthian church some of its members committed such serious sins of the flesh as adultery and incest. Now, while the blood of Jesus Christ cleanses us from all sin, this refers rather to the total effect upon Christians, in that they do not lose their salvation; but believers are not thereby relieved of their accountability for such sins. No sin in the Christian's life will prevent him from entering heaven, but in heaven he will have to give an accounting of all that has been done in the flesh, and his scars will be with him. That's why Paul bursts out in this verse, "If the dead rise not [that is, if our bodies do not rise], then we shall give ourselves over to indulgence in food and drink, since death means the end of our bodies and hence of physical enjoyment."

How important, then, is Paul's injunction to the Corinthians, "Flee fornication. Every sin that a man doeth is without the body; but he that committeth fornication sinneth against his own body . . . therefore glorify God in your body, and in your spirit, which are God's" (I Cor. 6:18, 20). Excessive indulgence in food and drink are also sins against the body.

Paul's first thought here is for the Christians. Remember that the resurrection is physical. You cannot indulge your body in sins, small or large, and expect to feel no effects in heaven. It seems to me that, even as Christians will not all have the same kind of bodies in heaven, so their enjoyment in their heavenly bodies will be proportionate to the holiness of their lives on earth. Those Christians who made physical sacrifices will have proportionately greater physical enjoyment in heaven. Those who gave their bodies over to self-indulgence and sin will have lesser joys.

As far as unbelievers go, the Bible teaches that they will undergo different degrees of punishment and suffering, even as there will be degrees of enjoyment in heaven for believers. Good works cannot secure heaven for anyone, for we are saved by grace through faith; but nevertheless every believer and unbeliever will be held accountable for the way he used his body on earth, and the results will be apparent in his resurrection body. How dare anyone say then, "Let us eat and drink" (that is, "Let us give ourselves over to gluttony"), when we know that such excesses will have their effect on our resurrection bodies?

WATCH THE COMPANY YOU KEEP

"Be not deceived: evil communications corrupt good manners" (I Cor. 15:33).

Corinth was notorious for being a city of great immorality and unbelief in the days of the early Church. The two usually go together. People with a profound faith in God are almost without exception moral; and immoral people are generally lacking in any vital religious convictions. If you do not believe in God, you will feel free to act in defiance of the absolute standards that He has ordained. You will set yourself up as the sole judge of what constitutes good and evil as far as you are concerned. You will accept the philosophy that right and wrong are relative matters; and neither God, the government, your parents, the church, the Bible, nor any other person can tell you what to believe and how to act. The result is moral chaos, which is just about what we find in society today, where each one wants to be a law unto himself.

Naturally, your philosophy of life determines your conduct. And when your conduct deviates from God's moral law and you become complacent about what He declares to be sin, it becomes difficult for you to believe in Him ever again. In departing from God's revealed truth, you have reached a state of degeneracy in which you cannot make proper or beneficial judgments.

That is why the Apostle Paul, faced with such a situation among the Corinthians, says to them, "Be not deceived: evil communications corrupt good manners."

The word "deceived" in Greek, *planasthe*, is from the verb *planaoo*, which means "to cause to wander." It is from this that we derive our English word "planet." Originally the Greeks called the heavenly bodies "planets" because they seemed to be moving or wandering about, instead of remaining fixed.

In the passive voice in which the verb is used here, *planaoo* has come to mean "to stray as a result of some influence upon one, to be deceived." Paul believes in an absolute standard, a straight course, from which man may stray—especially the one who professes faith in the Lord Jesus Christ, for it is primarily of Christian believers that Paul speaks here in I Corinthians 15. Do not deviate from the straight course, Paul tells the Corinthian Christians. The results could be tragic. Do not become a wanderer. Truth is to be found in only one place, the revelation God has given of Himself. Truth and doctrine are absolutes that you cannot trifle with. Truth is never relative; it cannot be adjusted to suit individual personalities.

This absolute truth about which Paul is speaking is the fact of the resurrection of the Lord Jesus Christ. There can be no "maybe" about it, he says. Either it is so or it is not. Paul has gone to great lengths to prove that Christ rose bodily from the dead. And now that He has risen, our bodies will also some day rise from the dead. This is absolute truth, based not on presumptive reasoning but on verified historical fact.

It seems, however, that the Christians in Corinth were tempted to listen to the speculations of the philosophers who abounded in that city. Instead of starting with a known fact, the resurrection of Jesus Christ, they started with a supposition based upon human reasoning—that it is impossible for men to rise from the dead. It is as though a scientist were to speak of biological impossibilities as if he had explored every possibility and knew with absolute finality whereof he spoke. But in our modern age we laugh as we read of what scientists of the past called unbelievable, impossible, and incredible. The germ theory, for instance, was bitterly attacked by the medical profession for many years. Vaccination to prevent communicable diseases was considered too dangerous ever to become practicable. Yet now these former impossibilities, and thousands like them, have become everyday realities.

Because we lack complete theoretical knowledge, we must rely on our scientific observations. This is what Paul told the Corinthian Christians to do. When there is a conflict between observation and theory, observation must win out. "Do not deviate; do not wander from observed facts," says Paul in effect. "Do not stand on a pedestal and declare, 'The resurrection of the body is an impossibility,' for in so doing you simply show how ignorantly opinionated you are. In fact, you will find yourself in real trouble."

And this trouble will be of your own making. Why? Observe that the verb *planasthe* is in the present indicative tense, which properly translated would make this verse read, "Do not keep on being deceived." The passive voice indicates that this deception is brought about by someone outside yourself. Paul tells these Corinthians not to get into such a frame of mind that they grow accustomed to being deceived, and do nothing about it. This is the master plan of the devil, gradually to brainwash you until you become insensitive to the fact that you are being deceived. In such a state of mind, even though you are on the wrong road, you insist that you are on the right one. You may even think yourself to be a Christian when you actually are not. These Corinthians to whom Paul wrote thought they could combine heathen philosophy with Christian doctrine, accepting only so much of either as commended itself to their human reasoning. Unfortunately they were playing fast and loose with a fundamental doctrine of the Christian faith, the resurrection of the body, without which they could not properly be said to hold basically to the truth at all. This is the kind of deception that Christians are in danger of becoming accustomed to, in this day of "anything goes" in so many modern pulpits.

To say that you are a Christian, yet not to believe in the bodily resurrection of all mankind that Christ taught, is like saying you have implicit faith in your wife or husband, but cannot always believe what they say. A Christian, by definition, is one who believes in and follows Christ. How then can you claim to be a Christian if you are not in complete agreement with what Christ taught? He predicted His own resurrection, He showed Himself alive to hundreds of witnesses after His death, and He proclaimed that both the just and the unjust would one day be raised from the dead to answer for the deeds done in the body. These are historically attested facts, not philosophical speculations or intellectual rationalizations. If you do not believe what Christ taught and demonstrated, yet persist in calling yourself a Christian, you have merely redefined the term to suit your own convenience. And if any preacher handles Scripture deceitfully, warping it from its plain intent, denying what Christ and His apostles believed and taught, you are not insulting him by saying he is not a true Christian. In fact, you would be insulting Christ Himself if you called anyone a Christian who refuted the very fundamentals of the faith He came to proclaim.

Then again, if you permit yourself to be brainwashed by such deceptive teaching, because it is clothed in fine-sounding words and seemingly intellectual phrases, you are in danger of being left spiritually bankrupt in your time of need, with nothing but a handful of philosophical speculations to sustain you. You will be like that goatherd, of whom Aesop speaks in one of his down-to-earth fables. It seems that this goatherd, having been caught in the mountains in a snowstorm, drove his flock into a large cave for shelter. There he discovered some wild goats who had taken refuge before him. The goatherd was so impressed by the size and looks of these goats, so much more beautiful than his own, that he gave them all the food he could collect. The storm lasted many days, during which the tame goats died of starvation. When the sun shone again, the wild goats ran out and disappeared in the mountains, leaving the disappointed goatherd to make his way home, a poorer, and one hopes a wiser man. So it is with all those who exchange the tried and true teaching of God's Word for the ear-tickling speculations of men.

Paul practiced what he preached, and in his defense of his ministry to the Corinthians we can discover a test for soundness in doctrine: "My speech and my preaching," he tells them, "was not with enticing words of man's wisdom, but in demonstration of the Spirit and of power: that your faith should not stand in the wisdom of men, but in the power of God . . . not in the words which man's wisdom teacheth, but which the Holy Ghost teacheth; comparing spiritual things with spiritual. But the natural man receiveth not the things of the Spirit of God: for they are foolishness unto him: neither can he know them, because they are spiritually discerned. But he that is spiritual judgeth all things" (I Cor. 2:4, 5, 13, 15a)—and that is what you must do, Christian, if you are to have a firm foundation for your faith and life. Paul indulges in a bit of irony toward those who believe they know better than God's revealed Word what He is like and what He requires of men. "For who hath known the mind of the Lord, that he may instruct him?" he asks with tongue in cheek. And then, with the conviction of firsthand knowledge, he adds, "But we have the mind of Christ" (I Cor. 2:16). Only if you take Christ at His word, in faith and obedience, can you echo this sublime affirmation of Paul.

WATCH OUT FOR BAD APPLES!

"Be not deceived: evil communications corrupt good manners" (I Cor. 15:33).

Popular proverbs speak volumes, containing as they do the distilled wisdom of the ages. The Apostle Paul on three different occasions quoted from the Greek philosophers (see Acts 17:28, I Cor. 15:33, and Titus 1:12). Here in I Corinthians 15:33 he resorts to a maxim of the Attic comic poet Neander, apparently much used in the schools and with which everybody was familiar: "Bad company corrupts good manners."

We see this to be as true in our own day as it was when Paul quoted it in his letter to the Corinthian church. If you want to grow in the Christian faith, have regular fellowship with believers. If you want to lose your conviction and sense of the reality of divine things, then habitually mix with those who never name the name of Christ. Your company grows upon you in a very subtle way. It also reveals to others just what kind of person you are. You cannot escape being affected by those with whom you associate. When you discover that you are in questionable company, get out. Don't be tolerant of an atmosphere that stifles your spiritual growth. Accept it as a proven fact that "Bad company corrupts good manners."

In the Greek text of this verse, the verb comes first, as it so often does for purposes of emphasis; so that the first word Paul uses here is *phtheirousin*, which means "to destroy by means of corrupting." There are two ways of destroying an organism: to crush the life out of it by a direct smashing attack, and the more subtle way of undermining and sapping its life by gradual and insidious processes. Take an apple, for instance. Its purpose is to feed and nourish you. Crush it under your heel and you have destroyed its usefulness. But leave it carelessly in a barrel where it comes in contact with a bad apple, and you have accomplished the same purpose only more gradually.

The militant atheist puts us on our guard at once. We naturally shun him, avoid him, exclude him from our circle of friends. But the man who never discusses religion at all, who smilingly and agreeably converses with us as though life had only one dimension — the human — and God had no place in the day-to-day affairs of men, can by his very attitude corrupt us by persuading us to leave God out in all our contacts with him. The Christian's business is to live in the world, but in such a way that he injects his convictions about Christ into all his contacts with the world; and not in such a way that he allows the world to live in him. A Christian is not one who practices peaceful co-existence with evil, but one who is pledged to war against evil. The moment good Christians cease to fight evil, corruption begins to set in.

Just what is it that corrupts a Christian's usefulness? Paul calls it *homiliai kakai*, translated "evil communications." The noun *homiliai* comes from the verb *homileoo*, which in its primary sense means "to speak." That's the word from which we get our English "homiletics" (the art of preaching). It's the art of knowing what to say and how to say it. But *homiliai* also means "associations, companies." I believe the Apostle Paul means both here. Evil speeches and evil associations cannot leave you unscathed. They will have a corrupting influence upon you. They will lull you into a false sense of security at first, making you believe you are so strong that evil cannot touch you.

But heed the admonition of Paul: "Let him that thinketh he standeth take heed lest he fall" (I Cor. 10:12). There isn't a Christian so saintly he can walk through fire and not be burned. Fire burns, and evil corrupts, whether through speech or association. Be careful what you choose to listen to, and whom you choose to keep company with. Of course, we must of necessity hear much that is evil in this world, and do business with all sorts and conditions of men. But when it comes to friendship and fellowship, we have no business exposing ourselves to "evil communications" or bad company.

Listen carefully to the counsel of God's Word. "Blessed is the man that walketh not in the counsel of the ungodly, nor standeth in the way of sinners, nor sitteth in the seat of the scornful" (Ps. 1:1). Observe the progressive deterioration indicated by the verbs. First you walk, then you stand still, and finally you sit down comfortably in the presence of evil. "Enter not into the path of the wicked, and go not in the way of evil men" (Prov. 4:14). "Be not thou envious against evil men, neither desire to be with them" (Prov. 24:1; see also I Cor. 5:9).

"But now I have written unto you not to keep company, if any man that is called a brother be a fornicator, or covetous, or an idolater, or a railer, or a drunkard, or an extortioner; with such an one no not to eat" (I Cor. 5:11). And again Paul says, "Be not unequally yoked together with unbelievers: for what fellowship hath righteousness with unrighteousness? and what communion hath light with darkness?" (II Cor. 6:14; see also II John 10).

The adjective Paul uses to indicate the character of these speeches or associations he tells us to avoid is *kakai*, "evil." There are two Greek nouns for evil, *kakos* and *poneeros* (singular masculine). *Kakos* indicates a person or thing that is inherently evil, but *poneeros* is that which, or one who, is not only evil but is not content unless it or he corrupts others. *Kakos* is passive evil, and *poneeros* is active evil. The devil is sometimes called *ho poneeros*, because not only is he evil, but he is also an evil doer, out to deceive.

In the proverb, "Evil communications corrupt good manners," however, the phrase that is used is *homiliai kakai*, speeches or associations that are simply evil without necessarily having an intent to corrupt. These are the most dangerous because they are the most subtle. They are not out ostensibly to destroy the good in you; they simply show indifference to your moral principles and sound doctrine. Against the enemy that is out to get you, you can take precautions; but your defenses are down against an enemy that seems to be harmless. If the serpent in the Garden of Eden had been hideous and repulsive, and had hissed at Eve with his fangs exposed, she would have run from him. But he was a creature of beauty, who spoke softly and agreeably, and by specious and persuasive arguments won her away from her clear sense of duty to God (II Cor. 11:14, 15).

It is a dangerous thing to be living in peace with your enemy without realizing your danger, since he has not openly declared war against you. This in my opinion is the great danger America and every other nation founded on Christian principles is facing today. We brace ourselves against our declared enemies, those who are *poneeroi*, or active propagators of evil. But we tolerate those who are *kakoi*, or simply evil in themselves. They will corrupt us from within simply by association, without our even realizing it. Heeding Paul's admonition may save your life, may save our nation, may save the whole world. God grant it. (See discussion in R. C. Trench's *Synonyms of the New Testament*, Eerdmans, 1953, pp. 315-18.)

STAND YOUR GROUND AND FIGHT

"Evil communications corrupt good manners"
(I Cor. 15:33).

A man may be an upstanding citizen, husband, and father, and still not know the difference between a salad fork and a meat fork. Good manners do not consist primarily in knowing which piece of silverware to use at table, but in gracious and considerate behavior toward others.

When Paul says, "Evil communications corrupt good manners," however, he is not talking about etiquette, but about the Christian's "manner of life." The Greek phrase is *eethee chreesta*, translated in English "good manners." The word for "manners," *eethee*, is the one from which we derive our English word "ethics." *Eethee* among the Greeks referred primarily to a place of customary resort, a haunt; hence a settled habit of mind or manners. (Harper, *The Analytical Greek Lexicon*, p. 185.) It refers to a person's moral makeup.

Thus Paul intimates that a Christian is a person with a definite way of life, of special customs and places of resort. This way of life will be quite different from that of persons who have not yet tasted of the grace of God. Where there is saving faith, there is always a change in one's life. If no change is evident, genuine faith does not exist. You may say you have faith, but if the pattern of your life, including your friendships and the places you frequent, has undergone no change, you may well question whether you are a Christian. A Christian is a moral person, whose principles are governed by the absolute standard set forth by God in His Word and are not determined by personal preference or considered merely relative.

Beware, says Paul, of evil speech and evil associations; they can corrupt your way of life. Beware when you no longer want to go where the Word of God is preached, where you have fellowship with other believers. Beware when you begin to let down the bars, and your habits of life become subtly altered. You are slipping.

Don't be afraid to be known as a person with definite Christian moral standards, patterns, and customs. Be known as a man of clean speech and purity of life, who embodies the positive virtues of love to God and neighbor, and on the negative side refrains from drinking, swearing, sexual immorality, greed, and all other vices. Remember, however, that a Christian is not merely a person who does not do a lot of sinful things, but is primarily one who embodies the positive active characteristics of the Lord he serves. If Christ were simply one who refrained from evil, He would have been a passive and pale character indeed. No, He "went about doing good," and enjoined a like manner of life on His disciples.

A woman who read my Gospel messages in the press wrote to ask how she could know whether or not she was a Christian. I wanted to give her a practical answer. "If you run after sin, you are not a Christian," I told her. "But if sin runs after you, don't be alarmed; just don't stand there and let it catch up with you."

You and I as Christians may sometimes be tempted into acts, thoughts, and omissions that are sinful. But beware the danger of dwelling in them. Sin can attack us and defeat us temporarily; but if not resisted it may dwell with us and corrupt our whole way of life.

The Greek adjective used for "good" in the phrase "good manners" or "way of life" is *chreesta*. We want to consider two Greek adjectives that may be translated "good"—*chreestos* and *agathos*, from which we get the nouns *chreestotees* and *agathoosunee*. The first word refers to goodness that is not aggressive. Something is *chreeston* or somebody is *chreestos*, good, when it or he possesses the harmlessness of the dove, and nothing of the wisdom of the serpent. A person is *agathos*, good, when he is active in the propagation of goodness. For instance, wine that has been mellowed with age is called *chreestos* (Luke 5:39). Christ's yoke is *chreestos*, good, because there is nothing harsh or galling about it (Matt. 11:30). (See R. C. Trench, *Synonyms of the New Testament*, Eerdmans, pp. 231-5.)

Thus the expression *eethee chreesta* means customs or ways of life that are good and harmless, but which lack aggressiveness in the conversion of evil doers. This is how we might describe most Christians. They are living a Christian life that harms nobody, that suffers the yoke of Christ with patience, but lacks aggressiveness. It is not militant but passive goodness. It does no evil but at the same time does not fight against evil.

Such passive Christians are most susceptible to the corruption that comes from evil speeches and associations. The best safeguard against being corrupted by the evil around you is to declare war against it. If your goodness is harmless but not aggressively wise, it is susceptible to defeat. A defensive army seldom wins a war. To win you must take the offensive. That should be the custom, the way of life, for the Christian. Take the offensive against evil. Put it on the run, rather than letting it put you on the run.

There is a great deal of difference in these two approaches to the Christian life. Which one is yours? Your goodness should have an edge against evil, a sharpness in it, a righteous indignation against sin, and a ready willingness to take up arms against it. God does not win His battles with an army of ascetics but with Christian soldiers who are courageous and willing to take a firm stand against the enemy. Fleeing evil is sometimes necessary when it attempts to seduce you; but standing your ground in Christ's strength and fighting entrenched evil around you and around the world accomplishes victory.

Animal trainers say that the secret of handling lions, tigers, and leopards is to keep them constantly afraid of you. The instant they get over their fear, they will attack. They are treacherous beasts and often gather courage for an attack when the trainer's eyes are turned away from them. One never knows when they will spring at their keeper if they have a chance to do it from behind.

Our fight with the forces of evil is like that. Satan

is always seeking to attack us from the rear or in ambush. He goes about like a roaring lion, seeking whom he may devour, but he is a great coward when faced with courage. "Resist the devil and he will flee from you" is as true today as it was when the Apostle James first made the declaration (James 4:7).

In the athletic world, physical courage is highly esteemed. A physical education teacher in a Philadelphia college used to require his students to cross a river on a rope stretched from shore to shore, holding on to another rope a little above the first one. He did this, it is said, in order to harden the nerves of his pupils. But why not test one's courage, and cultivate steady nerves, in more worthwhile ways?

Set the pupils, for instance, to escorting the blind and elderly across busy street intersections.

Encourage them to turn down their glasses at social functions.

Or give up smoking and not be afraid to say why.

Or speak up when someone is telling smutty jokes or taking the Lord's name in vain.

Or pray aloud in prayer meeting.

Or carry a Bible to church.

Or witness for Christ among their own friends and relatives.

Or—but why go on? You get the idea. A strong Christian life calls for courage at every turn, both physical and spiritual. No need to engage in athletic stunts to prove our courage. Life itself offers enough opportunities to do that in the situations that confront us day by day.

GETTING DRUNK WITH AN IDEA

"Awake to righteousness, and sin not: for some have not the knowledge of God: I speak this to your shame" (I Cor. 15:34).

Liquor can make you drunk for a few hours, but an idea can make you drunk for life. Ideas may sometimes be even more dangerous than liquor. They can become obsessions, fixations that will rob you of your ability to think straight and walk straight.

In the early days of the Corinthian church, some of its members became obsessed with the idea that it is impossible for men to rise from the dead. "How can a dead body ever resume the form it once had?" they reasoned. "Everybody knows it decomposes once the soul leaves it." But faith in the future life is not simply a matter of logic but also depends upon one's state of mind. From what the Apostle Paul says further in this epistle, we deduce that those who thought their bodies would never be resurrected were tempted to deliver them over to debauchery. He emphatically declares that it is possible for men so to live that their vision becomes blurred, their sensibilities dulled, and they themselves become incapable of great ideals and hope.

When Paul sought to convince these Corinthians that they were in error, he did not just set forth his opinion as against theirs. After all, one man has as much right to express his opinion and hold to it as another. What is needed is a determination of which opinions are based on fact and which are not. What seems true to me or you may not necessarily be true. There is an objectivity to truth, a standard against which to measure men's opinions. In the 15th chapter of I Corinthians, Paul seeks to determine the truth about this matter of the resurrection. Will our bodies one day be raised from the dead or not? How can we know?

Impossible, says one group. But before you make such a flat declaration, look at that unattractive insect upon the blade of grass. In just a few short days you will find that insect floating in the air, a beautiful gossamer creature with wings that rival the rainbow. Look at the dry root in the dark and cold of winter. When spring comes, out of that root will blossom forth a profusion of beautiful blossoms. Look at the egg, an inert and earthbound shape. Yet in it lies the eagle, that can wing and soar above all other birds, or the tiny hummingbird that remains poised in mid-air before some flower, defying the pull of gravity. The doctrine of the resurrection is not inconsistent with the analogies of nature or the experience of our common history.

Paul has developed his argument as follows: Has anyone ever risen from the dead? Yes, there is one—the Lord Jesus Christ. I can prove this through indisputable historical evidence. Therefore, since one man rose, it is possible that others will also—especially since Christ declares that they will. If He had not risen bodily from the dead by His own power, but had simply voiced this as an abstract teaching, His opinion would be no more trustworthy than yours or mine. But He speaks as one who has demonstrated this truth in His own life. The risen Christ is a reality. There were people living in Corinth at that time who had actually seen Christ after His resurrection. In fact, says Paul, of the more than 500 witnesses to the resurrected Christ, more than half were still living when he wrote this epistle. Can all these people be wrong? In the face of their testimony, how can you continue to maintain that it is a biological impossibility for the human body to be resurrected? If you do, you place yourself in the position of saying, "I'll hold on to my preconceived notions, and never mind the facts." That is how the mentally disturbed function. They are out of touch with reality. A false idea can lead you to a deplorable state. Watch out for ideas. They can make you drunk, intoxicating you with the heady wine of thinking you know better than anyone else.

The Corinthians who insisted on rejecting the doctrine of the resurrection, in spite of all the proofs presented by Paul, reminded him of drunkards. That's why he says in verse 34, "Sober up." That's the literal translation of the Greek word *ekneepsate*, and not "awake" as the Authorized Version has it. These people were not so much spiritually asleep as drunk with the idea of the supposed impossibility of the resurrection.

The verb is a compound, made up of the preposition *ek*, meaning "from," and the verb *neephoo*, "to be sober." The compound verb *ekneephou*, then, means "to become sober again," and it is in the imperative mood, indicating a command. "Become sober again," says Paul. These Corinthians must therefore have latched on to some new philosophical speculations that deflected them from the truth. This reminds us that Paul is writing here to Corinthians who had believed in Christ. In the first verse of this chapter he addresses them as "brethren." They were not strangers to the Gospel whom Paul was trying to win to a saving knowledge of Christ. They were Christians who had been influenced by a philosophy of men, an agnostic philosophy that declared that the resurrection of the body was impossible *per se.*

Furthermore the verb *ekneepsate* is in the active voice, which would indicate that the job of sobering up is your own responsibility. You cannot take a passive attitude, claiming that your backslidden state renders you helpless to change. "Get up," says Paul. No one can lift you out of your drunken supineness against your will. God will give you the power to get up, but you must first want to. All you have to do is by faith to place your hand in His, and He will make it possible for you to get on your feet.

Notice also that the verb *ekneepsate* is in the aorist imperative, which refers to a once-for-all sobering up. Get up from your drunken stupor and stay up. Make a determined act to come back to your sane mind in Christ. None of this getting up and falling down again, no more sobering up and then getting drunk all over again. A drunken man is often remorseful and full of good resolves as the result of a hangover; but once he has recovered he is soon back in his cups again. This sobering up of which Paul speaks requires a determined act of your will, not wallowing supinely in the gutter till a helping hand attempts to pull you to your feet again. Sober up and stay sober is Paul's message to the Corinthians and to you.

Are you drunk with the notion that you can discern what is and what is not inspired in the Bible, rather than accepting "all Scripture" as God's Holy Word? This is heady wine indeed, that promises to set you free from old-fashioned rigid ideas to a more liberal concept of the Christian faith. However, you may find it liberalizes you right into the gutter of no faith at all, as it has done for so many who have set themselves up as judges of that which should judge them.

Are you drunk with the idea that "God is dead," that He is not a personal God interested in individuals, but has left the determination of history up to the human race? This promises to set you even freer, allowing you to formulate your own standards of right and wrong, and to plan your own life, without reference to any objective standard. In reality it merely sets you free to anarchy, to a realization that life has only the meaning you assign to it; and in the end, if you are honest, you will find that you lack the capacity to assign any valid meaning to it at all.

If you must be intoxicated with an idea, let it be the exhilaration of knowing you are vitally linked with God Himself, through Jesus Christ His Son, the One who framed the worlds and who is so unimaginably great that Scripture refers in the most casual and off-hand way to the fact that "he made the stars also" (Gen. 1:16). If you had been an intimate associate of Einstein, of Leonardo da Vinci, or any of the "greats" of the past, you might well have something of which to boast. How much more when you are allied with the Creator Himself, and can call Him your friend! Someone has spoken of the "God-intoxicated man," and this is what every Christian should be.

CAN YOUR JUDGMENT BE TRUSTED?

"Awake to righteousness, and sin not: for some have not the knowledge of God: I speak this to your shame" (I Cor. 15:34).

If you want to know whether you are a Christian or not, just ask yourself two questions: "Do I believe with all my heart that Jesus Christ is the Son of God, who became man, died for my sins and those of the whole world, and rose again from the dead?" The second question is, "Do I seek to obey Him in my daily life?"

This does not mean that you need be theologically correct in all details, in order to be saved. But while certain beliefs are essential to salvation, certain disbeliefs can rob you of the joy of that salvation.

Take the Corinthians of Paul's day, for example. Nowhere do we find that they rejected the fact and importance of the bodily resurrection of Jesus Christ. They could not help accepting that, for it was a proven fact. No one can be saved without a belief in the resurrection of Christ as a historical fact. But certain persons in the church could not bring themselves to accept the projection of that fact to their own lives. Because they believed in Christ's resurrection, Paul calls them brothers. But their denial of the bodily resurrection of all men was robbing them of the joy and steadfastness of their Christian experience.

They had stood upon this resurrection doctrine some time in the past. That is why Paul says, "Sober up again," return to your senses. They had not lost their salvation, but they had certainly lost the joy and victory of it. Because they did not believe they would live again in resurrected bodies for all eternity, many of them were tempted to slip into sin, to eat and drink more than they should. The person who believes that he will live for eternity in a body that will bear the marks of his behavior while on earth, lives with utmost care and flees sin.

These Corinthian Christians fell into a backslidden state by first becoming drunk with a false idea and then following it to its logical conclusion. When you come to the place where you don't believe that there will be an accounting for the deeds done in the body in the world to come, you tend to become careless in your Christian walk. How many people would be moderate in eating and drinking if they felt no one would criticize them for being gluttons? And in the moral realm, how many honest cashiers would we have if they knew that no one was going to check up on them? Yet the principles we apply to safeguard ourselves, we deem harsh and unloving when God uses them. How inconsistent we mortals are!

When men begin to sin because they lose their belief in a resurrection or a judgment, then it becomes far more difficult for them to become moral and upright again. Sobering up from a state of being drunk with a false idea or a philosophical supposition is easier than sobering up from the resultant state of gross sinfulness.

A missionary was preaching on the resurrection

when the native chief cried out, "What are these words about the dead? The dead arise?" "Yes," said the missionary, "all the dead shall rise." "Will my father arise?" "Yes," answered the missionary. "Will all that have been killed and eaten by lions, tigers, and crocodiles arise?" "Yes, and come to judgment." "Hark!" shouted the chief, turning to his warriors. "You wise men, did you ever hear such strange and unheard-of news?" The chief then turned to the missionary and said, "Sir, I love you much; but the words of a resurrection are too great for me. I do not wish to hear about the dead rising again. The dead cannot rise; the dead shall not rise!" "Tell me, my friend, why not?" asked the missionary. "Because I have slain my thousands. Do you think I want *them* to rise again?" The Gospel was all right as long as it did not interfere with his sins.

Paul actually wants to remind the Corinthian Christians of how wonderful their former state of spiritual sobriety was. Come back to it, he says. Look at your present state and remember from whence you have fallen. This obsession with the idea that the body cannot rise has not added one iota of joy to your lives. You are living in a dream, under the shadow of a delusion. That's what happens to those who get drunk. They mistake temporary pleasure for lasting joy. They are divorced from reality.

Christ's bodily resurrection is real; and belief in the resurrection of the body means staying in your right senses and living a life pleasing to Him. Many people unfortunately take the opposite view—that the

Christian is a dreamer because he believes in a world to come, the resurrection of the body, and a day of judgment. Yet these are the realities, and disbelief in them is the dream.

Even in the Christian world, those who become obsessed with some strange idea will harp on that to the exclusion of the fundamental doctrines of Scripture. They actually attempt to convert people to that idea, to a strange doctrine instead of to Christ. As drunkenness in its extreme consequences can lead to blindness, so being drunk with such an idea can lead to spiritual blindness.

It does something else. It encourages people to live a life of sin. It is often sadly true that Christians who are off on some doctrine that may not be fundamental to their salvation, may also be off on questions of holy living. Intoxicated with an idea that gives them a feeling of superiority over common folk who have not "seen the light" as they have, they begin to deem themselves above the moral standards of common folk also. They may slip into liberties that sound Christians wouldn't even think of. Obsession with an off-color doctrine tends to steal away from the purity of a Christian life. It certainly did in Corinth among some of the Christians there. That's why Paul wants to correct their doctrinal errors.

Notice how he proceeds. First correct your doctrine, he tells them, and then your life will be straightened out. "Sober up again," he says. That's the first step. Then he adds, "and sin not." When you are mentally drunk, it is easy for you to fall into sin, so that you acquire a personal bias that may hinder your ability to appreciate great truths such as the resurrection of the body. Your convictions and feelings influence your actions. In turn your mode of life reacts upon the mind and colors your reasoning. Few opinions are formed as a result of logic alone. The pressure of personal inclination subtly deflects the logical process.

The International Bureau of Weights and Measures at Sevres, France, possesses a precision balance of extraordinary sensitiveness; the oscillations are observed through a telescope, and to guard against disturbances due to the warmth of the operator's body he is required to stand twenty feet away from the instrument. In our more honest moments, many of us would have to admit that in matters of Christian doctrine and conduct we sometimes believe only what we choose to believe.

A sense of objectivity and honesty with regard to our own motives is a wonderful faculty to cultivate. It would certainly humble us to understand how much of our dearly cherished and defended ideas are the result of our own personal predilections, and how few are arrived at as the result of a noble and unflinching determination to know and follow the truth, cost what it may. So often, we do not want to know the truth; we want only to be proved right.

Then, again, many of us may hesitate to affirm beliefs or adopt modes of conduct that run counter to those of our friends. Paul points this out in no uncertain terms to these erring members of the Corinthian church. Evil associations do indeed corrupt one's conduct. These Corinthians had suffered their minds to be corrupted through intimacy with the godless society from which they ought resolutely to have severed themselves. Their continued fellowship with skeptical, scoffing, sensual companions had debauched their personality, so that they were no longer competent to judge impartially a spiritual question. Their attitude toward the doctrines they had once embraced had become suspicious, critical, resistant.

If a cube of lead is placed on a cube of gold, the two metals slowly but inevitably begin to penetrate each other. In the same manner we tend to imbibe the spirit, to share the opinions, to partake of the qualities of our intimate associates. Though we may believe that our gold will enrich their lead, the opposite is far more likely to prove true—that their lead will debase our gold. That is why the Psalmist said, "Depart from me, ye evil doers, that I may keep the commandments of my God" (Ps. 119:115).

Astronomers once blamed the inaccuracy of the images viewed in their telescopes on atmospheric disturbances. Later investigation revealed that a good deal of the disturbance of telescopic images arises from currents within the telescope itself. But though we cannot altogether eliminate the conditioning of outside influences in our quest for truth, we must attempt to free ourselves as much as possible from the disturbing currents within—the moods, tempers, sympathies, and fears that falsely bias the soul.

QUESTIONS TO ASK YOUR PREACHER

"Awake to righteousness, and sin not: for some have not the knowledge of God: I speak this to your shame" (I Cor. 15:34).

How do you go about curing a drunk? The answer to that is, you can't. Before a man can lead a consistently sober life, he has to be motivated from within. He has to admit to himself that he has a real problem, and he has to want to lick it. Only then can anyone help him.

It is the same way when a man is drunk with a false idea. You can't change his opinions simply by telling him he is wrong. He will only become more firmly set against you, and more determined to defend his idea than ever. No, a man has first got to admit to himself that following his idea to its logical conclusion in his life has led to utter spiritual poverty; he must want to know the truth; and he must be willing to follow it once he is convinced of it.

The Apostle Paul understood this when he was writing to the Corinthians who had given up their belief in a personal resurrection and were reaping the consequences in a loss of spiritual fervor and purity of life. If he could just make them see the consequences of their folly, he felt it would jolt them into an awareness of their need. So he told them they were mentally drunk and therefore not in their right minds.

"Sober up," he says, and follows this with a most interesting adverb. In Greek it is *dikaioos*, the literal translation of which is "righteously or in a righteous manner." What does he mean by this? How many ways can a man sober up? There are two: in his own strength or in the strength of the Lord. The first is the way of self-righteousness, the second is the way of Christ's righteousness. Paul never preached that a drunkard can pull himself up out of the gutter or make a new man out of himself. He proclaimed that Christ is our righteousness. Left to ourselves, we cannot even think straight. What Paul means here is that man must be willing to let God lift him out of his predicament and set him on his feet.

After all, these Corinthians who had gone astray in their beliefs and conduct were originally saved through the righteousness of Christ, even as we who believe in Him today. We were guilty. He was just. We should have died for our sins. Instead, He died for us. If we accept what He has done, through faith in His atoning work, we acquire His righteousness. And likewise, if backsliders are to return to full fellowship with the Lord and be straightened out in their beliefs and practices, they cannot do it on their own, but must look to Christ in faith to do it on their behalf. When that happens, and they finally realize how mistaken they have been in their biased belief, their drunken ideas, they will quit their sinful life.

It is noteworthy that the first imperative Paul issues to these erring Corinthians, *ekneepsate,* "sober up again," is in the aorist tense, which refers to a once-for-all action. Get up and stay up, Paul admonishes them. Give up these Gnostic ideas about the impossibility of man's resurrection, once for all. Let yourself be brought to a new state of mind through Christ's righteousness. How wonderful that the righteousness of Christ suffices not only for the initial bringing of a sinful soul to Himself, but also for the restoration of that soul when it has wandered away from the truth.

Paul's second imperative is in the negative, *mee amartanete*, in the present indicative, which means "do not keep on sinning." Being liberated from false doctrines through the righteousness of Christ will also liberate you from a life of sin. This does not mean that there is no further possibility of your sinning, as would have been the meaning if the aorist tense had been used here, but that you will not continue in a life of sin. A person who firmly believes in the Biblical doctrine of the resurrection of the body finds it a strong deterrent to sin and an encouragement to a life of righteousness.

What do those who deny the resurrection of the body reveal about their own nature? They think they are showing that they know something that the common run of people do not. That's why those who proclaimed this idea called themselves the Gnostic philosophers, that is, the philosophers that know. But though they might have known many things, Paul says they lack knowledge of what is most vital: "For some have not the knowledge of God."

To declare that you know what doctrines are true and what are false, without knowing the One of whom those doctrines speak, is like trying to paint a picture of a person you have never seen, or telling someone how to be successful in business when you yourself have never made the grade. It is something like that little girl who baked a cake without benefit of a cookbook or her mother's advice. She knew nothing about proportions of flour, baking powder, sugar, salt, and milk, and never thought of eggs or shortening. When the cake came out of the oven, it was well rounded and nicely browned. She exhibited it to her family with pride as "a cake I made my very own self," but when she took her first bite of it she found it bitter with too much baking powder, and hard as a rock. That's pretty much how our own concoctions turn out in the spiritual realm, when we blithely assume we "know the recipe" without reference to the cook or the cookbook. You must first know God in Christ through receiving Him as Saviour and Lord, before you can have the spiritual discernment that will enable you to understand the doctrine revealed in His Word.

"Some have not the knowledge of God," Paul says. "I speak this to your shame." He is bringing a stinging indictment against those who were priding themselves on their superior knowledge. In parading their human knowledge they showed they were ignorant of the source of all knowledge, God Himself. He who knows God knows more than he who knows everything else, if that were possible, about what God has made. In fact, the most learned man, when He knows God, becomes aware of how little he knows; and, far from parading his human knowledge, humbly seeks to "think God's thoughts after Him."

Paradoxically, the more we discover, the more ignorant we find ourselves to be. A. G. Sherbourne, of

Science Service, says that "our present scientific knowledge could be placed in 10 million volumes and is increasing one million volumes a year. By 1977, we will find out more than we have from the beginning of time to the present." Knowledge has advanced more rapidly in the past 50 years than in the previous 5,000 years. It is doubling every 10 years. There is 100 times more to know today than there was in 1900. By the year 2,000, there will be 1,000 times as much to be learned as today. Man is mighty but God is the Almighty.

Observe that Paul does not say that all the Corinthian Christians to whom he is writing are ignorant of God, but only some of them. Who are these "some"? Undoubtedly those who did not believe the revelation of God about Himself and His plan for the future, especially the bodily resurrection of all men.

Why do you listen to people who do not know God, you who know Him? Is there anything they can really teach you about your eternal salvation and the world to come, about the resurrection and the judgment? These are beyond their ability to know. He who does not know God personally as his Father through the Lord Jesus Christ as his Saviour is unable to teach you anything about God or His plan. If you sit at the feet of such teachers, you ought to feel the shame of which Paul speaks in rebuking the erring Corinthians.

It might be a good idea for you to ask the one who preaches to you or who teaches your Sunday school class, "Do you really know God; not just things about God, but God Himself? Do you believe that Jesus Christ died for your sins, that He was buried and rose again bodily the third day? Do you believe that in the same manner all men shall rise from the dead?" If he says "No" to any of these questions, you as a born-again believer in Christ ought to be ashamed to sit under his preaching or teaching. Remember, "evil communications" corrupt that which is good. Even Christians can become drunk with false ideas. You cannot trust your own judgment in these matters, but must take a firm stand upon the revealed Word of God. If in anything your doctrinal beliefs differ from this standard, you lack a full knowledge of God, and should confess your spiritual ignorance with shame. "Awake to righteousness—sober up—and sin not."

WISE AND FOOLISH QUESTIONS

"But some man will say, How are the dead raised up? and with what body do they come? Thou fool. . . ." (I Cor. 15:35, 36a).

A newspaper column starts with the question, "Why should I believe in a God I can't see, just because some preacher tells me I should? What virtue is there in a faith like that?"

I for one have never held that the Christian religion should be accepted without inquiry into its credentials. Nor, when a person decides to become a Christian by receiving Christ as his personal Saviour from sin, do I believe he needs to set aside his mental powers. However, we all need to recognize the limitations of our finite minds, and to admit that, because of this, observable facts cannot always be fully explained.

In the 15th chapter of I Corinthians, when Paul had finished giving the proofs of Christ's bodily resurrection, and arguing from them the resurrection of the human body after death, he met head on with a typical objector. Verse 35 says, "But some man will say, How are the dead raised up? and with what body do they come?" The word "man" actually does not occur in the original Greek, but is understood in the indefinite pronoun *tis*, which means "a certain one, some one." Only to man has God given reason that includes the privilege of questioning. Man must satisfy his intelligence. The type of question you ask, however, will reveal your maturity or lack of it.

Children sometimes ask unanswerable questions just to get their parents' attention. Unfortunately, some who call themselves adults use the same device to occupy the center of the stage. A little boy drove his mother to distraction with questions one day. Finally she sent him packing off upstairs to bed. Later, feeling troubled, she tiptoed into his room, knelt beside his bed, and told him she was sorry she had been cross with him, adding, "Now, dear, if you want to ask one more question before you go to sleep, I'll try to answer it." Quick as a wink the youngster blurted out, "Mommy, how far can a cat spit?" Some theological questioning is just about as foolish. Be careful before you open your mouth that what you are about to ask does not make you sound foolish. That's exactly what Paul calls the man who asks these questions about the resurrection body, "Thou fool." The Greek word here is *aphroon*, which comes from the negative prefix *a*, "without," and the noun *phreen*, "mind." You are a man without sense, without reason, Paul says, if you think there can be an explanation in detail of all observable facts and the conclusions to be drawn from them.

A college professor, noted for his arrogance, shot questions in rapid succession at a raw freshman. "I understand you attend the class in mathematics?" "Yes, sir." "How many sides has a circle?" "Two." "Indeed!" said the surprised professor. "What are they?" "Inside and outside." Taking another tack, the professor continued, "And you attend the moral philosophy class. Have you heard lectures on cause and effect?" "Yes." "Does an effect ever go before a cause?" "Yes." "Give an instance," said the professor, beginning to sound irritated. "A wheelbarrow being pushed by a man." The professor, scratching his head and frowning, said snappishly, "You may go now." The question in this case might be, who was the fool and who the wise man?

The opposite of *aphroon*, "fool or foolish," is *phronimos*, meaning "sensible, thoughtful, prudent, wise." Paul implies that a man can use his mind either unwisely or prudently. Believing in the physical resurrection of the dead does not exclude the use of reason. In fact, reason dictates that you accept this truth, since it is based on the historical evidence of Christ's bodily resurrection, already amply attested by Paul.

Paul further implies that, if you think you can know all about everything, your powers of reasoning are foolish indeed. Man's wisdom and knowledge in this life are limited, and this limitation prevents your being able to determine all future possibilities, especially those that lie in the infinite wisdom of God. You are an intellectual fool when you say what can or cannot happen in the future—especially when the past has given a sample of such a situation in the divine person of a historically God-attested being called Jesus Christ. The man who can discern the limitations of his capability to know is *phronimos*, wisely intelligent.

I do not believe that the Apostle Paul includes himself in the category of those who ask these questions. His belief in the resurrection of the human body is beyond dispute. He merely wishes to anticipate the questions in the minds of those to whom he writes. He may, in fact, have encountered these very questions in personal debate from time to time. Where Paul indicates some sympathy with an objection, he says, "What shall *we* say" (Rom. 4:1; 6:1; 7:7; 8:31; 9:14, 30). But here he indicates no sympathy with the questioner. "These are foolish questions," he says in effect.

What are these two questions? First, "How are the dead raised up?" Second, "And with what body do they come?" Some scholars believe this is actually one question with two parts, the second being a little more specific than the first. The first asks how a dead body, decomposed into the physical elements of which it was originally composed, can be reconstituted. The second concerns the kind of body that those who are raised from the dead will have.

Let's get Paul's fundamental premise clear at the start. In speaking of man's future resurrection, he is not referring to a life that man will live on this present earth under the same laws of nature that now prevail. Man's resurrection concerns the life to come in an entirely new setting described in the Word of God as "a new heaven and a new earth" (Isa. 65:17-25; 66:22-24; Rev. 21, 22).

Originally "man was given dominion over the earth" (Gen. 1:26-28, Ps. 8:6). But when the first man rebelled against God, not only did he himself become the object of God's punishment, but his domain, the earth, was cursed because of him (Gen. 3:17). Paul declares that the whole universe became "the victim of frustration" (Rom. 8:20 NEB).

A new man in his glorified body will have a new

and redeemed creation in which to live compatibly (Rom. 8:21 ff). The two redemptions—of our bodies and of our world—according to Romans 8:21,. 23 will take place simultaneously. There will be a re-creation of our present bodies and a re-creation of our world in which these glorified bodies are to live. As J. A. Schep says, "The resurrection of the body as a glorified body of flesh is inseparably tied to the renewal and glorification of the cosmos." (*The Nature of the Resurrection Body*, Eerdmans, p. 218.)

Thus the question asked in I Corinthians 15:35 does not concern someone who has died and returned to the same world with the same mortal body, as in the historical instances of Lazarus, or the son of the widow of Nain, or the daughter of Jairus, and others (John 11; Luke 7:11-15; 8:41). These were miracles involving the return of the same unchanged life to the same unchanged environment.

Why does Paul consider these questions foolish? Because fundamentally we must be prepared to accept the idea that nothing is impossible. It may be impossible at a certain time, but that does not preclude its possibility in the future. Would your grandfather have believed that you could travel at 1,800 miles an hour? Paul wants the Corinthians to be intelligent enough not to say that bodily resurrection is impossible.

I have used this illustration before, but it bears repeating. A servant who had received a silver cup from his master accidentally dropped it into a vat of acid. The servant was dumbfounded when he saw the whole cup disappear. He immediately went to a fellow servant and told him that the silver cup was lost forever. "It can't be recovered. You can't even see it." The master, an educated man, came on the scene. He infused salt water into the acid, which precipitated the silver from the solution. Then by melting it and hammering the metal he restored the cup to its original shape. A skeptic who saw this was so struck by its analogy to the resurrection, which he had rejected as impossible, that he now believed it most credible.

An old writer says, "Faith and reason may be compared to two travelers: Faith is like a man in full health, who can walk his twenty or thirty miles at a time without suffering. Reason is like a little child, who can only with difficulty accomplish three or four miles. On a given day Reason says to Faith, 'O good Faith, let me walk with thee.' Faith replies, 'O Reason, thou canst never walk with me!' However, to try their paces, they set out together, but they soon find it hard to keep company. When they come to a deep river, Reason says, 'I can never ford this,' but Faith wades through it singing. When they reach a lofty mountain, there is the same exclamation of despair; and in such cases, Faith, in order not to leave Reason behind, is obliged to carry him on his back; and, oh, what a luggage is Reason to Faith!"

Why has God made faith the indispensable ingredient in man's approach to Him? Is it not precisely because man's reason can go only so far; and where reason comes up against an insurmountable obstacle, faith soars above it and apprehends God and heavenly mysteries by this divinely given faculty?

WILL OUR RESURRECTION BODIES BE EXACTLY LIKE THE ONES WE NOW HAVE?

"How are the dead raised up? and with what body do they come?" (I Cor. 15:35).

Is the body you now have the same body you have always had? Not really. The human body is always changing. It is not a constant and permanent thing like a statue, always continuing in the same state and consisting of the same particles of matter. The body is a successive thing, continually spending and continually renewing itself; every day losing something of the matter it had before, and gaining new matter; so that men may have entirely new bodies every seven years or so. In fact, a man's body undergoes several complete changes in his lifetime.

As our bodies grow from infancy to maturity, new matter is added to them over and beside the repairing of what is continually being used up; and, after a man attains his full growth, the amount of food he eats each day that turns into nourishment is compensated for by the waste matter carried off from yesterday's body. Thus we live in a constantly changing organism.

Now, at the resurrection, which state of our body will live again? Are we going to have the body of childhood, youth, adulthood, or old age? Are we going to re-acquire exactly the same body that we had at the time of death, with all its sickness and pain? None of us would like to contemplate that. And even if our bodies were in the best state we ever knew at death, that which is yet to come must surpass in quality anything that we have thus far known.

This ought to give us much comfort and encouragement. For isn't it true that one of the greatest burdens of human nature is the frailty and infirmity of our bodies, the necessities that frequently press them down, and the many diseases they are liable to? True, these infirmities are often God's messengers, sent to discipline us or to cause us to rely more on His strength and less on our own. But not one of us but would gladly be rid of our physical infirmities if we could. As Christians we submit to them with whatever grace God gives us, knowing that "all things work together for good to them that love God, to them who are the called according to his purpose" (Rom. 8:28). Nevertheless, many suffering ones look forward to the redemption of the body as a day of glad release.

None of us really know what the sinless body was like as God originally created it. Like the spirit, it was created in the very image of God. However, man was not made infinite like his Creator, but finite as a creature, and that he will always be.

There was nothing wrong with the flesh as God created it. But the first man sinned and brought upon himself and his descendants the natural consequence of death, as declared by God. As a result, his flesh and soul became sinful and liable to pain resulting ultimately in death, at which time the soul leaves the body and enters upon a separate existence. That is why, in Scripture, you will always find death exclusively connected with sin (Gen. 2:17; Matt. 10:28, Rom. 5:12, I Cor. 11:30-32, Heb. 9:27, etc.).

But in the resurrection, as we shall see through this unique passage in I Corinthians 15, man will possess a body-soul (spirit) personality. And his body, though individually identifiable, will not consist of the same kind of sin-dominated flesh that we now have, but of flesh that will never die or experience pain or, in its new environment, be subject to sin. Although many believe it will be of the same pre-sinful quality as originally created by God before the Fall, the redeemed body will actually have greater glory than did the bodies of Adam and Eve before the Fall, because man will not now be in a state of probation as before the Fall. Redeemed man in his new body and new environment will be incapable of wanting to sin. (See Tillotson's sermon entitled, "The Reasonableness of a Resurrection," in *The World's Great Sermons*, compiled by Grenville Kleiser: Funk and Wagnalls Co., Vol. II, pp. 135-154; and J. A. Schep, *The Nature of the Resurrection Body*, pp. 17-24.)

Our bodies as presently constituted are capable of living in our present world. If they were to be exactly reconstituted, they would be fit only for living in a cosmos such as we now know. In a poem written about the parting of the spirit and body at death, the spirit is represented as saying to the body, "When I would have started on the moon's track, on the comet's pathway, *you held me back*." How many careers have been hampered by illness; how often our plans and desires are thwarted by our bodily states.

But the time is coming, if we are careful to prepare ourselves for it, when we shall be clothed with another kind of body, free from all the miseries and inconveniences that flesh and blood as we now know them are subject to. The heathen in the early ages of the Christian Church believed this to be so impossible that they used to burn the bodies of Christian martyrs, and scatter their ashes on the wind, in derision of their hope of a resurrection. But saints and martyrs in all ages have died confident in the belief that "our vile body" shall be changed and "fashioned like unto his [Christ's] glorious body" (Phil. 3:21). When our bodies are raised to new life, they will become incorruptible. "For this corruptible must put on incorruption, and this mortal must put on immortality . . . then shall be brought to pass the saying that is written, Death is swallowed up in victory" (I Cor. 15:53, 54).

When this last enemy is conquered, there will be no "fleshly lusts" or brutish passions to fight against the soul; no law in our members to war against the laws of our minds (Rom. 7:23); no disease to torment us; no danger of death to amaze and terrify us. Then the passions and appetites of our outward man will be subject to our inward self, and our bodies will partake of the immortality of our souls. It is only a little while longer that our spirits shall be crushed and clogged with these heavy and sluggish bodies; at the resurrection they will be refined from all dregs of corruption and become spiritual, incorruptible, glorious, and every way suited to the activity and perfection of a glorified soul and "the spirits of just men made perfect" (Heb. 12:23).

Of course, man as he is now constituted cannot conceive of all that is in the mind of God as far as His future plans are concerned. Our finite minds, even enlightened by God's revelation, can go only so far in grasping the complexities of the infinite. Those who lack faith in God as Creator and Saviour, through Jesus Christ, must fall back on the limitations of unaided human reason. And then there are those Christians who, with a superficial literality of thought, fail to understand Paul's language regarding the resurrection body in this 15th chapter of I Corinthians. They firmly believe God is going to gather together every atom of our dead bodies and reconstitute them exactly as they were prior to death. While it is literally true that our bodies shall live again, Scripture does not require us to believe that God has to take exactly the same particles of all the physical substances of which our bodies are made and put them together again like a jigsaw puzzle. Let's not be like that woman who blithely stated that she did not believe in the resurrection of the body, because as the result of an accident she had left one leg in England, and she fully expected to die in the United States.

If you expect the same atoms to be brought together again, how would you expect this to happen in the case of a man eaten by cannibals? His flesh would have been digested and become part of the bodies of those very ones who dined upon him. In the resurrection, would their bodies be robbed of the necessary particles to reconstitute the man they had devoured? Do you see to what ridiculous extremes we would be led by an insistence that God work in accordance with what we believe must happen?

Of course, nothing is impossible with God. I would not find it difficult to believe that God is able to gather every fragment of bone, flesh, muscle, and sinew that made up our earthly bodies, to make up our glorified resurrection bodies. Men might conceive this impossible, but God can do it. The only reason I declare that it is not going to be so is that God's Word reveals that it will be otherwise. He, an omnipotent God who can create our bodies in the first place, can re-create them at the resurrection. Grant that God exists, and no difficulties remain.

Will resurrection be a greater wonder than creation? God created the world out of nothing. This seems to be even more marvelous than calling together scattered particles and re-fashioning them into what they were before, if that is what God wanted to do.

The identity of our body-spirit personalities will be preserved in the resurrection. But don't confuse personal individual identity with absolute sameness of substance and continuance of atoms. Since infancy we have all undergone great changes, but we have the same bodies and the same souls; we are the same people. The body in which we die will be the same body in which we were born, but not composed of the same particles. In the same manner, the body in which we rise will be the same body in which we die, greatly changed, yet in a manner that will not affect its identity.

NEW BODIES FOR OLD

"How are the dead raised up? and with what body do they come?" (I Cor. 15:35).

The Christians in the early days of the Corinthian church who had difficulty with the doctrine of the resurrection did not disbelieve in the survival of personality after death. Their difficulty was not with the survival of the human spirit, but with its rejoining a body. "What kind of body will it be?" they asked skeptically. Paul answers their question in a masterful and satisfying manner.

To confirm the meaning of the first question, "How are the dead raised?" Paul joins it to the second question with the adversative conjunction *de*, translated "and" in the Authorized Version, but which I believe should be translated "but." On the assumption that we accept the post-resurrection personalities as body-spirits, the difficulty is not with the identifiable spirit personalities but with the body connected with them. "But with what kind of body do they come?"

The pronoun *poioo*, "what, of what sort," speaks of the quality of the body (see also John 12:33; 18:32; Rom. 3:27; I Pet. 2:20). Agreed that it's going to be a body-spirit personality, but what will be the quality of the body? The Jewish tradition held that the blind, lame, dumb, and other afflicted men would be raised in the same condition in which they died. Paul sets out to prove that the quality of the body will be physical in its relation to the spirit, even as our present physical body is distinguishable from our soul or spirit. Yet though this resurrection body will be physical, its metaphysical characteristics will be different from the physical characteristics of our present bodies. The quality will be far superior anyway. How much or in what way superior, you and I with our finite minds cannot now understand. Paul shows us that it is reasonable, however, for us as believers to accept our inability to know fully, and this not because God is unable to tell us, but because we cannot possibly comprehend qualities of something to come that will be so different from—and yet a continuation of—the identity of our present bodies.

Observe that Paul says "they come" (*erchontai*), shifting from "the dead" (*hoi nekroi*) to the "body" (*soomati*). "They" are the formerly bodiless spirits whose individual glorified bodies have been raised and reunited with their spirits. Note that they are "coming": they possess the power of motion; they have bodily life. But this is a life that shall never cease; therefore their quality is different from that of our present corruptible bodies.

Now we know that all life must have a congenial and suitable environment in which to flourish. If this is so in this present world, may we not assume it to be so in our future state of never-ending existence? Fish are so constituted that they can live under water. You and I are not. As human beings we can live only in an environment that provides us with oxygen. In eternity, the conditions under which the resurrected ones live will be quite different from what we now know. Our body, as it is now, is not capable of living in such an environment, for it is subject to disease, decay, and death. It needs reconstituting. But He who originally created the body, and then made it reproduce from a sperm and an egg, is capable of reconstituting it from its present state to one that will fit its eternal environment.

If you believe God could create your natural body but not your eternal body, Paul argues, then you must be mentally deficient. As proof of the foolishness of this objection, Paul goes on to draw an analogy from a grain of wheat.

What do we know about the germination of seeds? Keep a grain of wheat in your pocket all your life and it will never change. But place it in a congenial environment, a furrow of earth, and it will sprout into a living sheaf of grain. Every kind of life requires its particular corresponding environment in order to achieve its full and predestined potential. You would really be just as foolish to expect your body, as now constituted, to be able to live in the world to come, as a farmer would be if he expected to produce a harvest of wheat by keeping bare grains stored in his pocket.

"How are the dead raised?" asks the skeptic of Paul. What's the mechanics of the resurrection? What's the process? Observe that Paul does not depict the skeptic as inquiring how the "bodies" are raised, but how the "dead" are raised. In the Greek, the dead are called *hoi nekroi*, all those who are not living in this present world, as you and I are now doing. This refers to personalities now in existence but under different conditions from the living ones on earth, *hoi zoontes*.

(See I Thess. 4:16, 17, where these two terms are used.) The only difference between the dead and the living is that the latter live in bodies as we now know them, and the dead live as spirit-beings, having left the body at death. We read in I Thessalonians 4:13-18 that, when the Lord comes again, two things will happen: The dead will be raised first, and then the living will be caught up with them. However, they will not go on living as presently constituted, for I Corinthians 15:51 tells us that we shall all be changed. We are not told *how* the bodies of those living when Christ returns will be changed; but the change will no doubt be equally as revolutionary as the re-creation of the bodies of those who died previous to the Lord's coming. We are not told the *how* of this either; but we do know the dead will rise with their personal identities preserved. However, their newly formed bodies will not necessarily be composed of the same atoms and particles as their corruptible bodies.

The personal identities of the dead are now preserved even without their bodies. These bodiless souls or spirits are here called "the dead." But they will be raised. The verb *egeirontai*, "are raised," in Greek indicates changing from a prone position to an upright one. Scripture abounds in references to death as going to sleep. People lie down when they go to sleep. But it is the body that lies down and not the soul. That the essential self lives on after the death of the body is demonstrated by the account of Lazarus and the rich man in Luke 16, as well as by Paul's declaration that when a Christian departs this life he goes to be with Christ (Phil. 1:23).

In answer to the question, "How are the dead raised?" Paul refers to the formation of a resurrection body to be indwelt by the spiritual living personality, thus forming the spiritual body of which he speaks in I Corinthians 15:44. It is not merely a soulless body that is formed. These are "the dead" who are now, even before the resurrection, alive as bodiless souls, but who will once again become body-soul personalities.

The Theological Dictionary of the New Testament (Gerhard Kittel), in its discussion of the verb *egeiroo* (to raise), says that it is used in relation to individual bodily resurrections (Vol. II, p. 335). For each one there will be an individual resurrection, a body formed, just as a body was formed at birth. The God who made it once can certainly remake it. There will be no uniformity of personalities then, even as there is none now with our present bodies, although there is uniformity of the type of material of which every body is made. And yet each body is distinguished from every other by its shape, form, characteristics, and identifications.

Could you, from the same raw materials, fashion over three billion bodies, all distinctly different from one another? God has done it. How? If you can answer that, then perhaps Paul could be expected to give an answer to how the dead will be raised, each to constitute a new and distinct body-spirit personality.

WHAT'S SO INCREDIBLE ABOUT THE RESURRECTION OF OUR BODIES?

"But some man will say, How are the dead raised up? and with what body do they come?" (I Cor. 15:36).

Don't treat this important question of your eternal future as a matter you can put off thinking about. Your future life must be determined here and now. Life eternal is not simply that which begins after death, but can and does begin in the present. You remember how the rich man in Luke 16:27-31 wanted to go back to earth after his death and warn his relatives of things to come, so that they could set their lives right with God while still in this present life? Your happiness or your misery here and now is conditioned by whether or not you believe in Christ, and that in Him the dead shall rise and exist as body-spirit personalities (that is, a "spiritual body"), with feeling, recognition, and ability to suffer or to rejoice.

Do you really live with your eyes fixed on that wonderful, glorious body with which you will come into a life so transcendent that it defies description? If you do, then two things should follow: 1) You will not value your present body so highly that you are not willing to sacrifice it for the Lord if need be; and 2) You will endure with patience the physical sufferings that God allows you to undergo in this world.

We thrill to Nathan Hale's patriotic declaration, "I only regret that I have but one life to lose for my country," yet all too often we make some slight infirmity of the body our excuse for not serving the Lord. We contemplate with awe the inspiring poems of Martha Snell Nicholson, so crippled by arthritis that she was bedridden for years, and seldom drew a pain-free breath. Yet her writings are fragrant with praise of her Saviour. Her secret? She "endured, as seeing him who is invisible" (Heb. 11:27). Through her poems and example she brought encouragement to thousands.

Yes, let us consider our body expendable, but when sacrificed for Jesus Christ it is never thrown away. One day the triumphant soul that goes to be with the Lord at death will receive a new and glorious body, and then the former pains and labors will be remembered no more.

Observe that in the questions, "How are the dead raised up? and with what body do they come?," both verbs are in the aoristic present tense (specific, applying to the time of the resurrection [see Robertson, p. 865] and hence the present tense is used in spite of the fact that the event is to take place in the future at the coming (*parousia*) of the Lord). A little later on in verse 50 and what follows, Paul uses the future tense, but now he uses the present. This is a future event but nevertheless it is of paramount importance here and now; for, among other things, what we shall be is determined by what we will to be here and now. And what we believe about Christ and about the resurrection of our bodies and the life to come determines our earthly conduct. Paul has just finished talking about this in verses 32-34.

The world is so full of conflicting ideas about the meaning of life that it's no wonder people are confused about what to believe. Set sail on the sea of non-Christian philosophical speculation, and you'll wind up going nowhere. Oh, you may find some congenial port that lets you feel you've really arrived; but sooner or later its fair promise will prove to be a mirage, and you will awaken to the reality of things as they are. Let it be now, rather than after death.

As Paul admonished the skeptical Corinthians, so I beseech all who are tempted to doubt God's Word: Stop listening to anti-Christian philosophical assumptions that one or another of the doctrines taught by Christ and His apostles are not true. By God's grace, you are intelligent enough to draw your own conclusions from the lessons of creation all around you. No need for college or university training to do that. An unbelieving university professor would have a harder time proving his unbelief reasonable than a farmer, for instance, would have proving his Christian belief well-founded. There are far more questions that would flood an honest, inquisitive mind that has assumed that everything in this universe made itself, than would trouble the person who believes that everything was made by someone greater than itself.

Paul looks the individual skeptic squarely in the eye and says, "Thou fool." The Greek word for "fool," *aphroon*, with which I Corinthians 15:36 begins, is singular in number. Paul is not addressing a group but the individual objector. In a group one is sometimes unduly influenced by others, and the personal God-given capability to think for oneself is lost.

A young woman, who had become badly confused

with regard to life's values, turned to psychotherapy for help. Here she found much of value in learning to understand her basic motivations. But whenever she voiced an ideal or a spiritual aspiration, the psychotherapist became uninterested. Such feelings were not "realistic," she was made to feel. Gradually the young woman became brainwashed into feeling that only people were real, and God was a projection of her own subjective needs and desires. She came out of psychotherapy to an empty world, in which God was unknowable.

But as the years passed by, her hunger for God did not diminish, and gradually she regained confidence in the fact that He was knowable, and that she was capable of knowing Him, apart from anyone else's opinions or pronouncements on the matter. She now believes, from having lived in both worlds—that of unbelief and that of faith—that apart from God her life has no meaning whatever; not because of what anyone has told her, but because it is absolutely incredible to her that all that she sees around her has no meaning, and that all men's hopes and aspirations for truth and personal fulfillment arise from nothing and are directed at no one. When she turned over her life to obey God wherever He might lead, she found faith in Him returning in a tide that bore her up out of suicidal despair to a renewed zest for life.

Mankind has experienced much progress as the result of individuals thinking for themselves. Don't say you believe the resurrection of the body is impossible because you heard someone else say so. Don't even believe it *is* possible because I say so, or any other person. Think it through for yourself. Examine the evidence. Read the Bible and ask God Himself to help you "know of the doctrine" whether it is true. Christianity is not a rubber stamp religion; it appeals to your individual thought and reason. When you believe, do so only after examination of all the data available. Make up your own mind through personal investigation.

Paul believed that, if people reasoned things out properly, they would be persuaded. In Acts 18:4 and 13, when he was preaching in the synagogue of Corinth, he did not ask the opposition to accept his message about Christ without due personal investigation. He "reasoned" with them *(dielegeto* in Greek, the very word from which we derive our English word "dialectic"). His preaching was a challenge to individuals to reason things out. Examine the mysteries of your darkness, he seems to be saying, and I'll examine the mysteries of my light. In both there are mysteries. But there are far more mysteries in darkness, unbelief, than in light, faith.

Did this reasonable approach produce results? Yes, he was persuading these people (vv. 4 and 13), *epeithen, anapeithei.* Those who believed as a result of Paul's preaching did so after having been persuaded that there was a greater weight of reasonableness on the side of belief than unbelief. They were persuaded in their own minds about the truth of the resurrection.

You as a doubter may begin to hope when you find yourself beginning to doubt your doubts. And you as a believer need not fear to find the most ultimately reasonable foundations for your belief.

A student oppressed with doubts went to an old experienced teacher for help. The old man refused to answer each specific question, saying, "Were I to rid you of these doubts, others would come. There is a shorter and more effective way of destroying them. Let Christ be to you really the Son of God, the Saviour, and His light will dispel the darkness, and His Spirit will lead you into all truth." No one can really rid you of the spirit of doubting but Christ Himself, as you seek Him with your whole heart, and follow where He leads.

DO YOU FIND THE RESURRECTION HARD TO BELIEVE? "BUT GOD. . . ."

"Thou fool, that which thou sowest is not quick-ened, except it die: and that which thou sowest, thou sowest not that body that shall be, but bare grain, it may chance of wheat, or of some other grain: but God. . . ." (I Cor. 15:36-38a).

The English Bible has Paul saying, "Thou fool," in I Corinthians 15:36. But in the Greek the order of words is inverted. "Fool," says Paul to the skeptic, and immediately adds *su,* "thou." Apply this to your-self. Don't excuse yourself on the ground that every-body else may be foolish. Why should you be a fool? Don't be like that doctor who got tired of hearing a scrub woman praising God as she washed the steps of the hospital. One morning as she was singing, "Oh, my soul, praise the Lord," he interrupted her with, "Listen, lady, I'm a doctor; I've dissected lots of bodies, and I never saw a soul." "Is that right?" answered the simple woman. "I thought you were a smart man who wouldn't expect to find a soul in a dead body. But I'm not dead; I'm alive." The doctor disappeared fast.

"Be not wise in your own conceits," says Paul in Romans 12:16. Don't get so puffed up with self-esteem that you end up being a fool. Don't say in effect, "I have dissected bodies and never found a soul." Just stop a minute and think. In dissecting bodies, did you ever find an imagination? A conscience? Did you ever find music? Are they then dreams, lies, wholly inconceivable because you did not find them?

Take a small seed in your hand. Can you see a tree in that? Suppose you had no experience of its ever becoming a tree; you would never believe it possible. But if you knew it had happened once, you would believe it could happen again. However, the proper conditions must be met. The seed must first be placed in an environment of soil, receive its proper nourishment, and then, through a process filled with mysteries, which even now are only imperfectly understood, it will spring up into the same kind of tree from which the original seed came—though the end result is in shape and function different from the seed. "Fool, thou, that which thou sowest is not quickened, except it die."

Note that Paul is not at all apologetic about his belief in the resurrection of the body. He faces the objector head on. He anticipates the challenge before it comes, and he swings in for the attack. As Spurgeon says, "No man has ever been convinced of a truth by discovering that those who profess to believe it are half ashamed of it, and adopt the tone of apology. He who realizes his strength attacks first and wins." This is the kind of strength Paul realized he possessed in his belief in the resurrection of the body.

I Corinthians 15:36 answers the first question of verse 35, "How are the dead raised up?" The response is, "Thou foolish one, that which thou thyself sowest is not quickened except it die." This is a down-to-earth practical demonstration of what is going on in nature. Here is something you observe constantly. You sow a seed by putting it into the ground. It must first die, and then it rewards you with a living plant. How does this take place? Can you or anyone else fully explain this philosophically, rationally? Do you refuse to eat the fruit of this seed until such time as you know in minutest detail how it grows into a plant? Hardly. You accept the generating power of nature. And when you sow wheat, you expect the same kind of plant to come up. But that plant does not contain every particle of matter that was in the seed. It contains the identity of the seed, but not the entire actual seed as it was put into the ground. Yet the plant resulting from that seed will produce seeds corresponding to that original seed, made of different yet identical material particles.

The plant in reality is that same seed which was placed in the ground, in different form. So will it be with your resurrection body. It will be the same body in the sense that it is your own body—yet no longer the seed, so to speak, but the plant. When your soul leaves your body at death, that spirit-less body is good for nothing but burial in the ground. There it can die and return to dust; and through death it will live again by God's power. You can do nothing about it yourself, of course. This death and resurrection of the body is foreordained of God. You could probably never even have thought of it. You, with all your intellectual pride, do not really control creation. You must obey it. If you don't, you will be the loser.

In contrast to that personal pronoun *su*, "yourself," with which verse 36 begins, we have the phrase "but God" (*ho de theos*) in verse 38. All you can do is sow the seed. You didn't make it; God did that.

You just put it in the ground to follow the God-ordained process of death and resurrection. You may prefer another method, *but God*. You may think the resurrection of your self-same body incredible, *but God*. Observe that which exists—the vegetation resulting from seed-sowing—and apply this to the resurrection of the body. How does this take place? "But God giveth it a body as it hath pleased him, and to every seed his own body."

Think, man. Nothing that you see or can handle made itself. The chair you sit on did not come into being of its own volition and power. Then why will you say that the sky above you is self-created, self-formed, and came about nobody knows how? If the glove you wear did not make itself, it ought to be foolish for you to believe that the hand is self-made. The only way to stop asking the "how" to which there can be no answer, at least in this life, is to add, "But God."

What Paul draws attention to on the one hand is the commonness of the experience of sowing seed and reaping a plant, and on the other the rarity of the experience of the resurrection, which took place only in the case of the Lord Jesus.

"Thou foolish one, that which thou sowest. . . ." The Greek verb is *speireis*, "you sow all the time." This is a common everyday experience. You accept it because you see it happening all the time. How true it is that there are many wonders in the world that you would not have believed by report, if you had not come across them by experience and observation. Had you lived fifty years ago, would you have believed that a picture could be taken by Telstar, a photographic communication satellite in the sky, which would then send back a clear picture on your television screen? In fact, would you have believed television? In the air there are only video waves, but on the television screen you see a person, an actual scene. Everything is wonderful until you are used to it; and the resurrection of the body owes the incredible portion of its marvel to the fact of your never having come across it in your observation, that's all. After the resurrection we shall regard it as a divine display of power as familiar to us as creation and providence now are.

If it did not happen so often, the springing of every seed out of the ground would amaze us, just as the prospect of the resurrection of our bodies does. If the birth of a child did not happen so often, it would equally astound us. The commonness of the experience has robbed it of its human incredibility and its divine and transcendent nature. It is only because we know it and see it so commonly that we do not recognize more fully the wonder-working hand of God in human births.

To the spiritually discerning, all so-called natural phenomena are mighty works of God, to be wondered at, and to move men's hearts to worship. One poet has expressed it this way:

> Earth's crammed with heaven,
> And every common bush's afire with God;
> But only he who sees takes off his shoes—
> The rest stand around and pick blackberries.

Can you discern the resurrection in the germination of a seed? Or do you merely pluck and eat the fruit to satisfy the needs of your present body, with no thought of that spiritual body to which God would call your attention?

HOW DEATH AFFECTS OUR PERSONALITIES

"But some man will say, How are the dead raised up? and with what body do they come? Thou fool, that which thou sowest is not quickened, except it die" (I Cor. 15:35, 36).

Those of us who have to go to work, or who send our children to school, find it a great help to turn on the radio every morning to get the weather report. But along with it we often hear other news items, and these are frequently of a tragic nature. It is not unusual to hear a newscaster say, "An airliner crashed at sea, and all passengers were lost." Our hearts go out in pity to their families, and we breathe a prayer for God to comfort and console them.

But what has actually happened to those who were killed in the crash? What, if anything, lies ahead for them? Scripture tells us that at death our personality or self is separated from our body. The body then begins that process of disintegration which will return it to dust, and the soul goes to one of two places: the unrighteous to a place of torment called Hades (see Luke 16:23, where the Authorized Version incorrectly translates it "hell"), and the righteous to be with Christ in Paradise (Luke 23:43).

But Scripture goes on to tell us that this is not the eternal state of the dead. Even as our present state of existence in a soul-body personality will one day come to an end, so will the single-soul-state of the dead. They will again become body-soul personalities, but with changes that will enable them to live in their new environment.

"But is this feasible?" asks someone. "Can there be

a new body for the now existing soul of the dead to dwell in?" The doubters in the early days of the Corinthian church said "No." But the Apostle Paul's answer is an emphatic "Yes." He argues that to say otherwise is foolish, since there is plainly an analogy between the physical and the metaphysical world. The only difference is that we observe these earthly types of the resurrection daily, while the phenomenon of man's bodily resurrection that is to come, we have not yet seen.

As an instance of what one may learn from nature, if he only has eyes to see, is the example of a man who looked into his tropical aquarium one day and saw on the surface a tiny creature, seemingly half fish and half snake, not an inch long, writhing in what seemed its death agony. With convulsive efforts it bent head to tail, now on this side, now on that, springing in circles with a force truly remarkable in a creature so small. "I was stretching out my hands to remove it," said the aquarium owner, "so that it would not sink and die and pollute the tank, when in the twinkling of an eye its skin split from end to end, and there sprang out a delicate fly with slender black legs and pale lavender wings. Balancing itself for one instant on its discarded skin, it preened its gossamer wings and then flew out of an open window. The impression made upon me was deep and overpowering. I learned that nature was everywhere hinting at the truth of the resurrection."

The resurrection of the body, however, is not based primarily on analogies from nature, but on Christ's demonstration when He rose from the dead with His body essentially the same as it had been before His death, yet with different and superior qualities. Thus in the physical world resurrection similar to that which the human dead body will experience is observed constantly; while in the case of the human body it has taken place only once—and He who experienced it, the Lord Jesus Christ, tells us that it will one day happen to all (John 5:28, 29). For anyone to say that it happened only once and cannot happen again is utter folly.

Christ has therefore brought a new estimate of death. He has invested it with a beauty and a peacefulness and a glory unknown before. This is what caused a Greek by the name of Aristeides to marvel, when trying to explain to one of his friends the reasons for the extraordinary success of Christianity. In a letter written about A.D. 125, he said: "If any righteous man among the Christians passes from this world, they rejoice and offer thanks to God, and they escort his body with songs and thanksgiving as if he were setting out from one place to another nearby." Is it any wonder that a religion like that swept paganism? Those believers who are gone before are not lost, not separated from us permanently; they are only waiting in another place nearby for us to join them again.

Who can deny that we humans owe this glorious hope to Christ and Him alone? He gave answers to our doubts and rest to our inquiries. The future state up to the time of Christ was vague and inconclusive, with a notion of a life to come founded on certain Old Testament passages that intimated both spiritual and bodily survival of personality after death, but which gave no explicit teaching on which to formulate a doctrine of resurrection. In the pagan world, the hope of immortality was merely guesswork, based greatly on the conclusion—thus far unfounded—that as there is resurrection in the physical world, so there must be in the metaphysical world, with human bodies coming through to a new and glorious existence.

But man's guesses are now replaced by glorious realities, though these are yet to be experienced by the human race. Christ was unique in predicting history before it was made, particularly in the striking prophecy of the unique redemptive history, namely, His own death and resurrection. He never failed in any of His prophecies. As someone has aptly said, "He alone discovers who proves."

For the person who is out of Christ, death is generally viewed with terror. It is said that the French nurse who was present at the death of Voltaire, being urged to attend an Englishman whose case was critical, said, "Is he a Christian?" "Yes," was the reply, "he is a Christian in the highest and best sense of the term—a man who lives in the fear of God. But why do you ask?" "Because," she answered, "I was the nurse who attended Voltaire in his last illness, and for all the wealth of Europe I would never see another infidel die."

Of course, among the unrighteous there are examples of heroism and martyrdom, but the motive is diametrically different from that of the Christian. It is pride that causes a man to suffer defeat manfully when he fails to conquer in the fight. Such a person succumbs without a tear and without a sigh because he wants to show himself a man to the very end. To others, death is viewed as a release from trouble, from suffering, from shame. But they have no prospect for the future, no joy, no hope, as does the Christian believer. For the non-Christian, death is an end; but for the Christian it is a beginning of a new life. No wonder the poet contemplating his own death could ask in wonder,

> Out of my prison bars,
> The dark clasp of earth—
> Why do they call this death?
> Death instead of birth?

Yes, it's Christ's resurrection that makes our own resurrection sure. Notice that the Apostle Paul first established the fact of Christ's resurrection (I Cor. 15:1-11) and then went on to expound the doctrine of our own bodily resurrection. Only then does he bring forth the analogy of the seed to establish his point that death is not terminal but germinal. He does not base the doctrine of the resurrection merely on a natural analogy, but begins with the fact of Christ's resurrection and His teaching on the resurrection of the body, and then proceeds with the analogies from nature. Nature can never lead you to the fullness of God's mysteries yet to come. But God's revelation in Christ can make natural phenomena confirm the higher reasonableness of God's revelation concerning things to come which escape our power to observe at present.

DOUBT HAS MORE DIFFICULTIES
TO EXPLAIN THAN FAITH

"And that which thou sowest, thou sowest not that body that shall be, but bare grain, it may chance of wheat, or of some other grain: But God giveth it a body as it hath pleased him" (ICor. 15:37, 38).

If you put a single seed into the hand of a child—and he must be a very little one—he might not believe that this hard, dry, dead-looking particle of matter could be a living thing again. Yet we know that, put into the earth for a few weeks or less, under the mysterious influences of God's sun and rain, it will spring up (we do not understand how), and there will be a stalk and leaves, and perhaps a flower. It has risen from the dead. Common sense would naturally ask, Is man—the most honorable of all earthly entities—to be an exception to the resurrection rule?

Suns set and rose before Christ; seeds decayed in the ground, and plants sprang up. But what was the impression that these generations of nature left on the heathen mind? They were seen, not as analogies, not as resemblances, but as contrasts to human destiny. How different man appeared, when compared to the sun and to the seeds and flowers. All else seemed to speak of incessant renewal, of continuous life; man alone was born to eternal, irrevocable death. "Suns may set and rise again," writes one, "but we, when our brief day has set, must slumber on through one eternal night." "Alas! the flowers and the herbs," moans another, "when they perish in the garden, revive again afterward and grow for another year, but we, the great and strong and wise of men, when once we die, sleep forgotten in the vaults of earth a long unbroken endless sleep." (Catullus, *Carm. 5;* Moschus *On the death of Bion,* 100 sq., as quoted by J. B. Lightfoot in *Cambridge Sermons,* London, 1890: pp. 75-6.)

How men craved for the assurance of things to come! You do, too, don't you? You look at nature on the one hand and at your own human aspirations and instincts on the other, and you wonder. Is there a similarity or a contrast? You stand by the sick bed of a loved one. You watch the bodily frame wasting away and your own heart sinks and your mind wonders. Can it be that this body that is waning away is similar to a seed that cannot come back to life unless it dies? That's true of plants in the physical world, but can it be true of bodies in the metaphysical? Then you consign that lifeless form to the slow disintegration of the grave. Can man's destiny end here, in the dust?

When Stephen, the first Christian martyr, died in the early days of his ministry, was his life really ended? Were his capacities, his affections, his aspirations doomed to this limited span of fulfillment? Men are anxious to make a name for themselves in this world, to leave behind them the memory of great accomplishments. We may say that Stephen did this, of course, but will there be no further unfolding of his life in time to come?

Up till the time of Christ, men's attempts at securing lasting remembrance on earth impelled them to erect stately mausoleums and towering pyramids; to inscribe their deeds on tablets, and have their likenesses reproduced in sculptured images. In this way a man recorded his stammering protest that he was still a man among men, that he was still alive. But all was vague, uncertain, faltering. Shelley's poem, "Ozymandias," speaks of the futility of such hopes of immortality.

> I met a traveler from an antique land
> Who said: Two vast and trunkless legs of stone
> Stand in the desert. Near them on the sand,
> Half sunk, a shattered visage lies, whose frown
> And wrinkled lip and sneer of cold command
> Tell that its sculptor well those passions read
> Which yet survive stamped on these lifeless things,
> The hand that mocked them and the heart that fed;
> And on the pedestal these words appear:
> "My name is Ozymandias, king of kings:
> Look on my works, ye mighty, and despair!"
> Nothing beside remains. Round the decay
> Of that colossal wreck, boundless and bare,
> The lone and level sands stretch far away.

From this fruitless striving and suspense, Christ set us free. His resurrection dispelled the mists that shrouded men's gropings after truth; and where before was an uncertain haze, there burst forth the brightness of the unclouded sun. Truth entered the hearts and lives of the uneducated and the scholar, the rich and the poor, the king and the slave. A little child can now grasp the idea of immortality with a firmness that was denied to the strongest intellect and the most patient thought before Christ. (See Lightfoot, *Ibid.*, pp. 62-79.)

Paul had every reason to call the person who objected to the possibility of man's resurrection a fool, after the overwhelming demonstration of Christ's resurrection. He is an even greater fool if he fails to see the analogy to such a resurrection in nature. If that was so 1900 years ago, how much more is he a fool now after such a fantastic increase in knowledge as that embodied in the discovery that $E=Mc2$, which tells us that energy—unseen by the human eye and without set form—can be changed into mass form, and vice versa. If a person was a fool in Paul's day for rejecting the resurrection on philosophical grounds, he is a thousand times a fool today as a result of our scientific discoveries.

Today as never before, if you are unable to refute the historicity of Christ's resurrection, what ground have you for declaring it could not conceivably have taken place? It is certainly far better attested than much of the contemporary history of its day, and by witnesses of unimpeachable character who gave their lives to back up their testimony. Thousands of impossibilities we assumed for the past have become realities of the present, and we cannot with such ground on which we stand assume any impossibility for the future. As F. Podmore says, in his *Naturalization of the Supernatural,* "The philosopher who, antecedently to experience, should venture to pronounce the word 'impossible,' even in the region of pure mathematics, would write himself belated" (that is, out of date). (Quoted by C. H. Robinson in his *Studies in the Resurrection of Christ, p. 97.)*

The Apostle Paul asked a most cogent question when, standing before King Agrippa, he said, "Why should it be thought a thing incredible with you, that God should raise the dead?" (Acts 26:8). Today he could ask it of a group of scientists with a much louder voice. There was a time when it was required of faith to give reasons. But now it is for doubt and unbelief to justify themselves. Why do you doubt? Give a reason for the doubt, fear, and unbelief within you. With our Gibraltar of Christ's resurrection and our current scientific discoveries in nature, it's not the Christian's responsibility to explain his faith to the doubter, but the doubter's to explain his unbelief. Doubt will be found, if sincerely examined, to have more difficulties to explain than faith. You belie your intelligence when you fail to see in the very body laid down in the grave the potential of a glorious body to come.

> Suns that rise and moons that fill
> Still must set, must vanish still;
> Stars that azure night renews
> Soon returning day subdues;
> Gardens that expand in flower
> Touched by vernal sheen and shower,
> Wither, and expire in death
> Under winter's icy breath.
> We that weaker seem than all,
> Victims of a deadlier thrall,
> Lights in outer darkness lost,
> Flowerets sealed in final frost—
> Yet, such hope benignant Heaven
> Deathless after death has given,
> We shall rise in fadeless bloom
> From the winter of the tomb.

YOUR RESURRECTION BODY
WILL BE A NEW CREATION

◄─────►

"And that which thou sowest, thou sowest not that body that shall be, but bare grain, it may chance of wheat, or of some other grain" (I Cor. 15:37).

Children love to plant seeds in a flower pot and watch them grow. You don't have to go to any expense to give them this pleasure. Grapefruit and orange pits, dried beans, and avocado pits, to mention just a few, will sprout even on city windowsills. And from these you can teach children not only elemental lessons in botany, but also the deeper truths of the resurrection.

In our study of I Corinthians 15:36-38, we have seen that a seed must die in the ground before God causes it to spring up into a plant; and that this plant will be consistent with the nature of the seed planted, yet different in form and function. To emphasize this difference between the seed and the plant as being similar to the difference between the body that is laid in the grave and the body that will one day be resurrected, Paul says in verse 37, "And that which thou sowest, thou sowest not that body that shall be, but bare grain, it may chance of wheat, or of some other grain."

The analogy here is that of your dead body to a seed, and of your resurrection body to the plant. There is nothing in Scripture that requires you to believe that the body you put into the ground is the selfsame body that will rise in the resurrection. Paul says that, with bodies as with plants, you don't bury that which is to be in the same form that it will eventually assume. A bare grain of wheat will produce a plant bearing many grains, but you don't sow the whole plant. You sow a seed and you get a corresponding plant.

It makes no difference what you sow. "That which thou sowest" *(ho speireis)* is not at all restrictive. As Paul says at the end of the verse, it may be a grain of wheat or a seed belonging to a different kind of plant. The point that he wants to get across is that there is a difference between what goes into the ground and what comes out of it, and that the difference between the human body buried at death and that body which is raised at Christ's coming is as radical as that between a seed and a plant.

Paul also wants to bring out the lesson that, even as in natural vegetation there is a new work of generation, a new begetting, each time a seed springs out of the ground, so it will be with our resurrection bodies. This is made clear by the Greek verb *geneesomenon,* or *gignomai,* the future participle of the verb *ginomai,* which in its primary sense means "to be born or begotten." It is the same verb that in John 1:3 and 12 is translated "made" and "become," referring in verse 3 to the creation of all things, and in verse 12 to the bringing into being of the "sons of God"—one the original creation, the other a spiritual re-creation or regeneration of man.

Now, in I Corinthians 15:37, in speaking of the "body that shall be," this same verb indicates a third and future act of creation, the creation of the resurrection body. You were created once a natural man or woman. When you receive Christ as your Saviour and Lord by faith, you are re-created in spirit. And after your death, in the resurrection that will take place at Christ's second coming, your body will be re-created by God into a new and glorious body like Christ's.

The verb *geneesomenon* is used to show that God does not need to form the new resurrection body out of the old buried, decomposed body. It is a new creation, which may be *ex nihilo* (out of nothing), yet bearing the same identity as the old body. This new creation will be fitted for a new environment, even as our present body constitutes a creation fitted to live in this present world. There can be no mixing of the two worlds. That which is now is not the same as that which is to be. Each body has its own environment; and as it took one creative act of God to form our present body, so it will take another divine creative act to form our resurrection body.

As I have said before, we must not think that the body as God originally created it was vile. True, Paul seems to say in the Authorized translation of Philippians 3:21 that God "shall change our vile body, that it may be fashioned like unto his glorious body." But the word "vile" is an unfortunate translation of the Greek word *tapeinooseoos,* "humiliation." This is the very word that the Virgin Mary used in describing her low estate in Luke 1:48. What Paul meant by the expression "our body of humiliation" is that, masterful though the body is, it is not the governing element in human nature. Man is something higher, something nobler, than the physical form with which he is intimately identified, though it is certainly part of himself. Man alone among the creatures enjoys this distinction of having a body on the one hand, and of being a conscious spirit on the other. And from the point of view of his higher, that is to say, his spiritual, existence, his body naturally enough seems to him to be a body of humiliation, which falls under all kinds of limitations and disabilities from which pure spirit is exempt.

Yet we are not to hold the body in contempt, for Christ Himself took upon Him our physical form; and yet what a difference between His glorified resurrection body and our present bodies. Nevertheless, He has promised us that the body has a splendid future in store. If we are in Him, He will one day change our body of humiliation so that it will be fashioned like His glorious body. It will be a true body still, but one that belongs to the sphere of the spirit.

It is difficult for us to understand how this poor body is to be wrenched from us at death and then restored to us in the resurrection, transfigured into one that is impervious to disease and superior to material obstacles in moving through space—the spirituality which awaits it without destroying it. (See H. P. Liddon, "The Glorious Destiny of the Human Body," in *The Churchman's Pulpit,* Vol. XIII, pp. 303-6.)

To make it absolutely clear that God is going to create a new body in continuation of our present body, Paul adds in verse 38, "But God giveth it a body as it hath pleased him, and to every seed his own body." Two truths are made clear by the word "giveth":

1) In the Greek, this verb *(didoomi)* in the New Testament is used with the idea of a gift and not merely a disposition (James 2:16, Kittel's *Theological Dictionary of the New Testament).* The body that we shall have in our metaphysical state will be a gift of God. It is not a reward that we deserve; for nothing that we are or do or possess is deserved. It is by God's grace.

2) God, in giving us anything, does not sidestep the natural processes of life. You have a child; you have brought it into the world. But don't forget that the very

ability you possess to bring forth children is God-given. God doesn't sidestep you to give you children descending from the sky. But be careful that you don't consider what you receive through nature—such as the plants that result from the seeds you sow—as your own unassisted achievement. All you can do is sow and cultivate. God must do the rest. And without His part, your part is worthless. Nevertheless, He expects you to sow.

"It seems to be a rule of the Divine procedure to work for man through man. Not through angels. They seem almost to be warned off from, rather than to be commissioned for, man's salvation. An angel was sent to Cornelius, not to preach the Gospel to him, but to tell him where he could find a man to do it!

"It is a marvel of marvels that God should entrust such a work into man's keeping. But He has chosen to do it. 'We are labourers together with' Him! 'It hath pleased God by the foolishness of preaching to save them which believe.' 'Go ye into all the world and preach the gospel to every creature.' " (F. H. Marling, "Labourers Together with God," *The Christian World Pulpit,* Vol. 6, p. 255.)

Paul propounds a searching question and gives a humbling answer that illustrates the proper relationship of God's work and man's. "Who then is Paul," he asks, "and who is Apollos, but ministers by whom ye believed, even as the Lord gave to every man? I have planted, Apollos watered; but God gave the increase. So then neither is he that planteth any thing, neither he that watereth; but God that giveth the increase. . . . For we are labourers together with God" (I Cor. 3:5-9).

YOUR RESURRECTION BODY WILL BE DIFFERENT FROM EVERYONE ELSE'S

"But God giveth it a body as it hath pleased him, and to every seed his own body" (I Cor. 15:38).

When you receive your new body in the resurrection, at the appearing of Jesus Christ, it will not have to be formed over a period of time, as our present physical bodies must be. There will be no nine-months' waiting and growing of the implanted seed. The Greek participle *geneesomenon*, speaking illustratively of the "body that shall be," denotes punctiliar action, indicating pictorially by means of a seed that this new body will be given by God instantly to believers. It is a direct creative act of God without the intermediary of man, in contrast to the procreation of our natural bodies. "God giveth it a body."

Whenever the Lord Jesus during His earthly ministry brought people back from the dead, He did it suddenly. When He called Lazarus out of the tomb, the men who withdrew the stone looked with awe into that dark vault, expecting to find what the sisters of the dead man had feared when they said, "Lord, by this time he stinketh; for he has been dead four days" (John 11:39). There lay the decaying body of Lazarus, until that moment when the Saviour spoke the word, "Lazarus, come forth!" Then his spirit entered his body, though no one saw it, even as no-one had seen it depart. In a moment that rotting, decaying body began to move in its grave-clothes. "Loose him," said the Saviour, "and let him go"; and instantly Lazarus came forth. And He who is now at the right hand of God, our risen Saviour, will one day call to the dead, and "all that are in the graves shall hear his voice, and shall come forth" (John 5:28).

Thus is the absolute power of God demonstrated. But Paul couples God's power, both in creation and resurrection, with His eternal will: "But God gives it a body as he willed." The verb *eetheleesen* here is in the aorist tense, which refers to an action in the past that is complete.

Very interestingly the same word is used in John 5:21, again dealing with the resurrection. "For as the Father raiseth up the dead, and quickeneth them; even so the Son quickeneth *whom he will.*" There seems to be complete harmony in the will and power of God.

"And to every seed his own body." The Greek word for "every" is not one that would emphasize totality so much as individuality within totality, "each one separately." God will not leave anyone without his own particular body. But this is not one mass-produced assembly-line body, exactly the same for all, but an individually distinctive body, even as we have today. There is a similarity between all human bodies, but there is also a distinctiveness to each individual body. No two bodies of the billions that have existed on this earth have been or are absolutely identical in looks and composition, not even those of identical twins.

Any botanist knows that no two trees have exactly the same number of branches, leaves, roots, etc. In a wheatfield, although you can tell that each stalk is wheat, out of the billions of stalks there are no two exactly alike. There is a similarity but also distinctiveness of kind and distinctiveness among individual plants. So will it be with our resurrection bodies. Basically they will be similarly constituted, but each one will be a distinct, personally identifiable body.

The word *idion,* "his own," means "pertaining to oneself, as opposed to belonging to another." Your resurrection body will have its own distinctive characteristics, just as your present body has. This will not be a distinction of kind but of personality attributable to the make-up and looks of the resurrection body. To have a resurrected human body is not all that is promised, but to have your very own resurrection body. There will be no elimination of your personality, even in its bodily characteristics, in the world to come.

This expression, "and to every one of the seeds its very own body," takes us back to the first chapter of Genesis to the original creation. God ordained at the very beginning that each plant should yield seed "after his kind" (Gen. 1:11). The apple tree will never give you orange seeds, or vice versa. Nor can a pig ever produce a cow or a monkey or a man. Don't overlook or forsake that which is evident—the creation of each species of plant and living animals and substances according to its kind—for some fanciful evolution from one kind to another. The Genesis account of creation clearly indicates that God meant each original "species" to reproduce in accordance with its nature. It does not tell us how many original species God created, but it does show quite plainly that there were definite limits to what biological changes could take place.

Mutations are one thing; evolution from one species to another is quite a different matter. Mutations are chemical changes in the genes that can result in permanent change in a given species, but they do not result in higher forms of life but in a deterioration of the species. As Henry M. Morris points out in his book, *The Twilight of Evolution* (p. 46), "The basic processes at the present time [i.e., in the world as we have always known it] are those of *conservation* and *deterioration,* not innovation and development."

In other words, a horse was a horse from the beginning. Any mutations have been only of a harmful nature. A horse will never evolve into a different kind of creature of a higher nature, but left to itself, apart from interference by man's breeding procedures, will always be a horse as God created him, subject to deterioration through chance mutations. We see no half-way creatures in today's world—no ape on the way to becoming a man, no reptile in the process of becoming a bird, no weed in the process of becoming a tree.

Again Morris claims that all we know of science and history can be understood either in the light of evolution or of creation and the fall—and that we choose which we will believe, not on the basis of "inductions from the facts, but rather on deductions" from our own basic presuppositions.

Why, then, do most modern scientists accept evolution, not as a theory but as a proven fact? Is it not precisely because they prefer a world in which God does not exist and hold them accountable to Himself, and therefore they welcome evolution as a way of explaining the universe without reference to its Creator? It is not the "facts" that we have to fear in examining the theory of evolution, but the state of mind that would lead men to make false inferences from those facts because they want to rule God out of the universe.

Oddly enough, in doing away with God as Creator, they have predicated another God, whom they call Nature. To "her" (and it is interesting that they use this personal pronoun) they attribute intelligence, good judgment, a

-622-

purposeful striving for progressively higher development; and they optimistically look forward to a time, perhaps eons in the future, when Nature shall have achieved some sort of perfection in man, beast, and all living things.

Pressed as to what they mean by Nature, they will substitute another word or phrase, such as "life force," but each time they will endow it with an intelligent determination to improve matters. This belief in a mythical creative intelligence called Nature would be appropriate in a child given to fairy tales and daydreams, but in mature men it seems almost incredible. Again we find a clue to such pseudo-scientific thinking in the fact that Nature has this convenient feature, that it makes no moral demands on its devotees.

Let me dispel one more fairy-tale, and that is that when we depart this life we shall become "angels." They are a different order of being altogether, and Scripture gives no basis for this notion. We shall have bodies in accordance with out "kind," with what we are, men and women redeemed by Jesus Christ, who will receive bodies "like unto his glorious body," which was recognizable to His disciples after His death and resurrection.

HOW NATURE HELPS US TO UNDERSTAND
THE RESURRECTION OF THE BODY

"But God giveth it a body as it hath pleased him, and to every seed his own body" (I Cor. 15:38).

In our previous study we saw that "Nature" as an intelligent force apart from God is a figment of men's imaginations. But nature with a small "n" is a convenient term to designate the observable facts in our world that operate in accordance with the laws that God has instituted. It is in this sense that I shall employ the term in this study.

First of all, let us be frank to admit that we can find nothing in nature that exactly corresponds to the resurrection of the body. Some comparisons come close, but they do not constitute perfect analogies. One must never press Biblical analogies beyond the intention of the writer. When Paul uses the analogy of the seed, for instance, he is simply telling us that what happens to the seed when it is sown in the ground is similar to what death does to the human body: "That which thou sowest is not quickened [does not become alive], except it die" (I Cor. 15:36).

However, there is this difference between the dead seed and the dead body: in the seed there continues to dwell a life germ, and the disintegrating particles become its food from which it builds itself up again; but in dead bodies no such life germ remains.

Sleep has been used as an analogy of death, yet this too is inadequate. When we go to sleep, our bodies are still alive, but in death the body begins to decay and will not awaken after a few hours of rest.

Then again, the development of insects has provided an interesting analogy. The larva has been compared to man in his present condition, the chrysalis to man in his death, and the imago, or perfect insect, to man in his resurrection. But even this analogy breaks down, for there is life in the chrysalis; we cannot mistake it for a dead thing. If we take it up, we shall find everything in it that will come out of it. The perfect creature is evidently dormant there. But if you could crush the chrysalis, dry up all its life juices, bruise it into dust, pass it through chemical processes, utterly dissolve it, and then call it back to being as a butterfly, you would have a perfect analogy of the resurrection. This, however, has never happened in nature as yet.

No, all that Paul wants to bring out in this analogy from the seed is that, as it must die to become a living plant, so also the human body must die before it can become the glorious resurrection body. The only exceptions to this will be those who are living on earth at the time of Christ's return. Death, therefore, is not the end of existence but the doorway to a glorified eternal existence for the believer.

A seed is not like a human body, nor a furrow like a grave, nor an ear of corn like our glorified flesh. But the terms are related in the sense that as the seed is to the ear of corn, so is the corruptible body to the incorruptible; and as the furrow to the wheat, so is the grave to our flesh.

What Paul wanted to stress to the philosophizing Corinthians is that there is the same order in nature as there is in revelation. We are subject to the same laws as the seed, as vegetation, as nature. You cannot escape natural law. Do what you will, go where you may, nature, as you call it, will deal with you and dispose of you according to the very same laws as we see in God's special revelation. These laws are facts in nature as well as doctrines of the Gospel, because both have the same Author, God. Look at the seed and the human body. Look at the springing up of the plant and the doctrine of the resurrection taught in the Word of God. You cannot miss the correspondence between the facts of nature and the doctrines of the faith. The marks of the same hand, the hand of the Creator God, are visible in both.

Paul here invests nature with a divine character in the true sense of being the God-ordained order of things. The seed behaves and develops the way it does, not because it chooses to, but because its Creator determined it should. The seed is "quickened," revived, after death. This word "quickened" in I Corinthians 15:36 is *zoo-opoieitai* in Greek, which literally means "to be made alive." It is in the passive voice, indicating that the little germ dormant in the seed, when put in the earth, cannot by itself spring up into the life of the plant, but must be given new life by a power outside itself. God operates in nature; nothing happens by itself. Life is in God and is not the absolute prerogative of anything or anyone else.

The verb "quickened" is the same as that used in I Corinthians 15:22, where Paul tells us that "all shall be made alive." This refers to the physical resurrection of our bodies. Here, too, the verb is in the passive voice, indicating that our bodies do not rise of themselves but are raised by the power of God. Death is now natural to man. It is a consequence—the consequence of his sin. But the resurrection of the body is supernatural, requiring the direct action of God. The Lord does not as a rule strike anyone dead. Men just die. But it takes God to raise them up. This applies both to their spiritual and physical resurrection.

To explain that the new body is indeed a gift of God, Paul says in verse 38, "But God gives unto him a body as he [God] desired." He does the same with every plant that He raises from a seed buried in the ground. If you are unable to see God in nature, you will find it even more difficult to see Him in His special revelation. True, nature is an inadequate revelation; but if you view it with intelligence you will be constrained to accept the revelation of the unseen world. Your observation of nature can make it the basis of faith. It consecrates the visible world as a type and sacrament of the unseen.

Paul points this out in Romans 1:19, 20: "Because that which may be known of God is manifest in them; for God hath shewed it unto them. For the invisible things of him from the creation of the world are clearly seen, being understood by the things that are made, even his eternal power and Godhead; so that they are without excuse." (See also Acts 14:17.)

Nature stops the mouth of anyone who would declare that the resurrection of the body is impossible. The refutative force of the argument from analogy is absolute. But in its constructive form it is only a presumption. Because the seed, when it dies, becomes a plant, it does not logically and irrefutably follow that something similar will happen to your dead body.

You cannot stop with what you learn from nature, for nature's revelation is insufficient to tell you of things unseen. Never take analogies from nature as the measure or limit of revelation. Christianity, considered from the viewpoint of having come on the temporal scene, is not as old as the creation, and is not revealed by it. Christ is alone in His revelation about what is going to happen to our dead bodies. The resurrection of the body is a doctrine peculiar to Christianity. The continuation of the existence of the soul was always taught, even by heathens, but they knew nothing of the resurrection of the body.

Evidence of this is found in the reaction of the Greeks on Mars Hill when Paul referred to the resurrection. They knew he was speaking of the body and not the spirit, for they would have agreed with him about the immortality of the latter. But they had never heard or even thought of the resurrection of the body. Reason in a measure teaches the immortality of the spirit, but it is the revelation of Christ alone that teaches and establishes the fact of the future immortality of the body. Christianity is a supernatural religion. It should never be allowed to merge or coincide with naturalism in our thinking. We must be very careful, therefore, that in studying the analogies from nature by Paul or any other Biblical writer we do not read more into them than is intended.

Do all the seeds that are buried in the ground spring up into plants? No, for much depends on the condition of the seed and the environment. If we were to depend on analogies completely, we could not say positively and unequivocally that the resurrection will apply to all dead bodies. But because this truth was revealed by Christ Himself, we can take it as absolute.

However, it is not necessary to believe that our risen bodies will contain the same particles of matter as those we now carry about with us. It is enough for us to remember that the very body in which the unrepentant sinner dies will be resurrected, and in this body he shall suffer in hell; and the very body in which you believe in Christ and in which you yield yourself to God will be resurrected and will be the one in which you shall walk in heaven.

In his poem about Childe Harold, Byron quotes him as saying:

> The thorns which I have reaped are of the tree
> I planted—they have torn me—and I bleed;
> I should have known what fruit would spring
> from such a seed.

What fruit will spring from your body after death? On that resurrection morning will it be raised in newness of life in Christ, or will it be raised only to be cast into the deepest hell for an eternity of conscious torment? Before it is planted in the earth, you should make that decision—now, today—for tomorrow may be too late.

WILL OUR RESURRECTION BODIES BE MADE OF THE SAME KIND OF FLESH AS THEY NOW HAVE?

"But God giveth it a body as it hath pleased him, and to every seed his own body. All flesh is not the same flesh: but there is one kind of flesh of men, another flesh of beasts, another of fishes, and another of birds" (I Cor. 15:38, 39).

"If a man die, shall he live again?" That question was asked by a man named Job thousands of years ago (Job 14:14). Men have been asking that same question and giving various answers to it throughout history. It remained for the Christian church in Corinth, in the First Century A.D., to ask its corollary: "With what body do they come?" (I Cor. 15:35). They did not doubt man's soul would continue to live on in eternity, but some of them could not accept the idea that the body would one day be raised to eternal life.

After pointing out to them that just as God could raise a plant from a seed buried in the ground He could also raise the dead to a state of material existence, Paul goes on to show them that God had given various kinds of flesh to the living bodies He created. He enumerates these as beasts, fishes and birds. Think of the multitudinous bodies to which God has given various kinds of flesh. Feathered bodies whose natural element is the air; furred bodies who live in lands of Arctic cold or tropic heat; scaly bodies that can survive only in the seas and rivers.

Each of these creatures might in its ignorance deny that the other elements existed or could sustain life. Even so, man in his willful ignorance may often deny that these bodies of ours will one day exist in a state they have not yet experienced. To deny the existence of what they have never seen is a form of blindness to which men are dangerously and sinfully susceptible. Who made these forms of life to differ from one another? Who created them all? Examine every insect, every mammal, every fish and fowl; note their infinite perfections and varieties; and confess at last that there is no explanation equal to God as their Creator.

Paul's argument is this: If God can form so many different kinds of bodies here on earth, all of flesh, yet all diversified, why should we question His ability to give the disembodied spirits of men bodies that are real, preserving the identity of their earthly bodies, made of flesh suited to their new other-worldly environment? If both a reptile and I can be said to possess the common bond of flesh, yet with my flesh differing from its flesh as much as my immortal spirit differs from its mortal life, why may there not be flesh in common between me as I am now and me as I am to be hereafter—but with my flesh then differing from my present flesh as much as my soul made perfect in holiness will then differ from my soul now, groaning under "the body of this death"? (Rom. 7:24.)

In I Corinthians 15:35-38, Paul told us that our dead bodies would be raised; different in some respects but yet the same in others; with such differences as it may seem good to God to make; with such sameness as shall identify me personally, in body and soul, to myself and to all my friends. When I die and become pure spirit, I know that I shall resume my bodily frame again; changed, much changed, in its structure and organization; yet so thoroughly one with the bodily frame that I lay aside now, that I must answer in that body for the deeds done in this. (See Robert S. Candlish, *Life in a Risen Saviour,* pp. 157-8.)

The same God who could give each of His creatures on earth a particular body of flesh to suit its ordained environment can give the proper kind of fleshly body adapted to man raised from the dead. Man will then be above what he is now, even as he is now above beasts, fishes, and birds.

The literal translation of the first part of I Corinthians 15:39 is "Not every kind of flesh [is] the same flesh." The verb is not there but is understood. It's a statement of fact negatively declared. The word *pasa*, "all," actually refers to the sum total of all substances that can be termed "flesh," but stresses particularly the idea of individual kinds of flesh. They have a common characteristic that binds them into one classification, "flesh," yet they are distinguishable by individual characteristics. The expression "the same," *hee autee*, actually means the same identical one. It refers to the identity of the flesh. The flesh of the present body and the flesh of the body that is to be have something in common that can group them in the same category, "flesh," and yet the flesh that is to be is sufficiently different that it cannot be mistaken as exactly the same in every detail.

Paul has told us in his analogy of the seed and the plant that there is an essential continuity and organic relation between that which dissolves in the earth and that which God causes to sprout forth from it. Now, as he applies that to our bodies, he wants us to understand that the new body of flesh will be distinguished by something new and richer which is missing from the present body. The individuality, however, will be preserved, for there is no such thing as a mass-produced resurrection body.

How do men, beasts, birds, and fishes differ from each other? In structure, quality, functions. But they are all essentially made of flesh, differing not in essence but in quality. And such will be the difference between our present body and the resurrection body.

But man is more than a body, of course, even though the body is all we ever see of him. Did you ever hear anyone say, "I *am* a body"? No one would think of talking about himself that way. He would say, "I *have* a body." The nature of man is a great mystery. For instance, in the expression, "I said to myself," who is the "I" and who is the "self"? However we may attempt to explain it theologically, man experiences himself as a trinity—body, soul, and spirit. This should not surprise us, for the Bible reveals that the whole Trinity, Father, Son, and Holy Spirit, was concerned in the creation of man. In Genesis 1:26 we read, "And God said, Let *us* make man in *our* image." I believe this included endowing man with a three-in-one personality corresponding to the triune nature of God.

God has embodied Himself, also. In one sense, the whole creation is the embodiment or expression of His personality. But God is not merely *in* creation; He is beyond it, outside it, above it. Creation is not God, for God is Spirit. Supremely He incarnated Himself in Jesus Christ, in order to reveal Himself to the world as the God-man who as Saviour and Redeemer came in the flesh to give Himself as "a ransom for many," that man might through Him be reconciled to the Father.

THE GLORY OF OUR RESURRECTION BODIES

"There are also celestial bodies, and bodies terrestrial: but the glory of the celestial is one, and the glory of the terrestrial is another. There is one glory of the sun, and another glory of the moon, and another glory of the stars; for one star differeth from another star in glory" (I Cor. 15:40, 41).

Voltaire, that strange combination of freethinker, deist, and rabid denouncer of Christianity, gives scant comfort to atheists and agnostics in some of his pronouncements. "The world embarrasses me," he said, "and I cannot think that this watch exists and has no Watchmaker." And in the same vein he confesses, "To whatever side you turn, you are forced to acknowledge your own ignorance and the boundless power of the Creator."

In this, though he little realized it, he was ironically in harmony with the whole tenor of Paul's arguments for the resurrection of the body in I Corinthians 15:35-44. After pointing out the analogy of God's raising a plant from a buried seed, and the further analogy of the various kinds of flesh God had given to the living bodies of bird, beast, and fishes that He had created, Paul asks in effect, "Do you still doubt that God can give the departed souls of men a suitable fleshly environment?" You have looked at the earth and have seen that men, animals, fishes, birds all have flesh, but each its own kind. Yet the same God made them all.

Now look up, Paul continues in verse 40. You will see bodies in the heavens different from those of earth. The sun, moon, and stars do not have flesh, but they are bodies composed of matter; and flesh is matter. Paul's chief concern here is to convince the questioning Corinthians that the future body will be material, and yet of such material as to fit it for its own new environment. Don't you think the God who clothed the sun and stars with matter is able to give us back our bodies after we die, the same as those we had yet different? Can He not form bodies for His saints to be raised up in, as well as for those who rejected Him and died in their unbelief? And since Paul is particularly interested in the resurrection of believers, he asserts that the same God who hangs the heavenly bodies in space can give the saints who died bodies differing from their earthly bodies as much as the glory of the celestial bodies differs from the glory of the terrestrial bodies.

Not only that, says Paul, but even among the stars and planets there are differences in glory. "There is one glory of the sun, and another glory of the moon, and another glory of the stars: for one star differeth from another star in glory" (v. 41).

See what God can do with matter? He can make a man, a beast, a fish, a bird, a sun, a moon, a star—the same God, out of the same matter. Is it so hard for you, then, to believe that God can find material bodies for glorified saints in the world to come? Have you ever stopped to think how many different kinds of bodies God has created out of the few elements of matter? As you look at what is, can you really and sincerely and intelligently conclude that God has exhausted His creative energy? Do you think He has completed His job; that He cannot form yet another type of body to fit the disembodied souls of men? Exercise your common sense as you observe the facts and fashions of nature.

The substance of the bodies celestial mentioned in verse 40 is definitely distinct from the substance of the bodies terrestrial, whether men, beasts, birds, or fish. They are both composed of matter, but there is a distinct difference between flesh and other matter. Paul emphasizes the contrast in glory between them: the contrast between the glory of creatures on earth and the glory of God's heavenly creations; and then between the heavenly creations themselves. These vary in brilliance and magnitude, and yet God who made the one made the others. It is as if Paul were saying that the same God who created the earthly body of flesh for man can also create the heavenly fleshly body for the resurrected man.

God, says Paul, has the power to create all kinds of glory in varying degrees. Should it then be impossible for Him to turn our present mortal earthly body of flesh into a heavenly immortal and glorious resurrection body of flesh?

Although I doubt there is any intended connection in Scripture between this passage and Daniel 12:2 and 3, I cannot help thinking of Daniel's words, "And many of them that sleep in the dust of the earth shall awake, some to everlasting life, and some to shame and everlasting contempt. And they that be wise shall shine as the brightness of the firmament; and they that turn many to righteousness as the stars for ever and ever." One cannot but think of the varying degrees of glory that the believers will enjoy in heaven, depending upon their fidelity to the Lord Jesus Christ while they were on earth. (See also Jer. 17:10, Matt. 16:27, I Cor. 3:8, II Cor. 5:10, II Tim. 1:16-18, and Rev. 20:12; 22:12.)

Perhaps you think it wrong even to suggest that faithful believers will be glorified in the life to come, as though rewards and honors were somehow inconsistent with our lot as creatures undeserving of anything but wrath, and saved only through the mercy of God. However, this is not what Scripture teaches with respect to the one who has become a child of God through faith in Christ. It not only speaks of rewards in heaven, but also encourages us to strive for them. Christ promises that those who are faithful in using their God-given talents for His service on earth will be elevated to positions of higher responsibility and honor in the life to come. There will be crowns, and stars in those crowns; there will be mansions, and positions involving rule and judgment for the redeemed of the Lord. There will be praise for work well done, and "an eternal weight of glory" for those who endured suffering for Christ's sake on earth (II Cor. 4:17).

However, the glory and rewards of the saints will in no wise detract from or compete with the exceeding and supreme glory of the Godhead, for there can be no comparison between them. The difference in degree is as great as that between the sunlight reflected in a drop of water and the sun itself. We shall not glory in our glory in heaven, if I may put it that way, but in the glory and majesty and power and dominion of Him who in His infinite love and generosity is pleased to reward His faithful servants so abundantly as to say, "Enter thou into the joy of thy Lord" (Matt. 25:21).

THE NECESSITY FOR THE RESURRECTION
OF THE BODY

"The glory of the celestial is one, and the glory of the terrestrial is another. There is one glory of the sun, and another glory of the moon, and another glory of the stars: for one star differeth from another star in glory" (I Cor. 15:40, 41).

We do not use words like "celestial" and "terrestrial" in ordinary conversation, so let's substitute their everyday equivalents to see what Paul is getting at in I Corinthians 15:40. Phillips translates it, "The splendor of an earthly body is quite different from the splendor of a heavenly body."

What bodies is Paul talking about here? What is he comparing? Is he speaking of angels as compared to men, or of the resurrected bodies of the redeemed as compared to the bodies we now have on earth? Since in the previous verses he has been trying to convince the Corinthian Christians that the dead shall live again in a material body, the same as, and yet different from, the one they now have, I believe it is the latter.

But surely this verse can also be taken in a broader sense, as teaching that everything else in heaven is glorious, and that this earth also holds its glories for those with eyes to see. The Lord Jesus Christ saw glory in the lilies of the field clothed by God's hand, and in the birds of the air, not one of whom could die without the pitying eye of God upon it. He enjoyed human friendships and appreciated human kindness. He ate and drank as normal men do, with enjoyment of God's blessings. He prized all that was excellent and good.

And the Apostle Paul followed his Master in his appreciation for all that was wholesome, good, beautiful, and worthy of admiration on this earth. His advice to the Philippian Christians bears this out: "Finally, brethren, whatsoever things are true, whatsoever things are honest, whatsoever things are just, whatsoever things are pure, whatsoever things are lovely, whatsoever things are of good report; if there be any virtue, and if there be any praise, think on these things" (Phil. 4:8). He remembered that though the Lord Jesus Christ suffered greatly, and experienced evil in its most excruciating form—being rejected by those for whom He had come to earth to make the supreme sacrifice of love—His earthly life was not without its glory, its blessed experiences, its deep and tender joys.

If any human being knew by personal experience how much wickedness, corruption, hardship, and suffering this life holds, it was Paul. And yet he did not pour out his denunciations of woe and doom on God's creation, nor constantly find fault with his lot. He believed that every evil that happened to him was a blessing in disguise. "All things work together for good to them that love God, to them who are the called according to his purpose" (Rom. 8:28). That was his daily motto, and not just a pious sentiment. He could sing in prison, with his feet in the stocks, and his back bleeding from the Roman lash. "I have learned," he said, "in whatsoever state I am, therewith to be content" (Phil. 4:11).

Paul regarded his body as the temple of the Holy Spirit, not to be despised but to be preserved holy and blameless for Christ's service. Those who despise the body and creation, and declare that all matter is inherently evil, despise the Creator and fall into the error of Gnosticism.

I have no patience with those who decry this world as wholly evil, while they stuff themselves with good food, wear fine clothing, and live in comfortable homes. This is mock piety, which the sincere Christian will turn away from as smacking of hypocrisy. We can see God's glory everywhere, in creation and redemption, and in His common mercies that fall upon the just and the unjust. But beautiful as creation is, wonderful as Christ's presence in the heart of the believer is, satisfying as communion with the Heavenly Father may be, and enjoyable and rewarding as His service is on earth, the glories of heaven will far surpass anything we have yet known here below.

Here creation is still under the curse that came upon it when Adam sinned, so that the elements are often hostile to man. In the heavenly kingdom, the lion will lie down with the lamb; nothing shall harm man or any other creature. Here we experience Christ's presence strongly at times, faintly at others, and sometimes not at all, depending upon the state of our faith. In heaven we shall see Him as He is, and so shall we ever be with the Lord. On earth our communion with God is often interrupted by circumstances and affected by our spiritual ups and downs. There we shall see Him face to face, and have unbroken fellowship with Him.

On earth our service for Him is accomplished often at the cost of great effort, of fatigue, and of striving against the powers of darkness. In heaven His service will be all pure delight, for we shall have entered into that "rest" which takes all striving out of our labor of love for Him. On earth we come to the end of each day conscious of how imperfectly we have fulfilled our high calling as followers of Christ; how far short we have fallen from the goal of being like Him. But in heaven there will be no more temptation, no more sin, no more backsliding, no more sorrow over the weakness of the flesh. Our glorified bodies will be impervious to such weakness as we have experienced here on earth.

Now what connection is there between the earthly glory we may know as God's children and the heavenly glory we shall know hereafter? Is it not just one more reinforcement of Paul's argument for the resurrection of the body? Man must have a body in the life to come, for if there is no resurrection—no embodied eternal life—then Jesus is still in the dust of Palestine, and there is no Gospel of hope. For the Gospel message is just this: that Christ did rise from the dead, and it is through His cross and vacant grave that we pass from earth to heaven. If we believe this, then there is no fixed gulf between this world and the next; but death is the ladder by which we pass from one to the other. Earth and heaven are as close as the human heartbeat. One moment it is functioning to keep us wholly earthbound; the next, it stops, and we are "with Christ"—"absent from the body" but "present with the Lord" II Cor. 5:8).

And finally, what we are on earth largely determines what we shall be in heaven. And even as among the stars one body differs from another in glory, I believe that among the resurrected bodies of believers there will be degrees of glorification, depending on the degree to which they were dedicated to God's glory on earth. (See "Celestial and Terrestrial," by Rev. Adam Scott, *Christian World Pulpit*, Vol. 37, pp. 152-4.)

WILL OUR INDIVIDUALITY BE PRESERVED IN OUR RESURRECTION BODIES?

"So also is the resurrection of the dead. It is sown in corruption; it is raised in incorruption: it is sown in dishonour; it is raised in glory: it is sown in weakness; it is raised in power: it is sown a natural body; it is raised a spiritual body. There is a natural body, and there is a spiritual body" (I Cor. 15:42-44).

When Christ returns to earth and our bodies are raised from the grave, in what way will the believer's body differ from his present body, and in what will it be similar? What kind of body will it be so that it can fit its new environment?

Paul has silenced the objector who says that it is impossible for the dead body to be raised, or for God to give new bodies of flesh to the disembodied spirits of men. Now he states what this new body will be like. "It is sown in corruption; it is raised in incorruption: it is sown in dishonour; it is raised in glory: it is sown in weakness; it is raised in power."

Corruption, dishonor, weakness. These are conditions of our present natural body. Paul groups them together in verse 44 when he says, "It is sown a *natural* body."

And in contrast here are the conditions of the metaphysical body, the spiritual body as he calls it: incorruption, glory, power. The contrast Paul is drawing throughout is not between a corpse (a dead body) and a living body, but between two living bodies. The corpse is corrupt, dishonored, and weak because that was its original condition as a living body. Death did not cause these conditions; it is the result of them. I die because of what I am in my body.

The expressions, "what is sown," "the bare grain," "this body of ours," refer to our present dying body while it is yet alive. Death and burial only make explicit what has been present all along—the conditions of corruption, dishonor, and weakness. Death is the final deterioration of a deteriorating state.

The word for "corpse" in Greek is *ptooma,* that is the lifeless matter placed in the ground. But that which is sown is not actually *ptooma,* or a "corpse," but *sooma* (v. 44), a "corpse" plus the "it" of verse 38. And it's that "it" that is going to be clothed with a new resurrection body, even as the unseen germ of the seed is clothed with a new plant body.

"So also is the resurrection of the dead." In the same manner as God does it in the present physical world, He can do it in man's metaphysical existence. "Just as simply" might be one of the meanings of the Greek adverb *houtoos,* here translated "so."

Look at the Genesis account of creation. Out of the formless void and darkness, God called light and life into existence simply by the Word of His mouth. Out of the dust of the ground He formed man's body, and infused it with life simply by breathing into its nostrils. How simply the Scriptures refer to the stupendous achievement of creating the infinite galaxies by saying, "He made the stars also" (Gen. 1:16). And you mean to say this God cannot call man's body back from the grave and re-infuse it with life, giving it a new and glorified substance that is flesh, yet of a different quality, and still preserving our individual identities? Of course He can, and He will.

This adverb *houtoos* connects what has preceded in verses 35-41 with that which follows in verses 42-44. If you were to look carefully at nature and the various creations of God, you would come to the conclusion that He is able to give new bodies to the disembodied souls or spirits of men. If He can do everything else, why not this?

Dr. W. W. Akers, a Rice University engineer working with surgeons to build an artificial heart, describes the human body as "the ultimate in technological perfection." If God could give man such a body originally, is it too much to assume that He can give us new and superior bodies in the life to come?

"Thus also [*houtoos kai*] is the resurrection of the dead." The word "also" in Greek is the conjunction *kai,* meaning primarily "and." In certain contexts it bears, however, the emphasis of the word "even." Even the resurrection of the dead can follow a process just as simple for God as the process of all His previous acts of creation. Don't consider this too hard for God to do. The Corinthians apparently did, but Paul is trying to show them how unwarranted this is. For God to have created what we see, He must be worthy of our faith that He is able to create our resurrection body also.

The word for "resurrection" in verse 42 is *anastasis,* which basically means "standing up." Again this must refer to the body, which has been lying down and dormant. The resurrection of "the dead ones" (*toon nekroon*) is the literal translation here. The idea is that each one will experience an individual "standing up," so to speak. This will not be on an assembly-line basis, any more than our individual coming into the world was a matter of impersonal mass production. God created an individual, and consequently one by one He brings us into this world. God did not create "humanity" as such, but men and women one at a time. So shall it be with our bodies.

The subject of the verbs that follow is "the body" *(sooma)* of verse 44. The body *is sown* in corruption; it *is raised* in incorruption. The body *is sown* in dishonor; it *is raised* in glory. The body *is sown* in weakness; it *is raised* in glory. The body *is sown* in weakness; it *is raised* in power.

This "life" or "spiritual body" will be clothed with an incorruptible material body. It will be a body of flesh, such as the Lord had when He rose from the dead. Is this contrary to the statement that "flesh and blood cannot inherit the kingdom of God" in verse 50? Not at all. Christ's resurrection body had "flesh and bones" (Luke 24:39), but they were "changed," even as ours will be changed to suit our new environment. Later we shall consider exactly what the expression "flesh and blood cannot inherit the kingdom of God" means.

LOOKING FORWARD TO THE DAY WHEN
MATTER WILL BECOME INCORRUPTIBLE

"So also is the resurrection of the dead. It is sown in corruption; it is raised in incorruption" (1 Cor. 15:42).

Did you ever see a farmer weep as he placed seed in the ground and covered it with the fresh-turned earth? Of course not, for that sort of burial causes no grief. The farmer knows that the buried seed will spring up into luxuriant vegetation in due course. Human burial is quite a different matter. It arouses far deeper emotions because of our attachment to the precious form laid in the grave. But for Christians this grief is tempered by the knowledge that those who die in the Lord are safe with Him, and that one day we will be reunited with them, not only in our spirits but in new and glorious bodies that will spring from the grave at our Lord's coming.

"So also is the resurrection of the dead," says Paul, referring again to his analogy of the seed. "It is sown in corruption; it is raised in incorruption" (I Cor. 15:42). This word "corruption" is from the same root form as that used in verse 33, where Paul told us that "evil communications *corrupt* good manners." (See also II Pet. 2:12.)

Now the Greek word for "corruption" *(phthora)* does not mean annihilation but decomposition, inevitable change. It is the opposite of *genesis,* which means coming into being. Our bodies do not come into being out of nothing, nor do they end in nothingness. They change their form, even as the sperm does in the process of becoming a human body. It is a reverse process of genesis. This change, or wearing out, or decomposition of our present bodies goes on all the time from the day we are born.

But when we are raised from the dead, our body state will have a permanence about it such as we do not know now nor can possibly imagine in our present circumstances of constant change. Observe that now we change inevitably, such change being built into the very structure of our body. But then we shall be changed once and for all.

When Paul says, "It is sown in corruption," what does the "it" refer to? In his analogy, "it" is the seed which the farmer sows in the ground. Then in verse 44 Paul spells out what the real "it" is. "It is sown a natural body," he says, referring to the physical body as we now know it.

But does Paul mean the lifeless body, or is he referring to that which is the life of the body? Is he saying that the dead body lying in the grave is that which is sown in corruption, or is he referring to something else? In Greek a lifeless body is known as *ptooma,* meaning "corpse, carcass." Eliminate life, and what remains is *ptooma,* a corpse. We are not in the habit of calling a human body a corpse before the life has left it. Unfortunately in some instances in the New Testament this word is wrongly translated as "body," as in Matthew 14:12 and Mark 15:45. This word *ptooma* never occurs in the entire 15th chapter of I Corinthians. The Apostle nowhere speaks of the resurrection of the "corpse."

I believe there is a reason for this. The body here does not stand merely for the carcass or corpse, but for the living body, for the entity, for the personality. That living "it" is the individuality surrounding each body, making it into a personality. This is analogous to the germ of the seed but yet so different from the seed that grows up into a plant.

That's what receives the new substance not contained in the decomposing materials of the seed but in the unseen yet life-preserving germ. But although there is no parallel germ remaining in the dead and decomposing corpse, yet the personality "it" of each human being after death is preserved.

That which surrounds this life element now is corruptible matter, subject to disease and pain; and finally the only thing that can be done with it is to bury it in the earth just as the farmer buries the seed. But it is a naked grain. Life goes on in a different, non-material form until such time as that personality "it" will once again be clothed with a material body identical to the one a person had before, not subject to the conditions of corruption and change. It is raised. What is raised? The "it" that makes the life of the body what it now is. The *sooma*, the living body is raised in incorruption.

The Greek word for "incorruption" here is *aphtharsia*, which means "not capable of deterioration." That which is divine is not subject to corruption. Our future resurrection body will be exempt from decay. It will be material, yet not subject to the same conditions of corruptibility and decay that everything material, even the created universe, is liable to constitutionally. All things now decay, but there will be a change in the very constitution of matter, especially of the matter with which our resurrection bodies will be constituted.

Observe how Paul phrases it. "It is sown *in* corruption; it is raised *in* incorruption: it is sown *in* dishonour; it is raised *in* glory: it is sown *in* weakness; it is raised *in* power." The Greek preposition translated "in" is *en*, which refers to the sphere in which anything exists. The present body is in a sphere of constant and unavoidable decay, dishonor, and weakness. It is the sphere of our present world. Our present bodies cannot constitute an exception to the general rule of the present state of our universe. But as there shall one day be a change of being, a change in the entire universe, to a state of perpetuity and incorruptibility, so shall there be a corresponding change in the body.

All along Paul has stressed the necessity of correspondence between the being and its environment. The seed belongs to the ground, and the plant to the open air. The fish needs the sea, and you and I need an environment that provides us with oxygen. Similarly in the new heaven and the new earth (Isa. 65:17-25; 66:22ff; Rev. 21 and 22), where there will be no decay of matter as there is now, the body must be so constituted as to be capable of living in an atmosphere of noncorruptibility. Even as our bodies now suffer and decay, so also the whole creation "travaileth in pain" (Rom. 8:21ff). The incorruptibility of our resurrection bodies will coincide with the incorruptibility of the entire universe. We shall be raised into a sphere of incorruptibility, a condition not susceptible to decay.

HOW YOU CAN HAVE VICTORY OVER THE
SINS OF THE BODY

"It is sown in dishonour; it is raised in glory: it is sown in weakness; it is raised in power" (I Cor. 15:43).

The Ancient Greeks were so enraptured by their contemplation of the smoothness and symmetry of the human body that they actually worshiped it. The heathen attributed more honor to the body that would ultimately perish than to the soul that would live on after death. The museums of the world contain many examples of Greek sculpture glorifying the human body. But while the statues are still in existence, the bodies represented by the statues have long since crumbled to dust.

The Apostle Paul told the first-century Corinthian Christians that not only were our present bodies subject to corruption, but that also inherent in their make-up were two other conditions—dishonor and weakness. By contrast, the resurrection body is possessed of honor and power. The cause of our present dishonor and weakness is corruptibility. It is an inherent condition of matter, while dishonor is a general mental reaction to such a condition. It is hard to sustain admiration for something that persists in decaying, no matter how good care we take of it. The final disposition of our present body will be six feet of earth. We do not keep decayed bodies in our living rooms. Yet we continue to build mausoleums and purchase expensive cemetery plots, as if they could preserve and give honor to the body from which the life has departed.

Like the human body, the bare grain in Paul's analogy

is also smooth and symmetrical. Yet it too must suffer corruption in the dust. The dishonor of the grain and the human body lies in this, that both must lose their present make-up if they are to be transformed into something far more admirable. There is a certain glory to the life of the body, to the personality as an entity, but not to the mere material with which it is clothed. Complete corruptibility is an inherent state of being. You cannot be 50% corruptible. But you can possess honor and strength to a relative degree. Men will apportion their honor of you according to their appreciation of the qualities you possess.

Of course, the body compels a great deal of admiration, even as the farmer cannot help admiring the smooth shiny seeds from which a beautiful field of wheat will one day emerge. If you fully understand what is in your body, how intricate, how methodical all its functions are, you cannot help but admire and honor it. You could not possibly create such a masterpiece. Scientists may make a living virus, but that's far from constructing a whole living body. But this wonderfully made body has been corrupted by your sin and mine. We have caused corruptibility to set in in the cosmos, which includes our bodies.

Incidentally, if scientists do someday manage to create life in the laboratory, will this pose any threat to our Christian faith? In the January 3, 1964, issue of *Christianity Today,* John R. Holum, an associate professor of Chemistry at Augsburg College, tells of a young Christian who asked his minister-father, "If scientists can create life in a test tube, who needs God?"

"If scientists eventually accomplish this," states Professor Holum, "technically it will be a truly great achievement. Philosophically and theologically, however, it would

-651-

create no new problems . . . .As Christians we acknowledge and worship the Lord of life, however life emerges . . . .Scientists may someday 'create life' (and speaking as a chemist, I think it would be fun to be part of that future team). But the source of that Life that is of transcending importance is our Lord Jesus Christ. That is the whole point."

Yes, man may create life, a living cell, but he cannot perpetuate it or give anyone eternal life. Originally it was man's moral attitude toward God—disobedience to His command—that brought about the physical corruptibility of the whole universe. We can incur no greater dishonor than to continue corrupting our bodies morally. However, the Gospel proclaims that when we are saved by receiving Christ as the atonement for our sins, we are delivered from our moral corruption. This spiritual redemption immediately brings a certain degree of honor to our bodies. They become the temples of the Holy Spirit (I Cor. 6:19).

Nevertheless, in spite of Christ's redemptive work, man's body still retains the corruptibility of matter brought upon him by the disobedience of the federal head of the race, Adam. This is the dishonor spoken of here by Paul. It is not dishonor willfully brought about by man now, but inherited dishonor consequent to corruptibility. Your body is therefore honorable. "Meats for the belly, and the belly for meats: but God shall destroy both it and them [that's their corruptibility]," says Paul to these same Corinthians in his First Epistle. "Now the body is not for fornication, but for the Lord; and the Lord for the body" (I Cor. 6:13). In other words, if you are a fornicator you bring added dishonor to your body.

But you can avoid further defilement, further corruption, further dishonor of your body. "And God hath both raised up the Lord, and will also raise up us by his own power. Know ye not that your bodies are the members of Christ? shall I then take the members of Christ, and make them the members of an harlot? God forbid" (I Cor. 6:14, 15). "And the very God of peace sanctify you wholly; and I pray God your whole spirit and soul and body be preserved blameless unto the coming of our Lord Jesus Christ" (I Thess. 5:23).

"It is sown in dishonor." Again the preposition *en* is used with the dative of the noun *atimia*, "dishonor," to indicate the present sphere in which our body exists and the ultimate end when life departs from it and it is placed in the ground. The whole world is in a fallen state, an atmosphere of corruption, which tends to perpetuate the further dishonor to our body and by our body. The temptations to make you sin against the body are everywhere. We live in an environment of dishonor, of corruption. But the risen Christ not only will raise our corrupt bodies, but gives them the power here and now to resist evil and to be victorious.

To a pastor's study one day came a young man from a good family. He was in the depths of despair, and confessed that he had practiced the most loathsome sins. He hated his own body, the instrument of his shame. He wanted to die, and would have put an end to his life if he could have been sure that death ended all. The pastor in recounting this incident said that he shuddered to think of what would have been the result of that interview if he had not been able, on the authority of God's Word, to call him to repentance and conversion in Christ, and to assure him of a gift of power that can give victory over all sins. One genuine experience of Christ is worth more than all the arguments of a pagan philosophy.

WILL MAN AND THE UNIVERSE EVER BE RESTORED TO THEIR ORIGINAL GLORY?

"It is sown in dishonour; it is raised in glory" (I Cor. 15:43).

When Paul tells us that the human body has been dishonored, what does he mean? The word "dishonor" in Greek is *atimia,* from the privative *a* meaning "without" and *timia,* which is a derivative of the verb *tima-oo.* The noun *timee* means a valuing by which the price is fixed. In Modern Greek it has also come to mean the price. *Timee,* "honor," is the value of anything, which determines the esteem and preciousness attributed to it.

Sometimes in a bargain basement you'll see a sign, "Soiled merchandise, greatly reduced in price." Something like that happened in the dawn of human history. God attributed great value to the human body as part of His creation. He honored it by imparting to it His own image. But man did not place an equal value on it. He reduced the price tag originally affixed to it, and, at the same time (since man was made to have dominion over the rest of creation), reduced the proper value of the whole creation in the sight of God and man.

But when the consummation of the age comes, when Christ returns and the resurrection of our bodies takes place, then God will restore the value of what He originally created. This is why the universe must be restored to its original glory, along with man.

"It is sown in dishonor," says Paul. Observe that the verb "it is sown," *speiretai,* is in the present indicative. In

Greek grammar, this is called the gnomic present, which means that it refers to all time. Although stated in the present, it is expressive of continuous action. Paul could have used the passive future here, *spareesetai,* if he had wanted to indicate that this sowing was limited to an instant act of the future. But he wants to tell us that this has been taking place from the very moment that Adam disobeyed God. The devaluation of the sanctity of the human body, and God's creation generally, is a process which began in the past, which takes place now, and which will continue till death. That's the terminus of the present body as now constituted. You will never again have a body like the one you now have, subject to the same conditions of existence. Your body personality, however, will be preserved. It will take upon it on the resurrection day a body that is incorruptible and glorious, and will live in an environment of glory.

Now what does the expression "in glory" mean? The Greek word for glory is *doxa,* from the verb *doke-oo,* meaning "to have an opinion, an estimate." *Doxa,* "glory," in Scripture always refers to a good opinion concerning anyone, and, as resulting from that, praise, honor, glory. (See Luke 14:10, Heb. 3:3, I Pet. 5:4.) It usually stands as the opposite of *atimia,* "dishonor." But both words contain the words that mean value: *timee,* or "esteem," and "opinion" (*doke-oo* in its verbal form). The glory of God, for instance, means man's true evaluation of God and consequently the worship and adoration of God. You cannot adequately worship God until you value Him for who and what He is.

Our bodies—and let's not forget that Paul in this entire 15th chapter of I Corinthians speaks primarily of the resurrection of the bodies of believers—will have a true and complete appreciation of God only when they are raised from the dead. One of the marks of sin upon man has been his loss of the ability to understand God for all that He is. Truly we know God, we see God the very moment we believe and our hearts, or our sinful natures, are purified (Matt. 5:8, John 14:19). But now we do not, we cannot really see God as He is. We see Him "through a glass, darkly; but then face to face: now I know in part; but then shall I know even as also I am known" (I Cor. 13:12).

God knows us fully, but we cannot know God fully this side of death. That full appreciation of God is yet to come. It will be realized on the glorious resurrection morning. Why should you or I fear death, then, as if it were the end of knowledge? No, it's the beginning of the full knowledge of God which we cannot realize in this world in this body of corruptibility and dishonor. "For we know in part, and we prophesy in part. But when that which is perfect is come, then that which is in part shall be done away" (I Cor. 13:9, 10).

Now why is it that the verb "is raised" (*egeiretai* in Greek) is in the present indicative gnomic, as was *speiretai*, "is sown"? Why not in the future passive, *egertheesetai*, which would localize the event of the resurrection in time and space? Why did the Apostle not say, "It shall be sown in dishonor; it shall be raised in glory"? No, he says "It is being sown in dishonor; it is being raised in glory."

The process for the believer has already begun. The true, although partial and incomplete, appreciation of God has already begun for those who have accepted Christ as God's answer to and remedy for man's fall. The corruption of man, and his wrong estimate (dishonor) of God and His dispositions toward him and His entire creation, began with the fall of man (see Gen. 1-3). The redemption of man, his salvation and his proper appreciation of God, began with Christ, and in every man begins with his acceptance of Christ. "He that hath seen me hath seen the Father," says Christ (John 14:9). The moment you as a sinner believe in Christ, you begin to see God, to have a proper although incomplete estimate and appreciation of Him. God becomes your father (John 1:12). You know that what He permits in your life is not intended to hurt you but to help you to achieve His eternal and ultimate purpose. You acquire an entirely new philosophy of life. You do not consider your present body as God's ultimate vessel of honor; that will be your resurrection body. You begin, however, to have a true and honorable estimate even of your present decaying but partially redeemed body. You do not curse God for permitting an injury to that body, but you praise Him. You can only do this if you transfer from the realm of spiritual death to the realm of spiritual life, where you will have a true sense of values, of God and His eternal plan for you.

This is the very reason why the Lord Jesus presented the result of belief in Him as part of the work of the resurrection. Read the 11th chapter of John carefully, which tells of the physical resurrection of Lazarus. Along with it you will find some pointed and relevant words of Christ concerning the beginning of spiritual life. "I am the resurrection, and the life: he that believeth in me, though he were dead, yet shall he live: and whosoever liveth and believeth in me shall never die" (John 11:25, 26). Even so our full knowledge and esteem of God will be made perfect on the resurrection day, with the resurrection of our bodies. But our partial yet redeeming knowledge of God begins here and now, and begins its perfections when our spirits go to be with Christ. It is finally completed on the resurrection day. From the moment we believe, we experience a life of constant resurrection, till the day when the change will be complete in an environment where God can be known in His fullness "in glory." And that will be when the life of each one of us will have a new body not subject to physical decay, as is our present body.

WHAT IS A SPIRITUAL BODY?

"It is sown in weakness; it is raised in power" (I Cor. 15:43).

Doctors say that the most frequent complaint they hear from their patients is "I'm always so tired!" How easily our strength gives out; how often we need to rest. Man is a weak creature when compared to the creatures of the animal kingdom or when pitted against the elemental forces of nature. Even such a soft and gentle thing as snow can stop him in his tracks.

The real strength of man lies not in his body but in his inventive soul. Because of this he can now control nature to a far greater extent than his ancestors, for instance, not because of superior physical strength, but because of his resourcefulness and the devices it has produced. But no matter how much man has compensated for his physical weakness, he often finds his body unequal to the execution of the impulses of his spirit. "The spirit is willing but the flesh is weak" is a common saying among us.

The Apostle Paul recognized this also. In the same masterful way in which he presented his first two couplets of contrast between our earthly and our resurrection body —"It is sown in corruption; it is raised in incorruption: it is sown in dishonor; it is raised in glory"—he now presents the third: "It is sown in weakness; it is raised in power." Here again the reference is to two spheres. Our bodies are now "in [the sphere of] weakness." In the resurrection they will be "in [the sphere of] strength."

The Greek word for "weakness" here is *astheneia,* which is made up of the privative *a,* meaning "without," and the noun *stheneia* or *sthenos,* meaning "strength," especially bodily strength. In Modern Greek, *astheneia* has come to mean "sickness." In New Testament times it was also used with that meaning. (See Luke 13:11, 12, John 5:5; 11:4, Gal. 4:13.)

The human body is comparatively strong when it obeys the laws of nutrition, rest, and exercise that God has instituted; it is weakened when it disobeys these laws. Our body's weakness began with Adam's disobedience and has continued ever since, reaching its culmination in death, at which time it becomes completely helpless. This weakness is the result of our inherent material corruptibility.

How joyfully then we ought to look forward to the day when we shall receive our incorruptible resurrection body. In contrast to our present inherent weakness, our body then will be characterized by strength. "It is raised in power," says Paul. The Greek word for power here is *dunamei,* not *sthenei* (which means "strength derived from our very body"), which would have been the exact opposite of *astheneia. Dunamis* is inherent power, power residing in something by virtue of its nature. This *dunamis* or "power" will be imparted by God to our resurrection body. The word *astheneia* used here of the weakness of our present body denotes the weakening of the life-power proceeding from the flesh. Our flesh now is characterized by *astheneia,* "weakness," due to our sinful nature. Our resurrection body will have a qualitatively different flesh, containing the God-given element of non-corruptibility.

We have said that the word *astheneia* basically means "sickness" even in Modern Greek. Our body now becomes sick by virtue of what it is; but our resurrection body will not get sick, because of what God will make it. It is suggestive that *dunamis* in the New Testament is also used to speak of a miracle, which indicates that it is influence proceeding from a supernatural force.

The strength of our body now is dependent upon food, exercise, and sleep. But our resurrection body will be independent of these material means of sustenance, although capable of enjoying them even as was the body of the risen Christ. It will have abilities that our present body does not. God has not revealed in detail all that we shall be able to do, but a glance at what Christ was able to do after His resurrection will give us some idea. His body broken upon the cross was a human body like ours, characterized by weakness and therefore subject to death. But His resurrection body was impervious to harm.

When Lazarus and others mentioned in the New Testament were raised from the dead, the act of death was simply canceled as though it had never been. They resumed their earthly existence just where they had left off, and in due time they died again. But with Christ, death was not simply canceled; it was allowed to have its perfect work. He did not return to the condition of mortal existence in which He had moved before, and in which you and I still move. After His resurrection, our Lord was no longer subject to the laws of the material order to which His earthly life was previously conformed. In our earthly life, our spirit is manifested through the body. In the life of the Risen Christ, the body is manifested through the spirit. No one sees Him coming, yet He "appears." He is "in the midst" of a group, and no one knows how or where He goes. Closed doors cannot keep Him out. He vanishes from sight after revealing Himself to His disciples; and finally a cloud receives Him into heaven.

What a marvelous glimpse of the potentialities of the resurrected body! Who ever thought that a human form could survive death, and in surviving change from a natural to a spiritual state of existence!

We conclude, therefore, that our resurrection body will be incorruptible, not subject to decomposition and decay, not composed of earthly particles ever changing and ultimately destined to return to the dust from which they came. Yet it will be material and at the same time indissoluble. It will be a visible body, tangible, able to feel and move. Whereas we are now inherently corruptible in body, we shall then become inherently incorruptible, and therefore glorious and able to act in opposition to the laws of our present natural order. Our body will finally become a suitable companion for our immaterial and ever-living soul.

This, as we have stated before, is a state that begins the moment we trust Christ as our Saviour and Lord. There is truth and practical reality in the words of Paul, "I can do all things through Christ which strengtheneth [*endunamounti*, a form of the same Greek word *dunamis*] me" (Phil. 4:13). In a sense, then, the life of resurrection and power begins the moment we believe; but it finds its completion with regard to the physical limitations of the body on the glorious resurrection day. Then no violence can either destroy or derange our body, no weapon can hurt us. Grosser matter, whether alive or dead, animate or inanimate, cannot affect us. Whatever the detailed make-up and capacities of our body, it is enough to know that this incorruptible and glorious body will be no clog or restraint, through its impotency, on the free soul; but able and strong, as its minister, to do its pleasure. (See Robert S. Candlish, *Life in a Risen Saviour,* pp. 178-9.)

HOW CAN A MATERIAL BODY BE SPIRITUAL?

"It is sown a natural body; it is raised a spiritual body. There is a natural body, and there is a spiritual body" *(I Cor. 15:44).*

To sum up the conditions of our present body—corruptibility, dishonor, and weakness—the Apostle Paul says that such a body is "natural." And to sum up what our resurrection body will be, with its conditions of incorruptibility, glory, and power, he calls it "a spiritual body."

The latest critical text of the Greek New Testament begins the latter part of I Corinthians 15:44 with an "if." *"If* there is a natural body, so also is there a spiritual one." No one doubts that there is a natural body. Paul argues here from that which is evident to that which is not yet evident but which has been revealed by God. If there is a body such as we know now, why shouldn't there be a body that is spiritual in the life to come? Again underlying Paul's argument is the assumption that the God who created one can create the other also.

Here is one instance where English is incapable of expressing the full meaning of the Greek words. In Greek, the word translated "natural," describing the condition of our present body, is *psuchikon,* the adjective form of the noun *psuchee,* commonly translated "soul." This is the same word from which we derive our English word "psychology." And the word translated "spiritual," *pneumatikon,* comes, of course, from the noun *pneuma,* meaning "spirit."

Does it surprise you that a word pertaining to the soul is translated "natural"? In fact, the literal translation would be "soulish." This requires some explanation. Man as we know him has two aspects of his personality or being—the material and the immaterial. The material is his body; the immaterial is spoken of in Scripture as his "soul" *(psuchee)* or "spirit" *(pneuma).*

All living creatures—birds, beasts, or fish—have a soul. Does a dog have a soul? Yes, indeed, but not in the commonly understood sense. In Greek, *psuchee,* "soul," sometimes means only life, that which animates the body or the entire person. It is the vital force that man has in common with the animals. The adjective *psuchikon,* "natural," refers to that which pulls man down to the animal level rather than raising him to the divine level. Sometimes man's entire immaterial nature is called his "soul" and sometimes his "spirit" in Scripture. These two words are used interchangeably. But living creatures other than man do not have a "spirit." This belongs to man alone. It is through his spirit that man knows God. And whenever man's immaterial nature is spoken of as soul it includes the spirit of man also.

At death, man's immaterial nature, consisting of soul and spirit, are separated from the material. The body, without that life principle which we call the soul, is a corpse, fit only for burial in the ground. In his earthly life, it is through his soul that man knows his environment; but it is through his spirit that he knows that which is above and beyond him.

In I Thessalonians 5:23 Paul speaks of man's (especially the Christian's, in this context) threefold nature thus: "And the very God of peace sanctify you wholly; and I pray God your whole spirit and soul and body be preserved blameless unto the coming of our Lord Jesus Christ." Spirit *(pneuma)* is that element in man that pulls him upward.

Soul *(psuchee)* is that element that pulls him downward to conformity with the animal kingdom. That has been our condition ever since Adam's fall. We all know the struggle that goes on between our spirit and our soul. This struggle is usually for the mastery of the body. The soul desires the body to conform to its animal instincts, and the spirit desires to pull the body away from the lower kingdom to the higher. Thus there is constant war between soul and spirit. As Dr. Guthrie once said, ' I do not affirm that the most advanced saint is altogether free from the bondage of sin, [but] the happiness of a child of God lies mainly in this: that sin, though it remains within his heart, has ceased to reign there, and that, made perfect at length in holiness, he shall enter by the dismal gate of death into the full and glorious liberty of the children of God."

The Lord Jesus was unmistakeably correct when He told us that no man can serve two masters with equal allegiance. Your body in its present state of corruption, dishonor, and weakness—being a natural body, a soulish body— will always prefer the lower master, the *psuchee* or soul, to the spirit. Its tendency is to save the animal soul. It cannot help it, since it is a natural body and therefore adapted to the purposes of the natural life. It is a body of or belonging to such a soul, congenial to it, accommodated to it, in harmony and sympathizing with it.

To your higher spirit, or soul as it is sometimes called, which is the inspiration of the Almighty giving you understanding, your present body stands far more distantly and doubtfully related. When required to serve this higher master, when he would make use of it, your body is by no means so much at home. It is not so ready to minister to it.

Of course, when you receive Christ as your Saviour

and Lord and are born again, your spirit begins to acquire the pre-eminence over your natural soul. As a Christian you experience victory over sin; but the struggle within you does not cease, even as it did not with the Apostle Paul, who confesses in the 7th chapter of his Epistle to the Romans, "I know that in me (that is, in my flesh,) dwelleth no good thing: for to will is present with me; but how to perform that which is good I find not. For the good that I would I do not: but the evil which I would not that I do. Now if I do that I would not, it is no more I that do it, but sin that dwelleth in me" (Rom. 7:18-20). Yet he did not accept this as the final verdict for the Christian, but affirmed that victory is indeed possible: "In all these things we are more than conquerors through him that loved us." Nevertheless, he recognized, as we all must, that even in our redeemed and victorious lives we carry about with us a natural body," a soulish body, that tends to pull us down.

Our complete transformation will take place only with the new resurrection body, which will be a spiritual body. There will then be no struggle between the animal and the divine in us. The body will never again serve the natural instincts that characterize us now, but will serve only the Spirit of God. There will be complete conformity to God's purposes. As there is a body that is prone to obey the lower principle now, so there will be a body, a spiritual body, that will be suited for and congenial to the higher spirit within us that is akin to deity.

NEW BODIES FOR A NEW WORLD

"There is a natural body, and there is a spiritual body" (I Cor. 15:44b).

Some people think that our resurrection bodies will be so purely spiritual that their very substance will be spirit alone. Is this a logical assumption? Let's examine Paul's use of the words "natural" and "spiritual" in reference to the body. We have seen that the word "natural" when applied to our present body means "soulish" in Greek. Now no one would contend that our present body is composed of "soul" or *psuchee*; and likewise no one should make the mistake of thinking that the "spiritual body" will be composed purely of spirit. What Paul means by these two expressions, "natural body" and "spiritual body," is that just as our present body is an organ for the soul or animal principle of life, so our resurrection body will be a proper organ for the spirit. Nor does he mean that, in the resurrection, the spirit instead of the soul will animate the body. In the resurrection we shall have a material body, a soul, and a spirit, but the body will be at the service of the spirit.

Not only will our resurrection body be so constituted that it will be the servant of the spirit rather than of the soul, but the whole new creation will provide the proper condition for this—a condition of incorruptibility, glory, and power. The condition of our present body will change, and the condition of our environment will be made new.

This helps to explain the 50th verse of the 15th chapter of I Corinthians, which we shall examine in greater detail later: "Flesh and blood cannot inherit the kingdom of

God; neither doth corruption inherit incorruption." We begin to comprehend that man, as he now is, corruptible, dishonored, weak—a frail, earthbound, perishable creature—cannot have a place in God's glorious heavenly kingdom. His human nature must first be changed so that he will be able to live in a world that is completely different from this present one—a new world in which sin, weakness, and death are unknown; where procreation of the race is no longer necessary; where there is no marriage; where the sustaining of life depends no longer on eating and drinking; and where God dwells among and in His people with all the fullness of His Spirit. (See Isa. 33:24, Matt. 22:30, I Cor. 15:28, Rev. 7:16; 21:1-4.)

To live in such a world, man need not be deprived of his body of flesh in which resides the image of God, any more than Christ needed to abandon His body of flesh. What man needs is a change in the conditions of his body and of his whole humanity; a change from corruptibility, perishability, dishonor, and all that belongs to this earthbound life, to indestructibility, immortality, glory, and all that is characteristic of a world that indeed may be called heaven on earth, and where the Spirit of God fills man's body and soul to the brim, as He does the new Adam, the life-giving Spirit. (See J. A. Schep, *The Nature of the Resurrection Body,* Eerdmans, p. 204.)

It is obvious that such a body of flesh is beyond adequate human understanding, just as is the glorious body of our Lord. The change of which Paul speaks is a divine miracle. When Paul says in Philippians 3:21, "Who shall change our vile body, that it may be fashioned like unto his glorious body," He adds emphatically that it will take place "according to the working whereby he is able even to subdue all things unto himself." Miraculous power is necessary, even as it was necessary in the formulation of our present intricate body in spite of its limitations.

For this resurrection body, as for hosts of other realities, there can be no scientific verification and understanding. There could be no scientific explanation of the material resurrection body of Christ going through walls and closed doors, and yet it was a reality. So was the verification of it as a body of flesh, by Thomas and others. To deny the possibility of a body of flesh that has all the characteristics described here, just because our scientific mind cannot conceive of such a body, amounts to thinking lightly of the power of that God to whom nothing is impossible.

In the words of H. Bavinck: "Almighty God who during this life, despite the constant flux of all the particles of our body, is able to preserve its identity from childhood to old age, possesses without doubt the power to do something similar through death."

One basic thought Paul was striving to drive home to the skeptical Corinthians—that a tremendous change must come about. This resurrection cannot be a mere repetition and continuation of the present body and life and blood; that is, man in his present condition is not able to enter the new resurrection world. Our future bodies will be spiritual, adapted to the eternal things in the midst of which our future life is to be passed.

But what is the purpose of these revelations about our future life? In the first place they teach us what is the right attitude about the body. Clement exhorted the early Christians, "Guard ye the flesh, that ye may partake of the Spirit." A life that is given over to the indulgence of the flesh cannot issue in a life in which the body will be the servant of the spirit. In some way our present body is connected with the body that is to be. Like comes from like, wheat from wheat, tares from tares: God gives to every seed its own body; the spiritual body to those who live to the Spirit. All labor now expended on the work of the Lord, all suffering patiently borne for Christ, is definitely leading up to the spiritual body.

We cannot say how our present bodies supply the germ from which the risen body is to spring; but we are sure of this, that as certainly as we commit the body of a faithful Christian to the grave, so certainly will God raise up a splendid and deathless companion for the redeemed spirit. (H. B. Swete, *The Life of the World to Come*, pp. 89-91.)

Robert Laidlaw, in his little gem of a tract, *The Reason Why*, asks: "Would it be kindness to transfer a poor ragged beggar into the glare of a beautiful ballroom? Would he not be more conscious of his rags and dirt? Would he not do his best to escape again to the darkness of the street? He would be infinitely happier there. Would it be kindness and mercy on God's part to bring a man in his sins into the holy light of Heaven if that man had rejected God's offer of the only cleansing power there is? If you and I would not wish our friends to see inside our minds now and read all the thoughts that have ever been there (and our friends' standards are perhaps not any higher than our own), what would it be like to stand before God, whose absolute holiness would reveal our sin in all its awfulness?

You cannot sow thistles and reap figs, the Bible says. You cannot live for the lusts of the flesh here, and expect to enjoy the things of the Spirit hereafter. "For he that soweth to his flesh shall of the flesh reap corruption; but he that soweth to the Spirit shall of the Spirit reap life everlasting" (Gal. 6:8).

WHAT WAS LOST THROUGH ADAM WILL
BE REGAINED THROUGH CHRIST

"And so it is written, The first man Adam was made a living soul; the last Adam was made a quickening spirit" *(I Cor. 15:45).*

One day you will be raised from the dead. You will have a new body. It will be a material body of flesh. But this flesh will not be the same kind as you now have, which subjects you to the laws of nutrition, sustenance, and reproduction. If you are a believer in Christ, you will receive an incorruptible, glorious, and powerful body. It will no longer serve the animal instinct that now tries to strangle you, but will serve your spirit, and the Spirit of your spirit, God.

This was God's original plan for you. But Adam's disobedience spoiled and changed it. This despoiled state, however, will last only until you close your eyes in death. Following that, you will exist in a bodiless state that will yet fully maintain your personality. Then, in the resurrection, the soul that animated your body, like the germ of the seed planted in the ground, will be clothed with a new body that God will create for you. It will maintain all your personality characteristics and yet will be material. God's original plan, frustrated by man, will not suffer ultimate frustration, even as righteousness will not forever be permitted to be trodden under foot.

This is what Paul has been telling the Corinthians in I Corinthians 15:35-44. Now he proceeds to bring to them the Adam-Christ parallel in verses 45-49. In this parallel he will show the Corinthians and us that God's plan as originally designed will be realized in principle. God does not work haphazardly. He follows a plan which He will execute.

Observe that verse 45 begins with exactly the same adverb as verse 42, where Paul says, "So also is the resurrection of the dead," expressing the analogy between the death and resurrection of the believer and a seed that is sown in the ground, grows up according to its kind, and yet, when it becomes a plant, is different in its make-up from the seed itself.

In verses 42-44, we have seen how Paul detailed the differences in the conditions of the resurrection body from our present bodies.

Now in verse 45 he again says *houtoos kai*, "so," or "thus," or "simply in the same manner." You have looked at the universe and found a variety of beings and degrees of glory. Isn't it logical to conclude that the same God who created these can bring about such changes in the conditions of the new resurrection body? This is simply according to His fore-ordained eternal plan, so that man may know that he cannot forever frustrate the Eternal. "And it was simply written" might be a correct paraphrase of the opening words of verse 45. The word translated "it is written" is *gegraptai* in Greek, which is in the perfect indicative passive, indicating that this plan was written in the past, but holds good in the present and will be realized in the future.

How often we humans change our minds as we find ourselves incapable of bringing to realization hopes expressed in the past. But God did not seek to provide Himself with an alibi against the possibility that He might find Himself incapable of fulfilling what He had foretold, in spite of the fact that His plan might seem fantastic and unrealistic to man. He wrote future events as "history in advance," so that looking back upon the written record we might have full confidence that what He promised He was able to perform. In giving us a written record, He invited our full confidence and trust. He was not like those modern politicians who merely deliver oral statements, and then, when these are reported in the press, say, "No, I never said that," as so many men do when found in a jam.

Man is destined to have two bodies, God's Word declares. One we know now. That's connected with the first Adam. One we shall know as a result of the resurrection of the dead. That's connected with the last Adam, Christ. The one is natural, the other spiritual.

Consider how these two different sorts of life—the natural and the spiritual—come to you. Where did they spring from? The life you now have has come down to you from the first Adam. The other, which you begin to possess from the moment you believe in Christ as your Saviour, and which finds its consummation in the resurrection, comes to you from the last Adam, Christ.

And you should mark that, even as there is an essential difference between the present body and the resurrection body, so also is there an essential difference between Adam and Christ. "The first man Adam was made *a living soul; the last Adam was made a quickening spirit.*" You, too, as a believer, are a living soul. You have been made so through Christ's resurrection, beginning in this life and to be completed when you receive your new resurrection body. In Ephesians 2:1-6 Paul tells us, "And you *hath he quickened* [the words in italics do not appear in the original Greek], who were dead in trespasses and sins; wherein in time past ye walked according to the course of this world, according to the prince of the power of the air, the spirit that now worketh in the children of disobedience....and were by nature the children of wrath, even as others. But God, who is rich in mercy, for his great love wherewith he loved us, even when we were dead in sins, hath quickened us [the same basic word used in I Cor. 15:45 to describe Christ as 'a quickening spirit'] together with Christ....and hath raised us up together, and made us sit together in heavenly places in Christ Jesus "

The statement, "The first man Adam was made a living soul," is taken in part from Genesis 2:7, the Septuagint Greek translation, which reads *Egeneto anthroopos eis psucheen zoosan,* "Man became unto a living soul." Paul adds that this was *the first man,* and that he was *Adam.* Here is the entire statement of Genesis 2:7 in the King James Version: "And the Lord God formed man of the dust of the ground, and breathed into his nostrils the breath of life; and man became a living soul." This verse gives us the second account of the creation of man. The first account is given in Genesis 1:26, "And God said, Let us make man in our image, after our likeness: and let them have dominion over the fish of the sea, and over the fowl of the air, and over the cattle, and over all the earth, and over every creeping thing that creepeth upon the earth."

The two accounts present man in two distinct and contrasting points of view: in his relation to God who made him (Gen. 1:26), and in his relation to the earth which is to be his domain. The first indicates his look and tendency upward and heavenward; the other, his bias downward and earthward. The one brings out what, in a sense, he has in common with God, in whose image and after whose likeness he is made; the other, what he has in common with the other animals that were formed, like him, from the dust of the ground. Formed out of such materials, made of the dust of the ground, man had the breath of life breathed into his nostrils by Him who formed him and made him. And so he became "a living soul."

Thus we see that man is made of matter that is animated by the soul that quickens and moves it. This life element, called *psuchee* or "soul," he holds in common with all living animals. But man has two advantages over the animal world: a spirit by which he knows God and an organism far superior to that of any animal. He has the hand with the opposed thumb that feels and holds; he has the mouth that speaks his thoughts. The instincts also of the natural man are more allied to his reasoning faculty than those of animals. Still, man's nature, as a being formed "of the dust of the ground," is substantially the same as theirs. Man shares with the animals a body animated by a soul; they are all soulish or natural bodies.

But man also bears the image and likeness of God. As Dr. J. H. Jowett says, "God called other creatures into existence by His Word, and so made them live; but man He inspired with His own breath, and so gave him a portion of His own Divine life. And corresponding to this difference of beginning was the after history. God blessed the living creatures which He had made, pronounced them very good, and bade them increase and multiply; but with man He *held communion.*" And he goes on to quote Thomas Erskine as saying: "If man is created for fellowship with God there must exist within him, notwithstanding all the ravages of sin, capacities which will recognize the light and life of eternal truth when it is brought close to him. Without such capacities revelation would in fact be impossible." (*Great Texts of the Bible,* ed. by James Hastings, Vol. 1, pp. 57-58.)

WHY SHOULD ALL MEN BE PUNISHED
FOR ADAM'S SIN?

"And so it is written, The first man Adam was made a living soul; the last Adam was made a quickening spirit" *(I Cor. 15:45).*

When God created man and set him in the Garden of Eden, he was placed on probation. Had he been faithful for a season, who knows but God would have caused a change in his living bodily frame that would have brought it into harmony with his nobler spiritual nature? God's ultimate purpose was a spiritual body for man such as all the redeemed will possess in their resurrection life. The heavenly element in man does not find itself at home when it has to dwell in a house of clay, in the "earthly house of this tabernacle" that may be "dissolved" at any time (II Cor. 5:1). There can be no incongruity in God's eternal purposes for man. The original body had to change, even as through death and resurrection our present soulish body has to change, if God's Spirit in us is to have His full and unrestricted way. Man cannot be godlike in his spirit and animal in his flesh.

Ah, if the first man Adam had not fallen! If only he had obeyed God. He could have been forever what he can only be hereafter through death and the resurrection. He could have been changed from "a living soul" to "a living spirit," and his body could have been changed from a soulish or natural body to a spiritual body. The spirit of man would then have been in command instead of his animal soul. Had Adam obeyed God, "the members of the human race would have gone on developing until they were transfigured into the presence of God; there would have been no death. Death to us has become natural, but the Bible reveals it to be abnormal. Adam refused to turn the natural into the spiritual; he took dominion over himself and thereby became the introducer of the heredity of sin into the human race, and instantly lost his control over the earth and air and sea. The entrance of sin means that the connection with God has gone and the disposition of self-realization, my right to myself, has come in its place." (Oswald Chambers, *The Psychology of Redemption,* p. 11.)

I Corinthians 15:45 begins with the words, "And so it is written." Paul found his quotation in Genesis 2:7, which tells us, "Man became a living soul." The Apostle shed some light upon this verse by adding the words "the first" and "Adam." "The first man Adam became a living soul." Although the word "man" in the Genesis passage is used in the generic sense, it has specific reference to Adam as God's first created human being. Paul adds the word "first" to indicate that Adam was the progenitor of all other men. Adam became a living soul and all others followed suit. He was the leader of an entire race. He became a sinner; therefore we are all sinners. If Adam had not sinned, it wouldn't have been necessary for Christ to come.

The quotation from Genesis refers only to Adam and not to Christ. It is Paul who adds: "the last Adam [became] a quickening [i.e., life-giving] spirit." Because there was a first Adam who sinned, there had to be a second or last Adam to undo the results of that sin. The first became the progenitor of a purely natural race, the other of a spiritual. From the one we received only a soulish or natural body; and from the other we shall receive a spiritual body.

"But, you say, was not the offence a very slight one to be followed by such a punishment? Slight? Ah! think again; it was the violation of the only express command God seems to have given him." Abraham had a truly severe test of obedience when he was told to offer up his only son as a sacrifice. The Lord Jesus Christ, the second Adam, had a truly severe test when He fasted for 40 days and then was tempted of Satan to relieve His hunger by performing a miracle to satisfy His own wants, apart from the will of God. "But Adam's test was the easiest that could have been invented, of loving and loyal obedience" to a simple command not to touch a certain tree in the garden, "and therefore the failure was the more shameful and criminal." (See James Large, *280 Titles and Symbols of Christ,* p. 409.)

The Authorized Version translates I Corinthians 15:45, "And so it is written, The first man Adam was made a living soul; the last Adam *was made* a quickening spirit." In the Greek, the second "was made" is not there, but is simply understood. The first "was made" is the Greek verb *egeneto,* exactly as we have it in John 1:14 where it speaks of the Word which "was made" (actually "became") flesh. This is a dynamic or deponent middle and really means that Adam came into being as a living soul (self). This refers to Adam coming into being as a living soul as a direct result of God's creation (Robertson, p. 811). This verb being of a middle deponent form means that God created Adam as a "soulish body," capable of becoming a sinful creature if he chose to disobey God. This Adam did, and so became a sinner of his own free agency in the probationary state in Eden.

How prone man is, however, to find excuses for his sinful actions. That's what the first Adam did when he succumbed to temptation. He attempted to throw the blame on his wife. It's the fault of the woman you gave me. Isn't that just like human nature today, blaming our short-comings on our wives or husbands, our parents, our teachers, our environment, and ultimately on God? Who is actually to blame for your sinfulness, for your natural body that seeks to gratify its animal instincts rather than God? Adam and you. And before you conclude that Adam alone is responsible for your predicament, ask yourself what you would have done in his place. Knowing yourself as you do, do you think you would have done any better?

This same verb *egeneto*, "became," must be understood as applying to the last Adam also, who is Christ. "The last Adam 'became' a quickening spirit." Christ became a life-giving spirit of His own free will and in His own power. Just as there was no coercion in the case of Adam, there was none in the case of Christ. One became a "living soul," a soulish or natural body spoken of in the previous verse, that is to say an individual whose propensities are sinful. But Christ, the last Adam, became a "quickening spirit."

What does that mean? The Greek word for "quickening" is *zoo-opoioun*, which means "life-giving." There is a difference between the words "living" (*zoosan*) in the expression "living soul" that pertains to Adam, and the word "life-giving" (*zoo-opoioun*) that pertains to Christ. Man received life from God, while Christ never received life from anyone. His life is from the beginning. "In the beginning was the Word . . . . The same was in the beginning with God . . . . In him was life" (John 1:1, 2, 4). If He had not given us life, we would never have had any. (For a full exegesis of John 1:1-18 see author's book, *Was Christ God?*, Eerdmans Publishing Co., Grand Rapids.)

HOW CHRIST GIVES US RESURRECTION
LIFE HERE AND NOW

". . . . the last Adam was made a quickening spirit" (I Cor. 15:45b).

In the course of recorded history the eternal Word, Jesus Christ, became flesh. He became, of His own volition and power, that which He was not in eternity. He took upon Himself a body, born of the Virgin Mary. He became what we are, with the exception of possessing a sinful nature (Heb. 4:15). But when Paul tells us that He became "a life-giving spirit," in I Corinthians 15:45, he does not refer to His becoming "flesh." This verse, therefore, must not refer to His incarnation but to His resurrection. It was then that His body changed from a soulish or natural body to a spiritual body. Before His resurrection, His body was subject to the laws of nature—the need for nutrition, rest, and so on. It was truly a body like ours. But after His resurrection His body was changed, as ours will be changed as a result of the resurrection, into a spiritual body.

The word "body" does not occur in verse 45 but is readily understood. When the first Adam became a living soul, he wasn't some ethereal, non-visible being, but possessed a body. Therefore "a living soul" in verse 45 and "a soulish (natural) body" in verse 44 must be equated.

Similarly the life-giving spirit of Christ in verse 45 must be equated with the spiritual body of verse 44. It is not pure spirit that is referred to, but a body that is not dominated by the soul in the sense of the natural, but by the spirit in the sense of the divine.

The last Adam, Christ, became a life-giving spirit at His resurrection and by His resurrection. In His incarnation He simply became, like all of us, a living soul. His incarnation was equivalent to Adam's creation, except that Christ was pre-existent as the Word, as bodiless Spirit. In His incarnation, Christ became what Adam was created to be prior to his fall and disobedience.

What the last Adam, Christ, had to do as the Word become flesh, as the incarnate God, was exactly what the first Adam was supposed to do and failed to do, to obey God. Christ, "being in the form of God, thought it not robbery to be equal with God: but made himself of no reputation, and took upon him the form of a servant, and was made in the likeness of men: and being found in fashion as a man, he humbled himself, and became obedient unto death, even the death of the cross" (Phil. 2:6-8).

But the last or second Adam had to do more than the first Adam was supposed to do. He also had to undo what the first Adam did, to expiate the guilt of the sin that the first Adam brought into the world, and to procure its cancellation forever by His atoning death. This was in addition to withstanding the temptation that the first Adam had failed to withstand. This is the fundamental reason why Christ was permitted to be subjected to temptation, even as the first Adam was.

In His life as the second or last Adam, Christ was a life-winner, a life-conqueror, but not yet a life-giver. In His earthly lifetime before His resurrection, He accomplished what Adam should have accomplished, obedience and victory over temptation. Then came the cross and the resurrection. The life-winner now becomes the life-giver. He did not die for Himself, for He was not a sinner. He died for the sin of the first Adam and all who belong to his sinful race. Had it not been for the sin of the first Adam, the life of Christ would have sufficed. But His death and resurrection were necessary for the sake of Adam and us, his posterity. His sacrifice was the very essence of unselfishness. He was under no obligation to die for His own sake. He did it for you and me, to free us from Adam's sin and our own.

A great many complain that Adam's sin still comes down upon the human race after all these years. They seem to think God is unjust to visit Adam's sin upon all humanity; but they forget that, the very day Adam fell, God gave us a Saviour and a way of escape; so that, instead of complaining that God is unjust, we ought to look on the other side and acknowledge what a God of grace and love we have.

Suppose you had been in Christ's place? How would you have treated your creature who disobeyed you, and the whole human race who had rebelled against you all along? You would have been tempted to remove the original rebel from the face of the earth. Christ came and lived among the rebels and then died for their redemption and salvation. Probably, since you would have had the power, you would have created another man. But God made possible the restoration of the fallen ones through the sacrifice of His Son, the Lord Jesus, the last Adam. He gave us the One who is life, to give us life—the life of the Spirit, which we had discarded in Adam. Through the disobedience of one, many were made sinners, but through the sacrifice of Another, many were made partakers of the life of the Spirit.

All that the first Adam could have gained, had he obeyed, would have been to become a living spirit instead of a living soul; to have his eyes permanently turned toward the heavenly instead of the earthly. But he could never have become a life-giving spirit, because, since there would have been no sin to atone for, there would have been no need.

The Greek word *zoo-opoioun* would literally imply that this life-giving, or in reality life-making, is not only a blessing that is in store for the far future resurrection life of our body but that it starts here and now. The verb is made up of *zoo-ee,* "life," and *poie-oo,* "to make." The participle *zoo-opoioun* is in the present tense, active voice, indicating a present and a never-ending accomplishment. The very moment you accept by faith what Christ, the last Adam, has done for you on the cross and through His resurrection, a new life is created within you.

If you could only realize the power in the resurrection of Jesus Christ. Listen to the same Paul who spoke about "the last Adam" who "became a life-giving spirit." "That I may know him, and the power of his resurrection" (Phil. 3:10). "But if the Spirit of him that raised up Jesus from the dead dwell in you, he that raised up Christ from the dead shall also quicken [the same Greek word, *zoo-opoieesei*] your mortal bodies by his Spirit that dwelleth in you" (Rom. 8:11; see also 11:15). "And you hath he quickened, who were dead in trespasses and sins . . . . and hath raised us up together, and made us sit together in heavenly places in Christ Jesus" (Eph. 2:1, 6; see also Col. 2:13). Observe that Christ has already done this. He has quickened us; He has given us His resurrection life. This is true even now in our mortal, soulish body, but after our resurrection He will make our present mortal, dishonored, weak, natural body into an incorruptible, glorious, strong spiritual body. Oh, blessed day, that begins for those who believe in Christ! The best is yet to come in the resurrection morning.

WHY THE CHRISTIAN HAS CONFLICTS

"The first man Adam was made a living soul; the last Adam was made a quickening spirit" (I Cor. 15:45).

The life of heaven begins here on earth for those who are redeemed by Christ. True, its full realization must await the second coming of our Lord, for, as Scripture tells us, "It doth not yet appear what we shall be: but we know that, when he shall appear, we shall be like him; for we shall see him as he is" (I John 3:2).

But observe the first part of the verse, "Beloved, NOW are we the sons of God." The life-making of the risen Christ can begin with you here and finally find its completion with the resurrection of your body if you die before Christ's return; or it will be changed to conform with His resurrection body and life. "It is the spirit that quickeneth," says Christ. "The flesh profiteth nothing: the words that I speak unto you, they are spirit, and they are life" John 6:63).

Is your physical frame spiritualized by the power of Christ's resurrection? Look to this last Adam, Christ, who has fulfilled the conditions of life that the first Adam failed to fulfill. He is not merely quickened; He did not just become alive Himself after He was laid in the tomb; but He became the only life-giving One. What He did for Himself, He can do for you. Remember that it is with special reference to that very body of yours of which you complain as "the body of this death" that the second Adam is a quickening spirit. Christ, the last Adam, is not like the first Adam, a mere creature, but He is a Creator, and one of the greatest proofs of this was His bodily resurrection. But this was not the last proof. He is the Life-giver now; He quickens our mortal bodies and He will in the end replace our corruptible bodies with incorruptible ones. He is the life-making Spirit. Every victory you have as a redeemed believer is due to the resurrection of Christ. But the final victory is yet to come.

The first Adam as a representative of man took away the spiritual possession of our personalities. He made us soulish, natural. Christ, the last Adam, makes us spiritual and will one day complete this work by subjugating all evil in us and around us. Then it will not be mere victory over evil but the very destruction of evil and the complete transformation of human nature into "a spiritual body," a body that is ever an obedient servant of the Spirit.

What a difference between the first and the last Adam! The first one sinned and immediately tried to find an excuse. The last Adam did not sin but became sin for us so that He could die for us and provide redemption. To find someone to blame for your sin is a human trait; but to die for the sin of another is a divine characteristic. The first Adam looked upon the tree and ate of its fruit and fell. The last Adam was nailed to the tree. The one brought a curse to us; the other lifted the curse from us.

There is some kind of finality about these two Adams as the representatives of the human race. The one who brought the curse upon us was first, and the one who took the curse away through the cross was the last. There shall be no return to the first Adam's life once Christ has taken possession. Otherwise there would be defeat for Christ, which is inconceivable for the One whom death could not hold.

Observe that later in verse 47 Christ is called "the second man." He is both the last and the second. There is no one who stood as a representative of the human race in the sight of God between Adam and Christ. All men intervening between them had Adam as a common ancestor. All men after Adam were copies of the first representative; differing indeed in detail of character and nature, but fundamentally alike, and presenting the same radical defects.

What Christian does not know this by experience? Who of us can say that his body is not natural, soulish? Every spiritual victory represents a struggle. If in the beginning of your Christian life you thought that now all your conflicts were over, you were soon undeceived. As Spurgeon says, it is as if a soldier going to the wars should expect a continual truce with the enemy; or as if a mariner going on a long sea voyage should expect nothing but fair and calm weather, without waves and storms. Even so, it is irrational for you as a Christian to expect exemptions from trial and temptation here on earth.

If you have enlisted as a soldier of the cross, don't expect a life of ease. If there is no war, there can be no victory. What we need is not freedom from conflict but greater faith in the Captain of our salvation. Our trials would not defeat us so often if we stayed our hearts and minds on Him. But do not be discouraged when you lose a battle; because Christ has won the war *for* you and will win it *in* you as you rely on His strength and look to Him to give you the victory.

Take heart from the fact that Christ introduced a new kind of man, not after the pattern of Adam, and became the head of a new family of man. He became the head of spiritual men. There shall never be a third Adam, for Christ was the last Adam; He is both second and last.

"Thus Adam and Christ divide all mankind between them, not only as the two types, but as the two authors of all human life. It is their life which is veritably in all the world by descent from them. As for the first man, we know, of course, that our creature life comes to us by hereditary transmission from him; his blood flows in our veins; his physical, mental, and moral characteristics are stamped upon every one of us. As for the second man, we know by faith that He is just as truly and as really in those who are His: 'I live,' says the apostle, 'yet not I, but Christ liveth in me'; 'we are members of His body, of His flesh, and of His bones': for this cause the Holy Ghost came down upon the believers, that we might share the spotless and victorious human life of Christ, even as we share the sinful and perishing human life of Adam by nature.

"We therefore have life from God by both of these—indirectly, through Adam, and from him polluted and mortal; directly, through Christ, and from Him pure and immortal,—both live on in us, the first man and the second man." (R. Winterbotham, *Sermons and Expositions*, p. 313.)

WHY MUST OUR BODIES CHANGE?

"Howbeit that was not first which is spiritual, but that which is natural; and afterward that which is spiritual" (I Cor. 15:46).

Despite the claims of the reincarnationists, only one Man who ever walked this earth had a former existence as a personality. Christ before His incarnation was essentially Spirit. "In the beginning was the Word, and the Word was with God, and the Word was God" (John 1:1). To understand what this means, we could paraphrase it, "Before there was any beginning, the Word had been."

This Word, this One who was Spirit, this intelligence in personality, "became flesh" (John 1:14). The immaterial always existing Spirit became a human being with a material body. Of course, He never ceased to be Spirit, for the infinite and eternal can take on finite form without losing any of the characteristics of eternity and infinity.

In I Corinthians 15:45, the Apostle Paul, speaking of Christ as the last Adam, says He "became a life-making spirit." Not "a life-giving body," mind you, for it was not Christ's material body or even His actual resurrection body that became life-giving to sinful men. How foolish then we are to deify material relics, such as a piece of the cross or the bones of saints. None of these material things can give spiritual life to man, nor can they procure his resurrection. Christ alone, in His essential deity as God-Spirit, can give life to the sinner. "He became a life-giving or life-making spirit," although of course He rose from the dead in His body. This was a spiritual body, however, not subject to the limitations of matter, having the qualities of spirit while at the same time being truly material.

But as far as the human race is concerned, Paul immediately goes on in verse 46 to declare that the natural comes before the spiritual. "Howbeit that was not first which is spiritual, but that which is natural; and afterward that which is spiritual." What does he mean?

Basically he is referring to our body and the coming resurrection. The human body as presently constituted is soulish or natural and therefore imperfect. But the resurrection body, the spiritual body, will be perfect. The perfect comes after the imperfect; the spiritual after the natural. Thus the resurrection body follows the general order of God's creation. It will be perfect.

We have said that Christ is a life-giving Spirit. But this creative Spirit made the natural body first, to be followed by a spiritual body in the life to come, although we may realize it to some extent here and now. "The decaying, the dying, the weak, the corruptible, in the proper order of events, was first. This order was necessary, and this is observed everywhere," says Albert Barnes.

This verse is actually the history of the planet and of man in miniature. We see the development of the physical world in the very first chapter of the Bible. "The formless void; the birth of light on the welter of chaos; the separation of material elements into sun and planets, sky and earth, sea and land, day and night; the birth of life, vegetable and animal; and at last man, an earthly creature, who was also a living spirit.

"Yes, the spiritual is built upon the natural, and could not come to itself as we know it without the natural, out of which it grows. Food must be there before digestion can begin; lips and tongue must come before speech and song; the canvas must be prepared before you can paint your picture; the candle must be lit before its flame can burn; the brain must be fashioned ere the mind can think; *the body of man must be prepared before the soul can realize itself within it.*" (E. Griffith-Jones, *The Unspeakable Gift*, p. 118.)

Certain fundamental elements emerge from Paul's statement that the spiritual follows the natural, that perfection follows imperfection. The first is that the natural is helpless to overcome its imperfections until the spiritual comes to help it. That's how it is with the human body in its present state. It will be sinful until the spiritual comes. It will be mortal until death and resurrection open to it the doors of immortality.

Second, the material has within itself the potential of spiritual life. "Its total story has not been told until a waiting impulse has been felt within it dimly conscious of incompleteness, until it has answered to the spiritual call and roused itself to life. The lips are not complete lips until they have spoken; the brain is not a whole brain till it has thought. So in the Bible the first Adam is full of blind reachings and desires, which the second Adam alone fulfills. The life of man here upon the earth is capable of a heavenliness which heaven alone can bring to its completeness. The whole secret of the physical has not been read until its power of becoming spiritual by service of the spirit has been discerned." (Phillips Brooks, *The Mystery of Iniquity*, p. 243.)

Man is not born a spiritual being. He is born a sinner after the first Adam—a soulish or natural man. "Behold, I was shapen in iniquity; and in sin did my mother conceive me," confesses the Psalmist (Ps. 51:5). And yet this fallen nature is illumined by self-conscious mind. That is why the natural can seek the spiritual, and why it is possible in this life—and more fully in the life to come—for the spiritual to take possession of the natural, just as the seed does of the unresisting soil. The natural man is not pure nature. Something has happened to him that has changed him from what he was intended to be. He has yielded his spirit to his soul. An anti-spiritual element is now in possession of the field; he is under the dominance of evil, of sin; he is a fallen creature.

No matter how the unbelieving world scoffs at the doctrine of original sin, the evidences of its truth are all around us. From his birth, a baby has to be taught to do what is "right." He instinctively knows how to do wrong. Left to himself, he would grow up completely selfish and amoral. You do not have to teach a baby how to throw a tantrum, how to grab what he wants, how to disobey. You have to teach him self-control, regard for the rights of others, and respect for authority. And you have no guarantee that your teachings will "take." We see on every hand manifestations of man's unregenerate sinful nature. The cry, "I want to be myself! I want to be free!" too frequently means, "I want to give free reign to the selfish and immoral impulses that have been welling up in me ever since I can remember—those impulses that have always rebelled against restraint—and which I see no need to yield to a higher power than my own." It is only the Spirit of God striving with man that awakens in him a desire for that which is spiritual.

WHAT IS THE PROPER ATTITUDE TOWARD OUR BODIES?

"Howbeit that was not first which is spiritual, but that which is natural; and afterward that which is spiritual" *(I Cor. 15:46).*

"Two mistakes have been made in the relation of the natural and the spiritual which have had disastrous effects in the world's history. There is the mistake of the carnal man, who pooh-poohs religion, and thinks it a weak and silly thing. . . . On the other hand there is the mistake of the religious man, who thinks that the only way to subdue the 'natural man' is to override and ignore him."

In the economy of God, the plant emerges from the seed; the seed first, then the plant. So shall it be with our resurrection body as a spiritual body. There must first be the natural body, then the spiritual body, because the spiritual finds its opportunity by the conquest of the natural.

Therefore we should not seek to exalt the spiritual by treating the natural with contempt. We are to treat this present life and this present body with respect. It is God who made the natural body first, and the spiritual can only be realized in the natural. It is only the natural as degraded by sin that we should denounce, not the natural as the potential servant of the spiritual. The materials of the spiritual life are all found in the natural order. It is sin that has spoiled nature, which alone is wrong, and by conquering sin the soul redeems the lower nature to its true uses and place in the universe.

What is this natural man whom the ascetic is tempted

to treat with contempt? It is the physical, the emotional, the intellectual, the volitional, the ambitious forces within us that make it possible for us to enjoy all such satisfactions as food, beauty, art, music, literature, nature, and our earthly loves and attachments. These are the forces—and these alone—through which the spiritual can express itself in this world. Unless the spiritual controls these passions, emotions, and faculties, the natural man is incomplete and has missed the highest of which he is capable. But if the natural did not exist, that which is spiritual could never fulfill itself, for it would lack any avenues for expression.

The unregenerate man often believes in giving free rein to the natural, frequently in disregard of the moral and social laws and the rights of others. He's here to have "a good time," and he regards the spiritual man as a weak and pallid individual who is afraid to indulge his appetites. As a result, he always remains half a man, "incapable of entering into any high conception of the natural life, and altogether to miss the possibilities of the spiritual life." Whether such a man ends up in the gutter or becomes a brilliant success in the eyes of the world, he is inwardly a crippled and dwarfed soul, with a dead spirit.

But the ascetic also does violence to God's intent for man when he treats the body with contempt, thinking that he is thereby becoming more spiritual. He who retreats from the world in order to avoid temptation will find that the occasions of sin are still with him. He must take his body wherever he goes; and solitude will not change his natural heritage from Adam. By denying the natural man his rightful and legitimate satisfactions, he may only be laying up trouble for himself when outraged nature rebels. This, we feel, has been the mistake of monasticism.

But they are just as mistaken who denounce even innocent pleasures as sinful. In trying to impose their harsh restrictions on society, they only cause it later to break out in extravagant excesses of vice, while they themselves become mean and embittered in spirit.

We should not go to either extreme, if we are to realize our full potential in this life. Body and soul must each be given its rightful place in this present world. "The right place for the spiritual man is to be the inspirer as well as the ruler of the natural man, and the right place for the natural man is to be the willing instrument and servant of the spiritual." Young people often think they must "give up" many things to become a Christian. But your natural instincts, talents, passions, can all be made to serve as vehicles for your new spiritual life. Once you are born again, the things which once led you into sin can now be turned to sanctified uses.

To quote Griffith-Thomas, "The sex instinct blossoms into the Christian home; the love of pleasure is clarified of grossness and lifted into an atmosphere of purity and true joy; the passion for power becomes a yearning for holy influence; selfishness rises into the pursuit of lofty personal ideals; the very passions become wings with which to rise into the regions of a true delight in God. Cleanse the heart of sin, and the whole man becomes the temple of the Holy Spirit, and 'all things are ours' in a higher and truer sense than the worldly man knows anything of "

The very reason God created the natural first is that it might exist for the spiritual. But judging by the way in which the natural man resists and rebels against the spiritual, this is not at all self-evident. "The natural man," says Paul, "receiveth not the things of the Spirit" (I Cor. 2:14).

The coming of the spiritual during our lives heralds a state of war, not of welcome. Its demands "are resisted, its authority spurned. 'For I know that in me—i.e., in my flesh—dwelleth no good thing: for to will is present with me, but to do that which is good is not.' And the reason is this: 'For we know that the law is spiritual; but I am carnal, sold under sin.' (Rom. 7:18, 14.) And so the spiritual can take possession and come to its own only by conquest." (*Ibid.,* pp. 168-9.)

"The idea is," says Albert Barnes, "that there is a tendency towards perfection, and that God observes the proper order by which that which is most glorious shall be secured. It was not His plan that all things in the beginning should be perfect; but that perfection should be the work of time, and should be secured in an appropriate order of events. The design of Paul in this verse seems to be to vindicate the statement which he had made, by showing that it was in accordance with what was everywhere observed, that the proper order should be maintained. This idea is carried through the following verses." (*I Corinthians,* p. 317.)

Thus man was made to have a bodily structure with physical vitality at first, and only for a season. To this God added a higher spiritual principle of life. But still God does not consider such a body suitable forever. Man should have one better, one more suited to his higher nature. This is only reasonable and in accordance with the general law of progress and development in all the works of God.

THE TWO SOURCES OF MAN'S ORIGIN

"The first man is of the earth, earthy: the second man is the Lord from heaven" (I Cor. 15:47).

The Apostle Paul believed and proclaimed that Christ was no mere earth creature, but the only person who had a material body yet had descended from heaven. He speaks of the two Adams, the first and the second; but one is a creature and the other the Creator. Lest there be any misunderstanding about the law of progress he spoke of in verse 46—that first comes the lower life and then the higher, first the natural and then the spiritual—he states in verse 47 that Christ had not evolved from the earthly natural Adam. "The first man is of the earth, earthy: the second man is the Lord from heaven." It is important to get the origins of these two representatives of the human race straight. Anyone who claims that Paul never taught the deity of Christ has overlooked the implications of this verse. In unequivocal terms Paul declares that Christ is not man evolved or glorified, but One descended from heaven.

John also affirms this in his Gospel (3:31), where he says, "He that cometh from above is above all: he that is of the earth is earthy, and speaketh of the earth: he that cometh from heaven is above all."

And then Christ Himself asserted it when he said, "For I came down from heaven, not to do mine own will, but the will of him that sent me" (John 6:38). Again "he said unto them, Ye are from beneath; I am from above: ye are of this world; I am not of this world" (John 8:23).

The declaration, "The first man is of the earth,

earthy," takes us back to Genesis 2:7, "And the Lord God formed man of the dust of the ground, and breathed into his nostrils the breath of life; and man became a living soul." The expression "the dust of the ground" in the Septuagint is the Greek phrase *choun apo tees gees. Choun* here means "dust," from which the word *choikos*, "earthy," is derived. It is the element—common dirt—with which the surface of our planet is covered. You might think that earth and earthy mean the same thing, but in Greek the first is *gees*, meaning "earth" as a planet, and the second is *choikos*, an adjective derived from the noun *chous*, meaning "soil, dust." In order to give a more literal translation we would have to render this clause, "The first man is of the [planet] earth, dusty or soily." In forming man, God started with the inanimate—the dust which He had already created and placed on this earth. Then God breathed life into this inanimate body and it became "a living soul."

Adam was the only man God ever created in this manner. For though Eve, too, had a special creation, Adam was the only one who had the distinction of being literally created out of the dust of the earth. He is our progenitor. All of us who followed as a result were born by means of a natural father and mother.

Also observe that in speaking of Adam's origin and Christ's, whereas "of the earth" stands in contrast to "of heaven," there is no adjective given in relation to Christ, the second Adam, to stand in contrast to *choikos*, "dusty or soily," which relates to the first Adam. What do you call the Christ who descended from heaven? Evidently Paul could find no adjective in the human language adequate to describe the second Adam. This adjective would have had to describe, not the earthly body of Christ prior to His resurrection, but after it. The contrast all along in this passage is between man's present body and the resurrection body, the one soulish and the other spiritual. Therefore, when Paul speaks of the first Adam, he presents him as the one responsible for all mankind having their present corruptible soulish bodies. When the second Adam, Christ, is presented, it is in His risen body. He became "a life-giving spirit." That was consequent to His resurrection. In His earthly life and body He was the life-giving God-man, fully human and fully divine.

Paul tells us that, as Christ rose, so shall we. It is the risen body of Christ that defies description, even as our forthcoming resurrection bodies. Man is now *choikos,* "dusty or soily." Our body is composed of material that originally came from the dust of the earth, and it will return to dust. But the body of Christ, risen from the dead, is not categorized. All that Paul gives us are a few functional adjectives, "incorruptible, glorious, strong, a spiritual body."

But these do not tell us what it will be made of. The elements of the resurrection body are completely unknown to the present order of things. That is why the exact make-up of our resurrection bodies defies description in this realm of time and space. Could anyone analyze the glorious body of the risen Christ? It offered itself for personal identification but not for analysis. It was material, yet it could move through solid walls. It could partake of food or dispense with it at will. In its release from such restrictions, it was everything our fondest imaginations could wish. What an expectation!

The resurrection body of the second Adam was not of the earth. It was a creation of heaven, even as His physical body prior to the resurrection had been, in the sense that He had a human mother but not a human father, being conceived "of the Holy Spirit" (Luke 1:35). He was unique in that He was partly of the earth and partly of heaven. But Paul is speaking only of His resurrection body when he describes it as "of heaven." He means that after He rose from the dead, He was entirely of heaven, just as we shall be in our resurrection body as believers, as the offspring of the second Adam. God will give us each a new body, without the necessity of using material substances as we know them here and now. As we are of the first Adam, "dusty," soulish, corruptible, dishonored, weak, we shall be of the second Adam, Christ, spiritual, heavenly, incorruptible, glorious, strong. Is there any element on this present earth that possesses such characteristics? No, we shall have new bodies altogether.

We have said that Christ's body in His incarnation was also of heaven, although earthy, corruptible, and weak—but never soulish. It had elements of the heavenly and elements of the earthy. But His incarnate body did not constitute the beginning of His existence. "He had been before there was any beginning . . . . He became flesh" (John 1:1a, 14a). He always was in heaven, His eternal dwelling place. He came down to earth and became what He was not before, a God-man. He came that He might occupy Adam's place and undo Adam's work. He assumed for a little while Adam's earthly status as a human body. But He did not retain it very long, for He was the Lord from heaven. His body in its corruptibility was not a fit permanent dwelling place for His Spirit, even as our present bodies are unfit for the supremacy of the Spirit. He had to assume a resurrection body, and so must we. We cannot be what we must be eternally in our temporal corruptible bodies.

Christ put on the first Adam's garment of a natural body only until He had redressed the wrong and repaired the evil of Adam's miserable fall. But when that end was accomplished, He put it off. He had to have another sort of body to wear as the Lord from heaven when, His work on earth finished, He passed into heaven again, a body, a corporeity, a living material organization, in which even the Lord from heaven, now risen and ascended to be the Lord in heaven, might feel Himself, as it were, at liberty and at home forever. (See Robert S. Candlish, *Life in a Risen Saviour*, pp. 215-16.)

CAN AN EARTHLY BODY LIVE IN HEAVEN?

"As is the earthy, such are they also that are earthy: and as is the heavenly, such are they also that are heavenly" (I Cor. 15:48).

"What are those slanted letters in the Bible for?" a youngster asked his father. He was referring to italics appearing in the King James Version. Most of us are accustomed to seeing italics used for emphasis, but this boy was puzzled as to why such unimportant words as "and" and "is" should be emphasized. The explanation, of course, is that the translators of the King James Version decided to use italics to indicate that such words did not appear in the original Greek or Hebrew, but were inserted by the translators to give the sense of a particular verse or passage.

Thus in I Corinthians 15:48, where the King James Version reads, "As *is* the earthy, such *are* they also that are earthy: and as *is* the heavenly, such *are* they also that are heavenly," we understand that the italicized verbs do not appear in the Greek. Literally this verse would read, "As the earthy [dusty] one, such also the earthy [dusty] ones; and as the heavenly one, such also the heavenly ones." Here we have two exact parallels and two opposites: earthy one—earthy ones, and heavenly one—heavenly ones.

Ours is a body of earth or dust [*choikos*], and that is where our present body will end, in the dust. *Choikos* is the identical word used in the previous verse with regard to Adam. But when it comes to the second Adam, Christ, whereas in verse 47 Paul speaks of "the second man . . . from heaven" (*eks ouranoon*), in verse 48 he uses the words *epouranios* and *epouranioi,* "heavenly one" and "heavenly ones." *Epouranios* is a compound Greek word made up of the preposition *epi,* meaning basically "on, upon," and *ouranios,* "heavenly." The expression is applied to God. He is our heavenly Father (Matt. 18:35, *Textus Receptus*).

Here the expression is used of Christ and those who are His. As He is heavenly, so are those whom He has redeemed. This does not mean that they descended from heaven. The origin was spoken of in verse 47 as being *ek gees* for Adam (from the planet earth), and as *eks ouranoon* for Christ (from heaven). Even redeemed human beings could not be said to have descended from heaven as Christ did. This would make us equal to Him. Even in our resurrection bodies we shall never be equal to Christ. He is the source of incorruptibility, glory, and strength; we become only the recipients. In Him was life (eternally); we have received it. He is from heaven, but we are from the planet earth.

Nevertheless, heaven is our destination. A fitting paraphrase might be "And as the heavenly one—the one who now dwells in heaven and is of the nature to fit such an environment—such also the heavenly ones—we who have been redeemed by Him and will acquire a resurrection body such as He did." But again let me stress that this does not mean we shall be equal to Him. We shall be with Him and like Him, but still dependent upon Him.

Epouranios, "heavenly," here, I believe, is what Christ was in His entire being before His incarnation. He was the heavenly Adam who came down to make us earthy ones heavenly. Christ brought heaven down to us. In a sense we, as Christians, are already living in heavenly places, as Paul expressed it so beautifully in Ephesians 1:3, "Blessed be the God and Father of our Lord Jesus Christ, who hath blessed us with all spiritual blessings in heavenly places in Christ." The Greek for "heavenly places" is *epouraniois,* exactly as in I Corinthians 15:48. These are not spiritual blessings that will be enjoyed in heaven, but the blessings of heaven brought to us here on earth. Becoming "heavenly" is becoming like Christ.

And this transformation begins here and now, the very moment we accept Christ. It is at that time that we become citizens of heaven. But our bodies continue to be *choikoi,* "dusty," subject to corruption. This state will completely change one day. As Christ is now in a heavenly state in His resurrection body, so shall we be. But for us to adapt to our new environment and be able to live in heaven, our present bodies must change. And this new body will be ours through the power and creativity of the second Adam.

Someone wrote me that I had no right to say that when Christians die they go to heaven, for nowhere in Scripture does it say so. True, it does not proclaim this in so many words. But in Acts 1:11 we read, "This same Jesus, which is taken up from you into heaven, shall so come in like manner as ye have seen him go into heaven." This tells us that Christ in His resurrection body is now in heaven. This is what is meant by the expression *epouranios,* revealing both His state—having a spiritual body that can travel through any substance or space without limitation— and His abode, heaven.

Paul was confident that when he died his spirit would go to be with Christ: "For I am in a strait betwixt two, having a desire to depart, and to be with Christ; which is far better" (Phil. 1:23). That is what lies in store for the believer at death. But where is Christ now? In heaven. Therefore that's where our spirits go. But the day will come when we shall be heavenly in our bodies also, at the resurrection, and shall dwell in heaven bodily as well as in spirit. Heavenly bodies are spiritual bodies and the place of their permanent abode is heaven. "Let not your heart be troubled," said Jesus, "ye believe in God, believe also in me. In my Father's house are many mansions: If it were not so, I would have told you. I go to prepare a place for you. And if I go and prepare a place for you, I will come again, and receive you unto myself; that where I am, there ye may be also" (John 14:1-3).

If you have any doubt as to the particular dwelling place of God, recall the Lord's Prayer, which begins "Our Father which art in heaven" (Matt. 6:9). Also observe that our being taken into Christ's dwelling place is connected with His coming again, which corresponds to what Paul has to say about the resurrection of our bodies in I Corinthians 15 and throughout. "Christ the firstfruits; afterward they that are Christ's at his coming" (I Cor. 15:23). See also I Thessalonians 4:13-18, but more especially verse 16, "For the Lord himself shall descend from heaven with a shout, with the voice of the archangel, and with the trump of God: and the dead in Christ shall rise first."

What a glorious end for earthy souls such as we are! Christ came down to earth from heaven. He lived on earth and died on earth. He rose with a spiritual body, and in that body ascended to heaven. From heaven He will come back to earth, at which time the dead bodies shall rise and the spirits of believers shall be united with spiritual bodies like Christ's, and with Him shall live in heaven forever. Only heaven is a fit place for a heavenly spiritual body, incorruptible, glorious, and strong. Do you have that blessed heavenly hope?

THE CERTAINTY OF THE CHRISTIAN'S RESURRECTION

"And as we have borne the image of the earthy, we shall also bear the image of the heavenly" (I Cor. 15:49).

It's one thing to speak in general terms about going to heaven; it's another to be able to affirm that you personally are going there. The Apostle Paul didn't have a "hope-so" salvation, and neither should you and I. It is the privilege of every born-again believer in Christ to be able to say with Paul, "I know whom I have believed, and am persuaded that he is able to keep that which I have committed unto him against that day" (II Tim. 1:12).

Dwight L. Moody once said, "The great trouble is that people take everything in general, and do not take it to themselves. Suppose a man should say to me, 'Moody, there was a man in Europe who died last week, and left five million dollars to a certain individual. 'Well,' I say, 'I don't doubt that; it's rather a common thing to happen,' and I don't think anything more about it. But suppose he says, 'But he left the money to you.' Then I pay attention; I say, 'To me?' 'Yes, he left it to you.' I become suddenly interested. I want to know all about it.

"So we are apt to think Christ died for sinners; He died for everybody, and for nobody in particular. But when the truth comes to me that eternal life is mine, and all the glories of heaven are mine, I begin to be interested. I say, 'Where is the chapter and verse where it says I can be saved?' If I put myself among sinners, I take the place of the sinner, then it is that salvation is mine and I am sure of

-705-

it for time and eternity."

Thus, when we come to the 49th verse of I Corinthians 15, we see that Paul can no longer continue speaking in general terms about man. He is one of them. He is a citizen of heaven. He is going to have a resurrection body. So in this verse he bursts out in an expression that is personal but at the same time inclusive of all believers: "And as we have borne the image of the earthy, we shall also bear the image of the heavenly."

The verb "have borne" is *ephoresamen* in Greek, which literally means "we dressed ourselves with, we put on." It is a form of the verb *phoroo,* which we use even today in Modern Greek; and similarly "clothing" or "dress" is *phorema.* Basically the verb *phoreoo* comes from *pheroo,* "to bear, to carry." Since it is in the aorist tense, it indicates an action that took place at a definite time in the past. What was it that we put on or dressed ourselves with at a definite time in the past? The image of the dusty one or the earthy one, the first Adam. What is this image? The Greek word is *eikona,* which does not refer to mere resemblance, in which case *homoiooma* (likeness) would have been used, but always presupposes a prototype, that which it not merely resembles but from which it is drawn. In the Greek text of the Septuagint translation of Genesis 1:26, both words are used. "And God said, Let us make man in our image [*eikona*], after our likeness [*homoiooma*]." The word *homoiooma,* however, by no means suggests that this likeness is derived. The *eikoon* is like the monarch's head inscribed on a coin, the sun's reflection in the water, a statue in stone or metal, a child in relation to his parents. This is the word used by Paul. He says we put on the "icon," the image of the earthy one, Adam. We look like him; our bodies are like his and related to his. They are dusty or earthy, soulish or natural. As he died, so shall we.

When did we acquire Adam's image? The moment that each one of us was born into this world, we acquired this tragic image, because Adam, our forefather, sinned. But even as we took upon ourselves the image of the earthy, so shall we take upon ourselves the image of the heavenly. This refers to the body that shall be ours in the resurrection. It will be Christ's gift to us, even as our present body, with all its limitations, is the curse passed on to us by Adam. The one fitted us for earth, and the other, the resurrection body, will fit us for heaven.

The King James Version uses the future tense here, *phoresoomen*, "we shall bear," but many manuscripts use the aorist subjunctive, expressive of the hortative, or the wish, *phoresomen*, "let us bear" or "let us put on" the image of the heavenly. But Paul is not dealing here with wishes and counsel but with statements of fact as to what is to be concerning the resurrection body. Therefore we must accept the future tense as the correct one in agreement with the general trend of thought of the entire passage. Paul is pointing to a definite time in the future when we shall wear the body of the heavenly, of Christ who is now in heaven, to fit us for our eternal heavenly home.

We first put on the image of the heavenly when we believe in the Lord Jesus Christ, but our bodies are still mortal. "Ye have put off the old man with his deeds; and have put on the new man, which is renewed in knowledge after the image [*eikona*] of him that created him" (Col. 3:9). The moment we receive Christ, our bodies come under His control. But the final and complete stamping of His glorious image on us is to come at the resurrection, when we shall receive a body like unto His.

In the days when any country boy could stand in front of a blacksmith's shop and watch with fascinated eyes what happened there, something analogous to the resurrection of the body occurred. The smith would put a rusty, cold, dull piece of iron into the fire, and, after awhile, take that identical piece of iron out of the fire, but now bright and glowing. Thus it will be with our bodies: they are laid down in the grave, dead, heavy, earthly; but at the general resurrection this dead, heavy, earthly body shall arise living, lightsome, glorious.

Why, then, set so much store by this earthly body, which is temporary and subject to temptation, weakness, and decay, in view of the heavenly spiritual body, incorruptible, glorious, and strong? Death is one gateway through which we pass in expectation of that new dress for heaven. Get ready for it and live in the constant anticipation of it.

WHY YOUR BODY OF FLESH AND BLOOD
WILL NOT ENTER HEAVEN

―――――◆―――――

*"Now this I say, brethren, that flesh and blood can-
not inherit the kingdom of God; neither doth corruption
inherit incorruption" (I Cor. 15:50).*

"Give me no nonsense!" Isn't that what everyone
says when seeking answers to ultimate questions of life and
death? "Tell me, do you believe there is any meaning to
life?" is the challenge the young man or woman throws out
to his peers and elders. And he begins to probe them as to
their basic philosophy. But at the first hint of phoniness,
the first unsupported assertion, he draws back in distrust—
disappointed and disgusted.

No nonsense! That's what the Apostle Paul seems to
be asserting in I Corinthians 15:50. "Now this I say, brethren." This is an expression he used in chapter 7, verse 29,
also. He uses it for emphasis. What he has said and what he
is going to say is of utmost importance. It is fundamental.
The verb *pheemi,* "say," in Greek also has the meaning of
"affirm" or "assert." Paul places his own intellectual acu-
men at stake here. It is as if he were saying, "Do you think I
am so easily fooled as to be taken in by a false idea of the
resurrection? What I have said, what I believe, has not been
lightly arrived at." Paul was a university man. He could not
be easily duped into believing what amounted to sheer fantasy. Anyone can propound a doctrine, but such declarations are usually worth only as much as the reliability of
the one who makes them. "Now this *I* say." Who? Paul, formerly a skeptic, a man whose mind has been trained to

accept no nonsense. This man declares the resurrection of the body to be no speculative doctrine but an absolute certainty.

In spite of the fact that Paul had reasoned hard and long with these Corinthian Christians, they still had doubts. He tried to straighten them out, to give them a sure reason for faith in the resurrection, but they were hard to convince. Despite that, he calls them "brethren"; he corrects them in love.

What is this declaration that he prefaces by staking his reputation on it? "That flesh and blood cannot inherit the kingdom of God; neither doth corruption inherit incorruption." Many have tried to use this verse to prove that our resurrection body cannot be material, and therefore our present bodies will not be raised. Such a deduction is based upon a wrong premise. In the first place, you cannot isolate this declaration from its context. The context declares that in heaven we shall possess a body called a "spiritual body," incorruptible, glorious, and strong. Paul cannot contradict in verse 50 all that he has tried to prove in the whole chapter. By denying that the resurrection body is material, Paul would of necessity have to deny that the risen Christ had a material body.

In bringing up this point, Paul is really answering the question of the skeptic in verse 35: "How are the dead raised up? and with what body do they come?" The skepticism of such a questioner is due to the basic misconception that this doctrine means that our body as presently constituted is the one that will live eternally after its resurrection from the dead. "If it's going to be my body, it's got to be the identical body," he says in effect. "No," says Paul, "not the way you mean it." The make-up of the new body must fit the new environment. You cannot have a new environment, the Kingdom of God, which is characterized by eternity and incorruptibility, peopled by corruptible bodies such as we now have. To understand verse 50 you must take it in conjunction with verse 51, "we shall all be changed." You've got to be changed to be suited to the world to come.

Furthermore, "flesh and blood" cannot mean the evil propensities of our moral character. Usually these would be expressed in Greek simply by the word *sarx*, "flesh," as in Romans 8:12, 13: "Therefore, brethren, we are debtors, not to the flesh, to live after the flesh. For if ye live after the flesh, ye shall die: but if ye through the Spirit do mortify the deeds of the body, ye shall live."

We find two exactly parallel statements in I Corinthians 15:50: (1) "Flesh and blood cannot inherit the kingdom of God," and (2) "Neither doth corruption inherit incorruption." This leads us to the conclusion that flesh and blood is equated with corruption, and the Kingdom of God with incorruption. This could also be expressed as "Corruption cannot inherit the kingdom of God." This is what Paul has been saying all along, that our present body—soulish, natural, corruptible, dishonored, weak—cannot possibly live in heaven. It must be changed into a spiritual body—incorruptible, glorious, strong. It is as if he were saying that fish cannot live on dry land, or that birds cannot live under the sea. The environment would be incompatible with their bodily structure and functions. Only spiritual, incorruptible bodies can live in God's eternal heavenly kingdom.

This is a law, declares Paul, and not a matter of choice. "Flesh and blood *cannot* inherit the kingdom of God." It is an absolute impossibility. *Ou dunatai* in Greek means "does not have the inherent capacity." Corruptibility and the kingdom of heaven are incongruous, incompatible. Everything here on earth—including our bodies—is corruptible because of Adam's sin.

The first statement of verse 50 is a setting forth of the universal law: "Flesh and blood cannot inherit the kingdom of God," and the second statement is an illustration of that law: "Neither doth corruption inherit incorruption." Flesh and blood is corruption. The Kingdom of God is incorruption. Therefore flesh and blood cannot inherit the Kingdom of God. The first proposition that we must examine then is: "Flesh and blood is corruption."

"Corruption" qualifies or explains or characterizes "flesh and blood" in the first clause. As we have said previously, however, corruption here must not be taken in a moral or spiritual sense. "Flesh" may be so taken (Rom. 8:12, 13), but not the expression "flesh and blood." Paul never uses the term "corruption" in I Corinthians 15 with a moral meaning.

As Robert S. Candlish says, "To say that bodies corrupted (morally) by sin or by the fall cannot enter heaven, would be simply an irrelevant truism, and would be held to be so by the parties with whom Paul is dealing. It is the admission or the assertion that flesh and blood, even in its best estate, is corruption, and cannot therefore inherit incorruption, which alone meets their view fairly, and lays the foundation for the inference or conclusion that what is composed of flesh and blood must be changed into something better. The corruption, then, here spoken of, is not an evil quality or effect superinduced on the bodily frame by sin; it is the essential property of flesh and blood as originally made." (*Life in a Risen Saviour*, pp. 222-3.)

WAS JESUS' RESURRECTION BODY BLOODLESS?

"Now this I say, brethren, that flesh and blood cannot inherit the kingdom of God" (I Cor. 15:50).

Some Bible scholars have tried to connect this verse with what the Lord Jesus said to Nicodemus in John 3:3 and 6: "Except a man be born again, he cannot see the kingdom of God . . . . That which is born of the flesh is flesh; and that which is born of the Spirit is spirit." These commentators then add, "Flesh and blood cannot inherit the kingdom of God." Yet these two portions of Scripture are not related at all. Christ was speaking to Nicodemus about man's spiritual rebirth as distinguished from his physical birth. The new birth is man's spiritual resurrection in this life. But even when a man is spiritually born again, he continues to have a corruptible body. I Corinthians 15, on the other hand, deals with the resurrection of the body and not the awakening of the soul.

The expression "flesh and blood" occurs in four other passages in the New Testament. Let's examine them to see what further light they shed on this expression.

In Matthew 16:17 we read, "And Jesus answered and said unto him, Blessed art thou, Simon Barjona: for flesh and blood hath not revealed it unto thee, but my Father which is in heaven." This was in response to Peter's great confession that Christ was the Son of the living God. "Flesh and blood" here means the natural man, as Paul so explicitly stated it in I Corinthians 2:14, "But the natural [*psuchikos*, "soulish," the same term used in I Cor. 15:44, 46] man receiveth not the things of the Spirit of God: for they are foolishness unto him: neither can he know them, because they are spiritually discerned." Flesh and blood does not mean the material substance of which the body is composed, for what reasonable person would suppose that matter could be capable of receiving a spiritual revelation? It refers rather to the whole body, both of believer and unbeliever, which for the believer is under the partial influence of the soul—the natural instincts—and for the unbeliever is under the complete domination of the soul—the fallen nature as compared to the spirit.

Again, in Galatians 1:15 and 16, we read, "But when it pleased God, who separated me from my mother's womb, and called me by his grace, to reveal his Son in me, that I might preach him among the heathen; immediately I conferred not with flesh and blood." This passage, like that of Matthew 16:17, deals with the reception of God's revelation by man, by Paul himself. Here "flesh and blood" means the natural soulish self, for surely the mere substance of the body cannot be conferred with.

And in Ephesians 6:11, 12, Paul admonishes the Ephesian Christians, "Put on the whole armour of God, that ye may be able to stand against the wiles of the devil. For we wrestle not against flesh and blood but against principalities, against powers, against the rulers of the darkness of this world, against spiritual wickedness in high places." Here again Paul refers to the soulish, natural self— not simply the particles that make up our material body, but the whole human organism as presently constituted. That is why no distinction is made between the corruptibility of the bodies of believers and the bodies of unbelievers. Both are corruptible, but as individuals the believers are redeemed, their corruptible bodies having become the dwelling place of the Holy Spirit, whereas in the unbelievers the Holy Spirit is completely absent. The believer has to fight against his soulish, natural body and against the evil outside himself.

Now let's look at Hebrews 2:14. Here the Apostle speaks of the human nature that the Lord Jesus assumed. "Forasmuch then as the children are partakers of flesh and blood, he also himself likewise took part of the same; that through death he might destroy him that had the power of death, that is, the devil." This, referring to the incarnate Christ, cannot possibly allude to moral sinfulness, because Christ was sinless. But He took upon Himself the same corruptible body—a body subject to death—as we now possess, with the exception of sin. His body died as ours will. It was subject to the same natural limitations as ours, prior to His resurrection. But after the resurrection, His body lost its corruptibility and became fit for heaven as a spiritual body. Christ was eternally a spirit. When He became flesh, He took upon Himself the form of man—body and soul. When He died, His spirit was received by the Father, as we see in Luke 23:46: "Father, into thy hands I commend my spirit: and having said thus, he gave up the ghost." But at the resurrection, His departed spirit returned, and He had a real, material body of "flesh and bones." "Behold my hands and my feet, that it is I myself: handle me and see; for a spirit hath not flesh and bones, as ye see me have" (Luke 24:39).

Immediately we ask, why flesh and blood in one instance and flesh and bones in the other? Did Christ's resurrection body consist only of flesh and bones without blood? There have been various explanations. One by B. F. Westcott (*The Gospel of the Resurrection,* p. 137) is that the expression "flesh and blood" was the common formula, which in the case of Luke 24:39 was replaced by "flesh and bones" because for the Jews the blood was the symbol and seat of corruptible life. Jesus' resurrection body had put on incorruption, and to indicate this Jesus spoke of "flesh and bones" instead of "flesh and blood." As someone suggested, the Jews expected the resurrection to start from the bones, as the imperishable element of the human body.

We are inclined to discount such an interpretation. It is true that "flesh and blood" was a common formula, but it did not denote the substance of man's body but man himself in the totality of his existence. In Luke 24:39 it is very particularly the substance of Jesus' body that is in dispute. Therefore the most natural explanation seems to be that Jesus referred to His flesh and bones because they were the most solid part of Him. They can be seen, touched, and handled, whereas the blood usually cannot.

It follows that the expression "flesh and bones" does not exclude the possibility that Jesus' resurrection body contained blood also. Flesh has blood in it. W. Milligan (*The Resurrection of Our Lord*, p. 241) remarks rightly that there is no reason why glorified flesh and bones should be possible, but not glorified blood.

Jesus' statement in Luke 24:39 that He "has" (Greek *echein*, "possesses") a body of flesh and bones is significant. It implies that such a body is an essential part of the risen Lord and excludes Westcott's accommodation theory, that the risen Lord was usually a spirit, but on occasion took on a body solely for the purpose of making Himself visible. He wanted them to be absolutely sure that His body after the resurrection was a material body. It was in this selfsame body that He ascended to heaven, and it is in this same body that He will return (Acts 1:11).

THE NECESSITY FOR PHYSICAL AND SPIRITUAL
CONSISTENCY IN THE KINGDOM OF GOD

"Now this I say, brethren, that flesh and blood cannot inherit the kingdom of God; neither doth corruption inherit incorruption" (I Cor. 15:50).

Most men would like to go to heaven when they die, if they didn't have to change in order to get there. Not only must they change spiritually but also physically. The Bible tells us that "Flesh and blood cannot inherit the kingdom of God; neither doth corruption inherit incorruption." What does this mean? That our present body (soulish and governed by its environment) is not fit for eternity, for the Kingdom of God. Why? Because it is corrupt, not in the moral sense but in the sense that it is perishable; it gets sick and weak and finally dies.

Our first proposition, then, is that flesh and blood are synonymous with corruption in this verse. And our second is that the Kingdom of God is synonymous with incorruption.

When the Apostle Paul equates the Kingdom of God with incorruption, he implies exactly the opposite of what the first proposition implies, that flesh and blood are destructible. The Kingdom of God here means the heavenly world in which believers shall live in their resurrection bodies. Scripture gives no detailed description of this heavenly state. But it does give one basic characteristic, that we shall be incorruptible in body in contrast to our present corruptibility. Now we are the sons of God in the flesh, but when Christ shall appear and we receive our changed and glorified bodies, we shall be like Him (I John 3:2).

A mortal body cannot live in an immortal world. "Flesh and blood cannot inherit the kingdom of God" because the one is corruptible and the other is not. Now observe the verb that Paul uses here, "inherit." When the lawyer in Luke 10:25 came to Jesus, he asked Him, "Master, what shall I do to inherit eternal life?" Why "inherit" rather than obtain or possess? When you inherit something, it is not because of what you have done or can do, but because of what you are in relationship to someone else. If you are a child, you inherit the result of your father's labors. You need not change to get such an inheritance. When the rich young ruler came to Jesus and asked Him the same question (Luke 18:18), he had no desire to change. He just wanted to do something extra in order to obtain eternal life, the life of God. But the life of God is not a mere additive to your present sinful life, producing a complacently accepted mixture of sin and righteousness. This change must of course take place in a man when he is saved and receives the life of God in himself, to make him fit to enter into his inheritance.

Just as oil and water do not mix, the old nature and the new cannot live in amicable compatibility. The unbeliever is sometimes quicker to recognize this than the inconsistent professor of religion. An atheist, on being asked by a professed Christian how he could live with his conscience in such a state of unbelief, retorted, "About as well as you who profess to believe in God seem to be able to live so much like the world. If I believed what you claim to, I'd think no sacrifice too great to live up to my faith."

The Kingdom of God in I Corinthians 15:50 involves a state of incorruption, the eternal glorious state of the believer. That state of incorruption is not something that is merely added without a change to our present "flesh and blood," the present make-up of our body. A change must occur in our present body in order for us to possess the eternal state of incorruption. It is exactly parallel to what happens to a man when God comes into his heart and life in and through Jesus Christ. He is changed when the Kingdom of God indwells him. He cannot remain the same spiritually corrupt individual and be said simultaneously to possess the Kingdom of God. "If any man be in Christ, he is a new creature" (II Cor. 5:17). In the same manner, "flesh and blood"—we as we are presently constituted as mortal beings —are not fit to live in the eternal state of immortality and glory. We need to be changed to fit our environment.

This declaration of the inability of our present state of being to live in the new eternal glorious environment of heaven is not a mere statement of fact, that the present body will not be able to live in a realm of incorruption, but it is a statement of principle, that it is so constituted that inherently it cannot. The Greek *ou dunatai* could be rendered "does not have the ability, the power." It is not merely that "flesh and blood *shall* not inherit the Kingdom of God" but "it is not able" to do so. Paul does not say that it cannot be changed and made fit for such an environment, but simply that it does not have the ability on its own.

In the Greek text we observe that the subject here is plural, "flesh and blood," but the verb is singular. Why a plural subject and a singular verb? Because flesh and blood stands for one thing, the present make-up of our mortal body. And no matter how much you tried, you couldn't change it. Go back to I Corinthians 15:38 and listen to

Paul's all-important declaration concerning the power that will effect this change. "But God giveth it a body as it hath pleased him." You cannot of your own power and volition change your physical make-up, but God, who created you to be what you are now, can create a body for you fitted for a new heaven and a new earth, for an eternal, glorious state.

And then Paul adds in a most natural way, "nor does corruption inherit incorruption." This is a statement of fact, not of principle like the first statement. It is not that "corruption is not capable of inheriting incorruption," but that "it does not" inherit it. Every body on earth is subject to decay. "He or she never ages" is a compliment in the realm of romance rather than of reality. All men change, all age, all move on to the disintegration of their material form.

The state of incorruption has never been added to the state of corruption. Matter as presently constituted disintegrates. But in the resurrection, our body—and all matter—will be so constituted that it will no longer disintegrate. Paul does not propound in the doctrine of the resurrection of the body something that is contrary to observable facts. He has bidden us look at the uniqueness of Christ and confess that it is inexcusable for anyone to state that there can be no resurrection of the dead. There can be, because Christ rose from the dead. But no one in an earthly body will ever escape disintegration. There has never been a corruptible body that has become incorruptible without undergoing a change in its very make-up.

WHO CAN UNVEIL THE MYSTERY OF THE FUTURE?

"Behold, I shew you a mystery; We shall not all sleep, but we shall all be changed" (I Cor. 15:51).

Have you ever wondered why nature works the way it does? What determines this constant cycle of coming and going—of birth, change, death, and final disintegration? You can learn in exhaustive detail how these laws of nature operate, but why they follow certain pre-determined patterns is beyond you.

Take your own body, for example. All of us wish we could retain the flush and vigor of youth, yet we realize that the body can never remain long in one state. Ultimately deterioration and disintegration set in. A mystery? Yes, and a most humbling one as we reflect on how little we know or can know.

As you reflect on the fact that you do not know why in the very nature of things and yourself there is disintegration and corruption, let this humility carry you one step further. Confess that no man has the right to say that there could not possibly be a state of incorruption for man and all things material, under a different set of circumstances.

After the Apostle Paul had told the doubting members of the Corinthian church that our present bodies could not possibly enter unchanged into a state of eternal incorruptibility, he paused to exclaim, "Behold, I shew you a mystery." "Look here (*idou*), I want to tell you something important," is the implication of the Greek text here. Then he goes on to speak of the transformation of our mortal bodies in time to come. Why does he call this a mystery?

The English word is a mere transliteration of the Greek noun *musteerion*. In ancient Greece a *mustees* was one who was initiated into and capable of receiving the secrets of the gods that could not be communicated to ordinary mortals. The believer in the revealed truth of God's Word is the Christian counterpart of this privileged character. He receives secrets from God that are hidden from those who have not been initiated into the life of faith. A mystery in this sense is a divine revelation. The unbeliever rejects it and therefore lacks insight into the knowledge that the believer is privileged to receive.

Under God, there is a body of truth that men can discover by their own intelligence unaided by God's special grace. But the honest person must admit that there is a greater body of truth that they cannot discover. The ultimate mystery of "Why" must forever escape the probings of man's unaided mind. Yet this great body of truth need not remain a total mystery. The big question is, who is going to reveal to you what you cannot discover for yourself? It is the One who knows more than human wisdom ever has been or ever will be able to find out. He demonstrated this by doing what no man has ever done—by dying and rising from the dead, never to die again. That is a historically demonstrated event, attested by many witnesses. If you are intellectually honest, you cannot brush aside the great weight of extraordinary evidence. Paul was convinced, and he was more intelligent and stubborn than most of us.

Look at Christ. He was no figment of the imagination. He died. He rose from the dead. And because He did, He is entitled to acceptance when He reveals to us that great body of truth that is beyond us. What He tells us about our future state of existence is still a mystery to us—it cannot be demonstrated in a test-tube—but we can accept it as true because through His resurrection Christ demonstrated that He is the truth—the whole body of truth, discoverable and revealed.

Therefore, though His revelations are mysteries to the human mind, the believer can intelligently accept them. Don't make pronouncements about the future life unless you have been initiated into the spiritual Kingdom of God. You must be born again, and only then will your eyes begin to see the truths that you could never see or accept before. The truths have been there right along, but the trouble has been with your ability to see and comprehend them. "The natural man," says Paul, "receiveth not the things of the Spirit of God: for they are foolishness unto him: neither can he know them, because they are spiritually discerned" (I Cor. 2:14).

A friend of mine went into a drugstore the other day and pointed to some toothbrushes on a rack. "Let me have a pink one," she requested. To her surprise, the clerk took down an orange one. "No, pink," she reminded him. This time he selected a lavender one. My friend began to sense the difficulty. "No, I said pink," she repeated pleasantly; and as the clerk's finger hovered uncertainly over the rack and neared the desired color, "That one," she declared emphatically. "I see you're color blind," she remarked as he wrapped her purchase. With a sheepish smile he confessed, "I always call blue 'green.' " But this same friend had a color-blind relative who doggedly insisted that certain colors were a figment of other people's imaginations, because he could not distinguish them. Do not be surprised, then, when those who do not know God cannot accept as real the spiritual truths He has revealed through His Word. The "eyes of their understanding" have never been opened.

The English translation of the first part of this 51st verse says, "Behold, I shew you a mystery." But the Greek text says, "Behold, a mystery unto you I speak." The verb "speak" here is *legoo* in Greek, which comes from the noun *logos,* meaning "intelligence, word, expression." *Logos* was John's word for the pre-incarnate Christ. The verb *legoo* means to speak intelligently in contrast to another Greek verb, *laleoo,* which does not necessarily presuppose thought behind the words expressed or the sounds made.

Thus Paul is saying to these Corinthians who were so proud of their natural knowledge, "Behold, I intelligently speak a mystery to you." It is as if he were declaring that intelligence and the acceptance and proclamation of God's revealed truth are not incongruous. "I am an intelligent man," he says in effect. "I have accepted the revelation of Christ concerning the unknowable, because He rose from the dead and has revealed Himself to me. Now I call upon you by faith to accept this unknowable truth and still not feel that you have to throw your intelligence overboard."

When the lawyer asked Christ what he should do to inherit eternal life, He said, "Thou shalt love the Lord thy God with all thy heart, and with all thy soul, and with all thy strength, and with all thy mind" (Luke 10:27). The climax was complete only when Christ added the intellect. Christians can intelligently believe what God says the future will hold for them.

YOU MAY NEVER DIE

"Behold, I shew you a mystery; We shall not all sleep, but we shall all be changed" (I Cor. 15:51).

When Jesus Christ comes back to earth the second time, there will be two classes of people here: the living and the dead. That is why the Apostle Paul says, "We shall not all sleep, but we shall all be changed." The word "sleep," of course, stands for physical death. And though Paul is primarily speaking of believers, as shown by the word "we," this also applies to the whole human race. All mankind will not have to die before Christ comes again.

What, then, will happen to the living and the dead? Paul tells us in I Thessalonians 4:16, 17: "The dead in Christ shall rise first: Then we which are alive and remain shall be caught up together with them in the clouds." Though Paul has been speaking about the believers' resurrection in this entire chapter, there is a parallel here for the unbelievers, though at a future time. Two kinds of resurrection are yet future: the resurrection of believers "unto life" and the resurrection of unbelievers "unto judgment."

That all the dead are to be resurrected is indicated by the words of Christ in John 5:28, 29: "The hour is coming, in the which all that are in the graves shall hear his voice, and shall come forth; they that have done good, unto the resurrection of life; and they that have done evil, unto the resurrection of damnation." The words "the hour is coming" should not lead us to believe that these two resurrections will be simultaneous. Scripture teaches that there is an hour for one and an hour for the other.

Paul clearly indicates that the resurrection of the believers is to follow immediately upon the coming of the Lord. "Christ the firstfruits; afterward they that are Christ's at his coming" (I Cor. 15:23). Also in I Thessalonians 4:15, 16 he says, "Even them also which sleep in Jesus will God bring with him . . . . For the Lord himself shall descend from heaven . . . . and the dead in Christ shall rise first." The Apostle John, who saw these future events in a prophetic vision on the Isle of Patmos, explains the purpose for the believers' resurrection in these words: "They lived and reigned with Christ a thousand years" (Rev. 20:4).

But when will the rest of the dead, the unbelievers, be resurrected? John tells us in the very next verse, "But the rest of the dead lived not again until the thousand years were finished." And speaking of the resurrection of believers, he emphatically states, "This is the first resurrection" (Rev. 20:5).

When the first resurrection occurs, the believers will have bodies that will be recognizable as their very own, but no longer corruptible, mortal, or limited to the capabilities of their present bodies. The bodies of both dead and living believers will be changed at the coming of the Lord. "We shall all be changed," says Paul in the last part of I Corinthians 15:51. The "all" here refers to living and dead believers, and the "change" will be primarily in the substance of their bodies.

The verb "shall be changed" in Greek is *allageesometha*, which is in the passive future, indicating that this change will be instantaneous. Secondly it will be brought about by someone other than ourselves, that is, by God. The verb *allasso* means "to make other than it is, to cause one thing to cease and another to take its place, to exchange one thing for another, to transform," that is, to take the disintegrated and the disintegrating mortal bodies and change them into incorruptible, glorious, strong bodies fitted to live in an entirely new environment. The natural body of the believer, whether dead or alive, will be changed into a spiritual body.

Paul stresses that death is not the only way in which this change can be effected. It may be that if sin had not entered the world this change could have been brought about in some other way. There have been two exceptions to the universal law that all must die before entering heaven. Enoch and Elijah did not die. But this does not mean that they were taken to heaven as they were. They can be considered an example of what is to happen to the believers who are still alive when the Lord returns. Their natural bodies must have been changed to spiritual ones when they were translated into the heavens. That is what will happen to the saints who remain alive until our Lord's coming. They will not be left behind when the dead are raised. As the dead will receive new bodies, so will the living ones exchange their natural bodies for spiritual ones. And in these changed bodies they will no longer be subject to death.

This change that will come upon all believers is not described in detail anywhere in Scripture. We are simply given the basic information that our bodies will be glorious, incorruptible, strong. Similarly, although the Lord told us about the many mansions He is preparing for us, He did not describe them. Other masters have been explicit, minute, detailed in their descriptions of the coming heaven, but the verdict even of John, Christ's most beloved disciple, is this: "It doth not yet appear what we shall be" (I John 3:2).

And here is the key to the whole silence. Before we

reach heaven "we shall all be changed." It is as if God said, "What is the use of describing the joys of heaven? They would not be joys to you as yet. You would not tell a child of the pleasure he will find in work, study, and duty as a man, because the pleasure of such pleasures is now beyond his comprehension. He will see the pleasure in these things only when he himself has been changed." (See George Matheson, *Moments on the Mount*, pp. 113-14.)

When Jesus rose from the dead, was He changed? Yes, indeed. His body may have seemed the same, for He showed Thomas His hands, and the nail-marks, and the open wound in his side. He was not a spirit, a ghost, for He had a real body. He said to His disciples once, when they were frightened as He suddenly appeared to them, "Handle me, and see; for a spirit hath not flesh and bones, as ye see me have" (Luke 24:39). And He also ate and drank with them. Yet in spite of His having the same body, He was very much changed. The risen body of Christ could do many things that ours cannot.

For instance, it is demonstrable that one solid cannot pass through another in the same way that light does through glass. But the changed body of Jesus could pass through closed doors. He could walk, and eat, and do all that His pre-resurrection body was capable of, after He rose from the dead. But He could now pass from place to place without walking when He chose, and suddenly appear here and there, vanishing away when he liked.

Suppose a visitor to our earth from another planet were to see a caterpillar on a rosebush, and that a conversation could take place between them. It might go something like this: "How ugly you are, and how gross, doing nothing but eat, eat, eat all day long," says the visitor. "True," replies the caterpillar, "but I won't always be like this. Some day I'll have beautiful wings, and fly from flower to flower." "A likely story," says the visitor with a laugh.

A few days later this stranger finds a hard brown chrysalis on the rosebush, and is surprised to hear the caterpillar's voice saying, "Now I'm worse off than before. You think I'm dead because I can neither move nor eat, but soon I shall have a resurrection and fly in the sun." "Poor deluded worm," says the visitor, "you'd better accept the fact that your life is over."

But about three weeks later the stranger, strolling in the rose garden, is surprised to hear the caterpillar's voice again. Looking for the chrysalis, he sees one beautiful wing and then another unfolding from its cracked shell. "You see," says the voice, "my resurrection has come," and spreading its wings the butterfly flits away to enjoy its wonderful new existence. (Adapted from "The Resurrection," by H. Martyn Hart, in *The Churchman's Pulpit*, Vol. 16, pp. 241-2.)

Now we are imprisoned in heavy earthbound bodies. One day, like the chrysalis, they will become inert—and the unbelieving will proclaim that that's the end of us. But the resurrection day is coming when we shall rise in newness of life, to receive bodies like Christ's, that will be as spiritual and able to move as quickly as our minds and souls are now.

THE INSTANT TRANSFORMATION OF BELIEVERS

"In a moment, in the twinkling of an eye, at the last trump: for the trumpet shall sound, and the dead shall be raised incorruptible, and we shall be changed" (I Cor. 15:52).

When the Lord comes again, how long will it take for the dead in Christ to be raised to receive their glorious bodies and for the living Christians to undergo a similar change? Paul answers this question in I Corinthians 15:52, "In a moment, in the twinkling of an eye."

The Scriptures do not tell us exactly when our Lord will return, although they do tell us of the signs that must precede His coming. And they stress the suddenness with which it will take place: "In a moment, in the twinkling of an eye." The Greek *en atomoo,* translated "in a moment," is literally "in an atom." The word "atom" is made up of the privative *a* (non) and the verb *temnoo* (to cut). An atom, therefore, to the Ancient Greeks was that which cannot be cut in two or divided. Democritus, the Greek philosopher, was the first man to use the word in this sense. Our scientific know-how has found out that the natural elements are not really composed of atoms in this sense at all, because they are being divided. But the atom at the time of the Apostle Paul represented not only an indivisible particle of matter but also, in reference to time, the smallest fraction conceivable. In an atom of time we shall be changed.

The verb "inherit" in the previous verse is in the aorist infinitive in Greek, *kleeronomeesai,* which refers not to a process involving a period of time but an instantaneous activity. There is no time at which the present body as is will be able to add to itself incorruptibility. But the change that the present body will have to undergo as an act of God will be instantaneous.

Paul does not specify the amount of time that it takes. God in His creation has set times for certain things to take place. There is a specific length of time for the seed to remain in the ground before it shoots up into a plant. There is a certain length of time that it takes for a human seed to grow into an embryo and then into a fully developed baby. There is a certain time that it takes for the earth to travel around the sun.

Where would our calculations be if it were not for God's precision timing? High tide and low tide are predictable to the minute. Sailors and fishermen depend on this information for plying their trade in safety. The movements of the sun, moon, and stars are predictable so far ahead that astronomers can tell you where they will appear in the heavens, and for how long, from any given spot on the globe, at any future date. Travelers, especially seamen, depend on this predictability for "dead reckoning." An almanac can accurately predict that Halley's comet will be visible again decades in advance. Eclipses are also predictable as to time of onset and duration. I could go on multiplying examples, but suffice it to say that God has things amazingly arranged so that we can depend upon His timing.

And, in regard to the great event of the human body changing to a state of incorruptibility, glory, and strength, Paul tells us that it will take place in the smallest conceivable amount of time—"in an atom" of time, whatever that may be. But it will not be so fast that the human eye cannot see it. This is what he implies by the expression, "in the twinkling of an eye." The Greek word for "twinkling" is *ripee*, a noun derived from the verb *riptoo*, "to throw, to cast, to hurl." It indicates rapid movement. How long does it take to cast your glance from left to right? Not long, especially if something startles you.

But I believe there could be an alternate expression, as "with the speed of lightning." This expression, and the previous one, "in an atom" translated "in a moment," are not used anywhere else in the New Testament. But why would the Apostle Paul use two expressions to convey one thought, that of speed or suddenness? Undoubtedly that is what the first expression, "in an atom," means. But the second, "in the twinkling of an eye," it seems to me has an added element—that of visibility. An eye's function is to see. The movement of the eye is fast for a purpose, to see things immediately as they happen. The great event of the resurrection of the dead and the change of living believers will not happen so fast that we cannot see it. It will be visible, just as visible as Scripture declares the descent of the Lord from heaven will be at His second coming. "For as the lightning cometh out of the east, and shineth even unto the west; so shall also the coming of the Son of man be" (Matt. 24:27; see also Luke 17:24).

Both believers and unbelievers will be able to observe this most momentous event of history, when the dead in Christ shall rise and the living believers shall be taken up from among their unbelieving friends and relatives. Heed the words of our Lord: "I tell you, in that night there shall be two men in one bed; the one shall be taken, and the other shall be left. Two women shall be grinding together; the one shall be taken, and the other left. Two men shall be in the field; the one shall be taken, and the other left "

(Luke 17:34-36). You who may have a husband, a wife, a child who is a believer, yet who persist in your unbelief, think seriously of this awesome separation. Just imagine a believing loved one taken up while you remain behind to go through untold and unprecedented suffering and trouble.

When the glorious body of the risen Christ ascended into heaven, those who stood around saw the event. Two angels spoke to them, saying, "Ye men of Galilee, why stand ye gazing up into heaven? this same Jesus, which is taken up from you into heaven, shall so come in like manner as ye have seen him go into heaven" (Acts 1:11). In other words, He will return physically and visibly. "Behold, he cometh with clouds; and every eye shall see him, and they also which pierced him: and all kindreds of the earth shall wail because of him" (Rev. 1:7). Will you be among the wailing ones or the rejoicing ones? You can make that choice here and now, depending on what you do with Jesus Christ, either receiving Him as your Saviour or rejecting Him.

What will you do with Jesus?
Neutral you cannot be.
Some day your heart will be asking,
"What will He do with me?"

GOD'S LAST CALL TO THE CHURCH

"*. . . . at the last trump: for the trumpet shall sound, and the dead shall be raised incorruptible, and we shall be changed*" (I Cor. 15:52).

The trumpet is not only a musical instrument but throughout history has been used as a medium of communication. In the armed forces trumpets are a sort of public address system by which the men are notified of the events of the day or are summoned to battle. A trumpet is blown to be heard. Thus, when the Apostle Paul says that Christ's coming will be seen all over the earth, he adds that "the last trump" shall announce it, indicating that it will also be heard. There will be a noise surrounding the event.

In the Old Testament, under God's command, trumpets were used to call the princes and the congregation together, to announce the journeying of the camps, and as an alarm or notification device. Trumpets were also blown in the days of Israel's "gladness," "set feasts," and over their sacrifices in the beginning of their months (Numbers 10:1-6, 10). I believe that it is in this sense of gladness for the Church of Jesus Christ that this last trumpet will be blown. Can there be any more joyous event than this, when the dead in Christ shall be raised incorruptible, and living believers shall be similarly changed? The Lord's trumpet will call all believers, dead and living, to join Him in possessing a glorious resurrection body. That's worth blowing a trumpet over, isn't it?

Of course, this is a symbolic representation and does not mean that the Lord will blow an actual brass trumpet.

It is what the trumpet does that is brought out here, a happy, glad summoning of all believers, dead and living, into Christ's presence.

Why does Paul call this "the last trump"? No doubt because it is the last time God's voice will be addressed to the believers in their bodiless state (for those who have died), and to the living in their mortal state. It is the last trumpet of God for the Church as it will be constituted at the coming of Christ. The word *eschatee*, "last," is not used in an absolute sense, for it is preceded by the definite article *tee*, which makes it relative in meaning. Other relative uses of this adjective are found in Luke 14:9, Matthew 5:26, and Rev. 15:1. For instance, Adam is called "the first," and Christ is designated as *ho eschatos*, "the last," which in reality means "the second." "The last day" (*hee eschatee heemera*), in John 6:39 "denotes that with which the present age, which precedes the times of the Messiah or the glorious return of Christ from heaven, will be closed." (Grimm-Thayer, *Greek English Lexicon of the New Testament*, p. 253.) Thus this is not the last trumpet in the sense that it is the last time God's voice will be heard, but it is His last voice or trumpet to the believers in the state in which they exist at His coming, at which time all believers, dead and living, will be changed.

This sounds forth a joyous note to the believers. In contrast, the seven trumpets mentioned in Revelation 8:2–11:15 will sound forth the judgments of God to unbelievers during the time of the Tribulation. We find a similar use of the trumpets in the Old Testament. In Numbers 10:9 we read of its use to arouse the hosts of Jehovah to war against their enemies. In Ezekiel 33:1-7 we read of the watchman's trumpet blown in faithful warning to deliver all who would take heed. So it is with the seven angels of Revelation. They will blow the very trumpets of heaven in judgment and protest against an earth become "as it was in the days of Noah . . . . as the days of Sodom," as Joshua and Israel blew the trumpets against Jericho. (See William R. Newell, *The Revelation,* p. 119.) These trumpets will follow the last one for the believers, but will not affect them in any way.

The fact that this great event will be instantaneous is confirmed by the verb *salpisee,* translated "shall sound." Undoubtedly the understood subject is "the trumpet," although this word does not appear in the Greek text. The verb is in the future, referring here to a one-time occurrence that is going to take place. It will blow; what God has promised will take place; the dead shall rise and the living be changed. This will be the signal that heralds the event.

This time Paul does not speak of dead believers as "those that are asleep," lest his previous statement be misunderstood. This time he says, "And the dead shall be raised incorruptible." The word *nekroi* (dead ones) is preceded by the definite article and has in this context a restrictive meaning. (See Robertson, *A Grammar of the Greek New Testament,* pp. 757-8.) A certain class of dead persons will be raised, not all of them, at this time. Only the believing dead, or, as he says in I Thessalonians 4:16, "*the dead in Christ* shall rise first."

What does Paul mean when he designates them as "dead ones"? Is he referring to their souls or their bodies? Undoubtedly the latter, because it is unmistakably of the body that he is speaking in this 15th chapter of I Corinthians. The question he is answering is that of verse 35, which says, "How are the dead raised up? and with what body do they come?" The soul does not need to be raised except in a spiritually regenerative sense. Thus we might paraphrase this statement, "And the dead bodies of the believers shall be raised incorruptible."

The verb "shall be raised" is in the future passive indicative, which here indicates three things:

1) That this will take place as a result of the power of God. This is not something that the corrupt particles of your dead body can do of their own volition, in their own strength, and at a time of their own choosing. There is an appointed time when this will happen, which has not been revealed. "But of that day and that hour knoweth no man, no, not the angels which are in heaven, neither the Son, but the Father" (Mark 13:32).

2) That it is going to be instantaneous, and not over a period of time. As Paul said, it will be "in an atom" of time, yet will be visible and audible.

3) That it is an absolute promise of God; there is no maybe about it. The dead shall be raised. This will happen whether we fully comprehend it or not, whether we fully expect it or not. Paul stresses that God not only can do this but also will do it. There are many things that God can do which He chooses not to do, but this one He both can and will do. God's promises are always absolutely trustworthy.

WILL WE BE LIKE ANGELS IN HEAVEN?

". . . . and the dead shall be raised incorruptible"
(I Cor. 15:52).

Fortunate indeed is the person who has never been so pressed beyond endurance in this life that he has not once entertained the thought of suicide. Nearly all of us have had days when we wondered if life was worth living. The young person shaken by disillusionment, the family broken up by tragedy, the older person who feels life has passed him by, are all tempted to give in to despair at one time or another.

It is then that a firm belief in the hereafter enables us to face the daily struggle with faith and a conviction that this life does not tell the full story: the ending comes hereafter, and that "Eye hath not seen, nor ear heard, neither have entered into the heart of man, the things which God hath prepared for them that love him" (I Cor. 2:9). Although this refers primarily to God's revelation of His mysteries to the believers in this life, it is equally true of the life to come, where the Lord Jesus has gone to "prepare a place" for us, that where He is we may be also (John 14:2, 3).

Look at your present body, pinch a fold of flesh between your fingers, feel the warmth of it as the blood courses through your veins. How incredible it seems in early youth that this vibrant organism shall ever cease to be, that it shall some day crumble to dust in the grave. If this were the end, how hopeless and meaningless it would all seem. And so it does to thousands who end their lives each year, believing that in death they will find annihilation and the end of all their woes.

But for those who unreservedly believe in the Lord Jesus Christ, and in His inspired Word, death and the dissolution of our present bodies only presage the sowing of a seed in the ground that will spring up into new and glorious life. Paul tells us that the dead bodies of believers will be raised "incorruptible." The Greek word is *aphthartoi*, meaning "not liable to corruption or decay."

However, some people conclude from Matthew 22:30, which is part of a reply our Lord gave to the Sadducees, that in the hereafter we will have no body and consequently will be "freed from the limitations which necessarily belong to bodily existence." Others think that in heaven we shall have "angelic bodies, made from the light and glory of God." And still others think Jesus was implying that all sexual differences will be erased in heaven, even going so far as to say that this applies to male and female souls as well as bodies. Let's examine this verse and related passages more closely to see whether they will bear out such interpretations.

First of all, to whom was Jesus speaking? We have said that they were Sadducees, which means that they did not believe in the resurrection. To trap Jesūs, they asked a hypothetical question about a woman married in succession to seven men, as to whose wife she would be in the resurrection. Our Lord replied, "In the resurrection they neither marry, nor are given in marriage, but are as the angels of God in heaven" (Matt. 22: 30).

Now in determining the meaning of Scripture we must be careful not to go beyond the intent of a given passage in relation to its context. All that this particular verse says, in relation to the discussion at hand, is that angels do not marry, and believers shall be like them in this respect in the life to come.

Luke 20:36 adds another way in which resurrected believers will be like angels, when it says of them, "Neither can they die any more: for they are equal to the angels." Again let us not go beyond the obvious intent of our Lord's words and read into them more than He said. Angels never die; and neither will resurrected believers.

Jesus rebuked the Sadducees in a manner that actually confirmed their hypocritical supposition about a coming resurrection. "Ye do err," He said, "not knowing the scriptures, nor the power of God" (Matt. 22:29). That means, "You Sadducees are in error in denying the raising of dead bodies from the graves, because this is promised in Scripture and will be accomplished by the power of God."

Look at Mark 12:25 and 26 for further confirmation of this fact. "For when they shall rise from the dead . . . . And as touching the dead, that they rise . . . ." In view of the whole discussion with the Sadducees, what else can these words mean except that our Lord taught that the dead will one day be raised in their physical bodies? Since their spirits have already ascended to God, what else could rise up?

The Pharisees had a different, yet equally erroneous, idea of the life to come. True, they believed in a physical resurrection, but, as their Rabbis stated, it was pretty much as a continuation of their present life, "only more beautiful and glorious, with greater fertility." The Lord Jesus brushed aside all such theories with the declaration that those who are raised from the dead "neither marry, nor are given in marriage; but are as the angels which are in heaven."

We conclude then that resurrected believers will be

like the angels in two respects: They will not marry and they will no longer be subject to death.

But what about I Corinthians 6:13, which says, "Meats for the belly, and the belly for meats: but God shall destroy both it and them"? Does this teach that in heaven we shall not have a physical body? Again, let us not try to make this verse say more than it actually does. It speaks of only one part of the body, one function, the digestive system. Our resurrection body will be like our Lord's, which could partake of food when He chose, but did not have to ingest food in order to live. The word translated "destroy" is *katargeesee*, which literally means "render inactive." In this verse I believe it means that our resurrected bodies will no longer be slaves to the necessity for food, as our present bodies are, which by then shall have been rendered inactive, in that the transformation to the resurrection body has taken place.

We see, then, that sexual functions, death, and the digestive necessities of the human body will cease in the life to come. God, who made us what we are, can make us what He has promised that we shall be.

(See J. A. Schep, *The Nature of the Resurrection Body*, Eerdmans, pp. 210-13.)

GOD'S TIME CLOCK AND OURS

"... and the dead shall be raised incorruptible, and we shall be changed" (I Cor. 15:52).

In our previous studies we have seen that, when Christ comes to earth again, and the dead in Christ are raised with a physical and immortal body, the living believers will have their bodies similarly changed. That is why Paul ends verse 52 with the words, "and we shall be changed." By the expression "and we" he means "we who are alive at the time."

But why is it that Paul speaks of the dead in the third person, while he speaks of the living in the first person plural, "we"? Was he under the impression that the coming of Christ was going to take place during his lifetime? If he believed and taught that, then his declarations in Scripture must lack divine inspiration and infallibility. If Paul was wrong in one thing, he could be wrong in others. How can we trust his doctrinal statements?

I believe critics have made too much of this. There is no place in Paul's writings that clearly and categorically states that he expected to be alive at the coming of the Lord. Paul was alive at the time he was writing, and it was only natural that he should speak of himself in that frame of reference, instead of placing himself among the dead. How can I speak of the dead and say "we" while I am still alive? But in projecting to the future, Paul includes himself among the living ones, since he is alive. "This is what will happen to all of us who will be alive." Paul did not want to divorce himself from this great event in which he looked forward to participating. Had he spoken of both groups, the dead and the living, then the critics would probably have hurled a more serious accusation at him, that he was uncertain as to his own fate, whether dead or alive. He knew, he was absolutely sure, that he was going to be changed, whether dead or alive, for he says in I Corinthians 15:51, "we shall all be changed." How could he leave himself out and say "they shall all be changed," as though he himself were in neither group? Hence the perfectly natural "we shall be changed," since he was a living person at the time of writing, and was speaking about what was going to happen to living believers at the time of the coming of the Lord for His saints, dead and alive.

Neither Paul nor any other inspired writer of Scripture has informed us, or even could inform us, of how remote or near this event was going to be. Only God in heaven knew that; and He had revealed it to no one. But since it was going to be such a glorious experience for the believers, they lived in full and hopeful expectation of it. When you desire something that is going to take place in the future, the telescope of hope can make it seem very close.

Peter, in urging men to repent, in Acts 3:19, 20, says "Repent ye therefore, and be converted, that your sins may be blotted out, when the times of refreshing shall come from the presence of the Lord; and he shall send Jesus Christ, which before was preached unto you." For the believer, whether Paul in his day or me in mine, the coming of the Lord and the resurrection have always been the greatest incentive to labor and suffer for the Lord. How often, in urging people to repent, we tell them to do so in view of the fact that if they don't they shall one day meet Christ as their Judge—and yet that event will not take place until long after the believers are taken from the earth. Present stimulation often results from the knowledge and expectation of future events, in spite of the fact that the exact time of their occurrence may be unknown. An everyday illustration of this is that men will take out the maximum amount of life insurance they can afford to protect their loved ones, knowing that their death is certain and could occur at any time, although no one has any certain knowledge of the exact date.

Thus it was perfectly natural for Paul, in looking forward to this instantaneous and practically simultaneous resurrection of the dead believers in Christ and the change of the living believers, to say, "we shall be changed." This was no demonstration of ignorance, but knowledgeable hope.

The early Church believed that the Lord would return unexpectedly, visibly, gloriously. "This attitude of waiting for the return of Christ was characteristic of the whole Apostolic Church and was encouraged by Christ and His Apostles," says W. J. Guest. "And the book of Revelation is full of the subject, beginning with 'Behold he cometh with clouds,' and ending with the words of the Lord Jesus—His last message to His Church—'Surely I come quickly'; and the Church's response, 'Amen. Even so, come, Lord Jesus.' " (Rev. 1:7; 22:20.) Guest goes on to tell us that there are about 318 passages in the New Testament that prove the early Church looked for "the speedy return of her Lord from heaven."

But when, at the end of two centuries of persecution, He still did not return, the Church allowed herself to be seduced by the Roman Empire into an alliance with the world, and gave up her earlier ardent expectation of a heavenly kingdom.

From that time on, the doctrine of the second coming

underwent various modifications and alterations. Some think that Origen, who died in A.D. 354, held that the passages describing the millennial reign of Christ were allegorical descriptions of the delights of the saints in the world to come. Augustine a century or more later taught that the Church was even then in the millennium. This view prevailed for a thousand years, during which the Church became more and more worldly. But at the end of that time, people began to doubt that this was indeed the millennium, and the thought of the return of Christ again began to permeate the life of the Church.

Another theory, which sprang up in the 17th century, is still quite popular today, and that is post-millennialism, which holds that the world will grow better and better until everyone is converted to Christ, and that this will usher in a thousand years of peace, at which time Christ will return. If this doesn't do violence to the Biblical emphasis on the imminence of His return, setting it so far off in the future that it becomes almost meaningless as something to look forward to, I can't imagine what would. Out of this proceeded another unscriptural notion, that Christ comes to us when we die, and that this experience is the second coming.

As we examine God's Word carefully, we see that the Lord's return is the blessed hope of the Church; that it could come at any time; and that we are to keep ourselves in readiness to meet Him. True, God's time-clock and ours may not be synchronous, for "one day is with the Lord as a thousand years, and a thousand years as one day" (II Peter 3:8); but there is nothing in Scripture to preclude His coming at any moment. "Watch therefore: for ye know not what hour your Lord doth come" (Matt. 24:42).

(See *Unveiled Mysteries,* by W. J. Guest, pp. 95-99.)

IS THE SOUL OF MAN IMMORTAL?

"For this corruptible must put on incorruption, and this mortal must put on immortality" (I Cor. 15:53).

Do you believe in the immortality of the soul? Men commonly use the word "immortality" to denote that which does not die but has everlasting existence. But the Bible teaches that "the soul that sinneth it shall die," yet goes on to say that the souls of the wicked are in everlasting conscious torment (Luke 16:24, Rev. 14:9-11). How can we reconcile these two statements? In order to clarify our thinking, it seems obvious that we must determine what the Bible means by its use of the word "immortality."

Let's go back a bit to I Corinthians 15:50, where Paul states that corruption does not inherit incorruption, and then note what he says in verse 53, that corruption must put on incorruption, mortality must put on immortality. Not wishing to speak in generalities, he points to his own mortal body and says, "For *this* corruptible must put on incorruption, and *this* mortal must put on immortality." It seems clear that he is saying here that our future permanent post-resurrection personalities will be clothed in a material body possessed of incorruptibility and immortality.

That is what the Greek verb *endusasthai*, "put on," indicates: that our body in its present form lacks incorruptibility and immortality, which our future post-resurrection body will possess. The verb *enduoo*, "put on," is used even in Modern Greek. It comes from the preposition *en*, meaning "in," and the verb *duoo*, "to plunge, to go down." *Enduoo*, therefore, means "to hide, put, envelope someone in clothes, to cover him with garments." *Enduma,* a derivative of this verb, means "garment, clothing" even today. The verb in this verse is an infinitive, grammatically speaking, in the aorist tense, but which, being an infinitive, must have its temporal bearing generally determined by the context, which is here future and refers to something that our present corruptible and mortal body will put on suddenly, at an instant of time, to fit it for its eternal heavenly environment. Though extremely quick, this change will be visible. Although *endusasthai* (put on) is in the middle voice, it has a passive sense, indicating that our present body will not put on incorruptibility and immortality of its own volition and power, but that this new garment will be God-given. (See Gerhard Kittel, *Theological Dictionary of the New Testament,* Vol. II, p. 320.)

There is only One who can clothe matter, including our material body, with these two qualities of incorruptibility and immortality, and that is God. He alone possesses these qualities and therefore He alone can dispense them. God never acquired incorruptibility and immortality; they are part and parcel of His eternal self-existence. But you and I do not possess such existence at present. Our bodies do decay and ultimately die. Our resurrection body, however, will be entirely different in this respect.

Nowhere in Scripture do we find the term commonly used by men, "immortality of the soul." The Scriptures do teach that the soul of man continues to exist after death, but this is a different matter, as I shall presently demonstrate. (In this connection, see Luke 16:19ff, 20:36, John 6:50; 8:51; 11:26, Rom. 2:7, II Cor. 5:1, I Thess. 4:17, II Tim. 1:10. In these verses eternal misery for unbelievers and eternal bliss for believers are also taught, as well as the resurrection of the body. These teachings take the soul's continued existence simply for granted. Its continued existence after death is never taught in isolation from other truths in Scripture.)

We have said that the Bible teaches that the soul can die, but by this it does not mean that it ceases to exist after the death of the body, because this would contradict the testimony of other portions of Scripture. How, for instance, could we reconcile the Lord's account of Lazarus and the rich man surviving their physical death, in Luke 16? How could Paul say that as soon as he departed from this earth he would be with Christ? (Phil. 1:23.)

Death basically speaks of separation. Physical death means separation of man's non-material nature from his material body. Therefore, when Scripture refers to the death of the soul or spirit of man, it must refer to separation also. But from what? From the Spirit of God. Spiritually speaking, then, man's soul is not immortal. It can die, it can be separated from the Eternal Spirit. But this does not mean the end of its existence. Here are some Bible verses that refer to death in this sense: Ezekiel 18:4, "The soul that sinneth, it shall die." Romans 6:23, "The wages of sin is death; but the gift of God is eternal life through Jesus Christ our Lord." Ephesians 2:1, "And you hath he quickened [made alive], who were dead in trespasses and sins."

Thus we can say that the soul or spirit of man, being mortal, capable of being separated from God, died as a result of Adam's sin. But, to those who repent and by faith receive Christ, He gives life, eternal life, the life of God which sinful man had lost. This means that, once man's spirit through faith is rejoined with God's Spirit, it will never be separated again. He who believes in Christ shall never die

(John 11:26). The mortality or immortality of the soul has nothing to do with its existence here or its continued existence hereafter. If your soul is separated from Christ here, it will be separated from Him forever. If it is united to Christ here, it will be with Him forever. The soul that believes does not receive immortality but eternal life, the life of God within, now and forever. Immortality, therefore, when applied to the soul of man in extra-Biblical language, actually is not merely the continued existence of the soul but the joining of the soul to God.

The word immortality in Scripture applies only to the body of man and not to his soul. This word occurs only in I Corinthians 15:53, 54, and in I Timothy 6:16. It is the Greek word for "deathlessness," *athanasia*. (In Romans 2:7 and II Timothy 1:10, where the Authorized Version has "immortality," it is actually another Greek word that is used in the original, *aphtharsia*, meaning "incorruption.")

We know that I Corinthians 15 deals with the resurrection, not of the soul but of the body. Now look at I Timothy 6:16. Paul had been speaking to Timothy about purity of life. He wanted him to keep the commandment "until the appearing of our Lord Jesus Christ" (v. 14). Then in verse 15 he presents the ultimate glory of Christ, "who is the blessed and only Potentate, the King of kings, and Lord of lords," climaxing with verse 16, "who only hath immortality." This can only mean the immortality of Christ's body. He has immortality not only for His own post-resurrection body in which He appeared to His disciples, but He can also grant immortality to our resurrection bodies as well. He "shall change our vile body, that it may be fashioned like unto his glorious body, according to the working whereby he is able even to subdue all things unto himself" (Phil. 3:21).

NEW BODIES FOR A NEW HEAVEN
AND A NEW EARTH

———◆———

"For this corruptible must put on incorruption, and this mortal must put on immortality" (I Cor. 15:53).

Many religious leaders in the past have made the claim, or their followers have made it for them, that they would never die. Yet the day inevitably came when they were consigned to six feet of earth like anyone else, and their bones now mingle with the dust of the ground. No one needs to tell us that our bodies are corruptible. Nature makes this fact only too apparent as the ruins of old cemeteries are dug up and the sad evidences of man's corruptibility come to view.

We have said that the only person who possesses incorruptibility and immortality is the Lord Jesus Christ, whose body did not see corruption. Observe what Psalm 16:10 has to say about Him: "Thou wilt not leave my soul in hell [hades, the dwelling place of the separated spirits, as in Luke 16:15ff]; neither wilt thou suffer thine Holy One to see corruption." That the word "corruption" here refers to the body of Christ is made clear by the Apostle Peter in his message at Pentecost: "He seeing this before spake of the resurrection of Christ, that his soul was not left in hell [hades], neither his flesh did see corruption" (Acts 2:31). This means that Christ as God eternal possesses immortality as far as His body is concerned independently of His incarnation. He has always had it. It is not an acquisition but an inherent quality.

In II Timothy 1:10 Paul tells us that when Christ

comes He will abolish death. "But [God's purpose] is now made manifest by the appearance of our Saviour Jesus Christ, who hath abolished death, and hath brought life and immortality to light through the gospel." We have seen that the Greek word for "immortality" here is *aphtharsia,* "incorruptibility." Only Christ brought this good news that one day we who believe shall possess a body that will be incorruptible—not subject to sickness, pain, and decay—and therefore immortal. That is, it will no more undergo separation from the soul as it did once at death.

It is therefore clear that the terms "incorruptibility" and "immortality" in I Corinthians 15:53 refer to the qualities that the Lord will impart to our resurrection bodies. They will not be subject to disease and decay: that's incorruptibility. They will not die, or be separated from their souls as once happened to those who underwent physical death: that's immortality. Immortality, therefore, in Scripture refers only to the resurrection body, not to the soul as it now exists.

We know that the soul never ceases to exist after its separation from the body, though for a time it must continue to exist without a body. But at the resurrection it will be joined again to a body that in every way is similar to its present body, being individually identifiable, but which will be clothed with the two qualities of incorruptibility and immortality.

This verse begins with the verb *dei,* translated "must." It means "it is necessary, there is need of." It is necessary, Paul says, for this body of ours to be clothed with incorruptibility and immortality in order that it may be fitted for its new eternal heavenly environment. And just as Scripture gives us promise of new bodies, it gives us a promise of new heavens and a new earth where these resurrection bodies will be fitted to live. Isaiah 65:17 says, "For, behold, I create new heavens and a new earth: and the former shall not be remembered, nor come into mind." Nor will you really remember your old bodies when you receive your new ones. Isaiah 66:22 goes on to tell us further of the preservation of the seed of the righteous: "For as the new heavens and the new earth, which I will make, shall remain before me, saith the Lord, so shall your seed and your name remain."

But have you thought what will happen to this present universe? Peter tells us, "The day of the Lord will come as a thief in the night; in the which the heavens shall pass away with a great noise, and the elements shall melt with fervent heat, the earth also and the works that are therein shall be burned up. Seeing then that all these things shall be dissolved, what manner of persons ought ye to be in all holy conversation and godliness, looking for and hasting unto the coming of the day of God, wherein the heavens being on fire shall be dissolved, and the elements shall melt with fervent heat? Nevertheless we, according to his promise, look for new heavens and a new earth, wherein dwelleth righteousness" (II Pet. 3:10-13).

This no doubt refers to the splitting of the atoms of the various elements, which will result in the dreadful catastrophes of atomic nuclear explosions. If man now has the capability of destroying his earth, how much more God the universe! But Scripture gives us His promise of remaking it all, to be an environment fitted for the eternal state of man.

Observe that all these events, the renewal of the universe and the necessity of creating new bodies that are incorruptible and immortal, are connected with the second coming of Christ. "And I saw a new heaven and a new earth: for the first heaven and the first earth were passed away; and there was no more sea" (Rev. 21:1). That is why Paul says in I Corinthians 15:53, "It is necessary, therefore, for this corruptible [body] to be clothed with incorruptibility and this mortal [body] to be clothed with immortality."

On the resurrection morning
   Soul and body meet again;
No more sorrow, no more weeping,
             No more pain!

Soul and body reunited
   Thenceforth nothing shall divide,
Waking up in Christ's own likeness
             Satisfied.

On that happy Easter morning
   All the graves their dead restore;
Father, sister, child, and mother
             Meet once more.

To that brightest of all meetings
   Bring us, Jesus Christ, at last,
By Thy cross, through death and judgment,
             Holding fast.

AN IMPOSSIBLE PREDICTION — OR IS IT?

"So when this corruptible shall have put on incorruption, and this mortal shall have put on immortality, then shall be brought to pass the saying that is written, Death is swallowed up in victory" (I Cor. 15:54).

The Old Testament prophets wrote some incredible things, humanly speaking. Who in his sane mind and knowledge of past experience would say that a day would come when death would be no more? No one. Of course, the prophets did not speak with merely human wisdom. Their predictions were not confined to the realm of the possible dictated by past experience, but encompassed that which transcends human possibility. A doctor can predict that a patient will die at a certain time; this is human wisdom based upon experience. But to predict that a man will not die at all or that, if he dies, he will rise again, transcends the realm of the naturally possible.

The element of divine inspiration in the prophetic utterances of the Old Testament cannot be easily dismissed. These men must have been either insane or divinely inspired. How can we determine which? Simply by the fact that these impossible predictions were fulfilled. It is not within the scope of this work to set about proving the fulfillment of all Old Testament prophecies. Suffice it to say that the New Testament constantly speaks of events taking place in Christ's lifetime that were the fulfillment of Old Testament prophecies concerning Him. The prophecies about the crucifixion are especially striking regarding details that no merely human wisdom could have foreseen

hundreds of years before they happened. Take these ex-
cerpts from the 22nd Psalm, for instance: "They pierced
my hands and my feet . . . . They part my garments among
them, and cast lots upon my vesture" (vv. 16, 18). Now
turn to the New Testament, and in Matthew 27:35 we read,
"And they crucified him, and parted his garments, casting
lots: that it might be fulfilled which was spoken by the
prophet, They parted my garments among them, and upon
my vesture did they cast lots."

In the 15th chapter of I Corinthians, the Apostle Paul
stresses that the death and resurrection of the Lord Jesus
were "according to the Scriptures" (vv. 3, 4). This means
according to the written prophecies of the Old Testament.
Christ's resurrection irrefutably proves the trustworthiness
and the divine inspiration of the Old Testament prophets.
That a historical being such as Jesus Christ would one day
die could have been predicted by anyone. But only a God-
inspired person could have predicted His humanly impossible resurrection. The very moment Christ rose from the
dead, humanity had the best reason possible for fixing its
attention on everything uttered by the prophets.

Paul states that one prophet said something similar
about death in relation to all humanity. This prophet was
Isaiah, who said that the time would come when physical
death would no longer be victor over men—that men would
die no more (Isaiah 25:8). Can you believe it? It's unreasonable, fabulous, fantastic. Call it what you will, and I'll agree
with you. It occurs to me that landing on the moon would
have seemed equally fantastic to a past generation, but can
you disbelieve it now? Times change. Who are we to exclude the possibility of further changes? If science has
taught us anything, it is that we can no longer say anything

is impossible.

And when it comes to the permanent resurrection of our bodies, it is all the easier to believe because of one verified instance of it, that of the Lord Jesus Christ. The prophets predicted His resurrection, and their prophecies came true. Now, says Paul, here is a prophet, Isaiah, who predicted over 700 years ago that centuries in the future death would be no more. Paul goes out of his way to make the resurrection of our bodies, as believers, to eternal life a reasonably and definitely believable fact of the future. Observe that in the first part of I Corinthians 15:54 he says that the day will come, at the second coming of Christ, when this corruptible body of ours shall be clothed with incorruptibility, and this mortal body shall be clothed with immortality. When our bodies are resurrected or changed at Christ's appearing (*parousia*) as predicted in verse 23, then our new bodies will die no more. They won't be subject to illness, either. They will be incorruptible and immortal, something they manifestly are not now.

"Then shall be brought to pass the saying" (literally, "Then [*tote*, an adverb of time] shall come into existence the word which is written"). The verb here is *geneesetai* in Greek, from *ginomai*, which means "to become, to come into existence, to begin to be." The written Word (*logos*) will then become a reality, even as in John 1:1 the Word became (the same Greek verb *egeneto*) flesh, became a visible reality. The non-material Word became material. Similarly the time will come when the word of the prophet Isaiah will begin to be verifiable, in the tangible bodies of the risen ones or the changed ones. These will begin a new state of being.

The words of these prophets are said to be "written"

rather than "spoken." How remarkable that God should see to it that the words of these prophets were not merely handed down as oral tradition but were preserved in writing. If you say something that later on proves to be damaging to your reputation, you can always change your mind and deny that you said it; but if you've put it in writing it is unalterable. So confident were these prophets of their divine inspiration that they wrote concerning events of the future without hesitation.

We have said that the word "then" (*tote*) in I Corinthians 15:54 is an adverb of time, but it should not be taken as referring to a period of time but to the smallest possible fraction of time, in continuation of the statement in verse 52 that our resurrection will take place in an instant, in the twinkling of an eye. The future tense of the verb *geneesetai* can be in agreement with this idea, and here certainly is, for it is in the aorist, referring as it does in this context to a specific time in the future. It will occur only once. It will not be protracted or intermittent. It will take place once and for all, and as a result neither corruptibility nor mortality will be the order of things any more.

> I will repudiate the lie
> Men tell of life; how it will pass
> As fragile flower, or butterfly,
> Whose dust shall nourish April grass.
>
> Since One, for love, died on a tree
> And in the stony tomb was lain,
> Behold, I show a mystery:
> All sepulchres are sealed in vain!
> —John Richard Moreland

THE LONELINESS OF DEATH

". . . . Death is swallowed up in victory" (I Cor. 15:54).

It is a regrettable fact that all literary works suffer in translation, and this is especially true of the Bible. Something is lost when you have to read the New Testament in English, for instance, instead of in the original Greek.

A case in point is the statement, "Death is swallowed up in victory," as the Authorized Version translates it. This is a quotation from Isaiah 25:8. Actually the verb is in the aorist tense here, indicating a definite act in the past, accomplished once and for all. "Death was swallowed up in victory" is what Paul says. Also he has changed the voice of the verb from active to passive. He seems to have rejected the Septuagint Greek translation which says, "Death has prevailed and swallowed man up."

The one who swallowed up death is none other than God Himself. It is He who permitted it in the first place, as the inevitable consequence of man's sin, and He alone can eliminate it. Isaiah predicted this some 700 years before the coming of Christ into the world, and Paul affirms that this prediction will be realized when the Lord returns to this earth and the bodies of the believing dead are raised.

Why does Paul speak of a future event as past? Undoubtedly, under divine inspiration, he anticipated it so vividly and realistically and was so certain of it that, as far as he was concerned, it was an accomplished fact. Death, which has been swallowing up people all through the ages, has itself been swallowed up. The tyrant is now subjugated.

Paul calls death "the last enemy" in verse 26.

Man's death, both spiritual and physical, is indeed an enemy as far as God is concerned. It grieves His heart more than anything else. It is a symbol of the moral fall of the human race. God cannot view man's death with anything but feelings of deep regret and hatred. He does not hate fallen men, because Christ said that "God so loved the world, that he gave his only begotten Son, that whosoever believeth in him should not perish, but have everlasting life" (John 3:16). He hates death, in spite of the fact that He fixed it as the inevitable consequence of sin. But it is illogical to blame Him for death, any more than it would be to blame a judge for applying the punishment fixed by law. It is the criminal alone who is to blame and who must be punished. Otherwise anarchy would reign.

But do all men consider death their enemy? Not really. It is not so regarded by those who commit suicide, thinking that thus they are ending their anxieties and sorrows. To them it seems a way of escape.

But for the great majority death is indeed considered an enemy. The instinct for self-preservation proves this. They hate it because of its very inevitability. It holds an aspect of terror. It produces in most of us an attitude of intense repulsion. We shrink from dying. We sometimes feel that, if the drawing of that last breath were with us, as with Christ, an act of the will, we should never dare to do it, it is so fearful.

Why do the majority of people hold life dear and regard death as an enemy? Canon Liddon gives some very penetrating answers to this question. He says it is because physical death separates us roughly and suddenly from all the objects and persons around whom our affections have entwined themselves. And this separation is likely to be felt more acutely the longer we live until, perhaps, the years immediately preceding the close of a very long life. Elderly people—as distinct from the very old, in whom the faculties are benumbed, and who are consciously tottering on the edge of the grave—elderly people do, as a rule, feel more attachment to persons and objects around them than the young; because in the young the affections have not yet had time to grow. A young man, it is true, gives up more of life when he dies voluntarily than an older one; but he can generally do it more easily because his affections have not bound him, like old ivy, so tightly to the fabric of earthly interests with which he is in daily contact. Death—we cannot doubt it—inflicts a sharp wound on the life of affection in proportion to the intensity and fervor of personal character.

Then again, looked at from the point of view of human nature, death means an introduction to loneliness and exile. Think of the child going to school away from the familiar environment of home. It is not easy to be all alone among strange faces and in new scenes, with new duties set before us, and new habits to form; alone, but with a memory—never so keen before—of all that we had left behind, of all whom we had loved, and from whom we now were parted.

The solitariness of the act of dying was that which most impressed itself upon the mind of the great Pascal: "I shall die," he said, "alone." So it must be. Friends may be standing or kneeling round, tending us with every care that natural kindliness or religious zeal can suggest; but the actual experience of dying and of that which follows death can be shared by no other; and until we go through it we cannot know or guess exactly what it is like. We only know that it means a wrench from all that has always been familiar; it means a plunge into the vast dark unknown world.

(See H. P. Liddon, *Sermons on Some Words of St. Paul*, pp. 154-58.)

> Alone! to land alone upon that shore,
> With no one sight that we have seen before:
> > Things of a different hue,
> > And sounds all strange and new;
> No forms of earth our fancies to arrange,
> But to begin alone that mighty change!
>
> Alone! to land alone upon that shore,
> Knowing full well we can return no more;
> > No voice or face of friend,
> > None with us to attend
> Our disembarking on that awful strand;
> But to arrive alone in such a land!
>
> —Faber

And yet this is not altogether a true picture, for the believer does not go through this experience entirely alone. True, no human being can accompany him on that last journey; but there is One who has promised never to leave him nor forsake him, and he can confidently say with the Psalmist, "Yea, though I walk through the valley of the shadow of death, I will fear no evil: for thou art with me" (Ps. 23:4).

IF CHRIST CONQUERED DEATH, WHY DO WE STILL DIE?

"So when this corruptible shall have put on incorruption, and this mortal shall have put on immortality, then shall be brought to pass the saying that is written, Death is swallowed up in victory" (I Cor. 15:54).

Men's consciences are at best uneasy things. It's a rare person indeed who is not troubled by a sense of guilt over his misdeeds and inadequacies at some time during his life. Some people have more sensitive consciences than others, of course. Yet it is almost universally true that, when a man faces death, his conscience tells him that beyond the grave lies an accounting for the life he lived on earth. This witness of the conscience is motivated by a deep-rooted conviction that man lives his life under the condition of moral responsibility, and that his death is a passing into judgment. "It is appointed unto men once to die, but after this the judgment" (Heb. 9:27).

Even for the Christian believer there is a constant sense of inadequacy, a feeling that he could have lived more worthily of the name of Christ. Therefore the judgment makes death somewhat unwelcome to him, because he longs for further opportunity to live a more purposeful life for Christ. Not that the hereafter, to the Christian, is dark. But, from the point of view of mere nature, death is an enemy that leads us away from the world that we know and love, into the loneliness of an unimagined and unimaginable exile.

Furthermore, it inflicts a wound—the exact sensations

of which we cannot anticipate—upon the composite being we have always recognized as ourselves. True, when the body is laid aside and decays in the grave, the undying spirit survives; but the spirit is only a part, though admittedly the most important part, of our complete identity. If death does not destroy man, it at least impairs and mutilates the wholeness of his nature. To see without eyes, to hear without ears, to think without a brain, to feel without the sympathetic action of heart and nerves, will be to have entered, for the time being, on a new existence. If we regard it as the act of an enemy violently to cut off an arm or a leg, even though he does not destroy life, we can understand why human nature should regard death as an enemy when it achieves so much larger a mutilation of our being; when it breaks up and destroys the body altogether, although it cannot touch that surviving spiritual essence that is the seat of personal life.

Why does Paul call death the *last* enemy in I Corinthians 15:26? In Greek the word is *eschatos* without the definite article, but the addition of the article in the translation is fully warranted. It would be incorrect to say "a last enemy," for only one can be "last." Death is the last enemy to be conquered by Christ. *Eschatos* is the word from which we derive the English noun "eschatology," and it is used to denote last in relation to time and not as to importance. Eschatology is the study of the last things that will take place in our world.

Death came in last as an enemy. It is the ultimate present consequence of sin. First came the devil, then sin, sickness, sorrow and ultimately death. This refers primarily to physical death, something which we, even as Christians, cannot avoid. Although we may recover from many illnesses in our lifetime, we cannot finally win in our struggle against death. The Lord does not always heal us, because some day we must die—unless of course we are caught up in the air to be with Him, if His second coming precedes our death.

While death will be the last enemy to be overcome, we must recognize that only Christ can overcome it. He did this for Himself and He will do it for us. Paul in writing to Timothy stressed the fact that, as far as Christ is concerned, He has already destroyed death. "Our Saviour Jesus Christ . . . hath abolished death, and hath brought life and immortality to light through the gospel" (II Tim. 1:10). And in Hebrews 2:14, 15 we read, "That through death he might destroy him that had the power of death, that is, the devil; and deliver them who through fear of death were all their lifetime subject to bondage."

As far as Christ is concerned, death has been abolished. But we still die. As believers in Christ, however, we do not die without hope. Death, our death, has lost its sting because of His resurrection. After our own resurrection, we shall taste death no more. It will be abolished, so that there will be no death for the resurrected glorious body of the believer, or for those believers caught up at the appearing of the Lord.

Because Christ has already taken the sting out of death for those who believe in Him, the Christian is not afraid to die. In this connection, it is interesting to note that the tense of the verb *katargeitai,* "is abolished," in I Corinthians 15:26, although referring to the future, is in the present indicative. Death will be destroyed completely after the return of our Lord, but its destruction has already begun. It is being abolished all the time. Its destruction is progressive, dating from the very moment of our Lord's resurrection. Christ has taken from death its tyrannical power by dying Himself. He has gone before us in every stage of our life, even to experiencing the very death that must be ours.

Our Lord enables His followers to conquer death by dissipating our ignorance about it. Without the Gospel, death and its surroundings are wrapped in mysterious gloom. Reason may attain to a certain conviction that man survives death, by reflecting that, if the accepted doctrine of the conservation of force is good for anything, it is as applicable to spiritual as to physical force. And since spiritual force cannot exist apart from a living person or subject, the conservation of spiritual force means the survival of personal life. However, without a resurrection of the body, this would be an incomplete survival of human identity. But our Lord throws upon death and all that follows it a much brighter light than any reason can supply. He has in very deed brought life and immortality to light. Can we doubt this information? Consider the credentials of the informant. He speaks not from conjecture but on the strength of experience.

The founders of other systems of religion can say, "Come after me, and I will show you the way to the good life." Jesus Christ alone can say, "I am the resurrection, and the life: he that believeth in me, though he were dead, yet shall he live: and whosoever liveth and believeth in me shall never die" (John 11:25). He alone can say, "Because I live, ye shall live also" (John 14:19).

DOES DEATH SERVE ANY GOOD PURPOSE FOR THE CHRISTIAN?

". . . Death is swallowed up in victory" (I Cor. 15:54).

Under Christ's voluntary and sacrificial death, and His attitude in death, lay a threefold conviction. In the first place, He was quite certain that death could not touch His personal existence. "To day shalt thou be *with me in paradise,*" He assured the believing thief on the cross (Luke 23:43). And His last words were, "Father, into thy hands I commend my spirit" (Luke 23:46). It was absolutely clear to His human spirit that, from the moment He bowed His head, and His spirit passed from His body, and His body lay a lifeless thing upon the cross, He would be living on.

And the same conviction came to His disciples. "For whether we live, we live unto the Lord; and whether we die, we die unto the Lord: whether we live therefore, or die, we are the Lord's" (Rom. 14:8). At the moment of death there is no real suspension of interior consciousness. One minute on that dying bed I may be conscious; the next, I am consciously free from the burden of the flesh in the presence of God. Whatever death does, it cannot really touch me. This is a great relief.

The Lord at His dying moment also had the absolute conviction that death not only did not touch his personality but also that it could not touch His union with God. Whatever is involved in the changed conditions of life, one thing never changes: as I live in my Father's hands here, I shall live in my Father's hands there. God will be to me then, only in a fuller sense than He is now, a supreme reality. "Father, into thy hands I commend my spirit." Never losing myself in suspension, I am alive in God.

And thirdly Christ had the conviction that the life into which He was passing was a life of peace and rest. "With me in paradise!" What paradise means we cannot entirely grasp while we are still here in the body; and, while all our knowledge comes to us as it does through channels of this body, we cannot get a definite realization of what life is there. But we can know this—that under those changed conditions the life of the Christian will be the life of rest. "Blessed are the dead which die in the Lord from henceforth: Yea, saith the Spirit, that they may rest from their labours; and their works do follow them" (Rev. 14:13).

While it is quite true that the imperfection in which we die here is turned into perfection in the life of paradise, it is also true that we are connected in paradise with the life of the past by memory; and we cannot retain that memory without a deepened sense of contrition. But along with it will come the joy of knowing that we are finally freed from the defilement, power, and penalty of sin.

When we hear our Lord say, "Thou shalt be with me in paradise," we realize what a weak thing death is. Yes, it is abolished, not as a reality, but as a reality before which I can any longer be troubled. More than that, death is the birth to incorruptibility. "O death, where is thy sting? O grave, where is thy victory?" (I Cor. 15:55).

I look into the face of Jesus and pray that God will give me grace to die consciously, that I may say with Christ, "Father, into thy hands I commend my spirit," and die in the consciousness in which Christ died. This is no interruption of my personal life; it is no passing from the enfolding arms; this is passing into rest.

(See "The Destruction of Death," by George Body, in the *Christian World Pulpit,* Vol. 67, pp. 260-2.)

But while we are anticipating this last victory over death, there are a lot of struggles that we must wage here and now till that day. As Spurgeon says, "You do not want dying grace till dying moments. What would be the good of dying grace while you are yet alive? A boat will only be needful when you reach a river. Ask for living grace, and glorify Christ thereby, and then you shall have dying grace when dying time comes. Your enemy is going to be destroyed, but not today. There is a great host of enemies to be fought today, and you may be content to let this one alone for a while. This enemy will be destroyed, but of the times and the seasons we are in ignorance; our wisdom is to be good soldiers of Jesus Christ as the duty of every day requires. Take your trials as they come, brother! As the enemies march up, slay them, rank upon rank; but if you fail in the name of God to smite the front ranks, and say 'No, I am only afraid of the rear rank,' then you are playing the fool. Leave the final shock of arms till the last adversary advances, and meanwhile hold your place in the conflict. God will in due time help you to overcome your last enemy, but meanwhile see to it that you overcome the world, the flesh, and the devil. If you live well you will die well. That same covenant in which the Lord Jesus gave you life contains also the grant of death, for 'All things are yours; whether . . . life, or death, or things present, or things to come; all are yours; and ye are Christ's; and Christ is God's' (I Cor. 3:21-23).

"Why is death left to the last? Well, I think it is because Christ can make much use of him. The last enemy that shall be destroyed is death, because death is of great service before he is destroyed. Oh, what lessons some of us have learned from death! 'Our dying friends come o'er us like a cloud to damp our brainless ardours,' to make us feel that these poor fleeting toys are not worth living for; that as others pass away so must we also be gone, and thus they help to make us set loose by this world, and urge us to take wing and mount towards the world to come. There are, perhaps, no sermons like the deaths which have happened in our households; the departures of our beloved friends have been to us solemn discourses of divine wisdom, which our heart could not help hearing. So Christ has spared death to make him a preacher to His saints.

"Without death we should not be so conformed to Christ as we shall be if we fall asleep in Him. If there could be any jealousies in heaven among the saints, I think that any saint who does not die, but is changed when Christ comes, could almost meet me and you, who probably will die, and say, 'My brother, there is one thing I have missed, I never lay in the grave, I never had the chill hand of death laid on me, and so in that I was not conformed to my Lord. But *you* know what it is to have fellowship with Him, even in His death.'

"Death, dear friends, is not yet destroyed, because he brings the saints home. He does but come to them and whisper His message, and in a moment they are supremely blessed.

"Have done with sin and care and woe,
And with the Saviour rest.
"And so death is not destroyed yet, for he answers useful purposes." (Spurgeon, *The Treasury of the New Testament*, Vol. III, pp. 210-11.)

CONQUERING THE FEAR OF DEATH

"... *Death is swallowed up in victory*" (I Cor. 15:54).

Many of our idiomatic expressions in English really do not make sense if you analyze them closely. Take the expression "swallowed up," for instance. Actually, we swallow downward rather than upward, don't we? The Greeks recognized this, and their word for this action reflects it more accurately. Where the Authorized Version says, "Death is swallowed up in victory," the Greek verb *katepothee,* "swallowed up," is actually derived from the preposition *kata* (down) and the verb *pinoo* (drink). It is "to drink down, to swallow down rather than up." It was also used to indicate the absorption of water by the soil. That which is swallowed down or absorbed does not exist as an active independent element any more.

Interestingly enough, in the majority of instances of the use of this verb in the New Testament, the object that is said to be swallowed down is an almost impossible item. In Matthew 23:24 we read about the swallowing of a camel by a human being—a natural impossibility. In II Corinthians 5:4 we are told that in our suffering bodies we wish that "Mortality might be swallowed up of life." In Hebrews 11:29, speaking of the Egyptians who tried to imitate the Hebrews as they passed through the Red Sea dry shod, the Apostle says that they were "swallowed up" ("drowned" in the Authorized Version, but the same Greek word, *katepotheesan*). Speaking of Satan who goes after his human victims, Peter presents him as "a roaring lion . . . seeking whom he may devour" (*katapiein*, swallow down),

(I Pet. 5:8). The lion actually does not devour human beings whole, but swallows them piecemeal. And finally the same word is used in Revelation 12:16 to represent the earth as swallowing up "the flood which the dragon cast out of his mouth."

God is going to swallow down death—an impossible feat—with the greatest of ease. Omnipotence can do with little effort that which is humanly and naturally impossible. Read the story of creation in Genesis and marvel once again at how God created this complex universe, including the complex organism of the human mind and brain, with simply a word!

Man can achieve, but he must start where God left off, and he must stop where God will begin. And God appointed death to be the inevitable fate of every human being. Man, no matter how smart you are, no matter how many doctorates you have in science or philosophy, you have to be swallowed down by death. You'd better find out what happens after that.

Every time a certain little boy went to a playmate's house, he found the child's grandmother reading her Bible. Finally his curiosity got the better of him. "Why do you suppose your grandmother reads the Bible so much?" he asked. "I'm not sure," said his friend, "but I think it's because she's cramming for her finals." Your finals may be closer than you think. There's only one book that can prepare you for them—that's the Bible, the written Word of God.

Although the English translation of the last part of I Corinthians 15:54 reads "Death is swallowed up in victory," in the Greek the verb comes first: "Swallowed up was death in victory." This is done for emphasis, to demonstrate the complete destruction of death. Paul does not speak of the checking of death but of its complete destruction, rendering it forever inactive.

The word "victory" presupposes a war, a struggle. When death acquired its victory over God's purpose for man, it was not as a result of a battle but of deceit. Satan did not declare war against God in the Garden of Eden but simply exercised fraud. He tricked man into sin. Death quietly took over the human race in consequence. It is in this manner that Satan has been working right along. This is the most dangerous technique—not open attack against God, because he knows that he cannot win—but subtle seduction of man to disobey God. There can be no quieter but more formidable enemy than death. Behind every casket lies Satan's apparent victory over God's eternal purpose for man. Satan carries on an undeclared war whose ultimate end for every man is death.

But the ultimate victory of God over death will not be quiet and undeclared. It will be open victory. In a moment, in the twinkling of an eye, at the last trump, the believers will find themselves in the body—a far better, stronger, more glorious body than the one they possessed previously. God wins with a declaration that death will not overtake man any more.

"Swallowed up was death in victory" is a declaration that not only does man's soul separated from his body share in this victory but also his entire personality as he was previous to death. If we were to be kept as spirits only after death, then death would not be completely overcome; it would be only a partial victory. Since the victory of death is the separation of our spirits from our bodies, the victory over death must entail the exact opposite—the joining of the body to the spirit, with the only difference being that this new body will be strong, glorious, and indestructible—a spiritual body.

Death like its master, Satan, stealthily watches to take its victims as a thief in the night. Quite often he gives no warning. Be prepared, therefore, to meet this enemy at any time.

Professor J. H. Huxley was a well-known agnostic. His nurse revealed that in the last moments of his life, as he lay dying, the great skeptic suddenly looked up as at some sight invisible to mortal eyes, and, staring a while, whispered, "So it is true."

Yes, it is true that the end of death will come; that when, through the resurrection, our glorious bodies are reunited to our souls, there will be no more separating of the two. There can be no greater victory than this. Man brought about his defeat through death, and God will bring about His triumph through the final and permanent abolition of death.

It is most interesting to note the Greek construction of this sentence: "Was swallowed down the death into victory." Note first of all that the word *thanatos,* "death," is preceded by the definite article. "The death" was swallowed down. It is the death imposed upon man as the consequence of his sin. It is not the spiritual death which implied separation of the spirit of man from the Spirit of God His Creator, but physical death.

Thanatos means both kinds of death in Scripture. For the spiritual meaning, look up John 11:13 and Hebrews 2:15; 5:7; 7:23. For the physical meaning, look up Genesis 2:17 and Romans 5:12, 14, 17, 21. When we believe in Christ, we are delivered immediately from the penalty of spiritual death, as we are told in John 5:24 and I John 3:14. But as believers we cannot escape the physical consequence of sin, which is physical death. Nevertheless, our death is far different from the death of the unbeliever. Once we receive spiritual life, we do not lose it. While we live on earth, Christ indwells our spirit-body personality. When the body and spirit are separated at death, Christ is no longer in us, but we are with Him (Phil. 1:23). And then, in the resurrection, we receive our full redemption when our bodies of humiliation are replaced by bodies similar to Christ's glorious resurrection body. When the Christian knows what awaits him, all fear of death as an inexorable tyrant disappears.

Someone asked an elderly believer what she would do in the hour of death, since Satan was so strong. "Well," she replied, "when two dogs are fighting over a bone, does the bone do anything? It doesn't fight; it just lies between them, and the stronger gets it. So when I come to Jordan, and Satan tries to get me, I'll turn him over to Jesus and just keep still, for Jesus my Master is stronger than Satan." This elderly saint of God fully understood what Paul declares in I Corinthians 15:54, "Was swallowed down the death in victory." Who won? Christ—with as much ease as we swallow down a pill. And indeed death is a bitter pill to swallow, but we may safely leave it to Christ, who gained the victory for us all.

YOUR OWN PERSONAL VICTORY OVER DEATH

"O death, where is thy sting? O grave, where is thy victory?" (I Cor. 15:55).

Death has often been personalized in poetry and literature, and nowhere more strikingly than in the Bible. In Revelation 6:8, for instance, we read, "Behold a pale horse: and his name that sat on him was Death." The Apostle Paul spoke of death as "the last enemy" in I Corinthians 15:26, and now, in verse 55, he addresses a rhetorical question to him: "O death, where is thy sting? O grave, where is thy victory?"

This is a quotation from Hosea 13:14, which in its original sense applies to the deliverance of the Northern Kingdom of Israel from its troubles. The literal translation is, "I will be thy plagues, O death; I will be thy destruction, O grave." The Septuagint Greek Version of the Old Testament is, "Where is thy judgment, O death? where is thy good, O grave?" Instead of "judgment" (*dikee*), Paul says "victory" (*nikee*), a difference of only one letter in the Greek. And then to make *nikee* agree with "victory" in verse 54, he changes it to *nikos*. This gives a different turn to the whole passage. Paul still uses it to express the overthrow of death generally, but that overthrow is now described not as in the Hebrew and Septuagint, as a punishment inflicted on death, but as annihilation of his power.

The change from "grave" in the King James version to "death" in most of the modern translations is justified, since the Greek word *hadees,* which occurs in the *Textus Receptus,* does not occur in most manuscripts, and Paul never uses the word. Therefore the text which we accept is, "Where thy, death, the victory? Where thy, death, the sting?" This is the literal translation in the exact order in which the words occur in the Greek text. The order of the words "victory" and "sting" has been reversed in the King James Version, although this does not affect the meaning in any way.

Paul does not deal with *hadees,* which in other books of the New Testament is presented as the dwelling place to which men's disembodied spirits went. It would have been contrary to the whole trend of his argument in I Corinthians 15 for him to speak of *hadees* as an enemy, for he does not deal with the period preceding the resurrection of Christ, when the spirits of believers and unbelievers went to *hadees.* (Luke 16:19ff indicates that Abraham's bosom was the designation of the place in *hadees* to which the spirit of righteous Lazarus went, and the place of torment in *hadees* was where the unrighteous rich man was consigned.)

After the resurrection of Christ, believers are never referred to as going to *hadees,* but as going to be with Christ (Acts 7:59, Phil. 1:23, Heb. 12:23). And Christ is in heaven (Mark 16:19, Luke 24:51, Acts 1:9, Heb. 4:14, I Pet. 3:22). Death is still an enemy of the Christian, for he still experiences it; but *hadees* is not, for the Christian does not go there. And it is with the external destiny of the Christian that Paul is primarily concerned in I Corinthians 15. His subject is the resurrection of the body, not the place where the soul dwells when disembodied. The resurrection is the answer to death, not to *hadees,* for there is no resurrection of the soul, but only of the body.

Paul is speaking from the viewpoint of the era of post-resurrection life. Death has already been abolished. The resurrection body is not only the possession of all believers, but also it will never know corruption and death any more. The victory over death is complete and eternal.

Death takes on an air of finality when it confronts man. Paul was close to death on numerous occasions. Speaking of his own circumstances he says that he was "in deaths oft" and that he died "daily" (II Cor. 11:23, I Cor. 15:31). And though Paul escaped death many times, he finally did die. But, because he died in the joyful expectation of the resurrection, he did not go as death's victim. On the road to Damascus he had seen Christ alive after His death. In truth we might regard the words of Christ to John—"I am he that liveth, and was dead" (Rev. 1:18)—as being spoken to Paul also. That is why Paul, while alive and facing death, could say, "Where, death, thy victory?" In all his perils he did not fear death.

It is as natural to die as to be born, and to the infant perhaps one is as painful as the other. This is the philosophic view of death. But the Christian, knowing that Christ arose and has earned the title to the keys of hell and death, no longer fears. Would you be afraid to enter a strange house if its doors were unlocked for you by your very own loving father? Can you enter into the feeling of the minister who said, "I have often laughed to see Death shake his dart at me"? This is what it means to have victory over death.

"O death, where is thy victory?" As Paul wrote these words, he may have been thinking of a death he could never forget—that of Stephen, the first Christian martyr. It was Paul, then known as Saul, who kept watch over the clothes of the persecutors who were stoning Stephen to death (Acts 7:58). He had had an opportunity to see with his own eyes how a Christian faced death, with a glow instead of with fear and bitterness. This may have been the beginning of his turn toward Christ.

I am writing these words after having just returned from the funeral of a 16-year-old nephew who was killed in an accident. I wish you could have seen the attitude of certainty and hope with which the father and mother greeted the hundreds of visitors who came to view their son's body. They demonstrated victory over death by their confidence that it had not spoken the last word. As I watched them standing by the body of their son, I said to myself, "Who can measure how many lives this death may reach for Christ?" Similarly, Stephen's death wasn't all defeat. There was victory in it for Paul, and who knows how many others? "O death, where is thy victory?" Do you realize that the death of every born-again believer is a victory for Christ? Do you have this confidence, or are you afraid?

Death for the righteous, those who have been justified by faith in Christ, does not entail meeting God for judgment, for the righteous have already been judged in Christ. The first physical death in the world did not come to Adam, the first sinner, nor to Cain, the first hypocrite, but to Abel, the innocent and righteous man. Remember that, when you see death come prematurely, as you think, to the righteous ones of earth. Do not think God is unjust, as though such an early death were somehow a punishment, and should not be inflicted on the Christian.

A young woman who lay dying sought to console her father, who was overcome with grief. "Dad," she said, "don't be so broken up. If I had received an offer of marriage from someone who was all you could desire for me, and whose station in life was far superior to mine, but who wanted to take me to live in a remote part of the world, don't you think you could have borne the separation, knowing all the advantages it would bring to me? But I am now being promoted to a situation incomparably beyond anything that could have happened to me in this world. Then why this reluctance to let me go? Our next meeting will be in far more wonderful circumstances, joyful, and everlasting." When the Christian thus regards death, he mourns not for the one who has passed to heaven's joy, but only for his own sense of loss. If he could only consider the other's joy, he might suffer far less acutely.

At the funeral of a minister, a little child was seen tripping light-heartedly through the cemetery at dusk. Someone asked, "Aren't you afraid of this place?" "Oh, no," she replied, "I only cross through here to get home." Death for the Christian is only a "crossing-through to get home." It is not ultimate and final death; it is only a seeming. Just as we say the sun sets, because that is how it looks to us, though it really does not, so with those who leave us. The sun greets us bright as ever in the morning, and so will they.

The Christian in death should not be like the child who is forced by the rod to quit his play, but like one who is wearied of it and is willing to go to bed. As William Cullen Bryant observes in his *Thanatopsis*,

So live, that when thy summons comes . . . .
Thou go not, like the quarry-slave at night,
Scourged to his dungeon, but, sustained and soothed
By an unfaltering trust, approach thy grave,
Like one who wraps the drapery of his couch
About him, and lies down to pleasant dreams.

A SURE AND CERTAIN HOPE

"The sting of sin is death; and the strength of sin is the law" (I Cor. 15:56).

Ignorance of the meaning and consequence of death can rob life of its joy. If your life is not an adequate preparation for making you victorious over death, you have not really lived.

"How hard it is to die!" remarked a friend as he watched by the bedside of a believer. "Oh, no, no!" he replied. "It is easy dying, glorious dying!" Looking up at the clock he said, "I have experienced more happiness in dying two hours this day than in my whole life. It is worth a whole life to have such an end as this. Oh, I never thought that such a poor creature as I could come to such a glorious death!" It was to such a victory that Paul was looking forward when he looked death in the eye and asked, "Where is thy victory?" May your faith in the living Christ give you the same assurance when you are called upon to view the lifeless body of a loved one, or when you look forward to the day when death will knock at your own door.

Two little birds had a nest in the bushes in the back part of a garden. Five-year-old Amy found the nest. It had four speckled eggs in it. One day, after she had been away for some time, she ran into the garden to take a look at the pretty eggs. What was her dismay to find only broken shells. "Oh," she cried, "the beautiful eggs are all spoiled and broken!" "No, Amy," said her brother, "they are not spoiled. The best part of them has taken wings and flown away."

So it is with death. The body left behind is only an empty shell, while the soul, the better part, has taken wings and flown away. How symbolic is the use of eggs at Easter time, portraying as it does this victory that the Christian experiences at death. Paul not only has this victory in mind but also the further and final victory of the soul when it is clothed with a resurrected body. For after all, the bird that came out of the shell is not mere soul, but soul and body. The victory, then, of which Paul speaks is not merely the freeing of the spirit from its corruptible body but the gaining by the soul of an incorruptible body. "Where, death, is thy victory?" Oh, if we could only enter into the triumph of this challenge.

Instead, to most people, death is a dreaded enemy. This dread is produced by its sting, which is the instrument of death. A sting is what makes a bee or scorpion dreaded. This is the meaning of the Greek word for "sting" here, *kentron*. The common feeling of mankind irresistibly proves that there is indeed a sting in death. In talking with our friends, we take pains to avoid the mere mention of the word. Many people put off making their wills and leave their affairs unsettled, causing great hardship to their families, simply because they cannot bring themselves to face the fact that they must leave this world and all their possessions. Doctors hesitate to tell an incurably ill person that he cannot recover. Few patients are willing to believe it, preferring to look forward to a return to health and strength than to approaching death.

How is it, then, that Paul demonstrated no fear of this universally dreaded enemy? It was because he was confident of the resurrection from the dead. Christ's resurrection had given satisfactory evidence of this to all His disciples; and

Paul argues from it, "If the dead rise not, then is not Christ raised: and if Christ be not raised, your faith is vain . . . . But now is Christ risen from the dead, and become the first-fruits of them that slept" (I Cor. 15:16, 17, 20). This resurrection has given us ground for the sure and certain hope that Christ will hereafter "change our vile body, that it may be fashioned like unto his glorious body" (Phil. 3:21).

Behind the fear of death lies something else—the fear of judgment. Paul makes this very clear in verse 56 when he says, "The sting of death is sin." If it were not for sin, death would not have been imposed on man in the first place. What makes death particularly horrible is what caused it. The word for "sin" in Greek is *hamartia,* "failure to hit the mark, to achieve." God's purpose for man in creation was that he should live forever in fellowship with his Creator. But man failed to achieve that goal because, by his own choice, he failed to obey God's simple and explicit command. For that choice God had to impose a consequence. As it was just for God to reward man with eternal life in the event of obedience, it was equally just to punish man with death in the event of disobedience.

God made the law and instituted the consequences of that law, not only in the spiritual but also in the physical world. The consequences in both realms are inexorable. Man is free to obey or disobey the law as he chooses, but he is not free to choose the consequences of his choice. As with the law of gravity man is free to fling himself from the top of a building, but must reap the injurious and even fatal consequences of his act, so in the spiritual world man is free to sin, but must face the consequence that "the soul that sinneth, it shall die" (Ezek. 18:4).

The death God imposed as the punishment of sin is

both spiritual and physical. Spiritual death was immediate: Adam died spiritually on the day he disobeyed God (Gen. 2:17), and hence all his descendants were born in the same spiritual condition (Rom. 5:12, 14, 17, 21), from which, however, those who believe in Christ are delivered (John 5:24, I John 3:14). For this to be made possible, Christ had to become man and bear the sins of the whole world (I Pet. 2:24).

But the second and more remote consequence of sin is physical death. It is primarily of physical death that Paul speaks here, since in this whole 15th chapter he deals with the resurrection of the body. In the Greek text the definite article precedes the words "death" and "sin." The literal Greek is, "And the sting of *the* death, *the* sin." It is the death of Adam, his physical death and ours, caused by *the* sin, his sin and ours. Sin therefore separated man's spirit from the Spirit of God and eventually separates man's spirit from his body. The death and resurrection of Christ reconciles the spirit of man to the Spirit of God, when man by faith receives Christ as his Saviour by appropriating what Christ did for him on the cross. The same death and resurrection assures the reunion of man's spirit to his own glorious resurrection body. This is the final restoration of man to God's eternal plan and purpose.

TAKING THE STING OUT OF DEATH

"The sting of sin is death; and the strength of sin is the law" (I Cor. 15:56).

Serpents can be rendered harmless by removing their sting. Similarly, it is possible for you and me in a sense to pull out the sting of death by accepting in faith Christ's work of redemption for us. If sin is the sting of death, then when sin is forgiven the sting of death is removed. It is then that you begin to be victorious over the prospect of physical death. When you receive Christ as your Saviour, then you take comfort from His Word, "He that believeth in me, though he were dead, yet shall he live" (John 11:25).

It is sin that makes death so frightening. If it were not for sin and the prospect of judgment, death would often be welcome as a relief from sorrow, poverty, or pain. Were it not for sin, there would be less occasion for grief and none for horror at the prospect of the spirit returning to God who gave it. But sin, which separated man from God, still makes us unwilling to approach Him. Death carries us into the immediate presence of our Creator; and, if we still bear the guilt of sin on our conscience, we regard our Creator, not as an innocent child meets a tender father, delighting to be restored to his arms, but as a disobedient son or daughter trembles at the approach of an offended parent.

This guilty fear of God was an immediate consequence of sin. When Adam and Eve sinned, they hid themselves from God in the Garden of Eden. If we can conceive of a man who had never sinned, death would hold no terrors for him. This same peace of mind can be yours when your sin is forgiven through Christ.

If you have no fear of death, one of two things must be true: either Christ has become your Saviour who has taken upon Himself the guilt and power of sin to hurt you, or your conscience is so seared and your heart so hardened that you have lost all understanding of the reality of your destiny. In the first case, you are aware of what awaits you; in the second, you are not. Nevertheless, the consequences of sin must be met, whether you realize it or not. Your state of being, resulting from the choices you have made, will be met by the inexorable purposes and laws of God.

But even for the Christian who knows that, on dying, he will go to be with Christ and will one day be raised in an incorruptible body, death is seldom joyfully welcomed. True, his sin is under the redeeming blood of Christ, and therefore the fatal sting of finality has been removed—he knows that death is not the end of everything. Nevertheless, it is an unpleasant experience. It is still an enemy simply because man, though redeemed, is not perfect. His imperfection is demonstrated to a great extent in the repulsion he feels toward death.

We have said that serpents can be rendered harmless when their sting is removed. Nevertheless, they are still snakes. This is how Paul presents death. For the Christian, even in view of the resurrection of the body, death is not exactly a pleasant experience even when the sting of sin and the fear of judgment are removed. It always entails separation from the known and loved associations of earth, but it can never separate the believer from God, for his soul lives on in a bodiless state in God's presence and his body will one day be regained in a glorious and incorruptible form. Therefore, though the Christian may face death with sorrow, he should not be overwhelmed by it.

The famed evangelist, Dwight L. Moody, once remarked in a sermon, "Some day you will read in the papers that D. L. Moody of East Northfield is dead. Don't you believe a word of it. At that moment I shall be more alive than now. I shall have gone up higher, that is all—out of this old clay tenement into a house that is immortal; a body that death cannot touch, that sin cannot taint, a body fashioned like unto His glorious body. That which is born of the flesh may die. That which is born of the spirit will live forever." And that is the sure and blessed hope the Gospel inspires. "O death, where is thy sting? O grave, where is thy victory? . . . . Thanks be to God, which giveth us the victory through our Lord Jesus Christ" (I Cor. 15:55, 57).

If it were not for sin, men would never have lost their relationship with God and they would never have died. Christ came to restore all who would by faith receive Him as their Sin-bearer. He came to undo the work of the first Adam. He resurrects the dead soul of man. That is the spiritual resurrection. Man becomes alive spiritually when he receives Christ as his Saviour. The sting of spiritual death is gone. That doesn't mean that the believer never has occasion to be sorry for sins caused by his soulish or natural body. We call to mind the sins that Paul had to rebuke in the early Corinthian Church, and how he later instructed that a certain penitent sinner be forgiven and taken back into fellowship "lest perhaps such a one should be swallowed up with overmuch sorrow" (II Cor. 2:7).

Sin cannot kill believers, but it gives them a hard time. The believer is sensitive to sin, while the unbeliever, being completely dead in sin, is far less sensitive to it, even to the point of being completely unaware of its presence.

Spiritual death is all around us. As Christians it can affect us but does not have the power to separate us from God's love. "In all these things we are more than conquerors through him that loved us" (Rom. 8:37). Spiritual death cannot have the victory over us, but it puts up a strong fight against us. The permanent condition of the Christian life is one of warfare and resistance against sin, both within ourselves and in the world around us. But we may confidently rest in the assertion of James, "Resist the devil, and he will flee from you" (James 4:7).

Every time you feel separated from God, sin is the culprit: Adam's sin originally, from which you inherited the sin-nature of your soulish body, and also your own personal sin. That's what is meant by "the sting of death is sin." Nothing hurts the sensitive believer more than a feeling of separation from God, compounded as it often is of the guilty knowledge that it has been brought about by his own sin. Your enjoyment of the presence of God in this life is directly proportionate to the absence of sin, to victory over sin, which actually means holiness of life.

Perhaps you wonder what sins are keeping you from full fellowship with God. You have committed no gross sins that you know of. But what about your complacency with worldliness, your quick temper, your fault-finding and detraction of absent friends, your neglect of prayer and Bible-study, your secularization of the Lord's Day? These will do for a start to provide you with food for thought as to why God does not seem as close to you as you would like Him to be. Confess and forsake these as sins, rather than regarding them as excusable weaknesses, and you will be on your way to that "holiness, without which no man may see the Lord" (Heb. 12:14).

WHAT MAKES SIN SINFUL?

"The sting of death is sin; and the strength of sin is the law" (I Cor. 15:56).

What makes sin sinful? I remember when I was in the army I was brought before my commanding officer because while I was on night duty I had opened a telegram I wasn't supposed to. Nobody had told me this. I thought it was part of my duty to open it and to communicate its contents to the officer on duty. I ended my defense with the words of Paul, "Sin is not imputed when there is no law" (Rom. 5:13). I was not punished. They saw the reasonableness of my contention that one cannot break a law that does not exist. No law, no sin.

In the Greek text, the definite article appears before the words "death, sin, and law" in I Corinthians 15:56, as if they were personified. "And the sting of the death the sin, and the strength of the sin the law." There is no flexibility as to the meaning of these terms. Each is clearly defined in the mind of Paul. "The death" is the spiritual separation of man from God and the physical separation of his body from his soul. "The sin" is man's missing the mark God set as the goal He had purposed for him in creation. "The law" is God's command to man. "The law" states two things: that we are to do or not to do certain things, and that if we fail to obey in any respect we will receive certain prescribed and appropriate punishments. Such punishments sting. Indeed, they must sting or the very establishment of law is ridiculous. The law that does not provide appropriate punishment for the lawbreaker is without strength. It is a dead letter, as so many of our laws have become.

Man has disobeyed and is disobeying God's law. He may think he is getting away with it, but the very fact that man dies and that death is such a dreaded enemy shows that God has put teeth in His law. As no one can escape the physical laws instituted by God, so he cannot escape God's spiritual laws. God ordained that two parts of hydrogen and one part of oxygen compose the substance we know as water. He makes it; you cannot; though you may put two parts of hydrogen and one part of oxygen together. God also ordained that the moment man touched the forbidden fruit he would die. And, in the very moment that he did this, he died spiritually; and ultimately he dies physically.

What is this law of which Paul speaks as constituting a check to sin? Many make the mistake of assuming that every mention of "the law" refers to the Mosaic Law or to the Ten Commandments. These are the summary of God's law, not the whole law in every respect. The law is not necessarily a specific command about a specific course of action that must be taken at a particular time but can also be a principle of discernment as to whether something is right or wrong. Man's conscience was originally the voice of God in his soul; and even now, in his fallen state, man has enough of this once holy function left to know the difference between right and wrong. It nags him with a persistent sense of guilt, which he may manage to put down while he is living, but which very often reasserts itself with terrifying force when he is dying.

This principle of discernment has been placed by God within the framework of human personality. A sense of guilt is the result of the innate knowledge of what should be done that we have failed to do. In His wisdom, God knew that man should be tested as to his willingness to obey. He gave him a specific command. Man disobeyed it. He became a fallen creature, and ever since he has been prone to disobey rather than to obey. Conscience witnesses to it every time. And so that God may not be accused of generalities, He delivered a set of specific commandments, obedience to which constitutes the yardstick of man's general obedience.

According to Paul, God is completely absolved of responsibility for man's sin. He made man capable of exercising the power of choice. For this we should be grateful. But He did not at creation make him prone to disobedience. He asked one thing of him—obedience to His law. And, that there might be no misunderstanding of what God expected man to do, He did not simply institute in man the principle of law and discernment of what is good and evil, but instead He gave a specific command. He said in effect, "Just don't eat of the fruit of this one tree." Now man did not need to eat of that fruit to keep alive and happy. The fruit in itself probably had no power of ill to affect man. It was not poisonous. The harm lay in man's beginning to question the reasonableness of God's command. "Why should He forbid me to eat of this one tree?" It might even have been exactly like many another tree in the garden. The fault lay in man's questioning God's wisdom.

You have experienced the same thing in family life. You tell a little child not to touch a certain bottle of pills that look to him like candy. The child immediately asks, "But why not?" In this case, of course, the harm of disobedience is twofold, for the pills themselves are inherently poisonous to a child. But to the child this is not obvious. You, of course, know why they must be forbidden. You know better.

Now, consider God, the infinite and eternal. Surely He knows better than man. The gap between His intelligence and ours is infinitely greater than that between a human father and child. God does not have to give reasons for His commands. The fact that He says so should be enough for those who are fully trusting Him. Don't think you must know the reason for everything God says and does. What makes you think the reasons are always humanly knowable? If you have a proper estimate of God's infinite wisdom in relation to your own limited intelligence and knowledge, you will concede that what He asks, does, and permits is for the best of all possible reasons.

One thing God does do, however, and that is He makes His commands so plain and clear that man may be inexcusable. His law is always sufficient for each circumstance so that man may judge the way that he should follow. The more specific the law the more specific the sin. The moment that Eve took of the forbidden fruit she sinned. There could be no evasion of responsibility. It was a specific command and a specific transgression.

God's law is full of such specific commands, both in nature and in human conduct. These are written and unwritten. They are in the Bible and they are in your own inherent make-up—call it conscience if you will. If it is an enlightened and true conscience, regulated by the Word of God, this index of consciousness will be basically true. But even if it is a seared and disordered conscience, there are enough remnants of discernment within your own consciousness to make you responsible before God for your attitudes and acts.

IGNORANCE OF THE LAW IS NO EXCUSE

"The sting of death is sin; and the strength of sin is the law" (I Cor. 15:56).

Listen to the words of Paul in Romans 2:12, 14, 15: "For as many as have sinned without law shall also perish without law: and as many as have sinned in the law shall be judged by the law . . . . For when the Gentiles, which have not the law, *do by nature,* the things contained in the law, these, having not the law, are a law unto themselves: which shew the work of the law written in their hearts, their conscience also bearing witness, and their thoughts the mean while accusing or else excusing one another."

The more specific the law of God the greater is the strength of sin. That's what Paul means. As you face death, your fear of it is in proportion to your knowledge of the measure in which you have failed God. And because we Christians also fail God we, too, fear death in varying degrees. Of course, our failure is not the same as that of unbelievers, who have rejected God Himself. Our failure is in the realm of falling short of God's expectations of us as believers. If during my lifetime I was able to give God more of my love, talents, time, and money than I did, my fear of death will be in proportion to my failure to measure up to what I knew He wanted of me.

Never forget what James 4:17 teaches: "To him that knoweth to do good, and doeth it not, to him it is sin." The Greek word for "sin" here is exactly the same as that in I Corinthians 15:56. God will hold you responsible for your attitudes and actions in proportion to the law that He has made specifically known to you. The words of Christ in John 15:22 are very revealing in this regard: "If I had not come and spoken unto them, they had not had sin: but now they have no cloke [or excuse] for their sin." This concerned those who were going to persecute His disciples. Because Christ had warned them specifically against this, their sin was greater.

Observe this fundamental truth. God delivers His law to man in various ways and measures. It is primarily in proportion to the measure in which He delivers His law that He holds man responsible, not in the measure that man decides to know, appropriate, and obey that law. Take the law of the State in which you live. By virtue of living in a particular State, you are under the responsibility of obeying the law of that State. If you disobey the law, your claim of ignorance of the law will not excuse you. It is incumbent upon you to know—to find out, in fact—the law as it applies to you. The existence of the law is the all-important thing as far as the judge is concerned. Your ability to know the law is sufficient to make you responsible.

Of course, you may choose to remain ignorant of the law, but that does not absolve you of the responsibility for obeying it. So it is with God's law. He instituted it, made it known through inspired men of His choosing who set it down in Scripture, and He gave you a certain ability to comprehend what He required of you. To say that you did not know what you should or should not do does not excuse you. The strength of sin is the law. The law therefore is the level of God's expectation of you as an individual. And of course what applies to individuals applies also to nations, for there is judgment of individuals and also for nations.

In fact, since death is mentioned here as the punishment for sin, Paul's declaration, "and the strength of sin the law," could be paraphrased "and the strength of the punishment—or death—the law." Your judgment primarily will be proportionate to your God-given opportunities to know and obey God's law, not merely as to your choice of knowing and obeying or disregarding His law. Increase in knowledge is based on your willingness to learn, whereas opportunity is God's provision of that which there is to learn and the ability to learn it. Make a clear distinction here.

This principle is well illustrated by the parable of the laborers in the vineyard in Matthew 20:1-16. Three servants were offered work at different hours of the day. Some therefore worked more hours than others, but they were not rewarded according to the actual number of hours worked but according to the opportunity afforded them. Thus our judgment of reward or lack of it will depend on the opportunity we had of knowing and obeying God's law. He who had an opportunity and did not use it will be judged accordingly; and he who did not have an opportunity—should there be such a one—will not be held responsible.

The intriguing word *dunamis* is used in this verse to show the strength of sin. It is the same word that is used in Romans 1:16 to describe the Gospel of Christ as "the power [*dunamis*] of God unto salvation." What is this power or strength? It is the ability to accomplish that which is intended. "The power of God unto salvation" is God's dynamic to bring salvation to man, to restore man to Himself. The Gospel, the Good News that Christ died for our sins, brings about man's reconciliation to God. The Lord provides the "dynamite," so to speak. But it becomes effective, it detonates, when you set it off by your repentance and faith. Then God's purpose for your redemption is basically accomplished.

The power of sin works in the same manner, though with opposite effect. It is set off by you and it separates you from God. There is only one way of bridging the gap, and that is through Christ. The law sends us to Christ to be justified, and then Christ sends us to the law to be regulated.

What is sin? It is any want of conformity to the law and will of God. Adam sinned because he ate of the forbidden fruit. What we are and are not supposed to do is not left to our subjective judgment. It is delineated by law. None of us can be a law unto himself. Yet this is the danger that threatens our society today, when large segments of the population are taking the law into their own hands and deciding what laws they will or will not obey. "What I think is right is law for me" is their attitude. This is not what the Word of God means by the word "law" here. "And the strength of sin is *the* law"—not your law or your circumstances. There is no room for situation ethics in God's Word. Sin is sin, and the law is the law, at all times. Situations don't change either the strength of sin or the law.

Sin is nothing to play with. It has the strength to defeat you if you get too close to it with excessive confidence in your own strength. A well-to-do man advertised for a chauffeur. Three applicants came. His first question was, "How close to the edge of a cliff can you drive without going over?" One man said, "A yard." Another said, "A foot." The third said, "I always try to keep as far away as possible." The third man got the job. He who underestimates the strength of an enemy is in danger of defeat. What Christ has accomplished for you, sin destroys, and Christ is the only One who can destroy the strength of sin.

ARE THE LAWS OF GOD OUTDATED?

"The sting of death is sin; and the strength of sin is the law" (I Cor. 15:56).

A little girl could not understand why her teacher kept marking her arithmetic examples wrong when they were almost right. One day the teacher sent home this note: "Please impress upon Cynthia the necessity of absolutely correct solutions. There is no such thing as an answer nearly right. The answer is either right or wrong."

There is an absoluteness about the law of God in the moral realm even as there is in the physical realm. Where would we be in our exploration of space if we could not depend on God's physical laws? His law in nature governs all our actions in the physical world. Why should we consider His moral law any less valid to guide all our actions in the spiritual world?

God's law in nature is distinguished by certain characteristics that also carry over into the spiritual world. These natural laws will therefore repay some study.

First, they are enduring. Only He who created them can supersede or overrule them to accomplish a desired purpose. When He does this, we call it a miracle. The resurrection body of Christ was not subject to the laws of nature. Neither will our resurrection body be. The miracle in the spiritual realm is that sin and death can have no dominion over the one who is spiritually risen with Christ.

Then God's natural law is inexorable and undiscriminating. It makes no exceptions. It is affected neither by age, ignorance, nor knowledge. It exacts its penalty from every violator. Natural law does not lessen its penalty because its violator is a child, or its violation is involuntary or in ignorance. Poison is not a bit less deadly because it was taken by mistake. If my arm is broken, it makes no difference whatever in the physical effects whether it happened in justifiable defense of my own person or in a criminal assault upon the person of another. If I am beheaded, the physical result is the same whether my name is haloed with the glory of a martyr or branded with the infamy of a culprit.

The general laws of nature march straight on, without discrimination in the execution of their effects, whether they bear upon man, woman, or the child that is too young to know about them. They are irresistible. Man may modify their effects for a while, but in the end they triumph. Physicians may stave off the too-early dissolution of the human body, but in the end the law of death prevails.

God's spiritual laws, too, are inexorable in their consequences. They are impartial, even as a mirror is impartial in revealing our cleanliness or lack of it—and for exactly the same reason, to show us our need of cleansing. As a mirror that reflects a dirty face sends us hurrying after soap and water to cleanse our skin, so God's spiritual law shows us our inner pollution and drives us of necessity to seek heart-cleansing and righteousness in Christ.

God's law defines and limits liberty so that even a child can comprehend it. When I was a child I used to cut across a vacant lot on my way home. I had no thought that I was trespassing. But what if the owner put up a sign, "No trespassing; violators will be prosecuted"? Law would then make me aware of transgression, and from then on the choice would be mine whether to obey or disobey. If I disobeyed, I could no longer plead ignorance, for the law existed and had been made plain.

Some people look upon God's law as entirely prohibitive. "Christianity is a series of 'don'ts,' " they say. God's Word is certainly a restraint; but it is such a restraint as the fence along a cliff's edge, which prevents a child from toppling over to his death. We acknowledge that most parental restraints have their source in love, with an eye to our well-being. So it is with our Heavenly Father, who requires certain things of us, not only to please Him but also to promote our own well-being and peace of mind; such as temperance, chastity, meekness, contentedness, and a regard for the rights of others. And all the vices He has forbidden us have a direct tendency to do us harm and disturb our minds, such as gluttony, drunkenness, anger, envy, and hatred.

To the man who knows Christ as his Saviour and Lord, the laws of God are no more burdensome than wings are to a bird. They are the means by which he soars into that joyous realm where he knows his actions are pleasing to God, and he can enjoy unbroken fellowship with Him.

Now the law reveals sin, but it does not save the sinner. It is like the rock in the river, which reveals the current by opposing it. An observer on shore can note the direction and velocity of the river's flow as it meets with the obstructing rock in midstream. Life itself is like a river—rolling downstream in unnoticed enmity against God until it meets with the obstruction of the law, which then makes known the force and direction of its flow. Sin is then seen for what it is. But as the rock in the river did not cause the disturbance around it, neither can it subdue it. And when sin in the human heart comes up against the law, the law simply reveals it without amending it. However, this revealing of sin is what makes the law "our schoolmaster to bring us unto Christ" (Gal. 3:24).

Man is different from all of God's other creatures in that he alone deliberately disobeys God's law. Nature never deviates from God's prescribed laws, but man in his unregenerate state finds it natural to go against what God commands. He wants to be morally unrestricted.

If there were no law, there would be no disobedience and therefore no sin. Why establish laws at all, then, since it may be argued that they are productive of sin? Law is a necessity without which there would be chaos. We acknowledge this in the physical realm. Where would we be without the law of gravity? And it is also true in the spiritual realm. How could society function without ethical and moral standards? About like Times Square without traffic lights!

God either had to give man omniscience to enable him to make his own laws, or He had to provide him with law. The first was impossible, for then God would have created little gods and not men, and how could there be "created gods"? What He actually did create were human beings who could not be trusted to exercise their power of choice wisely enough to make their own laws because of their limited knowledge. Therefore God had to make known to them what He required of them by way of duty to Himself and to their fellow men, so that they would have an absolute standard of right and wrong. And He had to impose sufficiently strong sanctions to make the law an effective brake on sin, so that society could function sufficiently well for the human race to continue. But the law makes no man righteous; it merely serves as a deterrent to sin, as a revealer of sin, and as a schoolmaster to bring men to Christ.

THE NECESSITY FOR A NEW NATURE

"The sting of death is sin; and the strength of sin is the law" (I Cor. 15:56).

Have you heard the story of the man who lived in a walled city and had never been outside the walls? For some infraction of the law, the magistrate of that city decreed that he must never go outside. Strange to tell, up to the moment the command had been issued, the man had been perfectly content and never thought of passing the border; but as soon as he was forbidden to go he pined, sickened, and finally died moaning over the restriction.

Man is often tempted to break the law merely because it is there. You may point out to him the way of uprightness, and tell him what is right and what is wrong, with all the wisdom and persuasion at your command, but unless you can give him a heart to choose the right and love the true, you have not done much to make him a law-abiding citizen. This is just the province of law. It can tell you what to do and what not to do, but it cannot make you obey.

In this way it can be said that the law gives strength to sin, by arousing a sinful man's desire to flout it. Nevertheless, law there must be. What man really needs is a new nature that does not rebel at God's law but obeys it without questioning the reasons for which God instituted it. For this he must have God within him. Victory against the strength of sin is possible only through Christ. Paul exclaims in I Corinthians 15:57, "But thanks be to God, which giveth us the victory through our Lord Jesus Christ." Sin loses its strength and God's law is obeyed when Christ indwells the human heart. In order for Him to be able to do this, very radical measures were needed. Satan, the instigator to sin, had to receive a death blow. The seed of the woman, the Lord Jesus Christ, had to "bruise his head," as the first prophecy of a coming Redeemer tells us in Genesis 3:15.

This brings to mind the story of the man with an axe who was attacked by a vicious dog, and in defending himself had to kill the animal. The owner was furious and asked the man how he dared kill his dog. The man replied that if he had not killed it the dog would have torn him to pieces. "Well," said the owner, "why did you hit it with the blade? Why didn't you just hit it with the handle?" "I would have," replied the man, "if it had tried to bite me with its tail."

So, when I have to deal with sin, some people say, "Why don't you go about it more diplomatically? Why don't you choose less offensive words to describe it?" And I answer, "I would, if it would bite me with its tail, but as long as it deals roughly with me, I will deal roughly with it; and any kind of weapon that will help to slay the monster, I'm going to feel free to use."

The victory against Satan was the victory against sin. And since the consequence of sin is death, Christ conquered sin by defeating death through His resurrection. It is the living Christ, therefore, who can continuously strike at sin and who will ultimately even cancel out physical death for us as He has already canceled our spiritual death. Paul states this very clearly in Romans 10:4, "Christ is the end of the law for righteousness to every one that believeth." When you believe in Christ, the law no longer strengthens your inclination to sin, for with your new birth comes an inherent inclination to righteousness. No man has a right to do as he pleases, unless he pleases to do right. As you grow in grace in the Christian life, you will more and more want to do right, so that there is truth in the aphorism, "Love God and do as you please."

When Christ takes His rightful place in our heart as Saviour and Lord, we will have no real struggle to conform to God's law, because then by nature we will have become the children of God. The law of God produces an irritation of man's fallen nature. But when man is transformed in his nature, he begins to live increasingly in harmony with the will of God. That's the way it was in Eden when man lived in innocence in his unfallen state. And that's the way it is when man lives the regenerated life in Christ and is renewed and led by His Spirit. Then there is no opposition between God's moral law and man's nature.

But with fallen and unreconciled man it is far otherwise. And it is otherwise with Christians who by willful disobedience and sloth have impaired their sensibility to sin. To such the moral law appears only as an outward rule, an unwelcome restraint upon all that they naturally desire to do and be. It is an unwelcome yoke that is inconsistent with the liberty of the passions; a continuous incentive to resistance until it is embraced voluntarily as a principle of life, until it expresses the bent and drift of the will. But until this blessed state is reached, law acts upon our fallen nature as a constant incentive to rebellion, and is thus the strength of sin.

Putting himself into the position of fallen man, Paul writes to the Romans, "I had not known sin, but by the law: for I had not known lust, except the law had said, Thou shalt not covet. But sin, taking occasion by the commandment, wrought in me all manner of concupiscence. For without the law sin was dead . . . . For sin, taking occasion by the commandment, deceived me, and by it slew me" (Rom. 7:7, 8, 11).

"Thus, in a sinful nature, sin is strengthened by the very presence and imperativeness of the Rule of holiness; and this makes it, for numbers of human beings, the sting of death. This sting is extracted when the moral Law has become, through regenerating grace, an inward principle, an instinct not to be distinguished from a man's average desire and will; but until this has been done, or when, through a lapse into willful evil, it has been undone, the moral Law cannot but be the strength of sin, and the minister of the sharpest pang to the thought and the experience of death." (H. P. Liddon, *Sermons on Some Words of Paul,* pp. 161-2.)

There is a wonderful contrast between the state of defeat because of the presence of sin and the state of victory because of the rule of Christ. This contrast is expressed by the use of the conjunctive particle *de,* "but," which joins verse 57 to verses 56 and 55. Sin brings death, *but* God gives the victory through Christ. You move from darkness to light, from death to life. In the words of the old hymn, you can say,

> Out of my bondage, sorrow, and night,
>   Jesus, I come; Jesus, I come;
> Into Thy freedom, gladness, and light,
>   Jesus, I come to Thee.
>
> Out of the fear and dread of the tomb,
>   Jesus, I come; Jesus, I come;
> Into the joy and light of my home,
>   Jesus, I come to Thee.

HOW CHRIST'S VICTORY CAN BE YOURS

◆

"But thanks be to God, which giveth us the victory through our Lord Jesus Christ" (I Cor. 15:57).

A Scotsman was once asked how many it took to convert him. "Two," he replied. "Two! How was that? Didn't God do it all?" "The Almighty and myself converted me," he said. "I did all I could against it, and the Almighty did all he could for it, and He was victorious."

Even so the Apostle Paul bursts out with a triumphant note of thanksgiving for the victory that he found in Christ. He had done everything he could to resist Christ, until finally the living Lord had to strike him down on the road to Damascus. No wonder he does not try to take any credit to himself. He says, "But unto God be thanks." He means God the Father in contradistinction to God the Son. The definite article appears before the word God here (*too theoo*). We could paraphrase it as, "But unto God the Father be thanks."

The word translated "thanks" in Greek is *charis*, which stands for "grace" in most instances in the New Testament. A similar use of the word occurs in Romans 6:17, where Paul deals with the subject of victory over sin, as he does here. "But God be thanked, that ye were the servants of sin, but ye have obeyed from the heart that form of doctrine which was delivered you."

The Greek word *charis* comes from the verb *chairein*, "to rejoice." Originally it referred to "that property in a thing which causes it to give a joy to the hearers or beholders of it" (Trench). Therefore it was the grace or beauty of a thing. Then it came to mean "the favor" and still later "the thankfulness that is aroused by the favor." In the New Testament the word is used not so much as the favor of man to man as the favor of God to man. And the response of gratitude or joy that it stimulates in man toward God is also called *charis*. It is the favor of the worthy to the unworthy, of the holy to the sinful. *Charis*, "grace," always implies a favor freely done, without claim or expectation of return, finding its only motive in the bounty and free-heartedness of the giver. (See R. C. Trench, *Synonyms of the New Testament*, pp. 166-8.)

What we offer back to God as thanks, therefore, is only what He has already given to us; it is grace of His grace. Of our own selves we cannot thank God. His grace seems to be made of rubber; when it touches us it bounces back. What a lesson we may learn from this! When we show a favor to someone, we benefit him. But the thanks that we receive in return is grace for us. There is never a giving without a receiving. As God always gives His grace to us freely without any expectation of return, let us do the same. Unavoidably He does receive a return, however, and so do we. And, when we get it without expecting it, we value it twice as much. Let us remember that grace bestowed produces joy, since joy is the primary meaning of the word *chairoo*.

An American admiral once had a small card printed and circulated among his subordinates and workers. On it in gray type was this background: "It Can't Be Done," and then, in bold black type across this was printed, "But Here It Is." As we look at sin and realize its strength, defeat would seem to be inevitable, were it not for Christ.

"But thanks be to God, which giveth us the victory through our Lord Jesus Christ." The phrase "which giveth us" is a present participle in Greek. A better translation would be "who keeps on giving us." This is not just one victory that God gives us but a constant experience of victory through Christ. We do not win the victory ourselves. We don't have the strength. He simply gives that to us. The verb here is *didonti*, from *didoomi* meaning "bestow, grant." It is given to us as a result of our attachment to Christ. Victory is the by-product of the close relationship maintained by the believer to his Lord.

Napoleon said, "Battles are won, not by men, but by a man." He was right in more ways than one. Victories are won, not by Christians but by Christ. And it is our privilege and joy to share in His victory. Like the small boy who jumped up and down shouting "We've won, we've won!" at a football game—though he was not a member of the team or of the school represented by the team—we too can rejoice in a victory with which we associate ourselves. We can live in joy and triumph. We can shout, "We've won!" over the victory that was accomplished by our Lord Jesus Christ on Calvary nearly 2,000 years ago.

In the darkest hour of the war with Germany, when the destiny of civilization was trembling in the balance, the Congress of Allied Women, meeting in Paris, adopted the ringing slogan, "Believe victory! Think victory! Preach victory! Live victory!" This is the slogan that the Apostle Paul wants us to adopt in view of the resurrection. It is so important to believe that victory is possible; but we must be clear in our minds as to how it can be won. There can be no appropriation of Christ's victory unless we have first appropriated His atonement, even as Christ could not be victorious over sin and death until He had first identified Himself with fallen man in taking upon Himself the sins of the world and offering Himself a sacrifice in our place, incurring the penalty of death on our behalf.

Can you look upon Jesus as standing in your place, to bear the wrath of God for you, and not be moved? When you, like Isaac, were bound to the altar, to be offered up to justice, Christ, like the ram caught in the thicket, was offered in your place. When like Jonah your sins had raised a fearful tempest, threatening every moment to bury you in a sea of wrath, Jesus Christ was thrown over in your place to appease that storm. Can your heart dwell for one hour upon such a subject as this and not melt? Can you, with the eye of faith, envision Christ as He was taken down from the cross, drenched in His own blood, and say, "These were the wounds that He received for me; this is He that loved me and gave Himself for me; out of these wounds comes that balm that heals my soul, out of these stripes my peace"? (Adapted from Flavel.)

Only when you have by faith repented of your sins and received the benefits of Christ's atonement can you share in the victory He has won for you over sin and death. The simplest act of faith, "O God, be merciful to me a sinner, and save me for Jesus' sake," will suffice, if you mean it with all your heart.

THE TRANSFORMING POWER OF
THE RESURRECTION

"Therefore, my beloved brethren, be ye stedfast, unmoveable, always abounding in the work of the Lord, forasmuch as ye know that your labour is not in vain in the Lord" (I Cor. 15:58).

How strong is your Christianity? Is it a feeble creed that keeps you constantly on the defensive against the attacks of unbelievers and the doubts of your own heart, or is it an overcoming power that enables you to meet triumphantly and courageously the mysteries and difficulties of your existence? Is it an extra burden that you must carry or is it God's power to carry you?

I do not mean to imply that we must not defend our faith against attack. Christianity can stand any intellectual and historical scrutiny because of Christ Himself. In fact, the Apostle Paul in this 15th chapter of I Corinthians was careful first of all to establish the historical veracity of Christ's resurrection. Our own certainty of a coming resurrection stands on the fact that Christ rose from the dead. But the penetrating question that Paul ends up with is, "What is this risen Christ accomplishing in and through you?" Let the resurrection not be a dead doctrine to you. Christ is alive and therefore must breathe in and through you.

One word of caution, however. The verbal defense of Christianity can be overdone. People are inclined to believe there must be something wrong if we are always anxiously defending our religion, as if it were something naturally weak that needed an immense amount of coddling to keep it alive. We must rid ourselves of this inferiority complex, and rejoice in the Gospel as "the power of God unto salvation to every one that believeth" (Rom. 1:16). Our faith should give us victory over the world, and it is as victorious people that we should face the world. Such a practical demonstration of the Gospel's redeeming power will prove its value far beyond any mere verbal defense.

No one need write a book to prove the value of the sun. It proves its worth by what it does. Without the sun our planet would be a frozen world spinning in perpetual darkness. We need no verbal arguments to convince us of the value of food, fresh air, exercise, and cleanliness. They prove their value by what they do. Should not our faith do likewise?

To demonstrate the power of the living Christ, Paul begins the 58th and final verse of this glorious resurrection chapter with the conjunction *hooste*, "therefore" or "consequently." This is the natural consequence of the resurrection in your lives, he tells the Corinthians. "Therefore, my beloved brethren, be ye stedfast, unmoveable, always abounding in the work of the Lord, forasmuch as ye know that your labour is not in vain in the Lord."

An atheist challenged a preacher to a debate before a great crowd of people. "I will agree," said the preacher, "if you will produce 100 people whose lives have been transformed by the power of atheism and who have in consequence made society a better place to live in. I in turn will agree to bring 100 such people whose lives have been transformed by the saving power of Christ, to give their testimony." Needless to say, the atheist declined.

Christianity is something more than a system of

beliefs, an argument, a philosophy; it is the life of Christ in human beings transforming them into new creatures who are moment by moment motivated by His power. Christianity involves a living Christ. As someone wrote me recently after being transformed as a result of reading our Gospel messages in the Greek press: "I never thought that a person like me could ever come to the point of loving my enemies." This is what John means when he says, "This is the victory that overcometh the world, even our faith" (I John 5:4). Faith is power within that demonstrates itself outwardly. If it does not do so it does not exist; it is what James calls "dead faith," which is good for nothing. The risen Christ enables us to overcome the world in our spirit, to be its masters and not its victims.

Charles Finney, a renowned evangelist of the past, was approached by a man at the end of one of his meetings at which he had preached on the verse, "The blood of Jesus Christ his Son cleanseth us from all sin" (I John 1:7). "Would you come with me to my place of business?" he asked. Another man overheard him and whispered to Mr. Finney, "If I were you, I wouldn't go. I'm not sure you would get out of there alive." But Mr. Finney went. He found himself in a notorious establishment. His heart was in his mouth when the man locked the door behind him and pulled a gun from his pocket. "Mr. Finney," he said, "this pistol has killed four men while I held it, and by proxy it has killed several others. Doubtless, sir, you know that you are in the den of the most murderous desperado in the country. I did not bring you here, however, to harm you, but to ask if such a blood-guilty man can be saved."

Mr. Finney quoted to him the verse he had preached on, "The blood of Jesus Christ his Son cleanseth us from all sin." The man turned, picked up a greasy pack of cards, and said, "Through the use of these, I have stolen thousands of dollars, and these have driven men to poverty, theft, murder, and suicide. Can your Gospel reach such a man as that?" Mr. Finney quoted his text again, "The blood of Jesus Christ his son cleanseth us from all sin."

With increased concern this poor prisoner of sin, crime, and the devil said, "I have neglected my family. I have beaten my wife, who has been true to me as an angel of God. I have kicked my own child about as if she were a beast. Now, sir, deal candidly with me and tell me, do you believe that such a profane, licentious, gambling, drunkard-making, wife-beating criminal has any right for mercy or grounds of hope?" Mr. Finney said, "You present a dark picture, but I am only authorized as a servant of God to quote my text, 'The blood of Jesus Christ his Son cleanseth us from all sin.'"

From the look of the alley the next day, it was apparent how the man spent the remaining hours of the night—throwing out bottles, cards, and other gambling equipment. In the morning, as he related later, he went home to his bedroom. His wife sent her namesake, Addie, a girl of eleven, to tell him to come to breakfast. He said, "Addie, darling, tell mama I don't want any breakfast." The little girl went running back, falling as she hurried to the kitchen, and exclaimed, "Oh, Mama, Papa called me darling!" When this happened for the second and third time, the wondering wife went up to see for herself. She saw her little girl sitting on her father's knee, and he was kissing her for the first time in his life. Looking up, he motioned for his wife to come, and pulling her down on the other knee he said, "Addie, it's been many years since you sat here, or received a caress or a kind word from me. I know you don't know what this means, and I hardly know myself, but I will need your help today as I have never needed it before. I have no barroom today; I have closed that hell-hole forever. I am going to sell most of my property and draw on my bank account until I have righted every wrong as far as possible, and paid back money that was not mine.

"You have a new husband this morning, our children have a new father, this community has a new citizen, right has a new friend, and the devil has a new enemy. And, with your permission, Mr. Finney will have dinner with us today, and he can explain it to you better than I can. He said, 'The blood of Jesus Christ his Son cleanseth us from all sin,' and God has given another miracle to the world, that Jesus had power on earth to forgive sins, even mine."

This is what a living, risen Christ can do in any life. Whether your sins are as gross as this man's, or the demeaning and seemingly petty ones of pride, cowardice, and self-centered living, you can be transformed. Say to yourself, "I believe Christ rose. Therefore what does that mean to me? A transformed life? Victory every step of the way? God grant it may."

WHO IS YOUR BROTHER?

"Therefore, my beloved brethren. . . " (I Cor. 15:58a).

Let a little difference arise in doctrine and practice between ourselves and our believing Christian neighbor, and we are all too prone to consign him to eternal hell. We refuse to call him brother. I once met a preacher of a denomination that believed in the atoning work of Christ, His deity, His second coming, and all the cardinal doctrines. However, his denomination held that unless one was baptized (presumably by his group) he could not be saved. I turned to him and said, "You have received the Lord Jesus Christ as your personal Saviour. You have been baptized. I have done exactly the same. You are my brother. Am I yours?" He hesitated for a moment and then said, "No, you are not." I thought to myself, "How narrow can you get?"

Paul severely rebuked the Corinthian Christians on many occasions. "And I, brethren, could not speak unto you as unto spiritual, but as unto carnal, even as unto babes in Christ" (I Cor. 3:1). In I Corinthians 15 he has dealt with those who on philosophical grounds could not accept the possibility of the resurrection of their bodies. It was not that they disbelieved in the reality of Christ's resurrection; otherwise Paul would not have counted them as brethren; for, as he stated in verses 1-4, the saving Gospel consists of faith in the death, burial, and resurrection of Christ. You cannot be a genuine Christian without believing that Christ died for your sins and rose again for your justification. A lack of faith in the future resurrection of your own body, however, while it will not deprive you of your salvation, does rob you of much joy and victory. Paul wrote this 15th chapter to prove that the Lord Jesus rose from the dead, and that this fact is sufficient basis for our faith in the resurrection of every human being. For the believer, this faith spells victory; for the unbeliever, judgment.

Now Paul never clubbed these Corinthians over the head in his endeavor to win them to the victory of faith in a future resurrection; he sought to win them with love. This is why, as he closes his argument for the resurrection, he calls them "my beloved brethren." What a great heart he had! You win people by declaring the truth in love, not by telling them they are anathema because they differ from you on matters not essential to salvation.

How divided the Corinthian Christians were, even in their loyalties to various personalities within the church! Yet the followers of Apollo and Cephas were still "beloved brethren" to Paul. When you fight with your brethren over minor points, just think of how those who have never heard of Christ would react to such bickering. This especially holds true on the foreign mission field, where Christ is preached to those who are total strangers to Him. Rightly did a missionary say, "We on the foreign field work as hard to hide the sectarianism in the churches of the homeland as you here in the homeland work to reveal these differences."

I don't say that we should not preach the truth as far as we can understand it through the enablement of the Holy Spirit, but let us never hesitate to call him who is saved our brother. Which is more precious to you, Christ or your denomination? Believe me, it is more important to have fellowship with those who are saved and belong to denominations other than your own than self-righteously to turn your back on all but your own group.

Paul was never pettily exclusive in his views. In verse 57 he did not say, "Thanks be to God, which giveth *me* the victory through *my* Lord Jesus Christ," but "which giveth *us* the victory through *our* Lord Jesus Christ." This, in spite of the fact that some of these Corinthians did not believe in a future resurrection, and that among them were some believers who had probably not been baptized, since Paul says, "I baptized none of you, but Crispus and Gaius. . . .And. . . . also the household of Stephanas" (I Cor. 1:14, 16). Yet he called all of them "my beloved brethren."

Have you heard the fable of the wolves and the dogs? It seems the wolves were afraid of the dogs, for they were many and strong, so they sent out a spy to observe them. On his return the scout said, "It is true the dogs are many, but there are not many who can harm us. There are dogs of so many sorts one can hardly count them, and, as they came marching on, I observed that they were all snapping right and left at one another, and I could see clearly that, though they all hate the wolf, yet each dog hates every other dog with all his heart."

How we need to take to heart the words of Paul to the Galatians: "For all the law is fulfilled in one word, even in this; Thou shalt love thy neighbor as thyself. But if ye bite and devour one another, take heed that ye be not consumed one of another" (Gal. 5:14, 15).

Not only did Paul consider the Corinthian Christians who disagreed with him his brethren, but he called them "beloved" brethren. The Greek adjective for "beloved," *agapeetos*, comes from the noun *agapee*, "love," denoting the highest kind of love. It is the love that pities and helps, the love that stoops over the weak and needy ones. It is loving a person, not because he deserves it or because of what you can get out of him, but because of what you can do to help him. To consider other Christians as your brethren is not enough; you must love them because they need you. And certainly these philosophizing Christians in Corinth needed Paul's correction in doctrine. But he rebuked them in love, and they accepted it because they knew he loved them.

However, let's not go to the other extreme and call everybody a brother, including those who lack saving faith in the Lord Jesus Christ. Who are our brothers? Those who have the life of the same Heavenly Father in them. And who have this life? Only those who have believed and received the Lord Jesus Christ. "But as many as received him, to them gave he power to become the sons [children] of God, even to them that believe on his name" (John 1:12).

I'd love to call you my brother, but you cannot become that until you believe on the Lord Jesus Christ and receive Him as your Saviour. I'll love you anyway, but I can only call you my beloved brother or sister when you and I have the same Father.

WHAT IS YOUR ULTIMATE GOAL?

"Therefore, my beloved brethren, be ye stedfast, unmoveable, always abounding in the work of the Lord...."
(I Cor. 15:58).

Does the thought of the future life immobilize you or spur you on to greater activity? Does the fact that you have made a profession of faith in Christ, and therefore have the assurance of heaven, cause you to have such a feeling of smug security that you feel you need do nothing more to "work out" your salvation—that is, put it into operation? The Apostle Paul wanted the Corinthians to realize that the prospect of the resurrection of their bodies and the reconstitution of their full personalities, which he discussed in such great detail in this 15th chapter of I Corinthians, should (and does) affect their daily lives.

He says in the 58th verse, "Therefore, my beloved brethren, be ye stedfast, unmoveable, always abounding in the work of the Lord, forasmuch as ye know that your labour is not in vain in the Lord." What he wants to bring out here is that, when you believe in the future resurrection, you will be made steady, unwavering, and fruitful in the Lord's service. It is as if he were saying that the resurrection is no "pie-in-the-sky" doctrine that bears no relation to actual life here and now. Though it is in the future, it has relevance to your present life because of the way it affects your attitudes and actions.

The resurrection implies a prior death. Paul stated that all men consider death an enemy, but it is less fearful to those who have the hope and knowledge of the resurrection. He now turns to a consideration of death as an end in the experience of a Christian that can bring great hope to him. It is as if he were saying, "Christian, cheer up, there is an end. But why dread it, when having an end in life is such a commonplace thing? We are accustomed to the idea that everything that begins must have an end, and often there is some comfort in it. What soldier would fight without the hope that there would be an end to the conflict in which he was engaged? What artist, or writer, or housewife, would start a task if they did not believe it would be finished sometime? God who wrote an end into the very character of nature and all of us—not extinction, but accomplishment—knew what He was doing.

The resurrection is the end that gives death its meaning and value, in that it is the final goal of all our labor. Let us look upon death, therefore, not merely as an enemy but also as a friend, for it is the doorway to the culmination of all present effort. What would be the use of enduring the difficulties of life if there were no end in sight? After all, the soldiers of Christ cannot fight forever. The end makes enduring endurable. If we today find the world a battlefield—as it most certainly is—and life in any respect a warfare, and if our arms grow weary and our hearts faint, we are still called upon to endure as soldiers tried and true. But we are not called to endure forever. There is an end in view.

People today set goals that they can achieve quickly. This is essential, but they should all be subject to that final goal called death as a gateway to the resurrection. When we have to travel long distances on a turnpike, the signposts along the way, that tell us how much farther we have to go, help to make the journey less tiring. Paul would have us think of death and the resurrection as the ultimate goal, and let our short goals give us the sense of moving toward the ultimate. In our daily work, we are to be concerned with what we have to finish that day, that month, that year, but we must also keep very clearly in mind what our lives must be used to accomplish, so that we will enter the gate of death with gladness rather than with remorse. John Stuart Mill declared that his life was changed by his suddenly asking himself the question, "Suppose I attain what I am now pursuing, what sort of man shall I be at the end?"

Our Lord Himself said, "He that endureth to the end shall be saved" (Matt. 10:22). Was he referring only to time here, to death itself as "the end"? I don't think so. The word "end" is often used to mean accomplishment or goal. And the word "saved" here does not refer to salvation from the penalty and power of sin, but to the accomplishment of that goal. This utterance occurs in the midst of Christ's predictions about the persecutions of His followers. Death may be considered by Satan as a punishment, the ultimate punishment upon the followers of Christ; but in reality it is not, for in it is the goal of your accomplishments.

In the midst of suffering, the day can seem so long that you say, "Will the sun never go down?" Take heart, you who are enduring to the end when the end never seems to come in sight. Patience, courage; there is an end. To all there comes a time when we can say, "I have fought my fight, good or bad; I have finished my course, whatever it may be; I have reached my end." There is comfort in this, though not in the end itself. A mere end in time is poor comfort. The end reached brings comfort only when it is purpose reached. To enable us to work and endure, we do not need to see the end actually completed before our eyes; we need rather to know that the work is to some purpose and will somehow reach its end.

Life has an ethical end as well as a temporal end. When the Lord sends His own servants into the world to endure, He has a purpose in view, and that purpose will yet be revealed and shall justify the endurance. He that endures to the end shall see the end, shall understand the meaning. And it is God's end, for the ultimate purpose after all is His—and this makes all our enduring worth while.

Knowing what our goal is and desiring to reach it doesn't necessarily bring it closer to us. Doing something does. Someone has asked the question, "Are you a pilgrim or a vagrant?" A pilgrim is one who is traveling with a destination in view. A vagrant is a mere stroller, with no settled purpose or goal. We need never be afraid of putting the goal too high. At least that way we'll get further than if we set an easy goal, and we'll put on muscle climbing toward it. The resurrection is the longest-range goal we can have. Let's not be discouraged by this, for we must have long-range goals that are certain of attainment in order to keep from being frustrated by short-range failures. "Therefore, my beloved brethren, be ye stedfast, unmoveable, always abounding in the work of the Lord, forasmuch as ye know that your labour is not in vain in the Lord."

BECOME AN ACTIVIST

". . . .always abounding in the work of the Lord. . . ."
(I Cor. 15:58).

Nobody likes to face the prospect of death, but we know it is inevitable. As Christians, however, we rejoice in the fact that one day our separated souls will be clothed afresh with new bodies whose qualities are far superior to those of our present bodies. What does this mean to you here and now? Does that hope make you a better man, a better woman, a harder worker?

The Apostle Paul closes his argument regarding the truth of the resurrection with the command to get going and accomplish something. The hope of the resurrection should not lead to inactivity but to hard work. This hope, he claims, puts energy into us to accomplish the tasks of life better. Who can work well if he thinks it is in vain? The soul can only work in hope and through hope. Hope is to end in service, is to be the very inspiration of service, and the guarantee of the reward of service.

This is the test of true religion. Do its doctrines motivate you to do anything about them, or just to sit and wait for the fulfillment of certain promises? True, the religion of Christ invites you to receive Him and by receiving Him gain eternal life. But that life begins here and now. It is not given merely for self-enjoyment but also for the joy that comes from the voluntary shouldering of a cross. The Christian life is not an armchair religion, an indolent acceptance of a freely offered salvation that leads to nothing. It is the cross, the spear, the blood, the loss, the love, the compassion that overcomes your pride and indolence and moves you to attend to the man whom you find bleeding on the road. The challenge of the Christian life is in service, in hard work, in doing more today than we did yesterday.

How significant that Paul's admonition to hard work for Christ in this life follows on the assurance of victory in the previous verse. In verse 57 Paul says, "Thanks be to God, which giveth us the victory through our Lord Jesus Christ," and immediately adds in verse 58 what this victory should inspire us to be and do: "Therefore, my beloved brethren, be ye stedfast, unmoveable, always abounding in the work of the Lord." Why did he do this? Because of the danger that, when we have victory assured, we are not likely to work as hard to achieve it. Paul recognizes this human trait and no doubt that is why he tells these Corinthians that, although Christ has won our victory, this in no way exempts us from doing our duty and putting our shoulder to the wheel.

It is just like our belief that God will save those whom He has foreknown and elected to be saved. We may be tempted to say, "Since God is going to save those whom He will, what is the need of my witnessing?" Simply because He has declared that the saving is His business and the witnessing is ours. Actually the same puzzle confronts us in the matter of our praying and the working out of God's will in our lives and in our world. As Andrew Fuller remarked in a letter to two relatives: "I used to think that the doctrine of election was a reason why we need not pray, and I fear there are many who split upon this rock, who think it is to no purpose to pray, as things will be as they will be. But I now see that the doctrine of election is the greatest encouragement instead of a discouragement to prayer. He that decreed that any should be finally saved, decreed that it should be in the way of prayer, as much as He that has decreed what we shall possess of the things of this life, has decreed that it shall be in the way of industry; and as we think of never being idle in common business, because God has decreed what we shall possess of this world's goods, so neither should we be slothful in the business of our souls, because our final state is decreed."

Actually, the assurance of victory ahead of time is a spur to make us work harder and with greater determination. If we felt that victory was in doubt, it would steal vigor and vitality from our fight. God has determined a course of events that He assures us of His benediction upon, once we have done our duty. His victory is offered to us on condition that we do our part.

Note here that, though Paul urges Christians to get busy in the Lord's work, his first concern is not in what we do but in what we are. That is because what we do springs from what we are. That is why his first command in verse 58 is "Be ye stedfast." The Greek word translated "be ye" is the present imperative *ginesthe*, which indicates, not a static state of being, but a continually progressive state: "Keep becoming stedfast." The verb is in the present indicative imperative, not in the aorist (past) imperative. There is no time in life when we can say, "Now I have reached the place where I need not watch out any more; there is nothing further I can grow into."

Those who believe that a Christian can be filled once and for all with God's Spirit or with any of God's blessings have a static Christianity and rob themselves of the blessing of growing. In the New Testament we find constant references to the disciples being filled with the Holy Spirit, not only once but on many occasions, in order to meet some difficult task with which they were confronted. (See Acts 2:4; 4:8, 31; 9:17; 13:9.) This constant infilling presupposes emptying, and the emptying occurs as we labor for Christ, as we bless others with the blessing with which we are blessed.

A little stream that flowed through a manufacturing town bemoaned its fate in having to carry off the foul waste materials of industry, which stained and polluted its entire course. Now there came a deliverer who said, "I will set you free and give you rest." So he stopped up the watercourse and said, "Now you may stay in your place. You won't flow any more where you can be enslaved and defiled." But the little stream soon found that it had only exchanged one evil for another, for its waters soon became stagnant, and began foaming and swelling and pressing against the dam that held them back. It was in the stream's very nature to flow on, and it never found rest until once again it was freed to pursue an active course along the channel that had been prepared for it. So we are made for activity, and when we are set free from the activities of our self-righteousness and the slavery of our sin, we must do something for Christ, and we shall never rest until we find that something to do.

THE CHRISTIAN'S CONTROL CENTER

". . .*be ye stedfast, unmoveable, always abounding in the work of the Lord*" (I Cor. 15:58).

The Christian life is the result of Christian belief. You cannot live like a Christian without being a Christian. Being a Christian is to believe that Christ died, was buried, and rose to save you. That is how the Apostle Paul began this great 15th chapter of I Corinthians. Now he ends his argument about the fact and doctrine of the resurrection of our bodies by saying that we ought to keep becoming (*ginesthe*) steadfast, unmoveable, and always abounding in the work of the Lord. This speaks of Christian growth—becoming something that you are not now. In the Christian life you never arrive at a position of full growth. As long as you live on this earth, you should continue to grow in grace and in the knowledge of the Lord.

We find a parallel here between our spiritual and our physical lives. Our entire physical self changes constantly. So does our spiritual self. And yet we are the same persons. Growth, becoming, does not hinder us from being our basic selves. That is what is implied by this 58th verse of I Corinthians 15. Keep becoming steadfast, unmoveable, abounding in God's work.

The Christian life is like riding a bicycle. You cannot move forward unless you steady yourself. When you ride a bicycle you sit steady, but you move forward. If you don't sit steady you'll wobble and not be able to move forward. This is exactly the meaning of the Greek word *hedraioi*, translated "stedfast." It is derived from the substantive *hedra*, which means "a seat." It means being settled in your spiritual and moral beliefs. It means secure but not stationary. You anchor yourself on the rock of Christ. Your resurrection is made possible because of His. And thus you will go places.

There is deep psychological insight in this statement of Paul's. Only he who is settled in his convictions and is not wavering will ever accomplish anything. Only he who believes in the resurrection of his body will work without fear. Only he who believes in victory will fight to attain it. Such work and warfare endanger life. But this, for the one who believes in the life after death, does not make him fearful. Courage is the product of faith. The Christian who believes in the resurrection is not afraid of the battle. He meets it head on and says with General Pompey of old, "It is a small matter that I should move forward and die. It is too great a matter that I should take one step backward and live." This same general, when hazarding his life on a tempestuous sea in order to be at Rome on an important occasion, said, "It is necessary for me to go; it is not necessary for me to live."

Paul speaks of victory through Christ in verse 57. This suggests a scene of warfare. The base is essential for the fighting soldier. The one who sits and plans the strategy is as important as the soldier who faces the enemy in the front lines—if not more so. The commands to the field must come from the headquarters, where the commanding officer sits. Otherwise confusion would result in the ranks of the fighting men. The supply base for ammunition is absolutely essential. The fighting man is totally dependent on this. So is the soldier of the Lord. He dares not cut his communication with the seat of command. Defeat would be the result.

A beautiful illustration of our dependence on a solidly established base while we are moving at a distance is the journey of Apollo 11 to the moon. A space station in Houston, Texas, was the seat of command. The three spacemen dared not disregard it as they circled around the moon and as two of them landed on its surface. Thus Paul tells the Corinthians that any work they undertake must be based on the firmness, the absoluteness, the dependability of the Lord Jesus Christ. He arose; He did what He said He was going to do; He told us that we shall rise. That is our control center. We can depend on it. We dare not disregard it. It is a matter of life and death.

As I was viewing this feat of man at the time Neil Armstrong was landing on the moon, I was impressed by the remark made by one news commentator: "These men cannot remain on the moon. They must follow instructions. They do not have only themselves to think of but also the entire project." Think of that, Christian, when you are tempted to act independently of the control center, Christ the Lord. You do not have only yourself to think of, but Christ and His Kingdom.

Where would the plane be if the pilot decided to disregard the guidance of the control tower? How many collisions we would have! How many calamities! As there is absolute necessity of control in our space explorations and air travel, and even in our daily driving under the direction of red and green lights on the highway, so there must be someone sitting in a control tower, as it were, directing our spiritual and moral behavior and work. Relative success depends on the observance of absolute principles. This is as true in the spiritual world as in the physical. The same God who made dependable physical laws also made absolute spiritual laws. It is foolhardy to obey the physical and disregard the spiritual. Success in any work for Christ depends fully on obedience to Him and His absolute laws. The forsaking of the steady and absolute means failure and destruction. Unfortunately that is the course followed by some in our society today who want to place all our actions on a relativistic, situational basis, instead of on principles and absolutes set up, not by us, but by Him by whom all things consist.

A friend of the late Professor Foster, of the University of Chicago, says that he asked the brilliant apostle of relativism a few months before his death what he was doing. "I am hunting for the absolute in history," Foster replied. "And have you found it?" "No," he said, "but I am convinced that if it cannot be found that means the death of religion." He was absolutely right. But, had he searched the 15th chapter of I Corinthians and all the historical evidence for the resurrection of Christ, he would have found the absolute.

You may be able to arrive at it as a reasonable deduction from the evidence of what is. But God did not wish man to rest only on human deductions, or to base his worship on probabilities. That is why the eternal and infinite *Logos*, the Word without shape and form (John 1:1), took upon Himself flesh and form (John 1:14), so that we could see Him and hear Him. He rose from the dead to prove that He was absolute among us. As long as His resurrection can stand, you can depend on Him as being the absolute foundation of your faith.

This is the conclusion Paul was leading to. He wanted to say "therefore," which he does in verse 58, just as you would in proving a theorem in geometry. Before you can say "therefore" (QED), you have to give the reasoning that led you to that confident conclusion. Paul did just that. The "therefore" of verse 58 refers to the entire chapter as well as to verse 57. You have to have a foundation before you can build.

Listen to this same Apostle: "Be not moved away from the hope of the gospel" (Col. 1:23). "As ye have therefore received Christ Jesus the Lord, so walk ye in him: rooted and built up in him, and stablished in the faith, as ye have been taught, abounding therein with thanksgiving" (Col. 2:6, 7). Of the early Christians it is written, "They continued stedfastly in the apostles' doctrine and fellowship, and in breaking of bread, and in prayers" (Acts 2:42). May this also be said of us. With all our scientific progress, we stand helpless before a human corpse. Christ rose from the dead. This is the rock on which we stand. Begin there. Let that be the control center of all your activity in this life. It will suffice for the after life as well.

NOTHING YOU DO FOR GOD IS EVER WASTED

". . .be ye stedfast, unmoveable, always abounding in the work of the Lord, forasmuch as ye know that your labour is not in vain in the Lord" (I Cor. 15:58).

Why does the Apostle Paul tell Christians not only to be "stedfast" but also "unmoveable" in doing the Lord's work? Why this second term? "Keep becoming stedfast," he says, and then move on from a safe and absolute base or control center and keep becoming "unmoveable." The word is *ametakineetoi*, which means "not capable of being moved." It's a compound form of the same word from which we derive the English word "kinetics," the branch of dynamics treating of the changes of motion produced by forces. It's also the word from which we get "cinema," moving pictures.

What did Paul imply by saying that we ought to grow "unmoveable"? Is there a basic difference between the two adjectives? *Hedraioi*, "steadfast," means "firmly imbedded, secured, rooted." We lay a foundation on a piece of property before erecting a building, so that it will stay put in one place. We realize that that's the only way we can build on it. But Paul wants us to recognize that there are outside influences which will purposely try to move us from that one safe position on which we are seated. This Greek word, which is a verbal adjective, is passive in form, whose meaning therefore indicates that there are outside agents which will try to move us. He was speaking out of his own personal experience. He knew that the devil, the world, our own subtle desires, would desperately try to unseat us. The deeper our roots go, the more we can withstand the attacks that originate from our environment.

Paul could look all kinds of trouble in the face everywhere and say, "The Holy Ghost witnesseth in every city, saying that bonds and afflictions abide me. But none of these things move me, neither count I my life dear unto myself, so that I might finish my course with joy, and the ministry, which I have received of the Lord Jesus, to testify the gospel of the grace of God" (Acts 20:23, 24). Can you speak so confidently in view of the resurrection? How we need to heed the advice of the Epistle to the Hebrews: "Be not carried about with divers and strange doctrines. For it is a good thing that the heart be established with grace" (13:9). God's grace is the cement that holds you to the unmoveable rock of Christ.

Firmness in doctrine, stability in Christ, does not result in stagnation but in abundant activity. "Always abounding in the work of the Lord." "Abounding" in Greek is *perisseuontes*, meaning "surpassing that which is required of us, or necessary." Your love for anyone can be realistically measured by how much you are willing to do for that person. If just enough, your love is not similar to God's love. How disappointed God must be in children of His who do just enough to prove their standing with Him. Given people who cannot do enough for God, we would have a spiritual revolution in this world.

We are to abound "in the work of the Lord." This is rather a broad term. What is the work of the Lord? I can't tell you. All I can say is, we must never limit it to our own narrow, exclusive, denominational interests. The work of the Lord is as large as His whole wide world. Whatever glorifies God is His work. Whatever brings His love and His salvation to humanity is His work. Remember, it is not your work. You are doing His work. Never be unduly possessive of your Christian vocation. Realize that what He permits you to do, important or seemingly unimportant, fits into His plan for the total accomplishment of His purpose.

The word for Lord is *Kurion*, meaning "Master." It indicates not only possession but also superiority. The victory is His, declares verse 58. You are only a cog in the wheel. Now observe the constancy of our abounding in the work of the Lord, as indicated by Paul's use of the word "always." There isn't a time when we can claim that we have done enough for God. In whatever circumstances we are found we can abound.

This is not always going to be easy. It will often be fatiguing. This is exactly what is indicated by the word *kopos*, "labour," in the last phrase of this glorious chapter. "As ye know that your labour is not in vain in the Lord." *Kopos* means "toil implying weariness." Working for the Lord is often tiring. But if people are willing to get tired for material reward, we who are the Lord's must be willing not merely to work for Him but to get tired in His service. What makes this fatigue and toil tolerable? The knowledge that what we do for Him is not in vain. Everything we do for God must have a purpose. Don't work hit or miss. Have a plan, have a goal. Then spare no trouble in accomplishing it.

The participle "knowing" is the Greek word *eidotes*, not *gignooskontes*. The first word which is used here comes from *oida* and indicates knowing by reflection; the second, from *gignooskoo*, which Paul didn't use here, knowing by experience. This word *oida* expresses an intrinsic truth. You don't need to experience the fruitfulness of your labor for the Lord. The fact that it is for Him makes it instantly worth while. The participle *eidotes*, "knowing," is in reality the perfect tense of an old verb, *eidoo*, unused in the present tense, meaning "to see," and may be literally translated "having seen, therefore realizing." This realization comes before the abounding service for the Lord. Since we know that nothing that we do for the Lord is ever wasted, we shall do it with zeal, devotion, and sacrifice. Again this is a demonstration of belief leading to activity. Note that the participle *perisseuontes*, "abounding," is in the present tense. The realization that our labor is not in vain comes first, and then our abundant service.

The word for "in vain," *kenos*, means "without effect, fruitless." It is important to note that this is in the present tense. "Knowing that your labor *is* not fruitless, empty, in the Lord," here and now. True, you will only know the full results of your toil for the Lord in the world to come, and meanwhile you may be kept in the dark as to the effectiveness of what you are doing. Don't be discouraged. Your labor of love will bear fruit as long as it is an honest endeavor "in the Lord."

The resurrection of our bodies being presented so certainly by Paul in this chapter may unconsciously transfix your eyes upon what is yet to be, and thus you may neglect what there is to be done here and now. That is why Paul closes his presentation on the resurrection, not by pointing to what is to be looked for in the future, but to what is to be done now so that others may be won to Christ. The world may not always understand why you are doing what you are doing for God, but as a missionary to the lepers said, "I gladly do it for Christ. I have no thought of any reward other than His smile of approval upon me." That's really enough, both for the here and the hereafter.

BIBLIOGRAPHY

I. COMMENTARIES, ENCYCLOPEDIAS, EXPOSITORY AND OTHER REFERENCE WORKS FOR ENGLISH READERS

Alford, Henry, *The Greek Testament,* Vol. I. Chicago: Moody Press, p. 133.
Analytical Greek Lexicon, The. New York: Harper and Brothers, p. 185.
Chafer, Lewis Sperry, *Systematic Theology,* Vol. VII. Dallas, Texas: Dallas Seminary Press, 1950, pp. 63-4.
Cremer, Hermann, *Biblico-Theological Lexicon of New Testament Greek.* Edinburgh: T. & T. Clark, 1954, p. 541.
Grimm-Thayer, *Greek English Lexicon of the New Testament.* Edinburgh: T. & T. Clark, 1956, p. 253.
Hodge, Charles, *Systematic Theology,* Vol. II. New York: Scribner, Armstrong, and Co., 1874, pp. 594 ff., 630 ff.
Jelf, William Edward, *A Grammar of the Greek Language,* Vol. II. London: John Henry and James Parker, 1861, p. 490.
Kittel, Gerhard, editor, *Theological Dictionary of the New Testament,* Vol. I. Grand Rapids, Michigan: Wm. B. Eerdmans Publishing Co., 1964, pp. 394-6, 483-4, 590.
_____*Ibid.,* Vol. II, pp. 23-4, 166, 320, 335, 465-6.
Liddell, H. G., and Scott, R., *A Greek-English Lexicon.* Oxford: Clarendon Press, 1958, p. 1160.
Robertson, A. T., *A Grammar of the Greek New Testament in the Light of Historical Research.* New York: George H. Doran Co., 1923, pp. 333-4, 757-8, 811, 814, 816 f., 880.
Trench, Richard C., *Synonyms of the New Testament.* Grand Rapids, Michigan: Wm. B. Eerdmans Publishing Co., 1953, pp. 166-8, 231-5, 315-8.
Vine, W. E., *An Expository Dictionary of New Testament Words.* Old Tappan, New Jersey: Fleming H. Revell Co., 1966, p. 81.

II. LEXICONS, ENCYCLOPEDIAS, AND REFERENCES, FOR GREEK READERS, FROM CLASSICAL AND KOINE GREEK TO MODERN GREEK.

Byzantiou, S. D., *Lexikon tees Helleenikees Gloossees (Lexicon of the Hellenic Language).* Athens: Koromeela, A., 1852.
Demetrakou, D., *Lexikon tees Helleenikees Gloossees (Lexicon of the Greek Language).* Athens: Demetrakou, 1954.
Enkuklopaidikon Gloossologikon Lexikon (Encyclopedic Glossological Lexicon). Athens: Morfootikee Hetaireia.
Enkuklopaidikon Lexikon Eleutheroudaki (Eleutheroudaki, Encyclopedic Lexicon). Athens: Eleutheroudakis, 1927.
Iooannou tou Chrusostomou Ta Hapanta (Complete Works of John Chrysostom). Kalaraki: Michael and Nikolas Galanos, 1899.

Liddell, H. G., and Scott, R., *Greek-English Lexicon,* as Translated and Enriched by Xenophoon P. Moschos and Michael Konstantinides. Athens: John Sideris.

Megalee Heleenikee Enkuklopaideia (Great Greek Encyclopedia). Pursos (Pyrsos), Athens: Heelios.

Neooteron Enkuklopaidikon Lexikon Heeliou (New Encyclopedic Lexicon "Heelios"). Athens: Heelios.

Papaoikonomou, George L., *Lexikon Anomaloon Rheematoon (Lexicon of Irregular Verbs).* Athens: Kagiaphas.

Stamatakou, J. D., *Lexikon Archaias Helleenikees Gloossees (Lexicon of the Ancient Hellenic Language).* Athens: Petrou Deemeetrakou, 1949.

III. REFERENCE WORKS CONTAINING CHAPTERS ON I CORINTHIANS 15

Andrews, C. F., *Christ in the Silence.* London: Hodder & Stoughton, 1933, pp. 271-2.

Angus, Joseph, *Future Punishment.* London: Hodder & Stoughton, 1871, pp. 42, 45, 56.

Barclay, William, *The Letters to the Corinthians.* Edinburgh: The Saint Andrew Press, 1958, pp. 152-180.

Barnes, Albert, *Notes on the New Testament (I Corinthians).* Grand Rapids, Michigan: Baker Book House, 1949, p. 317.

Beet, Joseph Agar, *A Commentary on St. Paul's Epistles to the Corinthians.* London: Hodder & Stoughton, 1885, pp. 263-306.

Bengel, John Albert, *Gnomon of the New Testament,* Vol. III. Edinburgh: T. & T. Clark, 1863, pp. 316-342.

Body, George, "The Destruction of Death," *The Christian World Pulpit,* Vol. LXVII. London: James Clarke & Co., 1905, pp. 260-2.

Brooks, Phillips, *The Mystery of Iniquity.* London: MacMillan and Co., 1894, p. 243.

Brown, E. F., *The First Epistle of Paul the Apostle to the Corinthians.* London: Society for Promoting Christian Knowledge, 1923, pp. 248-289.

Calvin, John, *Commentary on the Epistles of Paul the Apostle to the Corinthians,* Vol. II. Grand Rapids, Michigan: Wm. B. Eerdmans Publishing Co., 1948, pp. 5-66.

Candlish, Robert S., *Life in a Risen Saviour.* Philadelphia: Lindsay and Blakiston, 1858, pp. 157-8, 178-9, 215-6, 222-3.

Chambers, Oswald, *The Psychology of Redemption.* London: Simpkin Marshall, Ltd., distributor, 1941, p. 11.

Chavasse, Francis James, *Parochial Sermons of Bishop Chavasse.* London: Society for Promoting Christian Knowledge, 1938, pp. 165-6.

Clark, John, *Sixteen Sermons.* Cambridge, England: John Clark, 1829, pp. 1-153.

Cochrane, James, *Discourses on Some of the Most Difficult Texts of Scripture.* Edinburgh: Paton and Ritchie, 1851, pp. 104-22.

Dawson, W. J., "The Grace of God," *The Christian World Pulpit,* Vol. LII. London: James Clarke & Co., 1897, pp. 200-2.

Dods, Marcus, "The First Epistle to the Corinthians," *The Expositor's Bible,* W. Robertson Nicoll, editor. London: Hodder & Stoughton, 1900, pp. 326-86.

Edwards, Jonathan, *The Selected Works of Jonathan Edwards,* Vol. I. The Banner of Truth Trust, London: pp. 152-62.

Edwards, Thomas Charles, *A Commentary on the First Epistle to the Corinthians.* London: Hamilton, Adams & Co., 1885, pp. 385-460.

Exell, Joseph S., *The Biblical Illustrator, I Corinthians,* Vol. II. London: Wilkes & Co., pp. 380-558.

_____*Ibid., Acts,* Vol. I. London: James Nisbet & Co., pp. 102-5.

Foster, Henry J., *A Homiletic Commentary on the Epistles of St. Paul the Apostle to the Corinthians.* New York: Funk & Wagnalls Co., pp. 317-59.

Frick, Philip L., *The Resurrection and Paul's Argument.* Cincinnati, Ohio: Jennings and Graham, 1912, pp. 11-348.

Godet, F., *Commentary on the First Epistle of St. Paul to the Corinthians,* Vol. II. Grand Rapids, Michigan: Zondervan Publishing House, 1957, pp. 321-450.

Goudge, H. L., *The First Epistle to the Corinthians.* London: Methuen & Co., 1911, pp. 137-66.

Greenhough, J. G., *Sunset Thoughts: or Aftermath.* London: Arthur H. Stockwell, pp. 140-8.

Griffith-Jones, E., *The Unspeakable Gift.* London: James Clarke & Co., p. 118.

Grosheide, F. W., *Commentary on the First Epistle to the Corinthians.* London: Marshall, Morgan & Scott, 1954, pp. 346-95.

Guest, W. J., *Unveiled Mysteries.* Worcester, New York: Press of the Worcester Times, 1904, pp. 95-99.

Hart, H. Martyn, "The Resurrection," *The Churchman's Pulpit,* Vol. XVI, J. Henry Burn, editor. London: Francis Griffiths, 1911, pp. 241-2.

Hodge, Archibald Alexander, *Outlines of Theology.* Grand Rapids, Michigan: Wm. B. Eerdmans Publishing Co., 1949, p. 428.

Hodge, Charles, *An Exposition of the First Epistle to the Corinthians.* Grand Rapids, Michigan: Wm. B. Eerdmans Publishing Co., 1950, pp. 308-60.

Holum, John R., "If Scientists Create Life," *Christianity Today,* Jan. 3, 1964, Vol. VIII, No. 7. Washington, D. C.: Christianity Today, Inc., p. 3.

Horne, C. Silvester, "The Kingship of Christ," *Christian World Pulpit,* Vol. XXXII, London: James Clarke & Co., 1887, pp. 245-7.

Horton, Robert F., *The Trinity.* London: Horace Marshall & Son, 1901, pp. 39-54.

Hughes, Hugh Price, *The Philanthropy of God.* London: Hodder & Stoughton, 1890, pp. 175-84.

Inge, W. R., "The Sin of Self-Satisfaction," *The Christian World Pulpit,* Vol. CVIII. London: The Christian World, Ltd., 1925, pp. 121-2.

James, John Angell, "Our Risen Lord," *The Pulpit,* Vol. LXIX. London: John M. Robeson, 1856, pp. 365-71.

Jones, J. D., *Things Most Surely Believed.* London: James Clarke & Co., pp. 84-8, 95-100.

Jowett, J. H., "In the Image of God," *The Great Texts of the Bible (Genesis to Numbers),* James Hastings, editor. Edinburgh: T. & T. Clark, 1911, pp. 57-8.

Kling, Christian Friedrich, *The First Epistle of Paul to the Corinthians,* translated by Daniel W. Poor. New York: Charles Scribner & Co., 1868, pp. 306-53.

Lange, John Peter, *A Commentary on the Holy Scriptures,* Vol. VII of the New Testament, translated from the German by Philip Schaff. New York: Charles Scribner & Co., 1868, pp. 306-53.

Large, James, *Two Hundred and Eighty Titles and Symbols of Christ.* Grand Rapids, Michigan: Baker Book House, 1959, p. 409.

Laurin, Roy L., *Where Christian Life Matures.* Findlay, Ohio: Dunham Publishing Co., 1957, pp. 268-311.

Lenski, R. C. H., *The Interpretation of I and II Corinthians.* Minneapolis, Minnesota: Augsburg Publishing House, 1961, pp. 623-755.

_____*The Interpretation of St. Paul's Epistles to the (Ephesians).* Columbus, Ohio: The Wartburg Press, 1946, p. 404.

Lewis, C. S., "Hope," *A Reader's Notebook,* Gerald Kennedy, compiler. New York: Harper and Brothers, 1953, pp. 126-7.

Lias, J. J., *The Cambridge Bible for Schools and Colleges, The First Epistle to the Corinthians,* J. J. S. Perowne, editor. Cambridge, England: Cambridge University Press, 1899, pp. 141-63.

Liddon, H. P., "The Glorious Destiny of the Human Body," *The Churchman's Pulpit,* Vol. XIII, J. Henry Burn, editor. London: Francis Griffiths, 1910, pp. 303-6.

_ _ *Easter in St. Paul's,* pp. 1-15, 25-33, 44-7.

_____*Sermons on Some Words of St. Paul.* London: Longmans, Green, and Co., 1898, pp. 154-8.

Lightfoot, Joseph Barber, *Cambridge Sermons.* London: Trustees of the Lightfoot Fund (MacMillan and Co.), 1890, pp. 63-79.

MacLaren, Alexander, *Expositions of Holy Scripture (St. Paul's Epistles to the Corinthians, to II Corinthians V).* New York: A. C. Armstrong & Son, 1910, pp. 195-200, 209-12.

_____*Triumphant Certainties.* London: Christian Commonwealth Publishing Co., Ltd., pp. 140-51.

McPheeters, Julian C., *The Epistles to the Corinthians.* Grand Rapids, Michigan: Baker Book House, 1964, pp. 69-73.

Marling, F. H., "Labourers Together with God," *The Christian World Pulpit,* Vol. VI. London: James Clarke and Co., 1874, p. 255.

Martin, R. P., *Bible Study Books, I Corinthians-Galatians.* Grand Rapids, Michigan: Wm. B. Eerdmans Publishing Co., 1968, pp. 46-52.

Matheson, George, *Moments on the Mount.* London: James Nisbet & Co., 1886, pp. 113-4.

_____*Searchings in the Silence.* London: Cassell & Co., 1895, pp. 187-9.

Merrill, S. M., *The New Testament Idea of Hell.* Cincinnati: Cranston & Stowe, 1878, pp. 17-8.

Meyer, Heinrich August Wilhelm, *Commentary on the New Testament, Epistles to the Corinthians,* Vol. II, Translated from the German by D. Douglas Bannerman & W. P. Dickson, Edinburgh: T. & T. Clark, 1879, pp. 34-108.

Milligan, William, *The Resurrection of Our Lord.* New York: The MacMillan Co., 1917, p. 241.

Minton, Samuel, "The Last Enemy," *The Christian World Pulpit,* Vol. V. London: James Clarke and Co., 1874, pp. 305-6.

Morgan, G. Campbell, "The Christian Empire," *The Christian World Pulpit,* Vol. XC, 1916, London: James Clarke and Co., pp. 290-3.

_____*The Corinthian Letters of Paul.* New York: Fleming H. Revell Co., 1946, pp. 182-207.

Morris, Henry M., *The Twilight of Evolution.* Philadelphia: The Presbyterian and Reformed Publishing Co., 1963, p. 46.

Morrison, G. H., *Sun-Rise: Addresses from a City Pulpit.* London: Hodder & Stoughton, 1904, pp. 300-10.

Newell, William R., *The Book of the Revelation.* Chicago: Moody Press, 1935, p. 119.

Nowell-Rostron, S., *St. Paul's First Epistle to the Corinthians.* London: The Religious Tract Society, 1931, pp. 202-25.

Olshausen, Hermann, *Biblical Commentary on St. Paul's First and Second Epistles to the Corinthians,* Translated by John Edmund Cox. Edinburgh: T. & T. Clark, 1855, pp. 235-64.

Pfeiffer, Charles F., and Harrison, Everett F., *The Wycliffe Bible Commentary.* Chicago: Moody Press, 1968, 1255-9.

Pulpit Commentary, The, Vol. XLIV, H. D. M. Spence and Joseph S. Exell, editors. New York: Funk & Wagnalls Co., pp. 483-549.

Robertson, F. W., *Expository Lectures on St. Paul's Epistles to the Corinthians.* London: Smith, Elder and Co., 1866, pp. 241-93.

Robinson, Charles H., *Studies in the Resurrection of Christ.* New York: Longmans, Green and Co., 1911, p. 97.

Sadler, M. F., *The First and Second Epistles to the Corinthians.* London: George Bell and Sons, 1898, pp. 258-97.

Schep, J. A., *The Nature of the Resurrection Body.* Grand Rapids, Michigan: Wm. B. Eerdmans Publishing Co., 1964, pp. 17-24, 204, 210-3, 218.

Scott, Adam, "Celestial and Terrestrial," *The Christian World Pulpit,* Vol. XXXVII. London: James Clarke and Co., 1890, pp. 152-4.

Seiss, Joseph A., *Lectures on the Epistles,* Vol. I. Philadelphia: General Council Publication House, 1915, pp. 459-71.

_____*Ibid.,* Vol. II. pp. 268-80.

Smyth, Newman, *Newman Smyth's Works (The Reality of Faith).* London: Ward, Lock & Co., pp. 142-52.

Sparrow-Simpson, W. J., *Our Lord's Resurrection.* Grand Rapids, Michigan: Zondervan Publishing House, 1964, p. 120.

Spurgeon, C. H., "Cheerful Voluntariness," *The Christian World Pulpit,* Vol. LVIII. London: James Clarke & Co., 1900, p. 398.

_____*The Treasury of the New Testament,* Vol. III. Grand Rapids, Michigan: Zondervan Publishing House, 1950, pp. 210-7.

_____*The Treasury of the Old Testament,* Vol. II. Grand Rapids, Michigan: Zondervan Publishing House, 1951, p. 52.

Stanley, Arthur Penrhyn, *The Epistles of St. Paul to the Corinthians.* London: John Murray, 1882, pp. 283-327.

Sumner, John Bird, *A Practical Exposition of the Epistle of St. Paul to the Romans and the First Epistle to the Corinthians.* London: J. Hatchard & Son, 1843, pp. 440-69.

Swete, Henry Barclay, *The Appearances of Our Lord after the Passion.* London: MacMillan and Co., 1910, pp. 82-5.

_____*The Life of the World to Come.* New York: The MacMillan Co., 1918, pp. 89-91.

Thomas, John, *The Mysteries of Grace.* New York: Hodder & Stoughton, pp. 87-8, 318-28.

Tillotson, John, "The Reasonableness of a Resurrection," *The World's Great Sermons,* Vol. II, compiled by Grenville Kleiser. New York: Funk & Wagnalls Co., 1908, pp. 135-54.

Tymms, T. Vincent, "The Private Relationships of Christ," *The Christian World Pulpit,* Vol. LXX. London: James Clarke & Co., 1906, pp. 316-8.

Vine, W. E., *I Corinthians.* London: Oliphants, Ltd., 1951, pp. 202-28.

Wenham, Alfred E., *Ruminations on the First Epistle of Paul the Apostle to the Corinthians.* London: Alabaster, Passmore & Sons, 1912, pp. 148-68.

Westcott, Brooke Foss, *The Gospel of the Resurrection.* London: MacMillan & Co., 1874, p. 137.

Winterbotham, R., *Sermons and Expositions.* London: Henry S. King & Co., 1874, p. 313.

Zodhiates, Spiros, *The Labor of Love.* Grand Rapids, Michigan: Wm. B. Eerdmans Publishing Co., 1960, pp. 25-31.

_____*Was Christ God?* Grand Rapids, Michigan: Wm. B. Eerdmans Publishing Co., 1966, pp. 23-7, 47-52.

I
INDEX OF SUBJECTS

INDEX OF ENGLISH WORDS

Greek	English	I Corinthians		Page
a (alpha) privative	without, un, not	15:43 15:52	654,	659 730
achri	as far as, until	15:25		398
agapee	love	15:57		815
agapeetos	beloved	15:57		815
agathos	good (in an active sense)	15:33		555
agathoosunee	goodness (active)	15:33		555
allassoo *(allageesometha)*	change (transform)	15:51		726
ametakineetos *(ametakineetoi)*	unmoveable	15:58		830
ana	up	15:6c		116

anapeithoo
    (anapeithei)
	persuade to a
	    different opinion
		15:36		597

anastasis	standing up (resurrection)	15:42-44		644
aneer (andros)	man (distinguished from woman)	15:24		328
anisteemi	to raise up	15:6c 15:20	note	116 269
anthroopos *(anthropoo)*	man (generic)	15:21 15:45 (Gen. 2:7)		289 674
aparchee	first fruits	15:20, 23		257
aphroon	fool (foolish)	15:35, 36a 15:36	594,	578 595

aphtharsia	incorruption (not
	    capable of
	    deterioration)
		15:42
		15:53
		(Rom. 2:7)
		(II Tim. 1:10)
			749,	648
				749
				
				751

aphthartos *(aphthartoi)*	incorruptible	15:52		739
apo	from	15:47 (Gen. 2:7)		697

apollumi (apoolonto,
    apollumenoi,
    apoleetai,
    apollontai)
	destroy utterly,
	    kill, perish,
	    be lost
		15:18
		(I Cor. 1:18)
		(II Cor. 2:15; 4:3)
		(II Thess. 2:10)
		(John 3:16; 17:12)
		(II Pet. 3:9)
				227